For
THE SON OF MAN

Preface

When we began the task of producing *Modern Management Accounting,* we determined that it would serve future managers as well as future accountants. Consequently, the reader will find the book emphasizing the usefulness of accounting in making decisions. However, we found that utility could not be fully described without some attention to procedural matters. Managers cannot wisely use information without knowing where it comes from or what its weaknesses might be. Similarly, accountants cannot responsibly produce information without knowing why and how it will be used. We have exerted a great deal of effort to assure that neither aspect is neglected or overemphasized.

We also believed that the distinction between management and financial accounting, while useful for several reasons, cannot always be precisely drawn. This belief was confirmed by a survey which we conducted of over 100 accounting departmental chairpersons, regarding which topics should be included in the text. Their responses indicated that managers do need to have some exposure to financial accounting. Thus, we have chosen to include several topics that other authors may have deleted. The two most compelling justifications for our choice are (1) that today's managers are more or less obligated to report to outside parties, and (2) that financial statements can contain usable information that is not available elsewhere.

The material in the text is structured to allow flexibility in application, and is suitable for a variety of course formats. An introductory chapter provides definitions and describes the business environment and accounting's role within it. The text is divided into five major sections; and there are two appendices at the end of the text.

The first major section, Management and Financial Statements, contains four chapters that deal with the interface between financial and management accounting. These chapters cover the meaning and content of the financial statements, their analysis, and the effects of inflation on their informational content. The Statement of Changes in Financial Position is used as a vehicle for describing working capital management.

Because so much management activity is directed toward cost control, we present a second section of four chapters concerned with cost behavior, cost analysis, accumulation of cost information, and using cost information to make decisions. Special attention is given to helping the student understand how the various classifications of costs and cost concepts may properly be used in the management decision process. Because the only costs that can be controlled are *future* costs, most of the remaining chapters deal with planning.

The four chapters in Section 3 thus primarily focus on planning for the short run. Chapter 10 looks at responsibility and internal controls as means to assure that plans are made and supervised, and also contains a discussion of social responsibilities. Chapters 11 and 12 present conceptual and procedural information about budgeting; and Chapter 13 shows that planning is virtually useless without a comparison with the actual results obtained. The student is taught how a manager can monitor operations so that efforts are continually being directed toward achieving the company goals.

Section 4 deals with more long-range matters of planning, covering the major topics of capital budgeting, financing arrangements, and the relationship of taxes to business decisions. In this section we rely heavily on compound interest fundamentals, which are explained in depth in Chapter 14.

The last two chapters (Section 5) contain surveys of two subjects that should be understood by all managers and accountants: mathematical decision models and computers. The material is presented in a style designed to facilitate a quick grasping of the fundamentals without confusing the reader.

Finally, for those students needing an introduction to double-entry accounting systems, there is a highly accelerated but thorough coverage of the accounting cycle presented in an appendix to the text. Although a high degree of competence in these techniques is not at all necessary to use this book, some knowledge will help the reader to follow some of the discussions.

Perhaps the most enjoyable part of writing a preface is that we finally have the opportunity to tell everyone how much we have depended upon other people throughout the production of the book. First, we want to thank all our students who provided us with the motivation. Their patience and helpful advice during the testing of preliminary chapters was very encouraging and satisfying. Gratitude goes especially to three of our professional colleagues: Reed H. Randall, of the University of Utah, who, except for editorial changes for stylistic consistency, wrote Chapter 18; Kenneth J. Hanni of the University of Utah, who rendered much helpful advice on Chapter 17; and John McDonough, of the University of California, Los Angeles, whose thorough criticism and enthusiastic support revived a first version with several flaws.

No one but an author can fully appreciate the effort made by the editorial staff in finally bringing a project to fruition. Special thanks to Steven Lock, Editor; Gerald Rafferty and Colette Conboy, of the Goodyear production department, for their hours of patient assistance and a multitude of helpful criticisms and suggestions.

We could not have begun our work if it had not been for the support provided by the administration of the College of Business of the University of Utah, especially our Chairman, Art Johnson, and our deans, George Odiorne, Joseph Peery, and Blaine Huntsman. And, for their incredible patience in preparing the many versions of the manuscript, a bouquet of appreciation goes to Melissa Whitehead, Donna Porter, and Liz Porter.

We also gratefully acknowledge the assistance of the American Institute of Certified Public Accountants for permission to quote from official pronouncements and to use problems (in whole or in part) from past Uniform CPA Examinations. Similarly, we acknowledge the permission of the Institute of Management Accounting to use (in whole or in part) problems from past CMA Examinations. The problems used from these sources are labeled appropriately in the text.

Last, and greatest, we thank our families, especially our wives, Nadine and Diana, for their kindness, support, sacrifices, and love.

A. Tom Nelson
Paul B. W. Miller

Salt Lake City, Utah
November, 1976

Contents

CHAPTER

1

Introduction to Management Accounting

Businessmen of all kinds frequently stress the importance of accounting knowledge. A popular definition of *accounting* explains this significance.

Accounting is a service activity. Its function is to provide quantitative information, primarily financial in nature, about economic entities that is intended to be useful in making economic decisions.[1]

Few organizations, business or otherwise, operate without decisions being made. If one organization has more good decisions made on its behalf, it usually follows that it will be more successful. The lifeblood of good decisions is the information available to the decision maker about the probable results and ramifications of the alternative courses of action. There are many types and sources of information available, but the financial information provided by accounting processes is very significant, if not critical, in most cases.

THE USERS OF ACCOUNTING

Virtually every participant in economic activity consumes accounting information of one kind or another. We will look at some important classes of users.

[1] Accounting Principles Board, *Statement No. 4: Basic Concepts and Accounting Principles Underlying Financial Statements of Business Enterprises* (New York: American Institute of Certified Public Accountants, 1970), p. 17.

Managers

There are literally millions of organizations in the United States. Many operate for the purpose of earning profits, but others strive for different objectives. Many organizations are owned by individuals or groups of individuals; many others are agencies of the various levels of government. Regardless of the size, form, or purpose of each of these organizations, decisions must be made about the acquisition and subsequent use of scarce resources. The individuals responsible for making and implementing decisions are called *managers*. Each manager has a unique approach and each needs information to assist his decision making. Accounting systems can provide much of this useful information.

Investors

Private organizations depend on investments to begin, maintain, or expand operations. These investments may involve loans or acquisition of an owner's interests. Lenders *(creditors)* and owners *(equity holders* or *stockholders)* expect and receive organizational reports which assist them in deciding whether or not to remain as investors. Reports also assist *potential* lenders and owners in selecting the most promising use of their money. Accounting systems produce most, but certainly not all, of the information provided to investors.

Government agencies are "owned" by the public. Many of them must submit reports of their activities to the citizens or to the proper officials. Recently, there has been a significant growth in the use of accounting information in the evaluation of public agencies.

Employees

It is not uncommon, and certainly not unwise, for employees to receive and use financial information about their employers. Based on accounting reports, decisions are made, for example, about such matters as continued employment, adequacy of pension plans, and wage contracts. Many workers are also stockholders, and thus have a dual interest in accounting information.

Regulatory Agencies

Regardless of the need for it, there is substantial regulation of business activity by local, state, and federal agencies. Although many nonfinancial aspects are under regulation (such as employment practices, occupational safety, and environmental impacts), many facets of the firm are regulated through accounting reports (such as minimum wages, pension plan funding, and prices charged to customers). One agency, the Securities and Exchange Commission, was established to regulate the manner in which financial information is reported. Other agencies that utilize financial information in their activities are the Federal Reserve Board, the Federal Power Commission, the Interstate Commerce Commission, and the Justice Department. Comparable agencies also exist at the state level.

Taxing Authorities

If the founders of our country thought poorly of "taxation without representation," they should see what it is like *with* representation! Countless types of taxes are levied on individuals and organizations in our country. Income taxes, sales taxes, property taxes, use taxes, franchise taxes, estate taxes, gift taxes, and excise taxes are just a few. Taxes are collected by cities, counties, port authorities, and school districts, as well as by the federal government. Most tax assessments are based on some type of accounting information submitted by the taxpayer.

THREE TYPES OF ACCOUNTING

As shown, there are many varied demands for accounting information. To the naive observer, it would appear that one accounting system could provide all the information needed by all the users. However, because of the different purposes served, there are three general types of accounting information: *management, financial,* and *tax.*

Management Accounting

Managers have access to a wide range of information from which they can freely pick and choose among the possibilities in order to get the data they feel are most useful for a particular decision. Consequently, management accounting information tends to be less structured and less precise than the other two types. Although the emphasis is on the future, the past is by no means neglected. Management accounting reports tend to be very "narrow" in scope, and are seldom useful for anything other than the specific decision for which they are prepared.

The primary objective of this text is to describe situations in which management accounting information can be helpful, and to show how the information is gathered and interpreted.

Financial Accounting

In making presentations to nonmanagers, a firm must be extremely careful not to delete any potentially worthwhile information nor to include any potentially misrepresentative statements. Consequently, management accounting reports, which are prepared for the firm's internal consumption by persons who have a great deal of other facts at their fingertips, are generally inadequate in terms of meeting the needs of the relatively uninformed investors, employees, and regulatory and taxing agencies. Thus most firms *must* maintain *financial* accounting systems to provide reports for nonmanagers. Because of the need for impartiality, these "financial statements" tend to be highly structured, conservative, and past oriented. Numerous court cases have shown that there is little benefit in presenting unduly optimistic financial accounting reports.

Throughout this text, the authors are committed to the approach that modern managers need a minimum amount of knowledge about the fundamental concepts (and, to a lesser extent, the procedures) underlying financial accounting and the financial statements. There are several reasons supporting this point of view.

First, financial statements provide at least some information that is useful in managing. The manager must be able to distinguish the useful from the useless, then the statements can be applied in a satisfactory manner. Familiarity with the financial accountant's objectives and constraints will place the information in a more proper perspective.

Second, today's social and political environment is placing demands on the annual reporting mechanism, including the financial statements. No modern manager can safely ignore nor simply delegate the reporting responsibility to the "Accounting Department."

Finally, alternative solutions to a major management problem can produce different results in the annual statements. If sufficiently significant, the selection among the alternatives can affect, for example, the firm's apparent debt capacity, its dividend-paying ability, and even the market value of its stock. Thus, the potential impact on the statements must be considered as one of the variables in many management decisions.

Clearly, today's manager cannot function without knowledge of the strengths and weaknesses of financial accounting reports. Consequently, the first section of this text is devoted to describing the statements—their uses and their limitations—from the *manager's* point of view.

Tax Accounting

Finally, modern organizations must maintain a third accounting system for reporting to taxing authorities. Because tax laws are intended not only to raise revenue but also to redistribute wealth and to accomplish other economic policies, their provisions frequently call for accounting procedures quite different than those used in management or financial accounting systems. Consequently, no manager can afford to be ignorant of tax considerations in planning for the future. See Chapter 17 for a further discussion of this topic.

AN OVERVIEW OF ACCOUNTING

Now that we are aware of the role of accounting in our society, let's look at it more closely. In particular, we will examine the functions, the instruments, and the rules of accounting.

Functions of Accounting

In the opening paragraph, we made the broad statement that the function of accounting is to provide information. In particular, providing information involves three activities: *recordkeeping, simplification,* and *summarization.*

Because of the human's finite capacity for remembering facts, virtually all information about an organization is *recorded* in one form or another. The Incas stored information on knotted strings. Ink and paper sufficed for centuries. Recently, we have seen the development of electronic storage devices involving magnetic fields and surfaces. In accounting, we are concerned not so much with the medium in which the record is stored, but with the organization of the records. Accountants have developed techniques for storing and retrieving financial data.

Accounting systems are intended to *simplify* the information provided to the user; only certain *relevant* aspects of events should be recorded. Specifically, accountants convert every event or condition into monetary terms. For example, if a red truck is purchased, the accountant records its cost, not its color nor its horsepower. Other systems may record these facts because they are relevant to certain other decisions. But accounting systems simplify the information by concentrating on what is relevant to *economic decisions.*

The third function of accounting systems is to *summarize* the facts in order to facilitate the comprehension of complex series of events. For example, 5,000 steps may be involved in the production of a machine. If the accounting system is properly structured, we will be able to state that the cost of producing the machine was between $3,550 and $3,750. This information is more helpful than describing total payroll and raw material costs incurred during a time period when this machine and others were produced. Summarizing the facts helps to determine the selling price of the machine and whether or not to produce another one. A yearly income statement is more helpful (in some cases) than day-by-day descriptions of activities because it provides an *overall* summary of performance.

Instruments of Accounting

Information tends to be very abstract. We therefore try to *symbolize* information so that we can communicate and work with it more easily. For example, the *numeral* 8,231,969 is easier to deal with than the *quantity* 8,231,969. Try to imagine this quantity of dollar bills or automobile tires as a physical amount rather than an abstract number.

Perhaps the most complex symbol accountants use is the balance sheet. This arrangement of words and numerals may be no more than three or four pages; yet it may attempt to describe a large firm that sells thousands of products in hundreds of countries, employs thousands of workers, and occupies hundreds of large buildings.

The basic building block in the accountant's symbolization process is called the *account*—a representation of a thing *(asset, liability, owners' equity)* or an event *(revenue, expense).* An account is extremely abstract and is concerned only with the monetary aspect of the thing or event. As the monetary amount is increased or decreased, the balance of the account is increased or decreased. Thus, an account is much more than a bookkeeping device; it is the basis upon which all accounting information is built. Careful selection of which accounts to include in a system can lead to useful information; imprudent selection can lead to worthless information. Decisions of this kind separate the "accountant" from the "bookkeeper."

Rules of Accounting

Perhaps no other aspect of accounting is more universally misunderstood than its *rules,* or *principles.* These guidelines are extensive and intricate but are nonetheless based on common sense and compromise. Although it may sometimes seem that their only function is to provide employment for accountants, the reason for their existence is *communication.* It is essential to realize that the rules of accounting have pragmatically developed throughout history. Consequently, they are open to further changes as new remedies for their inadequacies are found.

The expression "generally accepted accounting principles" denotes the extensive set of rules, procedures, and conventions accountants use to prepare their reports. The "general acceptance" comes from two major sources: common usage by a large group of people and authoritative pronouncements. The role of the latter has grown dramatically since the late 1950s. This fact is significant for today's student because many more changes can be expected. At the time of this text's publication, the three major authorities are the Financial Accounting Standards Board (FASB), the Securities and Exchange Commission (SEC), and the Cost Accounting Standards Board (CASB). The FASB receives its authority by common consent among the members of the financial community; the SEC and the CASB are empowered by Congress to promulgate rules. The FASB and the SEC are concerned with financial accounting, whereas the CASB deals with accounting procedures used in government contracts. Rules for tax accounting come exclusively from tax laws and their interpretation by the Internal Revenue Service (IRS) and the courts.

Naturally, there is a great deal of congruence between tax rules and financial accounting rules (although there are significant differences as well). But there is no absolute authority that creates rules for management accounting. Each manager and his accountant are free to set up and use whatever system of internal accounting they desire. Unwise choices of information may lead to poor decisions, inadequate profits, or even bankruptcy. Consequently, there is a surprising amount of uniformity in management accounting, which arises from common sense rather than from authoritative edicts. Although we will present alternative approaches to solving a particular management problem, the final choice is based on the decision maker's *own* evaluation of the relative advantages and disadvantages of the alternative techniques.

In the following paragraphs, we will briefly discuss some of the broader general rules of accounting. The impact of each depends on the type of accounting system involved.

SEPARATE ENTITY

Accounting reports are almost always prepared as descriptions of an economic unit or its activities. The nature of the decisions determines the particular unit or entity. If a manager is concerned with the performance of the Polishing Department, he does not want a report describing the operations of the entire factory. Similarly, if a bank is evaluating an independent businessman's credit standing, it would want information on all his activities, not just his insurance agency, or his law practice, or his personal investments. Accounting systems are therefore established to gather and report information about all possible existing entities. This may be an expensive, but *essential* requirement.

TIME PERIODS

For convenience, many reports are constructed at regular intervals. This routine not only promotes efficiency but also reflects the existence of cycles in many business situations. As a consequence, accountants devote much effort to determining not only *what* has occurred, but also *when* it occurred.

An offshoot of this rule is extremely significant in describing net income. The *matching concept* calls for the comparison of rewards *(revenues)* with the efforts *(expenses)* to earn them. If the rewards exceed the efforts by a sufficient amount, *success* is achieved. There is some difficulty in applying this concept because efforts may cover several time periods, and rewards may not be easily tied to the efforts.[2]

MONETARY UNITS

In establishing and operating an account, the magnitude of the event or thing is expressed in terms of a unit of money. The reason behind this convention is the *common denominator* effect of money as a universal descriptor of value. Two significant problems arise from this rule.

First, we must decide what magnitude the number should assume initially and at later dates. In financial accounting, the first problem is solved by using *historical cost*. Management accountants cannot afford such a simplistic approach, as will be seen in later chapters.

Second, we must decide which monetary unit should be used. This problem arises when a firm has transactions occurring in different national currencies, or over time, when the value of a single currency changes.

---

[2] For example, sales may be generated over several years by a single two-month advertising campaign; or a machine may last several years after the date of its acquisition. In both cases, we will probably find it useful to assign the effort to several time periods.

VERIFIABILITY

All information included in reports should be as *factual* as possible to provide a solid basis for decision making. Because financial accounting reports go to outsiders, there is a great deal of emphasis on this aspect and estimates are kept to a minimum. Because managers are mainly concerned with the future, management accounting systems tend to incorporate less factual material. The manager must never mistake opinion for fact, however.

SIGNIFICANCE

Perhaps the most pragmatic of all the rules is the one of *significance,* or *materiality.* Simply, this rule states that insignificant (immaterial) items should not be reported separately. In application, this allows the accountant to take shortcuts and even to leave errors uncorrected if no one will be misled by the resulting information. Not unexpectedly, problems do arise in deciding what is significant or insignificant.

CONSISTENCY

Because accounting reports are frequently compared with similar reports from previous periods, they should be prepared in a consistent manner. Of course, changes for the better should be implemented. Notice that this rule does not extend to cover consistency among firms, but only deals with consistency within a single firm.

CONSERVATISM

The rule of conservatism has enjoyed an important place in financial accounting because it acts to defend the firm against claims that it fraudulently overstated its success or likelihood for success. Simply, this rule calls for the selection among accounting alternatives of the one that has the least beneficial effect on the report. In management accounting, there is no similar external influence that would cause conservatism to be used. Indeed, a manager might choose to have the most optimistic representation instead of, or even in addition to, the most pessimistic.

In closing, we must say that this preceding list is not exhaustive; we have presented only a few of the rules. There are other general rules that might be mentioned, and countless other specific rules that fall under the canopy of "generally accepted accounting principles."

THE ACCOUNTANT

Accounting could not be carried out if there were no *doers* to accumulate, simplify, and summarize the information. Just as there are different types of accounting, there also are different types of accountants with various job descriptions. A useful way to classify them is by their employment.

Public Accountants

The public accountant is an individual who is either self-employed or affiliated with other public accountants. He, or his firm, offers services to the public at large for a fee. The public accountant is a professional, as attorneys or doctors with public practices are.

In order to protect the public against incompetency, each state has established procedures to recognize individuals as *Certified Public Accountants*. The CPA is licensed by one or more states after a rigorous examination of his skills, character, and experience. The certification is a desirable goal for all accountants, whether or not they are in public practice, because it is a widely recognized label of competence and reliability.

Public accountants and their firms offer a mixture of four services. CPAs are most frequently called upon to *audit* the financial statements of their clients in order to add credibility to these statements. *Tax return preparation* and *tax planning* constitute the second major service. Based on their extensive experience, many public accountants offer *management advisory services*. Many individual accountants and smaller firms provide simple *bookkeeping* services. Typically, CPAs do not provide this service because their skills demand too much money to make it economical for their clients.

Government Accountants

Although accountants employed by the government are "public servants," they are not usually referred to as *public* accountants because they do not offer their services directly to the public. There are numerous agencies of local, state, and federal governments that hire accountants. *Tax specialists* are employed to write, interpret, and enforce revenue laws. *Auditors* verify whether or not other agencies are carrying out their duties as established by law. *Budget specialists* assist in the preparation and analysis of planned and actual expenditures of public monies. Numerous other accountants are engaged in other rapidly growing aspects of public service.

Management Accountants

In contrast to public and government accountants, management accountants are affiliated with a single, privately owned firm. Their services are consumed by their employer alone. They may be CPAs even though they are not in public practice. Beginning in the early 1970s, the Institute of Management Accounting (IMA), an agency of the National Association of Accountants (NAA), was specifically founded to award the *Certificate in Management Accounting* (CMA) to individuals who pass a rigorous written examination and meet other requirements. The CMA is not granted by a government body and the holder is not authorized by law to do anything that the nonholder cannot do. The certificate is nonetheless desirable because it denotes competency in a wide variety of skills.

On the whole, management accountants tend to be very specialized. *Internal auditors* examine not only accounting procedures but also managerial effectiveness. *Budget specialists* serve the same function in corporations as they do in government. *Cost accountants* establish and operate systems to determine the cost of producing the firm's products. Larger firms employ *tax specialists* who become intimately familiar with tax laws and make suggestions for minimizing taxes. *Financial accountants* design and operate procedures to prepare the firm's financial statements. Because these accountants lack independence, their statements are audited by public accountants to determine whether or not they comply with generally accepted accounting principles.

It is essential to recognize that the management accountant is *not* a manager. His task is to provide objective information that will assist managers in arriving at the best solutions to their problems. In organization theory, the accountant holds a *staff,* or *advisory,* position rather than a *line,* or *decision making,* one. In practice, this rule is frequently broken, with mixed results. Confusion arises occasionally from the simple fact that the chief management accountant is called the *controller,* despite the fact that he exerts no control over anything except his own staff.

Management accountants, then, are typically in a position to provide requested information or suggestions, but they should rarely establish managerial policy or strategy.

SUMMARY

This introductory chapter is intended to present information and opinions as to what accounting is and how it works. In fundamental terms, accounting provides useful information for those who make economic decisions, including not only managers but also present and potential investors, employees, regulatory agencies, and taxing authorities. Conflicting interests and necessities have brought about the development of three overlapping disciplines of accounting: *management, financial,* and *tax*.

Regardless of the orientation, accounting provides information through processes of *recordkeeping, simplification,* and *summarization*. The chief technique by which accounting serves these processes is *symbolization* of things (assets, liabilities, owner's equity) and events (revenues, expenses).

Accountants work through rules that have developed through compromise and pronouncement. Different interpretations of these *principles* exist among the three disciplines. Several of the more significant, broader rules are: *separate entity, time periods, monetary units, verifiability, significance, consistency,* and *conservatism*.

Accountants can be classified by type of employer: *public, government,* and *management* accountants. Within each category, there are various types of specialists, including experts in auditing, budgeting, and taxes. After a thorough screening process, some accountants receive the designation of Certified Public Accountant from the state government. Another form of recognition is the Certificate in Management Accounting, issued by the non-governmental Institute of Management Accounting.

The accountant's position within a firm should generally be advisory in nature. He may participate in the decision-making process through suggestions, fact finding, and analysis; but he usually should not have final decision-making authority.

QUESTIONS

1. For what purpose does accounting exist in today's business world?
2. Name five types of users of accounting information. Describe briefly why they find the information useful.
3. Name three types of accounting information systems. Why are they different?
4. What are three specific purposes achieved by accounting systems?
5. Why is it necessary to use symbols when describing a firm?
6. What do accounts symbolize?
7. What are "generally accepted accounting principles"?
8. Why is it useful to have information about separate entities?
9. Why is it useful to have reports issued periodically?
10. What is achieved by having reports prepared in monetary units? What problems are encountered in implementing this principle?
11. Why is it useful to have reports that are verifiable? That contain significant information? That are consistent? That are conservative? Are there any disadvantages in these rules?
12. What does it mean to be a Certified Public Accountant? What services are offered by a CPA?
13. What specialties are found among government accountants?
14. What specialties are found among management accountants? What does it mean to receive a Certificate in Management Accounting?
15. What is the role of the management accountant in the organizational structure of a firm?

PROBLEMS

P1-1 Management use of accounting. Sam Browning had started as a small businessman with a few customers who wanted custom cabinets built in their homes. Because of his pleasant personality, high quality craftsmanship, and promptness in meeting schedules, his reputation spread and the demand for his services grew so much that he found it essential to open a small shop, which was eventually replaced by a factory. Browning is now planning to undertake a substantial expansion of his present facilities, using a large loan from a local bank.

a. What kinds of accounting information systems are probably used in Browning's company? To whom does the information go?

b. In what order is it likely that these systems came into existence? How do they differ from each other?

c. What advantages would Browning realize from having an outside auditor examine his system?

P1–2 *Using accounting rules.* For each of these situations, identify which accounting rule or rules would apply, and explain whether or not the rule is being properly applied.

a. Stewart Samuels is a restaurateur who has become very successful through hard work and careful attention to quality and service. He recently opened a second restaurant in another section of town, but has elected to do all his purchasing and cash disbursements out of the original location. He sends food to the second location according to telephoned requests, and writes payroll checks without noting which restaurant the employee works in. Utility and insurance bills are combined for both locations in order to reduce the number of checks written.

b. Matthew Milton operates a small real estate sales and management agency, and has experienced a modest degree of success. His banker recently asked for a set of accounting reports. Milton has undertaken this task himself and has relied upon his memory and his knowledge of appraisal techniques to develop the reports, which will not be audited.

c. Jim Wiley has complained about the uncertainties of his business environment. He writes reasonably successful gothic novels, which usually take place in European locations. He travels abroad, doing background work, for eight to twelve months at a time. He then returns home for two or three years to write his manuscripts. Particularly, he complains that he incurs losses for several years because there are no royalties coming in prior to the publication of his books. However, when the royalties do arrive, he has few expenses to subtract from them.

d. Randy Reed is a consulting engineer and enjoys a reputation as being a good "detail" man. This attribute is reflected in his accounting records which contain very precise entries and are based on carefully computed rates and meticulously generated schedules. For example, his records show that his desk originally cost $184.63 and that over the last five years it has depreciated to a book value of $92.32.

P1–3   ***Financial versus management accounting.***   Mr. Green I. Shade has been the accountant of your father's successful retailing firm for a number of years. You are a recent graduate of the state university's business administration program, and you have been hired as a vice president. You have asked Mr. Shade to provide you with some management accounting information so that you can get around to making several important decisions, but he has responded with a twisted smile of superiority and a shaking of his head. In reply to your latest request, he said, "You should realize that this is only July and you'll have to wait at least until March before I can tell you what the business is doing and where it stands. I don't want to confuse you with the technical jargon, but it's enough for you to understand that our statements are prepared once each year, *after* the year is over. In order to tell you how much income we made in the first half of the year I'd have to either drastically modify our accounting system or make several estimates. The first choice is expensive and violates the general principles of accounting, and the second alternative would be inaccurate. I've kept my job by being accurate *to the penny*! So, you see, there's really nothing I can do to help you."

a.   Do you think Mr. Shade understands the differences between financial and management accounting?

b.   What rules of accounting should be considered in this situation? Are there any *tradeoffs* to be made?

c.   Do you think there is anything you can say to Mr. Shade to change his attitude?

P1–4   ***Using accounting rules.***   In going over some of the statements of your father's firm (see P1–3), you notice that: dividends from a family trust are included as other income; back taxes levied against the firm for the last five years are included as expenses; and insurance and gasoline on your car have been reported as business expenses because they were paid by your father out of company funds. You also notice an expense item labeled *Miscellaneous*. Based on what you have seen in this chapter, are these practices consistent with good accounting theory? Identify which rules seem to have been broken.

Section 1

Management and the Financial Statements

Historically, the financial statements were invented and produced to provide management with information about the firm's performance and condition. In this century, we have seen outsiders' interests in the statements increase, and, ironically, the reduction of their internal usefulness. This section is based on the observation that the manager must be familiar with financial statements for three reasons. First, they contain useful managerial information. Second, management needs to anticipate outside reaction to the statements. They can then take the actions needed to favorably alter future statements or provide *additional* information to clarify the situation. Third, corporate management must regularly report to the stockholders. Without knowledge of the statements and new developments in reporting, management cannot meet these responsibilities.

Chapter 2 provides a capsule description of the main financial statements, Chapter 3 shows several approaches to interpreting them. Chapter 4 analyzes the statement of changes in financial position, emphasizing the management of working capital. Finally, Chapter 5 covers the subject of inflation and the topic of accounting in terms of general purchasing power.

Financial Statements: The End Products

The end products of the accounting system are called *financial statements*. These statements serve the manager in much the same manner as instruments and gauges in an automobile serve the driver. Just as each gauge provides essential data regarding a particular aspect of the automobile's condition or performance, financial statements provide important data regarding the condition and performance of the firm. Managers use this information in evaluating past performance, in predicting future events, and in the decision-making process.

Financial statements also provide useful information for persons not involved with management. Essentially, managers have responsibility for certain assets and they provide reports concerning their effectiveness in using the assets to produce new wealth. Financial statements are the usual medium for reporting to owners, creditors, employees, and government agencies.

Although many firms issue *interim* statements every three or six months, the *annual report* is viewed as the most significant. Annual reports are primarily directed to stockholders but they are usually also available to the interested public, especially potential stockholders. (Specially produced reports, conforming to legal requirements, are submitted to government agencies as necessary. Lenders of large amounts may receive other special reports.)

THE ANNUAL REPORT

The annual report of a corporation usually begins with a letter from the president, summarizing the year's activities.[1] The report uses tables, graphs,

---

[1] When accountants speak of a "year," they usually refer to the company's *fiscal* or *accounting* year, which can be any consecutive 12 months or 52 weeks. It is advantageous for a firm

pictures, and other descriptions of company activities which management believes will be of interest to the readers. For example, it is common to describe new products, new operating divisions, research and development, new construction, new foreign operations, and pollution abatement efforts. Much of this material is designed to convey a favorable public image and consequently may reflect management bias. This portion of the annual report is presented without outside verification.

Financial accounting information is presented at the end of the annual report, generally in three parts: *financial statements, notes to the financial statements,* and the *auditor's opinion,* which is prepared by an independent CPA.

The financial statements of a typical annual report consist of a *balance sheet,* an *income statement,* a *statement of retained earnings,* and a *statement of changes in financial position.* To facilitate comparison, the balance sheet and the income statement frequently present data for the current and the next previous years. It is not unusual to find five- or ten-year summaries of significant financial facts compiled from previous annual reports.

THE BALANCE SHEET

The balance sheet is frequently referred to as a *position statement.* Its purpose is to describe a firm's financial position, or condition, as of a given moment, normally the close of business on the last day of the accounting period. It presents a "picture" of the firm's financial position, similar in concept to a still photograph. It lists balances, as of the closing date, of all asset, liability, and owners' equity accounts *(real accounts).* The statement presents the *size* of these accounts at the particular moment, and does not show anything concerning the *changes* in these accounts from a previous point in time. Consequently, the revenue and expense accounts *(changes* in owners' equity) do *not* appear on the balance sheet.

The balance sheet, then, is *not* the financial position but only a *report* on the financial position because the accounts from which the balances are taken are only symbols. A doctor may collect evidence regarding your health from an X-ray and incorporate it in his report. He then draws an expert's opinion on the state of your health from the report. The report is *not* your health; it is a description of your health through symbols. Likewise, a balance sheet is only a report on the financial *health* of a business—described in symbols and prepared by an *expert.*

Although there are a variety of ways to classify the accounts on a balance sheet, common practice classifies assets as *current, fixed,* and *other;* liabilities are designated as *current* or *long-term.* The classification of owners' equity depends on the form of the business organization (which will be discussed later in this chapter). A balance sheet prepared on this basis is shown in Exhibit 2-1.

---

to select a fiscal year that ends during the low point of its business activity. This arrangement makes it easier to compile the necessary reports from the accounting system.

Current Assets

Current assets have been defined as

> cash and other assets that are reasonably expected to be realized in cash or sold or consumed during the normal operating cycle of the business or within one year if the operating cycle is shorter than one year.[2]

Current assets, then, include cash, accounts receivable, notes receivable, marketable securities that are to be sold within one year, inventories, and prepaid expenses. It is common (but not essential) to list current assets on the balance sheet in the order of the ease with which they can be converted to cash.

The term *cash* is applied to all funds (checks, bills, and coins) that are on hand as well as those that are readily available from a bank account. Although it may clutter the statement, some companies show detailed classifications of cash, such as undeposited receipts, change funds, payroll bank accounts, and general bank accounts. Only cash which is available for use in the ordinary course of business should be included under this heading. Sums which are not readily available, or those which will not be used in ordinary business transactions (such as the cash surrender value of life insurance policies, or amounts held in special funds), should be listed as investments. Significant overdrafts in bank accounts (credit balances) should not be subtracted from other cash accounts but should be shown on the balance sheet as current liabilities.

Companies maintain cash balances in order to provide a *reservoir* from which bills can be paid, to take advantage of special opportunities, and to provide for unexpected emergencies. Although some cash is required to meet these needs, excess cash should not be accumulated. Because cash is a nonearning asset, management should try to put excess sums in the form of marketable securities.

Accounts receivable are amounts owed *to* the company from the sales of goods or services in the ordinary course of its business. These amounts are generally evidenced only by routine sales slips or sales invoices and may or may not earn interest. Some receivables are also nonearning assets and management should therefore adopt credit terms and collection policies that will minimize the time it takes to turn receivables into cash.

In those industries where it is common to sell goods on installment contracts, the resulting receivables are generally classified as current assets even though they may not be collected in full during the next year. They may be designated as *installment accounts receivable,* in order to distinguish them from other receivables.

Notes receivable are similar to accounts receivable, except that they are written promises which mature at specified future dates and virtually always earn interest. Notes often arise in settlement of an account by a customer who wishes to protect his credit record but does not have the cash to make payment within the original terms of sale.

[2] Accounting Principles Board, *Statement No. 4: Basic Concepts and Accounting Principles Underlying Financial Statements of Business Enterprises* (New York: AICPA, 1970), p. 94.

Exhibit 2-1
SATELLITE DISCOUNT STORES
Balance Sheet
December 31, 1977

Assets

Current assets:

Cash			$ 1,120,000
Accounts receivable	$520,000		
Notes receivable	140,000	$ 660,000	
Less: Allowance for doubtful receivables		(10,000)	650,000
Marketable securities			490,000
Merchandise inventory			13,320,000
Prepaid expenses			140,000
Total current assets			$15,720,000

Fixed assets:

Land			$ 890,000
Land improvements		$ 20,000	
Less: Accumulated depreciation		(10,000)	10,000
Buildings		$ 450,000	
Less: Accumulated depreciation		(180,000)	270,000
Equipment		$ 3,300,000	
Less: Accumulated depreciation		(1,270,000)	2,030,000
Intangibles			100,000
Total fixed assets			$ 3,300,000

Other assets:

Investments			$ 240,000
Deferred charges			10,000
Total other assets			$ 250,000
Total assets			$19,270,000

It would be unrealistic to assume that all receivables will ultimately be collected. Consequently, most businesses set up an *allowance for doubtful receivables,* to provide for losses which may arise from customers failing to pay their accounts. The allowance is a *contra,* or negative, asset and is deducted from the receivables on the balance sheet in order to show the net amount of cash likely to be collected.

Marketable securities include such things as stocks, bonds, and treasury bills, which have been acquired by the company and held for a short term (generally less than a year). These investments can usually be converted quite readily to cash and thus serve as a backup reservoir to the cash account.

Inventories include goods which have been acquired or produced for sale to customers. A merchandising firm, such as Satellite Discount Stores, generally has only a *merchandise inventory* account of finished products, ready for sale. A manufacturer, on the other hand, generally has three inventory accounts, each representing the cost of goods in various stages of the manufacturing process. *Raw materials* are goods which have been acquired for

Exhibit 2-1 (cont'd.)
SATELLITE DISCOUNT STORES
Balance Sheet
December 31, 1977

Liabilities and Stockholders' Equity

Current liabilities:

Accounts payable		$ 4,280,000
Notes payable		350,000
Current maturity of long-term debts		110,000
Accrued salaries and wages payable		1,200,000
Accrued interest payable		180,000
Federal and state income taxes payable		380,000
Total current liabilities		$ 6,500,000
Long-term debt:		
Sinking fund bonds—8%, 25-year		$ 420,000
Promissory notes—7%, 20-year		220,000
Mortgage payable		70,000
Total long-term debt		$ 710,000
Other liabilities:		
Deferred federal income tax liability		$ 10,000
Total liabilities		$ 7,220,000
Stockholders' equity:		
Paid-in capital:		
5% preferred stock, $1.00 par value	$ 40,000	
Common stock, $0.50 par value	560,000	
Paid-in capital in excess of par—Common	2,730,000	
Other paid-in capital	650,000	
Total paid-in capital		$ 3,980,000
Retained earnings		8,100,000
		$12,080,000
Less: Treasury stock (60,000 common shares, at cost)		(30,000)
Total stockholders' equity		$12,050,000
Total liabilities and stockholders' equity		$19,270,000

use in the production process. *Finished goods* have been completely process-ed and are now ready for sale. The *goods-in-process* inventory consists of materials in various stages of completion (somewhere between the raw and the finished state).

In a sense, inventories are the lifeblood of a business because they are the major source of revenue. Their value is realized, however, only when they are sold. Thus, management should make every effort to "move" inventory as rapidly as possible.

Prepaid expenses are unexpired costs for which cash has been paid in advance. They usually expire and are *charged off* as expenses in the next accounting period. Some examples of prepaid expenses are rent, insurance, advertising, and office supplies.

Fixed Assets

An asset is classified as *fixed* if it is *not* current and if it is *used* in the operation of a business. The word "used" is emphasized because this characteristic is the major factor that determines whether a noncurrent asset is categorized as *fixed* or *other.*

A fixed asset may have a limited or an unlimited life. It may be *tangible* or *intangible* in nature. Some *tangible* fixed assets are land, land improvements, buildings, machinery, and other equipment. Some *intangible* fixed assets are patents, copyrights, franchises, trademarks, and goodwill. The same basic rules are followed in showing *tangible* and *intangible* assets on a balance sheet: They are both carried at *unamortized cost.* As discussed in Chapter 1, the difficulties of determining the *current value* of assets prevent the accountant's use of that figure in the balance sheet. This reliance on historical costs can weaken the usefulness of the information contained on the balance sheet. To overcome both problems, unaudited footnote disclosure of current values can be provided, and is required for the largest companies.

On the balance sheet, the most permanent *(perpetual life)* assets are commonly listed first, followed by those less fixed in nature *(depreciable).* For example, land, buildings, and equipment would probably be listed in that order, because the land will last longer than the buildings and the buildings longer than the equipment.

The fixed asset caption *Land* is used to describe sites that are currently in use by the firm, such as a parking lot or the site of an existing building. This category generally should not be used to describe property that is held strictly for future use or for sale.

Land improvements include sidewalks, asphalt paving, landscaping, and similar items which increase the value of the land. The costs of these improvements are generally not included in the Land account because of their limited lives.

Buildings should include only those structures currently in *use* by the business, such as offices, factories, warehouses, and sales floors.

Equipment includes productive resources used in the factory, such as office machines, materials handling equipment, and vehicles. The term *machinery* is often used to separately designate factory or production equipment.

Because buildings, machinery, and equipment are subject to depreciation, we generally find the balance of the *accumulated depreciation* shown on the balance sheet. This account is a *contra* fixed asset account, and represents the amount of the asset's costs which has been apportioned to past accounting periods. The difference between the balances of the asset account and the accumulated depreciation account is referred to as the *book value* of the asset.

Intangibles are generally grouped under one subheading on the balance sheet. Theoretically, intangibles may have perpetual or limited life, but financial accountants are required to assume that they have a limited life and to amortize their cost.[3] Unlike the treatment of tangibles, the amount shown for intangibles on the balance sheet is only the net remaining unamortized cost.

[3] *APB Opinion No. 17* states that ". . . the value of intangible assets at any one date eventually disappears and . . . the recorded costs of intangible assets should be amortized by

Other Assets

Any assets which are neither current nor fixed may be listed as *other assets*. The most common are long-term investments, but this classification may include such items as cash surrender value of insurance policies and land held as a future building site.

The caption *deferred charges* basically consists of long-term prepayments. These costs will be charged off against the income of future periods as the benefit they acquired is used up.

Current Liabilities

Current liabilities are obligations of the firm that will be satisfied within a relatively short period of time. The AICPA has provided the following definition:

> Current liabilities include those [liabilities that are] expected to be satisfied by either the use of assets classified as current in the same balance sheet or the creation of other current liabilities, or those expected to be satisfied within a relatively short period of time, usually one year.[4]

Accordingly, current liabilities include accounts payable, notes payable, and accrued payables.

Accounts payable usually constitute the most significant current liability of a firm. This account symbolizes the debts that the company has incurred as a result of purchasing goods on credit.

Notes payable represent the firm's short-term obligations which result from borrowing funds. These obligations usually bear interest and are supported by a written promise to pay at a specified date.

Balance sheets often include a number of *accrued* liability accounts, which arise when the company adjusts its accounts to match expenses with revenues. Examples of accrued liabilities are wages payable, rent payable, federal and state income taxes payable, and similar items.

Current maturities of long-term debts should be included among the current liabilities. For example, mortgage installments that fall due within one year should generally be treated as current liabilities, whereas the remaining installments should be regarded as long-term liabilities.

Long-Term Liabilities

Those liabilities that mature after the current period are designated *long-term liabilities*. This category includes debts which are not due for at least one year, for example bonds payable, mortgages payable, and contracts payable.

---

systematic charges to income over the periods estimated to be benefited . . . and should not be written off in the year of acquisition . . . the period of amortization should not, however, exceed forty years." Accounting Principles Board, *Opinion No. 17: Intangible Assets* (New York: AICPA, 1970), p. 339.

[4] Accounting Principles Board, *Statement No. 4: Basic Concepts and Accounting Principles Underlying Financial Statements of Business Enterprises* (New York: AICPA, 1970), p. 94.

Corporations often incur long-term debts in the form of *bonds*. The 8 percent sinking fund bonds of the Satellite Discount Stores are an example of a *general credit bond*. Long-term debts may be evidenced by *promissory notes,* which originate by borrowing from banks, insurance companies, or other financial institutions. The *mortgage payable* is a long-term obligation for which the company has pledged certain fixed assets as collateral to assure the lender that cash will be made available at the maturity date, even if the property must be sold.

Owners' Equity

There are three major forms of free enterprise businesses: sole proprietorships, partnerships, and corporations. The only accounting differences between the forms are seen in the owners' equity *(capital)* section of the balance sheet.

PROPRIETORSHIPS

The capital section of the balance sheet of a firm owned by a *sole proprietor* consists of only the owner's *Capital* account. The balance of this single account equals the *net* of all investments, withdrawals, and retained income. The account symbolizes the owner's claim against the entity, and thus that portion of his wealth "tied up" in it.

PARTNERSHIPS

Where convenient, the balance sheet of a partnership shows a capital account for each partner. Each of these accounts is similar to the capital account used in the proprietorship. In order to simplify, the balance sheet of a partnership with a large number of partners generally shows only one caption, *Partners' Capital.*[5]

CORPORATIONS

Primarily because of legal requirements, such as those governing the payment of dividends, corporations use several *Stockholders' Equity* accounts. The two major types of owners' equity in the corporation are *paid-in capital* and *retained earnings.*

Paid-in capital represents the claims against assets arising from investments by owners. It is usually segregated into a number of different accounts, which specify the particular source or nature of the claim.

Corporations issue documents known as *stock certificates,* which serve as evidence of ownership in the enterprise. These certificates are often assigned an arbitrary *par value,* which is shown in a *Capital Stock* account. When the stock is issued at a price higher than the par value, the additional amount invested is shown in the *Paid-in Capital in Excess of Par* account (some-

---

[5] Some partnerships have several hundred partners. Peat, Marwick, Mitchell, and Co- Partners, a large public accounting firm, for example, has over 750 partners.

times called *Premium on Stock*). Some companies have more than one class of stock, each representing a different claim on the assets and the earnings. Thus, we may see *Common Stock* and *Preferred Stock* accounts.

When a company acquires previously issued shares of its own stock, the amount paid is recorded in the *Treasury Stock* account. Because acquiring its own stock reduces the claims of the selling owners, the Treasury Stock account is treated as a *contra* account and deducted from the stockholders' equity.

Retained Earnings are normally shown in a single account, which represents the net unsatisfied claim of the owners against the firm's assets arising from profitable operations since its formation. If the balance is negative, the account is referred to as a *deficit* and is shown as a deduction from paid-in capital.

Some companies prefer to "earmark" retained earnings by setting up several retained earnings accounts and indicating the reason why assets were kept (such as, *Retained Earnings Appropriated for Bond Retirement*) rather than distributed to the stockholders.

You should not be confused by the *Retained Earnings* account title. Retained Earnings is *not* an asset account and does not reflect the amount of "funds" the company has. Remember that the asset side of the balance sheet shows the nature of the assets; the Retained Earnings account merely shows a portion of the owners' claims on the assets.

THE INCOME STATEMENT

The income statement describes the results of the operation of a business for a *specified period of time*. By identifying a firm's revenues and expenses, the income statement provides a summary of certain types of events that occurred during the specified period. It helps answer such questions as: Are we earning profits or incurring losses? Why? At what rate? What contributed to our progress? What held us back?

To continue our earlier analogy, the income statement is like a motion picture. Unlike a snapshot that only shows a position at a given moment, the movie shows what took place along the way to that position. Revenue and expense accounts are set up to describe certain aspects of the business activity during the particular period, and their balances are summarized and presented in the income statement. *Net income* is equal to the difference between revenues and expenses.

Because there are different approaches to earning income, we find that there are different ways to construct income statements. Three general types of firms are those that (1) provide services, (2) sell merchandise, and (3) manufacture and sell products.

A Service Enterprise

An income statement for a service enterprise is generally the least complex. This type of organization earns revenue by providing various *services* to the public, in contrast to a merchandising firm that sells *goods*. The income

Exhibit 2-2
SPEEDY CAR WASH
Income Statement
For the Month Ended June 30, 1977

Revenues:			
Washing revenue		$5,250	
Waxing revenue		1,050	
Total revenues			$6,300
Expenses:			
Washing expenses:			
Water	$290		
Washing supplies	420		
Washing wages	800		
Depreciation washing equipment	150	$1,660	
Waxing expenses:			
Waxing supplies	$380		
Waxing wages	450		
Depreciation waxing equipment	120	950	
Other expenses:			
Building rent	$500		
Manager's salary	800		
Miscellaneous expenses	220	1,520	
Total expenses			4,130
Net income before taxes			$2,170
Income taxes			630
Net income			$1,540

statement of the fictional Speedy Car Wash is shown in Exhibit 2-2. Itemized revenues are listed first; detailed expenses are then deducted to arrive at net income before taxes. Finally, income taxes are deducted to compute the net income. This statement provides management with useful information regarding operations. It can be seen, for example, that waxing cars provided only one-fifth as much revenue as did washing cars.

It is helpful to classify expenses according to sources of revenue. The manager can then get some idea of which services are making the greatest contribution. Speedy Car Wash performs two major services: washing and waxing. Accordingly, an attempt has been made to classify expenses according to one of these activities. In doing so, we find some joint expenses that cannot readily be identified directly with either activity (for example, rent on the building in which both activities occur). These joint expenses have been shown as other expenses.

A Merchandising Concern

The income statement of a merchandising concern primarily differs from that of a service enterprise in the portion known as the *trading section*. This difference may be seen in the income statement of Satellite Discount Stores (Exhibit 2-3). The trading section has been identified in the left margin and is more detailed than those usually found in reports to outsiders.

The income statement of a merchandising firm opens with the sales account. This figure reports the amount of revenue that has been earned from

Exhibit 2-3

SATELLITE DISCOUNT STORES
Income Statement
For the Year Ended December 31, 1977

Gross sales		$64,520,000	
Less: Sales returns	$ 710,000		
Less: Sales discounts	510,000	(1,220,000)	
Net sales			$63,300,000
Cost of goods sold:			
Merchandise inventory (January 1, 1977)		$12,200,000	
Purchases	$46,100,000		
Less: Purchase returns	(1,600,000)		
Net purchases	$44,500,000		
Freight-in	2,020,000		
Net cost of goods purchased		46,520,000	
Goods available for sale		$58,720,000	
Merchandise inventory (December 31, 1977)		(13,320,000)	
Cost of goods sold			(45,400,000)
Gross margin			$17,900,000
Selling expenses:			
Sales salaries and commissions	$ 6,900,000		
Advertising expense	1,300,000		
Freight-out and delivery expense	640,000		
Depreciation expense, sales equipment	600,000		
Sales supplies expense	480,000		
Depreciation expense, store building	80,000		
Total selling expenses		$10,000,000	
Administrative expenses:			
Executive compensation	$ 1,960,000		
Office salaries	1,700,000		
Office supplies expense	600,000		
Insurance expense	440,000		
Depreciation expense, office equipment	300,000		
Depreciation expense, office building	40,000		
Total administrative expense		5,040,000	
Total operating expense			(15,040,000)
Operating income			$ 2,860,000
Nonoperating items:			
Deduct: Interest charges		$ (70,000)	
Add: Interest income	$ 24,000		
Dividend income	6,000	30,000	
Net nonoperating items			(40,000)
Net income before taxes			2,820,000
Income taxes			(1,320,000)
Net income			$ 1,500,000

The left margin is labeled "Trading section" spanning the Cost of goods sold area.

Earnings per common share: $1.41

the sale of merchandise. Certain deductions from revenues, such as sales returns and sales discounts, are subtracted from this amount to arrive at *net sales*.

Next, the cost of the merchandise sold during the period (*cost of goods sold*) is deducted. This amount is generally the most significant expense incurred by a merchandising firm, often totaling several times the sum of all other expenses combined. Because control of this expense may be the key to profitability, management is generally interested in a detailed breakdown of this amount. Thus, merchandise inventories, purchases, purchase returns, freight-in, and similar items appear in this section.

Then the cost of goods sold is deducted from net sales to arrive at *gross margin.*[6] This figure is also closely watched by management. It can best be evaluated, however, by expressing it as a percent of net sales—thus, the expression: Our gross margin last year was 42 percent. By expressing the margin as a percentage, management can make meaningful comparisons among operating divisions, as well as among different years. The use and limitations of this ratio will be discussed in Chapter 3.

A listing of expense accounts follows the trading section of the income statement. A common practice in preparing an income statement for a merchandising company is to separate the expenses into *selling* and *administrative* classifications. Selling expenses are directly related to getting the goods from the firm to the customer. All other expenses are administrative.

The income statement of the Satellite Discount Stores has another feature that differs from the simplified Speedy Car Wash statement (Exhibit 2-2). *Operating income* has been computed by considering only those revenues and expenses concerned with the *normal* operations of the business. Those items that do not pertain to operations (in this instance, interest income, dividend income, and interest charges) have been shown separately under the heading *nonoperating* items. This practice is often followed to more accurately analyze and evaluate the profitability of operations.

A Manufacturing Enterprise

The income statement for a firm that manufactures its products differs from a merchandising company's only in the trading section. Specifically, the section shows the *cost of goods manufactured* instead of *purchases.* The computation of cost of goods manufactured figure is presented in a separate schedule that details manufacturing costs (see Chapter 8).

THE STATEMENT OF RETAINED EARNINGS

The *statement of retained earnings* is relatively simple and summarizes the changes that occurred in the corporation's retained earnings during the accounting period. These changes come from three sources: (1) adjustments from prior accounting periods (which must be explained in detail in a footnote); (2) the net income for the period as reported on the income statement; and (3) dividends declared during the accounting period.[7] The beginning retained

---

[6] Gross margin is sometimes referred to as *gross profit.* The latter term is discouraged because it is easily confused with net profit—the difference between revenue and all expenses. Actually, the margin can hardly be referred to as profit because it is only the difference between the primary revenue (sales) and the primary expense (cost of goods sold).

[7] Prior to 1967, it was acceptable for the statement of retained earnings to contain many other items (such as gains and losses from the sale of fixed assets) which must now be described as *extraordinary items* in the income statement. This format is required by the *APB Opinion No. 9,* and came about because many corporations had used the statement of retained earnings as sort of a "garbage dump" to more discreetly disclose those items they apparently did not want to include on the income statement.

Exhibit 2-4
SATELLITE DISCOUNT STORES
Statement of Retained Earnings
For the Year Ended December 31, 1977

Retained earnings, January 1, 1977		$7,120,000
Add: Net income, per income statement		1,500,000
Total		$8,620,000
Less: Dividends		
5% Preferred stock (5% × 40,000 shares		
outstanding × $1 per share par value)	$ 2,000	
Common stock (1,120,000 shares		
outstanding × $0.40 per share)	448,000	(450,000)
Less: Adjustments for prior periods		
Additional depreciation (net of taxes)		(70,000)
Retained earnings, December 31, 1977		$8,100,000

earnings balance should agree with the one reported on the previous year's balance sheet, and the ending figure should agree with the amount shown on the current balance sheet. The statement of retained earnings for Satellite Discount Stores is shown in Exhibit 2-4. In many annual reports, the statement of retained earnings and the income statement are combined.

THE STATEMENT OF CHANGES IN FINANCIAL POSITION

The *statement of changes in financial position* is a relatively new addition to annual reports. As a result of reader demands for the information it contains, its presentation in the financial section of the annual report is required by generally accepted financial accounting principles. The Accounting Principles Board (APB) took this major step because many firms did not provide the information, and because of the lack of consistency in the practices used by those that did include it in the report.[8]

In its simplest sense, the statement is intended to describe how the firm's assets and equities arrived at their present balances from their previous ones. For reasons which we will discuss in Chapter 4, the format of the report provides lists of *sources* and *uses* of *working capital* (which is measured by subtracting current liabilities from current assets). Because one of management's primary activities is controlling the nature and amount of working capital, the statement is useful internally and externally for evaluating past results prior to planning future activities. To complete Satellite's annual report, the statement of changes in financial position is shown in Exhibit 2-5.

---

[8] *APB Opinion No. 19* states: "When financial statements purporting to present both financial position (balance sheet) and results of operations (statement of income and retained earnings) are issued, a statement summarizing changes in financial position should be presented as a basic financial statement for each period for which an income statement is presented." Accounting Principles Board, *Opinion No. 19: Reporting Changes in Financial Position* (New York: AICPA, 1971), p. 373.

Exhibit 2-5

SATELLITE DISCOUNT STORES
Statement of Changes in Financial Position
For the Year Ended December 31, 1977

Working capital generated by:		
Operations		
Operating net income	$1,500,000	
Add: Expense that did not use working capital:		
Depreciation	1,020,000	$2,520,000
Proceeds of sale of fixed assets		430,000
Collection of long-term notes receivable		20,000
Total working capital generated		$2,970,000
Working capital used for:		
Payment of dividends		$ 450,000
Reclassification of long-term debt		100,000
Acquisition of fixed assets		1,184,000
Acquisition of investments		200,000
Total working capital used		$1,934,000
Net increase in working capital		$1,036,000

NOTES TO FINANCIAL STATEMENTS

It is impossible to completely describe all economically significant events and conditions in terms of dollars in the financial statements. Thus, in addition to the president's letter, most financial statements are accompanied by footnotes which disclose facts that do or could have important effects on the company's financial position or the results of its operations. These notes serve either (1) to provide *a more detailed explanation* of an item in the statement, or (2) to disclose significant information that is *not* in the accounting system, and thus *not* in the body of the statement. Although financial accountants consider the footnotes to be a vital part of the statements, many readers pay little or no attention to them because of their apparent complexity and unfamiliar language. This could lead to unfortunate results because significant facts are described in the notes, such as current and pending law suits, major accounting policies, potential tax liabilities, executive stock options, pension plans, and leasing arrangements.

The following example from an actual footnote should demonstrate why so many are not read:

Effective January 1, 1976, in accordance with the Financial Accounting Standards Board statement on translation of foreign currency transactions and foreign currency financial statements, the Company's inventories denominated in foreign currencies have been translated into U.S. dollars by using historical exchange rates, and translation gains and losses have been reflected in the income statement. Although this statement also requires that financial statements for prior periods be restated to reflect the retroactive application of these accounting principles, it is the opinion of management, with the concurrence of its independent auditors, that such restated interim financial statements for 1975 would not be comparable with the current interim financial statements. Under these new accounting rules, the Company's exposure to foreign currency movements is increased, so the scope and nature of appropriate hedging activities is now substantially enlarged from those appropriate under former rules. Retroactive restatement of prior earnings for a quarter, without a hypothetical adjustment for the effects of an expanded hedging program, would be misleading. Accordingly, the 1975 interim earnings are as originally reported.

THE AUDITOR'S OPINION

The financial statements presented to nonmanagers are usually accompanied by an auditor's opinion similar to the following:

> We have examined the balance sheet of the Satellite Discount Stores as of December 31, 1977, and the related statements of income and retained earnings and changes in financial position for the year then ended. Our examination was made in accordance with generally accepted auditing standards, and accordingly included such tests of the accounting records and such other auditing procedures as we considered necessary in the circumstances.
>
> In our opinion, the aforementioned financial statements present fairly the financial position of the Satellite Discount Stores and the results of its operations and the changes in its financial position for the year then ended, in conformity with generally accepted accounting principles applied on a basis consistent with that of the preceding year.[9]

This type of opinion is presented as the result of an audit conducted by an independent CPA firm. Although the auditors are hired by the directors or stockholders and paid by the company, the CPAs must be given "free rein" to conduct the examination and to determine the scope of the audit. They are required by law and by a code of ethics to conduct their examination according to standards set up to protect the public.

It may be interesting to examine the auditor's opinion in several corporate reports; you may find that the reports are almost identical. Is anything wrong ever uncovered? Actually, the auditor invariably finds a number of improper items (such as an expense charged to the incorrect account) and calls them to the attention of the client. Because most managements would like a "clean" report, they agree with the CPA and make the changes necessary to bring the statements in line with generally accepted accounting principles. Thus, the statements presented in the annual report have been *adjusted* so that they do "present fairly" the financial position and the operating results. The auditor does not, of course, require changes if the amounts are immaterial.

[9] Committee on Auditing Procedure, *Statement on Auditing Standards: Codification of Auditing Standards and Procedures No. 1* (New York: AICPA, 1973), p. 81.

On occasion an auditor issues a *qualified* opinion; the "opinion paragraph" should be similar to the following:

Although the proceeds of sales are collectible on the installment basis, revenue from such sales is recorded in full by the Company at time of sale. However, for income tax purposes, income is reported only as collections are received and no provision has been made for income taxes on installments to be collected in the future, as required by generally accepted accounting principles. If such provisions had been made, net income for 1979 and retained earnings of December 31, 1979, would have been reduced by approximately $542,000 and the balance sheet would have included deferred income taxes of approximately $542,000 and current liabilities would have been increased and working capital would have been reduced by the same amount.

In our opinion, except that provision has not been made for additional income taxes as described in the preceding paragraph, the aforementioned financial statements present fairly . . . .[10]

In this instance, the auditor's findings were such that his revising the statements was not sufficient. The events were of such significance that the auditor felt it was necessary to place a limit on the meaning of his opinion.

A *disclaimer* is issued by the auditor when the client limits the auditor's examination, or when he finds things so bad that he cannot render an overall opinion. Again, because of management's need for the "clean" report, cooperation is usually given in the recordkeeping procedures and no limits are placed on the scope of the audit.

Note especially that the auditor does not guarantee the accuracy of the financial statements. If he were to guarantee them without risk, he would have to examine every document and every phase of the business. The cost of such an examination could never be justified in terms of the benefits achieved. The auditor generally limits his audit to: (1) compliance with generally accepted auditing standards and (2) tests he deems necessary under the circumstances. His report represents *only* an expert's opinion on the fairness of the presentation, and is not a certification of truth.

SUMMARY

In this chapter we have been concerned with the end products of a financial accounting system: the four financial statements normally presented in a corporation's annual report.

The *balance sheet* describes the company's financial position *at a given moment of time*. It contains a list of the assets (resources), liabilities (outsider's claims on those assets), and owners' equity (the owners' claims against the assets).

The *income statement* presents the results of operations (revenue and expenses) for a *period of time* (the fiscal or accounting period).

---

[10] Committee on Auditing Procedure, *Statement on Auditing Standards,* pp. 88, 110.

The *statement of retained earnings* itemizes the changes in the retained earnings *during the accounting period*. These changes represent either profits (increases in retained earnings), dividends (decreases in retained earnings), or adjustments to prior periods' earnings.

The *statement of changes in financial position* reports on the sources and applications of the firm's *working capital* (current assets minus current liabilities).

These financial statements are accompanied by notes which clarify the statements and present additional economically significant facts. When an *auditor's opinion* is also presented it indicates that the statements have been examined by an outside expert. An unqualified report informs the reader that the statements present a *fair,* or reasonable, picture of the company. The auditor's opinion is not a guarantee that the statements are precisely correct. The auditor's opinion relates solely to the financial statements and notes thereto and *does not* apply to the president's letter to the annual report.

QUESTIONS

1. Name the primary financial statements prepared by most companies. What types of accounts are reported on each?

2. Why do most corporations prepare annual reports? To whom are these reports directed? What sort of information do they contain?

3. What type of accounting information is contained in a typical corporate report? What assurance does the reader have that this accounting information is free from management bias?

4. Which statement is often referred to as a *position statement*? What account classifications are contained on this statement?

5. Why do firms generally attach notes to published financial statements? What is the nature of the items disclosed?

6. Distinguish among current, fixed, and other assets. Could a single item, such as land, appear under different classifications on two different balance sheets?

7. How should the current installment on a long-term debt be classified on a balance sheet?

8. On the balance sheets of a partnership and a corporation, how do the owners' equity sections differ?

9. What is a *contra* asset account? Give several examples of *contra* asset accounts. How should such accounts be shown on a balance sheet?

10. What is the nature of the retained earnings account? Why don't partnerships and proprietorships have retained earnings accounts?

11. In what way does the income statement of a merchandising concern differ from that of a service enterprise?

12. What is the difference between the operating income and the net income of a firm?

13. What is gross margin? Why is this figure of such importance to a merchandising firm?

14. What accounts enter into the calculation of a company's cost of goods sold? In what section of the income statement does the cost of goods sold account appear?

15. Assume that a company had cost of goods sold of $920,000; beginning inventory of $27,500; selling expenses of $89,000; and goods available for sale of $999,900. What was its ending inventory?

16. The first paragraph of the auditor's report states the "scope" of the audit. What sort of things does the auditor state he has done in the scope of his audit?

17. The second paragraph of the auditor's opinion expresses an *opinion*. To what extent does this opinion represent a *guarantee*?

18. Distinguish between an auditor's report in which the auditor issues a *qualified* opinion and one which represents a *disclaimer*.

EXERCISES

E2–1 *A simple balance sheet.* From the following correct account balances of Saturn Corporation shown as of December 31, 1977, prepare a balance sheet.

	Debit	**Credit**
Accounts payable		$ 100
Accounts receivable	$ 200	
Building	5,000	
Capital stock		4,000
Cash	500	
Equipment	2,000	
Inventory	800	
Mortgage payable		3,000
Retained earnings		1,400
	$8,500	$8,500

E2–2 *The balance sheet equation.* Determine the missing amounts in the following sets of figures. Each line represents a separate balance sheet.

	Assets	**Liabilities**	**Owners' Equity**
a.	$ 10,000	$ 3,500	?
b.	$ 82,900	?	$ 47,300
c.	?	$ 11,900	$ 23,410
d.	$117,772	$120,400	?
e.	$ 59,800	?	$ 48,940
f.	?	$ 47,720	$111,552

E2–3 *An income statement.* From the following data, prepare an income statement for Darling Stores, Inc., for the month of May 1977.

Advertising expense	$ 500
Beginning merchandise inventory	1,000
Ending merchandise inventory	1,200
Income tax expense	1,300
Merchandise purchases	8,000

Sales	$14,500
Salesmen's commissions	1,450
Store rent	300
Office salary	800
Other expenses	400

E2–4 **The trading section.** Prepare the *trading* section of an income statement from these *selected accounts* from the ledger of Harvey's Haven at March 31, 1976, the end of the company's fiscal year. A physical count at that date disclosed an ending inventory of $42,000.

Freight-in	$ 8,200
Freight-out (delivery expense)	6,300
Merchandise inventory (March 31, 1975)	37,000
Purchases	195,000
Purchase returns	6,000
Sales	273,000
Sales discounts	2,000
Sales returns	4,000
Salesman's salary	13,000

E2–5 **Preparing the statements.** Fred Ellsworth has a small business called Fred's Flower Service which provides gardening services to homeowners. He rents all his tools and equipment. These accounts were taken from the company books at the end of July:

	Debit	Credit
Accounts receivable	$1,100	
Capital stock		$2,000
Cash	3,200	
Dividends	500	
Employees wages	600	
Equipment rental	300	
Income tax expense	200	
Retained earnings		1,800
Tree-trimming revenue		800
Yard service revenue		1,300
	$5,900	$5,900

Prepare the following statements for Fred's Flower Service:

a.   Income statement

b.   Statement of retained earnings

c.   Balance sheet *(Hint:* You will have to use your answer from *b.)*

E2–6 **Classifying assets.** Classify the following accounts as (a) current assets, (b) fixed assets, or (c) other assets. List the accounts under each heading in the order in which they should properly be shown in a balance sheet.

1. Accounts receivable
2. Cash
3. Copyright

4. Deferred charge
5. Equipment
6. Factory building

7. Investment in bonds
8. Land (on which building sits)
9. Land (held for future building site)
10. Merchandise inventory

11. Notes receivable (due in 30 days)
12. Notes receivable (due in 3 years)
13. Patents
14. Store building

PROBLEMS

P2–1   *Classifying statement items.* Using the classifications for various sections of the balance sheet and the income statement, arrange the following accounts in proper statement form and indicate on which statement and under which heading each would appear. Classifications for the income statement should include: Revenues, Cost of goods sold, Administrative expenses, Selling expenses, Other income, and Other expenses.

1. Copyrights
2. Accounts receivable
3. Accounts payable
4. Sales
5. Cash in bank
6. Delivery wages
7. Interest earned
8. Mortgage payable (5 years)
9. Capital stock
10. Retained earnings
11. Depreciation expense, office building
12. Purchase returns and allowances
13. Land (held for future use)
14. Revenue received in advance
15. Accumulated depreciation, office building
16. Patents
17. Current installment on mortgage

18. Dividend income
19. Interest payable
20. Equipment
21. Federal income tax liability
22. Property taxes, office building
23. Prepaid rent
24. Unexpired insurance
25. Ending inventory
26. Long-term investments
27. Accrued salaries
28. Administrative salaries
29. Land
30. Freight-in
31. Commissions earned
32. Interest expense
33. Freight-out
34. Salesmen's commissions

P2–2   *Preparing financial statements.* The correct account balances of Wilkenson Widget Corporation as of December 31, 1977, are shown below.

	Debit	Credit
Accounts payable		$ 22,320
Accounts receivable	$ 59,200	
Accumulated depreciation, building		15,350
Advertising expense	5,920	
Building	250,000	
Capital stock		200,000
Cash	12,922	
Depreciation expense, building	10,000	
Freight-out	2,300	
Insurance expense	4,800	
Interest expense	950	

	Debit	Credit
Inventory (December 31, 1976)	$ 22,489	
Land	40,000	
Long-term investments	22,921	
Miscellaneous expenses	3,200	
Mortgage payable		$ 20,000
Purchases	110,300	
Purchase discounts		1,492
Retained earnings (December 31, 1976)		54,141
Sales		285,300
Supplies	3,255	
Supplies used	11,111	
Taxes	7,300	
Transportation-in	1,995	
Wages and salaries	29,940	
	$598,603	$598,603

Inventory (December 31, 1977): $29,585

Required:

a. Prepare an income statement in good form.

b. Prepare a balance sheet in good form. (*Hint:* You will have to adjust the retained earnings balance.)

P2–3   The trading section.

Part 1:

Determine the missing amounts in the following sets of figures. Each vertical row represents a separate situation. Use a minus sign to indicate a loss.

	a	*b*	*c*	*d*	*e*	*f*
Sales	70,000	105,000	125,000	(8)	90,000	(14)
Beginning inventory	40,000	45,000	60,000	40,000	(11)	40,000
Purchases	30,000	(4)	(6)	70,000	60,000	50,000
Ending inventory	(1)	55,000	40,000	35,000	45,000	30,000
Cost of goods sold	55,000	60,000	(7)	(9)	(12)	(15)
Gross margin	(2)	(5)	55,000	40,000	40,000	40,000
Expenses	20,000	25,000	35,000	35,000	(13)	(16)
Net income (loss)	(3)	20,000	20,000	(10)	20,000	−5,000

Part 2:

The following account balances are found in the ledger of a merchandising concern:

Sales	$13,220
Purchases	9,860
Sales returns and allowances	420
Purchase returns and allowances	160
Freight-in	190
Freight-out	320
Purchase discounts	130

Selling expenses	$ 650
Inventory (August 1, 1977)	5,140
Inventory (August 31, 1977)	5,560

Prepare the *trading section* of the income statement.

P2–4 Preparing financial statements. The correct account balances for the Watts Watts Manufacturing Company are presented on page 39. Required:

a. Prepare an income statement in good form.

b. Prepare a classified balance sheet in good form. (*Hint:* You will have to adjust the retained earnings balance.)

P2–5 Preparing financial statements. The following data were taken from the accounts of the Success Corporation. Except where otherwise noted, the figures all represent correct balances as of December 31, 1977.

Accounts payable	$24,950
Accounts receivable	41,490
Accrued salaries	1,860
Accumulated depreciation, store fixtures	2,790
Advertising	880
Allowance for doubtful accounts	7,090
Bad debt expense	870
Cash	8,690
Common stock ($50 par value)	33,300
Depreciation expense, store fixtures	780
Freight-out	730
Income tax	1,500
Land	24,820
Long-term investments	10,460
Merchandise inventory (January 1, 1977)	47,420
Merchandise inventory (December, 31, 1977)	48,720
Mortgage payable	26,280
Office expenses	2,220
Office salaries	11,540
Prepaid rent	850
Purchases	23,360
Rent revenue	1,960
Retained earnings (January 1, 1977)	44,550
Sales	82,680
Salesmen's commissions	38,890
Store fixtures	7,850
Store rent	2,040
Transportation-in	1,070

Required:

a. Prepare an income statement for the year ending December 31, 1977.

b. Prepare a classified balance sheet as of December 31, 1977, in good form.

(P2–4)   **WATTS WATTS MANUFACTURING COMPANY**
Adjusted Trial Balance
June 30, 1977

Cash	$118,690	
Marketable securities at cost (market value, $125,870)	123,950	
Accounts receivable	86,430	
Allowance for doubtful accounts		$ 9,760
Prepaid insurance	1,840	
Investment in stock of Lance Company*	98,650	
Land	57,130	
Buildings	148,960	
Accumulated depreciation, buildings		66,540
Equipment	251,720	
Accumulated depreciation, equipment		43,600
Goodwill	72,000	
Cash surrender value of life insurance on company officers	7,780	
Accounts payable		40,930
Notes payable		16,500
Accrued wages and other expenses		21,370
Estimated income taxes payable		25,900
Notes payable (due June 30, 1980)		350,000
Capital stock ($10 par value)		325,000
Premium on stock		23,600
Retained earnings (June 30, 1976)		42,430
Gross sales		1,253,800
Sales returns and allowances	18,180	
Sales discounts	9,930	
Merchandise inventory (July 1, 1976)	148,640	
Purchases	771,460	
Purchase returns and allowances		18,580
Freight-in	20,930	
Salesmen's salaries	36,800	
Advertising	17,890	
Shipping department expense	19,130	
Delivery expense	16,720	
Depreciation, store and equipment	2,990	
Officers' salaries	31,640	
Office salaries	18,900	
Taxes	6,170	
Insurance	1,820	
Utilities	8,440	
Depreciation, office and office equipment	4,350	
Interest and dividends on investments		5,250
Rent revenue		4,800
Interest expense	12,750	
Estimated income tax charges	134,170	
	$2,248,060	$2,248,060

Merchandise inventory (June 30, 1977): $202,500

*Lance Company stock is being held as a long-term investment.

P2–6 *Preparing the income statement.* The following amounts were taken from the books of the Eldon Corporation. The accounts are listed in alphabetical order.

Advertising	$ 680
Bad debts expense	210
Depreciation expense, delivery equipment	300
Depreciation expense, office	1,600
Freight-in	230
Freight-out	960
Income tax	8,960
Insurance expense	70
Interest earned	210
Interest expense	70
Merchandise inventory (beginning)	1,730
Miscellaneous selling expenses	270
Office salaries	3,800
Purchase returns and allowances	2,000
Purchases	29,000
Rent revenue	1,300
Sales	?
Sales discounts	300
Sales returns and allowances	200
Salesmen's commissions and salaries	2,700
Store rent	2,450
Taxes (other than income)	380

Net income after taxes was $13,400, and the ending merchandise inventory was $1,850.

Required:

From the given facts, you are to prepare an income statement in good form. Notice that you will have to compute the amount of gross sales.

P2–7 *Identifying errors.* You are the auditor of Giggit Corporation and you locate the following in the company accounts as of December 31, 1977:

1. An error was made in counting the December 31, 1977, merchandise inventory. The merchandise stored in one entire room of the warehouse building was omitted from the count causing the inventory on that date to be undervalued by $32,000.

2. The company has charged all freight bills (for both freight-in and freight-out) to the Freight-in account. Your examination of the supporting freight invoices disclosed that $10,900 pertains to freight-in and $8,440 pertains to freight-out.

3. A purchase discount in the amount of $200 has not been recorded. The offsetting error is in the Accounts Payable account.

4. A purchase in the amount of $770 was made (and received) in 1977 but was not recorded until January 1978. The purchase

was properly recorded but in the wrong accounting period.

5. In extending the inventory figures at the end of 1976 (December 31, 1976) a math error was made: 500 giggits which actually cost $10 each were shown in inventory at a cost of $1 each.

6. The company purchased land during 1977 for $10,000 and erroneously charged the amount to the Purchases account instead of to the Land account.

Required:

a. Describe the effect (overstatement or understatement and amount) of each error on the 1977 net income.

b. Describe the effect of each error on the retained earnings reported at the end of 1977. (For example, is the retained earnings figure in error? If so, by what amount?)

c. Explain which, if any, of the above errors, if not corrected, would affect the income reported for 1978. How?

P2–8 **Identifying errors.** Mr. I.K. Knowitall is the sole owner of the Big Sky Gas station. Early in January he decided to make an addition to his station and went to the local bank to borrow the money. The banker, Mr. Bright, said, "We'd be happy to do business with you, but we'll need to have a look at your financial statements in order to agree on the amount and terms of the loan. If you'll bring me your balance sheet and income statement for this past year, I'll look them over so we can talk further about the loan."

Mr. Knowitall had never had a balance sheet or income statement, but didn't want the bank to know this so he replied, "OK, Mr. Bright, I'll have to dig them out of my files and that might take a little time. Will it be all right to bring them to you next week?" Mr. Bright agreed, and Mr. Knowitall went back to his station to "find" the balance sheet and income statement.

Mr. Knowitall had taken bookkeeping in high school and so he thought he knew all there was to know about preparing financial statements. He rummaged through old records and found that he had bought the station for $125,000 just 2 years earlier. He paid $25,000 cash and signed a 15-year mortgage note for the balance. The station was expected to last 40 years with a $25,000 salvage value. When the business was formed (2 years ago), Mr. Knowitall also contributed an old tow truck which had a market value of $2,500 at that date. He estimated the truck had an additional 10 years of useful life with no expected salvage value. Additional tools and equipment for doing motor tuneups and minor auto repairs were purchased just 1 year ago at a cost of $1,500. This equipment should last 5 years with no salvage value.

The annual statement from the mortgage company shows that $9,680 interest has accrued against the mortgage note. In addition, a $3,470 principal installment will be due in 1 month. The remaining $93,300 balance on the note will be paid off in installments, payable from 1 to 13 years hence. There are 3 fulltime employees besides the owners. An examination of the cash records for the past year discloses the following:

Receipts:

Gas	$110,000
Lubrication	20,000
Oil and tires	40,000
Tuneups	60,000

Disbursements:

Owner's drawings	$ 15,000
Employees' wages	30,000
Gas	100,000
Oil and tires	22,000
Grease	5,000
Parts	10,000
Utilities	3,600
Insurance	2,400

The Cash account had a balance of $5,000 at year's end. Mr. Knowitall estimated inventories were about $51,000 at the end of each of the last 2 years. At year's end, customers still owed balances in the amount of $10,000 on charge sales. No charge sales were made during the company's first year in business. Experience of other stations in the area shows that about 2½ percent of customers' accounts prove uncollectible. Of the $60,000 cash received for tuneups, $10,000 represents advances from customers for repairs which have not yet been performed. This work is expected to be completed within 2 or 3 months. The $2,400 insurance premium was paid 1 year ago and covers a 3-year period.

After much effort, Mr. Knowitall constructed the balance sheet and income statement shown on page 43.

As an afterthought, Mr. Knowitall decides that it might be a good idea to have an accountant check his balance sheet and income sheet before Mr. Bright sees them.

Required:

a. Prepare a corrected income statement.

b. Prepare a correct balance sheet. *(Hint:* You will need to "force" Mr. Knowitall's Capital account.)

c. Determine whether or not you would recommend that Mr. Bright lend Mr. Knowitall the money. Assume that Mr. Bright's requirement for loan approval is a current ratio (current assets divided by current liabilities) of 2.0 or more. Show calculations.

BIG SKY GAS
Balance Sheet

Current assets:		Current liabilities:	
Cash	$ 5,000	Accounts payable	$ 4,000
Accounts receivable	10,000	Accumulated	
Inventories on hand	51,000	depreciation	2,000
Accrued interest on		Reserve for bad debts	250
building note	9,680		
Fixed assets:		Long-term liabilities:	
Station	125,000	Current installment	
Equipment	1,500	on building note	3,470
Other assets:			
Tow truck	2,500	Owner's equity:	
Prepaid insurance	2,400	Owner's equity	197,360
	$207,080		$207,080

BIG SKY GAS
Income Statement
As of December 31

Revenues:		
Gas	$120,000	
Oil and tires	40,000	
Lubrication	20,000	
Tuneups and maintenance	60,000	
Total revenues		$240,000
Expenses:		
Knowitall drawings	$ 15,000	
Employees' wages	30,000	
Cost of gas	100,000	
Cost of oil and tires	22,000	
Cost of lubrication	5,000	
Cost of tuneups, maintenance, and parts	10,000	
Utilities	3,600	
Insurance	2,400	
Total expenses		188,000
Profit		$ 52,000

P2–9 *Auditing problems.* You are an independent CPA employed by the firm Scrooge and Morley, CPAs. You encounter the following situations (each independent of the other):

1. The company you are auditing has total assets of $15 million and a reported net income of $1.6 million. The president asked the purchasing agent to buy an automatic garage-door opener for $189 for the president's residence. He realized this was a personal expense but felt he could get a better price by buying it through the company. The garage-door opener was purchased by the company and then installed by the president's assistant on company time. The assistant earns $250 per week and spent

1 day on the project. The company accountant charged the opener to factory overhead and the assistant's wages to administrative salary expense.

2. Partridge Company shows merchandise inventory at the end of the audit period of $375,000 and total assets at that date of $2.5 million. A mistake is found in extending the inventory figures and you note that the correct calculations show an inventory at that date of only $251,000. Detecting this error you become suspicious about other figures in the inventory. You feel some inventory which is stored in a warehouse should be recounted. The president informs you that the materials in the warehouse are "classified" and refuses to give you access for security reasons. He indicates he will be happy to have company personnel verify the previous count. Regarding the extension error you found, the president feels that because the error wasn't found until the subsequent year that no adjustment should be made for the year in question. He explains that an appropriate adjustment will be made in the following year because that is when the error was discovered.

Required:

a. Indicate what accounting changes, if any, you would recommend to the company.

b. Indicate, for each of the unrelated situations, whether you would issue a *clean* report, a *qualified* opinion, or a *disclaimer*, assuming that the company refuses to make the changes you proposed in *a*. In each instance, explain the reasons for your choice.

c. Write a brief auditor's opinion to cover situation 1.

CHAPTER

3

Interpreting Financial Statements

In Chapter 2 we compared financial statements to the gauges on an automobile's instrument panel. But what value does a gauge have if the operator doesn't know how to read it? The fact that an unused instrument has no value is apparently what caused automobile manufacturers to replace some of them with "idiot lights." Because many drivers didn't understand how to read the gauges, the manufacturers felt it would be better to put in a light and to instruct the driver to "turn off the motor and get help if the light comes on."

Unfortunately, modern business is far too complex to operate with "idiot lights." A successful manager must rely on many instruments, and he *must* understand what each *will* and *will not* tell him. Operating a modern business more closely resembles the command of a modern spacecraft or a huge passenger jet than it does the operation of an automobile. Their instrument panels include a variety of switches, scopes, and gauges which monitor position and performance and which permit the commander to change the course of the craft. Often the flight control process is a team effort as it is with modern management.

The manager must understand the tools and resources that are available to assist him in managing and controlling the business. This chapter introduces the student to some refinements in financial statements and familiarizes him with their purposes and limitations. Mastery of business management will come only as the manager learns to control the operation of the business by successfully reading the instruments and reacting to their messages.

Our discussion will center on three major techniques that managers can use to gain insight into the operations of their businesses and to enhance the usefulness of the financial statements: *horizontal analysis, vertical analysis,* and *financial ratio analysis.*

45

HORIZONTAL ANALYSIS

Horizontal analysis is accomplished by listing financial statements for two different periods, or at two different points in time, and then computing the differences between the two statements. For example, suppose sales during the current year were $250,000, and $210,000 for the previous year. Horizontal analysis will show an increase in sales of $40,000, or 19 percent over the previous year.[1] Horizontal analysis can also be useful in comparing actual figures with budgeted figures. Suppose our company set a goal to achieve a sales volume during the year of $480,000. Actual sales for the year were $455,000, or 95 percent of our goal.

Horizontal analysis normally refers to complete comparative statements rather than to individual items such as sales. The figures from these statements are listed in adjoining columns, with the current figures first. A net dollar change column is then shown, followed by a percentage change column. The percentage change is calculated by dividing the net dollar change by the older of the two figures.

Exhibit 3-1 shows horizontal analysis applied to the balance sheet of the Millit Manufacturing Company. The change columns indicate the net changes that have taken place during the year 1977 in balance sheet accounts. The first of these columns shows the change in dollar amounts and the second shows the change in percentage terms. These latter figures are often useful to place the change in proper perspective. For example, we note a 46 percent increase in Millit's current assets during a period when the total assets increased only 16 percent. This would indicate a change of major proportions in the ratio of current assets to total assets. Further analysis discloses that the marketable securities account is the only current asset that increased at a rate greater than either total current assets or total assets. Although the change in the marketable securities account explains most of the increase in current assets, the rate (892 percent) is somewhat misleading because of the low base figure.

Exhibit 3-2 shows horizontal analysis applied to the income statement of the Millit Manufacturing Company. It is often informative to analyze such a statement in order to relate the percentage change in sales to other changes. For example, Millit Manufacturing Company experienced only an 11 percent increase in sales during 1977 and yet enjoyed a 24 percent increase in net income. Analysis of changes in other items discloses that depreciation remained almost constant, selling expenses increased 15 percent, administrative expenses increased 6 percent, while other expenses decreased 11 percent. These figures indicate that the company increased its profit rate by coupling an increase in sales with a less than proportionate increase in expenses.

---

[1] The student should be cautioned at this point that figures presented in conventional financial statements are *not* normally adjusted for price-level changes (see Chapter 5).

Exhibit 3-1
MILLIT MANUFACTURING COMPANY
Horizontal Analysis of Balance Sheet
December 31, 1976 and 1977

Assets	1977 (in thousands)	1976 (in thousands)	Amount of Change (in thousands)	Percent of Change
Current assets:				
Cash	$ 42,490	$ 47,630	$ (5,140)	(10.79)
Marketable securities	129,780	13,080	116,700	892.20
Accounts receivable	125,050	119,240	5,810	4.87
Inventories	104,090	92,840	11,250	12.12
Prepaid expenses	7,520	8,200	(680)	(8.29)
Total current assets	$408,930	$280,990	$127,940	45.53
Fixed assets:				
Land	$ 50,300	$ 50,300	$ -0-	-0-
Buildings and equipment	901,800	888,600	13,200	1.49
Less: Accumulated depreciation	(414,800)	(409,640)	(5,160)	(1.26)
Total fixed assets	$537,300	$529,260	$ 8,040	1.52
Other assets	$ 22,900	$ 24,100	$ (1,200)	(4.98)
Total assets	$969,130	$834,350	$134,780	16.15
Liabilities and Stockholders' Equity				
Current liabilities:				
Accounts payable	$ 86,450	$ 78,520	$ 7,930	10.10
Wages payable	6,680	1,640	5,040	307.32
Taxes payable	63,770	55,470	8,300	14.96
Total current liabilities	$156,900	$135,630	$ 21,270	15.68
Long-term liabilities:				
Bonds payable	$100,000	$ -0-	$100,000	-0-
Mortgage payable	54,300	55,110	(810)	(1.47)
Total long-term liabilities	$154,300	$ 55,110	$ 99,190	179.99
Total liabilities	$311,200	$190,740	$120,460	63.15
Stockholders' equity:				
Capital stock, $1 par	$ 50,000	$ 50,000	$ -0-	-0-
Other paid-in capital	63,300	63,300	-0-	-0-
Retained earnings	544,630	530,310	14,320	2.70
Total stockholders' equity	$657,930	$643,610	$ 14,320	2.22
Total liabilities and stockholders' equity	$969,130	$834,350	$134,780	16.15

In analyzing horizontally presented statements, the manager should carefully examine each relationship in order to gain insight into trends and areas of possible strength and weakness. He should ask such questions as: What is the meaning of this change? What would cause these relationships to occur? With increased knowledge about the relationship between accounting and management, the student will gradually develop the ability to pinpoint the most meaningful relationships and will learn how to react to a given occurrence.

Exhibit 3-2
MILLIT MANUFACTURING COMPANY
Horizontal Analysis of Income Statement
For the Years Ended December 31, 1976 and 1977

	1977 (in thousands)	1976 (in thousands)	Amount of Change (in thousands)	Percent of Change
Net sales	$942,040	$850,090	$ 91,950	10.82
Less: Cost of goods sold	529,990	479,310	50,680	10.57
Gross margin	$412,050	$370,780	$ 41,270	11.13
Expenses:				
Depreciation expense	$ 57,220	$ 57,710	$ (490)	(0.85)
Selling expense	37,020	32,060	4,960	15.47
Administrative expense	140,100	132,330	7,770	5.87
Other expenses	1,070	1,200	(130)	(10.83)
Total expenses	$235,410	$223,300	$ 12,110	5.42
Operating income	$176,640	$147,480	$ 29,160	19.77
Interest charges	3,080	750	2,330	310.67
Net income before taxes	$173,560	$146,730	$ 26,830	18.29
Income taxes	88,700	78,340	10,360	13.22
Net income	$ 84,860	$ 68,390	$ 16,470	24.08

VERTICAL ANALYSIS

Financial statements can also be analyzed *vertically*. Such statements are sometimes referred to as *common-size* because each item is expressed in terms of a percentage of a common base number. On a balance sheet, each component is expressed as a percentage of *total assets*; on an income statement *net sales* is used as the base. Vertical analysis is particularly useful for comparing several companies within the same industry or for comparing different divisions within a company because, despite differences in size, the analysis places them all on *comparable* terms. If vertical analysis reveals, for example, that advertising costs represent 2 percent of net sales in one branch and 5 percent of net sales in another branch, it has called management's attention to an area which may need investigation.

Millit's common-size balance sheet is shown in Exhibit 3-3 and its common-size income statement in Exhibit 3-4. Actually, these statements are nothing more than series of ratios. Note, for example, that only 4 percent of Millit's assets, as of December 31, 1977, were in the form of cash, while 55 percent of the firm's assets were tied up in fixed assets. We might ask questions about any item on the balance sheet: How do these figures compare with those of other companies in the industry? Does Millit Manufacturing Company have too large a proportion of its total assets invested in fixed assets? Does the company have a ratio of current assets to total assets that is too large? Does the firm have excess "liquid" funds? Why is there a large investment in current assets? Is inventory too large or too small? Later in this chapter we will discuss some *yardsticks* which might help the manager answer such questions.

Exhibit 3-3
MILLIT MANUFACTURING COMPANY
Vertical Analysis of Balance Sheet
December 31, 1977

Assets	(in thousands)	Percent of Total Assets
Current assets:		
Cash	$ 42,490	4.38
Marketable securities	129,780	13.39
Accounts receivable	125,050	12.90
Inventories	104,090	10.74
Prepaid expenses	7,520	0.78
Total current assets	$408,930	42.20
Fixed assets:		
Land	$ 50,300	5.19
Buildings and equipment	901,800	93.05
Less: Accumulated depreciation	(414,800)	(42.80)
Total fixed assets	$537,300	55.44
Other assets:	$ 22,900	2.36
Total assets	$969,130	100.00
Liabilities and Stockholders' Equity		
Current liabilities:		
Accounts payable	$ 86,450	8.92
Wages payable	6,680	0.69
Taxes payable	63,770	6.58
Total current liabilities	$156,900	16.19
Long-term liabilities:		
Bonds payable	$100,000	10.32
Mortgage payable	54,300	5.60
Total long-term liabilities	$154,300	15.92
Total liabilities	$311,200	32.11
Stockholders' equity:		
Capital stock, $1 par	$ 50,000	5.16
Other paid-in capital	63,300	6.53
Retained earnings	544,630	56.20
Total stockholders' equity	$657,930	67.89
Total liabilities and stockholders' equity	$969,130	100.00

FINANCIAL RATIO ANALYSIS

A *financial ratio* is merely a comparison, in ratio or percentage form, of two significant figures taken from financial statements. Actually, vertical analysis, discussed in the previous section, falls under the heading of financial ratios. For example, the number expressing cash as a percent of total assets, as in vertical analysis, might just as easily be called the *ratio of cash to total assets*. The number of possible financial ratios is virtually limitless; we will consider here only some of the more important ones.

Limitations of Ratios

A word of caution about the use of ratios, in general, is important at this point. Ratios must be used for what they are—*financial tools*. Too often they are looked upon as *ends* in themselves rather than as the *means to an*

Exhibit 3-4

MILLIT MANUFACTURING COMPANY
Vertical Analysis of Income Statement
For the Year Ended December 31, 1977

	(in thousands)	Percent of Net Sales
Sales	$942,040	100.00
Less: Cost of goods sold	529,990	56.26
Gross margin	$412,050	43.74
Expenses:		
Depreciation expense	$ 57,220	6.07
Selling expense	37,020	3.93
Administrative expense	140,100	14.87
Other expenses	1,070	0.11
Total expenses	$235,410	24.99
Operating income	$176,640	18.75
Interest charges	3,080	0.33
Net income before taxes	$173,560	18.42
Income taxes	88,700	9.42
Net income	$ 84,860	9.01

end. The value of a ratio should not be regarded as *good* or *bad* per se. It may be an *indication* that a firm is weak or strong in a particular area, but it must never be taken as *proof*.

Another weakness of financial ratios stems from the fact that they are generally computed directly from the company's financial statements, *without adjustment*. Conventional financial statements (prepared in accordance with generally accepted accounting principles) have a number of serious weaknesses that the manager must consider if his ratios are to be meaningful. For example, accepted accounting practice *does not* provide for inclusion of all leased properties as assets, nor of obligations arising from these long-term leases as liabilities in the financial statements.[2] Suppose you are the president of a company that operates two department stores. One store is leased and the other is owned. Managers are evaluated on the basis of the profits they generate in relation to the assets they have been given. Logic would dictate that both managers should be held accountable for their store buildings even though the leased one may not be shown on the balance sheet. Yet ratios calculated from conventional statements will not show this. Thus, the manager must be alert to deficiencies in accounting practice which may cause ratios to be uninformative.

A second weakness in conventional reporting stems from the problem generated by the changing value of the dollar, or *inflation*. Conventional financial statements are prepared under a constant-size dollar assumption, which, of course, is *not* valid. Ratios taken from conventional statements can be grossly in error because they have failed to consider the changing value of the dollar. (Some attempts to deal with this problem are discussed in Chapter 5.) Needless to say, managers must exercise care in interpreting

[2] The FASB issued an exposure draft on July 22, 1976, which, if adopted in its proposed form, will greatly increase lease disclosure. (See discussion of capital leases in Chapter 16.)

ratios calculated from figures which have not been adjusted for price-level changes. For example, in Exhibit 3-1, Millit's inventories increased by over 12 percent during 1977. It is quite possible (and even likely) that the physical volume increase in inventories was very small and that the apparent increase is nothing more than increases in the prices Millit paid for their inventories.

Certainly one of the most serious weaknesses of ratio analysis is the fact that ratios are a *composite* of many different figures—some covering a time period, others an instant of time, and still others are averages. It has been said that "a man that has his head in the oven and his feet in the icebox is, on the average, comfortable"! Many of the figures used in ratio analysis are no more meaningful than the average temperature of the room in which this man sits! A balance sheet figure shows the balance of the account at *one moment of one day,* and certainly may not be representative of the typical balance during the year. Such a sample may not be representative of the real situation for several reasons.

First, the balance may be as it is by chance—1 day out of 365. Second, the selection of the end of the fiscal year usually coincides with the low point in business activity. Third, the balance may not be representative because of pure manipulation—management may "window-dress" the year-end figures to look better.

Because of the limitations of financial ratios and the uncertainties surrounding the general business climate, some managers refuse to use ratios and, instead, rely solely on their own intuition. Like rheumatic weather forecasters, these managers disregard available signs, gauging a company's financial position solely by a "feeling in their bones." The following statement relegates this "hunch" method to its proper place:

> A man may say, if he likes, that the moon is made of green cheese: that is an hypothesis. But another man who has devoted a great deal of time and attention to the subject, and availed himself of the most powerful telescopes and the results of the observations of others, declares that in his opinion it is probably composed of materials very similar to those of which our own earth is made up; and that is also only a hypothesis. But I need not tell you that there is an enormous difference in the value of the two hypotheses. That one which is based on sound scientific knowledge is sure to have a corresponding value; and that which is mere hasty random guess is likely to have little value. Every great step in our progress in discovering causes has been made in exactly the same way as that which I have detailed to you. . . . It is in these matters as in the commonest affairs of practical life: the guess of the fool will be folly, while the guess of the wise man will contain wisdom. In all cases you see that the value of the result depends on the patience and faithfulness with which the investigator applies to his hypothesis every possible kind of verification. . . .[3]

---

[3] Thomas Henry Huxley, as quoted by Roger E. Ballard and Allan A. Gilbert, in "How to Quantify Decision-Making," *Business Horizons* (Winter 1958), p. 79.

So it is with the task of financial analysis: The manager is still working only with hypotheses to which he must apply every available test. Although ratios may never transform a given hypothesis into a fact, they may well distinguish the "fool" from the "wise man." If their limitations and weaknesses are properly considered, ratio analysis can be a useful management tool. There will probably never be a substitute for skilled judgment in the field of management, nor for the successful manager who will continue to utilize every available tool in exercising his judgment.

Statement analysis is meaningful only when approached from the standpoint of the individual who is taking a particular action (for example, investing, promoting, firing). What information from the statements will be meaningful in relation to a specific decision? What is the person trying to learn about the company or branch that he is attempting to evaluate? What ratios might assist him in this evaluation? The student should refrain from merely memorizing or applying a "cookbook" technique to the ratios cited here; instead, in each case, he should ask himself who might use this ratio and what the user would be trying to learn.

STANDARDS FOR COMPARISON

The manager must also have some means of evaluating the ratios which he calculates. How does he know if the value describes a good or a bad condition? At least four yardsticks are commonly used for comparison: (1) rules of thumb, (2) the company's own experience (prior years), (3) other companies in the same industry, and (4) a standard set by management (a budget).

Although widely used, many rules of thumb should be avoided. Financial analysis is an individual matter and a value for a ratio which is perfectly acceptable for one company or industry may be totally inadequate for another.

It is sometimes helpful to compare a company's ratios with those computed for the same company at an earlier date. Is a particular ratio improving over time? What trends in financial ratios are evidenced in a particular firm over a five-year period?

A third yardstick which might be useful in evaluating a company's ratios is how our firm compares with similar companies in the industry. Trade associations, government agencies, and financial advisory firms can often provide useful data for comparative purposes.

Finally, a company may compare its ratios with standards established by management; this practice probably provides the most meaningful comparisons. Simply because a ratio is better this year than it was last year does not mean that we can conclude it is good. Nor does the fact that our company's ratio is better than the industry average mean it is good. Where are our ratios compared to *where they should be?* This question can probably best be answered by comparing our ratios with carefully established management standards.

The discussion of ratios in this chapter is centered around the question: What are the ratios designed to measure? The major questions that may be partially answered by ratio analysis are:

1. How *balanced* is the company's *equity structure?*
2. How *profitable* is the firm?
3. How *productively* is the working capital being utilized?
4. What is the firm's *current debt-paying* ability?

The data from the financial statements of the Millit Manufacturing Company, presented in Exhibits 3-1 through 3-4, have been used to calculate the following illustrative ratios. Year-end ratios have been calculated as of December 31, 1977, and period ratios for the year 1977. In each case, the figures presented have been rounded to the nearest millions of dollars.

Balance of Equity Structure

Most firms operate with assets that have been furnished partially by creditors and partially by owners. Those assets contributed by creditors create liabilities *(debt)* and those furnished by owners (through *investment* or *earnings*) create owners' equity. Certain benefits and risks accrue to owners when debt financing is employed. A firm that does not have enough debt deprives the owners of desirable profits, while a firm that has too much debt subjects the owners to undesirable risks. Selecting the correct balance of debt and equity is, indeed, a delicate art.

The process of balancing the equity structure involves a concept known as *financial leverage* or *trading on the equity.* Financial leverage simply means that profits or losses are amplified by the existence of debt in a firm's capital structure. If a company can borrow at 10 percent interest and invest at 15 percent return, the difference is a net gain to the stockholders.

Financial leverage can also be employed by issuing preferred stock because dividends on preferred stock, like bond interest, are normally fixed in amount. If the company can put the assets provided by the preferred stockholders to work earning a return greater than that paid to the preferred stockholders, the extra earnings accrue to the common stockholders. Although the principle holds for either preferred stock or debt, the latter works better because interest is tax-deductible to the corporation, while dividends are not. This condition causes the *net cost* of borrowing at a given interest rate to be lower than the cost of paying dividends on a preferred stock bearing the same rate (say, 8 percent bonds compared to 8 percent preferred stock).

However, financial leverage is a double-edged sword. The practice will increase the rate of return to the common stockholders if the earning rate exceeds the borrowing rate but it will increase the loss per share (negative rate of return) if the borrowing rate exceeds the earning rate.

The concept is clarified in Exhibit 3-5. COMMCO, Inc., employs no financial leverage ($200,000 of common stock). BONDCO, Inc. ($100,000

Exhibit 3-5
Financial Leverage

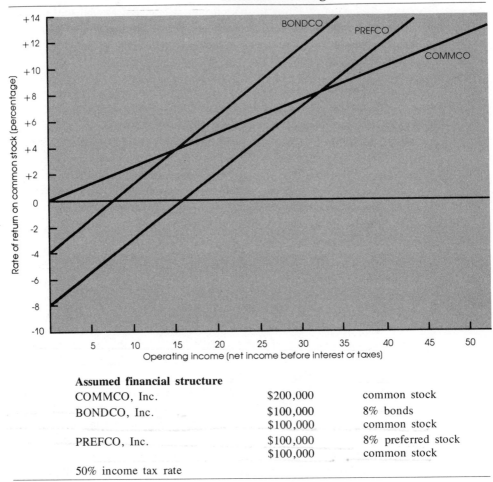

Assumed financial structure

COMMCO, Inc.	$200,000	common stock
BONDCO, Inc.	$100,000	8% bonds
	$100,000	common stock
PREFCO, Inc.	$100,000	8% preferred stock
	$100,000	common stock

50% income tax rate

of common stock plus $100,000 of 8 percent bonds), and PREFCO, Inc. ($100,000 of common stock plus $100,000 of 8 percent preferred stock) do use financial leverage. Note that the breakeven point between COMMCO and BONDCO is a $16,000 operating profit, which is just half of the $32,000 operating profit required to break even between COMMCO and PREFCO. This result arises because we assumed a 50 percent tax rate and it illustrates the tax advantage of debt over preferred stock. Note also the dual aspect of financial leverage. Above these breakeven points the common stockholders benefit by financial leverage; below these breakeven points they suffer from financial leverage. With an assumed operating income of $10,000, the existence of debt (or preferred stock) reduces the rate of return to common stockholders since COMMCO shows a return of 2.5 percent, while PREFCO shows a *minus* 3 percent, and BONDCO a 1 percent return.

On the other hand, when we assume an operating income of $40,000, the return to common stockholders of COMMCO is increased to only 10 percent, while PREFCO common stockholders enjoy a 12 percent return, and BONDCO stockholders a 16 percent return.

The same data are shown in the tables in Exhibit 3-6, for those readers who prefer that format.

In most instances, decisions regarding the firm's capital structure are made only by top management—generally the board of directors, or sometimes even the stockholders. Major new financing such as new stock issues or floating bond issues generally cannot be undertaken without the directors' or stockholders' approval. Dividend policies, which in turn determine the proportion of earnings retained in the business, are also set at this level. Thus, the operating manager is generally not concerned with establishing the capital structure but, instead, with the problems of *living within it*.

Several ratios may be used to evaluate the balance of a firm's equity structure. The most common are probably debt-to-equity, debt-to-total-capital, and times-interest-charges-earned.

Exhibit 3-6
Situation 1
(assumed operating income of
$10,000 is below breakeven points):

	COMMCO	PREFCO	BONDCO
Operating income	$10,000	$10,000	$10,000
Interest (8% of $100,000)	–0–	–0–	(8,000)
Net income before taxes	$10,000	$10,000	2,000
Income taxes (50%)	(5,000)	(5,000)	(1,000)
Net income	$ 5,000	$ 5,000	$ 1,000
Preferred dividends	–0–	(8,000)	–0–
Net income available to common	$ 5,000	$(3,000)	$ 1,000

Rate of return on common stockholders' equity	$\dfrac{\$5}{\$200} = 2\frac{1}{2}\%$	$\dfrac{-\$3}{\$100} = -3\%$	$\dfrac{\$1}{\$100} = 1\%$

Situation 2
(assumed operating income of
$40,000 is above breakeven points):

	COMMCO	PREFCO	BONDCO
Operating income	$40,000	$40,000	$40,000
Interest (8% of $100,000)	–0–	–0–	(8,000)
Net income before taxes	$40,000	$40,000	$32,000
Income taxes (50%)	(20,000)	(20,000)	(16,000)
Net income	$20,000	$20,000	$16,000
Preferred dividends	–0–	(8,000)	–0–
Net income available to common	$20,000	$12,000	$16,000

Rate of return on common stockholders' equity	$\dfrac{\$20}{\$200} = 10\%$	$\dfrac{\$12}{\$100} = 12\%$	$\dfrac{\$16}{\$100} = 16\%$

DEBT-TO-EQUITY AND DEBT-TO-TOTAL-CAPITAL RATIOS

The debt-to-equity and the debt-to-total-capital ratios probably most clearly show the extent to which a company is using financial leverage.[4] The ratios are two different methods of describing the same thing. Both attempt to measure the relative proportion of total assets supplied, respectively, by the owners and creditors. The debt-to-equity ratio is computed by dividing total liabilities by total stockholders' equity. The debt-to-total-capital ratio is computed by dividing total liabilities by total assets (which is the same as the sum of the liabilities and the stockholders' equity).

As with other financial ratios, it is neither possible nor desirable to establish a rule of thumb by which the acceptable proportions of debt and equity can be determined. This matter must be determined by the manager's careful, considered judgment, and will vary widely from firm to firm and from industry to industry. The primary basis for the determination consists of the amount and the stability of corporate earnings. In order to profit from financial leverage, management must be sure that the profits generated from the borrowed funds are sufficiently high and stable to more than cover the cost of such borrowing. Thus, the higher and more stable the earnings, the higher the ratio of debt-to-equity that is acceptable. Thus, we might expect a bank to have a very high debt-to-equity ratio because its earnings would be rather stable and predictable. A public utility would be expected to have a medium debt-to-equity ratio because, although less predictable than banks, utilities normally enjoy *fair* earnings (as determined by rate commissions). Finally, we would expect a steel manufacturer to have a relatively low debt-to-equity ratio because earnings of such companies are generally not too stable nor too predictable.

The debt-to-equity ratio and the debt-to-total-capital ratio for the Millit Manufacturing Company as of December 31, 1977, are calculated:

$$\text{Debt-to-equity} \quad = \quad \frac{\text{Liabilities}}{\text{Stockholders' equity}} \quad = \quad \frac{\$311}{\$658} \quad = \quad 0.47$$

$$\text{Debt-to-total-capital} = \quad \frac{\text{Liabilities}}{\text{Assets}} \quad = \quad \frac{\$311}{\$969} \quad = \quad 0.32$$

TIMES-INTEREST-CHARGES-EARNED

Another important ratio that describes the debt-paying ability of a firm is the *times-interest-charges-earned*. This ratio describes the amount of cushion available to long-term creditors by showing the relative sizes of net income and long-term interest payments. A high ratio indicates that the creditor is likely to receive his interest despite a decline in earnings. A low ratio shows that the creditor's position is not nearly as secure. A firm with a long history of relatively high and stable earnings could tolerate a lower ratio than a

---

[4] Unfortunately, practice shows that the terms *equity* and *capital* are used interchangeably. Our usage of *equity* means *stockholders' equity,* and *capital* means *total* assets.

company with highly variable earnings. Wide variations in this ratio over several periods could indicate an undesirable condition from the creditors' standpoint, and possibly that the company has too much debt.

The ratio is computed by dividing the net operating income[5] by the bond interest charges. For example, if net operating income is $40,000 and interest on bonds is $10,000, the interest charges have been earned *4 times*.

The situation is slightly more complex when there is more than one issue of bonds because a separate computation must be made for each issue. This is necessary because all bondholders do not have equal claims against the firm's assets. The issues that have prior claims (that is, those which will be paid interest first) are called the senior issues and those that have secondary claims are called junior issues. Where there is more than one class of bond, the net operating income is divided by the sum of the interest charges on the particular issue, *plus the interest charges on all prior issues.* Such a calcula-tion will reflect the fact that the security of a junior issue is closely linked to the size of the senior issues.

Sufficient detail is not given in the Millit statements to enable us to make separate times-interest-charges-earned calculations for each long-term obliga-tion. The overall ratio, however, shows an ample cushion:

$$\frac{\text{Operating income}}{\text{Interest charges}} = \frac{\$177}{\$3} = 59 \text{ times}$$

In evaluating this ratio, note that the $3 million interest seems low when compared with over $150 million in long-term debt. Further analysis will disclose that $100 million of new bonds were issued during the year. The low interest figure suggests that the bonds were likely issued near the end of the year; otherwise, the interest would be substantially more than $3 million for the year. This, in turn, suggests that the *times-interest-charges-earned* calculated above is considerably understated compared to what it would be if the annual interest on year-end debt were used. This illustrates the care the manager must take if he is to properly interpret financial ratios.

Profitability

Managers are typically under more pressure to achieve adequate profits than to achieve any other single company goal. How can we tell if profits are as great as they ought to be? Often we attempt to evaluate profitability by using ratios that relate profits to some other factor—for example, profits to assets, profits to equities, or profits to sales.

RETURN ON INVESTMENT

Return on investment (ROI) is probably the most important ratio to a manager. Managers are stewards, entrusted with certain resources (assets) with the expectation that they will generate an increase in those resources.

[5] Operating income is defined as the income before deducting interest and income taxes.

Generally, the greater the amount of assets entrusted, the greater the expected return. The return on investment is designed to reflect how well management does with this stewardship: How much did the manager accomplish in relation to what he was given?

The return on investment may be expressed in several different ways depending on whom is being evaluated and who is doing the evaluation. Two common ways of expressing return on investment are: (1) return on total assets, and (2) return on owners' equity.

RETURN ON TOTAL ASSETS

The return on total assets (sometimes called return on total *capital)* is a measure of a firm's general earning power. It measures the rate of return on utilizing a bundle of assets without considering whether these assets were financed by debt or equity funds. The return on total assets is computed by dividing the net operating income (income *before* interest, taxes, and dividends) by the average total assets.[6] The ratio attempts to isolate the return from operations from the income that has accrued from *trading on the equity.* It is a measure of management's effectiveness in employing the resources entrusted to them from *all sources.*

Operating income is used in this calculation (rather than net income) because the operating manager generally does *not* have control over interest, income taxes, or dividends. In most companies, the directors or owners determine the balance of the equity structure (and thus interest charges), the form of business (and thus the tax status), and the degree to which earnings will be retained (and thus dividends).

The return on total assets is particularly useful in comparing divisions within a company. Each division manager is given a "block" of assets which he is expected to effectively employ. The degree to which he meets this responsibility can be measured, to a certain extent, by calculating the rate of return on the assets he has been given. The performance of the managers can be compared in this manner. For example, assume Division *A* has assets of $500,000, and Division *B* assets of $800,000. During the year, Division *A* reports operating profits of $35,000, and Division *B* operating profits of $49,000. How did the managers do? Manager *A* earned a rate of return of 7 percent, while Manager *B* earned only 6.1 percent. Apparently Manager *A* was able to more effectively employ the resources entrusted to him than Manager *B*.

The major weakness in this ratio is that it compares *current earnings* with *assets valued at historical cost.* Suppose in our previous example that the assets in Division *A* are 10 years older (on the average) than in Division *B*. It is quite likely that we have overstated the rate of return in Division *A* because we have failed to account for the effects of inflation on asset values.

[6] Normally, when a ratio compares amounts from the income statement (in this case, operating income) with amounts from the balance sheet (in this case, total assets), it is best to use *average* balance sheet values. This is true because the income statement covers a *period* of time, while the balance sheet shows amounts at a *point* in time. To make the comparison meaningful we need the *average* balance sheet values for the period under consideration.

The return on total assets for Millit Manufacturing Company may be calculated as:

$$\frac{\text{Operating income}}{\text{Average total assets}} = \frac{\$177}{\dfrac{(\$834 + \$969)}{2}} = 19.6\%$$

RETURN ON STOCKHOLDERS' EQUITY

This ratio is calculated by dividing net income by the average total stockholders' equity. The ratio is designed to indicate how profitable the company is to the owners. It is another expression of return on investment but is used to evaluate how the *owners* are doing rather than to evaluate management. In addition to management efficiency, the owners' return is influenced by the capital structure and tax status selected by the owners. Thus net income is used in this calculation rather than the operating income.

Return on stockholders' equity also suffers from the weakness that balance sheet accounts (in this case owners' equity accounts) are shown at *book value*. Often, the *market value* of a share is far in excess of the book value, and so this ratio will not reflect the rate of return that a potential or current investor might expect to earn. The return on owners' equity ratio may be useful as a general indicator of profitability when used for comparative purposes rather than as an absolute rate. It could be useful, for example, in comparing the return of two companies within the same industry with assets of somewhat comparable ages. The return on stockholders' equity for Millit Manufacturing Company may be calculated as:

$$\frac{\text{Net income}}{\text{Average stockholders' equity}} = \frac{\$85}{\dfrac{(\$644 + \$658)}{2}} = 13.1\%$$

EARNINGS PER SHARE

One of the most frequently quoted ratios in investment circles is *earnings per share*. Managers are under continual pressure from stockholders, financial analysts, and other interested parties to increase earnings per share. In fact, this ratio has probably become the most important measure by which outsiders evaluate management. This statistic is calculated by dividing net income by the average number of shares of stock outstanding during the year. *Outstanding stock* refers to shares held by stockholders and does not include unissued or reacquired shares. For a company with more than one class of stock, separate calculations are made for each class. Earnings per share on preferred stock is calculated by using the preferred dividends instead of net income; earnings per share on common stock is calculated on net income less preferred dividends.

Because earnings per share data are so widely used in financial circles, the APB of the American Institute of Certified Public Accountants (AICPA) issued a lengthy opinion which placed requirements on the calculation of this ratio. The first requirement holds that "earnings per share amounts should . . . be presented for (a) income before extraordinary items and (b) net income. It may also be desirable to present earnings per share amounts for extraordinary items if any."[7]

The second requirement provides for dual earnings per share calculations —*primary earnings per share* and *fully diluted earnings per share*—for firms with complex capital structures. These companies have ". . . potentially dilutive convertible securities, options, warrants, or other rights that upon conversion or exercise could in the aggregate dilute earnings per common share."[8] If these convertible securities had been changed to common stock during the year, the number of shares would have been altered, as well as earnings per share. Investors should recognize the dilutive effect of these securities and this is the reason that the two earnings per share figures are required.

Because Millit does not have a complex capital structure, the 1977 earnings per share may be calculated as:

$$\frac{\text{Net income}}{\text{Average common shares outstanding}} = \frac{\$84,860,000}{50,000,000 \text{ shares}} = \$1.70 \text{ per share}$$

PRICE-EARNINGS RATIO

The price-earnings ratio is another index of profitability commonly used in financial circles. It is calculated by dividing the current market price per share of stock by some earnings per share figure, most frequently the last 12-months' earnings per share. Often this ratio has real meaning to the investor or potential investor because it relates earning power to current investment. It tells the investor what kind of return he can expect on his investment. Unlike the return on total capital, this ratio uses the current market value rather than the historical book value. As with earnings per share, the manager's main concern with this ratio is that he is constantly under pressure to take actions which will both increase the market price of the stock and increase earnings. It is really unfair to evaluate managers on the basis of the price-earnings ratio because stock market prices are influenced by many factors beyond the manager's control. It is generally impossible to tell whether a low price-earnings ratio is a sign of a bargain stock, a poor management, or a wide variety of other possibilities.

If the market price of Millit common stock were $28 per share on December 31, 1977, the price-earnings ratio at that date would be calculated as:

$$\frac{\text{Current market price}}{\text{Earnings per share}} = \frac{\$28}{\$1.70} = 16.5 \text{ times}$$

[7] Accounting Principles Board, *Opinion No. 15: Earnings Per Share* (New York: AICPA, 1969), pp. 220–21.
[8] *Ibid.*, p. 221.

YIELD

The yield on a stock is calculated by dividing the annual dividend per share by the current market price per share. This ratio tells the stockholder how much return he has received on his investment. Many companies choose not to distribute cash dividends to their stockholders in order to use their assets to earn more income. Thus, the amount of dividends per share can be substantially less than the earnings per share. The price-earnings ratio indicates how much is *earned* in relation to the market price, while the yield indicates how much is *paid out* in relation to the market price. Because directors (rather than managers) establish dividend policy, yield holds little significance for the typical manager.

Millit paid dividends of $1.41 per share.[9] Based on the assumed year-end price of $28 per share, this indicates a yield of 5 percent as:

$$\frac{\text{Dividends per share}}{\text{Current market price}} = \frac{\$1.41}{\$28} = 5\%$$

Productivity of Working Capital

A company's working capital consists of current assets less current liabilities (sometimes called *net* working capital). This working capital is the primary basis on which the company completes its *operating cycle*. Merchandise is purchased on credit, and cash is utilized to pay the liabilities thus created. The merchandise is sold (either for cash or on credit), the receivables (if any) are collected, and the cycle is ended. The working capital is the lifeblood of a business enterprise and must be kept circulating if the business is to be profitable. Generally, the faster the operating cycle occurs, the better, because it indicates that working capital is being well managed. If a company can shorten the cycle, and thereby increase the number of cycles per year, while holding profit margins and expenses constant, it will increase its profitability. For most merchandising companies, the control and movement of working capital are the keys to profitability.

There are a number of ratios designed to measure the effectiveness with which management controls working capital.[10] Some of the more important are inventory turnover, net sales to inventory, accounts receivable turnover, and average collection period.

INVENTORY TURNOVER

The inventory turnover may be used for evaluating the effectiveness of inventory management. The ratio is calculated by dividing the cost of goods

---

[9] Although the dividends for Millit Manufacturing Company are not shown directly on the financial statements, the amount may be calculated by comparing the net income ($84,860,000) with the increase in retained earnings during the year ($544,630,000 − $530,310,000) or $14,320,000. This difference ($70,540,000) amounts to $1.41 per share ($70,540,000/50,000,000 shares) and apparently represents the dividends paid during the year.

[10] The concept of working capital management is discussed more fully in Chapters 4 and 12.

sold by the average inventory. It is usually expressed in *turns* per year which indicates how many times the average inventory has been replenished during the period. The ratio is most accurate when the average inventory is calculated from monthly balances, since inventory levels may fluctuate greatly duɪ.ɪg the year. In fact, most companies deliberately select the end of their fiscal period, a point when inventories are at their lowest levels. This means that an average calculated only from the beginning and ending balances would be low and would produce an inventory turnover that is too high. When the inventory turnover is calculated from year-end figures, the resulting ratio should be reduced in order to more appropriately descɪibe reality.

Generally, management strives to get as many inventory turnovers as possible. The more sales that can be produced from a given investment, the better. In evaluating inventory turnover, however, the manager must be careful to investigate the cause of the turnover. A company or a division can increase its turnover in a number of undesirable ways. For example, the inventory will move faster if it is marked to sell at half the usual price—a practice which can create serious losses. Heavy advertising may increase turnover by increasing sales, but the increased revenue may be more than offset by the increased advertising costs. This situation again points out the importance of looking at a ratio in the light of other ratios and other data.

The inventory turnover for Millit Manufacturing Company for the year ended December 31, 1977, may be calculated as:

$$\frac{\text{Cost of goods sold}}{\text{Average inventory}} = \frac{\$530}{\frac{(\$93 + \$104)}{2}} = 5.38 \text{ times per year}$$

NET SALES TO INVENTORY

The ratio of net sales to inventory is designed to measure the same thing as the inventory turnover—how well the inventory is managed. It is calculated by dividing net sales by average inventory. This ratio is often used instead of the inventory turnover for situations in which financial statements do not detail the cost of goods sold. This ratio does *not* yield the actual inventory turnover but is merely an indication of the dollar sales produced from the average inventory. If relevant data are available, the inventory turnover is probably a more effective tool.

The 1977 net sales to inventory for Millit may be calculated as:

$$\frac{\text{Net sales}}{\text{Average inventory}} = \frac{\$942}{\frac{(\$93 + \$104)}{2}} = 9.56 \text{ times per year}$$

ACCOUNTS RECEIVABLE TURNOVER

The accounts receivable turnover is calculated by dividing net sales by the average balance of accounts receivable. This ratio is used as a guide in evaluating the relative collectibility of receivables. A company usually strives for as many turnovers as possible in order to tie up a minimum of funds in receivables.[11] The 1977 receivables turnover for Millit may be calculated as:

$$\frac{\text{Net sales}}{\text{Average receivables}} = \frac{\$942}{\frac{(\$119 + \$125)}{2}} = 7.72 \text{ times per year}$$

AVERAGE COLLECTION PERIOD

Probably the most useful indicator of accounts receivable management is found in the average days' sales uncollected *(average collection period)*. This period is calculated by dividing the number of days in the accounting period by the receivables turnover. This ratio expresses the average days it takes to collect an account and, like the receivables turnover, is designed to analyze the collectibility of accounts. By expressing the collection period in terms of days, the ratio makes it easy to compare this figure with a company's sales terms, which is an effective evaluation of the success of a company's credit policy. For example, if a company offers terms of "2/10, n/30" (2 percent discount if paid within 10 days, the bill is due net—no discount—within 30 days) and has an average collection period of 60 days, then it appears that management has been imprudent in granting credit, or unsuccessful in collecting its accounts, or both.

Millit's average collection period during 1977 was 47 days, as shown below:

$$\frac{\text{Number of days per period}}{\text{Receivables turnover}} = \frac{365 \text{ days}}{7.72} = 47 \text{ days}$$

Current Debt-Paying Ability

An important consideration in evaluating a company's financial position is its ability to meet obligations as they mature. Probably the best way to evaluate a firm's debt-paying ability is to prepare a projected cash-flow statement (a procedure described in Chapter 12). A more expedient practice is to use ratios that give a rough idea of current debt-paying ability. The two ratios most commonly used for this purpose are the *current ratio* (working capital ratio) and the *quick ratio* (acid-test ratio).

CURRENT RATIO

One of the most widely used financial ratios is the current ratio. Its purpose is to indicate the firm's general debt-paying ability within the near future, usually 1 year from the date of computation. The current ratio is calculated by dividing current assets by current liabilities. For example, if a firm has current assets of $3 million and current liabilities of $1 million, its current ratio is 3-to-1. If the ratio is less than 1-to-1, it may show that the firm is in a critical position of liquidity. To the extent that the ratio exceeds 1-to-1, there exists some cushion of current assets over current liabilities.

[11] Uncollected accounts receivable are really interest free loans to the customers.

Almost as well-known as the ratio itself is the often suggested *rule of thumb ideal*: the 2-to-1 ratio. The student has previously been warned against blindly following such rules.

Because it has been used so widely and because of the application of rule of thumb standards, the current ratio has often been abused. To begin with, it has been implied that the higher the ratio, the sounder the company. Actually, this is far from the truth. A ratio may be too high as well as too low. A management which accumulates excess cash and cash equivalents will soon build up a high current ratio. This condition may well be a sign of *stagnation* rather than of astute management. During the post-Second World War era, for example, Montgomery Ward accumulated large amounts of cash in anticipation of a depression which never occurred. In this instance, the high current ratio was probably not a sign of an alert and progressive management.

Another weakness in the current ratio is the fact that inventory and marketable securities figures used in the calculation are costs, not the realizable values. The latter amounts of cash will be available to repay the debt, and thus would provide a better indication of current debt-paying ability.

Sometimes the current ratio is misinterpreted because the manager fails to analyze its components. This problem is not a weakness of the ratio itself, but of the manager, and is an example of confusing the means with the end. An increased current ratio may be caused by a business slowdown as excess inventory is accumulated and the collection of accounts receivable slows. On the other hand, inventories may be intentionally accumulated, to provide a basis for enlarged sales volume in the future. The manager must carefully investigate the situation to discover what is really behind the reported figures.

Millit's current ratio, as of December 31, 1977, is calculated as:

$$\frac{\text{Current assets}}{\text{Current liabilities}} = \frac{\$409}{\$157} = 2.6$$

QUICK RATIO

The quick ratio, sometimes called the *acid-test ratio,* is another, more precise indicator of a company's ability to meet current debts. It is similar to the current ratio except that only those assets that are considered liquid (readily convertible into cash) are included in the numerator. Those assets most generally treated as *quick* are *cash, receivables,* and *temporary investments.* Excluded from this classification are such current assets as *inventories* and *prepaid items* which cannot be converted into cash in a short time in the ordinary course of business.

The quick ratio is calculated by dividing the total quick assets by the total current liabilities:

$$\frac{\text{Quick assets}}{\text{Current liabilities}} = \frac{\$297}{\$157} = 1.89$$

Comparative Data

Financial analysis is often most meaningful when the figures of one company are compared with those of other companies in the same industry. There are a number of sources to which one can turn to get the necessary figures, including agencies of the federal government, trade associations, and private financial advisory companies. For many years Dun & Bradstreet has distributed an annual publication, *Key Business Ratios*. For each industry, Dun & Bradstreet shows the upper quartile, the median, and the lower quartile for each of fourteen key ratios in different lines of business. The ratios are calculated from the sampling of corporations with owners' equity in excess of $35,000.[12]

SUMMARY

In this chapter, we have introduced some tools of financial analysis: *horizontal analysis, vertical analysis,* and *ratio analysis.* Horizontal analysis involves comparison of statements at two points of time or two periods of time. The difference between the two statements, for each item listed, is calculated and expressed in both dollar and percentage terms. In vertical analysis, each item in a statement is expressed as a percentage of a total. On the balance sheet each item is expressed as a percentage of total assets, and on the income statement as a percentage of net sales. This places companies and divisions of different sizes on a common basis for comparison. Ratio analysis involves the expression of figures in ratio form between two financial statement items which are felt to be meaningfully related.

Each of these techniques can be beneficial tools if they are properly used and if their weaknesses are fully understood. The techniques described here must be used for what they are: *limited financial tools.* No ratio may properly be viewed as being good or bad per se; rather, each must be considered one of many indicators to be evaluated together.

The student should attempt to view each particular financial ratio from the standpoint of the user of the financial statement, whether he is a manager, stockholder, creditor, potential investor, potential lender, or someone else. What information does the statement reader seek? What ratios might assist him in reaching the required decision? Ratio analysis can be meaningful only if it is approached in this manner. The ratios discussed in this chapter may assist in answering the following questions:

1. How well-balanced is the company's equity structure?
2. How profitable is the firm or the division within the firm?
3. How effectively is working capital being utilized?
4. What is the firm's current debt-paying ability?

[12] A current copy of this publication can be obtained by writing Dun & Bradstreet, Inc., Public Relations and Advertising, 99 Church Street, New York, NY 10007.

QUESTIONS

1. What are the differences in the procedures for constructing horizontal and vertical analyses? What is the special purpose of each?

2. In comparing the change between year 19X1 and 19X2, which year is used as the base year? If an item appeared at $75 in 19X1 and $100 in 19X2, what was the percent change?

3. In vertical analysis, which items on the balance sheet equal 100 percent? Which item on the income statement equals 100 percent?

4. What are the relative advantages of presenting changes in percentage terms as opposed to presenting them in absolute figures? What are the disadvantages of using percentages?

5. What is a financial ratio? Are financial ratios always expressed in ratio form?

6. What are the four major questions to which ratio analysis provides a partial answer?

7. How is the price-earnings ratio calculated? What effect do dividends have on a company's price-earnings ratio?

8. What do yield and the price-earnings ratio have in common? What is the main difference between what is shown by these two ratios?

9. What is the working capital of a firm? Of what importance is the working capital?

10. In evaluating a company's inventory turnover, what are some of the other ratios that might be useful?

11. How is the accounts receivable turnover calculated? What would a rising accounts receivable turnover indicate? In what other manner can the collectibility of receivables be evaluated?

12. What danger do you see in using *year-end* figures to calculate the average inventory to be used in computing the inventory turnover?

13. It has been said that a current ratio should not fall below 2-to-1. Comment on the danger of using such rules of thumb.

14. The current ratio of Armore Company is 3-to-1, and the current ratio of Segmore Corporation is 7-to-1. Evaluate the following statement: The current position of the Segmore Corporation may be considered the sounder of the two.

15. Which assets are *quick assets*? Which current assets are not considered *quick assets*?

EXERCISES

E3–1 *Simple ratios.* From the information that follows, calculate the firm's: (a) current ratio, (b) quick ratio, (c) debt-to-equity ratio, (d) debt-to-total-capital ratio.

Accounts receivable	$ 10,000	Accounts payable	$ 6,000
Cash	23,000	Common stock	63,000
Merchandise inventory	81,000	Mortgage payable	20,000
Notes receivable	12,000	Retained earnings	34,000
Prepaid insurance	6,000	Wages payable	9,000
	$132,000		$132,000

E3–2 Simple ratios. From the data given in E3–1 and the following additional data, calculate: (a) inventory turnover, (b) receivables turnover, (c) average collection period, (d) net sales to inventory.

Inventory one year earlier	$ 49,000
Gross sales	500,000
Sales returns	20,000
Accounts receivable one year earlier	16,000
Notes receivable one year earlier	20,000
Gross margin during current year	40 percent

E3–3 Simple ratios. The income statement of the Vida Pep Health Stores is presented below:

VIDA PEP HEALTH STORES
Income Statement
For the Year Ended October 31, 1978

Sales		$500,000
Cost of goods sold		300,000
Gross margin		$200,000
Selling expense	$60,000	
Administrative expense	50,000	110,000
Operating profit		$ 90,000
Interest charges		20,000
Net income before tax		$ 70,000
Income tax		25,000
Net income		$ 45,000

These average figures apply for the same year:

Total assets	$400,000
Total liabilities	90,000
Average inventory	32,250

Calculate the following ratios: (a) debt-to-equity, (b) times-interest-charges-earned, (c) return on stockholders equity, (d) inventory turnover, and (e) return on total assets.

E3–4 Simple ratios. Using the data about Vida Pep Health Stores given in E3-3 and the additional information presented below, calculate the following financial ratios: (a) yield, (b) earnings per share, (c) price-earnings ratio. The most recent price of the stock is $25 per share. Number of shares outstanding at October 31, 1977 was 10,000 shares and at October 31, 1978 was 20,000 shares (10,000 shares issued May 1, 1978). The dividends paid during the year ended October 31, 1978 amounted to $1 per share.

E3–5 **Ratio algebra.** Reconstruct the balance sheet of Big Rock Corporation at the end of the current fiscal year based on the following trial balance and current financial ratios:

Cash	?	
Accounts receivable	?	
Inventory	?	
Fixed assets	$500	
Current liabilities		$400
Bonds payable		600
Capital stock		200
Retained earnings		?
	?	?

Current ratio	3:1
Inventory turnover*	4
Receivable turnover**	10
Gross margin	40% of sales
Sales	$2,000
Net income	10% of sales
Beginning retained earnings	$150

* Year-end inventory was equal to average inventory.
** Year-end receivables was equal to average receivables.

E3–6 **Ratio algebra.** Reconstruct the income statement (in summary form) for the month of August for Wright Pencil Company based on the following information:

Ratio of net income to sales	10%
Gross margin (% of sales)	25%
Times-interest-charges-earned	10
Cost of goods sold	$4,500
Selling expenses	300
Administrative expenses	500

PROBLEMS

P3–1 **Horizontal analysis.** Prepare a horizontal analysis showing changes in terms of both dollars and percentages, using the balance sheet of Maltese Imports, Inc. for December 31, 1976 and 1977 presented on page 69.

P3–2 **Horizontal analysis.** Prepare a horizontal analysis showing changes in terms of both dollars and percentages, using the income statement of Maltese Imports, Inc., for the years 1976 and 1977 presented on page 70.

MALTESE IMPORTS, INC.
Comparative Balance Sheet
December 31, 1976 and 1977

Assets	1977	1976
Current assets:		
Cash	$ 6,500	$ 4,900
Marketable securities	18,900	21,300
Accounts receivable	44,600	39,500
Short-term notes receivable	14,000	13,600
Inventory	4,300	3,800
Prepaid expenses	1,600	2,400
Total current assets	$ 89,900	$ 85,500
Long-term notes receivable	$ 22,300	$ 20,700
Fixed assets:		
Building	$ 80,600	$ 80,600
Less: Accumulated depreciation	(37,500)	(33,500)
Equipment	58,400	72,500
Less: Accumulated depreciation	(21,600)	(30,700)
Land	60,000	60,000
Total fixed assets	$139,900	$148,900
Total assets	$252,100	$255,100

Liabilities and Stockholders' Equity		
Current liabilities:		
Accounts payable	$ 10,300	$ 78,300
Accrued payroll taxes	400	300
Current portion of long-term debt	1,700	1,500
Total current liabilities	$ 12,400	$ 80,100
Long-term debt (net of current portion)	$ 17,000	$ 18,700
Stockholders' equity:		
Common stock, $5 par value	$150,000	$140,000
Paid-in capital	12,000	10,000
Retained earnings	60,700	6,300
Total stockholders' equity	$222,700	$156,300
Total liabilities and stockholders' equity	$252,100	$255,100

P3–3 *Vertical analysis.* Using the information given in P3–1 and P3–2 for Maltese Imports, Inc., complete the following:

a. Prepare a comparative balance sheet and income statement in good form, using vertical analysis.

b. Explain why these statements are often referred to as *common-size* statements.

c. Calculate the firm's current ratio as of December 31, 1976 and December 31, 1977. Would you say the ratio improved during the year?

MALTESE IMPORTS, INC.
Comparative Income Statement
For the Years Ended December 31, 1976 and 1977

	1977	1976
Sales (net)	$478,400	$428,000
Less: Cost of goods sold	390,500	357,300
Gross margin on sales	$ 87,900	$ 70,700
Operating expenses:		
Selling expenses:		
Advertising	$ 16,300	$ 15,100
Salaries and commissions	15,200	14,700
General and administrative expenses:		
Office expenses	8,100	7,700
Salaries expense	5,500	4,900
Depreciation expense	5,600	5,000
Repairs and maintenance expense	700	1,100
Utilities expense	3,900	3,800
Insurance expense	1,800	1,700
Taxes and licenses expense	1,200	1,000
Miscellaneous expense	800	900
Total operating expenses	$ 59,100	$ 55,900
Operating income	$ 28,800	$ 14,800
Non-operating items:		
Interest expense	$ (900)	$ (1,100)
Interest income	1,600	1,700
Gain (loss) on sale of equipment	39,500	(2,600)
Total	$ 40,200	$ (2,000)
Income before taxes	$ 69,000	$ 12,800
Income taxes	14,600	2,100
Net income	$ 54,400	$ 10,700

P3–4 Understanding ratios.

Part 1:

Using the comparative data for Maltese Imports, Inc., in P3–1, compute the following financial ratios as of December 31, 1976 and December 31, 1977 (rounded to the nearest hundred):

a. current ratio

b. quick ratio

c. debt-to-equity

d. debt-to-total-capital

Part 2:

a. What do the four ratios listed have in common?

b. Which ratios may be used to evaluate the firm's current debt-paying ability? How do the two years compare in this respect?

c. Which ratios may be used to analyze the extent of leverage being used in the firm?

d. Which ratio can be read directly from a *common-size* balance sheet?

P3–5 Understanding ratios.

Part 1:

Using the comparative data for Maltese Imports, Inc., given in P3–1 and P3–2, compute the following financial ratios for the year ended December 31, 1977 (rounded to nearest tenth):

a. inventory turnover
b. return on stockholders' equity
c. receivables turnover
d. average collection period
e. return on total assets
f. times-interest-charges-earned

Part 2:

a. Why may the accuracy of the inventory turnover, as calculated, be questionable?
b. Why wouldn't a high inventory turnover, taken alone, be an encouraging indication of performance?
c. Which of the first two ratios calculated above would probably be more meaningful or useful to a manager? Why?

P3–6 Vertical and horizontal analysis. Comparative data for the Knotwhole Corporation appear below:

KNOTWHOLE CORPORATION
Comparative Income Statement
For the Years Ended December 31, 1977 and 1978

	1978	1977
Gross sales	$978,500	$894,200
Sales returns and allowances	6,300	5,700
Net sales	$972,200	$888,500
Cost of goods sold	681,850	623,300
Gross margin	$290,350	$265,200
Operating expenses	175,300	163,550
Operating income	$115,050	$101,650
Nonoperating charges	240	570
Net income before taxes	$114,810	$101,080
Income taxes	57,500	50,700
Net income	$ 57,310	$ 50,380

Required:

a. Prepare a *common-size* income statement for the Knotwhole Corporation for each of the two years.
b. Prepare a comparative income statement in which the net change is shown in dollar and percentage terms for each item in the income statement.

WATERBURY MANUFACTURING COMPANY
Comparative Balance Sheet
December 31, 1976 and 1977

Assets	1977 (in thousands)	1976 (in thousands)
Current assets:		
Cash	$ 5,850	$ 6,080
Short-term marketable securities at cost		
(approximate market value)	3,960	9,950
Notes and accounts receivable	21,980	19,100
Inventories	16,680	12,620
Total current assets	$48,470	$47,750
Fixed assets:		
Buildings (net)	$ 870	$ 640
Machinery and equipment (net)	2,840	1,860
Land	440	370
Total fixed assets	$ 4,150	$ 2,870
Total assets	$52,620	$50,620
Liabilities and Stockholders' Equity		
Current liabilities:		
Notes payable	$ 6,330	$ 5,480
Accounts payable	16,090	14,140
Accrued taxes	3,850	4,110
Total current liabilities	$26,270	$23,730
Long-term debt:		
Bonds payable	$ 4,760	$ 4,280
Mortgages payable	2,510	2,900
Total long-term debt	$ 7,270	$ 7,180
Stockholders' equity:		
Common stock, $10 par	$ 2,970	$ 2,950
Capital surplus	3,540	3,540
Retained earnings	12,570	13,220
Total stockholders' equity	$19,080	$19,710
Total liabilities and stockholders' equity	$52,620	$50,620

WATERBURY MANUFACTURING COMPANY
Comparative Condensed Income Statement
For the Years Ended December 31, 1976 and 1977

	1977 (in thousands)	1976 (in thousands)
Sales	$161,690	$155,920
Cost of goods sold	142,560	144,700
Gross margin	$ 19,130	11,220
Operating expenses	11,640	11,410
Net operating income (loss)	$ 7,490	$ (190)
Federal income tax	3,880	105*
Net income (loss)	$ 3,610	$ (85)

*Tax refund arising from loss carryback.

P3–7 *Horizontal analysis.* Prepare balance sheets and income statement for Waterbury Manufacturing Company, using horizontal analysis and showing changes in terms of both dollars and percents, based on the comparative statements on page 72.

P3–8 *Computing and using ratios.* Using the data for the Waterbury Manufacturing Company given in P3–7, calculate the following financial ratios, and explain what they should indicate to management:

    a.   As of December 31, 1976 and 1977:

        1.   Current ratio
        2.   Acid-test ratio
        3.   Return on total assets
        4.   Return on owners' equity
        5.   Debt-to-equity ratio

    b.   For the year ended December 31, 1977:

        1.   Inventory turnover
        2.   Receivables turnover
        3.   Average collection period

P3–9 *Computing and using ratios.* Using the data for the Waterbury Manufacturing Company given in P3–7, calculate the following measurements for 1977 and explain what they should mean to management:

    a.   price-earnings ratio
    b.   net sales to inventory
    c.   yield
    d.   earnings per share on common stock
    e.   times-interest-charges-earned

The company has included interest charges in the operating expenses. The interest charges during the year 1977 amounted to 8 percent of the total long-term debt at December 31, 1977. The company's stock sold as high as $95 per share and as low as $58 per share but closed the year 1977 at $62 per share. The company paid 50 percent of the 1977 earnings as dividends during that same year.

P3–10 *Applying ratios to management analysis.* Each of the following situations is independent of the others:

    1.   You are president of a department store chain that has 10 retail outlets, all constructed during 1970 and 1971. You are interested in evaluating the performance of each of the store managers.

    2.   You are a retired businessman living in Florida and your cash requirements remain rather constant from year to year. You have $25,000 to invest in the stock market and are looking for a "good" stock for your investment.

3. A company has applied for a 60-day loan which they say they will have no trouble repaying because of their strong working capital position.

4. You are president of a large furniture store for which your son-in-law manages the credit department. You have had difficulty collecting some of the bills lately and it has been suggested that the credit department has been lax in granting credit.

5. You are considering investing in a bond which "guarantees" interest at 10 percent. A friend advises you that even though the interest is "guaranteed" the company must be profitable or they won't have the funds necessary to pay the interest.

6. You are president of a rapidly growing company. As you walked through the warehouse the other day you noticed that it was full. You also noted some goods outside on the loading dock. This has made you wonder if the company is accumulating too much merchandise.

Required:

In each of the situations described above indicate:

a. Which ratio would be most useful

b. Why you selected that ratio

c. How the ratio is calculated

P3–11 *Using leverage.* A group of local doctors is contemplating forming a business to sell recreational equipment but are uncertain of the form the capital structure should take. Two plans have been proposed: The first, proposed by Doctor Van Order, calls for the doctors (owners) to supply the entire initial investment. This plan is advocated because ". . . that way the business will be entirely ours and we won't need to worry about any outsiders."

The second plan provides for a combination of debt and equity financing. Under this plan, 60 percent of the initial investment would come from the doctors and the balance from issuing 8 percent bonds (at face value). Dr. Dolowitz supports this plan because ". . . there is no need to tie up all our money when we can use someone else's."

A management consultant is hired to make a market survey and provide other data to assist the doctors in reaching a decision. He estimates annual sales will average $500,000 per year and operating profits (profits before interest and taxes) will average $80,000 per year during the next 5 years. Since the recreation business is quite cyclical he predicts 2 years when operating profits will be only $30,000; 1 year in which the operating profits will be zero; and 2 years when operating profits will be $170,000 per year. It is estimated an initial investment of $800,000 will be required. The doctors plan to pay all profits out as dividends in the year earned, and maintain the assets of the business at the $800,000 level throughout the 4-year period. Income taxes on the business are estimated at 50 percent of net income before taxes.

Required:

a. Prepare a projection of income and calculate the projected rate of return for each of the 5 years assuming the first plan is followed.

b. Prepare a projection of income and calculate the projected rate of return for each of the 5 years assuming the second plan is followed.

c. Which plan would you recommend? Why?

CHAPTER
4

Analyzing Changes in Financial Position

In 1971, another financial statement was added to annual reports by *APB Opinion No. 19* in order to provide the readers with a more complete description of the firm's activities during the fiscal year. The *statement of changes in financial position* is designed to describe the operating and nonoperating events that contributed during the year to the firm's status as of the balance sheet date. Prior to the issuance of this opinion, many firms had published one version or another of the statement, but there was virtually no uniformity among the formats, the contents, or even the names that were used.

In this chapter, our objective is to describe why there is a concern with the information provided by a statement of changes in financial position and to show what this statement contains. On the way to this objective, some background on preparation of the statement is given, and the reader should be able to solve relatively simple problems after completing this chapter. More detailed descriptions of preparation techniques are available in financial accounting textbooks.

CHANGES IN FINANCIAL POSITION

In the most abstract sense, the financial position (or *condition*) of a firm is its ability to continue operating in its environment. In simple terms, the firm will continue to operate if it has sufficient assets to pay its debts as they come due, and if it can earn sufficient profits to satisfy its owners. In this sense, the concept of financial position includes many factors, ranging from available cash to marketing programs to employee satisfaction. Financial accounting extracts a small set from among these attributes to construct the *statement of financial position* (also called the *balance sheet*), which lists the assets owned and the claims against the firm. Because of the nature of financial position, it is virtually always in the process of *changing*. Although it might be possible to monitor these changes on a continual basis, there probably would not be much benefit in doing so. However, managers and outside interests will want to know what significant changes in the firm's position have occurred. This information can be used to project future events and to evaluate management's past performance.

Comparative Balance Sheet

One source of information about changes in financial position over a period of time is a pair of balance sheets, one from the beginning and the other from the end of that period. However, there would be a limit on what this analysis would show. While we might know the beginning and ending balances of cash, or inventory, or fixed assets, or mortgages payable, or stockholders' equity, we could not positively conclude that the balances moved smoothly and evenly from the first to the last amount. For example, the balance in the Notes Payable account could be as follows:

December 31, 1980	December 31, 1979	Change
$100,000	$120,000	- $20,000

We might be making an error if we concluded that the firm paid off $20,000 of loans and undertook no new borrowing. Indeed, the firm may have paid $70,000 and borrowed $50,000, or even $170,000 and $150,000, respectively. Thus, while a properly constructed balance sheet can describe the asset base of the firm for paying its debts and earning profits, it is primarily a *static* representation (a still photograph), and cannot provide complete information about what happened in an intervening period.

The Income Statement

The income statement is intended to report on the firm's success in earning profits for its owners. It does provide information about *one* change in financial position—it describes increases (revenues) and decreases (expenses) in the owners' equity account arising from operating activities. However, the income statement is inadequate for describing all the changes in financial position. For example, if cash is borrowed from a bank and invested in machinery, no reference to this event will be reported on the income statement, except possibly for interest and depreciation expenses. The next balance sheet will reflect the changes in assets and liabilities, but other borrowings and other asset purchases (as well as debt repayments and asset sales) will cloud the picture of what really happened. Because of these inadequacies, neither the balance sheet nor the income statement is sufficient for describing the changes that occurred in the time period.

The Statement of Changes in Financial Position

The *statement of changes in financial position* is designed to summarize those significant events that affected the firm's condition during the specified time period. Although several options exist, the most effective format seems to be the one that uses a *working capital* basis for describing the events. Briefly, this approach shows the events that acted as *sources* and *uses* of working capital, as well as other events that affected the financial position. After a discussion of working capital and its management, we will return to a more complete discussion of this statement.

WORKING CAPITAL

Chapter 3 provided a definition and computation of working capital as the difference between total current assets and total current liabilities. From management's point of view, working capital represents not only a cushion against bankruptcy but also the means of taking advantage of opportunities. If funds are available, for example, a new asset can be acquired or a new marketing program can be undertaken. Unless managers can assure that enough funds are available, profits will probably be lost. Having *too much* working capital results in an undesirable situation because opportunities for earning a higher rate of return elsewhere may be missed. Clearly, the management of working capital is an important task in the administration of any organization. It is equivalent in rank to any other problem of management and cannot be neglected without running a high risk of disaster.

Sources of Working Capital

Before working capital can be managed, it must be acquired. Consequently, after selecting a marketable product and establishing the firm, the owners must go about generating working capital before operations can be started.

Initially, the owners are the obvious source of working capital. An original owner (whether proprietor, partner, or stockholder) nearly always will surrender something of value to the firm, which in turn is nearly always a current asset, such as cash. If a fixed asset, such as land, or a building, or a patent, is contributed, the firm will still need working capital to pay its bills. It is not unusual to find a stockholder investing *services* in the firm, such as legal or accounting work. Although no working capital flows into the firm from these services, at least none flows *out* to pay the fees. Thus the services may be equivalent to a working capital contribution; however, the firm will need to have an actual inflow from some of the owners.

Working capital can also be obtained by borrowing from some outside source. A short-term debt (due in 12 months or less) would not generate working capital because the transaction would increase both current assets and liabilities by the same amount. Thus, in general, we look to *long-term* borrowing as a source of working capital.

Fixed or other noncurrent assets can be used to generate working capital by selling them for cash or for a short-term receivable. Notes and accounts receivable can be converted to cash by such devices as discounting, factoring, assigning, and selling. In the strict sense, a short-term receivable *is* working capital, and its conversion to cash does not generate additional working capital. But it is hard to pay a payroll or the rent with someone else's promise to pay, with the result that steps frequently are taken to turn the receivables into spendable cash.

The fourth major source of working capital for a firm is its marketing operations. By selling goods or services, current assets (cash or receivables) usually flow into the firm. But assets also must be distributed in order to initially acquire or construct the product. Other expenses must be eventually paid for with cash. Notice that working capital is *used* in supporting operations, even if cash does not immediately flow out. For example, the use of electricity usually creates a new current liability which is not paid until the bill comes due. The increase in the current liability *decreases* working capital.

These, then, are the four sources to which management of new and old firms must look: investment by owners, borrowing, sale of noncurrent assets, and operations. Working capital may infrequently come from other sources, such as gifts and grants, but we will not devote any further discussion to them.

Uses of Working Capital

The reason for generating working capital is to use it for some productive and profitable purpose. If the prospects for its successful use are not good, then it is unlikely that any working capital would be provided by owners or lenders. Consequently, management of working capital involves not only planning and accomplishing its generation but also planning and controlling its use.

Owners invest working capital in a firm with an expectation of eventually getting it back. Corporations pay *cash dividends* in order to keep the owners satisfied in this respect. Occasionally, stock is reacquired by the corporation through purchase or redemption. In either case, the owners are paid with working capital, which reduces the amount available for other uses. In order to conserve cash, some firms distribute stock dividends to the stockholders. One cost associated with this approach is that the shares could have been sold to someone else for cash, and it may be eventually necessary to have the charter amended to create more new shares if more cash is needed from new owners.

Lenders are usually very explicit in stating the terms under which they expect to have working capital returned to them. Because of the legal powers that creditors have, a manager should assure that sufficient working capital is available to meet the payment schedule required by the loan. Technically, the payment of only *long-term* liabilities consumes working capital, and, furthermore, it would be unusual to pay a debt before it is due.

However, the reclassification on the balance sheet of a long-term debt as a current liability is required when it is known that it will be paid within 12 months. Thus, working capital is used when the reclassification occurs, and the actual cash payment reduces current assets and current liabilities by the same amount. Clearly, managers must plan to have sufficient working capital as cash on hand to face the debt-servicing requirements.

Another significant use of working capital is the acquisition of noncurrent assets, such as machinery, land, or long-term investments. If the acquisition is paid for with cash, there is clearly a use of working capital involved. If the funds are borrowed on a long-term basis, both a generation and a use of working capital occurs. On the other hand, if the funds are borrowed on a short-term basis (even on credit terms extended by the seller), there is only a use of working capital, just as if cash had been spent from available funds.

Finally, working capital can be used to pay for operating activities, as previously mentioned. Debts to suppliers and workers can bring a firm to the brink of bankruptcy just as quickly and effectively as a defaulted mortgage.

These, then, are the four uses of working capital: payments to owners, debt repayment, noncurrent asset acquisition, and operations. Occasionally, working capital is decreased by other causes, such as thefts, gifts, or calamitous natural disasters. The infrequency of their occurrence is sufficiently small to justify no further discussion of them.

THE STATEMENT OF CHANGES IN FINANCIAL POSITION

We explained earlier that the statement of changes in financial position presents a summary of the sources and uses of a firm's working capital in a particular time period. With the background provided in the preceding discussion, we can now go into more detail. Exhibits 4-1 and 4-2 present the basic financial statements for Bright Enterprises. From this and other information, we will be able to develop the statement.

Schedule of Working Capital Account Balances

According to *APB Opinion No. 19*, the statement of changes in financial position should include a description of the balances of the individual working capital accounts. Exhibit 4-3 presents this information for Bright Enterprises. Notice that working capital increased because of changes in cash and accounts payable. Working capital decreased because of changes in accounts receivable and notes payable. The total decrease of $2,500 will be explained in the rest of the statement of changes in financial position.

The purpose of including information about the individual working capital accounts is to show whether or not any one of them is getting out of proportion. For example, if the cash balance of a firm was decreased through excess purchases of inventory, the total working capital figure would be unchanged; however, the firm could be in a precarious liquidity situation. Thus, both managers and outside analysts benefit by having information about the separate accounts.

Exhibit 4-1
BRIGHT ENTERPRISES
Comparative Balance Sheet
December 31, 1979 and 1980

Assets	1980	1979
Current assets:		
Cash	$14,000	$ 8,000
Accounts receivable	10,000	12,500
Prepaid rent	3,000	3,000
Total current assets	$27,000	$23,500
Noncurrent assets:		
Equipment	$35,000	$30,000
Less: Accumulated depreciation	(13,000)	(10,000)
Investments (at cost)	6,000	7,000
Total noncurrent assets	$28,000	$27,000
Total assets	$55,000	$50,500
Liabilities and Owners' Equity		
Current liabilities:		
Accounts payable	$ 4,000	$ 5,000
Notes payable	7,000	–0–
Total current liabilities	$11,000	$ 5,000
Long-term liabilities:		
Notes payable	$18,000	$22,000
Owners' equity:	$26,000	$23,500
Total liabilities and owners' equity	$55,000	$50,500

Exhibit 4-2
BRIGHT ENTERPRISES
Income Statement
For the Year Ended December 31, 1980

Sales		$64,500
Expenses		
Salaries	$42,000	
Rent	3,000	
Depreciation	3,000	
Other	1,500	
Income taxes	8,500	
Total expenses		58,000
Net operating income		$ 6,500
Gain on sale of investment		1,000
Net income		$ 7,500

Sources of Working Capital

The statement of changes in financial position provides information about the events that generated working capital for the firm during the year. As shown, there are four general categories of sources: (1) contributions by owners, (2) borrowing, (3) conversion of noncurrent assets, and (4) operations.

Exhibit 4-3
BRIGHT ENTERPRISES
Schedule of Working Capital Account Balances
As of December 31, 1979 and 1980

	1980	1979	Change in Working Capital
Current assets:			
Cash	$14,000	$ 8,000	$ 6,000
Accounts receivable	10,000	12,500	(2,500)
Prepaid rent	3,000	3,000	–0–
Total	$27,000	$23,500	$ 3,500
Current liabilities:			
Accounts payable	$ 4,000	$ 5,000	$ 1,000
Notes payable	7,000	–0–	(7,000)
Total	$11,000	$ 5,000	$(6,000)
Net working capital	$16,000	$18,500	$(2,500)

CONTRIBUTIONS BY OWNERS

If an owner (proprietor, partner, or stockholder) invests current assets in a firm to increase his ownership interest, working capital for the firm has been generated. If he loans funds on a short-term basis (less than 12 months), no working capital has been generated. Good financial management seeks to balance the amounts of creditor and owner contributions in order to achieve higher profits without endangering the firm's solvency. The statement of changes in financial position can provide useful information about changes in the "mix" of debt and equity. For Bright Enterprises, there is no clue from the balance sheets as to whether or not the owner made a contribution to the firm. The underlying records would have to be examined in order to know for sure. But we will assume that he did contribute $1,000 in cash when the firm needed it.

For corporations, increases in the balance of the Capital Stock account would *suggest* that stockholders had contributed certain assets during the year. However, the balance can be increased by stock dividends, which do not affect assets at all, or by contributions of noncurrent assets, which would not have added to working capital. Also, if the only information available is the comparative balance sheet, there is no assurance that an increase in the Capital Stock account was not a net result of several transactions that individually increased or decreased the balance by several amounts.

The statement of changes in financial position is intended to provide information about such events, simply because they are not described anywhere else.

BORROWING

Working capital can be generated by borrowing current assets in exchange for a promise to pay back the amount borrowed after more than one year. Thus, current assets are increased but current liabilities are unchanged, so that working capital is increased. Borrowing on a short-term basis increases current assets and current liabilities equally and does nothing to increase net working capital. Borrowing on an installment basis with payments to be made over the next several periods increases both current assets and liabilities, but the former is increased more than the latter, and working capital is generated.

Again, a comparative balance sheet cannot tell the reader everything that happened concerning long-term borrowing. Some long-term debts may have been paid in cash and replaced by other, less expensive loans for the same amount, but no change would have appeared in the two balances. Any change that does appear could be only the net result of several transactions.

For Bright Enterprises, the decline of long-term debt from $22,000 to $18,000 can be traced to: (1) reclassification of a $7,000 note payable as a current liability, and (2) borrowing of $3,000 from a bank. Although the amounts shown on the comparative balance sheet decreased by $4,000, the underlying evidence shows that the firm generated $3,000 of working capital through borrowing. The underlying evidence can be found in the firm's journal and ledger.

CONVERSION OF NONCURRENT ASSETS

The firm's holdings of noncurrent assets, such as fixed assets and investments, frequently constitute a potential reservoir of working capital. If they can be sold for cash or exchanged for some current asset, working capital will be created. Or, if a current liability can be settled by giving up a noncurrent asset, net working capital will be increased. Clearly, not all noncurrent assets are readily convertible to current assets. Specially designed machinery, land, intangibles, and investments in wholly owned subsidiaries are generally more difficult to dispose of than others, and generally are not purchased with eventual sale in mind.

In measuring the working capital generated from the conversion of a noncurrent asset, the amount used is the *proceeds* of the sale rather than the *gain* or *loss* from the sale. Thus, if a machine is sold for $1,000 cash, the amount of working capital provided is $1,000, whether or not the book value of the machine is $100, $1,000, or $10,000. The event would be reported on the income statement as either a $900 gain, no gain, or a $9,000 loss, respectively. The treatment of the event is different on the income statement and the statement of changes in financial position because the information is used differently.

In examining the comparative balance sheets for Bright Enterprises, we cannot come to any positive conclusions concerning the conversion of either equipment or investments to cash. The Equipment account balance *increased* by $5,000, but a sale may have occurred and thereby reduced the amount of the increase from, for example, $13,000 to $5,000. The balance in the Investments account declined by $1,000, which could be the result of one event or of many. Furthermore, we cannot determine how much working capital was generated from the transactions. From underlying facts, we have discovered that no equipment was sold, and that an investment which originally cost $1,000 was sold for $2,000 (the difference between the cost and the proceeds was reported as an extraordinary gain of $1,000 on the income statement).

OPERATIONS

In most cases, the largest portion of working capital is generated through the marketing operations of the firm. Specifically, the sale of a product or service brings in cash and accounts receivable. In order to simplify the presentation of the information on the statement of changes in financial position, only the *net* amount of working capital generated or used by operations is shown, rather than listing the amounts of each separately.

There are two ways in which the net amount can be calculated. The first is technically more accurate, but it is more time consuming to produce and yields more detail than is conveniently read. The second approach produces the same result as the first, but involves fewer computations. It is preferred for this reason, and also because its starting point (net income) appears on the income statement. In order to assure that the reader can better understand the second method, we will examine both approaches.

Under the first, or *long*, approach, we have to examine each revenue and expense item in the original records of the firm in order to determine whether or not the event generated or used working capital. Virtually all sales transactions create working capital through either an addition to current assets or a decrease of current liabilities. It would be very unusual to find a sales transaction that added to noncurrent assets (such as a long-term receivable) or settled a long-term liability.

Many expenses reduce working capital. The cost of goods sold represents the reduction of inventory. Other expenses require an outlay of cash, the creation of accounts payable, or the consumption of prepaid expenses. However, depreciation of tangible fixed assets (and amortization of intangible fixed assets) involves the reduction of a noncurrent asset and does not reduce working capital.

Under this item-by-item approach, the following summary could be prepared for Bright Enterprises:

Working capital provided by:		
Sales		$64,500
Working capital used for:		
Salaries	$42,000	
Rent	3,000	
Other	1,500	
Income taxes	8,500	55,000
Working capital provided by operations		$ 9,500

In this particular example, there was not much difficulty in applying this approach, but imagine the more realistic situation where literally thousands of transactions would have to be analyzed.

The second, or *shortcut,* approach takes the reported net income from operations and adds to it those expenses that did not use working capital. Any revenues that did not generate working capital (which are very rare) would be deducted. For example:

Net income from operations	$6,500
Add: Depreciation expense	3,000
Working capital provided by operations	$9,500

A potential disadvantage of the shortcut approach is the appearance that depreciation and other noncash expenses are sources of funds. The naive observer might conclude that the greater depreciation expense is, the greater the working capital flow will be. Notice that if depreciation expense is increased, net income is decreased, and the working capital provided is exactly the same.

It is equally important to recognize that "net income" is *not* a "source" of working capital. *Net income* is a measure of the excess of rewards over efforts made to earn the rewards. It is a *result,* not an *event,* and it cannot accomplish anything in terms of providing working capital. *Operating activities* are events, and they are the sources and uses of funds. The net income figure appears in the statement of changes in financial position by tradition and to associate the statement with the income statement. For these reasons, the shortcut is used much more frequently in published statements than the long approach.

Notice that the shortcut computation of *working capital provided by operations* would have to alter the reported total net income if the gain or loss from the sale of a noncurrent asset were to be included in the figure. The income statement of Bright Enterprises showed a "net operating income" before considering the gain on the sale of the investment. If this distinction had *not* been drawn (that is, if only net income of $7,500 was reported), the following analysis would have to be made:

Net income	$ 7,500
Less: Gain on sale of investment	(1,000)
Add: Depreciation	3,000
Working capital provided by operations	$ 9,500

The adjustment is made because the sale of noncurrent assets is technically not an *operating* activity.

Uses of Working Capital

After describing the sources and amounts of working capital available to the firm during the year, the statement of changes in financial position next describes the purposes to which the working capital was applied as well as the amounts spent. The three major uses are: (1) distributions to owners, (2) debt repayment, and (3) acquisition of noncurrent assets. As we described earlier, the working capital used to pay for operations is deducted from the amount generated, and is not considered to be a separate use.

DISTRIBUTIONS TO OWNERS

Dividends, usually in the form of cash, are distributed to owners in settlement of their claims against the firm that have arisen from its successful earnings efforts. Dividends (or *withdrawals* for proprietorships and partnerships) are a major use of working capital, and the market value of the stock is frequently based on the firm's dividend-paying record. Consequently, if a manager fails to provide sufficient working capital for the distributions to the owners, he will be in an uncomfortable position. As mentioned earlier, a stock dividend does not constitute a use of working capital because no current assets are distributed.

From an extremely technical point of view, the *declaration* of a cash dividend is the event that actually uses working capital because this action creates a new current liability. And, when the dividend is finally paid, working capital is not affected because both cash and a current liability are reduced. This technicality does not alter the fact that distributions to owners must be considered in working capital management.

Other distributions to owners may occur through infrequent (but normal) circumstances, such as when treasury stock is acquired on the open market or when a particular partner or stockholder is "bought out."

It is not apparent from the balance sheets alone how much cash was withdrawn by the owner of Bright Enterprises during 1980. The basic records show that, over the year, $6,000 was paid to him.

DEBT REPAYMENT

If a noncurrent liability is settled by paying the creditor with current assets, the result is a decrease (or a *use*) of working capital. However, we should ask: Why would a liability be paid if it is noncurrent? Presumably, there would have to be some advantage in early retirement, such as avoided interest or a discount. If the loan can be settled for less than the amount shown on the balance sheet, the transaction will result in a gain, which would be reported on the income statement. However, the statement of changes in financial position would report only the amount paid as a use of working capital.

To repeat the point made earlier, cash does not have to flow out of the firm to cause a use of working capital. Reclassification of a long-term liability (or a portion of a long-term liability) as current results in a decrease of working capital, even though no cash is paid. And, when the new current liability *is* paid, no change in working capital results.

For Bright Enterprises, an analysis of the records would show that the Notes Payable disclosed under current liabilities on December 31, 1980, were signed in 1978, but will come due on May 1, 1981. Consequently, they are not long-term liabilities on December 31, 1980, and must be reclassified. Their conversion to the current designation has the effect of reducing working capital by $7,000.

ACQUISITIONS OF NONCURRENT ASSETS

The third major purpose to which working capital is applied is the acquisition of noncurrent assets, such as fixed assets and investments in stock. If the seller "finances" the acquisition by accepting a down payment with future payments over several periods, working capital is decreased to the extent of the down payment and the current liabilities. If assets are acquired through the issuance of stock, no working capital is used.

The records of Bright Enterprises show that the only noncurrent asset acquired during the year was an item of equipment purchased for $5,000 in cash.

Other Changes in Financial Position

A major disadvantage of the construction of the statement of changes in financial position on a strict working-capital basis is that some events can dramatically affect the firm's financial position without changing working capital. Although these events are relatively rare for most firms, they can be expected to occur occasionally, and, when they do, they are usually very significant. Some of these events are:

1. Acquiring assets by borrowing (on a long-term basis) from the seller
2. Acquiring assets by issuing stock to the seller
3. Acquiring assets by leasing over several years
4. Acquiring assets by exchanging other assets
5. Retiring debts by distributing noncurrent assets
6. Retiring debts by issuing stock
7. Distributing new stock to stockholders
8. Distributing noncurrent assets to stockholders

It should be quite apparent that the reader of the financial statement would want to be informed about events of this kind.

Practice varied before *APB Opinion No. 19,* which brought more consistency to the published statements. Under the provisions of the opinion, these "other events" can be disclosed in one of two ways: (1) They are listed in a separate section of the statements as "events affecting financial position that did not affect working capital." Or, (2) Each one is listed as *both* a source and a use of working capital. There is no substantial difference between the two, and there is little possibility that a reader would be misled by the choice of one over the other.

To keep the example simple, no events of this kind occurred at Bright Enterprises during 1980.

Exhibit 4-4 presents the main portion of Bright Enterprises' statement of changes in financial position, which lists the *events* that occurred during 1980 and their effects on working capital. Notice that the reported decrease in working capital of $2,500 corresponds to the change described in Exhibit 4-3 (page 82), which would be an integral part of the entire statement of

Exhibit 4-4
BRIGHT ENTERPRISES
Statement of Changes in Financial Position
For the Year Ended December 31, 1980

Working capital generated by:		
Operations:		
Net operating income	$6,500	
Add: Expense that did not use		
working capital: Depreciation	3,000	
Working capital from operations		$ 9,500
New contribution by owner		1,000
New borrowing		3,000
Proceeds of sale of investment		2,000
Total working capital generated		$15,500
Working capital used for:		
Distributions to owner		$ 6,000
Reclassification of long-term debt		7,000
Acquisition of new equipment		5,000
Total working capital used		$18,000
Net decrease in working capital		$ (2,500)

changes in financial position. We have followed the traditional approach of showing "working capital from operations" in the first position in the "sources" section. Any other location would be acceptable, especially if operations were not the source of the greatest amount of working capital.

PREPARATION OF
THE STATEMENT OF CHANGES IN FINANCIAL POSITION

To this point, we have emphasized the meaning and the format of the statement of changes in financial position. Managers will be able to understand and use the statement more wisely if they have an idea about its preparation. Those readers who will become accountants are certain to encounter more detailed descriptions than the following, but this introduction should provide a valuable background for that advanced study.

It is important to keep in mind that the preparer of the statement has access to a great deal of detailed information from the records of the firm. Before the issuance of *APB Opinion No. 19,* it was not unusual to find the external analyst attempting to construct the statement only from the comparative balance sheet and income statement. A rough approximation *can* be put together on that basis, but we must emphasize that such "detective work" is not necessary.

Schedule of Working Capital Account Balances

The computation of the change in working capital is easily accomplished by taking the differences between the beginning and ending balances of the current accounts. The source of this information is the ledger. The balance sheet may show this information but the details may not be available.

Sources of Working Capital

The first step in preparing the statement is to identify the sources of working capital and to measure their results. For each of the following items, we have shown the location of the required information:

Source	Information Location
Contributions by owners	Capital stock accounts in the ledger: Specifically, credit entries should be analyzed to determine the reasons for the increase and should be traced to the journal in order to determine the working capital added by the transaction.
Borrowing	Long-term liability accounts in the ledger: Specifically, credit entries should be analyzed to determine the reasons for the increase.
Conversion of noncurrent assets	Noncurrent asset accounts in the ledger: Specifically, credit entries should be analyzed and traced to the journal in order to determine the working capital added by the transaction.
Operations	Income statement, if depreciation and nonworking capital expenses are itemized; if not, the ledger must be consulted.

There are numerous systematic approaches to compiling the statement from the information sources, including *reversing of T accounts* and different forms of *work sheets*. All of them really serve only as well-structured analytical tools to assist the identification of every significant event that affected the firm's financial position during the year. Because our emphasis in this chapter is more on understanding the meaning and usefulness of the statement of changes in financial position, we have elected not to cover the details of any of these techniques.

From the analysis of these four general source areas, we should have developed a measure of the total working capital generated during the time period. The analysis should also have revealed whether or not there were any nonworking capital transactions, such as the acquisition of a fixed asset by issuing stock.

Uses of Working Capital

The next step in the preparation procedure is to determine how working capital was used during the time period, apart from the supporting of operations. Again, we identify the best source of the desired information:

Use	Information Location
Distributions to owners—dividends	Retained earnings accounts in the ledger: Specifically, debit entries should be analyzed to determine the reasons for the decrease. Also, the retained earnings statement would show dividends paid.

Use	Information Location
Distributions to owners—retirement of stock	Capital and treasury stock accounts in the ledger: Debit entries should be analyzed and traced to the journal to determine the working capital used in the transaction.
Debt repayment	Long-term liability accounts in the ledger: Specifically, the debit entries should be analyzed to determine the reasons for the decrease.
Asset acquisitions	Noncurrent asset accounts in the ledger: Specifically, debit entries should be analyzed and traced to the journal to determine the working capital used in the transaction.

The result of the analysis should be a measure of the amount of working capital that was used and what it was used for.

This information should be combined with the sources of working capital data. The difference between the amount generated and the amount used *should* correspond to the net increase or decrease in working capital found in the first step. If the amounts do not agree, we can be certain that at least one error, either arithmetical or conceptual, has been made. If the amounts do agree, we can be reasonably certain that the preparation is substantially complete and correct. It would be wise to double-check the procedures to have added assurance that a counterbalancing error has not occurred somewhere in the process.

Finally, the preparer should ask whether or not there have been any of those events that did not affect working capital that have escaped his attention. The analysis of the nonworking capital accounts should have revealed these events, but not necessarily. Because those events are unusual in nature and, when they occur, financially significant, it seems highly unlikely that they would escape the preparer's attention. The minutes of the board of directors' meetings should provide further assurance about the completeness of the analysis.

THE CASH BASIS

Heretofore, we have dealt exclusively with describing the changes in financial position in terms of working capital. The description can also be accomplished in terms of the cash account. The end result is usually a more complicated statement, and its analysis and preparation are also more complicated.

Cash is generated from basically the same four sources as working capital: (1) contributions by owners, (2) borrowing, (3) conversion of noncash assets, and (4) operations.

The determination of *cash from operations* is necessary because many sales do not generate cash directly; and many expenses do not use cash directly (cost of goods sold and insurance are good examples). Cash is usually the asset borrowed by the firm or invested by the owner, so no serious problems are encountered in this area except for including new accounts payable. The generation of cash from conversion of noncash assets

Exhibit 4-5
BRIGHT ENTERPRISES
Statement of Changes in Financial Position (Cash Basis)
For the Year Ended December 31, 1980

Cash generated by:			
Operations:			
Net operating income		$ 6,500	
Add: Expenses not using cash: Depreciation		3,000	
Add: Collection of receivables in excess of sales:			
Receivables from 1979 sales collected in 1980	$ 12,500		
Less: Receivables from 1980 sales *not* collected	(10,000)	2,500	
Deduct: Payments on payables in excess of purchases:			
Payables from 1980 purchases *not* paid in 1980	$ 4,000		
Less: Payables from 1979 purchases paid in 1980	(5,000)	(1,000)	
No change in prepaid expenses:			
Expenses for 1980 which were paid for in 1979	$ 3,000		
Expenses for 1981 which were paid for in 1980	(3,000)	–0–	
Total cash provided by operations			$11,000
Cash contributed by owner			1,000
New cash borrowing			3,000
Proceeds from sale of investment			2,000
Total cash generated			$17,000
Cash used for:			
Distributions to owner		$ 6,000	
Acquisition of new assets		5,000	
Total cash used			11,000
Net increase in cash			$ 6,000
Event affecting financial position that did not affect cash:			
Reclassification of long-term liability as current liability		$ 7,000	
Schedule of change in Cash Balance:			
Ending balance, December 31, 1980			$14,000
Beginning balance, January 1, 1980			8,000
Net increase in cash balance			$ 6,000

is more complicated because it must include collection of accounts receivable or other current assets.

Cash is used in much the same way as working capital. However, we have to account for the acquisition of noncash assets, which can include prepaid expenses, inventory, and accounts receivable. The payment of current liabilities is also a use of cash that is not a use of working capital.

A *cash flow analysis* is generally prepared internally in order to evaluate the performance of those persons responsible for managing cash. The detail of tle schedule makes it less useful for outsiders, especially when the schedule of working capital accounts accompanies the statement of changes in financial position prepared on the working capital basis.

Exhibit 4-5 shows the cash basis statement of changes in financial position for the year ended December 31, 1980, for Bright Enterprises. Even a short analysis will show that it contains more detail than the working capital approach seen in Exhibit 4-4. The collection of more receivables than were offered resulted in an addition of $2,500 to cash, but paying off more payables than were established used up $1,000 of cash. Depreciation expense is not a source of cash, but is merely entered on the statement because we followed the *shortcut* approach. The rest of the statement is virtually identical with the working capital basis except for the section labeled: *Event affecting financial position that did not affect cash.* The reclassification of the current maturity of the long-term debt was a use of working capital, but it did not reduce the cash balance. The event nonetheless had an effect on the description of the financial position of the firm presented on the balance sheet.

PROJECTED CHANGES IN FINANCIAL CONDITION

Perhaps the most extensive use of statements describing the events of the past is in projecting the events of the future. The past is gone and nothing can be done to change what did happen. However, we can learn from the past in order to better adapt to the future.

Internal users take the historical data and apply them in the context of their knowledge about what the management expects to accomplish in the future. The result of the analysis is called a *capital budget,* which will be discussed in more detail in Chapters 11, 12, 14, and 15. A capital budget serves not only as a guideline for future action but also for evaluating what actually happened after the future time period has passed.

The outside analyst can use the past statements to arrive at a less concrete prediction of the future. Nonetheless, the statement should assist him in making a well-informed decision. In the long run, the more informed decisions that are made, the more likely it is that the decision maker will be successful.

AN EXTENDED ILLUSTRATION

In order to show a more realistic statement of changes in financial position, to demonstrate the preparation of a statement, and to allow the reader to consolidate his newly acquired knowledge, the next few pages demonstrate the development of the statement of changes in financial position (on a working capital basis) for Century 21 Corporation. The comparative balance sheets for July 31, 1979 and July 31, 1980, appear in Exhibit 4-6. The income statement for the period between those dates appears in Exhibit 4-7.

Using information from the books of Century 21 Corporation (many of the facts are reflected in these statements), we can prepare the statement of changes in financial position. There are five basic steps that we will follow:

1. Determine the change in working capital.
2. Determine the sources and amounts of working capital generated.
3. Determine the purposes and amounts of working capital used.
4. Identify any other changes in financial position.
5. Prepare the statement.

Exhibit 4-6
CENTURY 21 CORPORATION
Comparative Balance Sheets
July 31, 1979 and 1980

Assets	1980	1979
Current assets:		
Cash	$ 17,992	20,443
Accounts receivable	56,130	49,299
Less: Allowance for doubtful accounts	(1,291)	(1,060)
Inventories	64,592	59,287
Prepaid insurance	1,824	1,599
Total current assets	$ 139,247	$ 129,568
Noncurrent assets:		
Machinery and equipment	$ 45,475	$ 48,146
Less: Accumulated depreciation	(28,914)	(25,200)
Building	40,000	40,000
Less: Accumulated depreciation	(18,500)	(17,300)
Land	2,391	1,091
Patent	2,000	–0–
Total noncurrent assets	$ 42,452	$ 46,737
Total assets	$181,699	$176,305
Liabilities and Stockholders' Equity		
Current liabilities:		
Accounts payable	$ 14,061	$ 11,933
Notes payable	9,013	7,902
Accrued taxes payable	7,752	11,859
Total current liabilities	$ 30,826	$ 31,694
Long-term liabilities:		
Bonds payable	$ 1,910	$ 2,559
Stockholders' equity:		
Preferred stock	$ 2,000	$ –0–
Common stock	55,000	50,000
Retained earnings	91,963	92,052
Total stockholders' equity	$148,963	$142,052
Total liabilities and stockholders' equity	$181,699	$176,305

Exhibit 4-7
CENTURY 21 CORPORATION
Income Statement
For the Year Ended July 31, 1980

Sales		$269,086
Cost of goods sold		(127,851)
Gross margin		$141,235
Selling expense*	$ 48,722	
Administrative expense*	75,317	
Depreciation	5,914	
Income taxes	6,200	(136,153)
Net operating income		$ 5,082
Loss on sale of machine		(171)
Net income		$ 4,911

*Excluding depreciation

Exhibit 4-8

CENTURY 21 CORPORATION
Schedule of Working Capital Account Balances
As of July 31, 1979 and 1980

	1980	1979	Change in Working Capital
Current assets:			
Cash	$ 17,992	$ 20,443	$ (2,451)
Accounts receivable	56,130	49,299	6,831
Allowance for doubtful accounts	(1,291)	(1,060)	(231)
Inventories	64,592	59,287	5,305
Prepaid insurance	1,824	1,599	225
Total	$139,247	$129,568	$ 9,679
Current liabilities:			
Accounts payable	$ 14,061	$ 11,933	$ (2,128)
Notes payable	9,013	7,902	(1,111)
Accrued taxes payable	7,752	11,859	4,107
Total	$ 30,826	$ 31,694	$ 868
Net working capital	$108,421	$ 97,874	$ 10,547

Step 1

From the comparative balance sheet, the changes in working capital for fiscal year 1980 can be found. Exhibit 4-8 shows the schedule of the working capital accounts. Steps 2 and 3 will show why the balance increased by $10,547.

Step 2

The four most commonly encountered sources of working capital are: contributions by owners, borrowing, conversion of noncurrent assets, and operations. We can go directly to the ledger of Century 21 to find out what happened during the year.

CONTRIBUTIONS BY OWNERS

When owners invest in a firm, the balance of the owners' equity account is increased. Thus, we can look at the various *capital stock* accounts to determine whether any new credit entries were made during fiscal year 1980. Our search would reveal two such entries: one to preferred stock for $2,000, and one to common stock for $5,000. In order to find out *why* the entries were made, we must turn to the journal.

In this case, we find that the preferred stock had been issued to the holder of a patent in return for the patent rights, which were recorded as a fixed asset. The apparent value of the patent was $2,000. Technically, the event did not generate working capital but it did affect financial condition. For this example, we will elect to treat the event as a source *and* a use of working capital (see page 87).

The $5,000 credit to common stock arose from the issuance of stock in return for $5,000 cash. This event did generate working capital for that amount.

BORROWING

Any new long-term borrowing would have been recorded as credits to the long-term liability accounts. Our search of Century 21 reveals that no events of this type occurred during fiscal year 1980.

CONVERSION OF NONCURRENT ASSETS

When assets are sold or otherwise disposed of, the event is recorded as a credit to the appropriate asset accounts. By going to the journal entry, we can find out how much working capital was provided. For Century 21, we find a credit of $5,171 to the Machinery account. From the journal, we discover that the asset had been depreciated by $1,000 up to the date that it was sold for $4,000. The difference between the selling price and the asset's book value ($5,171 less $1,000) produced a loss of $171, which was reported on the income statement in Exhibit 4-7. Our interest is in the fact that the event generated $4,000 of working capital.

OPERATIONS

The most complicated phase of the search for sources is to determine the working capital provided by operations. We will elect the shortcut approach because of its common usage. An examination of Century 21's revenue and expense accounts reveals that the only nonworking capital item is depreciation expense, which is shown on the income statement as $5,914. Thus, the working capital from operations:

Operating income	$ 5,082
Add: Nonworking capital expense	5,914
Working capital from operations[1]	$10,996

We have found the following amounts for sources of working capital:

Owner contribution (issue of preferred stock)	$ 2,000
Owner contribution (issue of common stock)	5,000
Sales of noncurrent assets	4,000
Operations	10,996
Total	$21,996

Step 3

Now, we can find out where this working capital went. The three major uses are: distributions to owners, debt repayment, and acquisition of noncurrent assets.

---

[1] This figure can be found also by subtracting the working capital expenses ($127,851 plus $48,772, plus $75,317, plus $6,200) from the revenues received as working capital ($269,086):

Working capital revenues	$269,086
Working capital expenses	258,090
Working capital from operations	$ 10,996

DISTRIBUTIONS TO OWNERS

Payments of assets to owners would be recorded as reductions, or debits, to the owners' equity accounts. To be certain that working capital (rather than fixed assets or capital stock) was distributed, the journal entry should be consulted. For Century 21 Corporation, the only debit to any stockholders' equity account was a $5,000 entry to Retained Earnings, which the journal shows to have been recorded for a cash dividend. Thus, $5,000 of working capital was distributed to the owners.

DEBT REPAYMENT

Any decreases in long-term liabilities would be recorded in those accounts with debit entries. Advance payments and reclassification of long-term debts as current liabilities would be the most likely events which would lead to a reduction in the account balance. For Century 21, a $649 debit was recorded to *Bonds Payable* during fiscal year 1980. The journal reveals that this amount of cash was paid to retire some bonds whose face value was also $649.

ACQUISITION OF NONCURRENT ASSETS

When new assets are acquired, debit entries are recorded in the asset accounts. To find out if and how much working capital was used for this purpose, these debit entries for a particular year can be traced through the journal for more information. Three of Century 21's asset accounts were debited during the year: Patents, Land, and Machinery. The entry to patents has been discussed earlier; it resulted from the issuance of capital stock. As part of our selection of format, this item must be shown as a use of working capital, even though no working capital was spent.

The journal shows that the other assets had been purchased with cash: land for $1,300, and machinery for $2,500.

At this point, our investigation has shown that working capital was used as follows:

Distributions to owners	$ 5,000
Debt repayment	649
Acquisition of asset (patent)	2,000
Acquisition of asset (land)	1,300
Acquisition of asset (machinery)	2,500
Total	$11,449

In order to test our procedures for completeness, we can see if the change found in step 1 corresponds to the difference between the amount found in steps 2 and 3:

Step 1: Increase in working capital	$10,547
Step 2: Working capital generated	$21,996
Step 3: Working capital used	(11,449)
Increase in working capital	$10,547

Thus, we can be fairly certain that we have discovered all events that used and generated working capital during fiscal year 1980.

Step 4

As a step of "caution," we would want to take a second look through the basic records to see if any event may have escaped our attention. As we saw in steps 2 and 3, a careful analysis would reveal events like the stock-for-patent exchange, and any special searches for them would be unnecessary. Just by looking through again, we produce an added measure of security.

Step 5

Finally, we can prepare the statement of changes in financial position. Century 21 Corporation's statement is shown in Exhibit 4-9. The information shown on it has been described in the preceding paragraphs. The schedule of working capital balances in Exhibit 4-8 would be an integral part of the statement.

SUMMARY

In this chapter, we discussed the statement of changes in financial position, which reports the *events* that occurred during the specified period and their effects on the firm's ability to pay its debts and to earn profits. Both managers and outsiders can find useful information about what happened in the past and what will happen in the future.

Exhibit 4-9
CENTURY 21 CORPORATION
Statement of Changes in Financial Position
For the Year Ended July 31, 1980

Working capital generated by:		
Operations:		
Net operating income	$5,082	
Add: Expenses that did not use		
working capital: Depreciation	5,914	
Working capital from operations		$10,996
Proceeds from issuing preferred stock		2,000
Proceeds from issuing common stock		5,000
Proceeds from sale of machine		4,000
Total working capital generated		$21,996
Working capital used for:		
Payment of dividends	$5,000	
Retirement of bonds	649	
Acquisition of patent	2,000	
Purchase of land	1,300	
Purchase of machine	2,500	
Total working capital used		11,449
Net increase in working capital		$10,547

The nature of the statement is to describe the amounts of working capital generated and used by the firm. There are four major sources of working capital: owners, lenders, buyers of noncurrent assets, and customers. Working capital goes to owners, lenders, sellers of noncurrent assets, and other suppliers. The amount of working capital needs to be managed to assure that bills and debts are paid, opportunities are taken, and profitable investments are made.

The information on which the statement of changes in financial position is based can be found in the ledger accounts. It is possible to prepare a statement (on the basis of conjecture) from the comparative balance sheets and the income statement. This effort is unnecessary because *APB Opinion No. 19* requires that the full statement of changes in financial position be included and audited with the other statements.

As an alternative to the working capital basis, a cash basis can be used to construct the statement. The result is a more detailed presentation, which is generally more useful for managers than it is for outsiders.

QUESTIONS

1. What is a firm's "financial position"? How do comparative balance sheets and income statements fall short of describing *changes* in financial position?
2. What is "working capital"? Give two reasons for having it available.
3. Explain the disadvantage of having *too much* working capital on hand.
4. Describe the four major sources of working capital available to the firm.
5. In what sense is an owner's contribution of services to the firm equivalent to the contribution of cash?
6. Does short-term borrowing increase working capital? Explain.
7. Describe the four major purposes accomplished by spending working capital.
8. Is the payment of a short-term loan a use of working capital? Explain.
9. What does the schedule of working capital account balances show?
10. What are the major sections of the *statement of changes in financial position?*
11. What is the difference, if any, between the *gain* on the sale of a fixed asset and the *working capital generated* by that sale?
12. Describe two ways to find the amount of working capital generated by operations.
13. Is *net income* a source of working capital? Is *depreciation* a source of working capital? Explain.
14. Is it a use of working capital to reclassify a long-term liability as current? Explain.

15. Give several examples of significant events in a firm's life that can affect its financial position without affecting its working capital. How are they disclosed by the firm?

16. Identify the location in the ledger where information about these events can be found:
    a. contributions by owner
    b. borrowing
    c. conversion of noncurrent assets
    d. operations
    e. dividends
    f. retirement of stock
    g. debt repayment
    h. asset acquisitions

17. How does the *cash basis* differ from the *working capital basis*?

18. Identify five steps in producing a statement of changes in financial position.

EXERCISES

E4–1 *Schedule of working capital accounts.* From the following excerpt of the comparative balance sheet for Baggly's Trading Post, prepare a schedule of working capital accounts, showing the change in working capital for the year.

	December 31	
	1981	**1980**
Accounts payable	$ 7,500	$ 9,000
Accounts receivable	12,000	13,500
Cash	4,200	2,900
Fixed assets (cost)	60,000	48,000
Accumulated depreciation	28,000	35,000
Inventory	35,200	40,000
Notes payable (current)	17,600	12,000
Notes receivable (long-term)	1,800	3,500
Prepaid rent	200	600
Marketable securities (current)	2,600	2,600
Retained earnings	35,300	20,400
Wages payable	700	–0–

E4–2 *Schedule of working capital accounts.* From the following account balances in the books of Gordon's Beanery, prepare a schedule of working account balances showing the changes in working capital for the year ended July 31, 1980.

	1980	1979
Taxes payable (current)	$ 800	$ 1,000
Sales revenue	93,600	87,000
Prepaid insurance	4,200	4,000
Notes receivable (long-term)	6,000	3,800

	1980	1979
Notes payable (current)	$11,000	$ 8,000
Inventory	2,900	750
Cash	3,600	3,600
Capital stock issued	9,500	9,500
Building	24,600	24,600
Accumulated depreciation	12,300	11,100
Accounts receivable	2,600	1,800
Accounts payable	4,100	4,000

E4–3 **Working capital generated.**

Part 1:

From the information presented below, calculate the "funds pro-vided by operations" during the past year, using (a) the *item-by-item analysis*, and (b) the *shortcut* methods:

OZARK COMPANY
Income Statement
For the Year Ended December 31, 1981

Sales		$800,000
Cost of goods sold		450,000
Gross margin		$350,000
Depreciation expense	$ 44,000	
Other expenses	100,000	144,000
Operating profit		$206,000
Loss on sale of equipment		15,000
Net income before taxes		$191,000
Income taxes		91,000
Net income		$100,000

Part 2:

The loss on the sale of equipment was computed as:

Assets received by Ozark	$ 70,000
Book value of equipment	(85,000)
Loss on sale	$(15,000)

Ozark received these assets from the buyer: $40,000 cash, a $20,000 6-month note, and a $10,000 24-month note. The equip-ment originally cost $150,000 and had been depreciated by $65,000.

Required:

What was the amount of working capital generated by the sale?

E4–4 **Working capital from operations.** From this income statement, determine the working capital generated from operations using (a) the item-by-item analysis, and (b) the shortcut method:

OLD DOMINION, INC.
Income Statement
For the Year Ended October 31, 1980

Sales		$287,000
Cost of goods sold		
Beginning inventory	$ 43,000	
Purchases	214,000	
Ending inventory	(52,000)	205,000
Gross margin		82,000
Expenses		
Salaries	$ 24,000	
Building rent	18,000	
Equipment depreciation	43,000	
Patent amortization	17,000	
Interest expense*	5,000	107,000
Net loss		$ 25,000

*Cash paid	$6,000
Bond premium amortized	(1,000)
Interest expense	$5,000

E4–5 *Statement of changes in financial position.* From the comparative balance sheet below, prepare a statement of changes in financial
position, including a schedule showing the working capital account
balances.

BRYCE COMPANY
Comparative Balance Sheet
June 30 and September 30, 1982

	September 30	June 30
Current assets	$ 2,600	$ 2,000
Land	12,000	10,000
Building	60,000	40,000
Less: Accumulated depreciation	(8,500)	(8,000)
Total assets	$66,100	$44,000
Current liabilities	$ 2,200	$ 1,500
Bonds payable	11,000	12,000
Capital stock	20,000	16,000
Retained earnings	32,900	14,500
Total liabilities and equities	$66,100	$44,000

The ledger and journal revealed the following information:

1. One parcel of land was bought for cash; none were sold.
2. An addition to the building was completed and paid for in cash;
   no credit entries were recorded in the Building account.
3. One bond payable for $1,000 was retired by paying the face
   value in cash to the holder.
4. One hundred shares of stock were issued for $40 cash each.
5. The only entry to the Retained Earnings account was for the
   excess of the revenues over the expenses.

E4–6 *Statement of changes in financial position.* Lattigo Divers, Inc., began operations in January of this year when the Lattigo family members contributed various assets in exchange for capital stock, and borrowed cash from the bank, which was used, in part, to buy a boat. The balance sheet at January 15, 1981, appears as follows:

Current assets	$ 1,000	Note payable	$40,000
Boat	50,000	Common stock	46,000
Investments	35,000		
Total	$86,000	Total	$86,000

During the year, various events occurred that caused changes in the firm's financial position:

1. Equipment was acquired by exchanging some of the investments. There was no gain or loss.
2. Half of the note payable was paid by distributing common stock to the bank.
3. Diving operations yielded profits of $17,000.
4. A cash dividend was paid to the stockholders.

At the end of 1981, the balance sheet appeared as follows:

Current assets	$14,000	Current liabilities	$ 5,000
Equipment	15,000	Note payable	20,000
Less: Accumulated			
depreciation	(1,000)		
Boat	50,000		
Less: Accumulated		Capital stock	66,000
depreciation	(4,000)	Retained earnings	3,000
Investments	20,000		
Total	$94,000	Total	$94,000

Required:

Prepare a statement of changes in financial position for Lattigo Divers, Inc., for the period from January 16, 1981 to December 31, 1981. Your statement should include those events that did not affect working capital, and treat them as both sources and uses of working capital.

E4–7 *Cash from operations.* From the income statement of the Ozark Company shown in E4–3, and from the following account balances, find the net amount of *cash* provided by operations during 1981.

	December 31, 1981	January 1, 1981
Accounts receivable	$70,000	$60,000
Inventory	86,000	77,000
Prepaid expenses	4,300	4,000
Accounts payable	42,000	49,000
Accrued interest payable	800	1,000
Accrued taxes payable	24,000	20,000

PROBLEMS

P4–1   *Statement of changes in financial position.*   From the facts that appear below, prepare a statement of changes in financial position for the Cambridge Corporation for the year ended December 31, 1982 (including a schedule of working capital accounts):

CAMBRIDGE CORPORATION
Comparative Balance Sheet
December 31, 1981 and 1982

	1982	1981
Current assets	$219,300	$175,000
Plant and equipment	235,400	183,600
Less: Accumulated depreciation	(102,800)	(97,300)
Delivery equipment	42,800	47,000
Less: Accumulated depreciation	(15,260)	(13,800)
Land	19,900	24,200
Goodwill	–0–	460
Total assets	$399,340	$319,160
Current liabilities	$102,700	$ 86,400
Bonds payable	105,000	75,000
Capital stock	132,800	113,500
Retained earnings	58,840	44,260
Total liabilities and equities	$399,340	$319,160

Other facts:

1. For $25,000 cash, a machine was sold that had originally been purchased for $75,000, and depreciated by $47,000 at the time of sale. The loss on the sale was *extraordinary*.

2. For $126,800 cash, other machinery was purchased.

3. For $260 cash, a delivery truck was sold that had originally been purchased for $4,200, and depreciated by $3,940.

4. No new delivery equipment purchases were made.

5. For $8,000 cash, a piece of land was sold that had cost $4,300. The gain on the sale was *extraordinary*.

6. Bonds Payable were increased by new borrowing of $45,000 cash.

7. Bonds Payable were decreased by $15,000 by an exchange of the bonds for new shares of stock. There was no gain or loss on the exchange.

8. Capital Stock on the books at $10,000 was retired by a cash payment equal to the book value.

9. Capital stock was issued in exchange for $14,300 cash.

10. Ordinary earnings for the year were $27,760. Depreciation and amortization expenses for the year were:

Plant and equipment	$52,500
Delivery equipment	5,400
Goodwill	460

11. A cash dividend was declared, payable for an amount equal to half of the ordinary earnings.

P4–2 **Statement of changes in financial position.** Following are the comparative balance sheet and income statement for the Bullock Company:

BULLOCK COMPANY
Comparative Balance Sheet
October 31, 1979 and 1980

	1980	1979
Cash	$ 45,641	$ 32,951
Accounts receivable	70,806	52,926
Inventory	71,810	75,270
Equipment	69,253	63,673
Less: Accumulated depreciation	(26,683)	(23,573)
Building	130,000	130,000
Less: Accumulated depreciation	(45,500)	(39,000)
Land	50,865	62,865
Patent	21,140	22,650
Total assets	$387,332	$377,762
Accounts payable	$ 48,275	$ 52,870
Accrued selling expenses payable	2,595	4,620
Accrued administrative expenses payable	2,400	2,102
Mortgage payable	100,000	100,000
Common stock	172,935	166,575
Retained earnings	61,127	51,595
Total liabilities and equities	$387,332	$377,762

The ledger and journal revealed these other facts:

1. A piece of equipment was sold for a price that produced the $200 loss seen on the income statement. Its original cost was $1,600, and its book value at the time of sale was $700.

2. A parcel of land that originally cost $12,000 was sold for cash at a price that yielded the gain of $320 seen on the income statement.

3. There was only one entry in the Common Stock account, resulting from the issuance of stock for cash.

4. Dividends of $3,240 were declared and paid in cash.

5. New equipment was purchased during the year for $7,180 cash.

6. The accrued expenses payable are current liabilities.

Required:

Prepare a complete statement of changes in financial position, including a schedule of the working capital account balances.

BULLOCK COMPANY
Income Statement
For the Year Ended October 31, 1980

Sales		$446,510
Cost of goods sold		
Beginning inventory	$ 75,270	
Purchases	374,476	
Ending inventory	(71,810)	377,936
Gross margin		$ 68,574
Expenses		
Selling	$ 23,604	
Administrative	12,863	
Equipment depreciation	4,010	
Building depreciation	6,500	
Patent amortization	1,510	48,487
Operating income before taxes		$ 20,087
Income taxes		7,435
Operating income after taxes		$ 12,652
Extraordinary items:		
Gain on sale of land	$ 320	
Loss on sale of equipment	(200)	120
Net income		$ 12,772

P4–3 *Statement of changes in financial position.* The financial statements of the Adderly Company are shown below:

ADDERLY COMPANY
Comparative Balance Sheet
December 31, 1981 and 1982

	1982	1981
Cash	$ 31,500	$ 20,100
Accounts receivable	33,400	35,500
Inventories	35,563	25,432
Prepaid insurance	1,400	1,200
Office equipment	35,445	32,750
Less: Accumulated depreciation	(18,210)	(16,150)
Delivery trucks	33,020	26,430
Less: Accumulated depreciation	(13,126)	(10,940)
Building	85,300	85,300
Less: Accumulated depreciation	(25,590)	(21,325)
Land	26,365	15,190
Total assets	$225,067	$193,487
Accounts payable	$ 47,104	$ 56,520
Accrued selling expenses payable	1,875	2,910
Mortgage payable (current)	20,000	–0–
Mortgage payable (long-term)	30,000	50,000
Common stock ($125 par)	75,000	50,000
Premium on common stock	8,200	6,200
Retained earnings	42,888	27,857
Total liabilities and equities	$225,067	$193,487

ADDERLY COMPANY
Income Statement
For the Year Ended December 31, 1982

Sales		$559,967
Cost of goods sold		
Beginning inventory	$ 25,432	
Purchases	479,446	
Ending inventory	(35,563)	469,315
Gross margin		$ 90,652
Expenses:		
Administrative	$ 12,300	
Selling	25,000	
Insurance	5,100	
Office equipment depreciation	3,455	
Delivery trucks depreciation	5,286	
Building depreciation	4,265	55,406
Operating income before taxes		$ 35,246
Income taxes		14,590
Operating income after taxes		$ 20,656
Extraordinary loss on		
sale of delivery equipment		625
Net income		$ 20,031

The ledger and journal revealed these additional facts:

1. There was one credit entry each to the Common Stock and Premium on Common Stock accounts, which arose from the issuance of 200 shares at $135 each.

2. A delivery truck was sold for $515, producing the extraordinary loss of $625 seen on the income statement. Its original cost had been $4,240.

3. Two delivery trucks had been purchased during the year for $5,415 cash each.

4. A debit entry to the Land account arose from the cash acquisition of a neighboring parcel. No land was sold during the year.

5. There was a credit entry to the Office Equipment account for $1,395, and a debit entry to Office Equipment Depreciation for the same amount. The entry in the journal showed that the particular item was worn out and discarded in the trash.

6. A debit entry to the Office Equipment account recorded the acquisition of several items for $4,090. This amount was credited to Accounts Payable, and was still unpaid.

7. A $20,000 payment on the mortgage is due March 1, 1983.

8. A dividend of $5,000 was declared and paid in cash.

Required:

Prepare a statement of changes in financial position, including a schedule of the working capital account balances.

P4–4 *Statement of changes in financial position.* The management of Wichita Pipeline Company is considering future expansion of plant facilities. In order to obtain new property, buildings, and equipment, more working capital must be acquired. A report is needed showing how net working capital has increased or decreased during the past year, 1983. Financial statements regarding the company are presented on pages 107 and 108.

WICHITA PIPELINE COMPANY
Comparative Balance Sheet
December 31, 1982 and 1983

Assets	1983	1982
Cash	$ 45,600	$ 40,300
Marketable securities	32,700	26,700
Accounts receivable (net)	112,000	97,800
Inventories	88,900	85,400
Prepaid expenses	3,800	3,200
Equipment	107,900	91,400
Less: Accumulated depreciation	(25,600)	(22,900)
Buildings	206,000	206,000
Less: Accumulated depreciation	(92,700)	(82,400)
Land	120,000	120,000
Goodwill	6,000	8,000
	$604,600	$573,500
Liabilities and Owners' Equity		
Accounts payable	$120,800	$114,300
Accrued expenses payable (current)	2,800	3,200
Current portion of long-term debt	25,000	30,000
Long-term debt	155,000	180,000
Common stock ($50 par value)	200,000	175,000
Paid-in capital in excess of par	13,000	13,000
Retained earnings	88,000	58,000
	$604,600	$573,500

The ledger and journal revealed these facts:

1. Short-term marketable securities were acquired for $6,000 cash.

2. A credit to the Equipment account of $14,300 recorded the sale of an item whose original cost equaled that amount. The item had been depreciated by $12,900 when it was sold. The sale caused the $3,000 gain on the income statement.

3. Three debit entries to the Equipment account recorded the acquisition of three items of equipment for $4,399, $13,501, and $12,900. All but the last item had been paid for entirely in cash. The balance owed ($5,000) on the last one is included in Accounts Payable, and is due on January 20, 1984.

4. Of the $30,000 current maturity at December 31, 1982, one-half was paid in cash, and one-half was paid by issuing stock.

The par and fair market values of the shares were the same on that date.

5. Another $10,000 entry to the Common Stock account recorded a cash sale of stock.

6. No dividends were declared or paid on the outstanding stock during the year.

7. A total of $25,000 of the long-term debt will become due and payable during 1984.

WICHITA PIPELINE COMPANY
Income Statement
For the Year Ended December 31, 1983

Sales			$575,000
Cost of materials used			
Beginning inventory		$ 85,400	
Purchases		363,500	
Ending inventory		(88,900)	360,000
Gross margin			$215,000
Expenses:			
Pipeline:			
Wages	$68,950		
Building depreciation	10,300		
Equipment depreciation	12,000		
Repairs and maintenance	710		
Utilities	1,360		
Lease rentals	1,420		
Payroll taxes	1,267	$ 96,007	
Selling:			
Advertising	$ 3,400		
Salaries	30,700		
Payroll taxes	564		
Insurance	4,400	39,064	
General and administrative:			
Office miscellaneous	$ 1,200		
Salaries	20,100		
Payroll taxes	369		
Goodwill amortization	2,000		
Contributions	800		
Equipment depreciation	3,600		
Office rent	2,400		
Interest	360	30,829	165,900
Operating income before taxes			$ 49,100
Income taxes			22,100
Operating income after taxes			$ 27,000
Extraordinary gain on sale of equipment			3,000
Net income			$ 30,000

Required:

Prepare a complete statement of changes in financial position for 1983, including a schedule of the working capital accounts.

P4–5 **Statement of changes in financial position.**   A series of successful contract negotiations has brought the management of the Woolley Blanket Company to the realization that some working capital is going to have to be raised in order to pay for a badly needed expansion of capacity.

An early contact with the bank yielded the fact that a statement of changes in financial position will be needed, as well as the balance sheet for the last two years and the latest income statement.

Your task is to construct the necessary statement of changes. The statements on pages 110 and 111 and other data from the records are available for your assistance.

The ledger and journal revealed the following:

1. Cash dividends had been declared and paid during the year in the amount of $1,380.

2. The debit side of the Equipment account showed that new items had been acquired for a total of $6,560.

3. The credit side of the Equipment account showed that old items costing $3,280 had been sold. The journal revealed that the selling price was $1,530.

4. The Accumulated Depreciation account for equipment showed a debit of $500 (for the sold items) and a credit of $670 (for the year's expense).

5. The debit side of the Buildings account showed that a new building costing $8,000 had been purchased.

6. The credit side of the Building account showed that an old building costing $4,000 had been sold. The journal revealed that the selling price was $755.

7. The Accumulated Depreciation account for buildings showed a debit of $1,245 (for the sold structure) and a credit of $825 (for the year's expense).

8. The interest expense included a $20 amortization of the bond discount:

Cash paid	$665
Discount amortization	20
Total expense	$685

9. The Common and Preferred Stock accounts showed credits of $1,000 and $5,500, respectively. Both amounts had been promised, but were as yet uncollected on December 31, 1980. The amounts due were included in Accounts Receivable.

10. The Land account was debited for the purchase of a parcel for $800 cash.

11. The mortgage arrangement calls for $500 to be paid every April 21.

WOOLLEY BLANKET COMPANY
Comparative Balance Sheet
December 31, 1979 and 1980

	1980	1979
Current assets:		
Cash	$ 5,835	$ 6,565
Marketable securities	10,000	7,500
Notes receivable	2,690	1,240
Accounts receivable	19,925	12,335
Interest receivable	800	720
Inventories	32,900	24,875
Prepaid expenses	2,725	1,365
Total current assets	$ 74,875	$54,600
Fixed assets:		
Land	$ 4,800	$ 4,000
Buildings	36,000	32,000
Less: Accumulated depreciation	(8,220)	(8,640)
Equipment	16,830	13,550
Less: Accumulated depreciation	(4,850)	(4,680)
Total fixed assets	$ 44,560	$36,230
Total assets	$119,435	$90,830
Current liabilities:		
Accounts payable	$ 6,840	$ 5,650
Accrued expenses payable	12,316	1,870
Notes payable	1,560	2,010
Current maturity of mortgage payment	500	500
Total current liabilities	$ 21,216	$10,030
Long-term liabilities:		
Mortgage payable	$ 2,500	$ 3,000
Bonds payable	10,000	10,000
Less: Bond Discount	(160)	(180)
Total long-term liabilities	$ 12,340	$12,820
Total liabilities	$ 33,556	$22,850
Stockholders' equity		
Preferred stock	$ 24,700	$19,200
Common stock	33,000	32,000
Retained earnings	28,179	16,780
Total stockholders' equity	$ 85,879	$67,980
Total liabilities and equities	$119,435	$90,830

Required:

a. Prepare the statement of changes in financial position.

b. Do you see any apparent strengths and weaknesses in Woolley's situation? The bank loan would be for $40,000. The proceeds would be used to finance acquisitions of buildings, equipment, and inventory. The loan would be repaid after 5 years.

WOOLLEY BLANKET COMPANY
Income Statement
For the Year Ended December 31, 1980

Sales		$153,000
Cost of goods sold		
Beginning inventory	$ 24,875	
Purchases	90,025	
Ending inventory	(32,900)	82,000
Gross margin		$ 71,000
Expenses:		
Rent	$ 6,000	
Repairs and maintenance	8,000	
Depreciation	1,495	
Interest	685	
Selling and administrative	28,665	44,845
Other income: Interest earned		560
Operating income before taxes		$ 26,715
Taxes on income		10,686
Operating income after taxes		$ 16,029
Extraordinary losses:		
On sale of building	$ 2,000	
On sale of equipment	1,250	3,250
Net income		$ 12,779

P4–6 *Cash from operations.* Using the information given in P4-2, prepare a schedule showing the cash generated by operations.

P4–7 *Cash from operations.* Using the information given in P4-3, prepare a schedule showing the cash generated by operations.

P4–8 *Cash basis.* Using the information given in P4-4, prepare a statement of changes in financial position on the cash basis.

5

Accounting and Inflation

Virtually all accounting reports, whether internal or external, depend on monetary quantities to relay economic facts to decision makers. These quantities are the bases for various analytical techniques, many of which involve manipulation of the data by addition, subtraction, multiplication, and division. It seems self-evident that before we add two numbers to obtain a sum, we should make sure that they are consistent with each other. For example, if the width of a table is 60 centimeters and its length is 40 inches, there would be little significance in adding these two quantities together to get 100 "somethings." If an automobile has its gasoline consumption efficiency described in kilometers per liter, the result is not directly comparable with other cars rated in terms of miles per gallon (especially when we realize that there are "U.S." and "Imperial" gallons).

In preparing financial statements and other reports, it has been traditionally assumed that every unit of a currency is exactly alike, whether it is present or past. However, one does not need to be an economics expert to be aware that today's dollar does not buy what it used to. In this chapter, our objectives are to describe purchasing power and price indexes, and to show how price indexes can be used to produce more helpful accounting reports.

To deal with this problem of inconsistent units, accounting experts have urged the publication of supplementary data based on the conversion of the different dollars to one particular dollar. At the time of this writing, the use of the described procedures is not mandatory. However, we feel that the information is sufficiently useful to justify describing its preparation.

PURCHASING POWER

The value of anything can be described in terms of what can be acquired in exchange for it. In primitive societies, a person's wealth was equated with the number of horses or other worldly goods that he owned. Although this system may suffice for a small group, we can see problems of precision arising because not all horses are of equal desirability. A 1,000-acre parcel of land in the desert may not be as valuable as half an acre in a city. Perhaps in recognition of the measurement problem, more advanced cultures described wealth in terms of a more standard, invariable commodity, such as a given quantity of gold or silver. From this practice, there developed the concept of money as a *medium of exchange* and a repository of value. We can see a vestige of this custom in the name of the British "pound sterling," which used to have the value of one pound of sterling silver.

In an ideal situation, the unit of money would be forever constant, much as a foot is always 12 inches in length. But money is not fixed in supply, nor is the demand for it constant. And we find that today's dollar, for example, is not "worth" what it was a year ago. When we complain of the "shrinking" dollar, we are not complaining of a physically smaller dollar bill, nor of the fact that we receive only 90 cents when we ask for change. Our complaint is more substantive, because we have found that the dollar will not buy the same quantity of goods that it used to.

Financial statements and other accounting reports are intended to describe various aspects of a firm, such as its wealth or its successful operations. The asset side of a balance sheet, for example, is basically a list of various items the firm owns, and the remaining value available from them for the managers. Under traditional financial accounting rules, the "value" is frequently the original cost, expressed in *original dollars*. Thus, we find that the dollar sum called "total assets" really can be a sum of numbers of different-size monetary units if the individual assets are acquired at different times.

To use an obvious analogy, in Exhibit 5-1, we show the balance sheet of a businessman who operates in the United States, Great Britain, and Germany. Consequently, he deals with different customers in different currencies. His balance sheet does not balance because the monetary units are not the same size. If it is known that 1 deutsche mark (DM) is worth $0.40, and that 1 pound sterling (£) is worth $2.00, then the account balances can be converted into the equivalent amount of purchasing power in one consistent

Exhibit 5-1
INTERNATIONAL BUSINESSMAN, INC.
Original Currency Balance Sheet
December 31, 1977

Cash	$ 1,000
Accounts receivable	$ 14,000
Investments (at cost)	DM 9,500
Fixed assets	£ 8,000
Accumulated depreciation	£ (2,000)
Total assets	? 30,500
Current liabilities	DM14,000
Long-term liabilities	£ 6,500
Stockholders' equity	$ 12,200
Total equities	? 32,700

Exhibit 5-2
INTERNATIONAL BUSINESSMAN, INC.
U.S. Dollar Balance Sheet
December 31, 1977

	Original Currency	Conversion Ratios	U.S. Dollars
Cash	$ 1,000	——	$ 1,000
Accounts receivable	$ 14,000	——	14,000
Investments (at cost)	DM 9,500	$0.40/DM1	3,800
Fixed assets (at cost)	£ 8,000	$2.00/£1	16,000
Accumulated depreciation	£ (2,000)	$2.00/£1	(4,000)
Total assets	? 30,500		$30,800
Current liabilities	DM14,000	$0.40/DM1	$ 5,600
Long-term liabilities	£ 6,500	$2.00/£1	13,000
Stockholders' equity	$ 12,200	——	12,200
Total equities	? 32,700		$30,800

currency. Exhibit 5-2 shows the conversion into U.S. dollars. The reader should perform the appropriate conversions to construct the balance sheet in DM and £. The figures for total assets should be DM77,000 or £15,400. This converted balance sheet is more meaningful, and the computation of ratios will produce logically consistent numbers.

For example, the current ratio before conversion was a meaningless 1.07, or ($1,000 + $14,000)/DM14,000. After conversion into dollars, the ratio is more consistently computed as 2.68, or ($1,000 + $14,000)/$5,600. The debt-to-total-capital ratio before conversion coincidentally has a value very close to the value when all the numbers are in dollars. The ratio before conversion is (DM14,000 + £6,500)/?32,700, or 0.63. The combination of monetary units makes the ratio take on a ridiculous value. Nonetheless, the converted ratio value is ($5,600 + $13,000)/$30,800, or 0.60. This example shows that erroneous methods can accidentally produce correct decisions. In the long run, the greatest likelihood is that we will make more bad decisions than good ones.

Let us look now at the balance sheet of a domestic firm, as shown in Exhibit 5-3. Are there any monetary unit problems here? Suppose that the investments had been acquired in 1972 and the fixed assets in 1970. Also, what if the stockholders' equity was derived from an investment by stockholders in 1969 and 1977 and from successful operations every year since 1971? We find that through the effects of inflation, the balance sheet account balances are composed of different-value dollars.

If we use the symbol $\$_{(n)}$ to stand for the dollar from the end of the year n, such as $\$_{(77)}$ for the dollar from the end of 1977, the balance sheet in Exhibit 5-4 will appear to be as inconsistent as the one in Exhibit 5-1. The different original dollars have different values and should all be converted to a single monetary unit of equal value, just as foreign currencies were converted to the U.S. dollar. In the next section, we will describe how purchasing power can be measured and value assigned to a particular dollar. Then, we will see how the account balances can be converted to a single, consistent unit of money and used to create more meaningful financial statements and other reports.

Exhibit 5-3
DOMESTIC BUSINESSMAN, INC.
Balance Sheet
December 31, 1977

Cash	$ 11,000
Investments (at cost)	19,000
Accounts receivable	23,000
Fixed assets (at cost)	100,000
Accumulated depreciation	(35,000)
Total assets	$118,000
Current liabilities	$ 17,000
Long-term liabilities	48,000
Stockholders' equity	53,000
Total equities	$118,000

Exhibit 5-4
DOMESTIC BUSINESSMAN, INC.
Original Dollar Balance Sheet
December 31, 1977

Cash	$(77)	11,000
Investments (at cost)	$(72)	19,000
Accounts receivable	$(77)	23,000
Fixed assets (at cost)	$(70)	100,000
Accumulated depreciation	$(70)	(35,000)
Total assets	$(?)	118,000*
Current liabilities	$(77)	17,000
Long-term liabilities	$(77)	48,000
Stockholders' equity	$(?)	53,000*
Total equities	$(?)	118,000*

*The symbol $(?) indicates that the quantity is a mixture of dollars with different values.

MEASURING PURCHASING POWER

The purchasing power of any currency unit is extremely difficult to measure. An approach that has been developed with a noticeable amount of success is the *price index*. The computation of a price index involves several steps, the first of which is the determination of the prices of a particular group of assets at several points in time. One of the points is selected as a *base*, and the prices from the other times are expressed as a *percentage of the prices at that base point*.

Let us construct a very simple price index by examining the behavior of the price of a standard wooden chair. Assume that our findings show the following facts about the price of a chair:

Year	Price
1920	$25
1950	40
1980	75

First, we will use 1920 as our base year, and our index will take on a value of 100 for 1920 (the price of the chair in 1920 is 100 percent of the price of the chair in 1920). For 1950, we will divide the price of the chair by the 1920 price ($40/$25), and convert the quotient to a percentage: 160. For 1980, with a base year of 1920, the index has a value of 300 ($75/$25).

Now, use 1950 as the base year. The size of the index in 1920 is 62.5 ($25/$40). For 1950, the index is 100. And for 1980, the index is 187.5 ($75/$40).

Finally, we can select 1980 for the base, and we can compute the 1920 index to be 33.3 ($25/$75), 1950 to be 53.3 ($40/$75), and 1980 to be 100 ($75/$75). The following table summarizes these computations:

	1920	1950	1980
Price of chair	$25	$40	$75
Price index values:			
Base year 1920	100.0	160.0	300.0
Base year 1950	62.5	100.0	187.5
Base year 1980	33.3	53.3	100.0

Notice that the relationship between any two years is the same, regardless of the base year. For example, we can say that the cost of a chair has tripled between 1920 and 1980 by looking at base years 1920 (300/100 = 3), 1950 (187.5/62.5 = 3), or 1980 (100/33.3 = 3).

Actually, it is somewhat imprecise to express a price index for a *period of time,* such as for a year or a month. Prices may change throughout the period, such that the *year's price* can be no more than an average in itself. To be most precise, a price index should describe the purchasing power of the dollar at a particular *point* in time, such as "midnight, December 15, 1979." Such precision is expensive, but u necessary because of the inherent inaccuracies in preparing a price index. We will not be too far off by assuming that an index value for a relatively short time period applies to each point in time within that period.

Two Kinds of Price Indexes

A *specific* price index, like our example, describes the change in the price of a single, reasonably unchanging item. There are numerous specific indexes, such as for machine tools, farm products, and common stocks of certain industries. A specific index is useful for describing the change in the economic value (relative scarcity) of the item, but it is unable to describe the change in the purchasing power of the dollar in the marketplace.[1]

A *general* price index, on the other hand, is intended to measure the change in the monetary unit's ability to purchase goods or services. The compiler of a general price index will determine the price of a much larger and more varied collection of purchased items.[2] This larger group is de-

---

[1] Indeed, without proper adjustment, a specific index may fail to distinguish between changes in the commodity's economic value and the dollar's purchasing power.
[2] The sample collection of items is often called the *shopping basket.*

signed to be a more representative sample of what a typical purchaser would buy, and it is hoped that a change in relative scarcity of one item will be matched by a similar but opposite change for another. Examples of general price indexes are the Wholesale Price Index (WPI), the Consumers' Price Index (CPI), and the Gross National Product (GNP) Implicit Price Deflator, which are compiled by the U.S. Departments of Labor and Commerce.

The Wholesale Price Index describes the relative amount of purchasing power of a dollar spent by a businessman in the wholesale market. The CPI describes the dollar's purchasing power in the marketplace of the individual and is based on a shopping basket that is significantly different from the one used in the WPI. The GNP deflator is perhaps the most ambitious and all-encompassing index, because it attempts to describe the change in purchasing power of the average dollar spent on anything anywhere in the entire economy.

Computational Difficulties

It is one thing to describe what a price index should do, but it is another completely different thing to produce an index that accomplishes that goal. We will briefly look at some of the problems.

THE SHOPPING BASKET

The index designer must determine which items are purchased by the "typical" buyer in the market. The task would be easier if buyer tastes stayed the same, with the result that the same items were bought year in and year out. Of course, the variety of goods that are purchased changes in accordance with perceived needs, changing tastes, fads, or even "scares." Thus, we see the composition of the *shopping basket* changing to keep up with the market. For example, very few inner tubes for auto tires are sold today, despite the fact that they were considered a necessity not too long ago. Relatively few black and white televisions are sold because consumer tastes have changed and they now prefer color sets.

It is also apparent that each of us has a different variety of goods that we buy according to our salary, culture, location, personality, and family size. By selecting a fairly large shopping basket sample, the price index preparer hopes to include the items that are purchased by all of us, in typical proportions. Such an ideal sample simply does not exist.

TECHNOLOGY

It was easy to develop a price index for chairs, but what about one for automobiles or refrigerators? Frequently, models vary drastically from one year to the next, with the result that items purchased five years apart can hardly be called by the same name. Technological improvements may even create completely new products that have never been in the market before. Also, models marketed in the same year frequently are quite distinct from each other.

For example, when we see that the price of this year's version of an automobile has been increased by $250, can we distinguish the effects of inflation from changes in quality? Not precisely, but we can make an approximation which will be fairly close. The point is that few things stay the same in the market when technology is changing.

LOCATIONS

Because of transportation costs, identical items may sell for different prices in different parts of the country. Also, human nature results in premium prices for certain items in some areas that far exceed the amount needed to reimburse the seller for transportation.[3] The condition is clearly not as noticeable in smaller countries, but it can produce significant effects in the United States and other geographically dispersed nations.

TIMING

The designer also must deal with the problem of selecting the frequency with which the index number should be computed. The Consumer Price Index is published monthly by the Department of Labor, whereas the GNP deflator is available only quarterly. The added expense of preparing the index more often must be compared against the benefit obtained from a more frequent measure of the change in the purchasing power. Clearly, this information is more beneficial in times of rapid changes than when prices are relatively stable.

To conclude these comments, we must acknowledge the *imprecision* of the price index. The final number is the result of combining numerous averages on a basis consistent with several assumptions. Thus, it is unwise to attribute *too much* accuracy to the final index figure, even if it is expressed as a number with one, two, or more decimal places.

USING PRICE INDEXES

With the measurements provided by the price index (PI) values, we can set about converting all the different dollars into one constant-size dollar, just as we converted the DM and £ balances into $ balances. The resulting numbers will still be the original cost, but instead of being expressed in "old" dollars, they can be expressed in "new" dollars.

The conversion process is based on a very simple algebraic equation called a *proportion*:

$$\frac{\text{Amount in \$}_{(now)}}{\text{Amount in \$}_{(then)}} = \frac{\text{Price index value—now}}{\text{Price index value—then}}$$

Through this equation, we can go about changing all the different-size "then" dollars to one constant value "now" dollar. The equation can be modified into the following useful formula:

[3] Diners on the East and West Coasts pay high prices for "Kansas City" beef, while Midwesterners crave Chesapeake Bay oysters.

$$\$_{(now)} = \$_{(then)} \times \frac{PI—now}{PI—then}$$

The ratio of price index values is a *conversion* ratio identical in concept to those that we saw for the foreign currencies. If we are converting to the present dollar (which is usually the most useful approach), the numerator of the ratio is always the most recent value of the price index.

To illustrate the formula's use, suppose that a firm acquired a truck near the end of 1973 when the price index equaled 120. If the general price index equals 150 at the end of 1977, we can use these index values to say that one $\$_{(73)}$ equals 150/120, or one and one-fourth $\$_{(77)}$. In turn, we can use this rate to convert the original cost in original dollars ($4,800) to the original cost in the later dollars:

$$
\begin{aligned}
\text{Cost in } \$_{(77)} &= \text{Cost in } \$_{(73)} \times \text{Conversion ratio} \\
&= \text{Cost in } \$_{(73)} \times 150/120 \\
&= 4,800 \times 1.25 \\
&= \$_{(77)}6,000
\end{aligned}
$$

It is essential to realize that, by using a general price index, we are *not* estimating today's value of the vehicle. The value is affected by the relative supply and demand for trucks like this one. What we *have* accomplished is the expression of the *original* cost in terms of $\$_{(77)}$, which is a unit of currency different from the one originally spent, just as a deutsche mark is different from a U.S. dollar.

This same conversion process can be applied to other items in accounting reports to achieve the goal of consistent measuring units. Let us go back to the Domestic Businessman, Inc., balance sheet in Exhibit 5-4 and see what changes we can make. Suppose that the price index had these values at the end of these years:

1970	100
1972	112
1973	120
1977	150

Exhibit 5-5 shows the conversion of the original dollar balances to the current dollar balances.[4]

Converting the Balance Sheet Accounts

The first step in the balance sheet conversion is to identify the *monetary* and *nonmonetary* items. The *monetary* balance sheet items are those assets and liabilities that are: (1) cash, or (2) to be collected as a fixed amount of cash, or (3) to be paid as a fixed amount of cash. In other words, the account balance is stated in terms of a fixed number of dollars, without regard to the value of the dollar. Thus, if a customer promises to pay us 1,000 dollars, we

---

[4] We could just as easily convert the original dollars to some other monetary unit, such as $\$_{(65)}$ or $\$_{(70)}$. Accounting authorities have recommended that the dollar from the most recent balance sheet date be used because of its relevance to current conditions.

Exhibit 5-5
DOMESTIC BUSINESSMAN, INC.
Purchasing Power Adjusted Balance Sheet
December 31, 1977

	Original Dollars	Conversion Ratios	Year-end Dollars
Cash	$(77) 11,000	(M)	$(77) 11,000
Investments (at cost)	$(72) 19,000	150/112	25,446
Accounts receivable	$(77) 23,000	(M)	23,000
Fixed assets (at cost)	$(70) 100,000	150/100	150,000
Accumulated depreciation	$(70) (35,000)	150/100	(52,500)
Total assets	$(?) 118,000		$(77) 156,946
Current liabilities	$(77) 17,000	(M)	$(77) 17,000
Long-term liabilities	$(77) 48,000	(M)	48,000
Stockholders' equity	$(?) 53,000	Various*	91,946
Total equities	$(?) 118,000		$(77) 156,946

(M)—Monetary items; no conversion necessary.

*The quantity of $(77) was found by subtracting the book value of the liabilities from the book value of the assets in terms of $(77).

will get 1,000 of whatever dollars are being used at the time we collect. Or, if we borrow 100 dollars, we will pay off the debt in 100 of the dollars that are current on the date of the loan's maturity.

The *nonmonetary* balance sheet items are those assets and liabilities that are *not* monetary items. Included in this category are inventories, investments, prepaid expenses, fixed assets (and accumulated depreciation), deferred revenues (such as advance deposits received from customers), and stockholders' equity. While each of these items can be described as a number of dollars, they are not: (1) cash, (2) to be received as a fixed amount of cash, or (3) to be paid as a fixed amount of cash.

Thus, in Exhibit 5-5, we find that cash, accounts receivable, current liabilities, and long-term liabilities are monetary items and are thus automatically expressed in terms of $(77) and do not have to be converted. The investments are disclosed in the traditional statements at their original cost, as measured in the original dollars from 1972. To convert to the original cost, as measured in the current dollar, the account balance is multiplied by (PI—1977)/(PI—1972), or 150/112, or 1.339.

The balances in the fixed assets and accumulated depreciation accounts are both carried in original dollars from 1970 and are converted by the ratio of the current index value to the value at the time of the asset's purchase (150/100). In this case, where all the assets were purchased at the same time, the same ratio could just as accurately be applied to the book value, $(70) 65,000, to arrive at the adjusted book value of $(77) 97,500.

Suppose, on the other hand, that there were two fixed assets acquired at different times and depreciated over different lives, such as:

Asset	Cost	Accumulated Depreciation	Book Value	Purchased in
A	$ 50,000	$25,000	$25,000	1970
B	50,000	10,000	40,000	1973
Total	$100,000	$35,000	$65,000	

Because the original dollars are $\$_{(70)}$ for A and $\$_{(73)}$ for B, the amounts cannot be converted with the same ratio. Instead, we have to go through a more complicated series of computations:

	Original Dollars	Conversion Ratios	Year-end Dollars
Asset A	$\$_{(70)}50,000$	150/100	$\$_{(77)}75,000$
Accumulated depreciation	$\$_{(70)}25,000$	150/100	37,500
Book value	$\$_{(70)}25,000$		$\$_{(77)}37,500$
Asset B	$\$_{(73)}50,000$	150/120	$\$_{(77)}62,500$
Accumulated depreciation	10,000	150/120	12,500
Book value	$\$_{(73)}40,000$		$\$_{(77)}50,000$
Total	$\$_{(?)}65,000$		$\$_{(77)}87,500$

Consequently, the conversion process will be more difficult for a firm with many assets of different ages. Nonetheless, the result of better information about the size of the sacrifice made to acquire the assets will generally be worth the effort.

Technically, it would be possible to do a similar item-by-item analysis of the dollars included in stockholders' equity, some of which would be from times when stock was issued and others of which would be from times when profits were earned. For simplicity, in this example we have departed from generally accepted accounting by combining the two components. In this case, and in dealing with retained earnings in real cases, the expedient (but accurate) approach is to *force* the answer by deducting the total other equities from total assets. This technique was used in Exhibit 5-5 when the liabilities total of $\$_{(77)}$ 65,000 was deducted from the total assets of $\$_{(77)}$ 156,946.

Converting the Income Statement Accounts

The balances of the income statement accounts frequently constitute a variety of sizes of dollars. Before the quantities can be meaningfully added to or subtracted from one another, they should all be converted to one common-size dollar. If ratios between income statement items and balance sheet items are to be computed, the revenues and expenses should be expressed in the same dollar that appears on the adjusted balance sheet.

The amounts shown on the income statement describe three kinds of events:

1. a constantly recurring revenue or expense (sales, salaries, and the like)
2. an infrequent, unusual revenue or expense (disposal of fixed asset, major repairs, and the like)
3. a current recognition of a previously received or paid item (rent revenue received in advance, depreciation expense)

In each case we should use the appropriate original value of the price index as the denominator of our ratio.

For the first type item, we find that, even for one year, there is really a large variety of dollars. If we make a sale each day of the year, we could have conceivably received 365 different kinds of dollars. But as we pointed out before, price index values are published only monthly or quarterly. We can gain a *close approximation* by utilizing these less frequent values, or by using an *average* price index for the year if the revenues and expenses occur continuously throughout the year.

Suppose that the price index moved evenly from 138 to 150 during 1977 and that Domestic Businessman, Inc., had sales of $120,000, as shown in Exhibit 5-6. If the sales occurred fairly evenly throughout the year, then the mixture of the various dollars can be converted to $(77) by using the *average* price index for the year[5] as the denominator of the conversion ratio:

$$\text{Sales in } \$_{(77)} = 120,000 \times 150/144$$
$$= \$_{(77)} 125,000$$

Thus, the 120,000 various-size dollars had purchasing power equal to 125,000 of the smaller year-end dollars.

Exhibit 5-6
DOMESTIC BUSINESSMAN, INC.
Original Dollar Income Statement
For the Year Ended December 31, 1977

Sales		$120,000
Expenses:		
Salaries	$74,000	
Depreciation	5,000	
Rent	5,000	
Miscellaneous	12,000	
Total expenses		96,000
Net income before taxes		$ 24,000
Income taxes		12,000
Net income		$ 12,000

The salaries and miscellaneous expenses shown in Exhibit 5-6 also occurred on an even basis, and they can be converted to the year-end dollars by the same ratio:

$$\text{Salaries in } \$_{(77)} = 74,000 \times 150/144$$
$$= \$_{(77)} 77,083$$

$$\text{Miscellaneous expense in } \$_{(77)} = 12,000 \times 150/144$$
$$= \$_{(77)} 12,500$$

As examples of income statement items that did *not* occur evenly throughout 1977, we can examine the rent and income tax expenses. If the rent was paid at the beginning of the year, it was a sacrifice of $(76)5,000, because there is no difference between the dollar at the end of 1976 and the

[5] Average = $\dfrac{(138 + 150)}{2} = 144$

beginning of 1977. Using the ratio between these price index values, we can see that the amount of purchasing power paid for the rent was:

$$\text{Rent in } \$_{(77)} = 5,000 \times \frac{\text{PI}-1977}{\text{PI}-1976}$$

$$= 5,000 \times 150/138$$

$$= \$_{(77)}5,435$$

Thus, the traditional income statement understated the rent expense by $\$_{(77)}$ 435.

Income taxes were paid by the firm at the end of 1977, on the basis of 50 percent of the taxable income, which must be computed under the traditional approach. Because of the timing of the payment, the purchasing power sacrificed was:

$$\text{Income taxes in } \$_{(77)} = 12,000 \times 150/150$$

$$= \$_{(77)}12,000$$

If the income taxes had been paid throughout the year on an estimated basis (the usual case in the real world), then it would have been appropriate to use the average value of the index for 1977.

The depreciation expense falls in the third category as the current recognition of a previously paid amount. Because the assets were purchased in 1970, the unadjusted cost and depreciation are stated in the original 1970 dollars. The depreciation expense can thus be converted as:

$$\text{Depreciation expense in } \$_{(77)} = 5,000 \times 150/100$$

$$= \$_{(77)}7,500$$

Other items that would be adjusted using older values of the price index would be prepaid expenses and revenues.

Exhibit 5-7
DOMESTIC BUSINESSMAN, INC.
Purchasing Power Adjusted Income Statement
For the Year Ended December 31, 1977

	Original Dollars	Conversion Ratios	Year-end Dollars
Sales	$\$_{(77A)}$ 120,000*	150/144	$\$_{(77)}$ 125,000
Expenses:			
Salaries	$\$_{(77A)}$ 74,000	150/144	$\$_{(77)}$ 77,083
Depreciation	$\$_{(70)}$ 5,000	150/100	7,500
Rent	$\$_{(76)}$ 5,000	150/138	5,435
Miscellaneous	$\$_{(77A)}$ 12,000	150/144	12,500
Total expenses	$\$_{(?)}$ 96,000		$\$_{(77)}$ 102,518
Net income before taxes	$\$_{(?)}$ 24,000		$\$_{(77)}$ 22,482
Income taxes	$\$_{(77)}$ 12,000	150/150	12,000
Net income	$\$_{(?)}$ 12,000		$\$_{(77)}$ 10,482

*The symbol for $\$_{(77A)}$ indicates "average 1977 dollars."

Exhibit 5-7 shows the income statement for Domestic Businessman, Inc., with the amounts adjusted to a single-value dollar. Notice that the adjusted net income figure is smaller than the unadjusted number, despite the fact that the adjusted revenue appears larger. The primary causes of the decreases can be found in the adjustments to the salaries and depreciation expenses. For firms with larger investments in fixed assets, the depreciation expense adjustment will cause a more dramatic decrease in the net income than is seen in this example. Also notice that the rate of income taxes as a percent of before tax income has increased from 50 percent to slightly over 53 percent. If the taxes had been paid on an estimated basis during the year, the effective rate would have gone even higher.

Missing from this illustration is a frequently significant item of income known as the *purchasing power gain or loss.* Traditional historical dollar accounting does not report this item, but it is measurable and reportable under purchasing power accounting.

Computing Purchasing Power Gains and Losses

If you were to buy a share of stock and watch its market value decrease, you would be very aware that you had suffered a loss. If you borrowed a cup of sugar from a neighbor when it was selling for $1.25 a pound and "paid" the loan when it was selling for $0.75 a pound, you would be aware that you had enjoyed a gain.

The same effects can be observed for those who hold cash (or its equivalent) or borrow cash when the price index goes up. In the first case, purchasing power is lost because each dollar of cash loses value. In the second case, purchasing power is gained because the loan can be repaid with relatively lower-value dollars. Indeed, the holder of a *monetary asset* (see page 119) suffers a purchasing power loss when inflation occurs. The holder of a *monetary liability* (see page 119) has a purchasing power gain when inflation occurs.

For a simple example, suppose that a Mr. Lender loaned $2,000 to Mr. Borrower on December 31, 1972, when the general price index equaled 112. The debt was repaid, without interest, on December 31, 1973, when the general price index equaled 120. Shown below is the analysis of Mr. Lender's loss:

	Original Dollars	Conversion Rate	Year-end Dollars
Purchasing power loaned	$(72)2,000	120/112	$(73)2,143
Purchasing power received	$(73)2,000	120/120	$(73)2,000
Purchasing power lost	$(?) –0–		$(73) 143

From the traditional accounting approach, Mr. Lender lost nothing from the loan. When we compare the inflow and outflow in terms of a constant measuring unit, we can see clearly that Mr. Lender lost $(73)143. A similar analysis would show that Mr. Borrower gained $(73)143 by paying back a smaller amount of purchasing power than he borrowed.

Let us suppose further that Mr. Lender charged 8 percent annual interest, so that Mr. Borrower repaid $2,160 on December 31, 1973. The analysis for Mr. Lender would be:

	Original Dollars	Conversion Rate	Year-end Dollars
Purchasing power loaned	$(72)2,000	120/112	$(73)2,143
Purchasing power received	$(73)2,160	120/120	$(73)2,160
Net purchasing power gained	$(?) 160		$(73) 17

In this case, Mr. Lender is better off by $(73)17, but his rate of return is less than 1 percent per year (17/2,143). Because of inflation, Mr. Borrower obtained a very cheap loan.

The procedure for finding the purchasing power gain or loss for a firm for a particular period of time is fairly complicated, though it is consistent with what we have seen above. After finding the quantity of monetary assets and liabilities at the first of the year, we determine the amount of purchasing power that came into the firm in the form of additional *monetary assets*. This amount would come from such events as sales for cash or credit, sales of fixed assets, and issuance of securities. A loan of cash would not add to the total of net monetary assets because it would increase a monetary asset (cash) by the same amount that it would increase a monetary liability (loan payable).

The next step in the computation is the tabulation of the purchasing power in the form of net *monetary assets* that went out of the firm during the year. These outflows would occur through such things as cash or credit paid expenses, purchases of nonmonetary assets, and payment of dividends. Paying off a loan would not reduce *net* monetary assets because it would lower monetary assets and monetary liabilities by the same amount.

The increases and decreases in net monetary assets are then added to and subtracted from the beginning balance to find the ending balance. If the situation develops that the firm was a net lender during the year while inflation occurred, the firm will have a purchasing power loss. It will have a gain if it is a net borrower.

Exhibit 5-8 shows the calculation of the gain for 1977 experienced by Domestic Businessman, Inc. In addition to the data from the balance sheet (Exhibit 5-5) and the income statement (Exhibit 5-7), the following facts are used:

1. December 31, 1976, balances in monetary items:

Cash	$ 3,000
Accounts receivable	20,000
Current liabilities	(18,000)
Long-term liabilities	(53,000)
Net liabilities	$(48,000)

2. Capital stock was issued for $10,000 cash in January 1977.

3. Cash dividends of $10,000 were paid in December 1977.

Exhibit 5-8

DOMESTIC BUSINESSMAN, INC.
Statement of Purchasing Power Gain
For the Year Ended December 31, 1977

	Original Dollars	Conversion Ratios	Year-end Dollars
Net monetary assets (liabilities):			
Beginning balance	$(76) (48,000)	150/138	$(77)(52,174)
Increases:			
Sales	$(77A)120,000	150/144	125,000
Capital stock issued	$(76) 10,000	150/138	10,870
Decreases:			
Cash expenses:			
Salaries	$(77A) (74,000)	150/144	(77,083)
Rent	$(76) (5,000)	150/138	(5,435)
Miscellaneous	$(77A) (12,000)	150/144	(12,500)
Taxes	$(77) (12,000)	150/150	(12,000)
Cash dividends	$(77) (10,000)	150/150	(10,000)
Ending balance	$(?) (31,000)		$(77)(33,322)
Purchasing power that would be owed			$(77) 33,322
Purchasing power actually owed			$(77) 31,000
Purchasing power gained			$(77) 2,322

The first column in the statement shows the amounts of the historical dollars that were on hand at the beginning and ending of the year and the historical dollars that came in and went out during the year. The second column shows the conversion ratios used to express the amounts of purchasing power listed in the first column into the common-size dollar from the end of 1977. The sum of the amounts in the third column, ($(77)33,322), is the amount of purchasing power that the firm *would owe* if it had to pay back the original purchasing power it borrowed. But, because only the original dollar quantity has to be repaid, the firm owes only the $31,000 shown as the sum of the first column. Thus, there has been a gain of $(77)2,322, as shown at the bottom of Exhibit 5-8.

In effect, the company owed $(77)52,174 at the beginning of 1977 and increased its holdings of net monetary assets by $(77)135,870 through its sales activities during the year and the issuance of stock in January. It reduced its net monetary assets by paying the four expenses listed with cash and by paying a dividend to its stockholders in December. The total reduction was $(77)117,018, which produced a net *increase* in net monetary assets of $(77)18,852. The firm's net monetary debt at December 31, 1977 should have been $(77)33,322, but it only owed $(77)31,000, so that its gain was $(77)2,322.

When the purchasing power gain is added to the net income reported in Exhibit 5-7, we can see that the total income for Domestic Businessman, Inc., was $(77)12,804, which appears to be better than the amount reported in the traditional statement. The significance of the difference between the two versions lies in the more consistent manner in which the purchasing power adjusted income was computed. The dollars of revenue and expense are all expressed in terms of the same monetary unit. The measurement of the purchasing power gain is also a significant step, in that an indication is given of the management's ability to deal with an inflationary environment while handling the firm's finances.

Budgets and Projections

The conversion of plans expressed in dollars into constant-size units of purchasing power is logically essential if actual results are to be compared with the budgeted figures. For example, the sales manager of Domestic Businessman, Inc., was to be rewarded if he met the goal for annual sales. If the 1977 goal had been set at $120,000 in December 1976, can we determine whether or not it was met?

Our analysis of the historical dollar data shows actual sales of $120,000, but the dollars are not the same size. Let's allow for the changes in the value of the dollar and see what happens to his bonus:

1. Convert the sales goal into $_{(77)}$:
$$\$_{(76)}\, 120{,}000 \times 150/138 = \$_{(77)}\, 130{,}435$$
2. Convert the actual sales into $_{(77)}$:
$$\$_{(77A)}\, 120{,}000 \times 150/144 = \$_{(77)}\, 125{,}000$$
3. Compare the goal with the actual:
$$\$_{(77)}\, 130{,}435 - \$_{(77)}\, 125{,}000 = \$_{(77)}\, 5{,}435$$

Thus, we can see that he fell short of the budgeted sales level by a substantial margin, and our finding is quite different from what we first thought.

IMPLICATIONS FOR MANAGEMENT

If purchasing power accounting becomes mandatory, there will be a significant impact not only on financial reporting but also on the financial markets and on management. Basically, the general purchasing power adjusted information will constitute a new set of standards for evaluating past performance and projecting future success. Although traditional statements will remain the primary reporting media, sufficient price-level information will be made available so that management will have to provide explanations for any materially different figures, especially if the difference is detrimental. The major result of this effort will be that management will be forced into devising and implementing strategies to cope with inflation, and thereby into producing reports that will not *require* explanation but will provide an opportunity to report good news. Astute managers will use price-level adjusted information whether external reporting is required or not, simply because it will allow them to be more informed about inflation's effects.

It is also conceivable that widespread usage of price-level adjustments will result in pressure on Congress to restructure income taxes to allow for inflation. Without revision, there is a continuing growth in income tax revenue from increases in reported income and from the fact that the tax rates get progressively higher as income gets higher. If businesses and individuals convert their income measurements to constant-size dollars, they will see that they a.e paying out a much larger share of their purchasing power in taxes. Consequently, substantial pressure may develop on legislative bodies to rewrite the laws to allow either restatement of reported income or adjustment of the tax brackets.

In any case, it seems likely that there will be an increase in management and outside interest in price-level adjustments and a number of changes in the practices of financial management and analysis.

OTHER ACCOUNTING EFFORTS DEALING WITH INFLATION

Despite the existence of the procedures described above, accountants and management have historically resisted adoption of purchasing power adjusted financial statements. Perhaps the most significant reasons were the difficulty of implementation, lack of reader sophistication, and the usual result of reduced reported net income. Over the last several decades, several alternative means to report price-level related effects in the statements have been proposed. We will look briefly at three of these: partial adjustments, replacement cost depreciation, and the LIFO inventory method.

Partial Adjustments

Some individuals argued for a compromise solution of the price level problem in which price index based adjustments would be applied to *only* fixed assets and depreciation. The justification for this approach was that these items are misstated more significantly on the traditional statements than any others.

Briefly, two points can be made refuting the validity of this approach. First, it is at best only a "piecemeal" approach to the problem and merely will add a new kind of inconsistency to the existing ones. Second, by ignoring the monetary items, we have failed to measure the *purchasing power gains and losses*. This approach received little support from the accounting profession.

Replacement Cost Depreciation

Other accountants and managers have suggested computing depreciation on fixed assets on the basis of the sacrifice that *would* have to be made at the present to acquire, or *replace*, those assets.

The classic example, and landmark case that invalidated this partial attempt to allow for inflation, involved the U.S. Steel Company in the relatively high inflation era following the Second World War. Like every firm, U.S. Steel's management had to face demands from laborers and stockholders for increased wages and dividends. In an effort to have more assets available to meet those needs, and to still maintain productive capacity by replacing fixed assets, an effort was made to use the current replacement cost of the assets as the basis for computing depreciation instead of the much lower original cost. The approach would have not only reduced the taxes paid out, but also more graphically demonstrated that profits were not as large as they seemed to be, and thus acted to relieve the pressures for higher wages and dividends. The effort was rejected by the court ruling on the tax question, and neither accounting practitioners nor an authoritative body accepted it for reporting to the public.

The primary reason for the rejection was the lack of verifiability, which could lead to manipulation of reported earnings through unscrupulous selection of the replacement value to be recorded. In the several decades since that time, we have seen the advancement of numerous eloquent arguments that "current" values lead to better descriptions of earnings and investments. The verifiability issue still acts as the stumbling block to general acceptance, however. There is certainly adequate reason that internal reports can be prepared on this basis and used by managers in making their decisions and evaluating their own performance. Information about replacement costs can be made available to outsiders in explanations of the financial statements, which would not be subject to an audit. At the time of this writing, the SEC has called for the publication of asset replacement costs in an unaudited footnote to the audited financial statements.

LIFO Inventory Method

Because of the relatively rapid turnover of inventory, the cost of goods sold is among the first income statement items to be affected by inflation. For example, firms that held petroleum products in their inventories when the international price of crude oil tripled and quadrupled found themselves deducting the lower original cost from the new higher sales revenues. The result was a substantial and even embarrassing increase in reported income. Critics spoke of "obscene" profits, and "windfall profits taxes" were discussed in Congress. But inflation itself exacted its own taxes because higher costs were incurred in replacing the inventory stocks. Thus, the higher profits were never realized in a form that would allow distribution of assets to stockholders as dividends.

The inventory accounting technique called *LIFO* (for *last-in-first-out*) produces an income description that more closely represents net income available to the stockholders than other approaches. Because the subject is discussed more extensively in Chapter 7, we will not go into any computational details here. The unavoidable consequence of LIFO is that it produces a low carrying value for inventory after an inflationary period. Thus, petroleum products would be disclosed on the balance sheet at prices prevailing when crude oil was $3 to $4 per barrel, even though new crude was $12 or more. Again, supplementary disclosures can make information about the replacement cost available, but the result is more effort and a higher probability of misleading the reader.

LIFO is perfectly acceptable for financial reporting as well as for tax accounting. The manager, however, must not accept the balance sheet figure as a valid description of the value of his investment in inventory.

COMPUTERIZED PURCHASING POWER ADJUSTMENTS

It may seem from the discussion in this chapter that the process for preparing purchasing power adjusted accounting reports can be rather time consuming and tedious. As we have learned in recent history, what is true for manual operations is not true for an automated system.

In a typical accounting system, events are recorded day by day, frequently utilizing a code, identifying the event by a number that can be translated into the date.[6] With surprisingly few complexities, the computer can be programmed to convert the dollars used to record each transaction into the dollars selected by the accountant as most appropriate for the reports. One efficient procedure would create a table of price-level values by date, which would be consulted for each transaction to find the proper ratio for the conversion. With the immense speed of the computer, there would be no need to work with average values, as the precise value could be found in the table just as quickly as the average. Once the data are available, statements could be prepared very quickly in terms of whichever dollar the accountant would care to select.

SUMMARY

In this chapter, we have been concerned with one aspect of inflation's impact on business. In particular, it has dealt with the problem of incomparability in the monetary units used to describe conditions and events in accounting reports. Inflation acts to change the value *(purchasing power)* of a unit of currency, with the result that combining dollars from different points in time on one report is like adding pounds sterling to dollars without making a translation.

Through values of a properly constructed general price index, conversion ratios can be found to express all the different dollars in terms of one constant measuring unit. The ratio's application depends upon the nature of the dollars originally used to record the facts. The usual effect of *purchasing power* adjustments will be to show larger numbers for fixed assets and stockholders' equity. The restated income from operations usually is a smaller number because of a higher depreciation charge. A very significant new income item is the purchasing power gain or loss from being a borrower or lender during inflation. One impact of this new measure could be to heighten management's interest in controlling its monetary assets and liabilities.

There are other methods of dealing with inflation, but they have tended to deviate more from usual cost oriented accounting practices and do not always distinguish the change in the value of money from changes in the value of the assets themselves.

[6] For example, transaction number 782120043 could be event number 43, on the 212th day (July 31) of 1978.

QUESTIONS

1. What is the concept of purchasing power?
2. In what sense does inflation cause a dollar (or any currency unit) to *shrink*?
3. What does a price index attempt to measure? What difference results from the choice of a particular base year instead of another?
4. Should a value of a price index be related to a *point* in time or a *period* of time? What is the usual practice?
5. What is the difference between a *specific* and a *general* price index?
6. What is the *shopping basket,* and what problems arise from its use in computing a price index?
7. Does changing technology affect a price index's calculation? How?
8. What are the characteristics that identify a balance sheet item as *monetary* or *nonmonetary*?
9. Identify which of the following items are *monetary*:
   a. investment in common stock
   b. bonds payable
   c. bonds receivable
   d. notes payable
   e. notes receivable
   f. cash on hand
   g. time deposits
   h. trucks
   i. accounts payable
   j. accumulated depreciation
   k. stockholder's equity
10. Because income statement accounts describe events that occur in a single time period, under what conditions is it misleading to fail to make price-level adjustments?
11. What are purchasing power gains and losses? Does the debtor gain or lose when inflation occurs? Why?
12. What reasons suggest the value of converting budgeted figures to a common purchasing power unit?
13. What is the weakness of partial price-level adjustments?
14. What are the strength and weakness of *replacement cost depreciation*?
15. How does LIFO soften the effects of inflation?

EXERCISES

E5–1 **Converting foreign currencies.**   A certain international business-man had projects going in three countries. He has prepared a balance sheet (on page 132), but is perplexed by what it shows.

    a.   What characteristic of the monetary units prevents the balance sheet from balancing as shown?

HUGH HOWARD, INC.
Balance Sheet
December 31, 1980

Cash	$ 1,000		Accounts payable	DM 9,000
Accounts receivable	£ 4,200		Notes payable	$ 8,000
Inventory	DM12,000		Capital stock	£ 20,700
Other assets	$ 50,000		Retained earnings	$ 11,200
	? 67,200			? 48,900

    b.   If $1 equals DM2.50, and £1 equals $2.00, prepare Mr. Howard's balance sheet in terms of:

        1. $ (dollars)
        2.   £ (pounds sterling)
        3.   DM (deutsche marks)

E5–2   *Computing a price index.*

    a.   If a widget cost $60 in 1960, $80 in 1970, and $120 in 1980, what was the widget price index in each of those years, where the base year is
        1.   1960
        2.   1970
        3.   1980

    b.   In order to answer *a*, what assumption did you make concerning technological advances in widget manufacturing?

E5–3   *Specific and general price indexes.*   From the facts about the costs of these four items in a family's spending for a year, determine (a) specific price indexes for each item, and (b) a general price index for the total, using 1970, 1975, and 1980, as base years:

	1970	1975	1980
Food	$ 8,000	$ 9,500	$12,000
Clothing	3,500	3,000	2,400
Shelter	6,000	6,000	6,000
Miscellaneous	2,000	4,000	3,500
Total	$19,500	$22,500	$23,900

E5–4   *Adjusting the balance sheet.*   The values of a general price index were observed for the following years:

	Average	End of the Year
1970	100	102
1975	122	125
1978	128	132
1979	137	140
1980	142	148

For each of the following items, (a) determine whether or not the account balance should be adjusted for changes in purchasing power, and (b) make the conversion into $_{(80)}$ where appropriate. All balances are as of December 31, 1980:

1. Cash in the bank $ 44,400
2. Accounts receivable $ 85,200
   (originated from sales occurring throughout the last quarter of the year)
3. Notes receivable $ 70,000
   (signed by a customer on December 20, 1979)
4. Investment in common stocks $ 26,400
   (valued at purchase price; date of purchase June 29, 1978)
5. Fixed assets—Building $250,000
   (original cost from December 15, 1970; depreciated over 20-year life, with no salvage value, on straight-line bases)
6. Accumulated depreciation—Building $125,000
   (see details in 5)
7. Current liabilities $ 47,000
   (from expenses incurred during December 1980)
8. Mortgage payable $200,000
   (remaining balance of loan made in January 1976)

E5–5 *Adjusting the income statement.* Based on the values of the general price index (where applicable) given in E5–4, for each of the following items, (a) determine whether or not the account balance should be adjusted for changes in purchasing power, and (b) make the conversion into $_{(80)}$ where appropriate. All balances are for the year ended December 31, 1980.

1. Sales $423,000
   (occurred evenly throughout the year)
2. Salaries expenses $ 65,500
   (occurred evenly throughout the year)
3. Interest expense $ 12,000
   (on a loan taken out January 1980; unpaid at present)
4. Rent expense $ 36,000
   (paid January 1980 for the entire year)
5. Depreciation expense $ 2,300
   (taken on a truck purchased in June 1978)
6. Income tax expense $112,000
   (paid in December 1980)
7. Repairs expense $ 26,800
   (paid March 24, 1980)

E5–6 *Using prices indexes.* Apply the following values of the general price index to each of the three situations below:

Year	Average	December 31
1975	94	100
1976	106	112
1977	116	120
1978	127	134
1979	141	148
1980	154	160

1. Mr. Victor Yougo purchased a piece of property on January 1, 1976 for $15,500. He sold it on June 30, 1980 for $20,250. Compute the gain or loss in terms of:
   a. $ (that is, unadjusted)
   b. $_{(80)}$ (that is, December 31, 1980)
   c. $_{(75)}$

2. Mr. Ludwell Jones has worked hard at his job and has taken pride in substantial raises received each year for the last several years. His salary for the calendar year has been:

Year	Salary
1977	$12,000
1978	$13,000
1979	$14,000
1980	$15,000

   Express his yearly salaries in terms of $_{(80)}$. Should he be proud of his record?

3. The Hussle-Bustle Corporation reported the following data on its income statement for 1980:

Sales (occurred uniformly)	$80,000
Salaries (occurred uniformly)	40,000
Rent (paid December 31, 1979)	10,000
Depreciation (asset purchased January 1, 1978)	15,000
Other expenses (occurred uniformly)	8,000
Income taxes (assessed at year-end)	40 percent

   a. Compute net income before and after taxes in terms of unadjusted dollars and $_{(80)}$. Delete the purchasing power gain or loss.
   b. Does there appear to be something inequitable in the assessment of income taxes?

E5–7 *Purchasing power gains and losses.* What is the amount of purchasing power gain or loss earned or incurred from holding the following accounts from a time when the price index is 112 to when it is 128? Express your answer in terms of the latter dollar.

   a. Cash — $ 75,000
   b. Accounts receivable — $ 20,000

c.	Temporary investment (at cost)	$ 18,000
d.	Inventory (at cost)	$ 33,000
e.	Prepaid rent	$ 27,000
f.	Accounts payable	$ 41,000
g.	Notes payable	$100,000
h.	Customer advances	$ 13,000
i.	Retained earnings	$ 62,000

E5–8 **Price indexes and budgets.** The budget for annual sales was prepared at the end of 1977, and projected total sales of $180,000. During 1978 the actual recorded sales were $190,000, and the price level moved from 123 to 137.

By how much (if any) did the firm exceed its budget in terms of constant-size dollars from:

a. the end of 1977

b. the average for 1978

c. the end of 1978

PROBLEMS

P5–1 **Converting foreign currencies.** Ken Outback is engaged in international trade with facilities, customers, and stockholders in the United States, Australia, and Canada. All three countries have the same name for their currency units, and some confusion has resulted in preparing the balance sheet of his company.

The following exchange rates are applicable:

$$\$_{(Can)}1.00 = \$_{(U.S.)}1.10$$
$$\$_{(Aus)}1.00 = \$_{(U.S.)}1.25$$

Convert the balance sheet balances for Outback's Company into (a) U.S. dollars, (b) Canadian dollars, and (c) Australian dollars:

Cash	(Can.)	$ 215,000
Inventory	(Aus.)	114,800
Inventory	(U.S.)	1,125,000
Accounts receivable	(Can.)	98,500
Fixed assets	(Aus.)	750,000
Accumulated depreciation	(Aus.)	(250,000)
Total		$2,053,300

Accounts payable	(U.S.)	$ 342,000
Notes payable	(Aus.)	670,000
Capital stock	(Can.)	400,000
Retained earnings	(Aus.)	153,000
Retained earnings	(Can.)	226,880
Retained earnings	(U.S.)	178,032
Total		$1,969,912

P5–2. **Purchasing power balance sheet.** Presented below is a balance sheet for the Ace Manufacturing Company, as of December 31, 1980. At this date, the general price index equaled 130.

Cash	$ 10,000	Accounts payable	$ 20,000
Accounts receivable	30,000	Notes payable[4]	80,000
Prepaid rent[1]	12,000	Stockholders' equity	122,000
Machinery[2]	100,000		
Investment[3]	70,000		
Total	$222,000		$222,000

1. The balance in this account represents what is left of a year's rent paid in advance on July 1, 1980, when the price index equaled 128.

2. The balance in this account is the net of the original cost less the accumulated depreciation. The three machines are being depreciated on a straight-line basis, with no salvage value. Other facts are:

Machine	Cost	Price Index at Purchase	Service Life	Years Used
1	$50,000	100	10	4
2	50,000	120	5	2
3	50,000	125	5	1

3. The balance in this account is the cost of two stock investments. The first was purchased for $50,000 at a time when the price index equaled 75. The second was acquired for $20,000 when the index was 120.

4. The balance in this account is the sum of two notes. One is for $20,000, and is due on July 1, 1980. The other is due one year later.

Required:

Prepare a purchasing power adjusted balance sheet for Ace Manufacturing Company, as of December 31, 1980, in terms of the dollars at the balance sheet date.

P5–3 **Purchasing power income statement.** The Neighborhood Laundramat Company prepared the following income statement for the year ended March 31, 1981:

Sales		$190,000
Expenses:		
Wages	$47,500	
Utilities	31,670	
Rent	63,340	
Depreciation	16,000	(158,510)
Net income before taxes		$ 31,490
Income tax expense (50 percent)		(15,745)
Net income after taxes		$ 15,745

During the fiscal year, the general price index moved at an even pace from 80 to 110. The operating expenses and the sales occurred in consistent amounts each quarter. The depreciation represents 1 year's usage of machinery that was purchased for $80,000 at a time when the same price index equaled 40. Income taxes are assessed at a rate of 50 percent of the historical dollar income.

Required:

Present the income statement of the Neighborhood Laundramat Company in terms of the dollars being used at the end of the income statement period.

P5–4 *Miscellaneous problems.*

Part 1:

From the following facts, determine the amounts that should appear on the purchasing power income statement of Derby, Inc., for the year ended December 31, 1980 (the year-end price index value was 150):

Quarter	1st	2nd	3rd	4th	Total
Average price index	110	120	130	140	——
Sales	$ –0–	$100,000	$250,000	$ 20,000	$370,000
Wages	50,000	50,000	55,000	45,000	200,000
Repairs	80,000	–0–	5,000	–0–	85,000
Rent	10,000	10,000	10,000	10,000	40,000
Income taxes	–0–	–0–	–0–	20,000	20,000
Net income (loss)	(140,000)	40,000	180,000	(55,000)	25,000

Part 2:

From the following facts, determine (a) the annual depreciation expense for 1980 and (b) the book value as of December 31, 1980 for these assets, in terms of $_{(80)}$.

Asset	Date Purchased	Price Index at Purchase	Service Life (in years)	Cost	Salvage Value
1	1/1/72	60	10	$18,000	$ –0–
2	1/1/76	80	5	20,000	4,000
3	1/1/77	90	6	13,500	2,000
4	12/31/78	100	3	9,000	–0–

Additional information:

1. Use straight-line depreciation.
2. Salvage value was estimated in terms of dollars at the date of purchase.
3. The price index at December 31, 1980, is 140.

P5–5 **Purchasing power gains and losses.** Loaner Company is managed by an individual who feels that sales can be increased by extending credit to customers but that being in debt is a sign of weakness.

Below are the firm's monetary items:

	January 1, 1980	December 31, 1980
Cash	$ 80,000	$100,000
Accounts receivable	140,000	180,000
Accounts payable	(18,000)	(20,000)
Notes payable	–0–	–0–
Net monetary assets	$202,000	$260,000

During the year, the following events occurred:

Sales revenue earned	$300,000	
Cash expenses paid	212,000	
Capital stock issued for cash	50,000	(March)
Capital assets purchased	80,000	(September)

These values of the general price index were observed:

January 1	100
March	105
Average for year	112
September	116
December 31	124

Required:

Using these facts, prepare a statement of purchasing power gain or loss for the Loaner Company for the year ended December 31, 1980.

P5–6 *Purchasing power gains and losses.* Barrow Company is managed by an individual who believes that bad debt losses can be eliminated by selling on credit only to some customers, and that borrowing is a sign of daring.

Below are the firm's monetary items:

	January 1, 1980	December 31, 1980
Cash	$ 40,000	$ 30,000
Accounts receivable	12,000	10,000
Accounts payable	(60,000)	(85,000)
Notes payable	(40,000)	(90,000)
Net monetary liabilities	$(48,000)	$(135,000)

During the year, the following events occurred:

Sales revenue earned	$310,000	
Cash expenses paid	200,000	
Cash borrowed on note	50,000	(March)
Capital assets purchased	150,000	(March)
Cash dividends paid	47,000	(December)

These values of the general price index were observed:

January 1	100
March	105
Average for year	112
December 31	124

Using these facts, prepare a statement of purchasing power gain or loss for the Barrow Company for the year ended December 31, 1980.

P5–7   *All-inclusive problem.* From the historical dollar comparative balance sheet, income statement, and other facts given below, prepare:

a. A statement of purchasing power gain or loss for the year ended December 31, 1980.

b. A purchasing power adjusted income statement for the year ended December 31, 1980.

c. A purchasing power adjusted balance sheet as of December 31, 1980.

MURPHY'S SOUP KITCHEN
Comparative Balance Sheet
December 31, 1979 and 1980

	1980	1979
Cash	$ 30,000	$ 20,000
Accounts receivable	70,000	55,000
Equipment[1]	130,000	150,000
Land[2]	40,000	40,000
Investments[3]	40,000	25,000
Total assets	$310,000	$290,000
Accounts payable	$ 65,000	$100,000
Notes payable[4]	80,000	70,000
Owner's equity[5]	165,000	120,000
Total equities	$310,000	$290,000

MURPHY'S SOUP KITCHEN
Income Statement
For the Year Ended December 31, 1980

Sales[6]		$134,000
Expenses:		
Wages[6]	$55,000	
Depreciation[1]	20,000	
Utilities[6]	12,000	
Property taxes[7]	4,000	91,000
Net income before income taxes		$ 43,000
Income taxes[7]		(18,000)
Net income		$ 25,000

Footnotes and other information:

The general price index moved evenly during the year from 100 to 120.

1. Additional data about the equipment:

Item	Original Cost	Price Index at Purchase	Service Life (in years)	Years Used
A	$160,000	60	20	12
B	70,000	90	10	2
C	20,000	90	4	2
	$250,000			

The equipment has no salvage and is depreciated on a straight-line basis.

2. The land was purchased when the price index equaled 60.

3. There are two investments (carried at original cost):

Item	Cost	Price Index at Purchase
D	$25,000	80
E	15,000	110
	$40,000	

4. There are three notes payable:

Note	Face Amount	Date Signed	Price Index at Signing	Due Date
F	$30,000	1977	75	1987
G	40,000	1978	80	1988
H	10,000	1980	110	1990
	$80,000			

5. Murphy invested an additional $20,000 cash early in January 1980.

6. Sales, wages expense, and utilities expense occurred evenly throughout the year.

7. Income and property taxes were paid in December 1980.

P5–8 *Computing real gains.* Mr. Long Green purchased a piece of rec-creation property for $20,000 cash at a time when the price index equaled 125. When he sells it, he will have to pay a capital gains tax of 20 percent of the difference between the proceeds of the sale and the $20,000.

Determine the sales price that will yield an aftertax gain of $20,000 of *current purchasing power* if the price index at the time of the sale is:

a. 125
b. 100
c. 160
d. 200

P5–9 *Price indexes and budgets.* Decker Enterprises prepared the following budget for the first and second halves of 1980. The amounts are expressed in terms of dollars from the end of 1979 when the price index equaled 120.

	First Half	Second Half	Total
Sales	$225,000	$350,000	$575,000
Rent	$ 20,000	$ 20,000	$ 40,000
Wages	45,000	60,000	105,000
Insurance	10,000	10,000	20,000
Advertising	70,000	110,000	180,000
Income taxes	40,000	75,000	115,000
Total	$185,000	$275,000	$460,000
Net income	$ 40,000	$ 75,000	$115,000

The observed results are:

	First Half	Second Half	Total
Average price index	122.5	132.5	——
Sales	$100,000	$500,000	$600,000
Rent	$ 20,000	$ 35,000	$ 55,000
Wages	40,000	75,000	115,000
Insurance	10,000	10,000	20,000
Advertising	90,000	90,000	180,000
Income taxes	-0-	115,000	115,000
Total	$ 160,000	$325,000	$485,000
Net income	$ (60,000)	$175,000	$115,000

From the given facts, it appears (superficially) that the budget was met. Convert the budget and the actual results into terms of dollars from the end of 1980 when the price index equaled 135. For each item, compare the actual with the budgeted amounts.

Section 2

Cost Analysis, Behavior, and Control

No other aspect of management deserves or receives more attention than cost control. In this section, several dimensions of cost behavior will be examined, as well as the procedures used to assign costs to products and services. Throughout the discussions we will emphasize the relevance of cost information to management decisions.

Chapter 6 introduces the concept and use of cost-volume-profit analysis. Chapter 7 deals with problems in assigning costs to inventories and in managing and controlling the inventory investment. Chapter 8 describes the principles and procedures of accounting for the costs of production. Chapter 9 focuses on identifying the particular factors (cost or otherwise) that are relevant and useful in decision making.

6

Cost–Volume–Profit Analysis

The term *cost* can be used in several different ways to mean several different things. In general, we can say that a cost is the *sacrifice made to acquire a benefit*. In the context of financial accounting, an asset's cost is thus the total of the expenditures made in the process of getting it ready to use. Before the asset is used to earn revenues, its cost can be labeled *unexpired*, and the balance sheet will show this amount as the asset's *cost*. Then, as revenues are earned (or benefits obtained), the cost of the asset is said to *expire*, and an expense is recorded. The asset's remaining cost (if any) appears on the balance sheet and the expense appears on the income statement.

The objective of managing a business can be described simply as assuring that the benefits achieved exceed the sacrifices made. In accounting terms, we can say that *the revenues should exceed the costs*. Thus, there should be no doubt that managers are very interested in cost behavior, cost control, and cost measurement, and that management accountants can assist managers in dealing with cost problems.

COST CLASSIFICATIONS

A very useful cost concept associates the reaction of production costs to variations in the volume of production.[1] Certain cost factors can be classified as *fixed*, because they do not react to changes in volume, while others are *variable*. Still others will display a combination of fixed and variable behavior, and can be called either *semifixed* or *semivariable*.

These classifications are meaningful only in relationship to a stated period of time. In the so-called *long run*, all costs are variable, because the manager will have enough time to change virtually every aspect of his firm. In

---

[1] We will look at some other ways that costs may be classified in Chapters 7 through 9.

the *short run,* certain aspects of the operation are essentially unchangeable. Also, it may be so inconvenient to change some aspects (such as the nature of the product) that they are also unchangeable. If we take the *short run* down to a *very* short interval, such as an hour or a day, virtually nothing can be significantly changed in that time span. For convenience, we will use one year as the length of the "run," but application of the system may call for some period longer or shorter than one year.

Fixed Costs

Fixed costs are those costs that remain fixed in total dollar amount regardless of the number of units produced. For example, the rent of a factory building would be the same whether the company produced only a few units or operated at full capacity. Although fixed costs remain constant in *total,* they vary inversely with production when expressed on a *per unit* basis. For example, if fixed costs for the month were $50,000 and the company produced 25,000 units, the *unit fixed cost* would be $2. But if the company produced only 10,000 units, the *unit fixed cost* would be $5.

Variable Costs

Variable costs, on the other hand, vary in total amount directly with production but are constant on a *per unit* basis regardless of volume. The cost of materials used in producing a product, for example, would be variable. If these costs amount to $10 per unit, then the total variable costs would be $100,000 if 10,000 units were produced, and $250,000 if 25,000 units were produced. Other variable costs might include labor used directly in producing a product and the electrical costs related to operating a machine.

Semifixed Costs

Many costs are actually *semifixed* or *semivariable.* These costs do not vary directly with production but vary on some other basis. For example, the heating costs of the factory might vary considerably from month to month— in this case, the costs vary with the outside temperature rather than with production. Because semivariable costs do not follow any regular pattern, accountants generally find it helpful to classify them as either fixed or variable according to the pattern that *best* describes their behavior. Or, sometimes these costs may be broken down into their fixed and variable components. Thus, all costs can be *classified* as either fixed or variable, even though their exact behavior cannot be determined.

COST-VOLUME-PROFIT *(CVP)* ANALYSIS

The fixed and variable cost classifications are particularly useful when considered in relation to volume and profit. By analyzing this relationship, we can estimate the expected profit at any level of production, calculate the point at which the firm will *break even,* and evaluate various production alternatives. This analysis is especially useful in evaluating the impact of proposed changes in production methods or marketing strategies.

Profit Calculation

In financial accounting, the difference between revenues and expenses in a given time period is called *profit.* If we assume that the entire output of a production process is sold in the same time period it is produced, we can say that the *revenues* minus the *costs* equals the profit for the time period. If we are engaged in management planning, we can make this timing assumption rather freely, whereas we cannot when we follow generally accepted financial accounting principles.

The relationships among these factors can be described in an equation:

$$\text{Profit} = \text{Sales} - \text{Expenses}$$

or

$$\text{Profit} = \text{Sales} - \text{Costs}$$

As shown, all costs can be classified as fixed or variable, so the equation becomes:

$$\text{Profit} = \text{Sales} - (\text{Fixed costs} + \text{Variable costs})$$

or

$$\text{Profit} = \text{Sales} - \text{Fixed costs} - \text{Variable costs}$$

If we assume that the unit sales price of the product is constant (a condition which is not always realistic), we can say that:

$$\text{Sales} = \text{Volume} \times \text{Unit sales price}$$

Similarly, if we assume that we can identify all variable costs as being truly variable, and therefore the same for each unit of product, we can say that:

$$\text{Variable costs} = \text{Volume} \times \text{Unit variable costs}$$

Our original equation can now be stated as:

$$\text{Profit} = (\text{Volume} \times \text{Unit sales price}) - (\text{Fixed costs}) - (\text{Volume} \times \text{Unit variable costs})$$

If we let

$$P = \text{Profit}$$
$$V = \text{Volume}$$
$$SP = \text{Unit sales price}$$
$$FC = \text{Fixed costs}$$
$$VC = \text{Unit variable costs}$$

the equation can be more compactly stated as:

$$P = V(SP) - FC - V(VC)$$

With this expression, we can substitute values for four of the five unknowns and then solve for the fifth.

Suppose that:

$$V = 20{,}000 \text{ units per year}$$
$$SP = \$45 \text{ per unit}$$
$$FC = \$300{,}000 \text{ per year}$$
$$VC = \$20 \text{ per unit}$$

We can then determine the estimated profit for the year:

$$P = 20{,}000(\$45) - \$300{,}000 - 20{,}000(\$20)$$
$$P = \$900{,}000 - \$300{,}000 - \$400{,}000$$
$$P = \$200{,}000$$

Profit Goal Achievement by *CVP* Analysis

We can also use this profit equation for profit planning by establishing a profit goal and then seeing how we can manipulate other unknowns to achieve this objective. To illustrate, assume that a firm has $1,000,000 invested in its factory and sets a goal of a 15 percent annual return. Fixed costs in the factory presently amount to $400,000 per year and variable costs run $15 per unit produced. In the past year, the firm produced and sold 50,000 units at $25 each and earned a profit of only $100,000. How can management achieve their profit goal of $150,000 (15 percent of the $1,000,000 investment)?

REDUCTION OF FIXED COSTS

Return to the equation:

$$P = V(SP) - FC - V(VC)$$

Now, let:

$$P = \$150{,}000 \text{ (the profit goal)}$$
$$FC = \text{the unknown}$$

and the other elements as given:

$$\$150{,}000 = (50{,}000 \times \$25) - FC - (50{,}000 \times \$15)$$
$$\$150{,}000 = \$1{,}250{,}000 - FC - \$750{,}000$$
$$FC = \$1{,}250{,}000 - \$750{,}000 - \$150{,}000$$
$$FC = \$350{,}000$$

Management could achieve the desired profit if they could achieve a $50,000 annual reduction in fixed costs (fixed costs are presently $400,000 per year and our calculations indicate they would need to be reduced to $350,000 per year to achieve the profit goal). A $50,000 reduction in fixed costs would amount to a 12.5 percent reduction.

REDUCTION OF VARIABLE COSTS

Suppose management feels they could better achieve their goal by a reduction in the firm's variable costs. Let us solve the equation with unit variable costs *(VC)* as the unknown:

$$P = V(SP) - FC - V(VC)$$
$$\$150,000 = (50,000 \times \$25) - \$400,000 - 50,000(VC)$$
$$\$150,000 = \$1,250,000 - \$400,000 - 50,000(VC)$$
$$50,000(VC) = \$1,250,000 - \$400,000 - \$150,000$$
$$VC = \frac{\$700,000}{50,000}$$
$$VC = \$14$$

The profit objective could be achieved by reducing variable costs by only $1 per unit or about 7 percent (variable costs presently amount to $15 per unit and would need to be $14 per unit to achieve this objective).

INCREASE IN SELLING PRICE

The profit objective might also be achieved by increasing the selling price while holding other elements of the equation constant:

$$P = V(SP) - FC - V(VC)$$
$$\$150,000 = 50,000(SP) - \$400,000 - (50,000 \times \$15)$$
$$\$150,000 = 50,000(SP) - \$400,000 - \$750,000$$
$$50,000(SP) = \$150,000 + \$400,000 + \$750,000$$
$$50,000(SP) = \$1,300,000$$
$$SP = \frac{\$1,300,000}{50,000}$$
$$SP = \$26$$

Thus, a $1, or 4 percent, increase in the selling price (from the present $25 to $26) would achieve the profit goal.

INCREASE IN UNITS SOLD

Finally, the profit objective might be met by increasing the volume of units sold (remember, units produced equal units sold in our model). Letting *V* (volume) be the unknown:

$$P = V(SP) - FC - V(VC)$$
$$\$150,000 = \$25V - \$400,000 - \$15V$$
$$\$25V - \$15V = \$400,000 + \$150,000$$
$$\$10V = \$550,000$$
$$V = \frac{\$550,000}{\$10}$$
$$V = 55,000 \text{ units}$$

Management would need to increase volume by 10 percent or 5,000 units (from 50,000 units to 55,000 units) in order to meet their goal.

IN CONCLUSION

The options management has in reaching their profit objective are summarized in Exhibit 6-1. They would need to carefully weigh these options in relation to the facts that would dictate which if any option could be followed in practice. What is the nature of the market? Will it sustain a 4 percent increase in selling price? How will competitors react? What is the nature of the fixed costs and variable costs? Can these be reduced by the required amounts without long-run repercussions (such as reduced product quality)? *CVP* analysis will not answer these questions. They must be answered by management in the light of the "real world." *CVP* analysis, however, can be useful in giving management insight into the nature of costs in relationship to volume and selling price. Management will then know *how much* of a change will be necessary to achieve a particular goal, and will be in a better position to evaluate the practicality of the change. Often, the ultimate solution will involve *some* change in several of the variables.

Exhibit 6-1
Summary of Profit Goal Alternatives

Strategy	Present Level	Desired Level	Required Change Amount	Required Change Percent
Reduction of fixed costs	$400,000	$350,000	$50,000	12.5
Reduction of variable costs	$15/unit	$14/unit	$1/unit	6.7
Increase in selling price	$25/unit	$26/unit	$1/unit	4.0
Increase in volume	50,000 units	55,000 units	5,000 units	10.0

The Breakeven Point

We may find it useful to know the level of sales that will just produce a zero profit. Any volume below this level will produce a loss, and any volume above it will produce profit for the time period. Our equation would be:

$$P = V(SP) - FC - V(VC) = 0$$

We can simplify:

$$V(SP) - FC - V(VC) = 0$$
$$V(SP - VC) = FC$$
$$V = \frac{FC}{SP - VC}$$

To distinguish this special *breakeven volume,* let us denote it by *BE,* and our equation becomes:

$$BE = \frac{FC}{SP - VC}$$

If we use the present levels in Exhibit 6-1:

$$FC = \$400,000$$
$$SP = \$25$$
$$VC = \$15$$

we can compute *BE*:

$$BE = \frac{\$400,000}{\$25 - \$15} = 40,000 \text{ units}$$

If we sell less than 40,000 units, we will fail to earn a profit.

This breakeven point in terms of physical volume can be converted to the breakeven point in terms of sales dollars simply by multiplying *BE* by *SP*. Thus, we will break even if sales for the period equal $1,000,000, or (40,000 × $25).

The Marginal Contribution

The amount by which the selling price per unit exceeds the variable costs per unit may be described as the *marginal contribution per unit,* and equals the amount contributed to the firm's fixed costs or profits by each unit sold. The marginal contribution may be used to calculate the breakeven point if we rewrite our equation as:

$$\text{Unit breakeven point} = \frac{\text{Total fixed costs}}{\text{Marginal contribution per unit}}$$

$$= \frac{\$400,000}{\$10 \text{ per unit}}$$

$$= 40,000 \text{ units}$$

The *marginal-contribution rate* expresses the marginal contribution as a percent of sales. The marginal-contribution rate for this firm is 40.0 percent ($10/$25). The breakeven point in terms of dollars may be calculated by using the marginal-contribution rate:

$$\text{Dollar breakeven point} = \frac{\text{Total fixed costs}}{\text{Marginal-contribution rate}}$$

$$= \frac{\$400,000}{.400}$$

$$= \$1,000,000$$

Multiproduct Cost-Volume-Profit

It is possible to perform a *CVP* analysis for a firm that produces and markets several products, provided that the sales mix remains constant or that we can forecast the sales mix. To illustrate, let us assume the following facts about the output of the Barker Bakery:

	Per Unit			Percent of
	Selling Price	**Variable Cost**	**Marginal Contribution**	**Total Units Sold**
Bread	$0.60	$0.36	$0.24	50
Cakes	$1.60	$0.80	$0.80	35
Pies	$1.40	$0.56	$0.84	15
				100

If we assume that the sales mix remains constant during the month, we can proceed as if all products are sold in packages that include 0.5 loaves of bread, 0.35 cakes, and 0.15 pies. The total marginal contribution of each package would then be $0.526, which is calculated:

$$0.5(\$0.24) + 0.35(\$0.80) + 0.15(\$0.84) = \$0.526$$

If the company has monthly fixed costs of $10,000, the breakeven point would be calculated:

$$BE = \frac{FC}{MC*}$$

$$= \frac{\$10,000 \text{ per month}}{\$0.526 \text{ per unit}}$$

$$= 19,011 \text{ units per month}$$

*MC refers to the marginal contribution per unit. In the case of a multiproduct firm the MC is the weighted average marginal contribution per unit.

The volume of output that would produce this zero level of profit would consist of 9,505 loaves of bread (50 percent of 19,011), 6,654 cakes (35 percent of 19,011), and 2,852 pies (15 percent of 19,011).

Of course, we can expand our model to predict profit or loss under different mix assumptions. For example, assume Mr. Barker receives a special order from a grocery chain to purchase 10,000 loaves of bread during August at $0.56 per loaf. He predicts that if he accepts this order, he will have the capacity to produce and sell the following mix (in order to increase bread capacity he must give up cake and pie capacity):

10,000 loaves of bread @ $0.56 each (special order)
6,000 loaves of bread @ $0.60 each
6,000 cakes @ $1.60 each
3,000 pies @ $1.40 each

If he does not accept the special order for the bread, he expects regular production and sales as follows:

12,000 loaves of bread @ $0.60 each
8,400 cakes @$1.60 each
3,600 pies @ $1.40 each

His *expected marginal contribution* under the two alternatives may be compared in the table on page 153.

	Accepting Special Order	Rejecting Special Order
Special bread	10,000 × $0.20 = $ 2,000	
Regular bread	6,000 × $0.24 = 1,440	12,000 × $0.24 = $ 2,880
Cakes	6,000 × $0.80 = 4,800	8,400 × $0.80 = 6,720
Pies	3,000 × $0.84 = 2,520	3,600 × $0.84 = 3,024
	$10,760	$12,624

We can see that accepting the special order will increase overall production, but it will also reduce profits. Rejecting the order will yield a contribution of $12,624 and a profit of $2,624 (contribution margin of $12,624 less fixed costs of $10,000), while accepting the order will yield only a contribution of $10,760 and a profit of $760 (contribution margin of $10,760 less fixed costs of $10,000).

Summary of *CVP* Assumptions

As we have illustrated possible management uses of *CVP* analysis, we hope you have kept these basic assumptions in mind:

1. All costs can be classified as either fixed or variable.
2. Variable costs vary at a constant rate over the full range of operations.
3. Fixed costs are truly fixed over the full range of operations.
4. Production equals sales (no change in inventory levels).
5. The efficiency level for labor and machinery remains constant.
6. Unit sales price is constant over the entire range of production (a condition peculiar to pure competition).
7. Sales mix is constant or predictable.

These assumptions, of course, limit the usefulness of *CVP* analysis. They do not, however, invalidate it. If the manager will keep the assumptions (and, in turn, the limitations) in mind as he makes his analysis, the results can be most useful.

The *CVP* Chart

In order to provide a more graphic description of their relationships, the revenues and costs at various sales volumes may be plotted on a *CVP graph,* or a *breakeven chart.* Such a chart is useful because it reveals the expected profit or loss at any attainable volume (including breakeven). The chart can be prepared by first plotting the variable cost curve. Where costs vary *directly* with volume (as we have assumed), this curve is a straight line that intersects the point of origin. It can be plotted by marking the total variable costs at any volume (other than zero) and drawing a straight line that intersects this point and the point of origin.

The fixed costs are added to the variable costs to arrive at the *total cost curve.* This curve originates at the point on the vertical axis that equals total fixed costs. It runs parallel to the variable cost curve.

Finally, the total revenue curve is plotted. This curve also intersects the

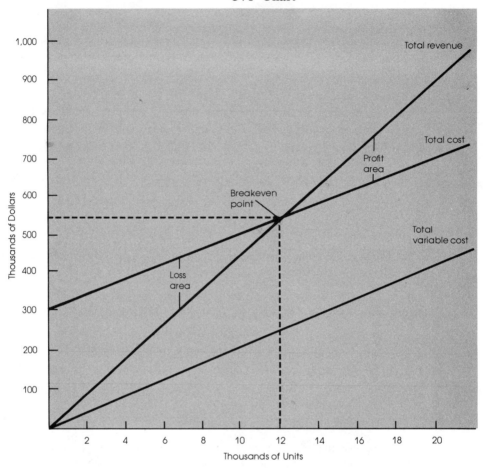

Exhibit 6-2
CVP **Chart**

Thousands of Dollars (vertical axis)

Thousands of Units (horizontal axis)

Total revenue

Total cost

Profit area

Breakeven point

Total variable cost

Loss area

point of origin, and is a straight line if all units are sold at the same price. It is plotted by fixing a point representing the dollar sales revenue at any volume (other than zero) and by drawing a line that intersects that point and the point of origin. The point at which the total revenue and the total cost curves intersect represents the volume at which the firm will break even. (Remember that we have assumed that all products are made and sold in the same period.) A breakeven chart based on the following assumed facts is shown in Exhibit 6-2:

Fixed costs	$300,000
Variable costs per unit	$20
Selling price per unit	$45

Exhibit 6-3 demonstrates that the size of the profit or loss at a particular volume can easily be calculated from the chart by drawing a vertical line through the total cost and total revenue curves at the given volume and then extending two horizontal lines to the vertical axis from the intersection points. The difference between the indicated amounts is the profit (if the volume is above the breakeven point) or the loss (if the volume is below the

Exhibit 6-3
Reading a *CVP* Chart

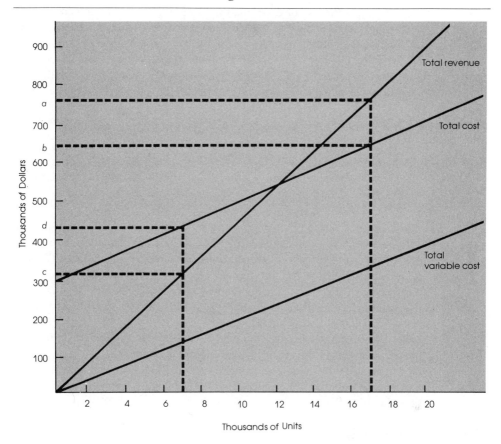

	17,000 units	7,000 units
Revenues ($45 per unit)	$765,000	$ 315,000
Variable costs ($20 per unit)	$340,000	$ 140,000
Fixed costs ($300,000 per year)	300,000	300,000
Total costs	$640,000	$ 440,000
Profit (loss)	$125,000	$(125,000)

breakeven point). In Exhibit 6-3, the profit at a volume of 17,000 units is $125,000 (*a* − *b*, or $765,000 − $640,000). The loss at a volume of 7,000 units is $125,000 (*c* − *d*, or $315,000 − $440,000).

CVP Charts for Planning

The *CVP* chart is best used in appraising various future alternatives that a company faces. By plotting these relationships under the various alternatives, management can make informative comparisons. For example, a proposed plant expansion may be evaluated by analyzing the impact of the expansion on the expected profits; or comparisons can be made to predict the results of automating certain steps in an existing production line so that higher fixed costs replace previously variable costs.

To illustrate the use of *CVP* analysis for planning, let us consider a problem being faced in the Eagle Manufacturing Company concerning automation of its assembly line. New equipment would be needed at a cost of $5,000,000, but it would last 10 years. By automating, variable costs per unit can be reduced by $2.50. Further, the capacity of the plant will be increased by 25 percent. The existing and potential situations are described as:

	Manual	**Automated**
Fixed cost per year	$1,000,000	$1,500,000
Variable cost per unit	$8.00	$5.50
Selling price per unit	$18.00	$18.00
Contribution margin per unit	$10.00	$12.50
Plant capacity	200,000 units	250,000 units
Breakeven point	100,000 units	120,000 units

The same data are plotted graphically in Exhibit 6-4. Notice that the total cost curve for the automated plant (TC_A) is flatter than the curve for the manual (TC_M). The only difference in the two total revenue curves (TR_M and TR_A) is their lengths for the different capacities. From the graph, we can observe that the profit under the manual system (TR_M minus TC_M) is greater than the profit under the automated system (TR_A minus TC_A) for any volume between 100,000 and 200,000 units. But, when volume exceeds 200,000 units (the manual capacity), the profit under the automated approach is greater. Thus, if management is reasonably assured that sales volume will be less than 200,000 units, the manual system should be kept. On the other hand, if the volume is likely to exceed 200,000 units each year, then automation should be undertaken.

Other Modifications

Numerous alternatives can be compared and evaluated by *CVP* analyses. Various price alternatives can be compared, plant expansion proposals can be evaluated, the best product mix can be selected, the impact of price changes can be appraised, and so on. The charts can also be modified to incorporate other than straight-line relationships. The revenue curve can be drawn to reflect a lower price per unit as sales are increased. The total cost curve can be redrawn with steps to reflect the fact that fixed costs cannot logically be expected to remain constant throughout the entire range of volume. Variable cost curves might also be drawn to reflect economies and diseconomies of scale.

The introduction of computers has made *CVP* analysis especially useful. Previously, it was necessary for a manager to rigidly adhere to a rather unrealistic set of assumptions (see page 153) because of the computational drudgery associated with changing a variable. A computer model, on the other hand, can easily be changed to accommodate a variety of modifications. The manager can experiment with various combinations of prices, volumes, and costs to predict the best cost-volume-price and, in turn, profit combinations. Once the computer program is prepared, it is a relatively simple and inexpensive task to change variables in the model.

Exhibit 6-4
CVP Chart Comparing Manual and Automated

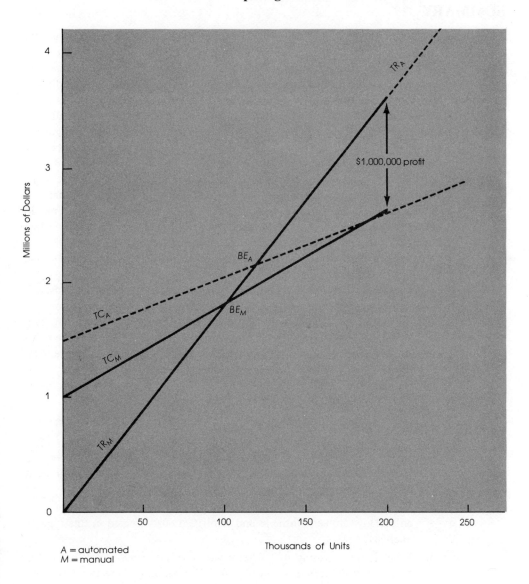

A = automated
M = manual

SUMMARY

The term *cost* is used in many different ways in accounting. Cost is usually defined as a *sacrifice* made to acquire something. We can identify and classify these sacrifices in many different ways to satisfy a variety of management needs. One particularly useful way of classifying costs is according to how they behave in relation to *volume* of output. Although many costs do not actually behave in this manner, management accountants normally assume just two types of behavior—*fixed* or *variable*. Fixed costs remain the same in total dollar amount at all levels of production; variable costs vary directly and proportionately with production.

After classifying costs as fixed or variable, the manager can get some valuable insight into cost-volume-profit relationships. This type of analysis, often referred to as *CVP* analysis, may be done by formula or by graph. In either case, four of the five elements of the profit equation are held constant while the other is manipulated to determine breakeven points, plan profit objectives, evaluate changes in production methods, set product prices, and the like.

A number of important assumptions must be made in *CVP* analysis: All costs can be classified as either fixed or variable; fixed costs remain constant over the full range of operations; variable costs vary at a constant rate over the full range of operations; production equals sales; efficiency level remains constant; sales price remains constant; the sales mix is constant or predictable. If these assumptions are properly considered by the manager, *CVP* analysis can be an extremely useful tool.

QUESTIONS

1. Define the term *cost*. Why are costs important to managers?
2. How do fixed costs behave with a given change in volume? In what sense may these same costs be classified as variable costs?
3. What use do accountants derive from classifying costs as fixed or variable? How are semivariable and semifixed costs treated in this type of analysis?
4. What is the meaning of the term *marginal contribution?* What is the meaning of the term *breakeven point?* Explain how these two terms are related.
5. What are some of the important assumptions made in breakeven analysis? What additional assumption is necessary in multiproduct breakeven analysis?
6. How may a breakeven chart or *CVP* graph be useful in the management decision process? Draw a breakeven chart and identify the total revenue curve, the total cost curve, the breakeven point, the profit area, and the loss area.
7. In what way might a breakeven chart be useful for more than the mere calculation of the breakeven point? Explain.

8. What effect would automating a plant have on a firm's breakeven point if the fixed costs increased while the variable costs decreased?

9. Calculate the breakeven point assuming fixed costs are $25,000 per year, variable costs $10 per unit, and selling price $15 per unit.

10. Draw a breakeven chart using the data given in question 9. Label the total revenue curve, the total cost curve, the breakeven point, the loss area, and the profit area.

11. Explain how cost-volume-profit analysis can assist management in profit planning.

12. Define *variable costs*. What is the "variable" with which these costs vary? What problems do you see in isolating variable costs when production does not equal sales?

13. Name four factors (variables) that management can adjust in the long run in an attempt to achieve profit goals.

14. List some costs which you would classify as *fixed* in a factory which manufactures automobiles.

15. List some costs which you would classify as *variable* in a factory which manufactures automobiles. How does the "time period" affect your classification of variable costs?

16. Because the goal of most business firms is to make a profit rather than to merely "break even," what significance does the "breakeven" point have to management?

EXERCISES

E6–1 **Finding desired volume.** Tantus Corporation directors have a stated profit goal for next year of a 10 percent return on the firm's net assets. Management estimates fixed costs will be $400,000 next year and variable costs will be $32 per unit. The product selling price is currently $55 per unit and that price is expected to hold constant throughout the coming year. Net assets are expected to be $3 million at the beginning of the year and $4 million at the end of the year. How many units must be sold next year: (a) for the company to break even and (b) to achieve the directors' profit goal?

E6–2 **Breakeven.** Compute the number of units that must be sold and the total dollar sales volume that must be achieved in order for the company to break even in each of the following situations:

1. Selling price is $12 per unit, variable costs $6.50 per unit, fixed costs $52,000 per year.

2. Fixed costs are $229,000 per year. The product sells for $17 per unit and variable costs are expected to be $11 per unit.

3. Variable costs are expected to be 60 percent of selling price, and fixed costs are estimated at $105,000 per year. Last year's

sales were $6,600,000, representing 110,000 units sold. Selling price is expected to be 10 percent higher next year.

4. Fixed costs are presently $59,000 per year and variable costs are $2.60 per unit. A new machine, with a 5-year life and no salvage value, will be purchased at the beginning of the year for $56,000. The machine will be depreciated on a straight-line basis. The average selling price of the product is $5.30.

E6–3   Multiproduct breakeven.   Chenok Products sells two products: Product A, which sells for $2.98, accounts for 72 percent of the units sold, and Product B, which sells for $4.50, accounts for 28 percent of the units sold. Fixed costs associated with manufacturing the products amount to $89,000. Variable costs of Product A are expected to be $1.12 per unit, and Product B $2.05 per unit. How many units of *each* product must be sold in order for the company to break even? What assumptions are implicit in your analysis?

E6–4   CVP *analysis of changes.*   Emmerson Kit Company is considering expanding plant capacity by constructing an addition to their factory. Fixed costs currently amount to $420,000 and are expected to increase by $125,000 if the plant addition is undertaken. The present plant capacity is 80,000 units per year. Capacity should increase by 50 percent with the new addition. Variable costs are currently $6.80 per unit and are expected to decrease by $0.40 per unit if the new addition is completed. The current selling price of $15.95 is expected to remain the same under either alternative. Draw a *CVP* graph for the current conditions and for the proposed expansion. What are the breakeven points under the two alternatives? Which alternative do you favor? Why?

E6–5   CVP *chart.*   The Lever Corporation has $385,000 in fixed costs. The product it produces is sold at $450 per unit. Variable costs for the product are $380 per unit. Prepare a breakeven chart for the company and label all parts. How many units must the company sell to break even? Verify the breakeven point by calculation.

E6–6   Finding the unknown.   Listed below are data relating to four separate companies.

	Company A	Company B	Company C	Company D
Annual fixed costs	$100,000	$60,000	$155,000	$?
Selling price per unit	$50	$7	?	$29
Variable costs per unit	$31	?	$46	$13
Breakeven point (units)	?	18,750	3,100	4,444

Required:

Complete the above table by filling in the spaces where question marks appear.

PROBLEMS

P6–1 **CVP** *analysis.* An examination of Vicker Corporation's records revealed the following:

Fixed costs	$485,000
Variable costs per unit	$12
Selling price per unit	$46

Required:

a. Compute the breakeven point in units and in terms of dollar volume.

b. If Vicker Corporation set a profit goal of $162,000 after a 50 percent income tax, how many units must be sold?

c. If variable costs increase to $18 per unit, what is the breakeven point in units and in terms of dollar volume?

d. If fixed costs increase by $132,000 and variable costs decrease by $2 per unit, what will the breakeven point be? (Disregard assumption *c.*)

e. Prepare a *CVP* graph under the assumptions in *d.* Label all parts of the graph.

f. List at least five basic assumptions that are normally made in *CVP* analysis. To what extent do these assumptions limit the usefulness of this technique?

P6–2 **CVP** *analysis.* T.B. Glenn and Company, maker of quality hand-made pipes, has experienced a steady growth in sales for the past five years. However, increased competition has led Mr. Glenn, the president, to believe that an aggressive advertising campaign will be necessary next year to maintain the company's present growth.

To prepare for next year's advertising campaign, the company's accountant has prepared and has presented Mr. Glenn with the following data for the current year, 1978:

Cost Schedule

Variable costs:	
Direct labor	$ 8.00/pipe
Direct materials	3.25/pipe
Variable overhead	2.50/pipe
Total variable costs	$13.75/pipe
Fixed costs:	
Manufacturing	$ 25,000
Selling	40,000
Administrative	70,000
Total fixed costs	$135,000
Selling price, per pipe	$25
Expected sales (20,000 units)	$500,000
Tax rate	40%

Mr. Glenn has set the sales target for 1979 at $550,000 (or 22,000 pipes).

Required:

a. What is the projected aftertax net income for 1978?

b. What is the breakeven point in units for 1978?

c. Mr. Glenn believes an additional selling expense of $11,250 for advertising in 1979, with all other costs remaining constant, will be necessary to attain the sales target. What will the after-tax net income for 1979 be if the additional $11,250 is spent?

d. What will the breakeven point in dollar sales for 1979 be if the additional $11,250 is spent for advertising?

e. If the additional $11,250 is spent for advertising in 1979, what is the dollar sales level necessary to equal 1978 aftertax net income?

f. At a sales level of 22,000 units, what is the maximum amount that can be spent on advertising in 1979 if an aftertax net income of $60,000 is desired?

(CMA Adapted)

P6–3 *Multiproduct* **CVP** *analysis.* Alfred Machinery Company manufactures three products: Alpha, Beta, and Gamma. During the past year Alpha accounted for 50 percent of units sold, Beta for 30 percent, and Gamma for the remaining 20 percent. Cost and selling price data regarding the products follow:

	Alpha	**Beta**	**Gamma**
Unit selling price	$ 620	$ 925	$ 1,220
Annual fixed costs	40,000	30,000	60,000
Unit variable costs	290	600	810

The fixed costs listed above represent depreciation of machinery and equipment which is used only on that particular product. In addition to these fixed product costs, the company has joint fixed costs (applicable to the company as a whole) which amount to $400,000 per year.

Required:

a. How many units of each product must be sold for the company to break even, assuming the sales mix remains constant?

b. How many units of each product must be sold in order to earn an aftertax profit of $100,000, assuming the sales mix remains constant?

c. Assume the sales mix changes to 10 percent Alpha, 40 percent Beta, and 50 percent Gamma. How many units of each product must be sold to break even?

P6-4 **CVP** *analysis of changes.*   Shapero Products Company has been in business for 10 years and has earned a profit in each year. The rate of profits, however, has not been satisfactory in recent years and management would like to take steps to increase profits by $100,000 per year. Since the company is now operating at only 80 percent of capacity, the sales manager has suggested that fixed costs be reduced to a level which will accomplish the desired profit. The production manager argues that the company's products are underpriced. He notes costs have been going up faster than selling prices and that "... anyone knows you must mark your goods up above cost sufficient to provide a fair return." The president thinks the goal could be achieved under the existing cost and price structure if the salesmen would just "get out and beat the bushes" and sell more units of product. The factory engineer has suggested that the assembly line be rearranged to reduce the variable costs of production. Data related to the past years' operations are:

Annual fixed costs	$1,500,000
Product selling price per unit	$72
Variable costs per unit	$28
Factory capacity (annual)	50,000 units

Required:

a.   Calculate the amount and percentage change which would be necessary to accomplish management's profit goal by:

1.   reduction of fixed costs alone
2.   reduction of variable costs alone
3.   increase in selling price alone
4.   increase in units sold alone

b.   What are some of the problems management might expect to encounter under each of the above alternatives?

c.   Suppose the company sells its product in a highly competitive market, the plant and equipment are under a 10-year lease agreement, and product quality is not very critical. Which option do you think would most likely achieve management's goal? Explain.

P6-5 **CVP** *graph.*   Sno Go Manufacturing Company produces and markets a snowmobile which it sells to dealers for $1,099 each and which has a retail price of $1,595 each. During the coming year the company expects fixed costs to amount to $1,000,000 for any volume up to 5,000 units. If production exceeds 5,000 units, the present plant capacity, fixed costs are expected to jump to $1,500,000 per year. The variable costs to produce 1 snowmobile are expected to amount to $488 per unit if 5,000 or less are produced. Because quantity discounts can be obtained, the variable costs can be reduced to $422 for all units produced in excess of 5,000.

Required:

a. Calculate the company's breakeven point assuming they will not exceed present plant capacity.

b. How many units would they need to sell in addition to the 5,000 units, the present plant capacity, in order to justify allowing the fixed costs to increase by $500,000?

c. Draw a *CVP* graph covering production of up to 10,000 units.

d. Refer to your *CVP* graph *(c)* and estimate the profit to be achieved at 8,000 units.

P6–6 CVP *analysis of changes.* Mano Motor Company has manufactured electric motors for nearly 10 years. During that time they have had little difficulty in operating at or near plant capacity and in selling their entire production. The selling price of a motor is currently $35, a price which has remained constant for the last 4 years. The company's fixed costs amount to $220,000 per year and variable costs are $17 per motor. The present plant has a capacity of 25,000 motors per year.

During the past year the market for electric motors has become quite competitive as energy conservation has cut back the sales of many products which use them. Mano's competitors have lowered the price of their competing motors to $32 and Mano expects to match this price. In addition, many of Mano's suppliers are talking of price increases, although they have not become effective yet.

Required:

a. Calculate Mano's profit at capacity under present costs and selling prices.

b. Calculate the breakeven point under present costs and selling prices.

c. Calculate the breakeven point assuming no changes except a price change to $32.

d. Calculate the breakeven point assuming no changes except for a 20 percent increase in variable costs.

e. Calculate the breakeven point assuming a 20 percent increase in fixed costs, a 20 percent increase in variable costs, and that the $32 motor price is matched.

f. Assuming no changes in selling price or costs but that Mano's decision to maintain the $35 selling price will reduce volume to 60 percent of capacity, calculate the profit.

g. Suppose management is given a choice between the following alternatives. Which should Mano select? Why?

Alternative	Selling Price Per Unit	Annual Fixed Costs	Variable Costs Per Unit	Unit Sales
1	$31	$220,000	$19	25,000
2	32	250,000	15	20,000

P6–7 Multiproduct breakeven. Sue Brennan and Patsy Zupon are roommates at State University. Because school spirit is growing, they decide to go into the business of selling pennants, caps, and pins that are imprinted with the school's slogan "Go Big Purple." In order to start the business, they must pay the University $100 for a business license and invest $500 in a booth. The university also requires a royalty of $0.05 for each item sold because all slogans used have been copyrighted by the university. Data related to the three products are:

	Selling Price Per Unit	Variable Costs Per Unit*	Fixed Setup Costs**	Commission to Salesmen	Sales Mix (Percent of Units Sold)
Pennants	$3.00	$1.40	$100	$0.30	30
Caps	$4.50	$2.00	$150	$0.40	25
Pins	$1.00	$0.60	$ 75	$0.10	45

*Manufacturer's invoice price only
**The manufacturer charges a fixed charge for setting up the machinery for the slogan for each item produced regardless of quantity ordered.

Calculate the number of units of each product the business must sell if the girls are to break even during the first year's operation.

P6–8 CVP analysis. Snap Courses, Inc., is considering publishing a new book to accompany Basket Weaving 442. Forecasted costs associated with this project are:

Machine setup time (36 hours @ $6/hour)	$216
Special binding machine (for this project only)	$395
Advertising costs	$400
Costs of paper and ink	$4.20 per book
Binding costs	$1.10 per book
Royalties to authors	10% of retail price

The book will have a retail selling price of $14. All copies will be sold directly to bookstores at a 25 percent discount off of the retail price. Course enrollments and textbook selection are very unpredictable so the publisher must plan to make this project pay based on sales projections for a single year.

a. Calculate the number of copies that must be sold in order to break even on the project.

b. Calculate the number of copies that must be sold in order to earn a before-tax profit of $10,000 on the project.

c. Assume Snap Courses pays income taxes of 45 percent of net income, how many units must they sell in order to earn an aftertax profit of $10,000?

d. What will the firm's profit (or loss) before taxes be if they sell 200 copies? If they sell 3,000 copies?

e. Would it be better to sell 500 copies with a retail price of $14, or 1,500 copies with a retail price of $10? Explain.

P6–9 *Multiproduct* **CVP** *analysis.* The Ecology Chemical Company manufactures fertilizer which it sells in 100-pound bags. Although the chemical content of each bag is identical, the fertilizer is sold under three separate brand names and through different channels of distribution. Brand "Super Green" is sold directly to retailers for $15 per bag. Brand "Better Green" is sold to wholesale distributors for $10 per bag, and brand "Green" is sold to a discount department-store chain for $9 per bag. The variable costs of producing each 100-pound bag are:

Materials	$2.90
Labor	2.20
Other variable costs	1.25

Annual fixed costs of production per year are:

Administrative salaries	$100,000
Building depreciation	40,000
Equipment depreciation	28,000
Fixed selling expenses	65,000
Other administrative costs	110,000

Brand Super Green is sold F.O.B. dealer (Ecology pays the freight to the dealer) and delivery costs average $0.60 per bag. In addition, Ecology's salesmen are paid a 10 percent commission on Super Green sales. Dealers are also given a rebate of $0.10 per bag as a local advertising subsidy.

Better Green is sold F.O.B. factory (the buyer pays the freight) and Ecology's salesmen are paid an 8 percent commission on these sales. Green is sold F.O.B. factory under a contract between the two company presidents and no salesmen's commissions are paid on these sales.

Each brand is packaged in a specially made bag with costs per bag as follows: Super Green $0.24, Better Green $0.20, and Green $0.18. During the past year sales were: 50,000 bags of Super Green, 90,000 bags of Better Green, and 40,000 bags of Green.

Required:

a. Calculate Ecology's profit (or loss) for the past year.

b. Assume that the sales mix (bags of each brand sold), selling prices, and costs remain constant. How many bags of each brand must the company sell this year in order to break even?

c. Suppose the total bags sold this year is the same as last year but that the mix shifts to one-third for each brand. Calculate the expected profit.

d. Explain why your answers to *a* and *c* are different even though the number of units sold remained constant.

Inventory Cost and Control

Financial accountants are preoccupied with costs because generally accepted income measurement depends on the assignment of costs to accounting periods. The matching concept (see Chapter 1) requires that a cost be assigned to the *period* (or periods) in which that outlay helped to produce revenue. Some costs (for example, the night watchman's salary) are reported as expenses in the period in which the services are received. Such *expired* costs are sometimes called *period* costs because they are recognized as expenses in the accounting period in which they are used up. Other costs (such as freight-in) are assigned to the *inventory* accounts when they are paid, and are not reported as expenses until the items are sold. These costs are known as *product* costs because they are assigned to a product (inventory) rather than expensed immediately. Product costs expire either in the present or in future accounting periods depending on when the inventory is sold.

In a very small business, measuring inventory costs and allocating them to the proper accounting period can be relatively simple. For example, John Price has a paper route with the Star Tribune. He buys his papers from the Tribune for $0.10 each and sells them to his customers for $0.15 each. Because he knows how many papers he needs each day, he carries an inventory for only an hour or two. All papers purchased one day are sold that same day so that no stock of goods (inventory) is required. Further, his only cost is for papers. Thus, he has no problem deciding which costs are product costs and which are period costs. If he sells 800 papers during a given week, his profit can be easily measured:

Sales (800 papers @ $0.15 each)	$120
Less: Cost of goods sold (800 papers @ $0.10 each)	80
Profit	$ 40

Virtually no business is able to anticipate its exact needs so completely. The manager of a grocery store, for example, does not know how many cans of beans will be sold during a given period of time. Furthermore, the bean supplier may be located a great distance from the grocery store (in another city, state, or even country). The grocer must therefore anticipate his need for a period of time, project the time required for delivery, and then allow for some margin of error in his estimates. In order to satisfy the needs of customers he must maintain an *inventory* of goods on hand.

There are several important accounting problems associated with inventories that managers should understand clearly. How is the quantity of inventory on hand at a particular date determined? What assumptions can be made regarding the flow of inventory costs? What effect do the different cost assumptions have on reported profits and financial position? Which costs should be inventoried? How can inventory values be estimated? Why and how are inventories controlled? In this chapter, we will try to answer these questions.

DETERMINING INVENTORY SIZE

Two common methods used to determine the size of the inventory at any particular date are the *periodic* and the *perpetual* systems. In a periodic system, the quantity is determined by an actual physical count of the goods at a particular date, such as the end of the year. In the latter case, records of purchases and sales are carefully maintained in order to provide the quantity on hand at *any* date during the year.

Periodic Inventory Systems

A periodic system has the advantage of simplicity of recordkeeping. No accounting records of quantities on hand, received, or shipped during the year are maintained under this system. Rather, when the information is needed for the preparation of financial statements, a physical count of all goods on hand is made. The taking of a physical count is a difficult and expensive task, because operations must be stopped and everything counted from "wall to wall." The count is not normally taken very often, usually only at the end of the fiscal period. Companies that carry many items of relatively low unit value typically use this physical inventory system because of the high cost of maintaining detailed records.

Perpetual Inventory Systems

Under a perpetual inventory system, the inventory manager maintains records that should reflect the quantity of goods on hand at all times. Each time a purchase or sale of an item is made, the change in the balance on hand is recorded on a stock record. This system, of course, requires a rather extensive set of records and procedures. Normally, it is practical only where the unit value of the goods is relatively high because of the high cost of keeping detailed inventory records. Generally, *sample* physical counts are made at regular intervals in order to verify the perpetual records. Because these counts can be made less frequently and can be staggered by type of goods, the expense is considerably less than is the case with a complete *wall-to-wall* count. Inventory control and the ability to prepare interim statements are the two chief advantages of the perpetual system.

ASSUMPTIONS REGARDING COST FLOWS

Once the quantity of goods on hand has been determined by either method, it is necessary to arrive at the cost of each item in order to measure profit and to assign an inventory value for the balance sheet. A paperboy is able to measure profit by comparing the cost of the papers sold with his sales revenue. Assigning costs to inventory can be relatively simple when all goods are purchased at a single price (as were the newspapers). But, what do we do when several different prices are paid for identical goods? *Which* costs pertain to goods sold and *which* pertain to goods still on hand? Suppose, for example, that Karl Kone sets up a business to sell transistor radios. During the year he makes the following purchases:

> 4 @ $6 each
> 4 @ $7 each
> 2 @ $8 each

Karl takes a physical inventory at the end of the year and learns he has 3 radios on hand. He now wants to measure his profit, and must assign costs to the 3 radios on hand and also to the 7 radios sold.[1]

To do this, Karl must make an assumption regarding *cost flows*. He will probably choose one of four common assumptions: *first-in-first-out* (FIFO), *last-in-first-out* (LIFO), *weighted average,* or *specific identification.* Generally speaking, the manager is free to select any of these methods but, once he has made the selection, he is pretty well tied to it. He cannot choose one assumption one year and another in a later year, without violating the consistency demanded by financial statement users.

Because our primary concern is to measure profit (performance), we are primarily concerned with *cost flows* rather than physical flows. The manager should select the cost flow assumption which he feels will result in the best matching of costs and revenues regardless of how the goods physically flow. For a better understanding, we will cite an example of how goods physically flow according to each assumption. As you read these examples, keep in mind that the assumptions made regarding *cost flows* need not parallel the physical flows.

---

[1] Because he had 10 radios available and only 3 are left, he *assumes* the other 7 were sold. This assumption is necessary under the periodic inventory system, unless other facts are known.

FIFO

The first-in-first-out (FIFO) assumption holds that the goods purchased earliest are the first to be sold. Therefore, the *most recent costs* should be assigned to the unsold goods (ending inventory). For this reason, the FIFO method is sometimes referred to as the *most recent invoice method* of assigning costs to inventories. Perishable products in a grocery store, such as milk, normally follow a FIFO physical flow (that is, the most recently purchased milk would be placed at the back of the cooler so that the customer would purchase the oldest milk first). Merchandisers are often cautioned to "rotate their stock." In many inventories, the best approach to physical flow management is the FIFO basis. As we noted in the previous section, this does not mean that FIFO necessarily provides the best *cost flow* description.

LIFO

Last-in-first-out (LIFO) assumes just the opposite physical flow; that is, the customer purchases the most recently acquired goods and leaves the oldest ones. Under this assumption, the inventory is priced from the oldest *invoices*. A bin of bolts in a hardware store is an example of a LIFO physical flow. As new bolts are purchased, they are emptied into the bin. When a customer purchases a bolt, he selects one of the most recently acquired ones from the top, leaving the oldest bolts in the bins. The ending inventory would always consist of old bolts, many of them the same, period after period.

Remember that the primary concern in selecting an inventory costing method should be *cost flows,* not physical flows. The manager should select that method which will provide the most meaningful financial statements, regardless of physical flows.

Weighted Average

The weighted average approach is based on the assumption that each sale contains a portion of the beginning inventory as well as a portion of each of the purchases made during the period. Gasoline purchased at a service station is an example: Each time new gasoline is placed in the tank by the distributor, it mixes with the contents of the tank. Each gallon pumped from the tank includes a fraction of each of the quantities previously placed in the tank.

Specific Identification

When specific identification of units sold and on hand can be accomplished by serial numbers or some other means of identification, no *assumption* about physical flow is necessary. New automobiles are easily inventoried in this manner by referring to the manufacturer's serial number. Documents related to both the purchase and the sale of a new car refer to this serial number, thus making it easy to determine the gross margin from the sale of any particular unit.

Comparison of Cost Flow Assumptions

When all units of a particular inventory item are purchased at the same price, the choice of cost flow assumptions makes no difference on either reported income or the balance sheet value. However, when the units are purchased at different prices, the choice of cost flow assumptions can have an effect on both net income and the inventory value shown on the balance sheet. Returning to our previous illustration, you will recall that Karl had purchased 10 radios:

$$4 \text{ @ } \$6 \text{ each}$$
$$4 \text{ @ } \$7 \text{ each}$$
$$2 \text{ @ } \$8 \text{ each}$$

His physical inventory shows 3 radios still on hand. If he assumes a FIFO flow, he should assign costs to the 3 units on hand from the most recent purchases. This would give him an inventory value of $23 (2 at $8 + 1 at $7) and a cost of goods sold of $45 (4 at $6 + 3 at $7). If he assumes a LIFO flow, he will show an inventory cost of $18 (3 at $6) and a cost of goods sold of $50 (1 at $6 + 4 at $7 + 2 at $8).

Under the weighted average assumption, he would calculate the weighted average cost of all items:

$$\frac{(4 \times \$6) + (4 \times \$7) + (2 \times \$8)}{10} = \$6.80$$

The inventory would then show a cost of $20.40 (3 at $6.80) and a cost of goods sold of $47.60 (7 at $6.80).

Under the specific identification method, the radios would be identified by a serial number. Let's assume the radios were numbered 1 through 10 and that the physical inventory showed No. 5, No. 6, and No. 9 were still on hand. Under these assumptions, the inventory would be shown at a cost of $22 ($7 + $7 + $8) and the cost of goods sold at $46 ($6 + $6 + $6 + $6 + $7 + $7 + $8).

The costs shown on the balance sheet and on the income statement under the four different cost flow assumptions may be summarized as:

	FIFO	LIFO	WA	SID
Inventory cost shown on balance sheet	$23.00	$18.00	$20.40	$22.00
Cost of goods (inventory) sold per income statement	$45.00	$50.00	$47.60	$46.00
Total inventory costs	$68.00	$68.00	$68.00	$68.00

Note that the total costs are the same under all four assumptions. There is a difference in how much of this cost is allocated between the ending inventory and the cost of goods sold, as illustrated in Exhibit 7-1. Note that the cost of goods available for sale (consisting of the beginning inventory, freight-in, and purchases) is charged partially to ending inventory and partially to cost of goods sold. An inventory valuation method which charges more of the cost to the ending inventory simultaneously charges less to the cost of goods sold and vice versa.

Exhibit 7-1
Inventory Cost Flow

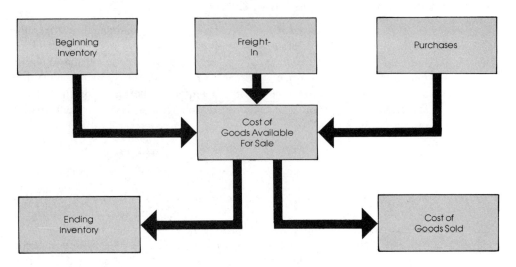

In periods of rising prices (as assumed here), the LIFO method allocates a larger proportion of the total costs to the income statement than FIFO, thereby showing the *least* profit. Because any of the assumptions may be used for income tax reporting (provided the same assumption is used for book purposes), the LIFO method results in a lower tax liability.

This result is particularly attractive to many managers and their accountants, and helps explain the popularity of LIFO in the 1950s and 1960s. Many companies switched from FIFO to LIFO during those decades in order to reduce their income tax liabilities. By increasing the cost of goods sold, LIFO reduces the company's reported and taxable profits, which in turn reduces the amount of income taxes assessed.

Note that the LIFO method places the manager in somewhat of a dilemma. This method will reduce current tax payments, thereby improving the company's cash flow (a desirable result), but it will also show reduced profits (an undesirable result). During the recession of the mid-1970s, many managers were again caught in this squeeze. Inflation was making the tax advantage of switching to LIFO very attractive. To do so would reduce cash payments for taxes (and possibly reduce demands by stockholders for increased dividends and workers for increased wages). On the other hand, the recession was producing lower sales, revenues, and profits. To reduce profits further by switching to LIFO might cause serious stockholder and investor reactions.

Another disadvantage of LIFO inventory valuation is the effect it has on the balance sheet. This method can result in showing the inventories on the balance sheet in terms of costs prevailing in earlier years. While LIFO inventory valuation improves the income statement, in the opinion of some people, it does so to the detriment of the balance sheet. Although this distortion may not be serious at first, it may become increasingly significant as time goes on. Each year the spread between the reported inventory cost and the current market price widens.

ESTIMATING INVENTORIES

Sometimes it is neither practical nor possible to calculate an inventory valuation, as just illustrated, thus making it necessary to estimate the value of the goods on hand at a particular date. For example, management may desire monthly financial statements (which in turn require monthly inventory figures) to evaluate performance more frequently, but does not wish to establish a perpetual system. Because of the inconvenience and high cost, a physical inventory is taken only once each year. How can management get the inventory figures to prepare monthly statements? The answer is to estimate them.

In other cases, inventory costs *must* be estimated because there is no other way to get these figures. For example, how else could we arrive at the cost of goods which were destroyed in a fire and for which we have no perpetual records?

The Gross Margin Method

The gross margin method utilizes the average gross margin from a *number of prior periods* to estimate the cost of goods sold. This figure is then deducted from the goods available for sale (beginning inventory plus net purchases) to arrive at the ending inventory. Basically, we assume that only two things can happen to acquired goods: They can be sold, in which event the costs are transferred to cost of goods sold; or they are still on hand (refer again to Exhibit 7-1).

To illustrate the gross margin method, assume that the inventory of the Eleven-Seven Store is destroyed by fire on the night of April 23, 1979. The company records, fortunately maintained in a fireproof safe, provide the following information:

	Net Sales	Cost of Goods Sold
1976	$ 55,000	$32,000
1977	62,000	37,000
1978	51,000	30,000
Total	$168,000	$99,000

Sales (January 1 to April 23, 1979)	$29,300
Purchases (January 1 to April 23, 1979)	25,400
Freight-in (January 1 to April 23, 1979)	1,100
Inventory (January 1, 1979)	7,200

The reports from prior years are examined and utilized to determine the *average gross margin* experienced by the firm. Note that net sales have averaged $56,000 per year ($168,000/3), while cost of goods sold has averaged $33,000 per year ($99,000/3). This means that the cost of goods sold has averaged about 59 percent of net sales ($33,000/$56,000), and gross margin has averaged about 41 percent of net sales ($23,000/$56,000, or 100 percent − 59 percent). Utilizing the past cost/selling price relationship, we can calculate the estimated value of the ending inventory as shown on page 174.

Beginning inventory		$ 7,200
Purchases	$25,400	
Freight-in	1,100	
Net purchases		26,500
Goods available for sale		$33,700
Cost of goods sold		
(59% of $29,300 net sales)		17,287
Estimated cost of ending inventory		
(destroyed in the fire)		$16,413

All the figures necessary to calculate the cost of the goods available for sale should be readily found in the company records. By first calculating that portion of the goods sold (utilizing the complement of the gross margin percentage), it is a matter of simple arithmetic to estimate the unsold portion (the ending inventory). The accuracy of the approach depends on the applicability of the past ratio to the particular set of goods on hand at the date of estimation.

The Retail Inventory Method

The retail inventory method is similar to the gross margin method because it also uses the relationship between cost and selling price as the basis for estimating the inventory's cost. The major difference between the two methods is that the gross margin method utilizes information from *prior periods,* whereas the retail method uses the costs and selling prices of the *current period.* Under the retail method, we keep more records, including the cost of goods available for sale in the period, the initial *markon* (the difference between the cost and the initial marked selling price), the *mark-ups* (subsequent increases in selling price), and the *markdowns* (subsequent decreases in selling price). With this information and the retail sales figures for the same period, we can estimate the cost of the ending inventory.

The retail method can also be used to convert a physical count from retail value to approximate cost. For example, when counting the items in the inventory of a department store, it would be easy for the employee to indicate the marked retail price of each item as it is counted. With this information, the retail value of the goods on hand can be calculated by multiplying the quantities counted by the selling prices. From this *retail value inventory,* we can approximate its *cost* by using the average cost to selling price ratio.

The technique also can be used to estimate the cost of inventories at dates when it is either undesirable (because of cost or inconvenience) or impossible (because of destruction or theft) to take a physical count.

The Retail Inventory Method Illustrated

The Hapco Company takes a physical inventory annually, but management desires monthly financial statements. The company records disclose the figures shown at the top of page 175.

Inventory at January 1: cost $25,000, marked selling price	$ 45,000
Purchases during January (cost)	165,000
Initial markon relating to purchases	45,000
Freight-in relating to purchases	10,000
Markups during January	4,740
Markdowns during January	4,000
Sales during January	180,000

The cost of the ending inventory can be estimated as follows:

	Cost	Selling Price
Beginning inventory	$ 25,000	$ 45,000
Purchases	165,000	210,000
Freight-in	10,000	
Markups		4,740
Total (basis of cost conversion factor)*	$200,000	$259,740
Less: Markdowns		(4,000)
Goods available for sale	$200,000	$255,740
Less: Sales		(180,000)
Estimated inventory at retail		$ 75,740
Estimated inventory at cost**	$ 58,320	

* ($200,000/$259,740) = 77%
** (77% × $75,740) = $58,320

Notice that the above calculations contained a small inconsistency between the computation and the application of the 77 percent ratio. The markdowns were deducted to find the retail value of the goods available for sale, but they were *not* deducted from the selling price that was used as the denominator. This inconsistency has the effect of reducing the cost percentage, and produces a smaller inventory value. In the opinion of many financial accountants, the lower figure represents a more conservative value that approximates the *lower-of-cost-or-market* required by generally accepted principles. Management should not feel obligated to use this convention for its internal reports, however.

MANAGING AN INVENTORY

For both retailing and production companies, the lifeblood of their operations is the inventory, because neither sales nor production can be achieved without goods or materials. Customers can be lost to more completely stocked competitors and production processes may be shut down if only one item of materials or supplies is not available when and where it is needed.

If the only objective of inventory management were to avoid shortages, there would be few problems other than finding the space for storage. Of course, there are economic considerations that place constraints on inventory size, and that cause the manager to seek optimum levels. In particular, *carrying costs* tend to rise as physical levels rise. If property taxes are assessed on inventories, it is wise to have a reduced level. Goods on the shelf are frequently subject to physical deterioration or theft. More subtly, a *technological* deterioration may occur through obsolescence. Insurance costs are clearly related to the size of the inventory. From a financial point of view, there is a cost of holding inventories because they do not normally increase in value as time passes. Thus, a large inventory will not produce a larger income than a smaller inventory that is *turned over* (sold or used) more frequently. But the larger inventory produces a larger cost because of the interest paid on loans to acquire it. Even if internal funds are used, there is a cost of interest income lost by being unable to invest the cash elsewhere. These costs become especially high when the money market is "tight."

From the other side, management must keep sufficient levels of inventory to avoid shortages. Also, more frequent ordering creates additional administrative costs and may cause quantity discounts to be missed. Special ordering of less demanded items is relatively expensive and should be avoided unless the customer is willing to absorb the costs as well as wait for the product. Prospects of inflation encourage large purchases and high stock levels to avoid more expensive replacement costs. Management is truly "squeezed" by all these factors.

In a simplistic sense, there are two approaches to solving the inventory problem: intuitive and scientific. In practice, there are probably as many approaches as there are managers. Less sophisticated managers depend on personal feelings and observations for signals of if and when an item should be reordered. Thus, inventory levels can easily be too low or too high. A small business with good customer relations and a nearby source of supply may do well under such an intuitive system. On the other hand, the lack of these two things can create a disaster. If a production facility is relatively flexible, it might be able to continue operating despite a "stock-out" of a particular input, perhaps by producing some other product. However, with a highly specialized line and a skilled payroll, there may be no alternative to a complete shutdown.

Scientific approaches to inventory management have existed since the late nineteenth century, but were not adopted widely until the 1950s. Basically, scientific management involves anticipation of the previously mentioned variables. Projections are made of such things as demand, supply times, holding costs, ordering costs, and the uncertainties associated with each of them. The "model" then produces an "optimum" answer for such things as the proper time to order an item as well as the proper size to order. (These techniques will be presented in more detail in Chapter 18.)

The information-handling abilities of computers has enabled and encouraged replacing intuitive with scientific methods. For example, an important part of scientific management is knowledge of the quantities on hand at a particular date and sold during a particular time period. A *perpetual* inventory system can provide this information, but it is extremely expensive to keep the records by hand. With proper programming and preparation of the data, a computer can perform many routine operations in addition to simply keeping a record of the quantity in stock. Reports can be prepared about slow or fast moving items; if desired, the system can calculate order quantities and even print purchase orders. We cannot emphasize sufficiently, however, the potential danger in turning too much control over to a machine.

Nonetheless, the computer has a great potential for providing inventory control and perpetual inventory information. Consider the use of retail data terminals (computerized cash registers) in connection with the new *Universal Product Codes* (UPC). UPCs, like the one shown in Exhibit 7-2, appear on most items purchased at a supermarket.

Businesses that use these codes need "point-of-sale" retail data terminals which can read the UPC. The information can then be transmitted to the computer where data regarding prices and quantities are stored. The computer can instantaneously make the necessary calculations to speed the customer on his way and at the same time adjust the inventory records and provide management with the data needed for inventory control.

Exhibit 7-2
An Example of a UPC

Inventory Control

The preceding discussion is based on a *macro,* or generalized, look at inventory problems from a higher management level. However, the solution to these problems must eventually be translated into *micro,* or specific, actions. It is only in very small firms that one individual is responsible for the entire inventory. Usually, there are many persons charged with inventory management. This approach tends to solve the smaller problems, but it creates another one in that their activities must be coordinated to assure that the entire firm's interests are being pursued.

Some of the variables that a manager may face in controlling his section of the inventory are:

1. Should an item be carried?
2. How many units should be carried?
3. Should an item be reordered?
4. When should an item be reordered?
5. How many units should be ordered?
6. What varieties (model, size, color, quality, etc.) should be ordered?
7. Is the item "moving" fast enough?
8. Is the item in the best location for likely sales?
9. Is the selling price too low or too high?
10. Is the item adequately protected against theft or damage?
11. Is the item displayed to its best promotional advantage?

Before he can put his talents to use in dealing with these problems, the manager needs data from some sort of inventory "information system." The structure and content of the system varies from firm to firm and from industry to industry. A high volume, discount store requires a different system than a low volume outlet. Trends and tastes in fashions are more volatile than those in lumber; thus, errors can be more costly. Even within a particular firm, some items of inventory may require more careful attention than others.

Inventory Control Illustrated

To illustrate how an inventory information system works, we will describe one used in a modern department store.[2] Castletons Inc. has 7 retail outlets located within a 50-mile radius of their central office and warehouse. Each merchandise purchase is made by a buyer through a common Purchasing Department. Each buyer handles certain classes of merchandise (such as shoes, coats, etc.) and is responsible for the quantities, colors, and styles distributed among the 7 stores.

As merchandise is received, the goods are counted and inspected to assure that everything agrees with the purchase order. An inventory control and price tag, such as the one shown in Exhibit 7-3, is prepared and attached to each individual unit. The numbers identify the style, stock number, color, class, season, and style of the particular item, as well as the vendor that supplied it. In addition, the same data are magnetically recorded on a thin layer of magnetic tape inside the tag between the layers of paper. The tags are prepared on a labelwriter similar to the one shown in Exhibit 7-4, which simultaneously prints the tag and codes the tape so that it can be read by the computer. After the tags are attached, the merchandise is distributed to the various stores according to the buyer's instructions. Prior to distribution, however, the tags are processed by a "wand" (a small reader which reads the magnetic symbols) so that the data will be stored in the computer.

Each store is equipped with several point-of-sale retail data terminals similar to the one shown in Exhibit 7-5, which also serve as cash registers.

Exhibit 7-3
Inventory Control and Price Tag

---

[2] The authors are indebted to Castletons Inc., Salt Lake City, Utah, for this example and the exhibits.

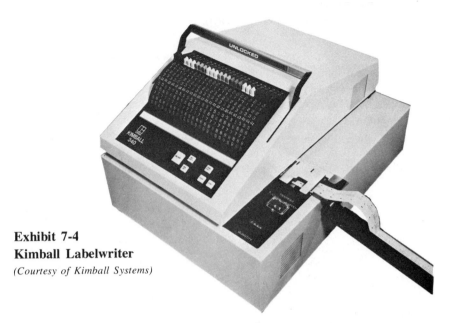

Exhibit 7-4
Kimball Labelwriter
(Courtesy of Kimball Systems)

When a customer makes a purchase, the clerk first passes the *wand* over the inventory tag to *read* all the data needed for inventory control. Next, customer data related to the sale are entered into the keyboard in much the same manner as with a conventional cash register. Calculations of discounts, sales taxes, change, and even verification of the customer's credit standing with Castletons can be accomplished by the terminal through its interface with the computer.

Exhibit 7-5
Sweda Point-of-Sale Retail Data Terminal
(Courtesy of Sweda International)

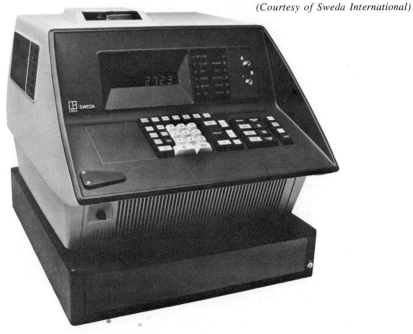

The computer is programmed to revise the perpetual account balance of each individual item of inventory based on the data read from the tags. A *stock control recap* (Exhibit 7-6), reflecting certain inventory control data as of the close of business on the previous day, is prepared each morning by the computer. These recaps are prepared for each buyer, (in this case Sandi Brey) and show nine data items for every item of merchandise for which she is responsible. The buyer can then use this information in making decisions regarding such things as transfers among stores, new orders, and price changes.

Exhibit 7-6

PAGE 2
DATE 02 23 77

CASTLETONS INC
Stock Control Recap From Terminals

SANDI BREY

VENDOR	STYLE	CLASS	COLOR	SEASON	STORE	SIZE	QTY	AMOUNT
0424	6059	1889	38	1	FH	50	1	21.00
0424	6153	1889	55	8	DT	13	3	20.00
0424	6158	1889	58	5	OL	11	6	19.00
0424	9244	1889	15	8	FP	11	1	18.00
0424	9254	1897	78	9	VF	90	1	35.00
0424	9928	1878	32	9	OL	90	2	15.00
0426	5232	1593	85	8	FP	90	1	14.99
0451	0112	1859	05	1	OG	60	1	7.00
0451	0112	1859	05	1	FP	60	7	7.00
0451	0140	1859	07	1	FH	80	1	7.00
0451	0150	1859	78	2	OL	70	1	7.00
0451	0150	1859	78	2	DT	60	1	7.00
0451	0150	1859	78	2	FP	70	1	7.00
0451	0153	1858	01	1	OL	70	4	13.00
0451	0201	1859	05	2	FH	80	5	9.00
0451	0201	1859	05	2	DT	60	1	9.00
0451	0742	1859	95	7	OG		1	3.50
0488	2501	1897	32	9	FP	50	1	50.00
0497	0111	1859	03	1	FP	70	1	7.00
0497	0115	1859	00	2	OL	80	2	7.00
0497	0115	1859	00	2	DT	70	1	7.00
0497	0118	1859	32	1	VF	70	3	9.00

SUMMARY

This chapter focuses on the *inventory,* perhaps the most important contribution to the day-to-day profitability of the firm. No manager can presume that inventory problems will go away or solve themselves. From the financial accountant's point of view, inventory must be properly measured if the firm's ability to pay its debts and earn profits are to be adequately described on the balance sheet and on the income statement.

In dealing with the management and the accounting problems, either a perpetual or a periodic recordkeeping system must be used to determine how many items are on hand. In order to assign costs to the inventory, some assumption about flows must be made. We described the FIFO, LIFO, weighted average, and specific identification methods. Occasionally, an estimated cost of the inventory is all that is needed or available. Two general approaches, the gross margin and the retail method, are briefly described.

In managing the inventory, numerous counteracting forces should be balanced. The costs of having too much must be weighed against the costs of having too little. The problem can be attempted on an intuitive or a scientific basis. Although the latter should be more helpful, it is expensive and by no means perfect.

QUESTIONS

1. Distinguish between period costs and product costs. Why is this distinction so important? Give some examples of each.

2. Distinguish between the two major methods of determining the quantity of merchandise on hand at a particular date.

3. What are the two primary methods used to estimate inventories? Why is it sometimes necessary or desirable to use these methods? What do the two methods have in common?

4. What similarity do you see between the two methods of estimating inventories? What is the main difference between them?

5. Why are markups considered and markdowns *not* considered in calculating the cost/selling price ratio for use in the retail inventory method? How do markdowns enter into the calculations?

6. What are the four assumptions regarding inventory cost flows that are used by accountants? Cite an example of the physical flow of goods for each of these assumptions. What is the primary criterion for selecting the appropriate cost flow assumption for a particular company?

7. Assume that a company purchased a single commodity at 3 different prices: $5, $6, and $7 per unit, in that sequence. At the end of the period, 1 unit was on hand. At what price should this be valued if the company uses FIFO costing? LIFO? Weighted average?

8. Refer to the data in question 7 and calculate the cost of the goods sold under: (a) FIFO, (b) LIFO, and (c) weighted average.

9. Which inventory cost-flow assumption best matches current costs with current revenue? Does this method always produce the *best* matching? Explain.

10. Which inventory cost-flow assumption do you feel is best from the standpoint of the balance sheet? Why?

11. What are the major advantages cited to support LIFO inventory valuation? What problem is LIFO really trying to overcome?

12. Why is inventory management important? What tools do modern managers have to assist them in this crucial task?

13. What sort of information might be useful to a manager in properly controlling his inventory? Would he keep the same sort of details regarding all units in his inventory?

14. During a period of rising prices (inflation), which inventory cost-flow assumption will produce the lowest profit? Which method will produce the lowest balance sheet value?

15. Jorgo Company's gross margin has averaged 35 percent for the past 5 years. Sales for the month of March were $90,000, purchases $52,000. The cost of the beginning inventory was $22,000. What was the approximate cost of the ending inventory?

EXERCISES

E7–1 Estimating inventory. On October 11, the Morton Furniture Company had a fire which completely destroyed the store and its contents. The company records, maintained in a fireproof vault, show that sales prior to the date of the fire amounted to $263,000. The balance sheet prepared at the end of the previous December showed an inventory of $41,000. Purchases during the past year amounted to $190,000 and Freight-in amounted to $6,000. The gross margin rate during the last several years has been 40 percent. What was the approximate value of the company's inventory at the time of the fire?

E7–2 Flow assumptions. Fife Pipe and Drum Company uses a periodic inventory system. At January 1 the company had 100 drums on hand at a cost of $12 each. Purchases during the year were:

March 8	400 @ $14 each
June 30	300 @ $15 each
October 26	500 @ $16 each

A physical count at December 31 shows 250 drums on hand.

Required:

Calculate (a) the cost of goods sold and (b) the cost of the ending inventory, under three separate assumptions: FIFO, LIFO, and weighted average.

E7–3 Estimating inventory. The Round the Clock Grocery store took a physical inventory at the end of the company fiscal year and, because the retail prices were readily available, priced the inventory at retail. The retail value of the year-end inventory was $180,000. At the beginning of the year the company had goods on hand which cost $120,000 and which were marked to sell at $175,000. During the year the company purchased goods at a cost of $700,000 and marked them to sell for $1,025,000. No markups or markdowns were made during the period. Estimate the cost of the ending inventory.

E7–4 Estimating inventory. The Big Bubba Snack Bar, adjacent to the campus, sells prepackaged sandwiches, drinks, and snacks. The company buys all products from a local food distributor and sells them to students at 50 percent above cost. Last night, after the football game, the snack bar was robbed. Since no cash was on hand, the hungry burglars stole all the food. Records indicate food which cost $200 was on hand at the beginning of the month, purchases amounted to $1,500 during the month, and sales up to the date of the theft were $2,100. What was the approximate cost of the stolen food?

E7–5 *Flow assumptions.* From the following information, calculate the cost of the ending inventory under each assumption: (a) first-in-first-out (FIFO), (b) last-in-first-out (LIFO), and (c) weighted average.

> Beginning inventory, 50 units @ $100 each
> January 3, sold 30 units
> January 10, purchased 80 units @ $200 each
> January 25, sold 40 units
> Ending inventory, 60 units

E7–6 *Estimating inventory.* Big Blue Company took a physical inventory on December 31, 1977, and, because the retail prices were conveniently marked on all items counted, priced the inventory at its retail value of $285,400. The company's independent CPA insists the inventory be valued at cost in the published financial statements. From data compiled from the company records you find the beginning inventory cost $190,000 and had a selling price of $300,000. Purchases made during the year cost $992,000 and were marked to sell at $1,560,000. Freight-in on these purchases amounted to $12,000. Markups during the year totaled $25,000; markdowns $35,000, and sales $1,564,000. What was the approximate cost of the ending inventory per the physical count? What was the approximate cost of the ending inventory per the retail inventory method? What was the approximate cost of the inventory overage or shortage?

PROBLEMS

P7–1 *Flow assumptions.*

Part 1:

Plastic Products closes its books quarterly and maintains a periodic inventory system. The following information is available for the first quarter of the current fiscal year:

	Quantity	Unit Price
Beginning inventory	150	$2.00
Purchases:		
January 15	150	1.90
February 12	75	2.00
March 8	100	2.10
March 29	100	2.20

Sales:	Units
January	100
February	175
March	100
Physical count	200

Required:

Compute the cost of the ending inventory and the cost of goods sold under each of the following methods:

a.   FIFO

b.   LIFO

c.   Weighted average

Part 2:

Assume that all sales were made at $3.00 per unit, and that operating expenses for the period were $300.

Required:

Compute net profit under:

a.   FIFO

b.   LIFO

Part 3:

Your calculations in Part 2 should indicate the significant effect on income which the choice of inventory valuation methods can have.

Required:

a.   Explain the significance of the choice between FIFO and LIFO.

b.   What is the cause of the variations?

P7–2   *Flow assumptions.*   Mr. Sharp and Mr. Grant are partners in Ace Specialty Company, a firm formed in 1973 to wholesale inexpensive flashlights. Because the flashlights are manufactured in Japan, it is necessary to buy in large quantities to get favorable prices and shipping rates. For this reason, the company makes 1 purchase per year, based on the sales forecast for the coming year. The flashlights are sold for $0.75 each to retailers as promotional sales items or to firms as advertising giveaways.

In January 1979, the bookkeeper presented the income statement for the previous calendar year to the owners for their review. They were happy to note that profits had increased to $14,470 from the previous year's $12,700. This came as a complete surprise, since the company's salesman had previously reported the number of flashlights sold had decreased slightly from 240,000 in 1977 to 239,000 units in 1978. Physical counts showed 20,000 flashlights were on hand December 31, 1977, and 21,000 flashlights were on hand December 31, 1978. The selling and administrative expenses remained about the same during the 2-year period. Selling expenses were $32,500 in 1977 and $32,000 in 1978, while administrative expenses were $10,000 in 1977 and $10,500 in 1978. Apparently, the profit increase was attributable to an increase in gross profit. "How could gross profit go up when our sales price has remained unchanged?" asked Mr. Grant.

The more the two partners studied the income statements, the more puzzled they became. Finally they called in Mr. Newly, the company's parttime bookkeeper, for an explanation. A very heated discussion followed, and finally Newly said, "As you know, I've been here for a little less than a year now. I have priced the inventory in the only correct way I know, at the price we paid during this last year. How else could one price it? Check it yourself, if you're so darn smart." After throwing the following summary of purchases on the desk, Mr. Newly stomped out of the office.

Year	Units Purchased	Unit Cost
1974	200,000	$0.42
1975	210,000	0.44
1976	230,000	0.48
1977	240,000	0.52
1978	240,000	0.52

Mr. Sharp and Mr. Grant know very little about inventory cost accounting, but they don't like Mr. Newly's attitude. Accordingly, they decide to hire an independent accountant to review their books and determine whether Newly is trying to put something over on them.

Required:

a. As the independent accountant, determine what caused the sudden decrease in cost of goods sold. Support your answer with income statements for the two years and necessary calculations.

b. Comment on the acceptability of the Ace Speciality Company's inventory costing practices. Does the firm have a choice of inventory costing methods when preparing annual income statements? Is the choice limited?

P7–3 **Estimating inventory.** On December 17, 1977 (the final day of test week), the Campus Bookstore suffered a fire that caused extensive damage. The building and its contents were covered by insurance. You are asked to prepare a report supporting your claim for merchandise destroyed, which will be submitted to the insurance company. A physical count indicates that books and other goods which cost $29,350 were not damaged by the fire, but that the balance of the goods on hand at the time of the fire was completely destroyed. The bookstore has followed the practice of marking all merchandise to sell at a price 25 percent above cost. From the bookstore records, which were in the vault of an adjoining building, you gather the following facts:

Inventory (December 31, 1976)	$172,391
Purchases (January 1–December 17, 1977)	524,300
Purchase returns (January 1–December 17, 1977)	10,200
Sales (January 1–December 17, 1977)	825,400
Sales returns (January 1–December 17, 1977)	12,700

Required:

Prepare a report, with detailed supporting computations, indicating the cost of the goods destroyed by the fire.

P7–4 Estimating inventory. On December 31, 1978, the Sentimental Card Shop took a physical inventory which was valued at a cost of $276.24. Mr. Love, the owner, thinks this inventory is much lower than it should be and fears that some theft has been involved. He furnishes you with the following data:

Inventory (January 1, 1978):	
Cost	$ 31,620
Selling price	45,675
Purchases:	
Cost	284,450
Selling price	562,110
Purchase returns:	
Cost	8,940
Selling price	15,635
Markups	12,000
Markdowns	15,000
Transportation-in	18,553
Sales	520,875
Sales returns	6,460

Required:

Calculate the estimated cost of the stolen goods (if any) using the retail inventory method.

P7–5 Flow assumptions. The Leaky Drain Plumbing Corporation has the following inventory record for 1978 on valve 404. The inventory on

	Purchases		
	Units	**Total Cost**	**Units Sold**
January 20	14,000	$30,800	9,610
March 4	10,000	23,500	8,485
April 10			6,230
May 31	8,000	19,200	5,540
July 3			5,630
August 26	13,000	32,500	8,254
October 1	14,000	35,700	8,660
November 20	13,000	33,150	9,041
December 21			9,430

January 1, 1978, was 5,320 units at a price of $2.00 each. (Where purchases and sales occur on the same day, assume that the purchases occurred first.)

Required:

Assume that the company uses the periodic inventory method and that the physical count agrees with the balance on hand shown on the inventory record card. Calculate the cost of the inventory at December 31, 1978, using:

a. FIFO method

b. LIFO method

c. Weighted average method

P7–6 Estimating inventory. On the night on July 4, Paul Revere's store caught fire. Everything except the accounting records, which were kept in a fireproof vault, was destroyed. Mr. Revere filed an insurance claim listing an inventory loss of $38,000. As a fire insurance adjustor, you called on Mr. Revere to verify his claim. From the accounting records the following information is available:

1.	Merchandise inventory on January 1 of the current year	$ 21,820
2.	Sales from January 1 through July 4	108,840
3.	Purchase returns for the same period	3,460
4.	Purchases from January 1 through July 4	57,910
5.	Freight-in from January 1 through July 4	2,160
6.	Sales returns for the same period	2,175
7.	The company indicates that gross margin this year is expected to be about the same as the average for the previous 5 years.	
8.	Facts from prior years:	

Year	Net Sales	Cost of Goods Sold	Operating Expense
1971	$ 80,000	$47,000	$30,000
1972	100,000	61,000	44,000
1973	120,000	80,000	56,000
1974	90,000	53,000	42,000
1975	110,000	70,000	51,000

Required:

Indicate your estimate of the cost of the inventory at the time of the fire. Show your computations.

P7–7 Flow assumptions. During its first year of operation, Winner Company made the following purchases of their chief product, *Pride.*

Month	Quantity Purchased	Unit Cost
January	800	$140
March	1,800	150

Month	Quantity Purchased	Unit Cost
July	1,100	$160
September	700	180
November	900	200

During the first 6 months of the year, Winner sold 2,000 units of Pride for $295 each. In late June management became concerned about the high rate of inflation and decided they would have to increase the selling prices (effective July 1) to $375. Apparently there was considerable resistance to the price increase in the marketplace as sales for the last half of the year amounted to only 1,200 units. Commissions of 8 percent were paid on all sales; other selling expenses amounted to $150,000, and administrative expenses to $110,000 for the year. The company estimates state and federal income taxes will amount to 50 percent of the profit reported before taxes.

Assume that a physical count on December 31 revealed 1,250 units of Pride on hand.

Required:

a. Prepare an income statement for the year assuming a FIFO cost flow.

b. Prepare an income statement for the year assuming a LIFO cost flow.

c. Prepare an income statement for the year assuming an average cost flow.

P7–8 Inventory management. Double Discount Centers is a small chain consisting of 6 locally owned discount department stores. Each store has 12 conventional cash registers. Physical inventories are taken monthly and a stock status report is prepared at that time.

These reports are discussed at monthly meetings and decisions are reached concerning replenishment, new items, and speeding the turnover of slow moving items. In addition, each buyer makes a weekly visual check to be sure that adequate supplies are on hand for all items for which he is responsible. When a customer complains about an item being out of stock, the buyer of that department verifies the shortage, gives the customer a rain check, and places an order.

For some time, the president of Double Discount has given consideration to the purchase of a computer system and remote terminal cash registers. The system would have scanners for reading UPC codes, and would print the product and price on the sales slip. He feels that this approach will increase the speed of checkout, give customers a better record of their purchases, reduce errors in recording sales, and provide valuable inventory control information. His main concern is balancing the costs against these benefits. The computer, terminals, and related equipment will cost approximately $150,000. He expects that he can get only $10,000 for his old registers. Operating costs are expected to be about $8,000 per year more than under the present system with the main increase coming in computer service costs.

About 60 percent of the goods carried by the stores have UPC codes which have been affixed by the product manufacturers. The others will be coded in the store. Because the present system requires that price tags be affixed to all merchandise, he contemplates a $20,000 per year savings by having to price and code only about 40 percent of the merchandise. These savings are somewhat uncertain in that a bill has been introduced in the state legislature which would, if passed, require stamping the price on all goods as a customer protection. Tagging the prices would not otherwise be necessary on the precoded items as the prices would be stored in the computer.

Not many firms in the area have had much experience with this type of system but the manufacturer indicates that it should substantially increase Double Discount's profits. The company president is interested in knowing how such an operation will increase the firm's profits.

Required:

a. List and explain the major advantages of the proposed system. Include an evaluation of any advantages cited in the problem plus any others that occur to you.

b. List and explain the major disadvantages of the proposed system.

c. What recommendation would you make to the president regarding the advisability of installing such a system? Why?

8

The Production Cost Information System

Information about the costs of producing a product is extremely useful, if not essential, in managing the production process. Information about the actual costs is used in preparing the financial statements, in addition to determining whether or not the process is operating as profitably as it should. Information about future costs is a vital input to the planning phase of management. The goal of the production cost information system is to provide the information needed for these purposes. The continuing emphasis in this chapter is on the manufacturing process, but the concepts are just as applicable in service operations. Our discussion centers on *actual* cost information, but information about projected costs is virtually identical in structure and composition.

We will show how the production line operates, and how the cost information system "shadows" the flow of labor, material, and overhead with cost flows.

THE PRODUCTION LINE

It is likely that each of us has seen one or more production lines in our lifetime. Even the simple routine of washing the dishes is a production process. Many products (such as automobiles, televisions, and shoes) are really processed on a number of production lines. Iron ore must be mined, transported, and smelted before it can be used. The ingot must be transported again, and transformed into a nut, a bolt, or a fender before it can become part of a truly finished product. The *cost accountant* is specially trained to devise an information system for compiling data about the costs of the output of a production line.

In the next few pages, we will use a highly simplified example of a production line for the construction of wooden crates, as diagrammed in Exhibit 8-1. Notice that the finished product comes from three sources: *raw* (or direct) *materials, direct labor,* and *overhead.*

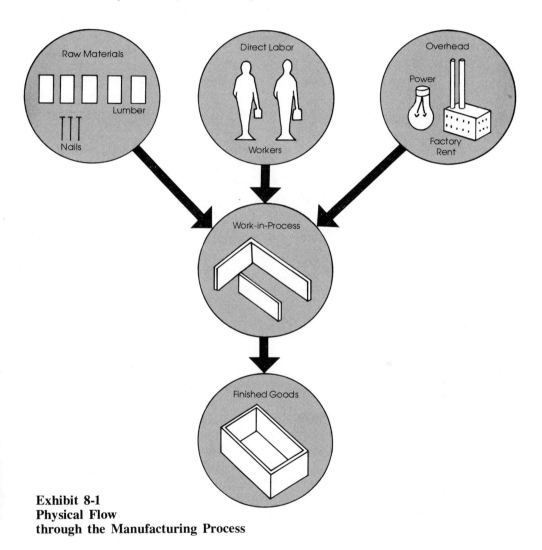

Exhibit 8-1
Physical Flow
through the Manufacturing Process

Raw Materials

Raw, or *direct materials,* are those physical items of input that actually become incorporated into the finished product. The modifier "raw" is somewhat broader than usual because this category includes all the materials used in production, whether in a natural state or changed by previous processing. This meaning is different than the common usage describing *natural resources.* Indeed, nearly all items described in business as "raw" materials are really finished products from some other production line.

Direct Labor

The efforts of employees who work directly on the product are appropriately identified as *direct labor*. Thus, the effort of a worker who fabricates or assembles the product (whether or not he uses a machine) is considered direct labor. On the other hand, the efforts of the foreman who supervises the work and the janitor who cleans up are *indirect labor*.

Other Overhead

There are many other resources and activities on the production line which also contribute to the manufacturing process. The factory building is a warm, dry, bright space where the manufacturing process can be accomplished. Machines are available to operate on the raw materials, and power is available to run these machines. Other employees provide information and other services that are indirectly useful for profitable production. These indirect resources and activities are collectively identified as *overhead*.

THE SHADOW PROCESS

A production cost information system might be described as the *shadow* of the manufacturing process. As the product is altered in production, the system accumulates data about the sacrifices associated with its conversion. These costs are classified under the same three headings just described for the physical process: *raw materials, direct labor,* and *overhead*.

Raw Materials

All identifiable costs of getting raw materials to the factory and available for use are assigned to those materials. These expenditures include the invoice price paid for the materials, freight, and any significant handling charges. Although the total cost could be symbolized by the balance of a single account, detailed records can be maintained in order to have information about the unit cost of each major type of material. As these materials are issued to the production line, their costs are assigned to a *Work-in-Process* account in accordance with data contained on the *issue slip,* which is a cost accounting source document, as well as a management control device. The balance of the Work-in-Process account is the sum of the costs of products that are still incomplete, and the account will receive several different types of debits as these costs are recorded.

Direct Labor

Direct-labor costs include the payroll related expenditures for all employees who work *directly* on the product. The caption appropriately includes the costs of such things as the employer's share of payroll taxes, vacation pay, various insurance premiums, and similar fringe benefits. It is frequently convenient to average these costs and express them on a *per direct-labor-hour* basis. *Timecards* or *timesheets* are maintained by employees and serve as the authorization for charging labor costs to the Work-in-Process account as well as informing supervisors about their workers' efforts.

Manufacturing Overhead

Manufacturing overhead costs include the expenditures for production efforts which do not conveniently fit into the raw materials or direct-labor categories. Included here are the sums paid for indirect labor, such as the foreman and the janitor; factory supplies used in the production process but not incorporated into the final product, (for example, sandpaper for a cabinetmaker); costs of operating machinery, including depreciation, power, and repair costs; occupancy costs, such as building rent or depreciation, property taxes, and fire insurance premiums; and accounting costs.[1] Like materials and labor, these costs also are charged to the Work-in-Process account. However, because it is often difficult to follow their actual contributions to the individual products, overhead costs are generally assigned to production on an average, estimated basis. We will discuss this recordkeeping procedure in more detail later in this chapter. It is sufficient for now to recognize that these overhead costs are production costs and therefore should be charged to the products if the unit cost is to be meaningful as a description of the full cost.[2]

Exhibit 8-2 illustrates this *shadow process* for our simplified example. Notice that as the physical goods move through the various stages of production, the accounting records accumulate information about the *costs* of this production.

SCHEDULE OF COST OF GOODS MANUFACTURED

The costs of production may be summarized on a schedule of cost of goods manufactured. When a firm has no in-process inventories such a schedule might look like Exhibit 8-3. The total on this schedule also appears on the income statement in place of the Purchases account of a nonmanufacturer.

In order to properly control production costs, the manager would normally want more detail than that provided in this simplified schedule. If changes occur in the level of raw materials or work-in-process inventories, this information must also be disclosed. Accordingly, Exhibit 8-4 shows a more typical schedule of cost of goods manufactured.

---

[1] For convenience, some direct efforts are assigned to overhead. For example, a supervisor may spend some time working on the product. Generally, it would not be worth the effort to isolate the direct and indirect portions of his salary.

[2] Many overhead items are fixed in relation to volume; thus, they do not represent *differential* costs for some decision situations. Consequently, some systems delete the fixed portion of overhead in order to provide a more relevant item of information for those decisions.

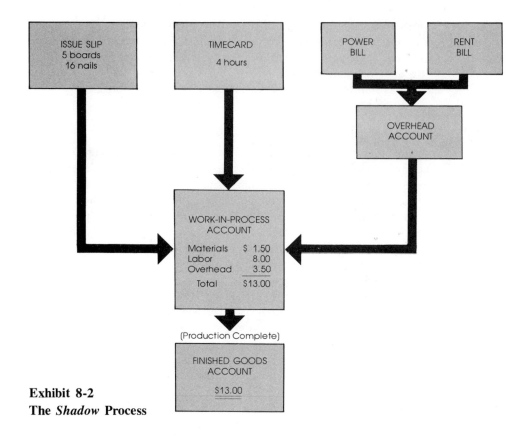

| MATERIALS | DIRECT LABOR | OVERHEAD |

ISSUE SLIP
5 boards
16 nails

TIMECARD
4 hours

POWER BILL

RENT BILL

OVERHEAD ACCOUNT

WORK-IN-PROCESS ACCOUNT

Materials	$ 1.50
Labor	8.00
Overhead	3.50
Total	$13.00

(Production Complete)

FINISHED GOODS ACCOUNT

$13.00

Exhibit 8-2
The *Shadow* Process

COST FLOWS

Before we look at the various forms of cost accounting systems, it will be helpful to show this *shadow process* in a less simplified flowchart. Exhibit 8-5 summarizes the production costs and illustrates how these costs flow through the cost information system. The various steps in the process are numbered and keyed to the transactions that follow. It will be helpful to refer back to this exhibit when we present the journal entries under the cost accounting systems described later in the chapter. The numbers in the flowchart correspond to the following transactions:

1. Purchase of materials
2. Payment of wages to factory employees
3. Payment of various overhead costs
4. Use of materials in the production process
5. Use of labor in the production process
6. Application of factory overhead to production
7. Transfer of completed products from production (work-in-process) to the warehouse (finished goods)
8. Delivery of finished products to customers

Exhibit 8-3

PRODUCT COMPANY
Schedule of Cost of Goods Manufactured
For the Month of June 1980

Raw materials used	$217,000
Direct-labor costs	242,000
Manufacturing overhead	116,000
Total cost of goods manufactured	$575,000

COST ACCOUNTING SYSTEMS

When the primary activity of a firm is the purchase and resale of finished goods, the cost flows through the inventory are relatively uncomplicated. The basic purchasing data can be used for financial accounting and management purposes without substantial modification. In contrast, the flows associated with manufacturing a product are more complex, and the accounting procedures must be more extensive if the information is to be useful. There are numerous questions that cost information can help answer, such as those dealing with income measurement, inventory investment levels, and control of the processes themselves. The system must cope with situations in which perhaps multitudes of material sources and workers' efforts interact, and information about them must be identified, sorted, stored, and summarized. Although it is quite likely that no two cost information systems are exactly alike, two basic approaches are used in practice. The selection between the *job-order* or the *process* system depends mainly on the nature of the production process itself.

Exhibit 8-4

PRODUCT COMPANY
Schedule of Cost of Goods Manufactured
For the Month of July 1980

Raw materials used:		
Beginning raw materials inventory	$ 22,000	
Raw materials purchased	185,000	
Raw materials available	$207,000	
Less: Ending raw materials inventory	16,000	$191,000
Direct-labor costs		211,000
Manufacturing overhead:		
Indirect-labor costs	$ 22,000	
Factory supplies used	17,000	
Factory depreciation costs	25,000	
Factory power costs	19,000	
Other factory costs	28,000	111,000
Total manufacturing costs this period		$513,000
Add: Beginning work-in-process		39,000
Total costs in-process during period		$552,000
Less: Ending work-in-process		47,000
Cost of goods manufactured		$505,000

Exhibit 8-5

Summary of Cost Flows in a Production Process

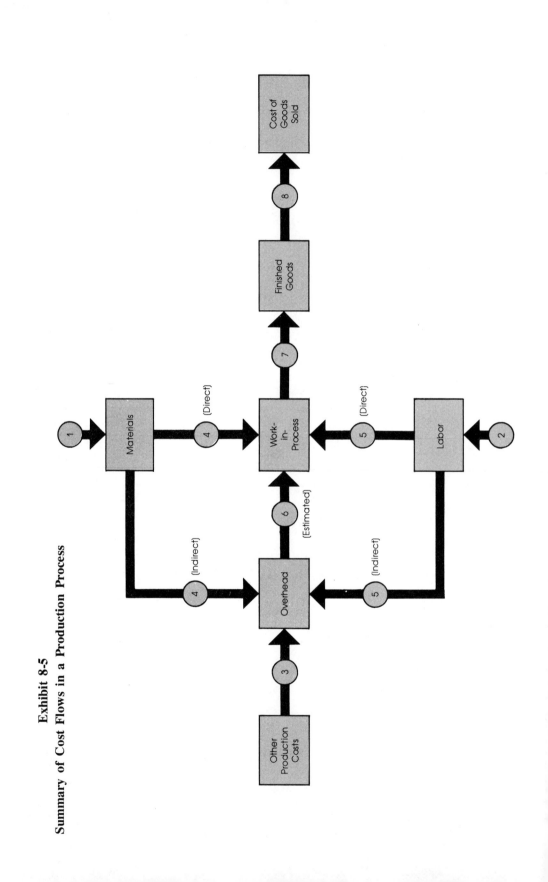

Job-Order Cost Accounting

The basis for a *job-order cost accounting* system is a production line that manufactures unique units of output or sets of unique items, each of which can be called a "job." This approach accounts for each project by accumulating the cost information as materials, labor, and overhead are applied to it. The costs are recorded, or *posted,* on a *job-order cost sheet,* which symbolizes the particular project. Thus at any point during production, this cost sheet shows the amount of costs accumulated in the job. The costs also are recorded in summary form in a Work-in-Process general ledger account for all jobs in-process. This account balance should at all times agree with the sum of the job-order cost sheets pertaining to jobs still in-process. When a project is completed, the balance in the account pertaining to that job is transferred from the Work-in-Process account to the Finished Goods account. These ledger accounts act as perpetual inventory records of the products. The individual job-order cost sheets serve as subsidiary records to these accounts. When the output is sold, the balance in the Finished Goods account is reduced, and the Cost of Goods Sold account balance is increased for the sum of the costs applied to the project.

Job-order costing is used to its best advantage (but not exclusively) where goods are produced to order, that is, where the product differs significantly from job to job. For example, the publisher of this textbook uses a job-order system to accumulate the production costs because no two publication projects require the same outlay of time, effort, and materials. Each is a separate, distinct project, and the cost accounting system is designed to accumulate the costs of production of each one.

STARTING THE PROJECT

As soon as a job is accepted for production, a *job order* or *work order* is prepared. This document describes the task to be performed, engineering specifications to be followed, and other data pertinent to the manufacturing process. It also contains appropriate signatures indicating that the project has been accepted and approved, and that responsibility has been assigned to a production manager. Typically, a section of the job order summarizes the actual costs assigned to the project. The accounting portion of a typical job order is shown in Exhibit 8-6.

ACCOUNTING FOR MATERIALS

In order to prevent improper and uncontrolled use, materials should be issued to the Production Department only on the basis of a properly approved job order. To authorize material issues, it may be desirable to forward a copy of the approved job order to the storekeeper. As an issue is accomplished, a *material-issue slip* is prepared, which indicates the unique *job-order number* and the quantity and costs of the materials. These issue slips serve as the basis for posting the costs of materials to the Accounting

Exhibit 8-6
Sample Job Order

JOB COST RECORD		CUSTOMERS ORDER NO.		JOB NO. 1001				

MATERIAL RECORD / **LABOR RECORD**

REQ. NO.	DESCRIPTION	PRICE	COST	DATE	EMP.	HOURS	RATE	COST
						TOTAL LABOR COST		

OVERHEAD COSTS

				DATE		HOURS	RATE	COST
		TOTAL				TOTAL OVERHEAD COST		
		LESS RETURNED MATERIALS		**COST RECORD**				
		COST OF MATERIALS		TOTAL MATERIAL COST				

OTHER DIRECT COSTS

REQ. NO.	DESCRIPTION	PRICE	COST					
	SUB CONTRACTORS COST			TOTAL LABOR COST				
				TOTAL DIRECT COST				
				TOTAL OH COST				
	SPECIAL EQUIPMENT							
				TOTAL COST				

PROFIT OR LOSS RECORD

				TOTAL SELLING PRICE				
	OTHER			LESS TOTAL COST				
				GROSS PROFIT				
		TOTAL DIRECT COST		LESS _____ % OF SELLING PRICE				
				NET PROFIT (LOSS)				

Department copy of the job order and also to the Work-in-Process account. Occasionally, materials cannot be economically identified with a project. For example, the cost of glue, nails, nuts, bolts, or screws may not be directly charged to a specific job, but might be more expediently classified as *overhead*.

ACCOUNTING FOR LABOR

Under a job-order cost accounting system, it is the usual procedure for workers to record the amount of time they spend on each particular product by using a time clock and punching a separate timecard (time "in" and "out") for each job. Under another arrangement, the worker submits a daily or weekly time report on which he identifies the amount of time he works on each project. These time reports are used by the Accounting Department for posting the direct-labor hours and costs to the individual job orders. All workers have some unassigned time which cannot be feasibly charged to a particular job. This time is recorded and the cost distributed on an average basis to the jobs later as an item of overhead.

ACCOUNTING FOR OVERHEAD

It is relatively simple to determine the quantities of direct labor and materials used in production and to identify them with a particular job. Overhead, on the other hand, is quite a different problem. It involves many cost items, each applied in production in a different manner and at a different rate. To individually account for and identify each cost with a specific job would be an expensive (if not impossible) task. For this reason, overhead is usually assigned to the jobs on an *estimated basis*. Later in the chapter we will discuss how a company selects the overhead basis.

Process Cost Accounting

For some production activities, it is useless or difficult to differentiate the various units of output. For example, can we distinguish among thousands of gallons of paint or rolls of paper towels? Even if we could, what would we gain? In situations where many identical units of output are produced by a uniform production *process,* we do not attempt to identify either specific units or costs of specific units. Instead, we assign the costs (labor, materials, and overhead) to the *process,* using *cost centers*. These costs are allocated among the units of output on an average basis, rather than on a specific basis.[3]

In designing a process cost accounting system, the first step is to identify the cost centers. There is a great deal of flexibility in this matter. A company could have 5 cost centers, each corresponding to a division; or 20 cost

---

[3] Thus, the difference between job-order and process cost accounting is a matter of convenience, not of concept. For example, should we treat an order for 50 chairs as a "job" or a "process"? The answer depends on other factors (like our accounting system) rather than the product itself.

centers, each corresponding to a department; or 100 cost centers, each corresponding to a section. The number of cost centers selected depends on the amount of detail desired and other management needs. Cost centers are normally established along organizational lines to facilitate control. Generally speaking, a greater number of cost centers results in a more expensive system. Management should carefully weigh the expense of creating additional cost centers against the potential benefit from increased detail.

ACCOUNTING FOR MATERIALS

Once cost centers have been created, procedures can be established to accumulate cost information. Each cost center can have one or more authorized persons who will draw needed materials from the storeroom. These issues are recorded, and the material-issue slip is used by the Accounting Department to assign the costs of the materials to the cost center, rather than to a job.

Because the costs of the materials cannot be directly allocated to specific units of output, they are indirectly assigned to them on an *average basis*. For example, if a cost center used $431,000 of materials in the production of 18,170 identical units, we would say the materials cost of each unit is about $23.72. In fact, one unit may have used $50.00 of materials whereas another unit used only $18.00. The process cost accounting system forces us to determine the *average* cost of units produced since we cannot produce the *specific* costs.

ACCOUNTING FOR LABOR

Generally, direct-labor-cost information can be accumulated more easily (but less precisely) under a process than a job-order system. Workers are generally assigned exclusively to a particular department. When the worker is assigned to that department, his payroll records can be coded so that his time and pay are charged to the appropriate cost center. When an employee works in more than one cost center, or is transferred, the Accounting Department should be notified so that his costs can be properly allocated. Costs associated with employees who work directly in production are treated as direct labor. The labor costs of cost centers that do not perform work directly on the products (such as the Janitorial Department) are treated as overhead costs.

ACCOUNTING FOR OVERHEAD

All other factory costs are called overhead and are accounted for in several different ways. Some can be identified with a particular cost center (for example, depreciation of a machine), while others pertain to the factory as a whole (for example, depreciation of the building). The entire efforts of some cost centers, such as the Maintenance or Personnel Departments, are usually treated as overhead. All costs can ultimately be charged to the products manufactured in the factory.

OVERHEAD ALLOCATION

Whether a company uses a job-order or a process cost system, expediency results in assigning overhead to the products on an estimated basis. The allocation can be accomplished by assigning either *actual* or *predetermined* overhead costs. Where actual costs are used, the company must wait until the end of the accounting period for all overhead costs to be recorded. This delay, of course, means that information about the cost of the products cannot be provided until sometime after the end of the accounting period. The untimely manner in which actual overhead costs must be assigned to production represents a serious limitation of this approach.

Overhead costs can be assigned to the products in a more timely manner on a *predetermined* basis. When this procedure is used, the overhead costs for the accounting period are estimated before the period begins. These estimated costs are then assigned to production as the products are manufactured, as if they were the actual costs.

Using an Overhead Allocation Basis

Because we cannot beneficially measure the actual overhead costs used in a particular phase of the production of a product, we select some appropriate means of approximating this use. Overhead costs may be assigned to specific jobs or cost centers (and thus eventually to individual products) according to one or more bases. Some possible examples are:

1. direct-labor hours
2. direct-labor costs
3. direct material costs
4. prime costs (material costs plus direct-labor costs)
5. machine hours

Management should select the approach that it feels produces the most useful allocation result. There is no universally *best* method because each company's circumstances are different. A company that is highly automated may find the machine-hour basis helpful, while a company which utilizes a great deal of direct labor and few machines may prefer the direct-labor-hour basis. Probably the most widely used are the direct-labor-hour and the direct-labor-cost bases.

When *actual* overhead costs are allocated, they are divided by the selected basis to get the actual overhead *rate*. Suppose, for example, that a company uses direct-labor costs as the basis for allocation. If actual overhead costs for the year totaled $1,750,076 and actual direct-labor costs totaled $829,420, the actual overhead rate would be 211 percent of direct-labor costs ($1,750,076/$829,420). The company would assign overhead to each job or process according to the dollar amount of labor charged to it. If Job No. 819 had been charged with $375 of direct labor, it would receive an additional charge of $791.25 for overhead.

If the company chooses to predetermine overhead, the rate is established by estimating the total overhead costs for a specified period, and dividing it by the amount of the base (hours or costs) that is expected to occur during the upcoming period. To illustrate, suppose that a firm allocates overhead on the basis of direct-labor hours, and forecasts overhead costs of $355,500 and direct labor of 150,000 hours for the coming year. The overhead rate of $2.37 *per direct-labor hour* was calculated as:

$$\text{Overhead rate per direct-labor hour} = \frac{\text{Estimated overhead cost}}{\text{Estimated direct-labor hours}}$$

$$= \frac{\$355,500}{150,000 \text{ hours}}$$

$$= \$2.37 \text{ per hour}$$

Thus, for every hour of direct-labor charged to a job or cost center on a time report, it would be assumed that $2.37 of overhead cost also occurred.

Under- or Overabsorbed Overhead

Where predetermined overhead rates are used, the cost accountant is faced with a special problem regarding the Overhead account. The *actual* overhead costs are added to this account as they are incurred. On the other hand, *estimated* overhead costs are subtracted from the Overhead account as they are assigned to Work-in-Process. This procedure may be seen more clearly by referring back to Exhibit 8-5. Transactions 3 (other overhead costs), 4 (indirect material), and 5 (indirect labor) each result in additions to the Overhead account. Transaction 6 reduces the balance of the Overhead account by an *estimated* amount, made on the basis of the *predetermined* overhead rate. Unless we make a perfect prediction, the Manufacturing Overhead account will be left with some balance at the end of the accounting period—either a debit or a credit balance depending on whether our estimate was too low or too high. If the balance is a *debit,* the amount is known as *underabsorbed,* or *underapplied,* overhead. If the balance is a *credit,* it is known as *overabsorbed,* or *overapplied,* overhead.

To briefly illustrate this point, consider these facts about a firm's overhead costs, which were assigned to products on a direct-labor-hour basis:

	Estimated	Actual
Total overhead	$355,500	$372,650
Total direct-labor hours	150,000	145,000
Rate per hour	$2.37	$2.57

Because the overhead *should* have been charged to the products at $2.57 per hour, it was underapplied at the rate of $0.20 per hour. A summary of the activity in the Overhead account would look something like:

Overhead

(Actual)	(Applied)
$372,650	$343,650 (145,000 × $2.37)
Balance $ 29,000	

The $29,000 debit balance is the amount that was underapplied; that is, an inadequate amount was assigned to the products. If the balance in the account had been a *credit,* we would have had *overapplied* overhead; that is, too much would have been assigned to the product.

In theory, this under/overapplied balance should be disposed of by assigning some portion to the products still in-process, some to the finished goods, and some to the goods that were sold, so that each total would include the overhead that would have been recorded in these accounts *if* our prediction had been perfect. If the balance in the Cost of Goods Sold account is substantially larger than the balances in the other two (typically the case), it is expedient to charge the entire under- or overabsorbed amount directly to the Cost of Goods Sold. This "closing" of the Overhead account is normally accomplished only once each year.[4]

Let us look at the difference between these two approaches in more detail. Suppose the following data were available about the products that were worked on during the year:

	Direct-Labor Hours Worked
Finished goods sold	120,000
Finished goods on hand	20,000
Unfinished goods on hand	5,000

Because overhead was underapplied at a rate of $0.20 per direct-labor hour, good theory would tell us to increase the recorded costs of these three categories by $24,000, $4,000, and $1,000, respectively. More expediently, we would simply increase Cost of Goods Sold by $29,000. Overapplied overhead would be treated in a similar manner, by decreasing the cost of goods sold.

Allocation of Shared Overhead Costs

In most factories and firms, there are some factors of overhead that are shared among the various jobs and departments. For two fairly obvious examples, the Building keeps all the departments out of the weather, and the Personnel Department hires employees for all parts of the firm. The cost accountant's task in connection with these shared costs is to assign them to the appropriate cost centers and eventually to the products in order to arrive at a meaningful and useful cost figure for the products.

The flowchart in Exhibit 8-7 represents the overhead cost flows through the departments into the products. Costs that can be uniquely associated with a particular department, such as supervisory salaries, depreciation of equipment, and supplies used, are frequently *separable,* and can be assigned directly to the user departments. The shared, or joint, costs can be distributed among the user departments in accordance with their consumption of the benefits.

---

[4] If interim (monthly or quarterly) financial statements are desired, then the balance in the Overhead account must be carried as a deferred charge (underapplied) or as a deferred credit (overapplied) on the balance sheet.

Exhibit 8-7
Overhead Cost Flows

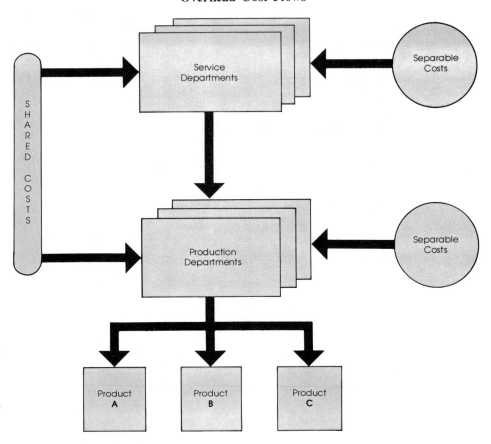

The next step in the process is based on the distinction between the *Service* and *Production Departments*. The former assists the latter in applying their efforts to the products.

BASES FOR ALLOCATING SHARED COSTS

In order to have a meaningful allocation of the costs shared by the departments, the accountant should select a *basis* for identifying the amount of a particular cost item consumed by each department. In mathematical terms, a department's usage is a *function* of the basis. For example, the amount of central-heating and air-conditioning costs incurred by a particular office would be very difficult to measure directly. However, an approximation can be made by using the volume of space occupied by the office in relation to the total volume heated or cooled. Thus, if the sales manager's office occupied 2,250 cubic feet out of a total of 225,000 cubic feet, we could say that he is responsible for 1 percent (2,250/225,000) of the total heating and cooling costs. In fact, his actual consumption will depend on a variety of factors, such as the size of the ducts, the thermostat setting, and the exposure of his office to sunlight. We could exert the effort necessary to have a more accurate allocation, but in general the return on the effort will not be worth it.

Listed are some typical categories of shared costs and allocation bases. If a firm can find a basis, other than one of these, that will do a better job of assigning the shared costs to the user departments, then it should be applied.

Cost Factor	Allocation Basis
1. Electrical power	Square feet occupied
	Engineering studies
2. Building depreciation	Square feet occupied
3. Machinery depreciation	Book value of machines
	(may be separable cost)
4. Repairs and maintenance	Book value of assets
	Square footage (may be
	separable for major repair work)
5. Payroll taxes and	Direct-labor costs
fringe benefits	assigned to department
6. Property taxes	Assessed value of assets in use
	Square feet occupied
7. Custodial	Square feet occupied
8. Fire insurance	Insured value of assets
	Square feet occupied
9. Telephone	Number of extensions (may be
	separable cost for long-
	distance calls)
10. Supervision	Number of employees

Exhibit 8-8 shows the allocation of the separable and shared costs for a given period of time. To simplify the illustration, only two shared cost items are included. In actuality, there could be tens or even hundreds of costs that are shared by more than one cost center.

Notice that the costs can be allocated on a *pro rata* fractional basis, or on a per unit basis. Thus, the Casting Department gets 2/15 of the total telephone cost, or two times the per telephone cost of $180 each.

Referring back to the flowchart in Exhibit 8-7, this schedule is represented by the arrows moving *into* the boxes symbolizing the Production and Service Departments. The next phase in the overhead allocation process is the distribution of the Service Department costs to the Production Departments.

ALLOCATING SERVICE DEPARTMENT COSTS

In effect, Service Department costs are shared among all the departments that consume their services. In our example, the Factory Office assists every other department in carrying out their assigned tasks. Indeed, the Factory Office would even help itself to operate more efficiently, just as the Custodial Department would have a person clean up its own facilities as well as

Exhibit 8-8

Shared Overhead Cost Allocation Schedule

	Total	Factory Office	Materials Handling	Custodial	Casting	Grinding	Finishing
Separable overhead costs	$203,265	$52,310	$56,062	$43,298	$19,560	$14,140	$17,895
Shared overhead costs (see below)							
Factory depreciation	43,200	800	1,800	600	7,520	20,800	11,680
Telephone	2,700	900	360	540	360	360	180
Total Overhead	$249,165	$54,010	$58,222	$44,438	$27,440	$35,300	$29,755

Allocation bases for common costs:
Factory depreciation:

Square feet occupied		108,000	2,000	4,500	1,500	18,800	52,000	29,200
Fraction of total		1,080/1,080	20/1,080	45/1,080	15/1,080	188/1,080	520/1,080	292/1,080

Can also allocate at $0.40 per square foot ($43,200/108,000 square feet)
Telephone:

Extensions used		15	5	2	3	2	2	1
Fraction of total		15/15	5/15	2/15	3/15	2/15	2/15	1/15

Can also allocate at $180 per extension ($2,700/15 extensions)

the other departments. In practice, there are three ways of allocating these shared costs:

1. The Service Department costs are allocated to the Production Departments only.

2. The Service Department costs are allocated to some Service Departments and to the Production Departments (*stepwise* allocation).

3. The Service Department costs are allocated among *all* user departments (*simultaneous* allocation).

Exhibit 8-9 demonstrates the allocation of the three Service Departments costs to the three Production Departments. Notice, for example, that none of the Factory Office costs are assigned to Custodial, and that none of the Custodial costs are assigned to the Factory Office. The allocation bases for assigning the Service Department costs are the same as those used for some of the other shared costs.

Exhibit 8-10 demonstrates the second allocation method, whereby some Service Department costs are assigned to other Service Departments. For example, Factory Office costs are allocated to the other 5 departments, but the Custodial costs (now increased from $44,438 to $53,501 by the allocations) are assigned only to the Production Departments. In effect, we go through a *series of steps,* and a department is "closed" when we have allocated its costs to the others. Even for ordinary firms, there may be as many as 15 or more steps to be followed before all the service costs are assigned to production. The selection of which departments are closed first should be based on an identification of those that provide the greatest amount of reciprocal service.

The third alternative recognizes the full amount of reciprocal service that all the departments provide for each other, and thus can be considered the most accurate. The mechanism for accomplishing this complete allocation of shared costs is a set of simultaneous linear equations. While this approach is conceptually superior to the other two, three reasons limit its usefulness: (1) the difficulty in implementation (a computer and a program are needed), (2) the underlying data about departmental usage are sufficiently limited in

Exhibit 8-9
Interdepartmental Cost Allocation Schedule
(to Production Departments only)

	Total	Factory Office	Materials Handling	Custodial	Casting	Grinding	Finishing
Total overhead	$249,165	$ 54,010	$ 58,222	$ 44,438	$27,440	$35,300	$29,755
Factory office	–0–	(54,010)	–0–	–0–	15,885	22,240	15,885
Materials handling	–0–	–0–	(58,222)	–0–	32,346	16,173	9,703
Maintenance	–0–	–0–	–0–	(44,438)	8,354	23,108	12,976
Production Department overhead	$249,165	$ –0–	$ –0–	$ –0–	$84,025	$96,821	$68,319

Allocation bases for Service Department costs:
Factory office:

	Total	Factory Office	Materials Handling	Custodial	Casting	Grinding	Finishing
Number of employees	106	6	10	5	25	35	25
Fraction of relevant total	85/85	–0–	–0–	–0–	25/85	35/85	25/85

Materials handling:

	Total	Factory Office	Materials Handling	Custodial	Casting	Grinding	Finishing
Cost of materials used	$103,000	$1,000	$2,000	$10,000	$50,000	$25,000	$15,000
Fraction of relevant total	90/90	–0–	–0–	–0–	50/90	25/90	15/90

Custodial:

	Total	Factory Office	Materials Handling	Custodial	Casting	Grinding	Finishing
Square feet occupied	108,000	2,000	4,500	1,500	18,800	52,000	29,200
Fraction of relevant total	1,000/1,000	–0–	–0–	–0–	188/1,000	520/1,000	292/1,000

accuracy to make a more detailed allocation virtually meaningless, and (3) the actually little practical difference in the results. For these same reasons, we have elected to delete any demonstration of this method. (References to current professional literature can be provided by your instructor.)

ALLOCATING PRODUCTION DEPARTMENT COSTS

The final step in the allocation of shared overhead costs is the assignment of the Product Departments' costs to the product. As discussed on pages 201–202, some basis should be selected that corresponds to the occurrence of overhead costs, such as direct-labor costs or machine-hour usage. It should be evident that the whole process of allocating shared costs is not necessary when there is only *one* product, because all the costs would eventually end up in the same place. However, when multiple products are manufactured, some allocation process will probably be useful.

Exhibit 8-10
Interdepartmental Cost Allocation Schedule (Stepwise)

	Total	Factory Office	Materials Handling	Custodial	Casting	Grinding	Finishing
Total overhead	$249,165	$ 54,010	$ 58,222	$ 44,438	$27,440	$35,300	$29,755
Factory office	–0–	(54,010)	5,401	2,701	13,502	18,904	13,502
Materials handling	–0–	–0–	(63,623)	6,362	31,811	15,906	9,544
Maintenance	–0–	–0–	–0–	(53,501)	10,058	27,821	15,622
Production Department overhead	$249,165	–0–	$ –0–	$ –0–	$82,811	$97,931	$68,423

Allocation bases for Service Department costs:
Factory office:

	Total	Factory Office	Materials Handling	Custodial	Casting	Grinding	Finishing
Number of employees	106	6	10	5	25	35	25
Fraction of relevant total	100/100	–0–	10/100	5/100	25/100	35/100	25/100

Materials handling:

	Total	Factory Office	Materials Handling	Custodial	Casting	Grinding	Finishing
Cost of materials	$103,000	$1,000	$2,000	$10,000	$50,000	$25,000	$15,000
Fraction of relevant total	100/100	–0–	–0–	10/100	50/100	25/100	15/100

Custodial:

	Total	Factory Office	Materials Handling	Custodial	Casting	Grinding	Finishing
Square feet occupied	108,000	2,000	4,500	1,500	18,800	52,000	29,200
Fraction of relevant total	1,000/1,000	–0–	–0–	–0–	188/1,000	520/1,000	292/1,000

PREDETERMINED DEPARTMENTAL OVERHEAD

The techniques just illustrated can also be used to estimate future departmental overhead rates. The same procedure is followed except that *estimated* overhead costs are used instead of *actual* overhead costs. Refer to Exhibit 8-10 and assume that the work sheet was prepared prior to the beginning of an upcoming year, based on estimated costs. The final figures in the work sheet would represent the estimated overhead costs of the three Production Departments (Casting $82,811, Grinding $97,931, and Finishing $68,423). A basis would then be selected for assigning these costs to the units of production, and this basis would be used throughout the year.

To demonstrate, suppose that extensive amounts of direct labor are used in the Casting and Finishing Departments but the Grinding Department is relatively automated. Further, suppose that all employees in the Casting Department are paid the same wage rate, but that wages vary from $2.50 to $11.50 per hour in the Finishing Department. Based on these facts, the company chose the following bases for assigning the estimated overhead costs to production during the upcoming year:

Department	Basis
Casting	Direct-labor hours
Grinding	Machine hours
Finishing	Direct-labor costs

To complete the illustration, assume that the company makes these estimates for the next year: 18,250 direct-labor hours in the Casting Department; 112,500 machine hours in the Grinding Department; and direct-labor costs of $235,000 in the Finishing Department. The departmental overhead rates would be:

Casting: $\dfrac{\$82,811}{18,250 \text{ direct-labor hours}}$ = $4.54 per direct-labor hour

Grinding: $\dfrac{\$97,931}{112,500 \text{ machine hours}}$ = $0.87 per machine hour

Finishing: $\dfrac{\$68,423}{\$235,000}$ = 29.1% of direct-labor costs

As products or jobs are processed in the various cost centers, data concerning the direct-labor hours in Casting, machine hours in Grinding, and direct-labor costs in Finishing will be accumulated. Then overhead costs will be assigned according to the predetermined rates.

Nonmanufacturing Applications

The preceding illustration of shared cost allocation deals with the overhead of a manufacturing concern. Many nonmanufacturing enterprises have similar problems for which this type of analysis can be useful. A department store, for example, may wish to make departmental income statements to evaluate the various operations. Because many costs, such as building rent, are jointly incurred by several or all departments, they may be allocated as overhead in a manner similar to that used in systems for manufacturing processes.

JOB-ORDER COST ACCOUNTING ILLUSTRATED

To show a job-order cost accounting system at work, we will describe a simple series of events. Each transaction corresponds to a step on the cost flowchart of Exhibit 8-11 and is numbered accordingly. This system flowchart is conceptually identical to Exhibit 8-5 except that accounts and job-order cost sheets are shown. Refer to the flowchart to more easily follow the accounting process.

1. Raw materials are purchased on account for $20,500.
    Journal entry: Materials   20,500
                            Accounts Payable   20,500
    Job-order card: No entry

2. The factory payroll for the month totals $15,325.
    Journal entry: Labor   15,325
                            Payroll Payable   15,325
    Job-order card: No entry

3. Overhead costs incurred during the month:
    a. Paid factory power bill of $2,300.
    b. Factory insurance expired during the month amounted to $1,450. The insurance had previously been recorded as prepaid.
    c. Rent for the factory building for the month is due but unpaid in the amount of $12,000.
    d. Machinery and equipment depreciation is $5,000 for the month.
    Journal entry: Overhead   20,750
                            Cash   2,300
                            Prepaid Insurance   1,450
                            Rent Payable   12,000
                            Accumulated Depreciation,
                                Machinery and Equipment   5,000
    Job-order card: No entry

4. Materials costing $14,100 were issued from the storerooms as follows: $8,000 to Job No. 501; $6,000 to Job No. 502; and $100 to Overhead (could not be identified with any particular job).
    Journal entry: Work-in-Process   14,000
                       Overhead   100
                            Materials   14,100
    Job-order card: At the end of each day the material-issue slips would be tabulated by job, and an entry showing the issue slip numbers and the costs of the materials used would be entered on each job-order cost sheet.

5. Job timesheets for the month are summarized as: 1,500 hours, $7,500 labor cost to Job No. 501; 1,400 hours, $7,000 labor cost to Job No. 502; 165 hours, $825 labor cost charged (as Overhead) to unassigned time.
    Journal entry: Work-in-Process   14,500
                       Overhead   825
                            Labor   15,325

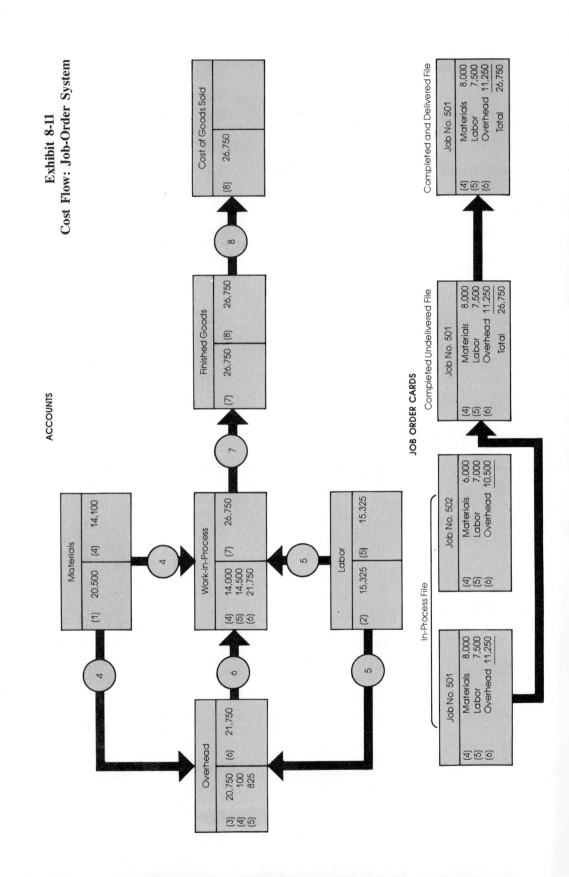

Exhibit 8-11
Cost Flow: Job-Order System

ACCOUNTS

Materials	
(1) 20,500	(4) 14,100

Work-in-Process	
(4) 14,000	(7) 26,750
(5) 14,500	
(6) 21,750	

Labor	
(2) 15,325	(5) 15,325

Overhead	
(3) 20,750	(6) 21,750
(4) 100	
(5) 825	

Finished Goods	
(7) 26,750	(8) 26,750

Cost of Goods Sold	
(8) 26,750	

JOB ORDER CARDS

Completed and Delivered File

Job No. 501	
(4) Materials	8,000
(5) Labor	7,500
(6) Overhead	11,250
Total	26,750

Completed Undelivered File

Job No. 501	
(4) Materials	8,000
(5) Labor	7,500
(6) Overhead	11,250
Total	26,750

In-Process File

Job No. 502	
(4) Materials	6,000
(5) Labor	7,000
(6) Overhead	10,500

Job No. 501	
(4) Materials	8,000
(5) Labor	7,500
(6) Overhead	11,250

Job-order card: The time tickets would be tabulated by job number and posted to the respective job-order cost sheets. The total charge to all job orders should agree with the debit to Work-in-Process.

6. Overhead is assigned to jobs at the estimated rate of 150 percent of direct-labor costs (150% × $14,500 = $21,750).

Journal entry: Work-in-Process 21,750
       Overhead 21,750

Job-order card: As direct-labor costs are posted to the job-order cost sheets in transaction 5 (above), 150 percent of this amount would also be posted as overhead costs.

7. Job No. 501 is completed and transferred to the warehouse.

Journal entry: Finished Goods 26,750
       Work-in-Process 26,750

Job-order card: The job order is removed from the *in-process* file and placed in the *completed* file. The total job cost recorded on the job-order cost card serves as the basis for the above entry.

8. The completed job (Job No. 501) is delivered to the customer, who is billed at the selling price of $55,000.

Journal entry: Accounts Receivable 55,000
       Sales 55,000
      Cost of Goods Sold 26,750
       Finished Goods 26,750

Job-order card: The job order is removed from the *completed* file and placed in the *delivered* file.

PROCESS COST ACCOUNTING ILLUSTRATED

The flow of costs under a process cost system is identical to that for a job-order system. However, a separate record is kept for each *cost center* rather than each job. The costs of materials, labor, and overhead flow through the various cost centers' Work-in-Process accounts to the Finished Goods account. In addition to these three cost elements, the various Work-in-Process accounts are charged with "prior department" costs, equal to the total materials, labor, and overhead accumulated up to that point in production. As the goods move from cost center to cost center, the costs of production are transferred in the accounts. The output of one cost center is effectively a material cost of the next one in the process.

The journal entries to record the acquisition of materials, labor, and overhead are the same with either process or job-order cost accounting. The difference comes as the goods are *used*. At this point, the costs are associated with a particular department or process (cost center), rather than with a particular job. Refer to Exhibit 8-12 and follow the transactions on the flowchart.

1. Raw materials are purchased on account for $20,500.

Journal entry: Materials 20,500
       Accounts Payable 20,500

2. The factory payroll for the month totals $15,325.

Journal entry: Labor 15,325
       Payroll Payable 15,325

Exhibit 8-12
Cost Flows: Process Cost System

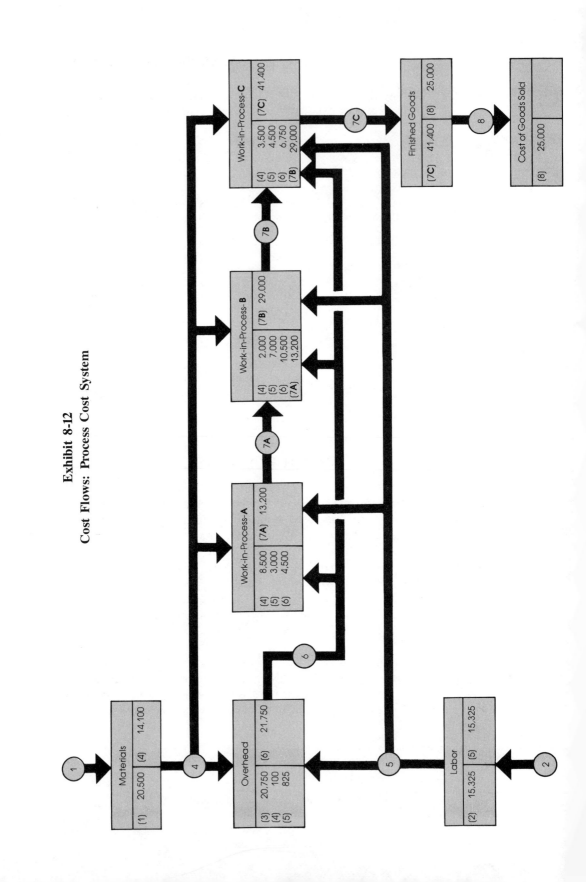

3. Overhead costs incurred during the month are:
    a. Paid factory power bill of $2,300.
    b. Factory insurance expired during the month amounted to $1,450. The insurance had previously been recorded as prepaid.
    c. Rent for the factory building for the month is due but unpaid in the amount of $12,000.
    d. Machinery and equipment depreciation is $5,000 for the month.

Journal entry:	Overhead	20,750	
	Cash		2,300
	Prepaid Insurance		1,450
	Rent Payable		12,000
	Accumulated Depreciation, Machinery and Equipment		5,000

4. The summary of materials used discloses that materials have been issued to production as follows:

Department A	$8,500
Department B	2,000
Department C	3,500
Jointly to all departments	100

Journal entry:	Overhead	100	
	Work-in-Process A	8,500	
	Work-in-Process B	2,000	
	Work-in-Process C	3,500	
	Materials		14,100

5. Employees are assigned to a particular cost center for the entire month, and their time is charged to that center. The labor summary for the month is:

Department A	$3,000
Department B	7,000
Department C	4,500
Unassigned	825

Journal entry:	Overhead	825	
	Work-in-Process A	3,000	
	Work-in-Process B	7,000	
	Work-in-Process C	4,500	
	Labor		15,325

6. Overhead is assigned to production at the rate of 150 percent of direct-labor cost.

Journal entry:	Work-in-Process A	4,500	
	Work-in-Process B	10,500	
	Work-in-Process C	6,750	
	Overhead		21,750

7a. During the month, Department A completed and transferred to Department B goods which had been assigned costs of $13,200.

Journal entry:	Work-in-Process B	13,200	
	Work-in-Process A		13,200

7b. During the month, Department B completed and transferred to Department C goods which had been assigned costs of $29,000.

Journal entry:	Work-in-Process C	29,000	
	Work-in-Process B		29,000

7c. During the month, goods which had been assigned costs of $41,400 were completed and transferred to the Finished Goods Inventory.

Journal entry:	Finished Goods	41,400	
	Work-in-Process C		41,400

8. Goods which cost the company $25,000 to produce were sold for $37,000 on account.

Journal entry:	Accounts Receivable	37,000	
	Sales		37,000
	Cost of Goods Sold	25,000	
	Finished Goods		25,000

EQUIVALENT UNITS

In the preceding illustration of process costing, the amounts transferred from center to center were given. You might wonder how the dollars of cost were allocated between the goods transferred and the goods still in-process. This assignment is accomplished through the concept of the *equivalent unit of production.*

Based on estimates of percentages of completion of the goods-in-process (which probably are imprecise), estimates are made of the *equivalent finished production. Equivalent unit costs* are calculated, and a total cost is assigned to the goods transferred. The technique assigns costs to various units according to their status in the manufacturing process. For example, a unit which is estimated to be 50 percent complete will have only half as much labor cost charged to it as one which is 100 percent complete.

In order to demonstrate a simple case of the application of the equivalent unit concept, suppose that the following facts are known about one particular step in a manufacturing process for a given month:

1. Materials are added to the product when the production process begins.
2. At the beginning of the month, 600 unfinished units of product were on hand. It was estimated that 33.3 percent of the labor and overhead necessary to complete them had been applied.
3. At the end of the month, 1,000 unfinished units of product were on hand. It was estimated that 25 percent of the needed labor and overhead had been added.
4. During the month, 10,000 units were completed and transferred out.

The following cost information was known for the same month:

Cost of goods on hand at the beginning of the month	$ 1,870
Cost of raw materials added	26,000
Cost of direct-labor added	30,150
Overhead costs assigned (130% of direct-labor costs)	39,195
Total costs	$97,215

Our objective is to determine how much of the $97,215 should be allocated to the 1,000 units still on hand and to the 10,000 units that were completed. A flowchart representation of the cost movements is shown in Exhibit 8-13.[5]

Because the goods are at different stages of completion in terms of *materials* and *labor and overhead,* two equivalent unit analyses must be pre-

---

[5] We have assumed a FIFO physical flow of goods. That is, the unfinished goods on hand were all completed and passed on to the next phase. Alternative, but more confusing, assumptions would be LIFO and weighted average. We have also deleted any consideration of lost or damaged units.

Exhibit 8-13
Cost Movement Flowchart

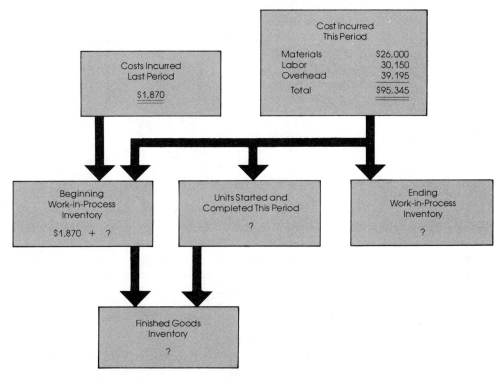

pared.[6] The equivalent unit calculations are shown in Exhibit 8-14. The first schedule tells us that we have used sufficient materials to produce 10,400 completed units. The second schedule tells us that we have used sufficient labor and overhead to produce 10,050 completed units. In other words, if all the work done this period had been applied to the full processing of units which were started *and* completed within the period, it would have produced 10,050 units of product. As it was, we had to use some of our efforts to finish up the 600 partially completed units on hand at the beginning of the period, and to start the 1,000 units still incomplete at the end of the period.

On the basis of these equivalent unit figures, we can calculate the various unit costs:

$$\text{Per unit material cost} = \frac{\$26,000 \text{ (Materials used)}}{10,400 \text{ (Equivalent material units)}} = \$2.50 \text{ per unit}$$

$$\text{Per unit labor cost} = \frac{\$30,150 \text{ (Direct-labor cost)}}{10,050 \text{ (Equivalent labor units)}} = \$3.00 \text{ per unit}$$

$$\text{Per unit overhead cost} = \frac{\$39,195 \text{ (Overhead applied)}}{10,050 \text{ (Equivalent overhead units)}} = \$3.90 \text{ per unit}$$

[6] Even this illustration is oversimplified. In fact, hundreds of equivalent unit schedules may need to be prepared when we consider the possibility that a firm might produce several products which go through a series of processes and which may vary in stages of completion for each product as well as for each process.

The amounts assigned to the completed goods and to the units in-process would be apportioned as follows:

	Amount	Beginning Inventory	Started and Completed*	Ending Inventory*
Beginning balance	$ 1,870	$1,870	$ –0–	$ –0–
Raw material used	26,000	–0–	23,500	2,500
Direct labor	30,150	1,200*	28,200	750
Manufacturing overhead	39,195	1,560*	36,660	975
	$97,215	$4,630	$88,360	$4,225

Cost of goods completed this period $92,990

*Number of equivalent units × unit cost

COMPUTERS AND COST INFORMATION SYSTEMS

It would be impossible to deal with computer applications in cost information systems in an entire book, much less in a few paragraphs. The volume of materials, labor, and other items through even a moderate-size production line is sufficient to cause paperwork headaches for managers and accountants alike. The computer was rapidly accepted as a productive partner in dealing with these problems.

Quite significantly, materials inventory management can be made more effective through automation because more accurate perpetual inventory data

Exhibit 8-14
Analysis of Equivalent Units: Material

	Physical Units	Percent Added This Period*	Equivalent Units
Beginning inventory	600	–0–	–0–
Started and completed**	9,400	100	9,400
Ending inventory	1,000	100	1,000
	11,000		10,400

*Inasmuch as materials are all added at the beginning of the period, no materials were added to the 600 units already in-process, and 100 percent was added for the 10,400 units started this period.

**If 10,000 units were completed and 600 of these were on hand at the beginning of the period, then 9,400 were *started and completed* this period.

Analysis of Equivalent Units: Labor and Overhead

	Physical Units	Percent Added This Period	Equivalent Units
Beginning inventory*	600	66.7	400
Started and completed	9,400	100.0	9,400
Ending inventory	1,000	25.0	250
	11,000		10,050

*The beginning inventory was 33.3 percent complete at the beginning of the current period, which means we added the other 66.7 percent of the labor and overhead during the period.

can be analyzed more quickly. Costly *stock-out* situations can be avoided more easily as potential shortages can be detected earlier. The movement of materials from the storeroom to the production line can be monitored more efficiently, and prepunched material-issue slips reduce the clerical efforts of storekeepers and foremen alike. They also add to the timeliness and accuracy of reports about the cost of goods in-process.

Earlier in the chapter, the employee time report was described and identified as a critical factor in the determination of product cost under a job-order system. Ingenious devices for input can alleviate the need for skilled machinists or other craftsmen to use expensive time and effort completing complicated timesheets. One design places an input terminal at each major work station, where the worker can use prepunched plastic cards or a small keyboard to notify the computer when he starts or finishes working on a particular job. This approach results in very accurate timing of work, as well as providing an efficient way for assigning costs to jobs. Foremen can more productively spend their time on the shop floor rather than the office, and worker productivity and morale increase as burdensome pencil pushing is avoided.

On a higher conceptual level, computerization can result in more useful analysis of cost reports because the information is more accurate and timely. Because bookkeeping tasks can be handled so quickly, many more different reports can be generated than is possible with manual systems. This aspect was neglected for many years, but interest increased as users matured. The underlying concept is the construction of an *integrated data base* in which all relevant facts are stored. Then by proper programming, various reports can be extracted as desired. Because the facts are already on file, the additional cost of an additional report is potentially very low. The flexibility produced by such a system is obviously quite high, and their number is growing as techniques become available.

SUMMARY

Production is the process of taking goods (materials) and converting them into finished products. The cost information system is a *shadow process,* which follows the manufacturing activities to accumulate the costs of production for use in management decisions and financial statements. The three categories of input and costs are: *raw materials, direct labor,* and *overhead.*

There are two approaches to designing cost accounting systems: *job-order* and *process.* The job-order system is useful if the company manufactures a unique product or batches of unique items. When a request for a product is received, a *job order* is prepared. The system is designed to accumulate the three kinds of cost for each of these separate jobs.

When it is difficult or impossible to distinguish among various units of output, it is appropriate to use *process cost accounting.* Under this approach, no attempt can be made to measure the specific costs of a particular unit of output. Instead, the costs are accumulated by *cost centers,* and assigned on an *average basis* to the various products produced in those centers. If several different products are processed in the same department or if units of the same products are in various stages of production, the equivalent units must be calculated. Costs are then assigned to the various products or departments based on the *equivalent* production.

In both job-order and process cost accounting systems, accounting for overhead poses special problems. Unlike direct material and direct-labor costs, which are more easily identified with a particular job or process, the flow of overhead costs is much more complex. For this reason, overhead is assigned to production on an estimated basis.

If *actual* overhead costs are to be assigned to the product, the period must be completed before a unit cost can be obtained. Alternatively, these costs may be estimated prior to the beginning of the year and assigned to products on a *predetermined basis*. The latter practice is followed more often because it furnishes more timely cost data. The disadvantage of this approach is that the costs are only estimates rather than objective data. There are several bases used to apply the overhead costs to the specific jobs or processes, including such measures as: the direct-*labor hours* used, direct-*labor costs* charged, direct *materials* charged, prime costs (material and labor) charged, or machine hours used.

QUESTIONS

1. Define the term *raw materials* as it is used in production cost accounting. Give an example of a raw material in an oil refinery, a steel mill, a television assembly line, a book publisher, a heavy equipment manufacturer.

2. Why has a production cost accounting system been described as a "shadow"? Explain how various production accounts correspond to the manufacturing process.

3. Are factory overhead costs expenses? Discuss the appropriateness of the following account titles: Factory Depreciation Expense, Direct Labor Expense, Materials Used Expense. Suggest better account titles.

4. Name the two major types of cost accounting systems. What types of manufacturing concerns would you expect to use each system?

5. What is the purpose of a job order? What sort of data is accumulated on the Accounting Department copy of the job order?

6. What is a *cost center*? What determines the number of cost centers in a manufacturing enterprise? What is the major limiting factor regarding the number of cost centers?

7. What is predetermined overhead? What are some bases which might be used to allocate the overhead costs to production?

8. If a company applies overhead on the basis of direct-labor hours and estimates overhead costs of $212,000 and direct-labor hours of 50,000, what is the overhead rate?

9. At what point in the flow of production costs are overhead costs recognized as expenses? Do you feel this practice assists in matching revenues and expenses? Why?

10. What is underapplied overhead? How should this amount be shown in financial statements prepared on a monthly basis? What disposition should be made of the amount at year-end?

11. Distinguish between a Service Department and a Production Department. Give several examples of each type of department. What is the ultimate disposition of Service Department overhead costs?

12. How do journal entries differ under the job-order and the process systems? In what way does the accumulation of costs differ under the two methods?

13. What is the equivalent production during the period if the beginning inventory consists of 600 units 33.3 percent complete, 6,000 units started, and 6,100 units completed, and the ending inventory is 50 percent complete?

14. Why is it necessary to calculate equivalent units under a process cost system? Under what circumstances can one prepare a single equivalent unit schedule to cover materials, labor, and overhead costs?

15. Are cost accounting systems peculiar to manufacturing firms or could they also be used by nonmanufacturers? Explain.

16. What types of overhead costs must be allocated? Name several such costs and indicate what you feel would be a fair basis for allocation.

EXERCISES

E8–1 Equivalent units. Pollard Products Company uses a process cost accounting system. At the beginning of January the company had 350 partially completed units in production which the foreman estimated were, on the average, 20 percent complete. During the month an additional 5,400 units were started in production. At the end of January there were 800 units still in-process which were estimated to be 25 percent complete. How many equivalent units did Pollard Products produce during January?

E8–2 Job-order journal entries. Niki Manufacturing Company uses a job-order cost accounting system, and assigns overhead to production at the rate of 150 percent of direct-labor costs. During the month they purchased $12,900 of materials and used $8,200 in production. Direct-labor costs for the month amounted to $11,800 and actual manufacturing overhead costs were $15,000. Job No. 909 for $900 and Job No. 910 for $1,600 were completed during the month. Job No. 909 was delivered to the customer for a total contract price of $1,300. Record general journal entries to summarize the above activities.

E8–3 *Predetermined overhead.* Drago Manufacturing accumulates overhead costs in three different *pools*: materials handling costs, factory service costs, and employee service costs. Separate overhead rates are calculated for each of these overhead pools and the costs allocated to production as follows:

Overhead Pool	Allocation Basis	Cost to be Allocated
Materials handling costs	Direct materials used	$44,000
Factory service costs	Direct-machine hours	98,700
Employee service costs	Direct-labor hours	85,000

During the month a total of $550,000 of direct materials were used; 125,000 direct-labor hours were worked; and the total machine time was 210,000 hours. Department K used $62,000 of direct materials, 15,000 of direct-labor hours, and 22,000 machine hours. Calculate the overhead rates for each of the *overhead pools*. What was the total overhead charge for Department K?

E8–4 *Equivalent units.* Galson Corporation purchased 50,000 gallons of raw materials at a total cost of $77,500. During the month of February, there were 30,000 gallons used in production. At the beginning of February, there were 240 partially completed units of output which were estimated to be 25 percent complete. At the end of February the company had 300 units in-process which were estimated to be one-third complete. The company completed 6,390 units during the month and transferred these to the finished goods inventory. Calculate the equivalent units produced during the month. What was the average cost of materials used in each finished unit?

E8–5 *Cost of goods manufactured.* Berry Fruit Packers, Inc., had beginning inventories of raw materials of $43 and work-in-process of $89. The ending inventory of raw materials was $26 and of work-in-process was $97. During the month of November the company purchased raw materials of $333, paid direct-labor costs of $422, and incurred manufacturing overhead costs of $555. Prepare a schedule of cost of goods manufactured for November. If the company had a beginning finished goods inventory of $177 and an ending finished goods inventory of $111, how much was the cost of goods sold?

E8–6 *Predetermined overhead.* Tatum Corporation predetermines its overhead rate at the beginning of the year based on estimates. The overhead rate being used during the current year is $8.80 per direct-labor hour. During June employees worked 72,500 direct-labor hours at a total cost of $362,500. The actual overhead costs incurred during the month amounted to $639,800. Calculate the amount of under- or overapplied overhead for June. How would this be disposed of at year-end? The actual direct-labor hours during July were

65,000, the actual direct-labor costs were $318,500, and the actual overhead costs were $561,300. Calculate the amount of the under- or overapplied overhead for July. What might have caused this condition (either over- or underapplied overhead)?

E8–7 *Allocation of shared costs.* The Rumplestiltskin Factory is organized into four departments. Two of these are service departments (Maintenance and Lunchroom) and two are production departments (Spinning and Weaving). All four occupy the same building and consequently share certain overhead costs.

These facts are known about the various departments:

	Total	Maintenance	Lunchroom	Spinning	Weaving
Square feet occupied	7,800	800	1,600	2,400	3,000
Ceiling height (ft.)	——	10	10	20	20
Number of employees	46	5	5	15	21
Number of telephones	8	2	2	2	2
Asset valuations (000's)	$80,000	$8,000	$4,000	$28,000	$40,000

During the last accounting period, the following shared costs were incurred:

	Amount	Allocation Base
Building depreciation	$ 23,400	Square footage
Heating and cooling	231,000	Cubic footage
Property insurance	216,800	Asset valuation
Telephone	1,458	Number of telephones
Employee recreation	56,580	Number of employees

Requirements:

a. Determine the amount of each type of shared overhead cost that will be assigned to each of the four departments.

b. Determine the amount of cost allocated to the two production departments from the service departments. Maintenance is allocated according to asset valuation and Lunchroom according to the number of employees.

  1. Allocate the service department costs only to the production departments.

  2. Allocate Maintenance to the other three, and then Lunchroom to Spinning and Weaving.

PROBLEMS

P8–1 *Job-order system.* The Long Horn Company uses a job-order cost system. At the beginning of the month, Order No. 510 was in-process with a total cost of $4,654.

The following costs were incurred during April:

Order No.	Materials Used	Direct Labor
510	$1,620	$4,500
511	2,308	7,084
512	952	1,648
513	1,475	3,070

At the end of April Order No. 513 was still in-process. Manufacturing overhead is applied to production at the rate of 75 percent of direct-labor costs.

Orders No. 511 and No. 512 were sold for $22,400 and $6,805, respectively.

Required:

a. Determine the total cost of each of the four jobs.

b. Prepare the journal entries to record all transactions for the month of April.

P8–2 *Process system journal entries.* The Stanekey Manufacturing Company utilizes a process cost-accounting system. On January 1 the following account balances appeared on the books:

Raw materials inventory	$10,000
Work-in-process A	2,000
Work-in-process B	4,000
Finished goods inventory	12,000

During the month of January the following costs were assigned to production in each department:

	Materials	Direct Labor
Department A	$6,000	$4,000
Department B	8,000	6,000

Overhead is applied at a rate of 150 percent of direct-labor costs. During the month, goods with assigned costs of $14,000 were transferred from Department A to Department B. Goods with assigned costs of $35,000 were completed in Department B and transferred to Finished Goods. Goods with assigned costs of $38,000 were sold on account for $60,000. Raw materials were purchased during the month at a cost of $10,000. Actual overhead costs totaled $14,500 (credit various accounts).

Required:

a. Compute the balances on hand at the end of the month for Process A, Process B, and Finished Goods.

b. Were overhead costs over- or underapplied? By how much?

c. Keying your entries to the flowchart shown in Exhibit 8-5, prepare all necessary journal entries for January pertaining to the production and sale of goods.

P8–3 **Equivalent units.** The Gulf States Manufacturing Company uses process cost accounting. On January 1 Department *B* had a beginning work-in-process inventory of $20,000, consisting of 8,000 units 60 percent complete as to labor and overhead and 40 percent complete as to materials. Production on 75,000 units was begun during the month, with $54,285 of materials added and $136,710 of direct labor and overhead added.

The work-in-process inventory of Department *B* on January 31 consisted of 3,000 units 25 percent complete as to materials, labor, and overhead. No units were lost in production.

Required:

a.   Determine the equivalent units of production for materials.

b.   Determine the equivalent units of production for labor and overhead.

c.   Determine the unit costs for materials, labor, and overhead.

d.   Determine the total dollar amount assignable to the ending inventory and to the goods completed.

P8–4 **Process system.** The Quad Company manufactures one product, *Quads*. The process begins in the Molding Department where all raw materials enter into production. The time required in this department is short and accordingly, the department normally has no goods-in-process at the end of the day. From the Molding Department, the partially completed Quads are transferred to the Assembly Department. All parts are placed in production at the beginning of the assembly process. This process requires more time and therefore partially completed goods are normally in the department at the end of each day. At the beginning of the current accounting period, the Assembly Department had 720 units on hand at a cost of $13,000 which the foreman reported were two-thirds complete. Transactions during the current period were as follows:

1.   Purchased $41,000 of raw materials on account.

2.   Used $33,000 of raw materials in production.

3.   Factory payroll costs for the period ($42,000) were classified as follows: direct-labor molding $12,000, direct-labor assembly $29,000, indirect-factory labor $1,000.

4.   Incurred additional factory overhead costs in the amount of $58,000 (credit various accounts).

5.   Applied overhead costs to production at the rate of 160 percent of direct-labor costs.

6.   Transferred all costs from the Molding Department to the Assembly Department.

7.   Completed 5,200 Quads and transferred them to the warehouse. The above transfer left 550 units which were 40 percent complete, in-process in the Assembly Department.

8. Sold 4,000 Quads on account at a price of $40 each. All Quads sold this period had been completed this period.

Required:

a. Determine the costs transferred out of Assembly and Molding, and the Cost of Goods Sold.

b. Prepare journal entries to record in summary form each of the above transactions.

P8–5 Allocation of shared costs. Data related to the Bigilow Bag Company overhead costs for the first quarter (January–March) of 1978 are summarized as follows:

	Number of Employees	Floor Space	Number of Phones	Direct Materials Used	Direct Overhead Charges
Factory office	15	16,000	15	$ 12,000	$23,250
Maintenance	9	10,000	6	10,000	9,450
Custodial	6	4,000	3	8,000	8,400
Department A	45	30,000	6	60,000	10,400
Department B	50	25,000	8	40,000	8,325
Department C	75	55,000	12	70,000	22,920
	200	140,000	50	$200,000	$82,745

	Allocation Base	Total Amount to be Allocated
Heat	Floor space	$ 18,000
Light and power	Floor space	48,000
Telephone	Number of phones	12,000
Factory depreciation	Floor space	35,000
Supplies	Direct material used	6,800
Property tax	Floor space	4,600
Fire insurance	Floor space	6,000
Other factory costs	Number of employees	16,600
Total		$147,000

Custodial	Direct material used
Maintenance	Floor space
Factory office	Number of employees

The company allocates service departments costs to the production departments in a stepwise fashion in the following order: (1) factory office, (2) maintenance, (3) custodial.

Required:

Prepare a schedule of shared overhead cost allocation. First allocate the above overhead costs to the various departments; then reallocate the service departments costs to the production departments (rounded to the nearest dollar).

P8–6 *Cost of goods manufactured.* Below is the adjusted trial balance of the Cactus Manufacturing Company. Accounts are listed in alphabetical order.

CACTUS MANUFACTURING COMPANY
Adjusted Trial Balance
December 31, 1977

Accounts payable		15,400
Accounts receivable	17,000	
Accumulated depreciation, factory machinery		34,200
Accumulated depreciation, office equipment		1,800
Advertising	5,400	
Cash	19,200	
Common stock		98,000
Depreciation, factory machinery	9,600	
Depreciation, office equipment	700	
Direct labor	95,600	
Factory heat, light, and power	8,400	
Factory insurance expired	500	
Factory machinery	175,800	
Factory supplies (January 1, 1977)	8,900	
Finished goods inventory (January 1, 1977)	33,600	
Freight-in	1,200	
Goods-in-process inventory (January 1, 1977)	18,700	
Indirect labor	18,700	
Machinery repairs	9,300	
Office equipment	6,800	
Office rent	3,300	
Office salaries	10,600	
Officers' salaries	19,700	
Other factory overhead costs	12,000	
Prepaid factory insurance	5,500	
Raw materials inventory (January 1, 1977)	21,200	
Raw materials purchased	81,400	
Retained earnings		47,500
Sales		419,400
Sales returns	2,000	
Sales salaries	31,200	
	616,300	616,300

Physical Inventory on December 31, 1977, disclosed the following goods on hand:

Raw materials	$20,000
Goods-in-process	14,000
Finished goods	35,000
Factory supplies	1,200

Required:
a. Prepare a schedule of cost of goods manufactured.
b. Prepare an income statement.

P8-7 Equivalent units of production. The Work-in-Process account of the Corbo Manufacturing Company showed the following amounts:

Work-in-Process (January 1, 1977)	$ 36,450
Materials used	230,650
Direct labor	165,727
Manufacturing overhead	45,052

At the beginning of the year there were 4,500 units in the Work-in-Process inventory; each unit was two-thirds complete as to labor and overhead. During the year, 35,000 units were started in the manufacturing process. On December 31, 1977, the work-in-process inventory contained 5,400 units; each unit was one-fifth complete as to labor and overhead. All the materials were put into the process at the start of production.

Required:

a. Make a schedule of equivalent units of production for materials and a second schedule for labor and overhead.

b. Make a schedule showing how the above costs should be distributed to the units in the beginning inventory, the goods started and completed during the period, and the goods in the ending inventory.

c. Prepare journal entries to transfer the appropriate costs from Work-in-Process to Finished Goods.

P8-8 Process system. The Early Bird Manufacturing Company makes alarm clocks. The several different models offered for sale are basically all variations of one "standard" and one "deluxe" model, with several different trim features. For many years the firm was operated as a partnership by Mr. Koch and Mr. Riser. Recently, Mr. Featherstone was admitted to the firm as a partner. The three partners decided that it would be advantageous to incorporate the business and thereby avoid some of the risks of partnership. They also felt a need for a good accounting system to provide information regarding their costs. You are hired to set up a cost accounting system for the company and to determine the unit cost of alarm clocks produced during October. After searching the records, you find the following information.

The company completed 20,000 clocks during the month of October, of which 40 percent were deluxe models. Each clock consisted of a molded plastic case and 3 molded knobs manufactured in the Molding Department; the clockworks, manufactured in the Stamping Department; and faces and hands produced in the Assembly Department. The parts were assembled into finished clocks by the Assembly Department and then stored and shipped by the Materials Handling Department. Cleanup, machine servicing, and other miscellaneous services common to all shops and departments were handled by the Custodial Department.

Materials costing $1.70 per clock were used in producing a case for each standard model, and materials costing $1.90 per clock were used in producing a case for each deluxe model. The material used to produce each knob cost $0.06.

The Stamping Department used $2.30 of sheet steel and steel rod, $0.70 of spring steel, $1.50 of phosphorous bronze, and $1.00 of sheet brass on each clock assembly. The Assembly Department added the face, hands, and various screws. Unit costs for materials used in the Assembly Department have not been calculated. However, materials which cost $32,320 were used by the department during the month. During that period, 20,000 clocks were completed, of which 2,000 were in-process (25 percent complete) at the beginning of the period. There were 3,500 units 20 percent complete at the end of the month.

Direct labor in all departments was paid at the rate of $7.80 per hour. It took 0.3 hours to mold a standard case; 0.4 hours to mold a deluxe case; 0.1 hours to mold 3 knobs; 0.3 hours to stamp the gears for each clock; 0.2 hours to make the springs for each clock; 0.5 hours to make the shafts; 0.75 hours to assemble the clockworks; 0.2 hours to install the case and put on the face and hands.

Overhead costs incurred during the month of October were:

Molding	$ 60,000
Stamping	100,000
Assembly	120,000
Materials handling	28,000
Custodial	32,000
	$340,000

The Custodial Department overhead costs are allocated equally to the other 4 departments, after which the materials handling costs are allocated to the Molding, Stamping, and Assembly departments in the ratio 3:2:1.

Overhead costs in the production departments (including that portion allocated from the service departments) are assigned to the clocks on the basis of actual direct-labor hours worked. During October, 8,800 direct-labor hours were worked in the Molding Department, 20,000 hours in the Stamping Department, and 19,000 hours in the Assembly Department.

Required:

a. Calculate the hourly overhead rate for each of the departments.

b. Calculate the equivalent production during the month in the Assembly Department and determine the materials cost per clock in the Assembly Department.

c. Calculate the unit cost of each deluxe clock and each standard clock.

d. Recommend a cost accounting system which you feel would be appropriate for this company.

9

Decision Related Cost Concepts

We have defined costs as the sacrifices made to acquire something. As we noted in the previous chapters, information about these sacrifices is useful for evaluating performance and for making decisions. Suppose, for example, that you are considering buying a duplex as an investment. You estimate that each of the 2 units should rent for $300 per month. Should you make the investment? You probably replied, "I don't know. I don't have enough information." Well, what sort of information would help you decide? Certainly, the most important data would pertain to *costs*. First, how much will the duplex *cost* to buy, and second, how much will it *cost* to maintain and operate? Given the latter information, you would have a much better chance of making the correct decision. Thus, we see that cost data can be very useful in the management decision process.

IMPORTANT COST CONCEPTS

Are all "costs" relevant in the decision process? The answer is *no*! One of the most important (and sometimes most difficult) tasks a manager faces is deciding *which* cost information is useful. In order to help you decide which information is relevant, we will examine some important cost concepts. Managers should be able to identify and distinguish among: differential costs, opportunity costs, imputed costs, sunk costs, out-of-pocket costs, replacement costs, and common costs.

Differential Costs

Probably the most important concept related to the decision-making process is that of *differential* costs. These are the costs which will be *different* under various alternatives—the sacrifices made by choosing one course of action over another. Suppose Bill Long is contemplating a trip to a city which is 80 miles from his home. He owns a car but the transmission is broken and will cost $200.00 to repair. The cost of gasoline to make the trip is estimated to be $5.00. He has considered renting a car at $20.00 per day plus $0.16 per mile (including gasoline). He has given some thought to hitchhiking. But to allow time to get to his destination, if hitchhiking, he will have to leave work at noon and thereby lose $20 in wages. Since he will also miss his lunch hour, under this alternative, he will need to stop at a restaurant and buy a $2.50 lunch. If he does not leave early, he can eat at the company lunchroom for only $1.00. The differential costs of each alternative may be calculated as follows:

1. Drive own car: $200.00 (cost of repair[1]) + $5.00 (gasoline) = $205.00
2. Rent car:
    $20.00 (daily charge) + (160 miles × $0.16 per mile) = $45.60
3. Hitchhike: $20.00 (lost wages) + $1.50 (extra lunch cost) = $21.50

In choosing among alternatives, it is the differential costs that are relevant in making the best choice. This is not to say that differential costs are the only relevant factors, for there often are important nonquantitative considerations. For example, Bill Long would likely consider the weather forecast as he makes his decision. If it is expected to be cold, windy, rainy, or otherwise unpleasant, he may reject hitchhiking even though it results in the lowest quantifiable cost.

Opportunity Costs

When we choose to follow one alternative, we are also choosing *not* to follow many others. By making a choice, we automatically elect to give up all the differential benefits that would have accrued had we chosen some other alternative. These foregone benefits are lost opportunities, and they should be considered as part of the cost of the decision. In our previous illustration, one of Bill Long's options was to hitchhike. If he selects this alternative, he loses the opportunity to earn $20. This $20 represents an opportunity cost.

It is frequently difficult to *quantify* opportunity costs, but it is never prudent to assume them away without *some* estimate of their size. When we have several alternatives, the relevant opportunity costs would be the benefits that would accrue under the next best alternative.

To further illustrate, assume that the Mantle Company decides to buy a new delivery truck with a list price of $4,500. The company's old delivery truck has a book value of $1,000; it may be disposed of by: (1) trading it in

---

[1] If Bill intends to get the car repaired anyway, the $200 repair cost is *not* a differential cost for this alternative. In that event the $200 cost would be incurred whether or not he makes this trip. It is *not* different under the various alternatives. Under this assumption, alternative 1 would have a differential cost of only $5.00.

on the new truck with a $1,200 allowance, (2) selling it in the secondhand market for $900, or (3) using it for a garbage truck, thereby saving the purchase of a $700 used truck for that purpose. If the company elects to trade the truck in, it is foregoing the $900 cash that it would receive under the second alternative and the savings of $700 it would enjoy under the third alternative. The relevant opportunity cost in this instance is the $900, because it represents the benefits foregone by not selecting *the next best alternative*. The $900 should be considered as much a cost of the new truck as the $3,300 cash payment.

Imputed Costs

Many opportunity cost measurements are easily obtained and require no special calculations. In the illustration just given, the figures for opportunity costs were obtained from *bona fide* offers or transactions. In many instances, however, the opportunity costs are not apparent and must be estimated or *imputed*. These costs are hardly ever recorded in the accounting records but should be calculated to assure that the best alternative will be followed. *Interest* is one of the most common opportunity costs requiring imputation. If the company plans to borrow, the actual interest can be calculated as an opportunity cost under the various alternatives. On the other hand, suppose the company does not plan to borrow but plans instead to use internally generated funds. Can it safely ignore the cost of money? Of course not. In this case, the company would need to impute the interest. The interest rate would be estimated by considering the alternate uses to which the money could be put. The concept of the time value of money (discussed in Chapter 14), will make it apparent that interest is an important consideration in deciding whether or not the funds will be borrowed.

Out-of-Pocket Costs

The term *out-of-pocket costs* is sometimes used to designate those costs that require actual cash expenditures. Sometimes these costs are more important than total costs, especially when available funds are extremely limited. In certain instances, management's best course of action may be to select the alternative that will require the least cash outlay instead of the one that will generate the most revenue. In these instances, the out-of-pocket costs are most significant. For example, suppose that an important machine on Delta Manufacturing Company's assembly line breaks down, costing the company $10,000 per day in lost sales. The breakdown has come at a most unfortunate time because the company is in a critical cash-flow position and banks are not willing to loan Delta any additional funds. The cash balance is down to $5,000 and no collections on receivables are expected for about 2 weeks. Management checks several suppliers and finds one who will sell them a new machine for $52,000 cash but will extend no credit. Another supplier will sell them the same machine for $60,000 but will require a down payment of only $3,000 with the balance to be paid in 12 equal monthly installments. In this instance, management would be wise to select the higher cost alternative because the out-of-pocket costs are lower. The additional costs are justifiable because of the revenue that can be earned in the meantime.

Replacement Costs

The replacement cost of an asset is the cost required to purchase an asset comparable to an existing one in the *current market*. Financial accountants use *historical* cost as the basis for recording assets, even though these costs are meaningful in relatively few decisions. The product pricing decision, for example, is one that must consider the replacement costs of assets. To illustrate, suppose that we have on our shelves an item of inventory that cost us $500 but, because of a manufacturer's price increase, would cost us $750 to replace. Which cost (the $500 historical cost or the $750 replacement cost) is relevant in setting the sales price? If we sold the item for $700, but replaced it for $750, we would sustain a loss of at least $50 (although the financial accounting records would reflect a $200 profit). Replacement costs cannot be ignored in the decision-making process.

Sunk Costs

As we have discussed various cost concepts that *are* relevant in decision making, you may have wondered what kinds of costs are *irrelevant*. Well, let's look at *sunk costs*—costs which have already been incurred and which cannot be affected by any possible future action. Sunk costs are simply "spent and gone." To illustrate, suppose that a company has a machine that was acquired 1 year ago at a cost of $10,000. Depreciation to date has only been $1,000; but, because of technological change, the machine has become virtually obsolete. The sunk cost in this instance is $9,000, the unrecovered portion of the original expenditure. This cost is irretrievable and therefore should not affect future decisions.

In choosing among alternative courses of action, sunk costs must be ignored. Management's attitude toward sunk costs may be summarized by the expression, "Don't cry over spilled milk." While the benefit of hindsight often provides reason to question the wisdom of some past decisions, the losses resulting from these faulty choices should not cause a compounding mistake. Management can proceed to select the best course of action by disregarding the sunk costs and considering only pertinent future costs.[2]

Common Costs

The search for cost information is sometimes more difficult when costs are shared by more than one process or product. For example, a department store may receive a truckload of different items to be sold. How should the

[2] A poker player's comment might be: "Don't throw good money after bad." If it is apparent that past investments have gone sour, new investments should be sought, regardless of how much was spent on the old.

shipping costs affect the selling prices? In many production processes, more than one product is produced from a single item of raw materials. A factory building may provide space for several production departments. How can these common costs be allocated among the different processes?

In meeting the needs of financial accounting, various allocation procedures have been developed, as described in the last chapter. We will now look in more detail at the situation where several (*multiple*) products can be made from a single process. The costs that occur *after* the products are separated from each other can be identified as differential and can be used accordingly.

To deal with common costs in the financial statements, financial accountants try to classify the various outputs as either *joint products* or *byproducts* in accordance with these two criteria: (1) Is the product easily marketed? (2) Does it significantly contribute to revenues? If the answer to each question is *yes,* the product is treated as a joint product.[3] If at least one answer is *no,* the product is considered a byproduct. The distinction between joint and byproducts is often difficult to make, and some firms actually see the classification change from year to year. A product may start out as a byproduct and evolve into a main product. A classic example is gasoline, which initially was a byproduct of the refinement of petroleum to obtain kerosene.

ACCOUNTING FOR BYPRODUCTS

Because of the materiality concept, financial accountants do not generally allocate *any* of the common costs to a byproduct, but assign the entire amount to the main products. Two equally acceptable methods are used to report the proceeds from the sale of a byproduct. Under one approach, the total proceeds are disclosed at the bottom of the income statement as *Other income.* Other accountants prefer to treat the net proceeds from the sale as a direct reduction of the Cost of Goods Manufactured, in which case the *income* does not appear as a separate item on the statement. Under the first procedure, the byproduct revenue increases profits in the period the *byproduct* is sold. Under the second, the profits are increased in the period the *main product* is sold.

ACCOUNTING FOR JOINT PRODUCTS

In order to determine the unit cost of the various common products, financial accountants generally agree that joint products should share the joint costs incurred up to the point when the products are separated. A common basis for sharing these costs is the *relative sales value* of the joint products. To illustrate, assume that the Economy Slaughterhouse purchases a 900-pound steer for $600. Production records indicate that the following joint products were produced from the carcass:

[3] The relative sales value is the more important of the two tests. Even if a product just *happens* (is not planned), it is generally treated as a joint product if it makes a significant contribution to revenue.

Product	Percent of Live Weight	Live Weight (Pounds)	Wholesale Price per Pound
Steaks	10	90	$1.90
Roasts	30	270	1.50
Hamburger	40	360	0.80
Waste	20	180	0.00
	100	900	

The $600 joint cost may be allocated to the end products according to their relative sales value as follows:

Product	Revenue Contribution*	Percent of Total Revenue**	Cost Allocation†
Steaks	$171.00	19.8	$118.80
Roasts	405.00	46.9	281.40
Hamburger	288.00	33.3	199.80
Waste	–0–	–0–	–0–
	$864.00	100.0	$600.00

*Percent of live weight × Live weight × Price per pound
**Revenue contribution/Total revenue
†Percent of total revenue × Total cost

The allocated cost per pound is calculated by dividing the cost allocated to each product by the number of pounds produced. Thus, the allocated cost of steak would be $118.80/90 pounds, or $1.32 per pound. None of the cost would be assigned to the waste. If the waste were to be sold, it would be treated as a byproduct and the proceeds reported according to the financial accountant's opinion.

COMMON COST INFORMATION AND DECISION MAKING

We cannot emphasize too much that allocated common costs are *irrelevant* to most decision situations, despite the meticulous manner in which they are computed. They are irrelevant because they are not differential. In producing steaks and roasts, hamburger is also produced. If we alter the mix of these products by grinding more hamburger or cutting less tender roasts, we have changed only the revenue from the steer, not the costs. Thus, the $600 cost is *sunk,* and the only relevant item of information is the amount of revenue that we can earn by selling the meat in various forms. The $600 would be *differential* only if we are deciding whether to spend it on beef, pork, chicken, or prepackaged cold cuts. We should anticipate which strategy will return the greatest amount of income in excess of the $600 and any later processing costs. Once our resources are committed to one of these purchases, we must then select which mix of output will produce the greatest amount of revenue.

APPLYING COST CONCEPTS TO DECISION MAKING

Now that we have analyzed some of the important concepts in the management decision process, let us turn to some cases which utilize these ideas.

Replacing Fixed Assets

From the very moment a fixed asset is acquired, the manager is faced with the question of whether and when it should be replaced by another one that will do a better job. This situation is especially apparent when technology is changing very quickly, but it exists in more stable environments, even where the asset was originally intended to be kept and used for a long period of time.

The manager's goal is to find the strategy that will produce the greatest overall benefit for the firm. He should examine the differential costs and benefits of the alternatives available to him. Unless carefully constructed, the cost analysis can lead to a faulty decision, and managers should be certain that they are not misled by a biased report prepared by a manufacturer.

Consider the case of the Pearson Company, which acquired a gasoline-powered forklift 3 years ago at a cost of $5,300. Because the lift was expected to last 10 years and to be sold at that time for $500, it was being depreciated at $480 per year.

Speedilift Company has brought out a new model electric forklift, which was originally listed at $6,000. The manufacturer's representative has made an offer to accept the older gasoline model as a trade-in from Pearson for $2,200, despite the fact that the old lift can be sold for only $2,000 in cash. A fair estimate of the new machine's salvage value 7 years from now (the end of the old lift's service life) is $2,200. If it is bought and kept its full service life of 10 years, it will be sold then for $1,500. Based on these facts and the original list price, the representative has computed the total amount subject to depreciation as $4,500 ($6,000 less $1,500) and divided it by 10 years, to get $450 per year. The following summary has been prepared to show the cost advantage of the new forklift:

Annual Operating Costs	New Lift	Old Lift
Gasoline	$ –0–	$ 600
Electricity	280	–0–
Maintenance	105	210
Wages	6,000	6,000
Insurance	60	100
Depreciation	450	480
	$6,895	$7,390

Thus, he has found a $495 cost savings each year, which will total $4,950 for the 10 years, and will more than recover the out-of-pocket costs of $3,800 necessary to buy the electric forklift. In examining this report, we can find several facts that have been treated improperly.

First, the actual cost of acquiring the new forklift is only $5,800, which is the sum of the $3,800 out-of-pocket cash payment plus the $2,000 cash equivalent value of the trade-in.

Second, the original cost of the old forklift is not differential in this decision situation. Notice that the original cost is not changed if we keep the old or buy the new. Thus, original cost depreciation on the gasoline forklift is irrelevant to the decision. The cost of keeping the old lift is an *opportunity* cost of lost cash. If we buy the new lift (by trade-in or by cash), we will receive $2,000 cash (or its equivalent) from the disposal of the old. Thus, if we elect to keep the old one, its relevant "cost" is $2,000.

Third, the manufacturer's representative has used incomparable service lives of *ten* years for the electric lift and *seven* for the gas lift. To have a fair comparison, seven years should be used for both, and the appropriate salvage values used.

Finally, there was no consideration given to the fact that the acquisition of the new asset will require an additional cash outflow. With the thought in mind that the cash could be invested elsewhere to earn a return, we should *impute* the cost of *lost interest income* under the two alternatives.

To accomplish imputation, we first estimate the average investment under each strategy, and then apply the usual rate of return earned on cash investments (we have assumed 8 percent per year). To find the average investment, we have elected to take the *arithmetic* average of the book values of the 2 lifts at the beginning and ending of the 7-year life. The computations are:

	Electric	Gasoline
Beginning value	$5,800	$2,000
Ending value	2,200	500
Total	$8,000	$2,500
Average investment (Total/2)	$4,000	$1,250
Imputed interest (8%)	$320 per year	$100 per year

Thus, if we buy the electric forklift, we will lose an average of $320 each year in income that could have been earned elsewhere (actually, we will lose more than that amount in the early years and less in the later years). Because the investment is smaller if we keep the old lift, we will lose only $100 each year (on the average) under that assumption.

With this information, we can now prepare a more proper differential cost analysis, as shown in Exhibit 9-1 on the following page. From this analysis, we can see that the additional cost of $2,100 to acquire the new forklift will result in an annual savings of $245 in operating costs. Because we will have these savings for only 7 years, the additional $2,100 will produce only $1,715 of savings, and we will be better off by $385 if we keep the old lift.

Another way to look at the facts would be to add a *cash value* depreciation to the annual operating costs:

	Buy Electric	Keep Gas	Difference
Annual cash costs (per Exhibit 9-1)	$6,765	$7,010	$(245)
Depreciation	514*	214**	300
	$7,279	$7,224	$ 55

*($3,600/7 years)
**($1,500/7 years)

Exhibit 9-1

	Buy Electric	Keep Gas	Difference
Purchase price:			
Cash paid	$3,800	$ –0–	$3,800
Cash value of old lift	2,000	2,000	–0–
Total	5,800	2,000	3,800
Salvage value (7 years)	(2,200)	(500)	(1,700)
Net cost	$3,600	$1,500	$2,100
Annual cash costs (savings):			
Gasoline	$ –0–	$ 600	$ (600)
Electricity	280	–0–	280
Maintenance	105	210	(105)
Wages	6,000	6,000	–0–
Insurance	60	100	(40)
Interest	320	100	220
Total	$6,765	$7,010	$ (245)

With this approach we arrive at the same conclusion: The electric forklift will end up costing us $385 more than keeping the gas lift ($55 per year × 7 years).

In order to keep the analysis relatively simple, we have made a number of assumptions and ignored various nonquantifiable aspects, such as safety, pollution, and changes in operating costs. The imputed interest approach is a relatively crude approximation and is not widely used. A superior analytical technique involving compound interest fundamentals is described in Chapters 14 and 15. The important points to take from this discussion are the needs to (1) identify all the differential costs, (2) produce estimates of their magnitudes, and (3) ignore nondifferential facts.

Accepting Additional Volume

Manufacturing firms occasionally must decide if a contract calling for additional production should be accepted. Before determining whether the selling price is sufficient, a careful analysis of the relevant factors should be useful. For example, a tire producer may negotiate a contract with a large department-store chain to manufacture tires to be marketed under the department-store brand name. The agreed contract price may be below the price at which the manufacturer sells similar quality tires to its own distributors, or, even below the manufacturer's total average unit cost. Without added information, accepting this new contract would seem foolish. However, careful analysis of the pertinent costs could possibly show that such action would tend to maximize the profits of the firm. In this situation, efforts should be made to determine which aspects of operations will be altered under the proposed contract. The relationship between the differential costs and revenues will be a key factor in the decision. If the differential revenues exceed the differential costs, then the contract should be accepted (regardless of the average unit cost), unless a better offer has been made.

In calculating the differential revenue, it is important to consider the impact of the proposed contract on the company's regular sales. Will the goods purchased under the contract be sold in a foreign market,[4] or will they be sold in direct competition with the manufacturer's regular output? Any decrease in revenue anticipated from regular sales should be subtracted from the contract price in computing differential revenue.

Consideration should also be given to the alternate uses of facilities. If the company has excess capacity and no other immediate prospects for utilizing these facilities, accepting additional volume could prove advantageous. If production is near full capacity, on the other hand, the additional volume could create bottlenecks and inefficiencies that could cause other costs to rise. For example, producing additional output may require overtime with a resulting 50 percent premium pay.

The application of these principles may be seen in a simple illustration: Peacock Electronics manufactures color television sets. Several years ago, Peacock invested substantially in a new plant to keep up with the demand for color sets. Recently, demand has leveled off, creating substantial excess capacity at the Peacock factory. The company's own sets are distributed through factory-authorized dealers, primarily in the Eastern and Midwestern sections of the country.

The Sunshine Department Store would like to introduce its own name-brand color set and offers Peacock $210 per set to produce it. The Sunshine set would be identical to the Peacock model NB-2525, except for minor trim and identification modifications. The Sunshine set would be distributed in numerous department stores located in 5 Western states, and no direct competition is expected. Without the contract, the Peacock plant would operate at only 75 percent of capacity.

Peacock has a modern cost-accounting system, and the controller estimates that the average unit cost of a model NB-2525 during the coming year should be $245 per set. This model is sold to Peacock dealers at a price of $299 per set. Other pertinent cost data are summarized in Exhibit 9-2.

Exhibit 9-2

Model NB-2525

Fixed costs (annual)	$2,100,000
Variable manufacturing costs	$193 per set
Expected production during the coming year	50,000 units
Variable selling costs	$10 per set

Sunshine Model

Additional fixed costs	$50,000
Contract price	$210 per set
Units contracted	8,000 units
Variable manufacturing costs	Same as NB-2525
Variable selling costs	None

[4] The term *foreign market* is used to denote any market in which the company does not currently sell its own product. For example, a manufacturer may be organized to sell his own product in only the Western portion of the United States. A contract with a firm selling only in the Eastern portion of the country, then, would be considered as pertaining to a foreign market.

Exhibit 9-3 summarizes the data (from Exhibit 9-2) to reveal the pertinent facts regarding the proposed contract:

Exhibit 9-3

Differential Revenue

8,000 sets at $210 each	$ 1,680,000

Differential Costs

Fixed cost increase	$ 50,000	
Variable costs (8,000 units × $193)	1,544,000	(1,594,000)
Net Differential Revenue		$ 86,000
Average Differential revenue per set ($86,000/8,000 sets)		$10.75

Although the contract specifies a price considerably below the company's total cost, the proposal could be accepted if other factors reveal that this return would be sufficient for the additional risks. This conclusion is reached because of the relationship between differential costs and revenues.

Make or Buy

Managers of manufacturing firms frequently face so-called *make-or-buy* decisions, especially for products that are assembled from many components. For each component the manufacturer should decide whether it will be in the firm's best interest to produce the component or to purchase it from an outside supplier. These are just a few of the many factors that must be considered in reaching a proper decision: Does the firm have the facilities to produce the part? Does it have the trained personnel and adequate experience with the product? Does it have sufficient volume to attain economies of scale? Can it maintain adequate control of quality if it purchases? What would be its position if the supplier were to suffer a strike? Will purchase make it overly dependent on its suppliers? The answers to some of these questions are hard to quantify; others readily lend themselves to incremental analysis.

A manufacturer of color television sets would encounter many make-or-buy problems. Suppose the management of Peacock Electronics has considered manufacturing picture tubes. At present, the company purchases them for $108 each. Peacock has ample space in the factory to produce its own tubes and sufficient experience such that no major technical problems are anticipated. Manufacturing the tubes will require special equipment that costs $750,000 and should be capable of producing 250,000 tubes; but, it is expected to have no salvage value. The cost of manufacturing 1 tube may be summarized below:

Direct materials	$ 20.00
Direct labor	40.00
Patent royalties	5.00
Depreciation on new equipment*	3.00
Factory overhead	80.00
Total	$148.00

*Notice that this per unit cost will vary as the output volume varies. A volume of only 100,000 units would cause this average cost to increase to $7.50 per unit.

The above figures make the present practice of buying seem very attractive. The unit cost to produce appears to be $148, as opposed to only $108 to buy. Careful analysis, however, might reveal the following pertinent facts: If the new equipment is acquired, the company will have to borrow the necessary funds at 6 percent interest, and variable overhead costs applicable to the tubes are expected to be $30 per tube (the balance of the overhead costs are fixed).

The expected tube-production costs can now be summarized in differential terms as:

Direct materials	$20.00
Direct labor	40.00
Patent royalties	5.00
Depreciation on new equipment	3.00
Variable factory overhead	30.00
Imputed interest*	0.45
Total	$98.45

* At a rate of 50,000 sets per year, the equipment should have about a 5-year life. Investment at the beginning of the first year will be $750,000 and zero at the end of the last year, or an average investment of $375,000. The average annual interest would be $22,500 ($375,000 × 0.06), or $0.45 per unit.

The preceding figures reverse the decision in favor of producing (if all the other factors are negligible), since the incremental unit cost to make is expected to be only $98.45 as opposed to the current purchase price of $108.

The incremental analysis used in the preceding illustration is a *short-run* solution to the problem of idle plant capacity. The solution points out how a company can temporarily utilize space and facilities that would otherwise go unused. It should be noted that in the long run all costs must be covered, and a company cannot indefinitely continue to make decisions based on this type of analysis. The long-run implications of a decision to produce its own tubes should be considered, such as the commitment of factory space for a five-year period.

Dropping a Department

Income statements can be prepared showing results for product lines or departments so that management can evaluate the profitability of the various operations. With this type of analysis, it is possible to find that one or more of the activities shows a loss. Consideration must then be given to whether or not this "unprofitable" operation should be eliminated. In making a decision, consideration should also be given to:

1. The costs and revenues that will be eliminated
2. The interrelationships among various products or departments
3. Nonquantitative factors, such as prestige and service

It is extremely difficult to measure the impact of the sales of one product on those of another. But, frequently, an item is sold at a loss in order to carry a "complete line." A grocery store, for example, may operate an unprofitable produce department because it is believed that customers may cease to patronize the store entirely if they cannot do all their grocery shopping in one stop. Careful consideration should be given to the interrelationships of the revenues of all products before any are eliminated simply because of an apparent lack of profits.

Sometimes companies retain unprofitable departments or products as a device to create *goodwill*. An automobile manufacturer may introduce a high-performance sports car, on which it never expects to break even, strictly to create or maintain a progressive image. Similarly, a shoe store may carry exclusive imports at a loss in order to establish its name. It is hoped, of course, that these products will contribute to long-term profit maximization, but their value in the short run may be difficult to establish. This strategy must be used carefully and wisely in order to avoid not only bankruptcy, but also violating various trade laws.

Perhaps the most important consideration in eliminating a department or product is the effect that such a decision will have on the company's overall profits. Some of the costs which are ordinarily assigned to a particular product or department will continue to be incurred even after that operation has been eliminated. Because these costs are not truly incremental, the elimination of an unprofitable department may even reduce the company's overall profit.

Consider the Waltham Department Store, which started business five years ago. Although operations as a whole have earned a profit in each of these years, the Children's department has yet to show a profit in any single year. A departmental income statement for the most recent fiscal year is shown in Exhibit 9-4.

Upon receiving the statement, management perceived that the Children's department might be dropped. To analyze the situation, the following cost related projections were prepared, showing the amount of savings for each type of cost:

	Savings
Advertising	$ 500
Sales salaries	20,000
Other selling expenses	1,000
Office salaries	1,000
Insurance	200
Other administrative expenses	100
Total	$22,800

The total costs of the Children's department are not eliminated because a portion of them is *fixed* and must be assigned to the other two departments.

Exhibit 9-5 shows the income statement of Waltham Department Store restated on the basis that would have been used if the Children's department had not existed in the preceding year. The combined total reflects the $22,800 cost savings listed, as well as the lost $32,000 gross margin contributed by the Children's department sales. Because the taxable income would have been reduced by $9,200, the income taxes would have decreased by half that amount, or $4,600. In allocating the expenses between the two remaining departments, the revised total was split in accordance with the same ra-

Exhibit 9-4

WALTHAM DEPARTMENT STORE
Departmental Income Statement
For the Year Ended January 31, 1980

	Men's Clothing	Women's Clothing	Children's Clothing	Combined Total
Sales	$251,000	$363,500	$75,000	$689,500
Cost of goods sold	149,200	222,300	43,000	414,500
Gross margin	$101,800	$141,200	$32,000	$275,000
Expenses:				
Selling expenses:				
Advertising	$ 2,000	$ 2,000	$ 1,000	$ 5,000
Delivery	8,000	9,000	8,000	25,000
Rent	18,000	20,000	12,000	50,000
Sales salaries	25,000	30,000	20,000	75,000
Other	5,000	7,000	5,000	17,000
Total selling expenses	$58,000	$68,000	$46,000	$172,000
Administrative expenses:				
Office salaries	$ 9,000	$ 9,000	$ 7,000	$ 25,000
Insurance	900	900	700	2,500
Heat and light	7,500	8,000	4,500	20,000
Other	1,000	1,000	500	2,500
Total administrative expenses	$18,400	$18,900	$12,700	$ 50,000
Total expenses	76,400	86,900	58,700	222,000
Operating profit (loss)	$ 25,400	$ 54,300	$(26,700)	$ 53,000
Income taxes (savings)	12,700	27,150	(13,350)	26,500
Net profit (loss)	$ 12,700	$ 27,150	$(13,350)	$ 26,500

tio seen in Exhibit 9-4. For example, the "Other selling expenses" would have been only $16,000 without the Children's department. This total was distributed in the 7/12 and 5/12 proportion used for this expense for these two departments in Exhibit 9-4 ($7,000 and $5,000). Regardless of how these joint costs are allocated, Waltham is $4,600 ($26,500 — $21,900) better off with the Children's department than if it had been eliminated.

Other Situations

In our discussion, we have shown several situations where total cost from the accounting records may be inappropriate for decision analysis. Differential costs, sunk costs, opportunity costs, out-of-pocket costs, and imputed costs were introduced as concepts that are important in the decision-making process. These concepts can be applied to many other types of decisions, including plant shutdown or abandonment, selling a product as it is or processing it further, or selecting the best method of manufacture. The illustrations were simplifed—each decision involved only two alternatives— in practice, of course, there may be many alternatives.

DIRECT AND FULL COSTING

It may be apparent that the cost accumulation techniques described in Chapter 8 do not necessarily provide measurements of the relevant costs that have

Exhibit 9-5

WALTHAM DEPARTMENT STORE

Departmental Income Statement (Pro Forma)

For the Year Ended January 31, 1980

	Men's Clothing		Women's Clothing	Combined Total
Sales	$251,000		$363,500	$614,500
Cost of goods sold	149,200		222,300	371,500
Gross margin	$101,800		$141,200	$243,000
Expenses:				
Selling expenses:				
Advertising	$ 2,250		$ 2,250	$ 4,500
Delivery	11,765		13,235	25,000
Rent	23,685		26,315	50,000
Salaries	25,000		30,000	55,000
Other	9,333		6,667	16,000
Total selling expenses	$72,033		$78,467	$150,500
Administrative expenses				
Office salaries	12,000		12,000	24,000
Insurance	1,150		1,150	2,300
Heat and light	9,677		10,323	20,000
Other	1,200		1,200	2,400
Total administrative expenses	$24,027		$24,673	$ 48,700
Total expenses		96,060	103,140	199,200
Operating profit		$ 5,740	$ 38,060	$ 43,800
Income taxes		2,870	19,030	21,900
Net profit		$ 2,870	$ 19,030	$ 21,900

been described in this chapter. In a conventional cost accounting system, we are concerned with accumulating and assigning *all* the costs of producing a particular product, and generally make no distinction among fixed, variable, differential, or sunk costs. This assignment is made because the financial accountant is primarily concerned with accumulating costs in a manner which will allow the matching of expenses and revenues according to generally accepted financial accounting principles. This practice is called *full* or *absorption costing,* reflecting the result that the *full* production cost of a period is *absorbed* by the output of that period.

In this chapter, we have shown that the relevance of particular items of information depends on the situation facing the decision maker. Accordingly, information provided by a full costing system is not always relevant for each decision considered by a business manager. In an effort to deal with a commonly encountered decision situation, many firms have developed and used a *direct,* or *variable,* costing approach.

The logic behind the direct costing approach is that there are two separate decisions concerning a firm's productive operations for a period of time: (1) What will the *capacity* of the factory be? (2) To what extent will that capacity be *utilized*?

The costs incurred under implementation of the first decision are basically independent of those incurred under the second. Once a capacity is achieved through investment in equipment and supervisory manpower, those costs are fixed and relatively difficult to change in the short run. However, there is a great deal more flexibility in setting the level at which that capacity is utilized.

242

In analyzing this decision, some managers have seen an advantage in isolating the fixed costs associated with the capacity decision, and in treating them as expenses of the time period in which the capacity was available for use. The remaining costs are all variable, and allow managers to come very close to measuring the differential cost of producing additional units. The variable costs are assigned to the product inventory and appear on the income statement *only* if the product is sold. Otherwise, they are carried forward and disclosed on the balance sheet as unexpired inventory costs.

In short, the difference between *full* and *direct* costing lies strictly in the treatment of the fixed costs of production. Under full costing, the fixed costs are assigned to the inventory (on an average basis), and reported as expenses in the period of *sale*. Under direct costing, the fixed costs are not assigned to the inventory, but are deducted as expenses completely in the period of *production*. To demonstrate this effect, consider the case of the Alexander Watch Company.

From the decision to provide the capability for the production of 200,000 watches per month, the firm incurs fixed costs of $1,500,000 each month through such costs as rent, property taxes, depreciation, and supervision. Each watch produced can be sold for $38, and has variable costs of:

Direct materials	$11
Direct labor	8
Variable overhead	5
	$24

Exhibit 9-6 shows what the operating results under the two cost accounting approaches would be if output and sales volume for July was 150,000 units and for August was 100,000 units.

For the per unit costs, full costing data show that the firm incurred a loss of $1 for every watch produced in August. A logical extension of this

Exhibit 9-6

	Full Costing		Direct Costing	
	July	August	July	August
Per Unit Data:				
Sales revenue	$ 38	$ 38	$ 38	$ 38
Direct materials	(11)	(11)	(11)	(11)
Direct labor	(8)	(8)	(8)	(8)
Variable overhead	(5)	(5)	(5)	(5)
Fixed overhead	(10)	(15)	–0–	–0–
Cost of goods sold	$(34)	$(39)	$(24)	$(24)
Gross margin	$ 4	$ (1)	$ 14	$ 14
Totals:				
Sales Revenue	$5,700,000	$3,800,000	$5,700,000	$3,800,000
Cost of goods sold	(5,100,000)	(3,900,000)	(3,600,000)	(2,400,000)
Gross margin	$ 600,000	$ (100,000)	$2,100,000	$1,400,000
Fixed overhead	–0–	–0–	(1,500,000)	(1,500,000)
Income before operating expenses	$ 600,000	$ (100,000)	$ 600,000	$ (100,000)

observation would have us conclude that it would have been better if no watches had been produced in August. However, if such a strategy had been chosen, Alexander Watch Company would still have had to pay the $1,-500,000 of capacity costs, and would have been in an even greater loss position.

Contrast this analysis with what the direct costing information shows. The *per unit* facts show that the firm is better off by $14 for *each* and *every* watch produced and sold. Thus, we can conclude that the decision to keep operating at the 100,000 unit output level was wise, because the firm is $1,400,000 better off than it would have been if no watches had been produced. The *per unit* cost and gross margin figures under direct costing are *descriptions of the differential cost and revenue to be encountered from the production of one additional unit*. The *per unit* figures under full costing are not as readily usable in dealing with the decision of producing additional units.

As further evidence of the usefulness of direct costing for some purposes, consider two particular watches: one is produced between 11 P.M. and midnight on July 31, and the other between midnight and 1 A.M. on August 1. Under direct costing, each of these identical watches will be assigned $24 of cost. But under full costing, the first watch will be said to cost $34 while the second is assigned a cost of $39. Such irregularity has great potential for hampering the meaningful interpretation of cost data in managing the production line. The information about the fixed costs relates to a separate decision, and can cause confusion and error if it is indiscriminately included.

Our example presumed that there were no changes in inventories, because each item was sold in the same month that it was produced. Of course, it is more likely that some items produced will not be sold until later, and some items that are sold will have been produced earlier. We turn now to a brief comparison of the three different situations concerning sales volume (S) and production volume (P).

PRODUCTION EQUALS SALES

As demonstrated in our example, there is no difference in total income under the two methods when the levels of output and sales are equal, because all of the period's fixed costs end up being deducted as part of the Cost of Goods Sold or as a separate expense.[5] Thus, under the appropriate conditions, when $P = S$,

$$\text{Full costing profits} = \text{Direct costing profits}$$

PRODUCTION LESS THAN SALES

When production does not reach the sales level, then some of the units sold must come from the inventory, and the cost of these items is part of the cost

[5] Our implicit assumptions are that (1) fixed costs in the preceding period are the same as in this one, and (2) production volume in the preceding period is the same as in this one. Under these conditions, the *fixed cost per unit* assigned to the Beginning Inventory is the same as the amount assigned to the Cost of Goods Sold and the Ending Inventory.

of goods sold. Under full costing, the Beginning Inventory cost includes some fixed costs from the previous period, and their deduction from revenue is effectively *postponed* one time period. Consequently, the Cost of Goods Sold under full costing is greater than the sum of the current fixed costs and the Cost of Goods Sold under direct costing, and the Net Income is less.

The first two columns of Exhibit 9-7 contrast the results of these two methods. Under the appropriate conditions, when $P < S$,

Full costing profits < Direct costing profits

PRODUCTION GREATER THAN SALES

When production exceeds the sales level, then some of the units produced are added to the inventory, and the cost of these items is not included in the cost of goods sold. Under full costing, the ending inventory cost includes some of the fixed costs of the current period, and their deduction from revenue is effectively *postponed* one time period. Consequently, the cost of goods sold under full costing is less than the sum of the current fixed costs and the cost of goods sold under direct costing, and the net income is greater. The last two columns of Exhibit 9-7 contrast the results of these two methods. Under the appropriate conditions, when $P > S$,

Full costing profits > Direct costing profits

Exhibit 9-7
Comparison of Full and Direct Costing Effects on Income

	$P < S$		$P > S$	
	Full Costing	**Direct Costing**	**Full Costing**	**Direct Costing**
Sales (units)	150,000	150,000	100,000	100,000
Production (units)	100,000	100,000	150,000	150,000
Sales revenue ($38 per unit)	$ 5,700,000	$ 5,700,000	$ 3,800,000	$ 3,800,000
Cost of goods sold:				
Variable costs ($24 per unit)	$(3,600,000)	$(3,600,000)	$(2,400,000)	$(2,400,000)
Fixed costs	(2,250,000)*	–0–	(1,000,000)**	–0–
Total	$(5,850,000)	$(3,600,000)	$(3,400,000)	$(2,400,000)
Gross margin	(150,000)	2,100,000	400,000	1,400,000
Fixed costs	–0–	(1,500,000)	–0–	(1,500,000)
Net income before operating expenses	$ (150,000)	$ 600,000	$ 400,000	$ (100,000)

    *When the production level is 100,000 units per month, the per unit average fixed cost is $1,500,000/100,000 units, or $15. Thus, with sales of 150,000 units in a particular month, the fixed cost portion of the Cost of Goods Sold is 150,000 units × $15 per unit, or $2,250,000 under full costing.

  **When the production level is 150,000 units per month, the per unit average fixed cost is $1,500,000/150,000 units, or $10. Thus, with sales of 100,000 units in a particular month, the fixed cost portion of the Cost of Goods Sold is 100,000 units × $10 per unit, or $1,000,000 under full costing.

It is important to recognize that a manager does not *have* to choose only one of these two costing methods. In order to comply with generally accepted financial accounting principles, full costing information must be used in assigning costs to inventories and to the Cost of Goods Sold. But if internally useful information about variable costs is desired, a direct costing system can be used. If only to avoid the additional expense, many firms have not used a direct cost system, but have been forced to make a more painstaking analysis of the available information. Others have designed systems that generate both measures. Each method has its merits in its own particular decision environment. The question to be considered is not one of "either-or," but of "when and how."

SUMMARY

Financial accounting information is primarily composed of historical facts. When speaking of *cost,* the financial accountant is concerned with a sacrifice that *was* made. The manager, on the other hand, is normally concerned with past costs only as they may indicate how costs might behave in the future. In decision making, then, the focus should be on the costs that we *expect to incur* under each of the alternatives under consideration. We have previously defined these as differential or incremental costs. Opportunity costs, imputed costs, out-of-pocket costs, replacement costs, and joint costs are only relevant when they are *also differential.* Sunk costs, on the other hand, are *not* relevant because they are *not* differential. They are the same under all alternatives and therefore should not affect the decision.

Because they represent differential facts, *replacement costs* are more relevant to managers than historical costs, which can at best serve only as estimators of future values. To emphasize their strict irrelevancy, historical costs are frequently referred to as *sunk* costs. They have been paid, and will not differ under any choice about future action.

Many costs are common, or *joint,* to several products or alternatives. In regard to any one product or alternative, these costs are not differential and should not be considered in decisions regarding that particular item. These joint products or proposals must be considered as a *package* and the joint costs considered as differential to that package in comparison to others.

In order to gather production cost information that more closely describes differential costs of using existing capacity, direct costing techniques have been developed. Direct costing differs from *full* costing in that the fixed costs of the period are not assigned to the product but are charged in total against the income for the year. Thus, the cost assigned to the product closely approximates the marginal cost of producing it. The technique is not currently accepted as part of financial accounting, but is quite useful in internal reports.

QUESTIONS

1. Are all costs relevant in the management decision process? Explain.

2. Explain why a manager might decide to produce and sell a product below *total cost*. Under what circumstances would this be a wise course of action?

3. Assume an asset that originally cost $15,000, is presently 50 percent depreciated, and could be sold today for $3,000. In deciding whether or not to replace this asset, how much of the cost is relevant? What are the relevant costs called?

4. Define an *imputed cost*. How are these costs treated in the decision-making process?

5. Should depreciation on an existing machine be considered as a relevant cost when deciding whether or not to produce a part to be manufactured on that machine? Explain.

6. What factors should be considered in deciding whether or not to eliminate an unprofitable product or department?

7. Are all variable costs incremental costs? Are all incremental costs variable costs? Explain the relationship of these two types of costs.

8. Explain how *time* is important in deciding which costs are relevant in decision making. Give some examples of costs that are relevant in the *long run* but not in the *short run*.

9. What are differential or incremental costs? How are these costs related to the management decision process?

10. Define opportunity costs. What applications do opportunity costs have to the decision-making process?

11. Are any costs other than those actually recorded on the books ever considered in decision making? Explain.

12. What are *sunk* costs? What attitude should the decision maker have toward sunk costs?

13. What costs are probably most important in decisions regarding the replacement of existing machinery? What nonquantitative factors might also be relevant?

14. What long-run factors should be considered in deciding whether to make or buy a required component for a manufactured product?

15. Will profit be maximized in all cases by eliminating unprofitable departments? Explain.

16. How are joint costs shared between joint products and byproducts? Distinguish between a joint product and a byproduct? Give an example of each.

17. Why do some managers prefer *direct* costing to *full* costing? Which costs are stressed in a direct cost system?

18. Indicate how profits will compare under direct costing and full costing when production equals sales. What about when production is greater than sales? What about when production is less than sales?

EXERCISES

E9–1 *Make or buy.* Scott Key and Lock Company currently manufactures part 4UP at a cost of $1.65. This cost is based on normal production of 50,000 units per year. The variable costs are $0.87 per unit, allocated fixed-factory costs are $30,000 per year and fixed costs associated only with part 4UP are $9,000 per year. The company is considering purchasing part 4UP from a supplier who has quoted a firm price of $1.25 per unit, which price he will guarantee for a 3-year period. In the event the part is purchased, the fixed assets which are used solely for production of 4UP will be sold for $1,000, a $10,000 book loss. Should the company continue to manufacture part 4UP or should it purchase the part from the outside supplier? Support your answer with calculations.

E9–2 *Dropping a department.* F-U-N Sporting Goods Stores presently has 6 departments, 5 of which are normally quite profitable. However, at no time in the company history has the slingshot department shown a profit. Last year the loss was $10,932 and management seriously considered dropping the entire department. The department has, of course, been charged with its share of the company overhead costs. Last year the slingshot department was charged $15,800 in company overhead, $9,600 salesman's salary, $151,000 for cost of goods sold, and $12,000 for the department head's salary. If the department is dropped, the department head will be discharged. The salesman will be transferred to another department where a vacancy has just been created by a resignation. The space freed by this decision will be utilized by the other 5 departments. Should the company drop the slingshot department? What other factors are relevant to the decision?

E9–3 *Changing product mix.* Porter Pot Company manufactures 5 sizes of flower pots with current selling prices and costs of manufacture shown below:

Pot Size	Number Produced	Unit Weight (in ounces)	Unit Selling Price	Unit Variable Cost	Unit Fixed Cost	Unit Profit (Loss)
AA	5,000	48	$3.10	$1.40	$0.40	$1.30
A	10,000	40	2.85	1.35	0.40	1.10
B	20,000	28	2.65	1.22	0.40	1.03
C	6,000	20	2.15	1.01	0.40	0.74
X	9,000	10	1.25	0.95	0.40	(0.10)

For years pot size X has been a loser and management is considering dropping the line. The sales manager objects because he feels pot

X is necessary to "carry a complete line." He expects sales of other pots to decline by 10 percent if X is eliminated. The production manager feels the whole problem is caused by the way the fixed costs are allocated—currently by dividing the total fixed costs ($20,000) by the number of pots produced (50,000 pots). The production manager feels the fixed costs should be allocated according to the weight of the pot. Should pot X be eliminated? Why or why not? Would your answer be different if the fixed costs were allocated according to weight?

E9–4 *Accepting a special order.* Zee Rock Company manufactures office copiers at a cost of $1,322 each and sells them to office supply companies for $1,995. They are currently operating at only 60 percent of the plant's 20,000-copier-per-year capacity. Since fixed costs amount to $6.3 million per year, the company president is concerned about this unused capacity. Kay Mark Company, a large retail chain, is anxious to offer a home copier to their customers. They offer Zee Rock $999 each for 5,000 copiers. These will be identical to the Zee Rock model except for a simple nameplate which can be produced at a cost of $1.10 per copier. Should Zee Rock accept the Kay Mark offer? Explain your answer.

E9–5 *Make or buy.* No Blow Company manufactures snow blowers for cleaning snow from sidewalks and driveways. The blower is currently powered by a Big Stratton 3-horsepower gasoline engine. The engines are purchased directly from the manufacturer at a cost of $45.45 each. No Blow uses 4,000 engines per year and expects demand to remain at this same level for at least 5 years. The production manager at No Blow feels the engine price is too high and believes that the company should manufacture their own engines. He notes the company currently has unused factory space but that special equipment costing $300,000 will need to be purchased. The equipment should last 5 years and is expected to have no salvage value. No Blow will need to pay royalties of $8 per engine produced and expects to incur additional variable costs of $22.22 per engine. Should No Blow manufacture their own engine or continue to buy from Big Stratton? What are some of the nonquantitative considerations?

E9–6 *Full and direct costing.* Moore Company produces monkey wrenches, which are sold for $24 each. Fixed production costs are $300,000 per month, and fixed administrative costs are $210,000 per month. The variable production costs are $5.10 per wrench, and variable selling costs are $2.40 per wrench.

At the beginning of May, there were no completed wrenches in stock. During May, 52,000 wrenches were produced, but only 32,000 were sold. During June, 55,000 were produced. All of them and the beginning inventory were sold in June.

Required:

In four parallel columns, produce income statements for both May and June under:

a.   the full costing approach

b.   the direct costing approach

PROBLEMS

P9–1   Replacing a fixed asset.   The Sentry Production Company owns a 4-year-old machine which cost $12,000. At the time of purchase, it was estimated that the machine would last 15 years and have a salvage value of $1,950.

A new machine has been developed that could reduce some of the operating costs. The new machine would cost $14,800 and is estimated to last 18 years with a salvage value of $2,200. A trade-in allowance of $7,395 would be given for the old machine. Assume an interest rate of 6 percent and that the new machine will have a salvage value equal to book value after 11 years.

	Annual Cost of Operation	
	Old	New
Operator's wages	$4,500	$3,900
Insurance	25	15
Maintenance	340	260
Part replacement	260	210
Depreciation	670	700
	$5,795	$5,085

Required:

Determine whether the new machine should be purchased. Show your analysis.

P9–2   Using differential costs.   The Schaeffer Pin Company is considering three alternative marketing strategies. The following information about the strategies for the upcoming year has been made available to the board of directors:

	1	2	3
Sales	$750,000	$800,000	$900,000
Costs:			
Materials	$100,000	$120,000	$120,000
Direct labor	225,000	280,000	290,000
Overhead:			
Indirect labor	75,000	35,000	50,000
Supervision	25,000	35,000	30,000
Rent	24,000	24,000	24,000
Insurance	5,000	5,000	5,000
Sales salaries	40,000	20,000	10,000
Sales commissions	37,500	80,000	120,000
Advertising	48,000	32,000	60,000
Total costs	$579,500	$631,000	$709,000

Required:

a. Define differential cost, and explain why differential costs are relevant to decision making.

b. In parallel columns, show the differential revenue and cost items for:

> Project 1 versus Project 2
> Project 2 versus Project 3
> Project 3 versus Project 1

c. From the data compiled in *B*, it should be apparent that Project 3 would be preferred to Project 1, and that Project 1 would be preferred to Project 2. Suppose that the additional volume required under Projects 2 and 3 would require Schaeffer to use a space in the rented factory that was being subleased to another company for $30,000 per year. Explain how this fact would change the analysis you prepared in *b* and the preferences described above.

P9-3 Accepting a special order. The Freezo Manufacturing Company makes refrigerators in a plant with a capacity of 100,000 units per year. The Whizo Distributing Company would like to add refrigerators under the tradename *Freezwhiz* to its line. It has offered to pay $270 apiece for 10,000 refrigerators.

Freezo Manufacturing Company sells its refrigerators to its dealers for $350 and has an average cost of $295, as follows:

Fixed overhead allocated	$3,150,000
Variable manufacturing costs	$235 per set
Expected production during the coming year	75,000 units
Variable selling costs	$18 per unit

If it were to produce the Whizo model, the Freezo Manufacturing Company would have additional fixed overhead costs of $180,000. Because of slight changes to the door design, the variable manufacturing costs would be $243 per set. Since Freezo Company would have a contract, there would be no variable selling costs involved.

Freezo Manufacturing Company and Whizo Distributing Company operate in different markets.

Required:

Prepare a schedule to show the profit or loss (total and per unit) that would result from the contract.

P9-4 Make or buy. The Mercury Manufacturing Company is presently purchasing part MM777 from an outside firm for $273.10. A study of plant activity indicates that part MM777 could be manufactured in the plant if a machine costing $630,000 were purchased. The machine could produce 105,000 parts and would likely have little salvage value. Direct materials needed to produce the part would cost $82.65 per unit; 22 hours of direct labor at $3.78 per hour are estimated to complete each part. Overhead is presently charged at a rate of 150 percent of direct labor; the company needs 15,000 parts per year.

Required:

a. Prepare a schedule to show the cost to manufacture the part, based upon the above facts. Should the company continue to purchase part MM777 or should it manufacture the part?

b. After careful analysis it has been determined that variable overhead applicable to the part will be only 110 percent of direct labor (the balance of the overhead is fixed). With this additional information, should Mercury Manufacturing Company continue to purchase the part or start manufacturing it? Show calculations.

P9–5   Allocating shared costs.   The Civet-Blivet Company manufactures blivets and has recently received an interesting offer from another firm to buy all of its production of a byproduct. The first phase of production passes a *Raw Mat* (in its natural state) through a trimming machine, where about 20 pounds of *Bye* are trimmed off. Each Raw Mat costs about $60, and each *Blivet* can be sold (after further processing) for $100.

For many years, the Byes had been dumped (at no additional cost) on vacant land, and quickly biodegraded. However, several years ago, a new product was invented, which uses the unprocessed Byes as a raw material. The maker of this product purchased packaged Byes in 20-pound lots for $1 per pound.

Before entering into this agreement, the bookkeeper of Civet-Blivet carefully computed the cost of each package of Byes in accordance with generally used accounting procedures. The cost of the Raw Mat was allocated between the Blivets and the Byes in accordance with their relative market value as shown below:

	Revenue	Fraction	Cost	Unit Cost
Blivets	$100	5/6	$50	$50 per blivet
Byes	20	1/6	10	$ 0.50 per pound
Total	$120		$60	

The packaging direct-labor per pound of Byes was figured to be $0.20, and overhead was allocated on the basis used for every other stage of production: 120 percent of direct-labor costs. The total cost of each pound of Byes thus equaled:

Material	$0.50
Labor	0.20
Overhead	0.25*
Total	$0.95

*One-fifth of the overhead is variable and the balance an allocation of fixed costs.

Because the $1.00 per pound price brought in a $0.05 per pound profit, which was $0.05 more than dumping it, the offer was accepted.

Recently, a second offer was received from another user of Byes, under which a price of $0.60 per pound would be paid for unpackaged Byes in their raw state. Volume is only sufficient to satisfy one of the offers. A conference was held to determine whether or not to accept this new offer.

The nearly retired bookkeeper said that it would lead to $0.10 profit instead of only $0.05, and all the trouble of hiring a packager and arranging the overhead would be saved.

The junior bookkeeper pointed out (tactfully) that the cost per pound would go *down* because the selling price per pound would decrease. He offered the following schedule, and concluded that the profit would actually be slightly less than $0.28 per pound:

	Revenue	**Fraction**	**Cost**	**Unit Cost**
Blivet	$100	100/112	$53.57	$53.57 per blivet
Bye	12	12/112	6.43	$ 0.3215 per pound
Total	$112		$60.00	

The marketing manager chuckled, and pointed out that the real profit was $0.60 per pound because they used to throw the Byes away.

The controller shook his head, and mumbled, then said rather forcefully, "We must not accept this new offer! We must continue selling the packaged Byes." The chairman of the board accepted this conclusion and rejected the new offer because he had confidence in the controller.

Required:

How and why did he come so assuredly to a decision contrary to the one recommended by the others? Did the chairman make a wise decision when he accepted the controller's recommendation? Support your answer with a schedule showing the costs you think are relevant in this decision.

P9–6 **Make or buy.** The Comfort Corporation, which produces and sells to wholesalers a highly successful line of summer lotions and insect repellents, has decided to diversify to stabilize sales throughout the year. A natural area for the company to consider is the production of winter lotions and creams to prevent dry and chapped skin.

After considerable research, a winter-products line has been developed. However, because of the conservative nature of the company management, Comfort's president has decided to introduce only one of the new products for this coming winter. If the product is a success, further expansion in future years will be initiated.

The product selected, called "Chap-off," is a lip balm that will be sold in a lipstick-type tube. The product will be sold to wholesalers in boxes of 24 tubes for $8.00 per box. Because of available capacity, no additional fixed charges will be incurred to produce the product. However, a $100,000 fixed charge will be absorbed by the product to allocate a fair share of the company's present fixed costs to the new product.

Using the estimated sales and production of 100,000 boxes of Chap-off as the standard volume, the Accounting Department has developed the following costs:

Direct labor	$2.00/box
Direct materials	$3.00/box
Total overhead	$1.50/box
Total	$6.50/box

Comfort has approached a cosmetics manufacturer to discuss the possibility of purchasing the tubes for Chap-off. The purchase price of the empty tubes from the cosmetics manufacturer would be $0.90 per 24 tubes. If the Comfort Corporation accepts the purchase proposal, it is estimated that direct-labor and variable overhead costs would be reduced by 10 percent and direct material costs would be reduced by 20 percent.

Required:

a. Should the Comfort Corporation make or buy the tubes? Show calculations to support your answer.

b. What would be the maximum purchase price acceptable to Comfort for the tubes? Support your answer with an appropriate explanation.

c. Instead of sales of 100,000 boxes, revised estimates show sales volume at 125,000 boxes. At this new volume, additional equipment (at an annual rent of $10,000) must be acquired to manufacture the tubes. However, this incremental cost would be the only additional fixed cost required even if sales increased to 300,000 boxes. (The 300,000 level is the goal for the third year of production.) Under these circumstances should Comfort make or buy the tubes? Show calculations to support your answer.

d. The company has the option of making and buying at the same time. What would your answer to c be if this alternative were considered? Show calculations to support your answer.

e. What nonquantifiable factors should Comfort consider in determining whether they should make or buy the lipstick tubes?

(CMA Adapted)

P9–7 Dropping a department. The income statement for the Jay See Department Store follows:

JAY SEE DEPARTMENT STORE
Income Statement
For the Year Ended June 30, 1978

| | Department | | | |
	A	B	C	Total
Sales	$550,407	$ 151,275	$552,945	$1,254,627
Cost of goods sold	396,430	96,354	418,703	911,487
Gross margin	$153,977	$ 54,921	$134,242	$ 343,140
Expenses:				
Selling expenses:				
Store rent	$ 35,000	15,000	$ 25,000	$ 75,000
Advertising	4,000	3,000	3,000	10,000
Salesmen's salaries	45,000	25,000	30,000	100,000
Delivery	12,000	8,000	23,000	43,000
Total selling expenses	$ 96,000	$ 51,000	$ 81,000	$ 228,000
Administrative expenses:				
Office salaries	$ 10,000	$ 10,000	$ 10,000	$ 30,000
Insurance	842	655	793	2,290
Heat and light	8,450	6,742	7,480	22,672
Telephone	4,000	4,000	4,000	12,000
Other	2,000	1,000	2,000	5,000
Total administrative expenses	$ 25,292	$ 22,397	$ 24,273	$ 71,962
Total expenses	$121,292	$ 73,397	$105,273	$ 299,962
Operating profit (loss)	$ 32,685	$ (18,476)	$ 28,969	$ 43,178

Since this is the fifth consecutive year that Department *B* has shown a net operating loss, the Jay See management has considered eliminating the department. It is estimated that 50 percent of the advertising costs charged to Department *B* could be eliminated, but that the balance represents an allocation of the companywide advertising costs. Likewise, $5,000 of Salesmen's Salaries charged to Department *B* represents that department's share of the company's sales manager's salary. The salesman will be discharged but the sales manager's salary will not be cut if Department *B* is eliminated. Management does not feel that the sales of either of the remaining departments will be adversely affected if Department *B* is eliminated. The controller estimates that the only other potential cost reductions caused by the proposed elimination would be:

Expense	Anticipated Reduction
Delivery	$2,965
Insurance	246
Other administrative	358

Required:

a. Prepare a differential cost analysis of the proposed elimination of Department *B*. Should it be eliminated?

b. Suppose that the elimination would reduce the sales volume of the other departments by 10 percent. Prepare another analysis to describe this altered situation. Assume no changes in the operating expenses would occur except those previously described.

P9–8 *Replacing a fixed asset.*   The Progressive Department Store has expanded during the last few years. Because of this expansion, its present delivery truck is unable to make all of the firm's deliveries.

The present delivery truck cost $6,850 when it was purchased 3 years ago. The store had planned to use it for 6 years, after which it expected the salvage value to be $850. The annual cost to operate the present truck follows:

Gasoline	$1,790
Maintenance	375
Operator's wages	3,780
Insurance	650
Depreciation	1,000
	$7,595

The Hare Delivery Company contracts to deliver for firms. For $6,022 per year the company will make 40 percent of the Progressive Department Store's deliveries. The rest of the deliveries would be made using the store's present delivery truck.

If Progressive wants to stop delivering, Hare will make all of the store's deliveries for $13,325 per year. In this event, the old truck would be sold for its fair market value of $2,480.

Progressive could purchase a new delivery truck large enough to make all of its deliveries. The new truck would have a list price of $12,960 and could be used for 6 years, at the end of which time the expected salvage value would be $1,900. The trade-in value of the old truck would be $2,480. The annual cost to operate the new truck would be:

Gasoline	$ 3,425
Maintenance	565
Operator's wages	3,780
Helper's wages (parttime)	2,300
Insurance	890
Depreciation	1,843
	$12,803

Required:

Which of the three plans should the Progressive Department Store adopt? Use a 6 percent interest rate and show all computations.

P9–9 *Allocating shared costs.* Warner Company manufactures 5 products from a single, common raw material known as "Ego." Last month they purchased and used 6,500 pounds of *Ego* at a cost of $0.52 per pound. Additional data relating to costs and production for the month are:

Product	Pounds Produced	Direct Costs of Production	Unit Selling Price
Abba	1,000	$500	$4.80
Dabba	1,600	900	3.70
Do	1,800	700	4.10
Zip	900	200	2.95
Bam	800	100	0.50

The production process is such that some of all 5 products must be manufactured but the foreman can control the proportions of the first 4 within the limits of ±20 percent of the above production. Because of its low selling price the production of "Bam" is always kept at the minimum possible within the constraints of the production process.

Required:

a. Assume that the company treats Bam as a joint product, and calculate the allocated cost per pound of each of the finished products.

b. Assume that the company treats Bam as a byproduct, and calculate the allocated cost per pound of each of the finished products.

c. If Bam has no established selling price, what is the minimum price you would accept from a customer offering to buy your entire production of Bam?

d. Explain why the minimum price calculated in c differs from the allocated unit cost of Bam calculated in a.

e. What would you do if the selling price of Bam fell below the figure you calculated in c?

P9–10 *Direct and full costing.* Production and cost data pertaining to Microw Company for the first quarter of the current fiscal year are shown below:

	June	July	August
Units sold	9,000	11,000	12,000
Units produced	10,000	12,000	14,000
Fixed production costs	$100,000	$100,000	$100,000
Fixed administrative costs	$ 80,000	$ 80,000	$ 80,000

Each Microw sells for $85. Variable production costs per unit are $15 for direct materials, $24 for direct labor, and $18 for variable overhead. The company pays 10 percent sales commissions on each unit sold. The company had 2,000 Microws on hand at the beginning of June which cost $65 each on a full cost basis, or $57 each on a direct cost basis (assume FIFO flow).

Required:

a. Prepare an income statement for Microw for each of the 3 months under the full costing method.

b. Prepare an income statement for each of the 3 months under the direct costing method.

c. Explain why profits may be different under the two (full and direct) costing methods.

Section 3

Planning for the Short Run

Few management activities promise to return as great a reward for the effort as does *planning* for the future. In this section, we look at those aspects of the firm and its environment that affect the manager's ability to plan and control the firm's activities over the relatively near future. A variety of conceptual and procedural matters are considered.

Chapter 10 establishes a foundation by identifying and defining internal and social responsibilities, and includes a discussion of internal controls that assist management in meeting those responsibilities. Chapters 11 and 12 deal more specifically with the planning process and the preparation of the budget, covering the steps from goal establishment to cash budgeting. Chapter 13 shows how budgeted and actual results can be compared and analyzed to help management improve the profit performance of the firm.

10

Responsibility and Control

In order to efficiently manage an enterprise, controls must be established and responsibilities defined and fixed. In this chapter we will discuss the nature and extent of the responsibilities of managers and accountants. We will also discuss some of the *principles* of control that should be adopted within a business enterprise.

Let us first turn to a brief definition of what is meant by *responsibility.* There are several ways this term may be used and it is relatively unimportant for us to draw fine distinctions among these usages.[1] In general, *responsibility* is a characteristic imposed upon a person from a higher level. If the person can meet the responsibility, he is *trustworthy,* and if he cannot, he is *irresponsible.* Responsibility involves a freedom of choice among alternative courses of action which might lead to the accomplishment of a goal. In turn, it must be accompanied by the *ability,* or the *authority,* to implement the selected strategy. Finally, the person who receives responsibility must be *accountable* for his actions. If this condition does not exist, there may be little incentive for him to perform responsibly. In business organizations, there are two primary types of responsibility: *administrative* and *social.*

Administrative responsibility exists among supervisors and subordinates, with the purpose of accomplishing the goals of the firm as efficiently and effectively as possible. An *organization chart* is a graphic representation of administrative responsibilities; Exhibit 10-1 presents one of these so-called *wiring diagrams.*

Social responsibility involves external influences, and is more complex. Social responsibility is imposed upon every "member" of society, whether individuals or institutions. Meeting these responsibilities may simply involve

[1] For example, we hear about such diverse things as responsible *positions, persons, actions,* or *decisions.*

Exhibit 10-1
An Organization Chart

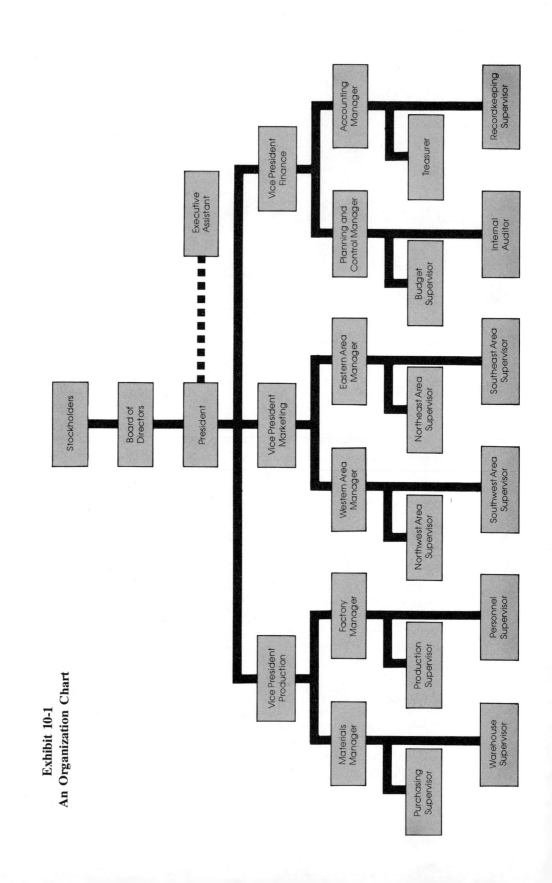

complying with laws created by the society. In the economic world, there are other matters that firms must deal with, which we might call *unwritten laws*.[2] Thus, many firms are concerned with the general welfare of their customers and employees, as well as their stockholders.

Let us look more closely at these responsibilities and examine their effects upon managers and management accountants.

ADMINISTRATIVE RESPONSIBILITY

As we stated, the purpose of establishing and enforcing administrative responsibility is to promote *efficiency* and *effectiveness* in management. To define these terms rather simply, efficiency is the ratio of output results to input efforts (the greater the efficiency is, the greater the ratio will be), whereas effectiveness is the adequacy of the output results. Thus, a manager could be efficient without being effective, or he could be effective and still be inefficient. While this difference may seem to be one of semantics, it is really quite significant in terms of creating an administrative responsibility system.

We also mentioned that responsibility must be accompanied by the authority to take action. One of the long-standing principles of management is that authority can be delegated to subordinates, whereas responsibility cannot. In the firm symbolized by Exhibit 10-1, the materials manager can authorize the purchasing supervisor to enter into purchase contracts. If the supervisor performs badly, he is accountable to the manager for his actions. However, the manager is responsible for the actions of his subordinates and is accountable to the vice president of production. If responsibility could be delegated, the supervisor would report directly to the vice president. Without stretching the imagination, we could see the poor supervisor finally trying to justify his actions to the stockholders. Clearly, this situation would be unworkable. Responsibility may be created at any level (such as from manager to supervisor), but it cannot replace existing responsibilities to higher levels.

To be effective, a management official should understand his position in the existing organizational structure. He must know what he is responsible for, and to whom he is accountable. He must know whom he has authorized to carry out certain tasks, and he must supervise their activities.

As we established in an earlier chapter, the function of the management accountant is to provide information to managers. Thus in the administrative context, the accountant should design an information system that will assist in evaluating performance and in meeting responsibilities. Indeed, many firms utilize *responsibility accounting systems* in addition to other accounting systems for other purposes.

Of course, the accountant must have a complete knowledge of the firm's organization and the relationships among the various levels of responsibility. He must determine the information needed at the various levels so that he can produce the desired reports. Most significantly, he must identify the

---

[2] Much of the social legislation of the late 1960s and 1970s converted unwritten laws to written ones.

factors at each level which are *controllable* by the person whose performance is to be evaluated. That is, if the manager does not have authority over
a particular factor, the adequacy of his performance should not be measured
by that factor. It would therefore be improper to evaluate the manager of a
production line on the basis of sales revenues because they are not subject to
his control. Nor would it be appropriate to chastise him if the total cost of
the raw materials used was greater than anticipated. While his crew may
have wasted some of the materials, it is also possible that the Purchasing
Department paid a higher price than was planned. In this situation, the
accountant must seek to measure which portion of the cost was controllable
by each of the managers. (A more complete discussion of this aspect of
management accounting appears in Chapter 13.)

The accountant's job is only partly finished when he designs the system
because it is his responsibility to implement, operate, and monitor what he
has designed. Thus, he must work closely with the managers at all levels to
assure himself that they understand the reports and that the reports produce
the appropriate input data. If the system does not work as planned, the
accountant must alter his design to accommodate the unexpected events.
This task is extremely difficult when a new accountant inherits an existing
system. In any case, efforts should be made to assure that all reports are
necessary and usable.

We must emphasize that a responsibility accounting system will be useful
if (and *only* if) the management of the firm is committed to it. Without this
commitment, reports will be ignored and inferior decisions will be made.
The accountant must demonstrate to the managers that the system does
produce good information. To establish a working system and to promote
commitment, the accountant should involve the managers in the design and
implementation efforts. This involvement should occur before, not after, the
system is established. In particular, the accountant and the managers must
work together to specify what items of information will be useful. The
accountant's task is to get as many of those items into the reports as he can
without spending too much money.

Furthermore, the accountant cannot assume that the system is perfect, and
he should seek suggestions from managers for modifications. Similarly, he
should suggest modifications in the firm's procedures where he has spotted
inefficiencies.[3] He should avoid "change for the sake of change," and he
should not request unsettling modifications in routine in order to simplify his
own work. Unfortunately, the tendency for each person to believe that *his*
job is the most important often creates friction among accountants and managers.

To briefly summarize, innumerable firms have found it useful to establish
administrative responsibilities in order to bring about efficient and effective
management. An important part of the responsibility system is the granting
of authority to the subordinate and the rendering of reports on success to the
superior. The accountant produces information that will help the subordinate

---

[3] Indeed, every employee of a firm has this responsibility.

describe his actions to his superior. The items described in *responsibility-accounting system* reports are the factors subject to the control of the subordinate. The accountant must construct the system carefully to see that it helps the firm achieve its overall goals. Thus, the information reported must be carefully compiled, complete, and as free from distortion as feasible. An accounting system that does not meet these criteria will be less than useful, and possibly even detrimental.

INTERNAL CONTROL

To assign and follow up on administrative responsibility, there must be a formal system of control. Otherwise, when something goes wrong, there may be no effective way to correct it; likewise, when something is done right we have no way of knowing whom to reward.

Controls may be classified into two major groups. *Production controls* are used to assure that products and services are being provided efficiently and effectively. Many of those procedures depend on information about costs, which we will discuss in Chapter 13. *Internal controls,* on the other hand, are used to assure that administrative policies are carried out properly and expeditiously. Let us look at some of the fundamentals of internal control and their effects upon managers.

In the context of financial accounting, a committee of the AICPA has defined internal control as:

> . . . the coordinate methods and measures adopted within a business to safeguard its assets, check the accuracy and reliability of its accounting data, promote operational efficiency, and encourage adherence to prescribed policies.[4]

ADHERENCE TO POLICY

From this definition then, the general objective of a system of internal control is to assure that the decisions (policies) of managers are properly implemented. In effect, the manager *indirectly* supervises his subordinates through the system, and is freed for nonroutine consultations, analyses, and decisions. The system assists managers at all levels in assuring that prescribed management policies are carried out.

EFFICIENCY

The internal control system should be constructed so that it imposes a minimum of administrative duties upon nonadministrative personnel. Furthermore, the controls should act to increase the amount of output obtained from the input efforts. In plainer language, the system should be free of unnecessary *red tape*.

---

[4] Committee on Auditing Procedure, *No. 1: Statement on Auditing Standards* (New York: AICPA, 1973), p. 15.

ACCURACY AND RELIABILITY

Accountants of every type are always concerned with gathering and reporting accurate and reliable information to assure that the best decisions can be made. An internal control system has the important objective of seeing that *good* information is relayed to the accountant. If no controls were exerted, the information could possibly contain inconsistencies and even simple errors in arithmetic. The controls should be aimed at eliminating errors and detecting the ones that are not eliminated. The significance of this function of internal controls is often understated.

SAFEGUARDING ASSETS

Because of the glamour and excitement associated with large frauds and thefts, the lay person tends to believe that the main purpose of internal controls is the prevention of these criminal acts. The need to safeguard assets cannot be ignored, but if employees are treated well and reasonably screened, it is highly unlikely that they will attempt to rip off the firm. Ironically, if an employee senses that he is not trusted, he may be more likely to plot against the firm than if he is left relatively uncontrolled. It is important to eliminate these feelings of repressions in order to avoid inspiring fraud.

Similarly, the manager should take reasonable steps to avoid leading an employee to commit a fraud. Sloppy cash-handling procedures may prove to be an irresistible temptation to a clerk or bookkeeper. If a fraud did occur in these circumstances, the manager would have to share the blame for not only the monetary loss but also the damage to the embezzler's personality and reputation. Of course, the best approach is the middle road of *sufficient trust* with *adequate control*. The specific solution will vary from situation to situation.

Assets should be safeguarded against not only theft but also misuse. While there may be no serious problems caused by an employee borrowing an office machine or a hand tool for temporary personal use, the picture may be altogether different if he borrows a company truck. Similarly, controls should be designed to prevent the misapplication of materials and supplies. For example, screwdrivers or wrenches should not be used to stir paint, and specially ordered stainless-steel wire should not be used to bale waste materials for easy disposal.

ECONOMY

Throughout the preceding paragraphs, we have implied that controls are necessary; but they cannot be achieved without costs. The task of the manager and the management accountant is to seek the greatest excess of benefits over costs. While safeguarding assets is important, we do not want to construct an expensive set of procedures that will reduce the efficiency of our production crews by wasting their time and even hurting their morale.

The system will involve taking risks, which should be evaluated carefully and objectively. It may be decided that certain losses can be accepted (such as office supplies taken for personal use) as a part of the expense of having employees. Of course, efforts should be made to prevent or to halt excessive abuses. The point to be made is that the costs of controls should not exceed the benefits.

Internal Control Guidelines

We turn now to a short discussion of some guidelines for setting up an internal control system. The student can find more complete information in standard auditing textbooks. We will describe some of the procedures commonly used in internal controls; specific cases may call for departure from these general guidelines.

ORGANIZATIONAL STRUCTURE

A well-designed set of administrative responsibilities can serve to prevent many errors and to detect the ones that do occur. The beginning point is the construction of an organization chart (see Exhibit 10-1) that describes the positions in the firm and their interrelationships. Unfortunately, many managers stop after they prepare the chart. Indeed, the chart is meaningless unless the people represented by the boxes understand what it means. Therefore, careful training of incoming personnel and continuous monitoring of the structure's efficiency are essential. Jobs may be added, deleted, or revised, if necessary. Above all, the manager must not presume that the chart necessarily represents actuality. Some testing and interviewing should be done to determine if the plan is effective. In reviewing the system of internal control, auditors often find the *actual* organizational responsibilities are quite different than those described by the company's formal organization chart.

COMPETENT PERSONNEL

The weakest link in the chain of control is frequently the people who fill the positions. Despite the obviousness of this point, many firms have performed poorly or even failed because of incompetency. We cannot begin to discuss this point completely in this context. However, the manager must realize that he should develop sound policies for not only hiring and training new employees but also retaining, firing, training, and promoting his present work force.[5] With competency, the number of mistakes should diminish greatly. Consequently, the internal controls can be simplified and made more economical.

[5] The student may be interested in reading *The Peter Principle* by Lawrence J. Peter and Raymond Hull, (New York: William Morrow, 1969). The theme of this highly entertaining book is that people tend to advance within a structure until they achieve their level of incompetency.

SEPARATION OF DUTIES

A frequently used internal control device is to have two people working separately at different aspects of the same task. When both have finished, there should be agreement in their results. This *double-checking* is very effective in detecting honest mistakes, and helps to prevent dishonest ones by requiring that two people collaborate in the illegality.

Frequently, it is a good idea to separate physical custody of assets from the accounting for their use. Records of the items in an inventory should be maintained by someone who has no access to those items. By the same token, the warehouse workers should not have access to the records. As a result, we can verify that inventory is being used properly if the balance on hand agrees with the records. If the quantities and records are managed by the same person, manipulations may cover thefts or other shortages.

Similarly, blank checks should be in the custody of someone who is not authorized to sign them. The bank statements and the cash records should be reconciled by a person who has no other responsibilities concerning cash. In this way, *all* checks and deposits cleared by the bank will be compared with the records by an impartial party (if we assume no collusion has taken place). Note that this procedure is very helpful in detecting arithmetic errors as well as intentional fraud.

Purchases of merchandise or other items should be approved by a supervisor before they are accomplished. Bills (invoices) from vendors should be compared with requests for purchases before they are paid. By having different individuals accomplish these tasks, it becomes more difficult for improper activity to take place.

As an extra dividend, separating the duties of clerks can lead to greater efficiency through specialization. For example, purchasing agents not only are independent of the using departments but also are very familiar with the nature of the markets in which they deal. Consequently, they know which firms are dependable, quick to deliver, or offer the best cash or quantity discounts. Similarly, if there is a separate bookkeeper for the accounts receivable, that person will be able to process transactions very quickly, and often serve as a storehouse of information about payment habits or any problems with particular accounts. This special knowledge can assist the manager in providing customer service and in avoiding additional bad debt expenses.

FORMS, PROCEDURES, AND OTHER AIDS

Hand in hand with separation of duties is the establishment of routine procedures for dealing with the vast majority of the firm's activities. Special blank forms should be used in processing these routine events to assure completeness and accuracy. The forms should include places for approving signatures, and should be designed to encourage their proper completion. Excessive complexity should be avoided. Color coding and sequential numbering can be used. Prenumbering allows us to account for each form and to be sure none are missing, thereby increasing the accuracy of the accounting systems.

Other devices may be used to speed up processing, or to make it more accurate. Simple office machines, such as typewriters, calculators, and check imprinters, can eliminate problems of illegibility and arithmetic errors. More sophisticated devices, including bookkeeping machines and computers, can greatly increase the efficiency, accuracy, and the timeliness of accounting reports. On a more mundane level, such things as floodlights, fences, night watchmen, sprinkler systems, and locks can protect assets against pilferage or fire. Well-constructed warehouses and storerooms can reduce losses through spoilage or other damage.

INSURANCE

Despite excellent controls, it is still possible that losses can occur. To reduce the impact of disasters, frauds, and other traumatic events, nearly every business shares the risks with insurance companies. Many firms may find that they are required to carry coverage by laws, loan agreements, or other contracts. Almost any loss can be insured against, if a person is willing to pay the price. We will briefly discuss four types of coverage commonly encountered in business.

Firms often acquire *life insurance* for key managers and major owners. In the first case, the proceeds can serve to compensate for lost revenues until the vacated position can be filled. In the second case, the funds can be used to settle any claims that the decedent's estate may have against the firm. In this way, the working capital can be maintained and the business can carry on more easily. Of course, a policy may serve both of these purposes if the key executive is also a major stockholder or partner.

Buildings, equipment, and other property (such as inventory) are insurable against *fire* damage. *Extended coverage* is available, and will provide payments for damage caused by such perils as wind, hail, rain, snow, explosion (not every explosion produces a fire), and even sprinkler leakage. Because they will have to be replaced at current market prices, it is appropriate to insure these assets at appraisal value rather than historical cost.

Nearly every fire insurance policy contains a *coinsurance* clause, which serves to encourage the insured to carry coverage equal to a certain percentage of the asset's current *insurable* value. For example, an 80 percent coinsurance clause would encourage the policyholder to insure a $500,000 building for at least $400,000. If the management chooses to carry less, they will find themselves bearing more of the loss than they would like.[6] In particular, the insurance company will pay only the percentage represented by the actual coverage divided by the required coverage. If the building were to be insured for only $300,000 the policy would pay only 75 percent ($300,000/$400,000) of the actual loss, *up to* $300,000. Thus if half the building were destroyed, only $187,500 would be paid. Even if actual damages exceed $400,000 no more than $300,000 would be paid.

As a result of coinsurance, it is good management practice to obtain insurance coverage through a reputable agency and to systematically review

---

[6] This sharing of the damages is the origin of the term *coinsurance.*

its adequacy. Although reduced coverage may be a worthwhile means of lowering costs, managers should avoid situations in which they find themselves *involuntary* coinsurers. Rising replacement costs may cause what was once adequate insurance to fall below the coinsurance rate. Indeed, the purpose of the clause is to encourage that coverage be updated frequently.

Many fire insurance policies also contain a *contribution clause,* which will allocate the loss among all the insurers if the same asset is covered by policies from more than one insurance company. This clause generally limits the total claims to no more than the market value of the asset, and thus discourages its intentional destruction through arson or other means.

Through the purchase of *fidelity bonds,* which are usually quite inexpensive, a company can insure against losses arising from dishonest acts of its employees. This policy not only reduces the monetary risk but also lets the employees know that they will be prosecuted by an impersonal insurance company in the event they are caught. A *position bond* covers losses caused by anyone who happens to be filling a particular job, such as cashier or treasurer. A *name bond* covers losses caused by a particular person regardless of his position.

Whereas a bond protects against willfully caused damages, *liability insurance* is intended to share the risk of losses caused by negligent acts of the firm's agents or employees, or by what turned out to be unsafe conditions or products. Thus, restaurants may have insurance against food poisoning, and amusement parks may desire protection against claims of injured customers.[7] Most states require that liability insurance be carried on motor vehicles and for workmen's compensation. If insurance is not carried, the firm will have to provide evidence that it is sufficiently able to meet any claims from its own resources.

There is certainly no reason that insurance should be obtained for every risk faced by a business. When a company decides to bear the risk, it is said to have *self-insurance.*[8] Careful managers should compare the chances of a loss (and its size) with the premiums that *must* be paid if a policy is obtained. As always, conservatism may enter as a factor in the decision.

REVIEW AND APPRAISAL

It would be an unusual internal control system that could adapt itself automatically to changes in the firm. Parts of the internal control system occasionally become obsolete or redundant, or a new activity may be left virtually uncontrolled. As a consequence, it is good management practice to examine the system frequently to determine if it is working as it should. The elimination of even such a minor item as an unneeded copy of a form may lead to significant savings in printing and employee effort.

The review should not be confined to a perfunctory study of diagrams.

---

[7] In either case, a court may rule out any awards to the injured on the grounds that he knew or should have known what he was getting into (or getting into him).

[8] This term is somewhat paradoxical, in that it means to share the risks with oneself.

Actual documents should be pulled from files and examined for completeness. Employees should be interviewed to detect areas for change, and their suggestions should be considered. Above all, procedures should not be continued simply because "that's the way it has always been done!" The *audit* is a popular review technique.

The Audit

An *audit* is an examination of evidence to be certain that actuality coincides with what is claimed to exist. A surprise quiz in your accounting class is a type of audit. Your teacher gathers evidence (your grade) about the state of your preparation. Furthermore, the possibility of a quiz encourages you to prepare more completely. Auditing has been applied extensively in the business world, and it appears that its use will continue to grow in the future. Audits are categorized according to the type of person who does the auditing. They are: *internal, government,* and *independent* audits.

THE INTERNAL AUDIT

An internal audit is accomplished by a person or group of persons that is employed only by the organization that is audited. The purpose of the audit is to verify for management that policies are being followed properly. Thus, the internal audit is really only a technique of internal control.

The scope of the internal audit may be quite broad, and usually reaches well beyond examination of the accounting system. There is a growing trend toward *performance audits,* which are designed to investigate the effectiveness of managers. The internal audit findings are virtually meaningless for anyone outside the firm because of the lack of perceived independence on the part of the auditor. Nonetheless, management can place a great deal of reliance on the findings, if the auditors are *organizationally* independent. The internal auditing departments of some firms report directly to the board of directors to assure that they are free of undue influence. Others work under the vice president of finance.

THE GOVERNMENT AUDIT

Some audits are performed by employees of a government agency, or by public accounting firms engaged by a government agency. For example, the Defense Contract Audit Agency performs audits of companies that are government contractors. The purpose of these audits is to determine the extent of the auditee's compliance with the requirements of a particular law. Consequently, the scope of the audit is extremely narrow, and the results may be meaningless for any other purpose. We are all familiar with tax audits and with bank examinations. Both of these government audits are involved mainly with accounting records. Government auditors also examine such things as employment practices, working conditions, and cost accounting methods used in government contracts. The audits not only determine whether the firm complied with the law but also encourage the firm to do so.

THE INDEPENDENT AUDIT

Chapter 2 introduced the reader to the most commonly encountered business audit, which is performed by an independent CPA. Despite the fact that he receives a fee from the auditee, the auditor is considered *independent* if he has a sufficient number of other clients and if he has no financial or personal interest in the firm that would compromise his ability to exercise objective judgment. The purpose of the audit is to add credibility to the firm's financial statements. To accomplish his examination, the auditor must do more than simply see if the ledger balances. Broadly stated, he must determine what reality is and then see if the firm's financial statements present a valid description of that reality. The validity of the description is defined by generally accepted accounting principles. Because of the imprecision involved in discovering reality, and because of the nature of the accounting principles, the auditor renders his *opinion* as to whether the statements are a *fair presentation*. This "fair" does not mean somewhere between "good" and "poor," but rather that the information has not been biased to meet the needs of only a few special readers.

If the auditor is satisfied with his findings in every *material* aspect, he will offer what is known as an *unqualified opinion*. His report will accompany the statements, and will attest to their propriety. If he is not satisfied with all that he finds, he can issue either a *qualified* or an *adverse* opinion.[9] Again, these reports accompany the statements, and, in this case, attest to their impropriety. Consequently, managers avoid these unfavorable opinions as if they were outbreaks of the plague!

If the findings are unfavorable, the client can take one of three actions: accept the opinion, fire the auditor, or amend the statements. Fortunately, the last course is chosen in nearly all cases. It does not do much good to fire the auditor, because the next one is obligated, by professional ethics, to contact the discharged one. He will have to duplicate the work of the first one (for a large fee), and is likely to produce the same result. While not totally unacceptable to the financial statement reader, an unfavorable opinion is hard to explain and may lead to difficulties with regulatory agencies.

The auditor is not allowed (by professional rules) to render a report that he has *no opinion* unless he has not completed his examination. Even if he discovers a serious error by accident, he cannot permit the statements to be published with his name unless that error is corrected.

Contrary to many preconceived notions, the independent auditor is not especially looking for fraud. His tests of the internal control system are intended to seek out errors in arithmetic, or, more significantly, in the application of the accounting principles. If he stumbles across an embezzlement, he will notify the client and await further instructions. His main concern remains with attesting to the fairness of the statements. However, the client may engage the auditor to produce a *management letter,* in which he will make comments about weaknesses in the control system and submit recommendations for improvement. It is usually in the best interest of the client to implement the changes, if only to reduce next year's audit fees.

[9] Chapter 2 presents examples of unqualified and qualified opinions.

Computers and Controls

Much to the embarrassment of the accounting profession, several rather large frauds have been carried out under the noses of auditors. In more and more situations, the thief is using a computer as an accomplice. When thousands of instructions are executed in a single second, just think how easily five or six crooked ones could be hidden! In the early stages of computer development, most applications were simply automated versions of manual systems, and ordinary auditors had few problems in adjusting their techniques. However, the computer industry continued progressing, and developed devices and techniques that bear little resemblance to the old ones. Auditors are catching up, but there still seems to remain a number of very large risks.

Perhaps the most useful tool in the internal control designer's "kit" is the *separation of duties*. If the programmer has no access to the computer, he cannot insert and remove special routines to accomplish the fraud. If the computer operator has no knowledge of the program, he is also prevented from fooling around with it. The computer can be programmed to keep records of all the operator's actions, a factor which also helps prevent manipulations.

Another useful tool is *surprise*. An auditor (usually internal) may have a program run at an unexpected time, and thereby hope to detect any unauthorized changes. He can test the program by running it with a set of real data, or with test data, or even by an instruction-by-instruction analysis. This last approach is the most expensive, but it is also the most effective in discovering any tampering.

Careful screening of the personnel in the data processing shop is also an important phase of control. Any audit tests should include careful scrutiny of any activities in the payroll or any other accounts of these employees. Frequent rotation of duties, while inefficient, may keep a programmer from having one program as his own, and it may deter the formation of collusive associations. These efforts may fail, if only because the typical electronic data processing (EDP) expert is above average in cleverness.

Thus, we can see that internal control over computer operations is quite complicated. However, the complexity should emphasize the need to be extremely careful. Unfortunately, it has been observed that many computer installations have next to no control at all. It does appear that some of the problems are being solved, but the entire area promises to pose a serious challenge for many years to come.

SOCIAL RESPONSIBILITY

The social responsibilities faced by the modern businessman are more complex than the administrative ones. Indeed, there are several levels that must be considered. First, the firm itself is a member of society and, as such, has many responsibilities. The manager, as the agent for the impersonal firm, assumes these responsibilities. Second, the manager is also a member of the society, and has the same obligations as any other member, without any regard to his administrative responsibilities. Finally, the manager has social responsibilities to the other members of the firm. For example, by hiring workers, he is obligated to provide safe working conditions, fair employment practices, and even unemployment benefits.

While these social responsibilities have always existed, and have always been significant, they have not always been recognized. The world has passed through several eras of *social awareness,* each building on the preceding one. Many people believe that the 1960s and 1970s witnessed some of the greatest efforts to recognize these responsibilities.

Social awareness has been brought about in many cases through legislation. In a sense, the government acts on behalf of society, and creates laws to cause men to do what they are not willing to do on the basis of economics. In the classic work, *Wealth of Nations* (1776), Adam Smith presented the argument that the "invisible hand" of self-interest would bring a society to the state of maximum well-being. Few serious economists now completely believe Smith's thesis. The consensus seems to be that the invisible hand may bring us close, but that government efforts will be necessary to arrive at the maximum. It is not our intent to present a solution to this disagreement (although you may wish to discuss it in class), but merely to point out that many social responsibilities have been converted into written and enforceable laws. Under a democratic system, the amount of social legislation (hopefully) varies inversely with the amount of voluntary action the business community undertakes to meet its social responsibilities. If a new law seems unavoidable, the socially responsible businessman should work with the legislative branch to help assure that the proposed controls will accomplish the desired conditions without prohibitive costs. This cooperation can include active *lobbying* or presentation of facts and opinions at public hearings.

The manager should also seek to comply with all existing laws that apply to his firm and to his own actions. Of course, through similar channels, he should seek to alter those laws which he feels are improper or unjust.

Events of the Watergate era showed that not all managers feel obligated to meet their social responsibilities. In some cases, they violate the laws hoping not to be caught, or else regard a bribe or a fine simply as a necessary business expense. Apparently, some managements see little difference between an illegal political contribution or a fine for price fixing and normal operating expenses such as employees' wages or rent expense. Other managers feel obligated to operate just barely within the law and disregard unlegislated social responsibilities. Extensive publicity of illegal political contributions, multimillion-dollar bribes to foreign governments and agents in foreign countries, and similar questionable activities all cause a general erosion in the public's confidence in our business institutions. SEC Commissioner A. A. Sommer, Jr., made these observations:

I think that confidence in our institutions and in the people who lead them is one of the essential cements of our society.

Our confidence in our business institutions and in its leadership is still unfortunately in the process of disintegration; how long that process may continue is a problem for all of us.

While the tragedy is unfolding, I think all of us who are in positions to influence the manner of unfolding should exercise our responsibility and our authority in the most cautious way. . . .

Businessmen have been singularly slow to raise their voices in criticism of the conduct of their fellow businessmen, conduct which inevitably hurts all businessmen. Not surprisingly, in the face of such silence Americans assume that the misdeeds are either condoned or are simply representative of practices universal in the business community. Such conclusions are unfair to the mass of businessmen who, despite the recent exposes, I am convinced are much more comfortable hewing to a narrow line of right than engaging in illegal payoffs, secreting caches of money, or bribing foreign officials.[10]

It would seem that unless businessmen respond to this public pressure for higher ethics in business, they may lose some of their freedoms. In Sommer's words:

Business constantly complains of the intrusion of government in its affairs. I can think of no better antidote to this tendency than strong action by businessmen to prove to legislators and regulators that they are truly concerned with the conduct of their fellow businessmen and that they are willing to move vigorously to identify those who do not share the highest ideals of American business. I would not suggest that Federal regulation will wither under such a sun, but I think that words of business will sound with a new sincerity if spoken by professionals wedded to a new business morality strenuously enforced in some meaningful way. . . .

Businessmen, government officials, all of us who share responsibility in this society, can contribute nothing more meaningful to generations to come than the gift of restored confidence in our nation, its institutions and its leaders. But such confidence must be earned and merited. I would hope that our business leadership will quickly erase the cancers in their midst and move swiftly and surely to a new day of responsibility and service.[11]

It is not always easy for a manager to meet all of his responsibilities. Sometimes he finds conflicts between his administrative and social responsibilities or even between social factors. For example, how should the manager of a pharmaceutical company price a new drug? He has a responsibility to stockholders to maximize profits (or at least generate a *fair* return) yet he has a responsibility to society to make the drug available to the masses to reduce suffering. A more complex situation is faced when the manager must

---

[10] From a speech to the Midwest Securities Commissioners Association, by permission of the speaker.

[11] *Ibid.*

decide between lower prices and unsafe working conditions, or destruction of the environment. There are no simple solutions; however, the businessman who seeks only to maximize his profits has an inadequate set of tools.

In Exhibit 10-1, we showed all authority in the firm coming down from the stockholders. If we were to expand the chart upward to include social responsibilities, we would show the stockholders to be subordinate to the society, and thus *accountable* to it for the actions of the corporation. Consequently, stockholders are faced with complex conflict situations. Their goal is to earn a satisfactory return on their investment, but they are also members of the society that may suffer as profits increase. Some stockholders react to the conflict by selling (or simply not buying) the stock, others vote to change the board of directors (almost always a futile effort), and others do nothing. Interesting conflicts arise when one individual is not only a stockholder, but also a customer, or even an employee. We cannot provide guidance to assist a person out of these problems, except to remind him of the need to meet his social responsibilities.

We can now turn to the accountant. With our expanded frame of reference, we have to consider not only the management accountant but also the independent accountant in public practice. The internal accountant faces essentially the same conflict as the manager. In order to assist the manager, he can attempt to gather information about the *social costs* of certain company policies and about the cost of modifying the policies to deal more responsibly with society. It would be expecting a great deal to suggest that the management accountant should speak out on apparent conflicts between his firm and society. He certainly has the same responsibilities as every other citizen but he may risk his livelihood if he becomes too vocal.

The independent CPA is subject to another set of rules, however. He has applied for and received special recognition from society (that is, the government) as a person with not only special skills but also unusual integrity. Despite the fact that he is engaged by his client's stockholders to audit a report of financial activities, many people believe that it is well within the scope of the auditor's duty to represent the interests of nonstockholders and to examine the adequacy of management efforts to meet their social responsibilities. Even though the accountant may lose his client, we can presume that he will have other clients to provide his livelihood. Furthermore, his certificate imposes an additional amount of social responsibility.[12]

While nearly all audit engagements presently involve the responsibilities of the firm's managers to the stockholders in terms of financial position and the results of operations, some audits tests the firm's compliance with legal agreements with nonowners, such as pension plans and bond covenants. It is possible that future auditors will be forced to change from these long-established practices. For example, generally accepted accounting principles some day may include the measurement of social costs. In addition, future

[12] It has been said that a CPA must never forget his middle name—*Public*. His obligation is *first* to the public, and then to special interest groups.

auditors may be required to expand the scope of the audit to include compliance with laws concerning such things as employment and promotion practices, environmental protection policies, working conditions, political contributions, and foreign bribes. While it may be argued that these areas have nothing to do with the financial statements, it may be countered that these factors certainly do affect the firm's ability to survive and earn profits, and thus do belong in the independent accountant's responsibilities.

We must emphasize that we do not have the answers to these extremely complex issues. It is not possible to dictate which specific actions should take place in all circumstances. Our purpose in this discussion is to make the student aware of some of the social responsibilities that he is likely to face in his business career. It is our personal feeling that it will be inadequate to simply rely on the law to define these responsibilities. It would be wise for all managers and accountants to participate in the political process in order to assist the creation of fair and reasonable laws. But even before laws are passed, all of us have an obligation to consider the well-being of the society as well as our personal wealth. Indeed, the continuation of the free enterprise system may hinge on how well you, as a future manager, fulfill your responsibilities. In the 1800s, Alexis de Tocqueville observed that: "America is great because she is good and if she ever ceases to be good she will cease to be great."

SUMMARY

This chapter has dealt with the rather broad subjects of responsibility and control. Responsibility involves authority and accountability. *Administrative* responsibility is used within the firm to aid its efficient operation. *Responsibility accounting systems* are designed to assist managers in evaluating their subordinates on the basis of factors *controllable* by them.

An *internal control* system can help assure the manager that his policies are being followed. Other objectives of the system are to promote (1) efficiency, (2) accuracy and reliability, (3) safeguarding assets, and (4) economy. Several guidelines should be followed in creating an internal control system, including the use of an organization structure, competent personnel, separation of duties, and insurance. A very widespread and significant tool for reviewing a firm's management and accounting systems is the *audit,* which can be performed by either *internal, government,* or *independent* auditors, depending on the nature of the audit.

Social responsibilities are broader than administrative responsibilities at several levels, such as the firm to society, the manager to society, and the firm to its workers. Some social responsibilities are difficult to enforce, but legislation has been written to enable society to control irresponsible activities. Perhaps the best enforcement comes from the consciences of the individuals involved. The future is sure to produce additional awareness of these obligations, and a good manager cannot afford to act as if they do not exist or are not important.

QUESTIONS

1. What is *responsibility*? Name and discuss three attributes of responsibility.
2. Distinguish between *administrative* and *social* responsibilities.
3. Can responsibility be delegated? Why or why not?
4. In designing a *responsibility accounting system,* what factors must the accountant identify? Why?
5. What is *internal control*? What are the objectives of an internal control system?
6. Name and briefly describe five guidelines within which the designer of an internal control system should work. Can he violate these guidelines?
7. What is *coinsurance*?
8. In general, what is an *audit*?
9. Compare and contrast these three kinds of audits: *internal, government,* and *independent.*
10. Why is the independent auditor's report expressed as an *opinion*?
11. What are the options of the manager in the event of a difference of opinion with the independent auditor?
12. What are the options of the independent auditor in the event of a difference of opinion with the manager?
13. Have computers made fraud easier or more difficult? What are some devices that the auditor can use to prevent or detect computer fraud?
14. What are the three levels of social responsibility that a manager of a firm might encounter? Are there any conflicts among them?

PROBLEMS

P10–1 Administrative responsibility. Examine this abstract (page 279) from an organization chart.

Suppose that the clerk made a significant error in interpreting a complex new section of the tax law. Because the clerk had proven competent in dealing with this specialized area of taxation in prior situations, and because of the complexity of the decision, the error appeared on the tax return, which was approved by the board of directors and submitted to the authorities. The error was discovered two years later, with a resulting large assessment for back taxes and penalties.

Required:

a. Discuss the arguments for and against assigning this responsibility to each person represented on the chart.

b. If the error were intentional, would your answer be different?

c. Is there a similarity between this situation and the famous My Lai massacre of the Vietnam War? (The student should recall who ended up in prison in that case.)

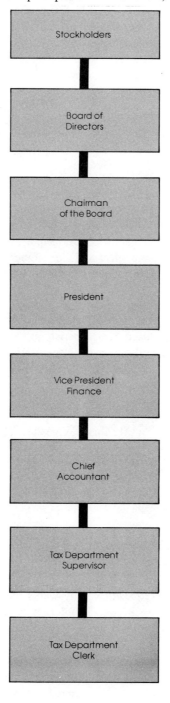

P10–2 *Responsibility accounting.* The Cardinal Company compensates its field sales force on a commission and year-end bonus basis.

The commission is 20 percent of gross margin (planned selling price less planned cost of goods sold), contingent upon collection of the account. Customer credit is approved by the company's Credit Department.

Price concessions are granted occasionally by top sales management, but sales commissions are not reduced by the discount.

A year-end bonus of 15 percent of commissions earned is paid to salesmen who equal or exceed their annual sales target. The sales targets are established by applying approximately a 5 percent increase to the prior year's sales.

Required:
a. What features of this compensation plan would seem to be effective in motivating the salesmen to accomplish company goals of higher profits and return on investment? Explain why.
b. What features of this compensation plan would seem to be countereffective in motivating the salesmen to accomplish the company goals of higher profits and return on investment? Explain why.

(CMA Adapted)

P10–3 *Participative management.* You are a member of the board of directors and a vice president of production. Your chairman has just introduced Mr. Robert Johnston as a newly hired expert in information and computer systems, and he goes on to say: "I have authorized Bob's hiring of three assistants for this project. They'll have six months to produce and implement a new management information system. I want all of you to cooperate with Bob by providing the data he wants and by not bothering him about what you want. In this way he can get his system together and running in as short a time as possible. Do you have any questions?"

Required:
In light of the topics covered in the chapter, what questions would you want answered?

P10–4 *Internal control.* Comment on the strengths and weaknesses of the following procedures in terms of meeting the objectives of internal control.
a. Whenever an item is needed from the supplies inventory, the requestor simply walks into the storeroom and takes whatever he needs. Reordering is handled by a secretary who walks through the room and notes which items are in low supply.
b. Whenever an item is needed from the supplies inventory, the requestor must fill out and have approved a triplicate requisition form. The form is handed to an inventory management clerk, who initials it and keeps one copy. The requestor carries

the remaining copies to the storeroom, where a clerk finds the item and delivers it. One copy is kept by him and the other is given back to the requestor. In the event the item is out of stock, the entire procedure must be repeated. Reordering is handled by the inventory management supervisor on the basis of the clerk's records.

c. Every tangible asset in the factory and offices is tagged with a metallic adhesive label, each of which shows a different number. At least once each quarter, the designated responsible person must submit a list of the assets in his custody and describe their condition. Any shortages or damages are investigated promptly and vigorously.

d. Accounting Department Supervisor *A* approves all requests for checks to be written. Clerk *B* records and writes the checks, except for the signature, and forwards them to Finance Officer *C,* who signs and mails them, and cancels the request form. Secretary *D* receives the bank statement and canceled checks from the mailman, and reconciles the bank's balance with the cash books.

e. Because of his knowledge of the market, the purchasing manager personally authorizes and places all orders for supplies, raw materials, and major asset acquisitions. Because he places the orders and has an office adjacent to the loading dock, he personally inspects each shipment received in order to verify its condition and completeness. If he is satisfied, he sends a request for a check directly to the cash disbursements clerk, who prepares it and runs it through a check-signer. The purchasing manager picks up the check in order to verify its amount, and then mails it to the payee.

P10–5 *Auditor's responsibilities.* Mr. Arnold Bixbee is the major stockholder, chairman of the board, and president of Shady Enterprises. As part of an agreement connected with a substantial loan, he has engaged you, an independent CPA, to audit the financial statements of the firm before they are submitted to the bank.

You are, of course, aware of the loan agreement, and learn that in addition to the provisions for repayment, it includes the following: (1) The current ratio must be maintained at a level no lower than two to one. (2) Earnings before taxes must be at least $200,000 a year. The income statement prepared by Bixbee shows a pretax earnings figure of $215,000. The following items appear on his balance sheet:

Cash	$ 15,000
Accounts receivable	45,000
Inventory	60,000
Total current assets	$120,000
Total current liabilities	$ 50,000

In the course of your audit, you make the following discoveries:

1. It appears that one of the receivables (for $5,000) will not be collected because of bankruptcy proceedings against a customer.

2. Because of a large number of obsolete items, the inventory should be carried at only $45,000.

3. The average cash balance throughout the year is $50,000, and current liabilities are usually between $80,000 and $90,000. Shortly before the balance sheet date, however, $35,000 in cash was paid to creditors 60 days ahead of schedule.

Required:

a. How will these discoveries affect the financial statements and loan agreement?

b. As the CPA, to whom are you responsible (name at least three parties)? If you could deal with each one *without* considering the others, what would be the best way to satisfy those responsibilities?

c. Assume that you have decided that you will issue a favorable opinion on the statements only if the assets are written down and the cash balance is reinstated. What can Mr. Bixbee attempt to do? What would you recommend that he do?

d. Suppose that it is discovered later that one of the employees had been stealing from the company. The effect on the statements of the thefts is negligible, but you are threatened with a lawsuit for malpractice. On what issue do you think the judge should decide the case? Explain your answer.

P10–6 *Internal control.* The Shoestring Company is faced with an interesting problem. Because of the limited budget, only three clerks work in the Accounting Department, but there are eight tasks to be performed. Each clerk is bright and capable, and you are sure that no two of them will ever collude to commit a fraud. However, you're not so sure about each of them acting independently. Given these jobs, assign them to the three clerks so that there will be an effective system of double-checking:

1. maintain general ledger
2. maintain accounts payable ledger
3. maintain accounts receivable ledger
4. prepare checks for signature
5. maintain disbursements journal
6. issue credits on returns and allowances
7. reconcile the bank accounts
8. handle and deposit cash receipts

Required:

What, if anything, could you do to prevent collusion?

(AICPA Adapted)

P10–7 **Internal control of EDP.** The Small Town Bank purchased a Big Town computer system several months ago, and because the volume was not too great, hired only one person to run the data processing shop. Included among her tasks were programming and operating the computer during the nightly updates of customer checking and savings accounts.

As the programmer, this person frequently alters the existing computer programs to make them "more efficient." She is also supposed to document all modifications to the programs, but has fallen behind because "there hasn't been enough time." The manager was told rather curtly that as long as the program was running there wasn't any need for documentation.

As the operator, this person also has access to the input data (compiled from checks, deposit slips, and withdrawal requests) and to the ledgers of the accounts, which are kept on magnetic tape.

Because she says she works "better" at night, and doesn't like somebody "looking over her shoulder," all the data processing is run after hours when the building is deserted. Suggestions that an assistant be hired have been coldly rejected by this person, despite the fact that she is frequently still on the job at 8 A.M. after coming to work at 10 P.M. the night before.

Required:

a. Identify the possible weaknesses in internal control of the data processing activities.

b. Is there *evidence* of fraudulent activity? Are there some signs that *suggest* it?

c. As manager of the bank, what steps should you take to strengthen the system? How would you deal with this person? How could you determine whether any defalcations had occurred?

P10–8 **Insurance.** At the suggestion of his recently graduated and newly hired nephew, the president of Old Fashioned Industries engaged the insurance consultant firm of Young and Eagar to make a complete study of the company's insurance protection. Al Codger, the president, is going over the findings with his nephew, Richard Snapper.

"Did you see this one? They say that we ought to be carrying life insurance on our key men! I can't see how that could possibly be justified on the income statement. They're just trying to sell more policies."

"And then they said our buildings are underinsured, too. The depreciated value, which our auditor makes us use on the balance sheet, is $100,000, but it would cost us $500,000 to replace them. I didn't think it would be legal to insure them for more than their book value, but these guys kept bringing up something called *coinsurance*. The last thing I want is two or three insurance companies *cooperating* on our coverage!"

"Have you ever heard of a fidelity bond? It seems to me that if somebody takes us for a bundle, it's up to us to track him down and get the money back."

"I guess this last thing is the most ridiculous I've ever heard. You know how customers like to come into the shop to see how we're putting everything together? It seems to me that if they get hurt doing that, then it ought to be their own fault and their own doctor bill! Same thing for the delivery men coming into the warehouse. They're husky guys and used to working in dangerous places. If somebody gets hurt, well, that's the breaks. It's got to happen sometime, don't you think? Anyway, your friends said that we ought to be buying insurance to protect *us* from injuries to *those people*!"

"I don't know where you heard about Young and Eagar, but I think we can do without their advice! Now go sharpen some pencils!"

Required:

Assume the role of Richard Snapper, and try to explain to your uncle why the recommendations deserve to be considered more carefully. Clear up any misconceptions that he seems to have.

P10–9 *Social responsibility.* At the executive dining hall, an interesting and heated conversation is in process. Ms. Jenny McDonald is heard to say: "I have always thought that the purpose of this company was to earn profits for the stockholders. Consequently, cutting our costs and raising our prices to the maximum the customers will pay are both legitimate and desirable tactics."

Mr. Ozzie Green responds: "On the contrary, the whole reason society lets us operate is because we provide a valuable service to the rest of the people. If we attempt to take advantage of the high demand for our product by raising prices, we are exploiting the market, and that's immoral. We should be doing everything possible to reduce our costs."

Mr. Bill Burton has been listening and fidgeting. He says: "Now, wait a minute! It is my opinion that the purpose of this corporation is to provide a source of income for the employees. We're the ones that do all the working! If it wasn't for us employees, none of those machines in the shop would be worth a darn, and there wouldn't be any dividends going out to the stockholders. It seems to me that the best strategy is to charge what the market will bear and distribute the minimum amount to the stockholders. Whatever is left over should be divided up among the workers."

Required:

a. Which of these points of view do you believe to be closest to the *truth*? Be prepared to discuss your answer with your classmates.

b. Suggest some compromises that might be made among these philosophies.

P10–10 *Social responsibility.* Imagine that you are affiliated with a company, and have worked closely with a high official of the firm.

Place yourself in the role of (1) an executive assistant to the official, (2) an internal auditor of the firm, and (3) an independent auditor of the firm.

In each role, describe how you would react to your accidental discovery that the official had:

a. Committed a felony not in connection with the line of business (for example, murder, extortion, robbery).

b. Committed a felony, or other questionable act, in connection with a business purpose (such as, paid a bribe, made an illegal contribution to a political candidate, accepted a *kickback,* signed a fraudulent tax return).

c. Made a decision and implemented a policy that would have negative social effects (such as, increased air or water pollution, increased unemployment, higher prices on necessities consumed by poor or elderly persons).

11

Planning Future Actions

An exhaustive examination of business successes probably would identify a large variety of methods by which prosperity was achieved. In addition to a willingness to take a risk and having some good luck, successful businessmen tend to show foresight and an uncanny ability to prepare themselves and their firms for future events.

To consistently succeed, today's manager should anticipate what lies ahead in the short and in the long run. By making this effort, plans can be made to capitalize on unique opportunities and to avoid pitfalls. But planning involves work and money. Furthermore, while most of us like to sit back and dream about the future, the task of formulating concrete actions to achieve those dreams can be rather distasteful. This chapter approaches the planning process on a relatively abstract level, with emphasis on establishing the context for planning as well as some of the broader alternatives available to managers. Chapter 12 presents more specific steps to be taken in preparing budgets.

THE STEPS OF MANAGEMENT

Planning for the future should be the primary activity of the manager. Even when he is examining evidence of past performance, his mind should be on what he can do in the future to improve on his past. Let's break the management process down into a series of steps, and see where planning and accounting information enter in.

Goal Setting

The first step in management is the establishment of *objectives* or the *setting of goals*. The classical economist assumes that the goal of the entrepreneur is to maximize his profits. Although this is a convenient assumption for analysis, it is too broad to be of value to the businessman. He needs to establish more specific goals concerning not only the fact that profits are desired but also the size of the profits, their timing, and the means by which they are to be accomplished. Some of the objectives, including such things as prestige, social responsibility, and security, have nothing to do with profits.

The size of the desired profits can be expressed as an absolute quantity, but this approach disregards the relationship between effort and reward. A more desirable way is to express a profit goal as a *return on the investment* (see Chapter 3). Profits can be described as a percentage of sales, but again we would be leaving out some of the effort.

It is essential to express the goal in terms of a *time frame*. To earn a million dollars is a worthwhile goal, and most of us would achieve it only if we could live several hundred years. Thus, our profit goal must be stated as a desired amount *within* a specified period of time.

If we fail to specify the means by which we intend to earn our profit, we still have no plans for the future. It is essential for a businessman to decide what *market* he is going to work in, and to identify how he intends to achieve his profit goal.

Examining Alternatives

The brief flowchart (Exhibit 11-1) indicates that once the manager has a set of goals,[1] he must go about finding alternative ways to accomplish them. The question of whether to purchase items or to make them would be answered at this stage. If he decides to be a producer, he has to select his production process (automated or labor intensive, for example) and establish other policies.

Some alternatives can be rejected outright as undesirable or unfeasible. The manager's toughest decisions will be the selection of the *best* alternative among the several that will essentially have the same payoffs. The variety of businesses which succeed in our economy is ample testimony that there are many different ways to reach the objective of earning profits.

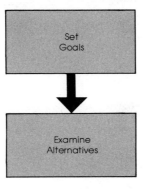

Exhibit 11-1

[1] The goals may be *self-developed,* or they might be *imposed* on the manager if he is under the employment of others.

Implementation and Evaluation

Once the most likely approach has been selected, the manager's next task is to implement it. This stage involves the acquisition of such things as building space, personnel, supplier contracts, and marketing channels. Many businesses falter before they ever begin operations simply because the manager is unable to obtain these fundamentals.

When the operations do get underway, the unwise manager begins to relax with the feeling that everything is moving smoothly. This fallacious attitude generally is based on the assumption that all his preceding decisions were correct. The more astute manager realizes that his planning decisions were based on conjectures and estimates, and that he must begin to evaluate actual performance in comparison with what he expected to happen. The evaluation should consider two questions: Did I select the best alternative? Did I select the best objective?

If the answer to either question is negative, the planning cycle must be picked up again at the appropriate spot. The flowchart in Exhibit 11-2 demonstrates the cyclical nature of the management process: The first phases (goal setting and alternative examination) should be recognized as *planning*. The evaluation phase should be seen as *controlling*.[2] Both are essential but interdependent. Planning is worthless if we do nothing to see whether we made the right decisions. Similarly, controlling is pointless unless we know what we are trying to achieve.

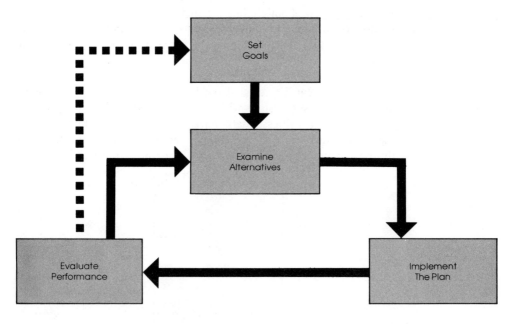

Exhibit 11-2

[2] The reader should note that we are dealing with production controls rather than internal controls (see Chapter 10).

The Role of Accounting Information

We have already seen some characteristics of accounting information and the techniques by which it is gathered. How does this information enter into the planning and control process?

The accountant, as well as economists, bankers, and marketing experts, should provide information that aids the setting of suitable goals. Projections of future sales, investments, and expenses must be processed to get an estimate of profits. Information about specific alternatives will come from these sources, and the accountant's task is to combine the data to produce meaningful reports.

Because he is dealing here with *internal* decisions, he is not confined to using and reporting only objective, historic measures. In many cases, the accountant will be called upon as a business expert to give his personal advice. However, this function is ancillary to his main job of providing useful and relevant reports which will assist management in selecting the best alternative.

The implementation of the chosen strategy occurs without significant input from either accountants or other information providing experts. The manager is, in effect, on his own for the time being. The accountant should be engaged in creating an *information system* to collect and summarize data about the success of the chosen plan.

The evaluation of the implementation depends heavily on the facts that the accountant can accumulate and report. Production accounting systems are especially suited for evaluation.

The flowchart in Exhibit 11-3 summarizes the planning-control cycle and the part played by accountants and other information providers. It must be emphasized that the accountant does not necessarily participate in manage-

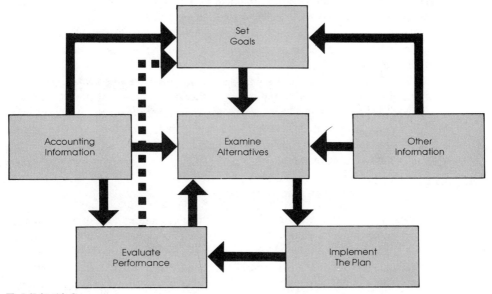

Exhibit 11-3

ment, and that his information does not necessarily prove that success or failure has been achieved or suffered.

This chapter and the next one will consider the planning phases of the cycle, while Chapter 13 will deal primarily with controlling.

BUDGETING

Perhaps the most significant management accounting document is the *budget,* which is a *numeric representation of the manager's plans for a specified period of time.* It is important to emphasize that the budget is *not* the plan, but only its representation. Responsibility for establishing the plan lies with the manager and his advisors, and the accountant's job is to express these projections in the budget. The manager who totally delegates the task of preparing the budget abdicates his responsibility for planning. On the other hand, if he fails to utilize his staff, he loses their specialized knowledge and skills, and can waste a lot of his own time and effort.

Even though a budget looks very much like an ordinary financial statement, it is really only a combination of hundreds of assumptions, projections, estimates, and compromises. It should never be used as a *precise* instrument for managing.

The Purposes of the Budget

Despite these imperfections, the budget can serve as an extremely useful tool for all managers. Let us look at some of the particular uses to which a budget can be applied.

COMMUNICATION

A budget can serve as a means of communicating information within a firm. It is especially useful for communicating expectations to lower level managers. For example, the district sales managers can be instructed as to what results are expected of them through the budget. The production manager knows how much labor he can consume from the allocation he receives in the budget.

The budget serves more subtly as a communicator over *time.* Without a written record, we might tend to forget the goals that we planned to achieve during a future month. There seems to be an innate tendency to forget what we expect of ourselves, especially when it looks like our expectations are too high. Frequent reference to the budget will remind us of our goals and our progress toward them.

COORDINATION

Whenever a manager is faced with managing two or more interrelated processes, he encounters the need to coordinate operations to minimize idleness and to maximize the utilization of *the available resources.* It may be possible for the manager of a small business to envision all the interrelationships that may exist between the purchasing and selling of inventory items, for example. As the size and complexity of the operations increase, however, it is frequently necessary to commit his plans to paper to see the situation more clearly. Consider the manager of a small manufacturing firm who may need to coordinate such things as raw material purchases, acquisitions of fixed assets, working capital matters, labor union negotiations, inventory levels, government regulations, and marketing.

As the size of the operation gets even larger, the number of factors is increased and their interrelationships grow more complicated and incomprehensible. *Coordination is essential when responsibility for different segments is delegated to separate individuals.* Without a concretely stated central plan, the manager is likely to find himself in a precarious situation. The budget can serve as the glue that holds it all together.

MEASUREMENT OF SUCCESS

Before we can consider ourselves successful at something, we need to define what *success* is. Very frequently, a businessman will feel that he is successful because he did "better" than the year before. If we determine success by comparing present performance against a previous period's performance, we have used an *historical measure,* which may prove to be inadequate. For example, the market for our product may have increased substantially, a condition which would have caused our profits to have been larger even if we did nothing new. However, in the absence of some measure of what "might have been," we could easily believe that our performance was outstanding.

Budgeted performance, on the other hand, is not an historical standard. It is a measure of what might have been against which we can compare our actual performance. It is imperfect because it is only an *a priori* estimate of future conditions and can be subject to manipulation. Nonetheless, the budget can be used as a success criterion, if done carefully and with additional data.

MOTIVATION

It is an unfortunate fact of human nature that many of us are hesitant to deal with the future and all its imponderables. But, if we are forced to prepare a budget for the coming year, we must come to grips with the future. Even if we fail to do excellent work, at least we have overcome our reluctance. Presumably, the more we anticipate future events, the better we become at doing it.

It is quite feasible to tie a reward system to a budget, and thereby motivate managers of subunits to achieve levels of output commensurate with the overall good of the firm. This approach puts an additional burden on the higher level manager because he has to prepare the budget more carefully and analyze it more flexibly.

Applications of the Budget

At this point, we will turn to a discussion of the areas of management to which budgeting can be applied. Chapter 12 will provide more details about the meaning and the preparation of the various parts of the budget.

OUTPUTS

After careful analysis of future sales possibilities, the manager will begin to plan *production* or *purchase requirements* to meet the expected sales figures. His efforts will be directed toward efficient acquisition of sufficient products to meet the anticipated demand. Without a budget, there would be only intuition and experience to establish production or purchasing needs. While these two factors *may* produce the desired results, the budget will nearly always do a better job.

INPUTS

Once the budget establishes a manufacturing firm's output requirements, the manager can go about planning for materials and labor acquisition to support the desired output levels. If he is able to plan far enough in advance, he can negotiate labor and material contracts at favorable rates because of the lack of pressure. On the other hand, if he deals with production problems on a crisis-by-crisis basis, he may find that he is forced into emergency materials purchases, overtime or less skilled labor, or even periods of no production because of the shortage of an essential item. In many cases, the budget helps managers avoid *offseason layoffs* and *peak period bulges* by spreading production more evenly through the year.

FACILITIES

In a similar fashion, good budgeting will inform the manager about the adequacy of existing facilities for his future needs. By spreading the work over the year, a smaller shop can handle as much production annually as a larger shop used seasonally. However, this approach will require the storing of additional materials and more units of the finished product. If space is not available, more will have to be rented or constructed. Additionally, increased inventory represents more noncash working capital, so that cash will have to be borrowed until sales can be made. We can see how a seemingly small decision can have a variety of effects. The preparation of a budget facilitates the anticipation of these interactions and assists in establishing coordination.

If special equipment needs are anticipated, the manager may seek a short-term rental instead of a purchase, or a purchase at favorable terms instead of a rush rental. Frequently, special equipment requires a highly skilled operator. The manager can begin to train one of his present workers instead of hiring a fully trained and more expensive temporary helper. If slack periods are budgeted, the manager can schedule *downtime* for preventive maintenance or for rearranging the production line.

ADMINISTRATION

The points brought out in the preceding paragraphs concerning production apply equally well to administrative activities. Needs for clerks, bookkeepers, secretaries, janitors, typewriters, office supplies, brooms, and the like, can be handled in a routine fashion through foresight and planning. Anticipation can lead to efficiency and higher profits in the office as well as in the factory. Bottlenecks in the flow of paperwork can create serious problems even in production. For example, if the Purchasing Department were understaffed, a purchase order might not be processed for several weeks, and thereby cause a delay in the receipt of needed materials and the ultimate stoppage of an assembly line.

CASH NEEDS

Frequently, firms go bankrupt despite their being profitable simply because they have an inadequate supply of a rare commodity—cash. By providing measures of future receipts and disbursements (routine and emergency), the treasurer can minimize the chances of running out of cash and, thus, the chances of being closed by anxious creditors. *Too much* cash is also undesirable because it is not capable of earning income. In the event of short-term borrowing, careful planning not only reduces interest charges but also creates a favorable impression on a lender. The subject of cash budgeting is discussed in more detail in Chapter 12.

CONTROL

Finally, a well-structured budget can lead to improved control of the firm. Because the manager has an indication of what *should* be done, the manager (with the accountant's help) can more easily spot what is being ineffectively done. One of the most popular (and most misunderstood) approaches to controlling with a budget is *management by exception.*

The purpose of this technique is to reduce the manager's wasted efforts by steering him quickly to those areas that deserve recognition as exceptionally good or bad. When *budgeted* quantities exist, the *actual* figures may be shown next to them in a schedule. Any large difference will stand out as an exception worthy of the manager's attention. Let us look at a hypothetical application of management by exception.

The schedule in Exhibit 11-4 is a summary of actual and budgeted payroll costs for the month of August. A report like this is sent to Arthur Johnston, the factory manager, each month. Through a *superficial* application of management by exception, Mr. Johnston would congratulate the Finishing Department foreman for his low costs, chastise the Maintenance foreman for his sloppy work, and ignore the foreman of the Inventory and Assembly Departments because they both show costs close to the budgeted figures.

However, suppose that the Assembly Department foreman had hired relatively unskilled workers at a lower hourly rate. Because the new men worked more slowly and had to be trained to use the machinery, the *actual* costs turned out to be close to the budget even though *output* was not. The Finishing Department costs were low because no work was coming out of the Assembly Department. However, costs in Finishing could have been lower if the foreman had not hired two additional workers under a contract that effectively prevented their being laid off. Maintenance charges were high because of the damage caused by the new workers in both Production

Exhibit 11-4
ABC MANUFACTURING
Payroll Report
For the Month of August 1980

Department	Budgeted	Actual	Over (Under) Budget
Inventory	$ 1,200	$ 1,200	$ –0–
Assembly	4,000	3,900	(100)
Finishing	4,000	3,200	(800)
Maintenance	2,000	3,000	1,000
Total	$11,200	$11,300	$ 100

Departments. Thus in this hypothetical situation, those items that varied from the norm were not necessarily the ones deserving reward or correction. This tool is only as good as the accounting system, the definition of exception, and the diligence of the manager.

Organization of the Budget

We will now examine how a budget might be prepared. There certainly are no hard and fast rules by which a manager *must* go about preparing or supervising the preparation of the budget. However, there are some generalizations that can be drawn to serve as useful guidelines. Depending on his managerial style, experience, staff, and complexity of his operations, he should select the approach that holds the greatest potential for success. Our intent is only to describe those methods which have been found useful in the past, and that should be useful in the future.

ASSIGNING PERSONNEL

It is essential that the manager of an entity assign his most qualified personnel to the preparation of the budget. In Exhibit 11-5, the extremely abbreviated organization chart of a medium-size manufacturing firm shows which people might be available.

The four vice presidents have responsibility for their respective functional areas. Each will delegate authority to his subordinates in order to get specific jobs done. The vice president for finance (or *controller*, or even *comptroller*) is responsible for providing whatever information is needed by anyone else

Exhibit 11-5

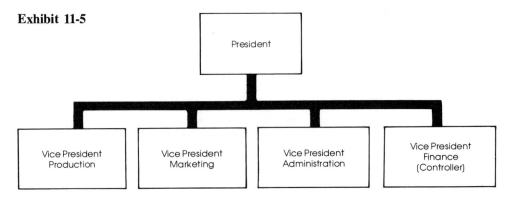

in the firm.[3] He makes decisions concerning the operations of his own department, but he only provides information for other departments. He fills a *staff* position, which means that he serves the *line* managers in an advisory capacity. He can make suggestions about management policies, but he should not establish any of them outside his own department. Because of their personal experiences and qualifications, some controllers' analyses and suggestions are accepted without question. However, a controller should not have authority to make decisions where he does not have the responsibility. Nonetheless, many managers make the mistake of assigning complete responsibility for the budget to the controller.

A better course of action is to establish a *budget committee* with representation from each of the functional areas. The controller may or may not serve as the chairman of this committee. In any case, his function should remain as information provider rather than policymaker. His department should *assist* the other managers in analyzing past results and in projecting future needs and goals. His staff will use their data management skills in combining the estimates from the various other managers. Some firms have a Budget Department to perform these tasks and to assist in evaluating actual results of the budget. However, because the vice president for finance is not accountable for the results, he should not be assigned the task of preparing the budget.

The committee will receive guidelines from the top manager or the board of directors, and attempt to translate them into more specific objectives. The means by which this translation takes place is the subject of the following section.

DERIVING THE BUDGET FIGURES

There are three ways that the budget committee can derive the estimates that appear in the final budget. Each approach has its advantages and disadvantages.

The committee may obtain the budgeted quantities strictly from the top level managers responsible for each major division of the firm. These figures are communicated downward to the lower level managers, who have virtually nothing to say about what is expected of them. For this reason, this type of approach produces an *imposed* (or top-to-bottom) *budget*.

On the other hand, the committee may seek out the information from lower level managers. Their estimates will then be coordinated and communicated upward to the higher levels. This approach is known as *participative* (or bottom-to-top), and has grown in popularity.

An advantage of the imposed budget is that the planning decisions are made by the managers who have a wider *perspective* of the firm's operations and the interactions of the different subactivities. In effect, the top managers see what resources the firm has available for the coming year, and allocate them among the various areas of responsibility. Additionally, the imposed

[3]For this reason, his title in some companies is Vice President for Information Systems.

budget is cheaper to prepare because of the relatively few persons involved in the process.

However, the imposed approach has two disadvantages. First, the upper level managers may not have precise knowledge of how the resources should be allocated in order to accomplish the firm's goals. By the nature of their positions, they are separated from the actual production and marketing processes, and may be without sufficient specific knowledge. Second, the imposition of budget figures may tend to reduce the commitment of the lower level manager to his job. If he has nothing to say about establishing his goals, then it is possible that he will not work as hard to achieve them.

The participative approach is aimed at eliminating these disadvantages. Because he takes an active role in establishing the budget figures, it seems only logical that the lower level manager will make special efforts to meet those goals. Because he is intimately involved in the day-to-day activities of his department, he knows best what his requirements and abilities are.

We must point out that there are two major disadvantages of this approach. First, the lower level manager may tend to inflate the importance of his own area of responsibility, and produce unrealistic demands. Simply stated, the approach is not based on an overall perspective.[4] Second, the participative approach may allow selfish interests to prevail. The lower manager may seek to make his job more "comfortable" by requesting more input than he really needs or by setting his output at an easily achievable level. From a practical point of view, the participative budget is more expensive to supervise and coordinate than the imposed one.

Because of these disadvantages, few firms use either a pure imposed or a pure participative budget. In practice there is generally an exchange of information between the higher and lower management levels. The first step is generally downward, to the effect that possible goals are communicated and the available resources delineated in accordance with an overall perspective. If this first "guess" is not acceptable to the lower levels, they are allowed and encouraged to suggest alternatives, either in terms of expectations or resources. Then, upper management seeks the additional resources or reduces their expectations. The output of this bargaining process is called a *negotiated budget*. It is hoped that this approach brings out the best of the other two. That is, it combines the broad perspective of top managers with the precise knowledge of line managers, and that it achieves a personal commitment from the line managers to reasonable goals. Obviously, these advantages can only be accomplished by a very expensive administrative process.

SELECTING THE TIME FRAME

In organizing a budget, it is essential to specify the time period within which the planned activity is to occur. The length of this *time frame* depends on the planned activity. For example, the foreman of a work crew may be told at the beginning of the day what his goals are *for that day*. A salesman may be

---

[4] In the vernacular, we would say that "he can't see the forest for the trees."

given a *monthly* quota. A production manager may be working with an *annual* plan. The vice president of finance may work within a *five-* or even *ten-*year span of time. In general, a shorter time frame requires more detailed information, because there is relatively less uncertainty in the near future.

The *frequency* with which a budget is prepared may or may not be the same as the period covered by the plans. If the frequency and the time frame are the same (an annual budget prepared once a year), we have a *static budget*. On the other hand, if the budget is prepared more frequently, we have a *rolling budget*. For example, in November 1980, we may prepare a one-year budget covering January through December 1981. Then in Feb-

Exhibit 11-6
FOUR SEASONS COMPANY
Rolling Budgets

	Prepared in November 1980				
	1st Quarter 1981	2nd Quarter 1981	3rd Quarter 1981	4th Quarter 1981	Total
Sales	$100,000	$120,000	$120,000	$140,000	$480,000
Cost of goods sold	(60,000)	(72,000)	(72,000)	(84,000)	(288,000)
Gross margin	$ 40,000	$ 48,000	$ 48,000	$ 56,000	$192,000
Administrative expenses	(20,000)	(24,000)	(24,000)	(28,000)	(96,000)
Income taxes (50%)	(10,000)	(12,000)	(12,000)	(14,000)	(48,000)
Net income	$ 10,000	$ 12,000	$ 12,000	$ 14,000	$ 48,000

	Prepared in February 1981				
	2nd Quarter 1981	3rd Quarter 1981	4th Quarter 1981	1st Quarter 1982	Total
Sales	$120,000	$120,000	$140,000	$140,000	$520,000
Cost of goods sold*	(80,000)	(80,000)	(93,300)	(93,300)	(346,600)
Gross margin	$ 40,000	$ 40,000	$ 46,700	$ 46,700	$173,400
Administrative expenses**	(18,000)	(18,000)	(21,000)	(21,000)	(78,000)
Income taxes†	(11,000)	(11,000)	(12,850)	(15,420)	(50,270)
Net income	$ 11,000	$ 11,000	$ 12,850	$ 10,280	$ 45,130

  * Increased purchase costs
 ** Savings through streamlined operations
  † Increased taxes (to 60%) effective January 1, 1982

	Prepared in May 1981				
	3rd Quarter 1981	4th Quarter 1981	1st Quarter 1982	2nd Quarter 1982	Total
Sales*	$132,000	$154,000	$154,000	$165,000	$605,000
Cost of goods sold	(80,000)	(93,300)	(93,300)	(100,000)	(366,600)
Gross margin	$ 52,000	$ 60,700	$ 60,700	$ 65,000	$238,400
Administrative expenses	(18,000)	(21,000)	(21,000)	(22,500)	(82,500)
Income taxes	(17,000)	(19,850)	(23,820)	(25,500)	(86,170)
Net income	$ 17,000	$ 19,850	$ 15,880	$ 17,000	$ 69,730

* Increase in sales achieved through increase in sales price without a decrease in volume.

ruary, we may prepare a new budget covering April 1981 through March 1982. In other words, an *annual* budget would be prepared every *three months* (see Exhibit 11-6). The main advantage of the rolling approach is that it constantly puts the planning process in a position that requires management attention and participation. If a static budget is prepared annually, there is a tendency to treat the process as a *once-a-year* task, with the result that the manager spends relatively little time looking ahead. A second advantage is that the rolling budget may be updated relatively easily to consider new conditions that develop during the year. Once a static budget is approved, there is a great deal of organizational friction that resists its revision.

The rolling budget is more expensive to produce and administer than the static budget. A subtle disadvantage may develop if the updating process is not carefully monitored. More specifically, it might be possible to revise the budgeted goals in an effort to cover mediocre performance rather than to adjust for an adverse turn of external events. Exhibit 11-6 presents a simplified example of a rolling budget prepared once each quarter for the following twelve months.

SELECTING AN ACTIVITY LEVEL

Chapter 6 drew a distinction between *fixed* and *variable* costs. The former remain constant regardless of the level of activity of the firm, whereas the latter increase or decrease in proportion to increases or decreases in activity. If a single activity level is selected for the budget, we are faced with interpretation problems if the *actual* activity is greater or less than the *projected* one. As an alternative to this *fixed* budget, we can construct a *flexible* budget, which is actually a series of budgets describing several possible levels of activity. Exhibit 11-7 presents a flexible budget for the

Exhibit 11-7
BINGO-BONGO BANJO COMPANY
Tuning and Tightening Department
Flexible Overhead Budget
For the Three Months Ended June 30, 1976

Level of activity		120 Percent		100 Percent		80 Percent	
Supervisor's salary	Fixed		$ 4,000		$ 4,000		$ 4,000
Building depreciation	Fixed		1,000		1,000		1,000
Machinery repairs	Fixed	$ 100		$ 100		$ 100	
	Variable	2,400	2,500	2,000	2,100	1,600	1,700
Supplies	Fixed	$ 800		$ 800		$ 800	
	Variable	5,400	6,200	4,500	5,300	3,600	4,400
Light and power	Fixed	$ 350		$ 350		$ 350	
	Variable	3,600	3,950	3,000	3,350	2,400	2,750
Custodial costs	Fixed	$ 200		$ 200		$ 200	
	Variable	4,200	4,400	3,500	3,700	2,800	3,000
Total costs			$22,050		$19,450		$16,850
Direct-labor hours			30,000		25,000		20,000

monthly overhead costs to be incurred in the Bingo-Bongo Banjo Company's Tuning and Tightening Department. The three levels of activity are expressed as 80, 100, and 120 percent of the "most likely" level of 25,000 direct-labor hours.[5]

The flexible budget is appropriate where the variable portion of the figures is relatively large. It is useful in planning because the manager is aware not only of the most likely level of input he will need to arrange, but also the level he *may* need if the production goes higher. He can thus begin anticipating the problems before the pressure of immediacy descends upon him.

A flexible budget is especially useful in our evaluation of past performance. If we have only the fixed budget, we might chastise our manager mistakenly for exceeding the expected cost figure, even though he actually performed better than we would have planned if we had anticipated operating 20 percent over budgeted activity. Thus, before we respond negatively to an actual overhead cost of $21,000 in Tuning and Tightening, we should see how many direct-labor hours were used. Similarly, before we applaud a total overhead of $17,000, we also should see what the cost should have been for the number of direct-labor hours actually worked.

Budget Difficulties

We would be telling only half the story of budgeting if we failed to point out some of the difficulties that a manager will face in preparing and implementing a budget. Let us turn to a discussion of some of these drawbacks.

THE NEW OPERATION

It is a formidable task to prepare a detailed budget for an organization that has never existed, or for a new division, product, or department of an existing firm. There are no historical records of the revenues that might be earned, the expenses that might be incurred, or the facilities that might be needed. This lack of information is the very thing that should force the new businessman to do some detailed planning and anticipating. How can a budget be prepared in this situation?

The advice of a *public accountant*[6] or a *banker* could be sought. The professional experiences of these persons are likely to include operations similar to the new one being considered. They can provide rough estimates of revenues and expenses and suggest areas that may lead to special problems, such as employee turnover, unreliable suppliers, or seasonal market behavior.

Trade associations have been formed among businessmen who operate in similar markets. These groups serve as forums for the exchange of ideas for the solution of common problems.[7] The prospective entrepreneur would be

---

[5] They could just as easily be expressed as 100, 125, and 150 percent of 20,000 direct-labor hours.

[6] That is, a CPA in public practice.

[7] An association for the purpose of *fixing prices* or *assigning markets* is not only unethical but also illegal.

wise to consult one or more of these associations to get information about likely revenues, expenses, and markups.

Additionally, the prospective businessman should adopt a *conservative* attitude. The old rule that, "if anything can go wrong, it will," applies especially to new operations. Managers tend to be overly optimistic about the potential for their products and the efficacy of their own management abilities.[8] The effort to be conservative should help counteract this fault. However, there will always be an element of risk that no amount of planning will ever eliminate.

THE IRREGULAR MARKET

The condition of the economic market for the product of a particular firm may virtually prevent any meaningful budgeting efforts. For example, farmers have been able to control many variables through hybrid seeds, fertilizers, and insecticides. But their crops may still be at the mercy of severe weather conditions. The market for their products also depends on the actions of their competitors at home and even overseas. Other firms, generally those dealing in specialized markets, may similarly find that their years are either "feast or famine" without any apparent, controllable factors.

In these situations, a carefully prepared budget may be "down the drain" if unseasonable weather or if a change in consumer tastes occurs. The need for *planning* is still essential, although it seems likely that a precise budget is nearly worthless. The planning might be manifest in a series of *contingency plans* which can be placed in operation as needed. Thus if a late spring thaw prevents the planting of one particular crop, the farmer should be ready to plant something else on short notice. Many specialty clothing stores acquire their merchandise *on consignment* rather than invest their working capital in what may prove to be unsellable items. If a particular style fails to be sold, it is returned to the manufacturer without cost, and replaced on the racks by another one that promises to be more popular.

In these situations, the manager probably should not devote much time, effort, or money to the preparation of a budget that will not be applicable.

LACK OF MANAGEMENT UNDERSTANDING

We encounter budgeting problems even in ongoing firms in stable markets. In many cases, the source of the problem is a lack of understanding of the fundamentals of budget preparation and utilization.

When a final budget figure is presented to a lower level manager, it should generally be treated as a *contract:* If he performs within that budgeted amount, he should be rewarded for having accomplished his goal. Of course, conditions and expectations may change, with the result that the previously agreed upon figure proves to be too small. The higher level manager should avoid the mistake of failing to renegotiate the budgeted

---

[8] Studies have reported that on the average, only *one* out of *fifty-eight* ideas for a new product is successful in the market.

amount. If the goal is changed unilaterally, the subordinate may find that he met a nonexistent standard and failed to meet the new one. His motivation for future periods could be diminished by this action. Thus, any budget allocation should be treated as a *commitment* which will not be revised by the manager without mutual consent.

For example, suppose that the sales manager promises a bonus to a salesman if he exceeds $100,000 of sales in a particular month. The manager should abide by his agreement, even if the salesman reaches his goal in only a week. On the other hand, it would not be wise for the manager to leave the goal at what turns out to be an excessively high level. It must be recognized that any budgeted figure is only an estimate, and is thus subject to error; but, modifications should not be made arbitrarily or unilaterally.

Some managers mistakenly consider budget figures as *exact* amounts. It may be appropriate, for example, to reward the salesman for only $90,000 of sales, even though the agreed upon goal was $100,000. It may be easier to interpret the budget with flexibility rather than to change the figure or to risk robbing the employee's motivation. Of course, wholesale disregard for budget limits should be avoided. In any case, decisions about performance should not rest simply on imperfect dollar measures.

In a properly constructed *responsibility accounting* system, performance measures must be correlated with *controllable factors*. For example, it would be improper to reward (or punish) a production manager because the level of sales went up (or down). It would be inappropriate to chastise the factory superintendent for an increased amount of property taxes or unemployment insurance. A salesman's performance should generally be measured by net sales (after sales returns) rather than gross sales or contribution margin. Gross sales can be inflated by *overselling* the product, so that it will be purchased but later returned by a dissatisfied customer. The use of contribution margin will encourage the selling of products with a high markup, but it also puts the salesman at the mercy of the Production or Purchasing Department.

If a budget is to be used as a standard of performance, the manager must be certain that his subordinates' activities are reflected appropriately by the items in the budget. Every effort must be made to identify and exclude those factors which are uncontrollable. Particular attention must be given to cost items that are composed of *allocated* amounts. As we saw in Chapter 8, a cost accounting system utilizes many compromises for the sake of expediency, with the result that an amount of overhead may include not only variable but also fixed costs. The manager must be careful that he grants or withholds rewards on a basis consistent with the *controllable* results.

In many larger firms (as well as government agencies), the budget ceases to be a *tool* for management. A budget may be prepared but used improperly. Or it may not be used at all. One of your authors knows of a circumstance where a small division of a multinational firm prepares an annual budget. The process consumes several weeks and requires the efforts of highly specialized engineers and scientists. When one of these men was asked why the budget was prepared, he explained that it was "to be submitted to the home office." Because no one ever bothered to follow up on it, there might as well have been no budget at all. The solution in this case is not to eliminate the budget but to institute its proper use.

In other cases, the budget may become an *end* in itself, rather than a *means* to the goal of profitable activity. The existence of this counterproductive attitude is evidenced by consistent disapproval of new projects because they are "not in the budget." If rewards or corrective actions are granted simply by analysis of final results in comparison with the budget, the manager is not using the planned figures properly. The budget is only a representation of future plans, and any use not consistent with that definition should be eliminated.

Some of the preceding comments deal with the situation in which the purpose of the budget is overlooked by a manager in an effort to appear to be managing. The existence of any of these behavior patterns is an indication that the budgeting procedures need to be revised and that manager should be counseled or, if necessary, replaced.

The best approach is to refer frequently to the budget as you would to a road map. While planning the trip, several routes are rejected as undesirable. However, once we get underway, we may find that traffic or road conditions make the preselected route unsuitable. Or we may see a scenic route that is not on the map. Similarly, because our budget is based on a preconceived plan, we should be ready to change it if actual conditions turn out differently or if an unanticipated opportunity develops.

LACK OF EMPLOYEE UNDERSTANDING

Difficulties may arise while using a budget not only *because* of management ignorance but also *despite* management's best efforts. If the employee (who may be a lower level manager) does not understand the budget, then it is likely that the firm will fail to accomplish what it wants to. The following paragraphs describe some of those problems.

Despite the fact that most of us work for someone else, we like to believe that we are independent and free to do as we would like. Add a budget to this picture and we develop two kinds of problems.

First, the person who prepares the budget may start to believe that he knows more than the person who receives the budget. A manager may suspect this attitude if requests for additional materials, supplies, or funds are returned from the Budget Department as "unnecessary and wasteful." Productivity may decline because these unbudgeted needs of the firm are left unsatisfied. The Budget Department should fill a *staff*, or advisory position, and should not be allowed to create policy.

Second, the worker who receives the budget may resent the intrusion upon his "kingdom," and express his feeling through counterproductive efforts (either consciously or subconsciously). Indeed, we may find that his goal is to be certain that the budget is *not* met. Rather than trying to produce a profit for the firm, he seeks to prove that he knows best by showing that the budget preparer was wrong.

The *participative* approach to budget preparation (discussed earlier in this chapter) attempts to deal with this problem by having the lower level manager provide input. However, the result may not always be what is intended. Imagine, for example, that a maintenance manager requests additional laborers but is turned down because of a gloomy economic forecast. He might try to *prove* that he needed the additional men by establishing strict safety rules which would reduce the output of his existing crews. Instead of *increasing* his personal commitment to the company's goals, the participation process would have the opposite effect.

Many firms operate under conditions of *budgetary slack:* Instead of seeking to maximize profits, they really only seek sufficient profits to satisfy the owners. When times are good, the slack tends to grow, and it shrinks when things get bad. Employees who participate in budget planning are likely to try to expand their own slack (and thus increase the chance of achieving their goals) by overestimating their needs or by understating their capabilities. A budget allocation is a measure of the *status* of the department or division head. Thus there will be another tendency to overstate one's needs. Furthermore, if the final budget is negotiated, the self-centered lower level manager's first request will be for what he is willing to get by with plus a sufficient cushion that he can later give up without really suffering.

In some circumstances, an employee may observe that he is rewarded simply for *setting* ambitious goals, whether or not he ever achieves them. The tendency in this case would be to underestimate the needs and overestimate the abilities. If very many budget figures are derived this way, the firm is likely to find itself with a great deal of productive capacity left idle because the lower levels could not deliver what they said they would.

A common starting point for budget preparation is the previous year's budget. Unfortunately, some top level managers fail to see the *tenuous* nature of the budget estimates. If Department A went over last year's budgeted expenditures, their reaction is to accuse A's manager of wastefulness and to set this year's estimate at last year's budgeted figure. On the other hand, if Department B failed to spend its entire allotment, the interpretation might be that this year's figure should be made smaller. While these actions may be appropriate in some circumstances, the decision rules must be more intricate. If these interpretations are always made, a department head will be certain that he spends at least as much as he is budgeted. This strategy assures that he will not have a cut, and may eventually lead to an increase.

In an effort to deal with this problem it is worthwhile to identify and evaluate (if only on a periodic basis) the contributions and needs of a segment of the organization without regard to any preexisting ideas. This *zero-level* analysis could show that an activity is no longer needed, or even that it is so valuable that it should be expanded.

A SOLUTION

When problems such as these arise from a lack of understanding, the only solution is to take steps to increase the comprehension of the budget's strengths and weaknesses. Other efforts deal only with the symptoms of the problems, and invariably fail or lead to further decreases in productivity.

The purpose of budgeting can be understood only through education and communication and through careful selection, advancement, and training of managers at all levels. The up-and-down channels of communication should be examined for effectiveness, so that budget administrators and managers understand each other's problems. Upper level managers should be honest in evaluating the budget requests from below, and should seek additional resources if it appears that profits can be increased.

In short, the budget can and should be the main tool for planning. It can meet this role best if its strengths and weaknesses are understood. Its major strength is that it can be flexible enough to deal with unforeseen difficulties or opportunities. It can achieve this flexibility only if it is placed in the hands of resourceful and responsible managers.

SUMMARY

This is the first of two chapters dealing with an essential element of successful management: *planning*. The first of two levels of planning occurs when the overall objectives of the firm are established. The second phase involves the selection of a particular course of action to be implemented in trying to achieve those goals. After *implementation*, the manager should determine if the goals were accomplished. He may leave the operations intact or he may seek to alter them. In either case, he is exerting *control*.

Accounting information is used in selecting the objectives and in describing the selected strategy. A *budget* is a numeric representation of management plans for a specified period of time. It is composed of estimates, and is thus subject to a number of weaknesses. It serves four major purposes within the firm: *communication, coordination, measurement of success*, and *motivation*. A budget can be applied in many ways: in particular, for planning *outputs, inputs, facilities, administration*, and *cash needs*, as well as for *control*.

In many cases, the preparation of the budget is turned over to a *budget committee* of line managers. The *controller* (the top accounting executive) should not be given full responsibility for the budget but rather should serve as chief advisor to the preparers. While he may be so respected that his suggestions are followed, final decisions must be made by the *line* managers. The controller may assume the task of compiling the estimates into a budget, but he should not be in a position to reject or accept any of these estimates. This separation is necessary because he is not accountable for the performance of the other departments.

Budget estimates may be prepared at the highest management levels and passed down from *top-to-bottom*. As an alternative to this *imposed* approach, we may see a *participative* plan whereby the estimates are derived at the lowest management levels and passed up from *bottom-to-top*. Many of the advantages of each of these systems are enjoyed under the *negotiated* budget.

A budget may be prepared only once or several times each time period. This second approach produces a *rolling* budget, which has the advantage of keeping the manager's thoughts on the planning phase of the management cycle.

In conditions where variable costs are high relative to fixed costs, some managers have found it useful to prepare several plans under different assumptions. This series of plans is called a *flexible* budget, and offers some advantages over the *fixed* budget prepared on a *best guess* about the future.

Budgeting has been recognized widely as a good tool, but it has sometimes been incorrectly applied. There are some conditions under which a normal budget simply cannot be prepared. Perhaps the greatest number of problems have arisen from misunderstandings between the manager and the managed. As is true in so many aspects of life, these problems can be alleviated through patience, effort, education, and communication.

QUESTIONS

1. What are the four steps of management? Discuss each of them briefly.
2. From where do the goals of a firm come? Are they ever changed?
3. What is the inadequacy of the goal of *maximizing profits?* What seems to be a more reasonable objective?
4. Distinguish between planning and control. Which, if either, is more important?
5. What is the function of the accountant in assisting the manager?
6. In the broadest sense, what is a *budget?* Name four things that a budget helps a manager accomplish.
7. Identify and comment briefly on five areas that can be included in a budget.
8. What is *management by exception?* How can it assist the manager? What are its weaknesses?
9. What role should be filled by the vice president of finance (controller)? Should he establish policy or prepare the budget? Why or why not?
10. Identify three approaches to preparing budget figures. What are the advantages and disadvantages of each?
11. Distinguish between static and rolling budgets.
12. What characteristics of cost behavior must be identified before a flexible budget can be prepared?
13. How can a budget be prepared for a new activity?
14. Does a relatively large amount of uncertainty in a firm's environment impair a budget's usefulness? Why or why not?

15. Briefly describe four things that can go wrong with a budget if the manager does not use it properly.

16. Briefly describe four things that can go wrong with a budget if the employee does not use it properly. Is misuse necessarily due to laziness or selfishness? Explain.

17. How can many of these problems (see questions 15 and 16) be avoided, or at least minimized?

EXERCISES

E11–1 **Budget concepts.** Pete Lester, the president of a fairly successful wholesaling operation, recently hired a new controller. Prior to this time, the previous controller had prepared tax returns and balance sheets once each year.

The new controller has suggested rather strongly that budgets be prepared and used to help Lester manage the business. He is rather dubious about this procedure, and has asked you, a close friend, for your ideas.

Required:

a. Discuss what can be gained by budgeting.

b. List and describe the business activities that could be budgeted for this firm.

c. Explain the pros and cons of letting the controller prepare and administer the budget without participation from line managers.

E11–2 **Budget concepts.** Bob Smith is a middle level manager in a fairly large and diversified manufacturing company. Six months ago, he and a small group of staff and line managers completed a lengthy and sophisticated analysis of the alternative approaches to organizing the production line in one of the company's plants under his control. He turned the plan over to the plant manager, and has been directing his attention to marketing and to some rather complex labor disputes.

This morning, he has received a report on the operation of the redesigned production line, and is distressed at the high costs being reported. A phone call to the plant manager produced this confused response: "My orders were to implement the new design according to the resources I had available. That is exactly what I have done, so I really am surprised that you are upset with the report. I have accomplished the objective in the time you allotted, and I thought I had done a good job."

Required:

In light of this discussion in the text and your own ideas, what error or errors of omission produced the cost overruns? Would a budget have prevented the poor results? Why or why not?

E11–3 **Budget concepts.** Comment on the weaknesses that are apparent in these two situations:

    a.   The sales manager has called the production manager concerning the company's plans. He is saying, "Look, I'm in the middle of setting our sales goals for the next couple of years. Tell me, given your current situation, what can we expect to have available in terms of units of product? I want to be sure that my sales estimates are smaller than your capacity."

    b.   The production manager of another company has called the sales manager concerning the company's plans. He is saying, "Look, I'm in the middle of setting our production goals for the next couple of years. Tell me, given your current situation, how many units do you expect to sell? I want to be sure that my production estimates are no greater than your expected sales level."

E11–4 **Budget concepts.** The managers at all levels of the Green Company are in the annual process of preparing the budget for the next fiscal year, which starts in about 30 days. The production supervisor is just closing a budget meeting with his foreman: "To summarize what we have decided, then, it is agreed that we will hire 10 new workers for the line, and one new foreman to oversee their training and to get them worked into our usual way of doing things. It looks like we'll need two new milling machines, as well as a grinder to replace the one that is worn out. The average of our estimates produces a budget projection of $350,975 in excess of this year's. I don't know about you, but I am really looking forward to finding out what level of output the budget is going to call for in the coming year. We made the target easily this year, and I think these additions will assure our success next year."

Required:

Comment on the situation that seems to exist in the Green Company. What, if anything, would you see as a potential change for the better?

E11–5 **Management by exception.**

    a.   Rearrange the information that appears below and on page 308 into an income statement that will enable the use of *management by exception* (you will need to define an exception first).

	Budget	Actual
Advertising expense	$ 5,000	$ 10,000
Cost of goods sold	41,000	76,250
Depreciation expense	8,000	7,000
Maintenance expense	5,000	2,000
Office wages	3,000	3,000
Officer salary	4,000	4,500
Rent expense	6,000	5,500

Sales	$100,000	$152,500
Sales returns	7,200	18,000
Selling commissions	10,000	15,250
Selling salaries	2,000	2,000

b. Identify the exceptions that seem to be *good*.

c. Identify the exceptions that seem to be *bad*.

d. Suggest some possible reasons for each of the exceptions. If you were the manager, what should you do before undertaking congratulatory or corrective action?

e. What are the strong and weak points of management by exception?

E11–6 Management by exception.

a. Rearrange the following facts into a format conducive to management by exception. They concern the annual costs of providing the physical facilities of a small factory.

	Budget	**Actual**
Repairs	$45,000	$30,000
Custodial supplies	17,500	12,000
Utilities		
Water	1,200	1,200
Lighting	18,300	24,800
Heating	11,800	9,200
Rent	24,000	24,000
Security	19,500	11,000
Wages		
Regular	40,000	30,000
Overtime	25,000	30,000

b. For each item in your analysis in *a*, suggest both a favorable and an unfavorable reason for the result.

c. If you were the manager, what would you do before taking action to commend or correct the responsible persons?

E11–7 Rolling budget.   Presented below is the first version of Frankfurt Industries budget for 1980:

	First Six Months	**Second Six Months**
Sales	$ 7,900,000	$ 9,500,000
Cost of goods sold	(5,700,000)	(6,900,000)
Gross margin	$ 2,200,000	$ 2,600,000
Administration expense	(1,200,000)	(1,300,000)
Selling expense	(700,000)	(900,000)
Income before taxes	$ 300,000	$ 400,000
Income taxes	(150,000)	(200,000)
Income after taxes	$ 150,000	$ 200,000

In May it was decided to adjust the original estimates for the second six months as follows:

Sales	Up 10%
Cost of goods sold	Up 12%
Administration expense	Down 5%
Selling expense	Up 15%
Income taxes	At 35% of income before taxes

Required:

a. What would be the revised amount of net income after taxes?

b. What are the strong and weak points of rolling budgets?

E11–8 Flexible budgets.

a. From the following facts, prepare a set of annual flexible budgets for sales levels of 10,000, 15,000, and 20,000 packages of Cheap Dip:

Selling price	$7.00 per package
Cost of goods sold	$4.00 per package
Administration expenses	$8,000 per year; $0.10 per package
Selling expenses	$3,000 per year; $0.70 per package
Income taxes	40% of net income

b. What is the average aftertax income per unit in each of the three cases?

c. If actual aftertax profits were $15,000 on sales of 16,000 units, was the company successful? Carefully support your answer.

E11–9 Cash flow concepts. Explain at least four general reasons in support of planning a firm's annual cash flow when the budget for the same year shows a substantial aftertax profit.

PROBLEMS

P11-1 Concepts of planning. Think of a special need of the students of your school that could be met by a small business operated by you and a few of your friends.

a. Establish a set of specific goals that would be appropriate for this small firm.

b. List several alternative approaches to accomplishing these objectives.

c. For one of these alternatives, identify the facilities, investments, and other inputs you would need, and suggest sources for each.

d. Identify the information you would need in order to determine whether or not you were successful.

P11–2   *Budget approaches.* Three executives are in the middle of a meeting devoted to planning this year's budgetary process.

Adams is saying: "As I see it, our job is to develop the budget figures up here and then just pass them on down to the lower levels. After all, we know what resources the firm has available and where we want to be going."

Benson follows: "I hate to disagree, but I really see it the other way around. I don't know of anybody who has a better feeling for what the firm can accomplish than those managers out there on the firing line. We need to seek their advice and estimates, and then do everything that we can to make available the resources that they need."

Carson is next: "Perhaps I am missing the boat someplace, but it seems to me that there ought to be some way for the people in the shop to express to us what they feel they can do. However, we are responsible for the firm, and we have to be sure that it stays out of trouble."

Required:

Comment on each of these three approaches, being sure to identify the strengths and weaknesses of each.

P11–3   *Management by exception.*

a. Rearrange the following information into an income statement presentation that will facilitate the use of management by exception:

	Budgeted for 1980	**Actual for 1980**
Sales	$4,269,000	$3,420,000
Sales returns	25,000	20,000
Cost of goods sold	3,415,000	2,650,000
Officers' salaries	200,000	200,000
Other salaries and wages	108,000	72,000
Depreciation, shop equipment	75,000	60,000
Office and shop rent	24,000	24,000
Depreciation, office equipment	14,000	12,000
Building security	14,000	6,000
Custodial services	20,000	13,000
Maintenance expenses	12,000	5,000
Property taxes	5,000	6,000
Property insurance	2,000	2,000
Liability insurance	2,000	–0–
Bad debt expense	3,000	1,000
Gain on sale of securities	–0–	10,000

b. Which of these items (select as many as you feel appropriate) would you choose to investigate first? Why?

c. Do the figures suggest an overall favorable or unfavorable picture? Why?

P11–4 *Rolling budget*. The Blue and Gray Company prepares a three-year rolling budget once each year. The following initial projections were made during 1980 (in thousands of dollars):

	1981	1982	1983	1984	1985
Sales	$150	$160	$160	$180	$200
Cost of goods sold	90	95	95	110	125
Selling expenses	15	15	20	20	25
Other expenses	10	15	15	20	20
Income tax rate	40%	40%	40%	40%	40%

Required:

a. Prepare income budgets for 1981, 1982, and 1983.

b. During 1981, the budget staff recommended the following revisions in the original data:

	1982	1983	1984	1985
Sales	Down 5%	Same	Up 5%	Up 10%
Cost of goods sold	Up 7%	Up 7%	Up 7%	Up 8%
Selling expenses	Same	Same	Up 4%	Up 5%
Other expenses	Same	Same	Up 3%	Up 3%
Income tax rate	Same	52%	52%	52%

Using these changes, prepare income budgets for 1982, 1983, and 1984 (rounded to the nearest thousand). (*Note:* In working *a* and *b*, it will be necessary for you to prepare budgets for the later years.)

c. During 1982, the budget staff recommended the following revisions in the previously revised projections:

	1983	1984	1985
Sales	Up 5%	Up 5%	Up 10%
Cost of goods sold	Same	Same	Down 5%
Selling expenses	Same	Down 5%	Same
Other expenses	Up 10%	Up 10%	Up 10%
Income tax rate	Same	Same	Same

Using these changes, prepare income budgets for 1983, 1984, and 1985 (rounded to the nearest thousand).

P11–5 *Flexible budgets*.

a. From the following projections, prepare a flexible budget for the factory of Wonder Widgets at 80 percent, 100 percent, and 125 percent of the most likely level of 100,000 units per year:

Labor:
Indirect: variable $1.00 per unit
            fixed $40,000.00 per year
Direct $6.00 per unit

Materials:

Indirect: variable	$0.50 per units
fixed	$11,000.00 per year
Direct	$7.50 per unit

Overhead:

Supervision	$45,000.00 per year
Maintenance:	
Building	$18,000.00 per year
Machinery: fixed	$15,000.00 per year
variable	$0.45 per unit
Tools	$0.04 per unit
Depreciation:	
Building	$50,000.00 per year
Machinery	$1.10 per unit
Utilities: fixed	$15,000.00 per year
variable	$0.06 per unit
Property taxes	$11,000.00 per year

b. If actual expenditures are $2,000,000 for production of 110,000 units, was the budget met?

c. If actual production were at 200,000 units, would it necessarily be proper to use the same data that were presented in *a*? Why or why not?

d. Under what conditions is a flexible budget useful?

P11–6 Flexible budgets. The Melcher Company produces farm equipment at several plants. The business is seasonal and cyclical in nature. The company has attempted to use budgeting for planning and controlling activities, but the variable nature of the business has caused some company officials to be skeptical about its usefulness. The accountant for one plant has been using flexible budgeting to help his plant manager control operations.

The company president has asked for more details. In preparing his report, the accountant has the following information available:

Normal monthly capacity of the plant in direct-labor hours is 10,000 hours, or 5,000 units of output.

Material costs	6 pounds @ $1.50	$9.00 per unit
Labor costs	2 hours @ $3.00	$6.00 per unit

Overhead (estimated at normal monthly capacity):

Variable (controllable):	
Indirect labor	$ 6,650
Indirect materials	600
Repairs	750
Total variable	$ 8,000
Fixed (noncontrollable):	
Depreciation	$ 3,250
Supervision	3,000
Total fixed	$ 6,250
Total	$14,250

Planned units for January:	4,000 units
Actual data for January:	
Hours worked	8,400
Units produced	3,800
Costs incurred:	
Material	$36,000
Direct labor	25,200
Indirect labor	6,000
Indirect materials	600
Repairs	1,800
Depreciation	3,250
Supervision	3,000
Total	$75,850

Required:

a. Prepare a budget for January, using the projected units of output as the activity base.

b. Prepare a report for January comparing actual and budgeted costs for the *actual* activity for the month, using hours worked as the activity base.

c. Prepare a report for January comparing actual and budgeted costs for the *actual* activity of the month, using units produced as the activity base.

d. Can flexible budgeting be applied to the nonmanufacturing activities of the company? Explain your answer.

(CMA Adapted)

P11-7 **Budget difficulties.** Identify the real problem in each of these five hypothetical cases, and suggest a solution:

a. An interoffice phone call to the factory supervisor has just been put through: "Steve? This is Sam Leonard in Budget. I just heard from a friend in Purchasing that you've just ordered another JL-1750 Automatic Bender. As you realize, of course, your budget allows you only three of these machines, and this one is number four for the year. I don't have anything to do with it, but if I were you, I wouldn't count on getting it at this point."

b. The department manager has called his assistant in for a brief conference. "Bob, it's that time again when we need to start thinking about our budget. Here's the budget for this year, and the amount we have spent so far. First, I want you to be sure that somehow or other we spend everything we're supposed to, and then I want you to prepare a new budget by adding 10 percent onto this year's figures. For example, requisition all those office supplies we haven't used yet, and we can store them in your office."

c. Roger Burns, sales manager for region 17B, is talking to his assembled staff: "Well, team, we just received word on the annual ripoff by the budget people! They say that we're supposed to cut down on our travel and entertainment expenses by 10 percent, while we have to get our sales up 15 percent. These amounts are entirely unreasonable, but what can you expect from a bunch of clerks who sit behind a desk all day? Laugh if you want, but I'm tired of it. So, I want you to keep on doing just what you have been, and we'll show them who can tell what to who!"

d. The factory manager is conferring with the supervisor of one of his smaller departments: "Well, Doug, I have some good news and some bad news. I know how pleased you will be to learn that your effort to streamline your shop and improve your crew's morale has not gone unnoticed. You have impressed a lot of important people. On the bad side, the company's sales have been below the budget, and we've been told to cut back. As you know, your department is not the most important one around here, so I'm asking that you lay off 20 percent of your crew by the end of the month. Then, we figure that you'll have to let the same number go by the end of the next month."

e. The chief accountant is counseling one of his section supervisors: "Tom, I guess you realize that it's awfully tough for us to justify our efforts through increased profits because nothing we do can affect sales directly. Consequently, even though some of the people up above have really liked those reports and analyses that you've been sending them, you have spent too much of our computer budget for the year. As much as I hate to, you're just going to have to cut down on your usage until we get our budget figures for next year."

P11–8 **Budget concepts.** The Cannon Company is a small-to-medium manufacturer of precision engineered components of various types of electronic devices. More by accident than design, annual sales have reached the $20,000,000 level, but indications of problems have begun to show.

The primary interest of Bill Cannon, founder and president of the company, has been research into and development of new construction techniques to improve the reliability and durability of existing component designs.

The marketing efforts have been handled by Tom Winder, who is an engineer, and who has assembled a sales staff with engineering backgrounds. With the exception of a 1-year government contract that brought in $4,000,000 for the delivery of a large quantity of identical components, the thrust of the marketing effort has been for the *sales engineers* to draw up unique specifications for each customer, with the result that much of the manufacturing consists of low-volume production runs, with high training and other setup costs.

The production line is supervised by Glenna Johnson, also an engineer, who has had significant experience in this field. Typically, she emphasizes promptness in filling a customer's order. She seldom takes a worker off a job to start another one, as she usually just assigns new jobs to whoever has completed the old one.

The inventories, which consist mostly of raw materials, are managed by Bert Randall, who also assists Glenna Johnson. Typically, he relies on quick delivery of materials by suppliers and orders according to the needs of each individual job. Over the last several years, the levels of physical inventories have declined steadily, and their dollar value even further because of the nature of the market.

George Campbell, the information system specialist and controller, has spent most of his efforts on the financial accounting system, and on the management of payroll, accounts receivable, and accounts payable.

Cannon and Campbell recently attended an executive development program on budgeting and the benefits it promises for firms with well-structured and divided responsibilities. They feel that their company might be better off if some budgets were prepared, but are not sure where to start.

Required:

a. What activities of the Cannon Company can you identify as *budgetable*? Are there any that you think cannot be planned? Explain.

b. An apparent problem in the firm is a lack of coordination among the functional areas. Can you suggest some revisions in policy to bring about coordination? Would a budget of some type be helpful? Why?

c. A management conference subsequent to the return of the two executives produced reactions from the various supervisors that Campbell should assume full responsibility for budgeting preparation and supervision. He is reluctant to do so, because the seminar leader had suggested strongly that the controller not be put in such a position. What should he say to argue against their proposal?

12

The Budgeting Process

Chapter 11 established that planning is an essential part of management and that a budget is a numerical representation of management plans. In this chapter, we will present more specific information on the preparation of several different types of budgets. In particular, we will look at sales, production, administration, and cash budgets.

BUDGETING SALES

Every activity of a profit oriented firm, from the hiring of a bookkeeper to the planting of a lawn to the building of a factory, must be directed to one overall goal—*sales*. If a product or a service cannot be produced at a sufficiently low cost so that it can be sold and profits can be earned, there is no economic reason for the firm to exist. Production or administrative activities cannot be carried out in a vacuum. Unless the firm's product can be sold, it should not be produced, and there is nothing to be administered.

Thus, the beginning point in the budgeting process is the development of the sales goals. This step is like the first one in the proverbial long journey: it not only starts us off but it also establishes the direction of the rest of the process. The usefulness of the entire budget depends on the reliability of our sales estimates. If it becomes apparent during this planning phase that we have to change the sales goals, we must often begin the entire process all over again because virtually every activity of the firm is tied to the level of sales. If our sales estimate is too low, profits will be lost because we will be unable to provide all the output our customers want. If our sales estimate is too high, we can encounter serious problems from incurring more costs than we recover. For these reasons, a great deal of effort should be expended on the preparation of the *forecast of sales*.

Much of the expertise for the preparation of a sales forecast is generally found within the marketing staff of the firm. This group will gather information from many sources, only one of which is the sales staff. For all but a very few firms, the state of the overall economy must be considered. The interdependence of our modern economy assures that no one is insulated against slowdowns and recessions. Marketing studies (especially consumer surveys and test markets) are done in order to determine whether or not the demand for a particular item exists, and, if so, how large it will be. The firm's experts will plot a strategy to acquire as much of that market as is feasible and profitable for the present condition of the firm or for its condition after a possible expansion. Various possibilities (such as price changes or specialization for particular submarkets) will be evaluated and accepted or rejected. From a group of alternative strategies, the budget committee will select the one to be used, and the planning phase will begin. An important factor in this decision will be the *price* at which the product will be sold. We will turn now to a discussion of the factors that will affect this pricing decision.

Pricing Factors

We will approach the pricing decision on three points: *market situation, cost recovery,* and *profit levels.*

MARKET SITUATION

In establishing a pricing policy, we must know if a market for our product already exists. If other companies are selling similar products, half of the pricing decision has been made for us. Unless we can create a higher level of perceived quality, it is unlikely that we can sell our product at a higher price than our competitors. We have to decide if we can achieve our sales goals by using the existing price or by using a lower one. The results of market surveys should help us make this choice. If we do decide to undercut the opposition, we have to weigh such problems as setting the price too low to earn a profit and our competitor's reactions.

On the other hand, if we are creating a new market, we have several additional factors to contend with. First, we have some freedom in selecting the price without any present concern for our competitors. In the long run, we can expect that competition will enter the picture. Thus we must build flexibility into our pricing system, so that we can respond quickly to any strategy that may be employed by other firms.

For a new product, there may be a tendency to "charge what the market will bear." While there are sound economic reasons for doing so, there may be social reasons for not following this strategy. Despite the fact that a person would pay all that he had in order to receive lifesaving treatments from a kidney machine, he will generally get by for much less. Consumers are quite sensitive to efforts at exploitation, and have been known to refuse to buy products that are priced unreasonably high over costs. Excessive prices also tend to attract competitors and government controls. For these reasons, this strategy is usually modified before it is applied.

Several firms have approached the pricing decision from another direction. They determine through market research first what the price of a new product should be in order to attract customers, and *then* they undertake to design the product so that it can be manufactured at a cost sufficiently low to assure a profit. This approach has been used successfully for not only small items (such as cartridge-loading cameras) but also large ones (such as specialty automobiles). This practice is certain to become more and more prevalent, especially as marketing research techniques become more common and more sophisticated.

COST RECOVERY

A rather uncomplicated law of economics holds that the sales revenues must exceed the cost of obtaining those revenues, if the firm is to survive. Two important questions must be answered, however: What is the cost of a product? By how much should the revenues exceed the costs?

Section 2 presented some rather detailed information about costs and how they are measured. It should be apparent that *cost* has several different meanings, and that the measurement of cost is frequently dependent on assumptions and compromises. How can we deal with these variables?

In the long run, our sales revenues must exceed our *total costs,* which include not only production efforts but also sales and administration activities. We can project these costs and divide them by the units to be produced in order to get an *average unit cost.* We could then add a *profit margin* to arrive at our selling price. But there are some problems that can develop out of this *cost-plus* strategy.

First, the approach almost completely neglects the competition. We simply assume that our present and future competitors have or will have essentially the same cost and the same profit margin that we do. To make a point by exaggeration, a firm might produce a book of matches at a cost of $0.15. After allowing for a "reasonable" markup, the matches would be offered for sale at $0.18 and none would be sold if the existing market price were only $0.05. In special situations, such as those that surround government contracts,[1] *cost-plus pricing* is used because there is no competition in the market once the contract is signed. In general, this approach must be supplemented by careful research of the market.

Second, we must consider the situation where more than one type of product is produced. How can we determine *the* cost of each of 5, 10, 100, or even 1,000 different items? We cannot achieve this allocation without some compromises, with the result that the cost of the *cost-plus* may not be meaningful.

---

[1] It was concern over the lack of control of the "cost" of "cost-plus" government contracts that led Congress to establish the *Cost Accounting Standards Board,* which has as its objective the determination and publication of cost accounting principles to be applied to government contractors. It is expected that the impact of CASB pronouncements will be profound because of the extensive number of firms that contract to perform services for or provide products to an agency of the federal government.

In the effort to deal with this problem, many modern businessmen have turned to *contribution pricing*. Instead of looking only to *total* costs, the decision maker looks at the *variable* cost of producing the item to be sold. The selling price is set at a level sufficient to recover *at least* the variable (marginal) costs. Any amount received in excess of the variable costs is recognized as a *contribution* to the fixed costs. In the aggregate, of course, profits arise only if the revenues exceed the sum of the variable and fixed costs.

Let us look at an example to see how contribution pricing works. Suppose that a special analysis prepared by the Hy-Heel Shoe Company accountant has reported the following data for the production of 50,000 pairs of shoes during the coming period:

Fixed costs	$100,000
Variable costs	250,000
Total costs	$350,000
Cost per unit	$7.00

If the desired profit for the year is $100,000, the selling price of each of the 50,000 pairs should be $9.00.

Suppose further that the firm receives a request for a bid from the Lite-Step Shoe Stores concerning the purchase of an additional 10,000 pairs of a special shoe that would be sold at retail stores in another part of the country. The plant has sufficient equipment to produce the shoes, which will not be sold until after the slowest part of the production year. What price should the Hy-Heel Shoe Company offer?

The answer, of course, is "as high as possible." But competition may exist, and a more appropriate price should be sought. Word reaches the manager that the Brass Buckle Shoe Factory will submit a bid in the neighborhood of $7.00 per pair. The vice president of marketing has recommended a $6.50 price, but the president has objected that a price that low "would not cover our costs, much less give us any profits."

To respond to this argument, let's turn to the *contribution margin*. How large will the contribution to fixed costs be if the shoes sell at $6.50 per pair?

Revenue	$ 6.50 per pair
Variable costs	(5.00) per pair
Contribution	$ 1.50 per pair

Thus, if the 10,000 pairs are sold at $6.50, there will be another $15,000 to cover the fixed costs. The total production can be summarized as follows:

	Regular	Special	Total
Revenue	$450,000	$65,000	$515,000
Variable costs	$250,000	$50,000	$300,000
Fixed costs	100,000	–0–	100,000
Total costs	$350,000	$50,000	$400,000
Profits	$100,000	$15,000	$115,000

Indeed, the firm will be better off for any sales price on this order in excess of $5.00, if no additional fixed costs are incurred. We could not afford to pursue this strategy for all units unless we had sufficient volume to cover the fixed costs and the desired profit. Suppose, for example, that all 60,000 pairs were priced to sell at $6.50.

	Regular	Special	Total
Revenue	$ 325,000	$65,000	$390,000
Variable costs	$ 250,000	$50,000	$300,000
Fixed costs	100,000	–0–	100,000
Total costs	$ 350,000	$50,000	$400,000
Profit (loss)	$ (25,000)	$15,000	$ (10,000)

The contribution margin ($1.50 × 60,000 units = $90,000) is inadequate to cover even the fixed costs, and provides no progress toward the desired $100,000 profit. Contribution pricing is clearly appropriate in cases where special orders can be used to occupy excess capacity. It is useful even if we would not be operating at all except for the special order. In this situation, any sales price in excess of the marginal cost would provide a contribution to the fixed costs.

In other special circumstances, the best strategy may be to *ignore completely* the cost of producing the item. Suppose the Hy-Heel Shoe Company discovers 5,000 pairs of high-button shoes in a remote corner of its warehouse. Would it be useful to determine the cost of those shoes from the accounting records? Even if there had been no inflation, the old cost figures would be meaningless. The only relevant facts are whether they can be sold or not, and who is willing to pay the most for them. The student should recall from the material in Chapter 9 that the old cost is a *sunk cost* and has no relevant bearing on our current pricing policy.

In dealing with joint products, their *cost* is estimated by an allocation of the total cost. The only relevant facts for pricing these items are the same two: Who will buy them and how much will they pay? In this case the costs are not sunk; they are simply unidentifiable and nondifferential. Our best strategy is to accept the best price from the potential buyers without regard to the allocated costs.

In summary, it is not sufficient to look only at the costs or the market value of our product. It is unlikely that we will be able to sell it at a price above an existing market level, and we should not undertake to produce anything if the incremental costs exceed the incremental revenues. If the product already exists, our choice is between selling or holding. The cost has become sunk. The only significant factor is whether there are buyers who might pay more than others.

PROFIT LEVELS

The third major point to be considered in establishing prices concerns the *amount* of profit that management would like to achieve in the upcoming time period. Classical economics assumed that the goal was to *maximize*

Exhibit 12-1

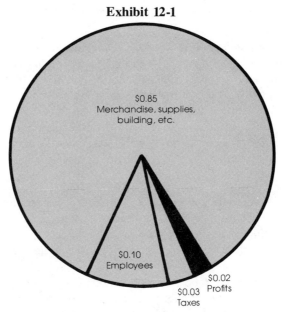

$0.85
Merchandise, supplies,
building, etc.

$0.10
Employees

$0.02 Profits

$0.03
Taxes

short-run profits, or to get as much as possible as soon as possible. Studies of organizations indicate that the real goal is to obtain *satisfactory* profits, which will be somewhat less than the maximum.[2] The size of profits that will satisfy a manager depends on a number of variables.

Two measures frequently applied in gauging the size of the profits are: *return on sales* and *return on investment.* The *return on sales* indicator is the ratio of net income to revenue. It represents the portion of each sales dollar that eventually ends up as profit. One chain of grocery stores has used the return on sales percentage in promotional efforts to show that profits were reasonable.[3] To illustrate the relationship, they used a *pie diagram* similar to the one in Exhibit 12-1. This 2 percent profit percentage can easily be misinterpreted.

A more appropriate measure of profit reasonableness is the *return on investment,* which is the ratio between net profits and the assets used to produce those profits. Suppose, for example, that the grocer has an average investment in inventory and facilities of $50,000. If his annual sales are $500,000 and he earns a 2 percent return on sales, his profit will amount to $10,000. Suppose also that a small manufacturer has facilities and inventory amounting to $50,000. His annual sales are only $60,000, of which 15 percent ($9,000) is profit.

If we look at return on investment, we will observe that the grocer earned at a rate of 20 percent ($10,000 income/$50,000 investment); the manufacturer earned at a rate of only 18 percent ($9,000 income/$50,000 investment). Whether either of these businessmen is exploiting his customers through excessive profits is a social judgment. It is apparent, however, that the return on sales percentage is not an appropriate measure for comparing firms in different industries.

[2] See J. G. March and H. A. Simon, *Organizations* (New York: Wiley, 1958), p. 169; and D. Katz and R. L. Kahn, *The Social Psychology of Organizations* (New York: Wiley, 1966), pp. 283–84.

[3] As described in *Consumer Reports* (February 1974), p. 105.

The discussion in Chapter 3 pointed out that despite the return on investment ratio's *conceptual* superiority, it is by no means *operationally* perfect.
The weaknesses of the ratio lie in the defects of the two numbers that are
used in its calculation: *net income* and *investment*. Because of the alternatives available for computing these numbers,[4] the budget committee should
establish clearly what is meant by the rate of return. From this point, the
desired amount of profit can be established, and a pricing policy selected.

Sales Volume

It is not sufficient to merely divide the total desired profit by the profit per
unit figure to arrive at the desired volume of sales. For example, suppose a
firm's management hopes to achieve an annual income of $100,000 by sell-
ing a product that sells for $1.00 more than its average unit cost. It would be
inappropriate to establish the desired sales volume as 100,000 units, *unless* it
is known that the firm could capture a share of the market sufficient to sell
that many units. Other problems arise when a firm markets several different
products, each of which makes a different contribution to profits.

Thus, the sales forecast should be stated initially in terms of potential
volume of units to be sold. When there are many products, the sum of their
profits can be compared with the total profit desired, and adjustments made
accordingly. It is the task and responsibility of the Marketing Department to
generate the sales estimates.[5] The controller (or his staff) will translate these
volume estimates into dollar figures. As always, the estimates should be
verified and adjusted if actual experience indicates that they are inappropriate.

Cost-volume-profit analysis (discussed in Chapter 6) is a good tool at the
initial stages of sales planning. From the information about costs and revenues, the budget committee can determine if the proposed volume will generate the desired profit.

The Sales Budget

The *sales forecast* is merely the estimate of the level of activity for the firm
during the coming year. It should not be confused with the *sales budget,*
which is the numeric representation of the Marketing Department plans for
the coming year. The amount of detail will increase as the budget is translated into specific plans for lower levels.

Exhibit 12-2 presents a hypothetical sales budget for the Marketing Department of Hy-Heel Shoes. Notice that the budget not only establishes *sales
goals* but also describes expenditures for accomplishing those goals. The
district sales managers should treat these allocations as authorization for

---

[4] There are a number of sources of variability in income measurement, such as alternative
  inventory and depreciation policies. Similarly, investment can be computed as original cost,
  original cost less depreciation, or even replacement cost. Additionally, both of these factors
  are subject to distortion from the price-level changes discussed in Chapter 5.

[5] As we mentioned earlier, the research should include projections about the total economy
  (perhaps international in scope), the industry, and then the firm's share of the market.

Exhibit 12-2

HY-HEEL SHOE COMPANY
Sales Budget
For The Year Ended December 31, 1980

	East*	Midwest	West	Total
District quotas:				
Unit sales:				
Product 1	10,000	30,000	10,000	50,000
Product 2	3,000	1,000	2,000	6,000
Product 3	25,000	5,000	10,000	40,000
Dollar sales:				
Product 1	$ 75,000	$225,000	$ 70,000	$370,000
Product 2	60,000	20,000	50,000	130,000
Product 3	100,000	40,000	80,000	220,000
Total Sales	$235,000	$285,000	$200,000	$720,000
Selling expenses:				
National office:				
Salaries				$ 20,000
Advertising				12,200
Travel				5,000
Entertainment				5,000
Total				$ 42,200
District offices:				
Salaries	$ 20,000	$ 16,000	$ 8,000	$ 44,000
Commissions	4,700	8,550	10,000	23,250
Entertainment	7,000	3,000	6,000	16,000
Travel	3,000	6,000	11.900	20,900
Samples	2,350	2,850	1,900	7,100
Total	$ 37,050	$ 36,400	$ 37,800	$111,250
Total Selling Expenses				$153,450

*Eastern regional quotas:	Northeast	Mideast	Southeast	Total
Unit sales:				
Product 1	2,000	5,000	3,000	10,000
Product 2	1,000	500	1,500	3,000
Product 3	15,000	4,000	6,000	25,000

making those expenditures. Their performance should be evaluated not only in terms of whether they met their quotas but also in terms of whether they exceeded their budgets. Each of these district budgets would be broken down into regional budgets, as was done for the unit sales quota for the Eastern district.

The sales *budget* also includes the expenses that are expected to be incurred in the efforts to make the sales. The national office will be responsible for supervising the field offices, and for promotional campaigns. The head of the office will travel about the country to visit the salesmen, and perhaps to participate in large transactions. Note that the districts do not have the same quotas, the same expense allowances, or even the same prices. Care must be taken to provide for the varying markets that each district represents. In the example, the salesmen in the West have lower salaries (only 4 percent of sales), but higher commissions. The Midwest salesmen do not spend as much on entertainment, but travel costs are higher (also for the West) because the customers are more dispersed. The performance in each district should be evaluated on the basis of what is expected of them, rather than on a national basis.

BUDGETING PRODUCTION

Once the sales forecast is produced, it is the task of the budget committee to prepare plans for making the product available for sale. Although the following discussion deals with the manufacturing context, the main principles also apply to the retailing situation.

Outputs

The sales forecast establishes the number of products that will be *sold*; the production budget must deal with the products that are to be manufactured. In the simplest case production output will equal sales. However, it is more likely that some of the items to be sold will come from the inventory of finished goods. It is also highly possible that some of the production output will be added to the finished goods inventory and sold at a later date. Thus, it is necessary to coordinate production management not only with sales management, but also with inventory management.

The flow of goods through inventory can be described in an equation:

Beginning inventory + Production output – Goods sold = Ending inventory

This expression can be more conveniently rearranged:

Production output = Goods sold + Ending inventory – Beginning inventory

This statement can be further simplified:

Production output = Goods sold + Change in inventory

In the simplest case, there is no change in the inventory, and the costs of production are equal to the costs of the goods to be sold. If the inventory is to be increased, production must be increased. If the inventory is to be depleted, then production output will be below sales volume.

We should examine the circumstances under which a firm would want to alter its inventory balance. If management believes that future sales will be growing, they will seek to utilize as much present productive capacity as possible in order to produce at the lowest cost possible. In a period of inflation (or prior to a period when inflation is *expected*), it may be wise to incur costs now and to earn revenues later.[6] The finished goods can be held in anticipation of being sold at higher prices. On the other hand, if a *decline* in future demand for a particular item is expected, it is appropriate to reduce the inventory of that product in order to avoid holding losses from declines in price.

---

[6]This decision should be made only after considering other factors, especially the costs of financing expanded inventories and providing storage space. Other factors that enter into the timing of production will be discussed later in this chapter.

Exhibit 12-3
HY-HEEL SHOE COMPANY
Production Budget (Units of Output)
For the Year Ended December 31, 1980

	Product 1	Product 2	Product 3
Inventory (December 31)	12,000	1,000	14,000
Inventory (January 1)	(10,000)	(3,000)	(14,000)
Increase (decrease)	2,000	(2,000)	–0–
Sales volume	50,000	6,000	40,000
Budgeted production	52,000	4,000	40,000

If several products are manufactured on the same production line and stored in the same warehouse, it may be desirable to adjust the *mix* as the markets change. For example, if sales of Product *A* are expected to slip, while demand for Product *B* grows, it would be reasonable to cut back on the production of *A* in favor of *B*. It would also be helpful to diminish the amount of *A* in the warehouse in order to make room for more units of *B*.

The schedule presented in Exhibit 12-3 is the overall production budget for Hy-Heel Shoes. If there were more than one factory, it would be necessary to assign a quantity of output of each product to the appropriate factory.

The publication of the production output budget accomplishes the *coordination* of the efforts of the production and sales divisions. The latter group knows what it is to sell and the former knows what it is to produce. Both groups will work to accomplish these goals as efficiently as possible. The establishment and use of these specific targets is much more effective than broad statements, such as "sell as much as you can," or "cut the costs of production."

In a retailing firm, the production budget is replaced by a *purchases* budget which designates the quantity of merchandise that should be acquired. The objective of this group is to buy the desired products at the best prices available.

Inputs

After coordinating plans for output, the next logical step calls for the production manager to begin formulating specific plans for accomplishing these objectives. He should anticipate the acquisition of direct labor, direct materials, and such items of overhead that are subject to his control.

In planning his needs for labor, the manager needs to examine such factors as the skill levels of his employees, recruitment of additional workers, furloughing of nonessential workers, training for special skills and safety, vacations and other times when workers will be off, and union contracts.

Many tasks in production require specially skilled employees. The manager should identify his needs for these workers and see whether his present payroll will provide. If not, he will have to consider training some of his presently unskilled workers for the more specialized jobs. As an alternative, he may consider hiring new people to do the work. On the other hand, if his payroll provides *too many* skilled employees, he must seek a productive way to use them or face the distasteful and socially undesirable step of laying them off.

The foreman may have to deal occasionally with what might be called the "mix" of his workers. When the same job can be done by more than one class of workers, he should seek out the best combination. For example, a task may be completed by either skilled, semiskilled, or unskilled workers. Consider the following facts about a particular phase in the production process:

Skill Level	Hours to Complete	Cost per Hour
A	6	$5
B	8	4
C	9	3

His best choice would be to assign the job to workers of skill level *C* because the total cost ($27) will be less than for *A* ($30) or for *B* ($32). In making this decision, he must consider alternative activities to which the workers can be assigned. If level *A* workers will be idle or assigned to less productive jobs, these costs must be compared with the savings. Chapter 13 will show a method of evaluating the foreman's choice of worker *mix*.

He must carefully consider the requirements of union contracts. If there are *jurisdictional* limitations on what types of job the members of a particular union can perform (for example, an electrician cannot do painting, and a painter cannot do carpentry), then the manager must very precisely identify what his needs are. Union contracts also contain provisions concerning overtime hours and vacations, which should be scrupulously observed in order to minimize problems with strikes and to maximize productivity.

In addition to direct labor, the manager must plan for his indirect labor needs, including supervisors, maintenance workers, warehousemen, and even floor sweepers. Many of the problems found in dealing with these employees are the same as we discussed in the preceding paragraphs.

Laborers cannot produce a product unless they have materials, and production planning requires anticipating the need for direct and indirect materials. If plans are not made, the manager must hope that the materials will be available whenever he needs them. While this procedure tends to minimize the costs of storing and handling materials, it may produce unnecessarily high purchase prices through rush orders and small quantities, or even costly slowdowns or stoppages because of shortages.

Some production managers tend to draw a line which separates them from material acquisitions. They believe that it is their job to put the raw materials together, but not to buy them. Their point of view is partially valid but their attitude may be counterproductive. Cooperation with the purchasing and warehousing people can reduce overall costs and help minimize shortages of essential items. Purchasing costs can be reduced, especially if requests from several production managers can be combined. With large quantities, fixed price contracts can be negotiated to assure the availability of the needed material without necessarily using up an excessive amount of warehouse space for storage. Such contracts also provide protection against inflation, but they involve the risks of missing out on lower prices or having useless materials on hand.

Exhibit 12-4
HY-HEEL SHOE COMPANY
Labor Budget
For the Year Ended December 31, 1980

Skill Level	Product 1	Product 2	Product 3	Indirect Labor	Vacation	Total
Hours						
A	–0–	2,500	1,000	2,200	300	6,000
B	8,000	1,000	1,500	1,000	500	12,000
C	500	2,000	1,350	3,000	150	7,000
Dollars						
A	$ –0–	$12,500	$ 5,000	$11,000	$1,500	$30,000
B	32,000	4,000	6,000	4,000	2,000	48,000
C	1,500	6,000	4,050	9,000	450	21,000
Total	$33,500	$22,500	$15,050	$24,000	$3,950	$99,000

Total Direct = $71,050   Total Indirect = $27,950

Materials Budget
For the Year Ended December 31, 1980

Material	Product 1	Product 2	Product 3	Indirect Materials	Total
Units					
A	15,000	7,000	8,000	–0–	30,000
B	8,000	2,000	10,000	–0–	20,000
C	3,000	1,000	1,500	2,500	8,000
D	–0–	–0–	–0–	8,000	8,000
Dollars					
A	$30,000	$14,000	$16,000	$ –0–	$ 60,000
B	12,000	3,000	15,000	–0–	30,000
C	3,000	1,000	1,500	2,500	8,000
D	–0–	–0–	–0–	2,000	2,000
Total	$45,000	$18,000	$32,500	$4,500	$100,000

Total Direct = $95,500

In addition to indirect labor and materials, the production manager may need to plan for other overhead items, depending on the extent of his control. For example, taxes and insurance will be controlled by others, and the production manager can do little to influence them. However, he can regulate the consumption of some electric power through careful management.

Maintenance expenditures pose an interesting problem: Not only too much but also too little can be spent on maintaining factory equipment. If little or no preventive measures are taken (such as cleaning and lubricating), costs will be reduced in the short run but increased substantially in the long run. Thus, higher level management should specify and enforce maintenance policies.

Exhibit 12-4 presents labor and material budgets for the Hy-Heel Shoe Company. Notice that the budgets are expressed first in hours and units of material, and then translated into dollars. Exhibit 11-8 presented an example of an overhead budget, so for the sake of brevity, we will not present this portion of the production budget for Hy-Heel Shoes.   *327*

Exhibit 12-5

HY-HEEL SHOE COMPANY
Production Timing Budget (Units of Output)
For the Year Ended December 31, 1980

	Product 1	Product 2	Product 3
First quarter	2,000	1,000	8,000
Second quarter	10,000	1,000	10,000
Third quarter	35,000	1,000	14,000
Fourth quarter	5,000	1,000	8,000
Total	52,000	4,000	40,000

Timing

It is not sufficient to know merely the amount of output that must be produced. The production manager also should anticipate the timing with which the outputs must be made available for sale. If the demand for the product is *seasonal,* it should be produced during the slack period to be certain that a sufficient amount will be on hand during the selling season. If the demand is more constant, the manager should find the optimum tradeoff between storage costs and setup costs. The *setup costs* are the expenditures incurred in getting the production system ready to produce a particular item. In some industries, these costs are low; in others, such as automobile fabrication, entire factories are closed down in order to change dies, tools, and work stations.

Strictly from the production manager's point of view, total setup costs are minimized when long production runs are used. However, this strategy increases the risk of running out of stock, because the entire inventory is not being replenished on a regular basis.

Labor hiring practices are affected by matters of timing. If production is constant, the manager will seek to hire stable workers that will stay employed. Their skill levels and wages will be high, but so should their productivity. If peak periods are encountered, the emphasis will be on less skilled, less permanent workers. This condition affects not only hiring and training policies but also the design of the production system.

The production timing budget for Hy-Heel Shoes is seen in Exhibit 12-5. The middle quarters are high in production of Products 1 and 3 because of the availability of unskilled workers. Product 2 is produced at a constant rate because of the need for highly skilled workers.

BUDGETING ADMINISTRATION

In all but the smallest firms, there is a separate group of employees which has the function of assisting the coordination of the activities of all the other departments or divisions. There may be only one person working as a combination secretary-treasurer-receptionist-supply clerk, or there may be literally thousands of highly trained persons acting to assist managers. We should plan and budget for this administrative staff for the same reasons that we plan and budget sales and production. If too *little* assistance is available, the managers may be distracted from important matters because they are required to spend too much time on clerical activities. Further, the decision

Exhibit 12-6
HY-HEEL SHOE COMPANY
Administrative Budget
For the Year Ended December 31, 1980

Officers' salaries	$ 40,000
Office salaries and wages	30,500
Office supplies	17,400
Depreciation	15,000
Travel	9,000
Donations	3,000
Others	11,000
Total	$125,900

process may be hampered because the manager may not have all the information he needs. If too *much* assistance is available, interference may develop from the presence of a large number of bored staff members seeking outlets for their energies.

Because administrative staffs, especially top executives, are often closely involved with approving the budget, there is an observed tendency for a great deal of slack (see page 303) to develop in the administrative budget. The proportions of these abuses can run the gamut from large expense allowances and plush carpeting to executive jets and lavish apartments. While these fringe benefits may be justifiable in small, closely held companies, they may be more questionable in large firms. In any case, the administrative expenditures reduce profits in the same manner as expenditures on production. Administrative inefficiencies should not be allowed to grow beyond reason.

Exhibit 12-6 presents the administrative budget for Hy-Heel Shoe Company. Because of the relatively small size of the operation, the budgeted amounts are fairly low.

BUDGETING ASSET ACQUISITIONS

Once the desired level of activity has been established, it is helpful to examine the adequacy of the existing facilities. In the event that new assets will have to be acquired, it is best to evaluate the profitability of proposed acquisitions. Chapter 14 and 15 will deal with this aspect of planning, which is known as *capital budgeting*.

BUDGETING CASH

The next step in the budgeting process is an important one. Even if it is apparent from the preceding steps that the firm will probably earn a profit, we must prepare a *cash budget*.

Modern financial accounting theory stresses the importance of good matching of revenues and expenses. The accrual approach is believed to produce a better measure of income than the cash basis. Nonetheless, we must be concerned with the amount of cash that flows in and out of the firm, as well as the amount that happens to be on hand at any particular time. There are two reasons that we must consider: *bankruptcy* and *idleness*.

If we have less than enough cash to keep the creditors satisfied, they have the right to take us to court in order to achieve satisfaction. If necessary, the judge can order us to liquidate our assets and use the cash to pay our debts. Needless to say, this action can be traumatic for a firm, and usually is the end of its life. Creditors are reluctant to file such a suit, and seek to avoid the necessity by not extending credit to firms with poor payment history. In other cases, *carrying charges* may be assessed against a delinquent account in order to encourage its payment. Clearly, in order to avoid interest charges and even dissolution, management must be certain that it has enough cash on hand to pay its bills on time. Significantly, the existence of an accrual accounting profit does not guarantee that adequate cash will be on hand.

Oddly enough, managers should plan to avoid having *too much* cash on hand. In order to be available immediately, cash must be kept on hand as currency or on deposit in a checking account. Unfortunately, in both of these places, there is no income earned by the cash. Unless it is invested somewhere, the cash will simply sit wherever it is and do nothing to add profit to the firm. So, the cash manager (usually the treasurer) must have neither too much nor too little. In the first case, he can cost the firm lost interest (an opportunity cost), and in the second, he can destroy the firm.

The first step, then, in preparing a cash budget is to establish the desired amount to have on hand. This *minimum balance* should be large enough to deal with emergencies in either expenditures or slow collections. Some firms establish a *credit line* with their banks, so that cash can be borrowed very quickly in the event of an unexpected need for it. Their minimum balances can be quite small.

The second step in cash budgeting requires the manager to identify all the *sources* from which cash flows into the firm. The primary source is the revenue generated by sales of the firm's product. Large amounts may flow in through borrowing or the issuance of stock. Other amounts may come as income from investments. Many firms (such as public utilities) require their customers to make *security deposits* against bad debts or damage. These payments bring cash into the treasury, even though they also create liabilities.

Once the sources have been identified, the manager must estimate not only the size of each cash flow but also its *timing*. Typically, sales are made on credit, with the result that the cash is received several weeks or even months after the transaction. By *factoring* or *pledging* accounts receivable, a firm accepts less than face value in order to have the cash sooner. The timing must be predicted very precisely in order to avoid running short. Consequently, many firms prepare monthly cash budgets, while others work on a weekly or even a daily basis. The lag of collections behind the sales can be estimated from past observations.

The third step in cash budgeting is the identification of the *applications,* or *uses,* of cash.[7] Cash flows out for such items as merchandise and mate-

---

[7] The reader may notice the similarity between the statement of changes in financial position prepared on a cash basis (see Chapter 4) and the cash budget. The former deals with the past while the latter projects the future.

rials purchases, payrolls, taxes, utility bills, insurance, asset acquisitions, debt repayments, and dividends. Again, we are concerned not only with the size but also with the *timing* of the outflows. Many firms strive to obtain excellent credit ratings so that they can get the maximum lag of their payments behind their accounting costs and expenses. Most purchases are made under credit terms that allow several weeks, or even months, to pass before the amount due must be paid. Other expenditures, such as payroll and utility bills, are paid currently. Still others, such as insurance, are paid in advance. The manager's task is to identify relatively precisely to whom and when the cash will be paid.

Finally, these predictions are brought together in the cash budget, and the results are analyzed. If there will be excess funds on hand, then plans should be made to find profitable *temporary* investments to occupy them. On the other hand, if shortages are predicted, the manager should begin shopping around for the least costly *short-term* loans. If there will be large and lengthy shortages, it will be wise to consider whether or not some drastic policy changes are in order. In addition, consideration can be given to altering the credit terms given to customers to encourage speedier collections (by cash discounts) or to encourage more sales (by more liberal credit extensions).

Firms that operate over large geographical regions have found it convenient and profitable to establish several bank accounts in order to speed up collections through reduced time in the mails. The disadvantage of this approach is that each account must have a minimum balance, and the total of all of them will be much greater than would be needed for one general account. To ease this problem, many banks offer *electronic funds transfers* (EFT).

Whether there is to be investing or borrowing, it is helpful for the manager to know what the future is likely to hold. This foreknowledge will allow him to enter the money market before he is desperate for some place to either invest or borrow. Because he can be more deliberate in his decision making, he is more likely to be able to find the best use of the surplus or the cheapest source of borrowed funds.

Exhibit 12-7

TWO-BIT COMPANY
Cash Budget
For This Month

Beginning cash balance	$ 2,000
Cash sales (20% of $10,000)	2,000
Receivables collection (80% of $9,000)	7,200
Investment income	50
Total cash available for use	$ 11,250
Cash purchases (75% of $11,000)	$ 8,250
Payroll	500
Asset acquisition	2,000
Total cash to be used	$10,750
Net cash available	$ 500

For a relatively simple example, let us consider the Two-Bit Company, a small retail operation. The managers believe that a $1,000 minimum cash balance is sufficient to meet any emergency. Some of its sales (20 percent each month) are made for cash, while the remainder (80 percent each month) are made on credit, and are collected in full during the month following the sale. In addition, $50 in interest from an investment is expected to come in this month. Purchases are paid in cash, and equal the cost of the next month's sales. The payroll is $500 each month. Occasionally, fixed assets are purchased to fix up the store. The following data are available from the accounts and the budget:

	Last Month (Actual)	This Month (Budget)	Next Month (Budget)
Sales	$9,000	$10,000	$11,000
Cost of goods sold (% of sales)	75%	75%	75%
Asset acquisitions	$2,000	$2,000	$ –0–
Ending cash balance	$2,000	?	?

From this information, we can prepare the very simple cash budget seen in Exhibit 12-7 (page 331). As a result of preparing this budget, the manager of the firm knows that he will have to do one or more of the following: (1) borrow $500, (2) reduce the minimum balance to $500, (3) postpone the purchase of the asset, or (4) liquidate part of his investment. In any case, he has a warning that certain risks lie ahead and he must begin to decide what he is going to do.

An Extended Illustration

Let us turn now to the Six-Bit Company, another retailing firm, and the data in Exhibit 12-8, which will assist us in preparing a cash budget for the firm.

From this information, we are to prepare a cash budget for the months of January, February, and March. Our first step is to determine when and how much cash will come in from sales. Exhibit 12-9 summarizes our computations. It can be seen that net cash proceeds in a particular month can be quite different from the sales for that month.

It is necessary next to compute the purchases that will be made in each month. To accomplish this calculation, we will need to project the ending inventories for January, February, and March. In addition, we will need the purchases from December ($39,000), and the beginning inventory for January ($32,000). The schedules in Exhibits 12-10 and 12-11 are helpful.

We can turn now to the hourly and commissioned payroll expenditures in Exhibit 12-12. Remember that 50 percent of the hourly expense is paid in the next month, and that the 10 percent commission is paid during the month *following the sale.*

Exhibit 12-8
SIX-BIT COMPANY
Data for Cash Budget

Cash sales	15% of month's sales
Credit Sales	85% of month's sales
Collection experience	60% in month of credit sale
	30% in month after credit sale
	8% in next month after credit sale
	2% uncollectible
	100%
Cost of goods sold	50% of month's sales
Ending inventory	80% of next month's cost of goods sold
Purchases payments	⅓ in month of purchase
	⅔ in next month
Payroll expenditures:	
Hourly	50% in month of expense
	50% in next month
Commission	10% of previous month's sales
Depreciation	$8,000 per month
Other cash expenses	$12,000 per month
Debt payments	$1,000 per month
Dividends	As declared
Minimum balance	$5,000

	Actual		Budgeted			
	November	**December**	**January**	**February**	**March**	**April**
Sales	$60,000	$70,000	$80,000	$70,000	$100,000	$75,000
Asset Purchases			$ 5,000		$ 5,000	
Dividends				$12,000		
Hourly payroll	$ 7,000	$ 8,000	$ 9,000	$10,000	$ 9,000	$ 7,000

All these items of information are combined in the 3-month cash budget (in Exhibit 12-13), which is based on a beginning balance in the Cash account of $5,000. Notice that depreciation does not involve a cash outflow, and it will not normally appear on the cash budget. If there is to be the minimum balance of $5,000 on hand at March 1, the firm will have to

Exhibit 12-9
SIX-BIT COMPANY
Projected Cash Collections

	January	February	March
Cash sales*	$12,000	$10,500	$15,000
Collections from credit sales** in:			
November ($51,000)	$ 4,080		
December ($59,500)	17,850	$ 4,760	
January ($68,000)	40,800	20,400	$ 5,440
February ($59,500)		35,700	17,850
March ($85,000)			51,000
Total	$62,730	$60,860	$74,290

*15% of total sales for the month
**85% of total sales for the month

borrow $7,577, or liquidate a temporary investment during February. After March $2,547 can be repaid or reinvested.

In summary, the cash budget is the final phase of the planning cycle. The function of this budget is to prevent one of two things: having idle cash, and running short of cash. It is necessary to establish a minimum balance, identify the sources of cash by amount and timing, and identify the uses of cash by amount and timing. From this information, contingency plans can be made for investment or borrowing.

Exhibit 12-10
SIX-BIT COMPANY
Projected Purchases

	Actual December	Budgeted January	February	March
Ending inventory*	$ 32,000	$ 28,000	$ 40,000	$ 30,000
Add: Cost of goods sold**	35,000	40,000	35,000	50,000
Less: Beginning inventory†	(28,000)	(32,000)	(28,000)	(40,000)
Purchases	$ 39,000	$ 36,000	$ 47,000	$ 40,000

*80% of the next month's cost of goods sold
**50% of sales
†The beginning inventory of one month is the ending inventory of the preceding month.

Exhibit 12-11
SIX-BIT COMPANY
Projected Payments on Purchases

Payments on Purchases	January	February	March
From purchases (Exh. 12-10) in:			
December ($39,000)	$26,000*		
January ($36,000)	12,000**	$24,000*	
February ($47,000)		15,667**	$31,333*
March ($40,000)			13,333**
Total	$38,000	$39,667	$44,666

*⅔ of prior month's purchases
**⅓ of current month's purchases

Exhibit 12-12
SIX-BIT COMPANY
Projected Payroll Payments

	January	February	March
Hourly payroll from:			
December ($8,000)	$4,000		
January ($9,000)	4,500	$4,500	
February ($10,000)		5,000	$5,000
March ($9,000)			4,500
Total	$8,500	$9,500	$9,500
Commissions paid*	$7,000	$8,000	$7,000

*10% of prior month's sales

Exhibit 12-13
SIX-BITS COMPANY
Cash Budget
For the Months January, February, and March

	January	February	March	Jan.-Mar.
Beginning cash balance	$ 5,000	$ 8,230	$ (2,577)	$ 5,000
Cash sales (Exh. 12-9)	12,000	10,500	15,000	37,500
Collections (Exh. 12-9)	62,730	60,860	74,290	197,880
Cash available for use	$79,730	$79,590	$86,713	$240,380
Payments for:				
Purchases (Exh. 12-11)	$38,000	$39,667	$44,666	$122,333
Payroll: (Exh. 12-12)				
Hourly	8,500	9,500	9,500	27,500
Commissions	7,000	8,000	7,000	22,000
Depreciation	–0–	–0–	–0–	–0–
Other expenses	12,000	12,000	12,000	36,000
Debt payments	1,000	1,000	1,000	3,000
Asset purchases	5,000	–0–	5,000	10,000
Dividends	–0–	12,000	–0–	12,000
Total cash to be used	$71,500	$82,167	$79,166	$232,833
Ending balance	$ 8,230	$ (2,577)	$ 7,547	$ 7,547

THE BUDGETED FINANCIAL STATEMENTS

After plans have been made for the firm's cash, revenues, costs, and asset acquisitions, it is possible to prepare *budgeted financial statements*. These statements will be identical to ordinary ones except that they will describe *expected* results of operations for the *coming* year, and *expected* financial position as of a particular *future* date. The cash budget is similar to an estimated Statement of Changes in Financial Position prepared on a cash basis. Exhibit 12-14 presents the summary of the expected costs of the goods to be sold by Hy-Heel Shoe Company. Exhibit 12-15 shows the budgeted Income Statement. (Because we have not adequately covered the topic of asset acquisition at this point, we will not present the budgeted Balance Sheet.)

These three statements are usually the leading items in what many companies refer to as the *master budget*. This collection of budgets is presented to the board of directors by the budget committee as its final act. Some firms choose to keep the entire master budget relatively confidential, and inform lower level managers about only the appropriations for their personal areas of interest. Other companies have the opposite policy of letting everyone know what is expected in the way of overall results. This strategy may be chosen in order to motivate lower level managers by showing them how significant their parts are within the entire firm. Also, it may be better to circulate the information *formally* because the "grapevine" will probably thwart any efforts to keep the figures secret. Additionally, secrecy may act to motivate the excluded managers in a negative direction. Again, we must warn that the best solution will vary from firm to firm, situation to situation, and person to person.

Exhibit 12-14

HY-HEEL SHOE COMPANY
Budgeted Cost of Goods Sold
For the Year Ended December 31, 1980

Finished goods inventory (January 1, 1980)				$ 51,750
Cost of goods manufactured:				
Work-in-Process (January 1, 1980)			$ 15,200	
Manufacturing costs:				
Direct labor*		$ 71,050		
Direct materials*		95,500		
Overhead:				
Indirect labor*	$27,950			
Indirect materials*	4,500			
Other sources	67,850	100,300	266,850	
Work-in-Process (December 31, 1980)			(14,000)	268,050
Cost of goods available for sale				$319,800
Finished goods inventory (December 31, 1980)				(57,300)
Cost of goods sold				$262,500

*From Exhibit 12-4 on page 327.

BUDGETING AND COMPUTERS

As is true in so many other areas in management accounting, the computer has had an effect on budgeting techniques. The computer certainly has not reduced the importance of the accountant in preparation of the budget, although his role has been altered.

Perhaps the most profound effect upon budgeting (and planning) has come through better *forecasting* techniques. Future events and their economic results can be predicted more systematically and accurately through the use of sophisticated statistical planning models. (More information on these models is provided in Chapters 18 and 19.) It would be impossible to gather and process the input data for these models without a computer.

Much of the accountant's "pencil-pushing" work in preparing the budget can be eliminated through properly written computer programs. For example, much of the manual effort involved in preparing the cash budget can be avoided. The computer is also especially useful in taking into consideration all the many interactions of the different phases of the budget cycle.

In a similar fashion, labor and overhead requirements can be consolidated much more quickly and accurately. The computer's speed allows more frequent comparison of actual results with the budgeted results, and thus promotes better management control of ongoing production processes.

The computer also encourages a more extensive application of *sensitivity analysis*. This procedure involves analyzing the effect on the outputs caused by variations in the inputs. For example, the computer reduces the amount of time needed to measure the effects on the profits of a change in the mix of the products to be manufactured. The shorter time allows (and even encourages) the budget committee to compare the results of several likely alternative strategies and to select the best one.

Exhibit 12-15
HY-HEEL SHOE COMPANY
Budgeted Income Statement
For the Year Ended December 31, 1980

Sales*		$ 720,000
Cost of goods sold**		(262,500)
Gross margin		457,500
Expenses:		
Selling*	$153,450	
Administrative†	125,900	(279,350)
Net income before taxes		$ 178,150
Income taxes‡		(71,260)
Net income		$ 106,890

  *From Exhibit 12-2
 **From Exhibit 12-14
  †From Exhibit 12-6
  ‡40% of net income before taxes

Finally, the computer also makes it more practical to prepare *frequent* budgets. If the computative steps are stored in a computer program, the budget can be prepared, for example, once each month instead of once each quarter or each year. The rolling budget can be prepared much more economically if the calculations are computerized. This simplification leads to more management involvement and better planning.

As a word of caution, the budget produced by the computer is only as valid as the data used by the program and the assumptions made by the programmer. Care must be taken to assure that too much significance or accuracy is not read into a budget simply because it appears on "computer paper." The element of human judgment is not eliminated by a computer. Indeed, judgment is the one thing that the computer cannot replace.

SUMMARY

This chapter is the second of two dealing with the important management activities of planning and budgeting. We examined the procedures for preparing budgets for three major areas: *sales, production,* and *administration.*

The first step in budgeting is the preparation of the *sales forecast* for the coming period. This projection of sales levels depends on the market situation. We described the factors that influence the establishment of selling prices because the *quantity* of products *to be sold* almost always depends on the price to be charged for them. The existing market price must be considered where one exists. In many cases, the businessman must turn to the *cost* of the product in order to establish a reasonable selling price. *Full accounting costs* may be misleading because of allocations of fixed costs. A useful alternative strategy is *contribution pricing,* which looks at the incremental costs.

The *sales budget* is an explicit plan that communicates to the sales manager what is expected of him and what he can spend to accomplish it.

Together with planned inventories, the sales forecast helps establish the level of *production*. The production manager must translate his output goals into input needs. By planning, he anticipates how many labor hours and units of materials he will consume. This advance knowledge allows him to establish plans for the timing of production. Thus, he is able to avoid rush purchases of needed materials or overtime labor costs.

The firm's *administrative* departments are not immune to budgeting benefits. Needs for office workers, supplies, and facilities should be anticipated and special efforts are needed to avoid excessive budgetary slack.

Although modern accounting emphasizes matching of expenses and revenues, we cannot afford to neglect cash flows. The *cash budget* is prepared to assure that we fall into the safe region between two dangers. If we do not have enough cash, we incur interest penalties and run the risk of bankruptcy. If we have too much cash, we will lose income because idle cash provides no return.

After all the supporting budgets are ready, the budget committee can prepare the budgeted financial statements for the coming period. The *master budget* will be presented to the board of directors, and will include all the budgets for the year. Whether or not the contents of the master budget are made known widely depends upon the desires of top management.

Finally, we discussed the effects of computers on budgeting. In addition to reducing clerical procedures, the computer encourages more use of sensitivity analysis and more frequent budget preparation. We can expect our sophistication in using computers to increase as our experience grows.

These last two chapters have dealt with the planning and budgeting activities of management and management accountants. Anticipating the future enables us to get the most out of it, and to avoid *some* problems. Budgeting is merely the effort of translating plans into written documents. While formal budgeting may take place only infrequently, planning should be continuous. A good budget system will allow the original plans to be changed when needed.

Additionally, a budget serves to *coordinate* the efforts of the various departments to assure that they are not counteracting each other. The budget communicates expectations to subordinates, and also acts as a very useful standard for evaluating actual performance.

QUESTIONS

1. What should every activity of a profit-making firm be directed toward?
2. What should be the first step in preparing a budget? Why?
3. What are three factors that affect the price a firm can put on its products?
4. Under what circumstances would it be appropriate to sell a product for less than its full accounting cost? For less than its marginal cost?
5. What is potentially wrong with setting a price at cost plus a percentage of cost?

6. How is the sales volume forecasted?

7. What is included in the sales budget that makes it different from the sales forecast?

8. In budgeting production output, what factors must be coordinated?

9. What are the three major inputs that must be considered in preparing a budget? What are the problems associated with each of them?

10. What part does timing play in planning production?

11. What is meant by the *mix* of inputs?

12. Why is it useful to budget administrative activities? Is budgeting slack more or less likely in an administrative budget in relation to other types?

13. What are the two things we attempt to avoid by budgeting cash?

14. What are the four steps of budgeting cash?

15. What factors affect the establishment of a minimum cash balance?

16. List some possible sources of cash. List some possible uses of cash.

17. How can a computer assist the manager in preparing a budget?

18. What is sensitivity analysis?

EXERCISES

E12–1 *Forecasting sales volume.* The marketing staff of the Piper Paper Products Company is formulating the sales forecast for 1981 for "Soakers," the company's disposable diaper. Their research has revealed the following:

Population of market area	12,400,000
Incidence of children in diapers	7.8 per 1,000 population
Observed usage of disposable diapers for these children:	
1 out of 5	80 per month
2 out of 5	30 per month
1 out of 5	10 per month
1 out of 5	0 per month
Possible market shares for Soakers:	

10% if sold at $2.50 per box of 40
15% if sold at $2.20 per box of 40
25% if sold at $4.00 per box of 80

Required:

Prepare a short table showing, for 1981, for *each* of the three marketing strategies:

a. Number of Soakers to be sold

b. Number of boxes of Soakers to be sold

c. The dollar sales volume (rounded to the nearest thousand)

E12–2 *Contribution pricing.* The Blass Furnace Company is a family-owned producer of small kilns used by hobbyists. Several years ago, the plant was expanded to an annual capacity of 10,000 kilns per year, although this year's production is expected to be only 6,000 units. The expansion was based upon an expected increase in local demand that never materialized.

Recently, a mail-order house with a national market offered to buy 2,000 kilns for $300,000. The chief accountant has presented a per unit cost in the past of $185, which was computed as:

Material	$65.00
Labor	40.00
Overhead	80.00

The overhead is allocated at a rate of 200 percent of direct-labor cost, but only $15 can be considered as the variable indirect costs.

Required:

a. On the basis of unit costs alone, should the offer be accepted? Support your answer.

b. On the basis of total costs, should the offer be accepted? Support your answer.

c. Suppose that Blass expected the local annual demand to reach 8,000 in 2 years, while the mail-order house expected to sell 5,000 kilns a year after two years. What other information would be needed before signing a long-term contract at $150 per kiln?

E12–3 *Rate of return.* Figures were recently published for the tennis sock industry, and showed that the industry leader, Forty-Love, had a rate of return on investment of 11 percent per year.

A small competitor, Deuce, recently entered the business after making a large investment in capital assets. Specifically, equipment that cost $2,750,000 had been depreciated on a straight-line basis down to $2,612,500. The firm's statements showed that only 7 percent per year was earned.

Another competitor, No-Fault, has a chairman of the board that is considering dropping out of the trade association. He feels that his report to them must have been lost, because his company's profit rate was 20 percent of sales, which is well in excess of the 11 reported by Forty-Love.

Required:

a. Suggest at least two reasons why Deuce's rate of return might be so much lower than Forty-Love's.

b. What error has the chairman of No-Fault committed?

E12–4 *Rate of return.* From the following facts, you are to compute these percentages of returns for each of the five firms and rank them from "best" to "worst" on the basis of:

a. return on sales
b. return on investment (use book value of assets)
c. return on investment (use original cost of assets)
d. return on investment (use book value of owners' equity)
e. return on investment (use replacement value of assets)

	Firm 1	Company 2	Organization 3	Entity 4	Corporation 5
Sales	$4,000,000	$4,000,000	$ 4,000,000	$4,000,000	$4,000,000
Net income	560,000	440,000	1,000,000	840,000	760,000
Assets (original cost)	6,250,000	2,600,000	7,200,000	9,400,000	6,400,000
Accumulated depreciation	2,500,000	850,000	1,650,000	2,400,000	3,850,000
Liabilities	650,000	–0–	550,000	4,600,000	–0–
Assets (replacement cost)	4,000,000	3,700,000	11,200,000	7,600,000	6,900,000

Round your answers to the nearest 1 percent.

E12–5 **Sales budget.** Green Witch Company markets a single product all over the country. The responsibility for marketing is assigned to three geographic regions: West, South, and North. The marketing staff is planning for 1982, which is the next upcoming year.

There are no expenses assigned to the national office. The following facts are known:

1. Total unit sales are expected to be 200,000 units
2. Total salaries are expected to be $90,000
3. Total travel costs are expected to be $40,000
4. Total other costs are expected to be $21,000

	West	South	North
5. Portion of unit sales	20%	25%	55%
6. Per unit sales price	$4.50	$4.00	$3.00
7. Sales commission rates (as percent of dollar sales)	10%	10%	5%
8. Salary distribution	30%	25%	45%
9. Travel distribution	40%	60%	0%
10. Other costs distribution	⅓	⅓	⅓

Required:
From the above facts, prepare a schedule similar to the one in Exhibit 12-2, that will show these budget items for each region and the company as a whole:

a. unit sales
b dollar sales
c. each expense
d. total expenses

E12–6 **Planning output and purchases.** The Dirk Kirk Works Company manufactures its product from two raw materials, A and B. Three units of A are added at the beginning and two units of B are added at the end of the process for each unit of output. Sales for 1980 are expected to be 120,000 units.

The following information is known about the inventories (physical units):

	January 1, 1980 (Actual)	December 31, 1980 (Budgeted)
Raw Material *A*	8,000	20,000
Raw Material *B*	19,000	15,000
Goods in Process*	5,000	2,000
Finished Goods	12,000	18,000

* After *A* is added, but before *B*

Required:

a. How many units of output will have to be completed in order to meet the sales and inventory goals?

b. How many units of output will have to be started in order to meet the sales and inventory goals?

c. How many units of raw materials *A* and *B* will have to be purchased in order to meet the production and inventory goals?

d. Give at least two possible reasons for management's choice to increase the finished goods inventory. What factors must be considered in ordering such an increase?

E12–7 *Planning labor usage.* The Bingham Manufacturing Company produces a product that requires a great deal of direct-labor input. The task can be performed by differently skilled persons, but with different hours per unit and different rejection rates:

Degree of Skill	Hours to Complete One Unit
Skilled	2
Semiskilled	3
Unskilled	5

Required:

a. If the cost per hour for the three types of worker are $10, $8, and $3.50, which type should the plant supervisor use?

b. Suppose that past history has resulted in these rejection rates by the quality control program:

Degree of Skill	Units Rejected
Skilled	1 out of 51
Semiskilled	1 out of 11
Unskilled	1 out of 5

If a rejected unit can be sold for the cost of the raw materials only, which level of worker should the plant supervisor use? (*Hint:* Find the number of units that must be completed in order to get 100 acceptable units.)

E12–8 **Cash budgeting.** The owners of Rhonda and Nettie's Tea House have prepared the following budgeted income statement for September:

Sales		$10,000
Cost of foods sold		(6,300)
Margin		$ 3,700
Expenses:		
Payroll	$1,800	
Rent	300	
Taxes	200	(2,300)
Net income		$ 1,400

All sales are made for cash, and the payroll is paid currently. The rent had been prepaid for the year in January, and the taxes are not due until November. Food is paid for during the month following its sale. Last month, the cost of foods sold was $7,500.

Required:

a. If the beginning balance in cash is $500, and the minimum balance is $350, how much, if any, cash can Rhonda and Nettie withdraw from their business?

b. If a profit is budgeted, why should we worry about the amount of cash that will be on hand?

E12–9 **Cash budgeting.** Sales for the Jenkins Toy Company in a typical month are 80 percent on credit, and 20 percent for cash. Of the credit sales, 40 percent are collected in the month of the sale, 40 percent in the month following the sale, and the remaining 20 percent in the month after that.

Merchandise purchases are paid for within 15 days, thus, 50 percent of a particular month's purchases are paid in that month, and 50 percent in the following month.

The employees are paid weekly. For a particular month, 75 percent of the payroll is paid out in that month, and the other 25 percent in the following month.

A cash dividend of $7,500 is expected to be paid in July.

A bank loan of $10,000 will be taken out in May. Funds from the loan, and from the bank account, will be used to buy an asset in June for $14,000. Depreciation expense in May and June will be $17,000, but it will increase to $17,500 for July.

Other cash expenses are paid in full in each month. The balance of cash as of May 1 is $5,000.

The actual and estimated amounts available are shown at the top of page 344.

Required:

From the provided information, you are to prepare monthly cash budgets for May, June, and July.

	March*	April*	May	June	July
Sales	$20,000	$10,000	$24,000	$12,000	$30,000
Purchases	4,000	5,000	4,000	5,000	6,000
Payroll	3,600	4,000	3,200	3,600	4,200
Other cash expenses	11,000	4,000	11,000	8,000	8,000

* Actual

PROBLEMS

P12–1 *Contribution pricing.* E. Berg and Sons build custom-made pleasure boats which range in price from $10,000 to $250,000. For the past 30 years, Mr. Berg, Sr., has determined the selling price of each boat by estimating the costs of materials, labor, and prorated portion of overhead, and then adding 20 percent.

For example, a recent price quotation was determined as:

Direct materials	$ 5,000
Direct labor	8,000
Overhead	2,000
Total cost	$15,000
Add: 20 percent	3,000
Selling price	$18,000

The overhead figure was determined by estimating total overhead costs for the year and allocating them at 25 percent of direct-labor costs.

If a customer rejected the price and business was slack, Mr. Berg, Sr., would often be willing to reduce his markup to as little as 5 percent over estimated costs. Thus, average markup for the year is estimated at 15 percent.

Mr. Ed Berg, Jr., recently completed a short course on pricing, which he wants to apply. Emphasis was placed on the contribution margin approach, and Mr. Berg, Jr., feels that it would be helpful in determining selling prices of their custom-made products.

Total overhead, which includes selling and administrative expenses for the year, has been estimated at $150,000, of which $90,000 is fixed. The remainder is variable in direct proportion to direct labor.

Required:

a. Assume that the customer in the example rejected the $18,000 quotation, and also a $15,750 second quotation (as low as Mr. Berg, Sr., would go) during a slack period. The customer countered with an offer of $15,000, which is being considered by Mr. Berg, Jr.

    1. What would be the difference in net income if the customer's offer were accepted?

2. What would be the minimum selling price that could have been accepted without reducing net income?

b. What advantages does the contribution margin approach to pricing have over the approach used by Mr. Berg, Sr.?

c. What pitfalls are there to contribution margin pricing?

(CMA Adapted)

P12–2 *Sales forecast and budget.* The Kitchen-Maid Manufacturing Company produces and sells two lines of home dishwashers, the Deluxe and the Special.

Of the new homes being built in Kitchen-Maid's marketing region, it is expected that 80 percent will have a dishwasher installed during construction. Of these homes, 30 percent will have a model comparable to the Deluxe, and 70 percent will have one in the Special's category.

It is also expected that, in any given year, 10 percent of the existing homes will add a dishwasher or replace an old one. The new or replacement machines will be 40 percent of the Deluxe class, and 60 percent comparable to the Special.

The marketing team of Kitchen-Maid expects to capture 25 percent of the unit sales of the Deluxe type machines sold, and 20 percent of the Special market.

The following additional facts about the coming year are projected:

1. Total advertising costs will be $430,000.
2. The three marketing areas are Anthonyville, Brewer, and Capston.

		Anthonyville	Brewer	Capston
3.	New home construction	5,000	12,000	20,000
4.	Existing homes	125,000	250,000	10,000
5.	Sales price per unit			
	Deluxe	$200	$200	$250
	Special	$140	$160	$160
6.	Sales commissions (as a % of dollar sales)	20%	25%	20%
7.	Advertising (as a % of the total)	20%	30%	50%
8.	Other selling costs (as a % of dollar sales)	10%	15%	20%

Required:

a. Prepare a sales forecast for the coming year, showing the physical units of Kitchen-Maid's dishwashers of each type to be sold in the three areas, and in total.

b.   Prepare a sales budget for Kitchen-Maid for the coming year, showing the dollar amounts of sales and sales related costs that are expected to occur in each area, and in total.

P12–3   Planning output. Fill in the missing amounts in these output budgets for the next three months (all numbers are units):

	June	July	August	Total
Ending inventory	?	?	?	13,000
Beginning inventory	14,000	?	?	?
Change in inventory	+3,000	+6,000	?	?
Sales	42,000	?	?	122,000
Production	?	57,000	?	?

P12–4   Budgeting output and input. The forecasted sales for the next 8 months for Easyrite ballpoint pens are:

	Units to be Sold
July	10,000
August	15,000
September	8,000
October	7,000
November	9,000
December	10,000
January	5,000
February	4,000

The manufacturer's policy is to try to have an inventory of finished goods on hand at the beginning of each month equal to 80 percent of that month's sales. The remaining 20 percent are manufactured during the month.

Since the fabrication process is very, very short, there are virtually no goods in-process inventories.

Each pen requires the following materials:

Plastic	3 units
Cartridge	1 unit

The supply of plastic is relatively stable, with the result that the inventory at the beginning of the month is considered sufficient if it equals 50 percent of that month's usage.

The supply of cartridges, on the other hand, is rather unstable, and the beginning inventory is considered sufficient only if it equals at least the usage of the current *and* the next month.

As of July 1, the following inventories are on hand:

Finished pens	7,990 units
Plastic	15,100 units
Cartridges	29,000 units

Required:

a. Prepare a schedule showing the number of pens that should be manufactured in July, August, September, October, and November in order to meet the sales and inventory goals.

b. Prepare schedules showing the number of units of each raw material that should be purchased in those 5 months in order to meet the production and inventory goals.

P12–5 Budgeting labor. The plant supervisor in charge of hiring personnel for the fabrication and packaging of the Easyrite ballpoint pens (see P12–4) received the forecasts of monthly production levels and went to work planning his actions for the next 6 months.

The production line uses three classes of workers, whose wages and average time to process *each* pen are shown below:

Worker Class	Hourly Wage	Per Unit Process Time
Assembler	$1.80	15 minutes
Tester	4.00	4 minutes
Packager	2.25	2 minutes

Because the plant is located in an area with many recreational facilities, the personnel supervisor encounters no difficulty in laying off workers and even has a waiting list of potential workers eager to work full- or parttime.

Once an employee is signed on for the day, he or she is entitled to a full 8 hours pay, although he or she may not have to work the entire day. The plant operates 8 hours per day, 22 days per month.

Required:

a. Prepare a schedule showing the number of minutes needed of each class of worker for the 6 months beginning July (the production forecast is found by solving *a* of the preceding problem).

b. Prepare a schedule showing the days and total labor costs for each class of worker for each of the 6 months beginning with July.

P12–6 Cash budgeting. The budget committee of Zack's of One Hundred Forty-Seventh Street prepared the following projections concerning the next 3 months:

	March	April	May
Merchandise purchases	$ 79,000	$ 85,500	$200,000
Equipment purchases		9,200	
Dividend payment		15,000	
Payroll expenses	10,000	11,000	12,000
Other cash expenses	5,600	4,700	6,200
Sales	109,000	122,000	185,000

Based on recent experiences, it is estimated that about 80 percent of the sales are on account. Of these, it has been seen that 10 percent will be collected in the month of sale, 75 percent in the next month, 14 percent in the second month, and 1 percent will be written off as uncollectible. The March 1 balance in Trade Accounts Receivables is $78,400, and a careful analysis indicates $5^,000 will be received during March, $11,500 during April, and $2,800 during May.

Merchandise purchases are on 30-day accounts, which causes them to be paid during the month following the transaction. The March 1 balance in Accounts Payable is $71,000.

The equipment will be paid for under C.O.D. terms. Employees are paid on the tenth of the month for services rendered during the second half of the preceding month, and on the twenty-fifth of the month for the first half. The balance in Payroll Payable on March 1 is $5,000. The Cash balance on March 1 is $16,300.

Required:

a. Prepare a schedule showing projected cash receipts (excluding investment liquidation) for March, April, and May.

b. Prepare a schedule showing projected cash disbursements (excluding investment of idle funds) for March, April, and May.

c. Prepare a schedule showing cash receipts, cash disbursements, investment, investment liquidation, and beginning and ending cash balances for March, April, and May. The minimum cash balance is $10,000, and investments can be liquidated to generate enough cash to reach the minimum. The maximum cash balance is $15,000, and cash in excess of that amount can be invested at once. Ignore interest income, as it is added to the investment account and is not realized as cash.

P12–7 **Expense and cash budgets.**   Data pertaining to the operation of Twin Cities Sales Company have been projected for 1980. Direct your attention to the following:

1. Net Sales for 1980 are estimated to be $5,400,000, with 10 percent of the total coming in December. Salesmen are paid an 8 percent commission in the month following the sale. December 1979 sales were $375,000.

2. In addition, the 40 salesmen are each paid a salary of $200 per month, paid on the tenth of the next month.

3. Administrative Salaries are estimated to be $12,000 per month, until April 1, when a 5 percent across-the-board raise will go into effect. These salaries are also paid on the tenth of the following month.

4. The Building Rent is $17,500 per month, and is paid on the first of the month; 30 percent of the space is used for offices, and the remainder is for sales.

5. The annual Fire Insurance premium was $4,500, and was paid on November 1, 1979. The state insurance commission approved a 6 percent premium increase, effective July 1 on all premiums due after that date.

6. The Office Equipment is recorded on the books at its original cost of $125,000, and the Sales Equipment at $640,000. All equipment is expected to last 10 years; none of it is to be retired this year, and no additions are planned. It is being depreciated on a straight-line basis with no salvage value.

7. Office Supplies on hand at January 1 cost $5,950. It is anticipated that $50,000 of supplies will be consumed and that the inventory will be increased to $7,000 on December 31, 1980.

8. The company has Prepaid Advertising at January 1 with a remaining cost of $15,400. It is expected that the account at the end of the year will show a balance of $10,000. Authorization has been given for cash expenditures of $122,850 on advertising contracts during the year.

9. Other cash expenses for administration are expected to be $45,200, and other cash sales expenses are budgeted at $73,150.

Required:

a. Prepare a selling *expense* budget for 1980.

b. Prepare a selling *expenditure* budget for 1980.

c. Prepare an administrative *expense* budget for 1980.

d. Prepare an administrative *expenditure* budget for 1980.

P12–8 *Cash budgeting.* Over the last few years, Programme Corporation has encountered cash-flow estimation problems, with the result that its relationship with its banker has been strained.

The controller has heard about mathematically modeling cash flows as an aid to better and easier forecasting. He has gathered the following facts:

1. Sales have been and are expected to increase at 0.5 percent each month.

2. Thirty percent of each month's sales are for cash, with the remainder on account.

3. Of the credit sales, 80 percent are collected in the month following the sale, with the other 20 percent in the month thereafter.

4. Gross margin averages 25 percent of sales.

5. Purchases in a particular month are equal to the needs of the following month, and are paid for in the month of purchase.

6. Monthly expenses are: Payroll $1,500, Rent $400, Depreciation $1,200, other cash expenses total 1 percent of sales. There are no prepayments or accruals.

Required:

Ignoring income taxes and other nonroutine cash receipts and disbursements, construct a mathematical model that will describe any month's net cash inflow in terms of sales for that given month. (In other words, the only independent variable will be the month's sales.)

(CMA Adapted)

P12–9 *Cash budgeting.* On April 1, 1979 the Kolor TV Sales Company applied to the Third National Bank for a short-term loan, which is to be paid back as surplus funds are accumulated. The loan officer has asked the company's manager to prepare a cash forecast in order to test his ability to plan, and, of course, to see how quickly the loan can be repaid. The budget is to cover the next 6 months (through September 30).

Kolor TV purchases its merchandise on terms that allow a 2 percent cash discount if paid within 30 days. All discounts are taken. Assume that all purchases are made on the last day of the month.

Sales are paid for under four-payment contracts. The first payment is due on delivery, and the others are due on the same date of each month thereafter.

Commissions to salesmen are 10 percent, and are paid in the month following the sale. Other selling expenses are paid in cash currently, and equal about 15 percent of sales each month.

Administrative expenses, including depreciation of $20,000, are $70,000 per month. The company has a policy of carrying a $25,000 minimum cash balance, and the balance as of April 1 is $28,000.

If a loan will be needed in a particular month in order to bring the cash balance to $25,000, the bank will make the money available on the first day of the month. Any repayments of the loan will be made on the first of the month. Interest will be charged at the rate of 1 percent per month, and will be computed on the balance outstanding during the month. It will be paid at the first of the next month.

Actual sales and purchases are:

	Sales	Purchases
January	$ 400,000	$ 300,000
February	500,000	400,000
March	500,000	800,000

Projected sales and purchases are:

April	1,100,000	1,000,000
May	2,000,000	500,000
June	1,500,000	400,000
July	800,000	200,000
August	500,000	200,000
September	500,000	200,000

Required:

Prepare the cash budget requested by the bank.

P12–10 *Budgeted income statement.* Allied Furniture Company manufactures and markets office desks. A reliable industry survey puts total demand in the nongovernment market at 1,200,000 desks per year. According to their own estimates, Allied has maintained a 7 percent share of the market in the past, but expects to increase it to 8 percent in the coming year. Additionally, Allied has a government contract that consumes about 40 percent of its annual sales. Despite the fact that the government and civilian desks are identical, the contract calls for a price of only $104 per desk, whereas the others can be sold competitively for $122 each.

The following projections about Allied's costs and expenses are made:

Fixed:	
Manufacturing	$1,500,000 per year
Administration	1,000,000 per year
Variable:	
Manufacturing	$75.00 per unit
Advertising*	0.50 per unit
Selling*	1.00 per unit

*Does not apply to desks sold to the government.

Applicable income taxes are expected to amount to 50 percent of net income before taxes.

The company has a beginning inventory of 10,000 desks (at a recorded cost of $83.00 each), and plans a year-end inventory of 10 percent of this year's sales. There are no in-process inventories. Assume a FIFO inventory flow.

Required:

a. How many desks should Allied plan to produce in order to meet its sales and inventory goals?

b. Prepare a budgeted income statement for the coming year.

13

Profit Improvement

We have just learned something about planning and budgeting. But what good does it do to plan and budget unless we periodically evaluate our actual performance in relation to the budget or plan? In far too many cases planning and budgeting are annual events—the budget is prepared and then set aside. These budgets are like New Year's resolutions that are made with good intentions but soon forgotten. If budgeting is to be effective it must be a *continuous process* and not a once-a-year task. It should be part of an overall process of *profit improvement*.

PROFIT IMPROVEMENT

Many managers simply "do the best they can" and then hope profits will reach a satisfactory level. A good manager, however, will not leave something as important as profits to chance. Instead, he will *plan* for profits, then monitor his achievement with a systematic program such as the one illustrated in Exhibit 13-1. The steps in this plan may be summarized as:

1. Set *specific* profit improvement objectives.
2. Establish accounting reports which will provide in a timely manner actual data (the data base) regarding performance in each of these objective areas.
3. Regularly compare the actual performance (data base) against the specific profit improvement objectives to determine the *objective variance*.
4. Subdivide the variances into specific problem areas according to lines of responsibility. Some *particular* manager should be responsible for each variance. While he must accept responsibility for the variance, he should

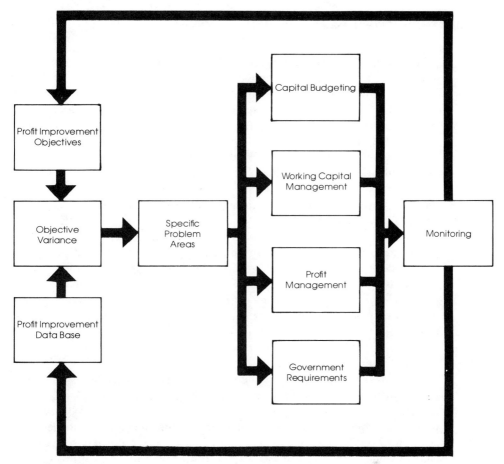

Exhibit 13-1
Profit Improvement System

be able to draw on the knowledge of experts in the company to assist his finding a solution to the problem.

5. A monitoring system is essential to provide a constant flow of information about the firm. As corrective action is taken, the monitoring system picks up the actual results and updates the data base to reflect the most recent performance. At the same time, action is taken to revise the objectives, where necessary, in order to make them realistic and attainable.

6. The cycle repeats itself with a revised objective and a current data base. Each time a cycle is completed, we would hope to see the objective gap close but, also, we would see new objectives set as the system uncovers new problem areas which require analysis. These new problems may show up at any point in the cycle. They may begin with management setting a new objective or subobjective, by a new fact being reported, or the analysis of an existing problem bringing to light an entirely new problem.

To illustrate the system, suppose that management sets a goal for the firm to earn a $2 million profit during the next year. In turn, they would set goals for each of the divisions which, if all of them were achieved, would reach this overall $2 million goal. These goals would then be compared with actual performance (the data base). This fact base tells us *where we are now,* whereas the objective tells us *where we want to go.* Let us assume that during the most recent 12-month period, the firm earned $1.5 million. Thus, initially, the firm has a $500,000 objective gap; that is, at the present level of performance they are $500,000 short of their goal. The objective of the profit improvement system is to close and ultimately eliminate this gap. To do this, management must analyze the variances and sort out specific problem areas. Often, this involves taking a very broad objective, such as the profit goal, and breaking it down into many parts. Suppose, for example, that we decide that a necessary condition in achieving the $2 million profit goal is to double the production and sales of Product *W.* In analyzing this problem, we observe that the process by which the product is manufactured relies on outdated and inefficient machinery. Should this equipment be replaced? If so, with what type? This situation is a *capital budgeting problem* and the responsible manager will need to compare the new costs with the expected savings and make a decision about the replacement.

If the manager decides to buy the new equipment after a careful analysis, the savings ultimately should contribute to narrowing the original objective gap. However, the decision may lead to a whole new set of problems for which new objectives must be set and facts accumulated. For example, the decision to acquire new equipment will increase the requirement for funds, and we will compare this revised capital budget with the available funds as described in the fact base. If we face a shortage, we must seek additional funds, and identify the possible sources, such as capital stock, leases, new debt, or internal financing.

So we see, as we take action to solve one problem, we may generate new problems. Our profit improvement system requires that each new problem be analyzed in essentially the same manner:

1. What is our goal (objective)?
2. What is our current status?
3. What is the size of the variance?
4. What is the cause of the variance?
5. What can be done to reduce the variance?
6. After implementing a new approach, what is the new variance?

RESPONSIBILITY CENTERS

It is important that the accounting system which provides data (as part of our profit improvement system) be designed to enable management to "fix" responsibility. That is, costs and other data in the data base must be accumulated according to *who is to be held responsible* for accomplishing a given objective. These organizational subdivisions are known as *responsibility centers.*

Management should assign responsibility for each objective so that one person can be held accountable for achieving the goal. It is equally essential that the monitoring system accumulate data which reflect the performance of each of these responsibility centers. For example, suppose we have an objective to reduce power costs in our factory to $25,000 per month, from the present level of $35,000 per month. Since we have a single power meter, the Accounting Department allocates the actual power costs to the various departments on the basis of the relative floor space occupied. This item in the fact base shows Department *B* used $6,241 of electricity last month. If the goal of $25,000 per month is also allocated on a square-foot basis then Department *B*'s share would be $4,460. Should top management now hold the manager of Department *B* accountable for this gap, and should he be charged with the responsibility for this apparent overage of $1,781? The answer to each question is *no*. Because there is only one power meter, it would probably be better to hold another individual responsible for power costs (like the plant superintendent), and have the monitoring system accumulate the *total* power *costs*.[1] Management can then more properly hold the plant superintendent accountable if the objective is not met.[2] If the company were to allocate the cost to several departments on the square-foot basis suggested earlier, the responsibility would *not* be fixed. Each of the department heads could blame the variance on the other department heads and excuse themselves on the grounds that the allocation system is unfair.

This inability to fix responsibility shows us that there can be virtually no meaningful allocation of costs to responsibility centers on the basis of averages. Each responsibility center should be charged only with those costs for which its supervisor reasonably can be held accountable. This procedure appears to conflict with what we saw in Chapter 8, where all costs were allocated to individual products. Actually, we have two accounting systems which are designed to accumulate the costs in two different manners: (1) to measure profit by assignment of costs to specific products (as we did in Chapter 8), and (2) to control costs by assigning them to particular responsibility centers.

This dual purpose of costing may be more readily understood by referring to Exhibit 13-2. Note that the total costs are the same in both cases ($55,100) but are merely accumulated in two different ways. The horizontal accumulation is by product, while the vertical accumulation is by responsibility center. In product cost accumulation, we would expect to see extensive allocation of indirect costs. For control purposes, we would find essentially no allocations. The method of accumulation in each case is established to accomplish a specific objective. Proper accounting for the purpose of measuring a product's cost may have no application from a standpoint of control.

---

[1] Or, alternatively, if we want to hold the individual department heads responsible, we would be better off to install separate meters for each department.

[2] His objective to keep power costs down, of course, *may* conflict with other objectives he has such as maximizing factory output. He must choose which objective is more important. If he chooses to increase production (which will increase power costs), then it will be necessary to revise the objective regarding power costs.

Exhibit 13-2
DUAL PURPOSE OF COSTING

| Product | Responsibility Center | | | | Total Product Cost |
	A	B	C	D	
1	$ 1,000	$ 1,500	$ 500	$ 800	$ 3,800
2	5,000	4,000	9,000	2,000	20,000
3	800	700	2,100	900	4,500
4	1,600	2,200	1,900	1,000	6,700
5	3,100	7,000	4,000	6,000	20,100
Total cost by responsibility center	$11,500	$15,400	$17,500	$10,700	$55,100

Types of Responsibility Centers

There are four general types of responsibility centers (from the least to the most complex): (1) nonmonetary centers, (2) expense centers, (3) profit centers, and (4) investment centers. In each case, a manager is responsible for one of these centers. The accounting system is then designed to accumulate data which will enable us to hold that individual accountable for any variance from the established objective.

NONMONETARY CENTER

The performance of some tasks cannot be measured in monetary terms. For example, how could we measure the output of the Accounting Department in dollars and cents? Instead, we may express our objective in terms of the *number of documents processed* each day by each accounting clerk. We could then devise a report which would accumulate facts regarding actual documents processed. These records could then be compared with the preestablished objective in order to evaluate performance. Assume, for example, that our objective calls for an accounts receivable clerk to handle 750 charge documents per week. The records maintained by the department supervisor show:

Employee	This Week	Average Year to Date
Uppin Adams	760	772
Knighton Day	500	480
Candy Kane	730	740
Zelda M. Works	780	775

Adams and Works are above the objective for both this week and the year to date. Kane is slightly below both objectives. Day is far below the objective but improvement is indicated for this week compared to his average year to date. Investigation may reveal that Day was hired only three weeks ago. His failure to meet the established objective can be explained by the fact that he is a trainee.[3] We will take a closer look at a nonmonetary responsibility center later in the chapter.

[3] This situation might result in the setting of a separate standard for a trainee, or management may simply choose to disregard the variances where they can be adequately justified.

EXPENSE CENTER

Sometimes it is not desirable or practical to measure output at all (either in monetary or nonmonetary terms). For example, how might we best evaluate the efficiency of the Custodial Department? Theoretically, we could place a dollar value on the output (sweeping the floors may be worth $3.00 per hour, washing windows $4.00 per hour, and so on) and judge the department in terms of the dollar value placed on these services. Or, we may ignore dollar value and try to measure output in some nonmonetary terms (according to number of offices cleaned per hour or number of square feet of windows washed per hour), as we did with the Accounting Department (a nonmonetary center) in the previous section. Both these methods, however, may result in more work than they are worth because we would need to keep detailed records regarding output. In this instance, we may choose to designate the department as an *expense center*. The responsible person is evaluated in terms of the expenses incurred by that department. A budget is prepared which establishes the objectives. A measurement of the actual expenses is then accumulated and compared to the budget. The department or individual is evaluated in ternˈs of how close actual performances come to the planned performance. Most expense centers are departments or operations whose output is difficult or impractical to measure. Our example showed how a Janitorial Department might be designated as an expense center because it would be difficult to evaluate performance based upon output.

PROFIT CENTER

In a profit center, the judgment about performance is based on the profits generated. The output and the input must therefore be measurable in terms of dollars. A Shoe Department in a department store could be designated as a profit center. Revenue could be measured for the department and direct expenses charged to the department. The difference between these numbers (technically contribution margin rather than profit) could be used to evaluate the department manager. On the other hand, the Accounting Department in the same store could hardly be treated as a profit center because its output can not be expressed in terms of revenue.

INVESTMENT CENTER

An investment center is a special form of profit center. In addition to revenues and expenses (profit), it may be useful to relate the amount of the investment the company has made in that center to allow evaluation in terms of the *rate of return* on the assets. Instead of looking only at profits, we can see how much profit was earned *in relation* to the investment. A large grocery chain might designate each of its stores as an investment center. The amount invested in one of the stores would vary according to size, locality, amount of inventory, and other factors. We would expect that a greater investment would yield greater profits. This rate of return might then be appropriately used as one basis for evaluating the performance of the various store managers.

Variance Analysis

As objectives are compared to the data base, *objective gaps* or *variances* are defined. Where these variances represent dollar amounts, often they may be broken into parts which will more clearly point to the problem area. To demonstrate, suppose we manufacture product Zee, which is made of material known as Omega. Engineering studies show that efficient production methods should consume 10 pounds of Omega per unit of Zee. The Purchasing Department advises us that if Omega is purchased from the best sources, in the proper quantity, and shipped to our factory by the most economical means, it should cost $3 per pound. From these data, we can set our objective as $30 for material costs per unit of Zee. Turning to our data base, we learn that during the past month we have produced 580 units of Zee and consumed 5,910 pounds of Omega, at a cost of $3.60 per pound. Calculations reveal an objective gap (negative variance) of $3,876:

	Pounds Used	**Cost per Pound**	**Total**
Objective	(580 × 10)	$3.00	$17,400
Actual	5,910	3.60	21,276
Variance from goal			–$ 3,876

Before we can find a solution to the general problem that seems to exist, we should break the variance down into specific components. Who is accountable for this variance and to whom can we look for a solution? Exhibit 13-3 helps us see how this variance can be analyzed into parts which will help us to fix responsibility. It shows that a variance has arisen because: (1) we paid too much (price variance), or (2) we used too much (quantity variance), or (3) we both paid too much and used too much (a combination price-quantity variance).[4] The formulas for calculating these three variances are shown at the bottom of the diagram.

The price variance (–$3,480) would be the responsibility of the purchasing agent. Did our purchasing procedures break down? Why did we pay more than our objective called for? Is our objective realistic or should it be revised?

The quantity variance (–$330) is the responsibility of the foreman. Were the workers careless in the use of materials? Did we have untrained workers? Was the quality of the product better than expected? Is our objective realistic or should it be revised?

Responsibility for the combination price-quantity variance (–$66) cannot be fixed on a single individual. It is obviously the result of two variables but normally will not be significant in relation to the other two variances. As we will see later, this variance is frequently combined with one of the other two as there is little to be gained from computing it separately.

Once we have answers to our questions regarding what caused the variances, we are ready to start through the cycle again. If our objective was not realistic, we should revise it. This new standard should then be compared with the updated fact base as the cycle repeats itself.

---

[4] The diagram is drawn to illustrate all negative variances (where we used *too much* and paid *too much*). The reverse could also occur (used less than our objective and paid less than our objective) as could other combinations.

Exhibit 13-3
Variance Analysis

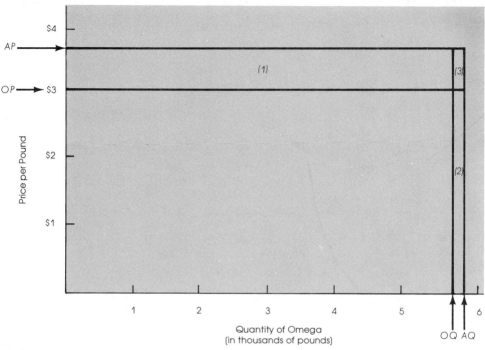

Variance

(1) Price variance = (Objective price – Actual price) × Objective quantity
($3 – $3.60) × 5,800 = –$3,480

(2) Quantity = (Objective quantity – Actual quantity) × Objective price
variance (5,800 – 5,910) × $3 = –$330

(3) Combination
price-quantity = (Objective price – Actual price) × (Objective quantity – Actual quantity)
variance

= (3 – $3.60) × (5,800 – 5,910) = –$ 66
‾‾‾‾‾‾‾‾‾‾
–$3,876

STANDARD COST ACCOUNTING

Some companies incorporate a similar variance analysis into a *standard cost accounting system*. These companies continue to maintain a full cost accounting system similar to those described in Chapter 8. The only difference is that the standard cost-accounting system accumulates *standard* costs, which can be defined as the amount that it *should* cost to produce a particular item under *ideal (but attainable)* circumstances. The purpose of a standard cost system is to facilitate *control* over the production process. The standards serve as our profit improvement objectives and are periodically compared with actual costs to evaluate efficiency. Differences between actual costs and standard costs are called *variances*, and serve as *flags* to management, indicating the areas that require special attention. Variances may occur in material, labor, and overhead costs.

359

Material Variances

Any input into the production process can be analyzed in terms of the three variances discussed in the previous section: (1) according to differences in prices (price variance), (2) according to differences in quantities (quantity variance), and (3) according to a combination of the two factors (price-quantity variance). Because the purpose of a standard cost system is *control,* little is gained by calculating the combination variance because: (1) responsibility for this variance cannot be fixed, and (2) the variance is normally insignificant in relation to either the price or quantity variance. For these reasons, the combination variance is frequently combined with one of the other variances and is not calculated as a *separate* variance. Common practice is to treat the combination variance as part of the price variance, although no strong reason can be seen for including it in one variance over the other. Where this practice is followed, the formulas for the material variances are:

$$\text{Material price variance} = (SP - AP) \times AQ$$
$$\text{Material quantity variance} = (SQ - AQ) \times SP$$

where:

SP = standard price per unit of material
AP = actual per unit price paid for materials purchased
SQ = standard quantity of materials per unit of output
AQ = actual quantity of materials

From these formulas, a positive sign signifies a favorable variance (better than standard performance), while a negative sign signifies an unfavorable variance (worse than standard performance).[5] The purchasing agent (who is responsible for purchasing) should be held accountable for the price variance while the foreman (person responsible for production) should be held accountable for the quantity variance.

Labor Variances

Labor costs may be analyzed in a manner similar to that just used for materials, except that the terminology is different. Because the price of labor is usually stated as an amount per period of time, the price variance is known as the *labor rate variance.* Likewise, since the objective of an analysis of the amount of effort worked is to evaluate the employees' efficiency, the quantity variance for labor is called the *labor efficiency variance.* The combination rate-efficiency variance is combined with the labor rate variance as:

[5] We need to be careful when referring to positive variances as *favorable* and negative variances as *unfavorable,* although the practice is common. Analysis of the variance is really necessary before we can judge whether the results are good or bad. For example, we might create a favorable (positive) variance by skimping on materials used and thereby produce an inferior product that results in lost sales. Such a practice should hardly be called favorable.

$$\text{Labor rate variance} = (SR - AR) \times AH$$
$$\text{Labor efficiency variance} = (SH - AH) \times SR$$

where:

SR = standard rate of labor per hour

AR = actual rate of labor per hour

SH = standard hours of labor (actual output × standard hours per unit of output)

AH = actual hours of labor worked to produce actual output

The personnel director (person responsible for hiring) is accountable for the rate variance while the foreman (person responsible for production) is accountable for the efficiency variance.

Mix Variances

When a firm uses more than one class of an input (either labor or material) and there is substitutability among these inputs, it may be helpful to calculate a *mix variance*. Such a variance will assist management in determining whether or not the inputs have been used in proper proportions. To calculate the mix variance we must first establish the standard proportions: What proportions will result in minimizing the product cost while maintaining desired quality in the end product?

Once this standard proportion has been established, we can compare actual with standard usage by calculating a mix variance. To illustrate, assume we are producing a product which utilizes three classes of workers. Each unit produced should use 5.2 hours in the following proportions:

Worker Category	Standard Hours	Percent of Total	Standard Rate	Standard Cost
Machining	2.4	46.15	$10.00	$24.00
Assembling	1.8	34.62	6.00	10.80
Polishing	1.0	19.23	4.00	4.00
Total per unit of output	5.2	100.00		$38.80

Average standard hourly rate ($38.80/5.2 hours) $7.46 per hour

Each of the workers is capable of performing any of the 3 functions but is most efficient in his particular specialty. Actual labor costs of producing 1,200 units in the month of November were:

Machinists	3,500 hours	@ $9.50 =	$33,250
Assemblers	2,200	@ 6.10 =	13,420
Polishers	800	@ 3.90 =	3,120
Totals	6,500 hours		$49,790

To calculate the mix variance, we first take the actual total direct-labor hours (6,500 hours) and figure out how many hours should have been worked by each class of worker according to our standard proportions. These figures, when compared with the actual results and multiplied by the standard rates, will give us the mix variances shown below:

	Standard Proportions	Actual Hours in Standard Proportions	Actual Hours in Actual Proportions	Difference	Standard Rate	Variance
Machinist	46.15%	3,000	3,500	−500	$10	−$5,000
Assembler	34.62	2,250	2,200	+50	6	+ 300
Polisher	19.23	1,250	800	+450	4	+ 1,800
	100.00%	6,500	6,500	0		−$2,900

These figures indicate that we incurred an extra $2,900 in costs during the period because we did not use the best combination (correct proportions) of workers. We used too much high cost labor (machinists) which cost us $5,000 extra. This amount was partially offset by utilizing less low cost labor (assemblers and polishers) which saved us $2,100. The net cost of using the wrong classes of labor was $2,900.

Where mix variances are calculated, the efficiency variance should be based on total hours used (6,500 hours) and the weighted-average standard rate ($7.46) as follows:

$$\text{Labor efficiency variance} = (SH - AH) \times SR$$
$$= (6,240 - 6,500) \times \$7.46$$
$$= -\$1,939.60$$

Separate rate variances could be calculated for each class of labor as:

$$\text{Labor rate variance (machinists)} = (SR - AR) \times AH$$
$$= (10 - \$9.50) \times 3,500$$
$$= \$1,750$$
$$\text{Labor rate variance (assemblers)} = (SR - AR) \times AH$$
$$= (\$6 - \$6.10) \times 2,200$$
$$= -\$220$$
$$\text{Labor rate variance (polishers)} = (SR - AR) \times AH$$
$$= (\$4 - \$3.90) \times 800$$
$$= \$80$$

Summary of variances:
Mix variances:

Machinists	−$5,000
Assemblers	+ 300
Polishers	+ 1,800
Rate variances:	
Machinists	+ 1,750
Assemblers	− 220
Polishers	+ 80
Efficiency variance:	− 1,940
Total*	−$3,230

*This total reconciles the difference between the standard cost of the actual output ($46,560) and the actual sums paid for labor ($49,790).

Generally, the foreman should be held accountable for the mix variance because he is responsible for using the inputs in the proper proportions. In our example, he has assigned skilled workers (machinists) to do relatively unskilled work (assembling and polishing). This deviation may be due to improper scheduling, lack of qualified workers (machinists and polishers), failure of suppliers to furnish requested inputs, or other causes. It should be noted that a variance analysis does not *explain* the variance gaps. It merely puts a measure upon them that assists management's evaluation of the performance of the responsibility center's head.

Overhead Variances (Two Variances)

There are many ways of analyzing the difference between actual and standard overhead. The simplest way, of course, is to have a single overhead variance. In a sense, this is what we did in Chapter 8 when we utilized a predetermined overhead rate. The entire difference between the actual overhead incurred and that applied to production was treated as over- or underapplied overhead. This difference could have been termed an *overhead variance*.

The single overhead analysis has limited usefulness because it does not provide management with any suggestions as to why the variances occurred and, therefore, does little to assist control.

In order to analyze the overhead in a more meaningful manner, the standard overhead rate should be divided into fixed and variable components. The variable overhead rate should remain constant regardless of the level of plant activity because, by definition, the total variable costs vary directly with production. The fixed overhead, on the other hand, remains constant in *total*. As the level of production increases or decreases, the fixed overhead rate in the opposite direction changes, as this constant sum must be spread over a greater or smaller number of units. The higher the level of production, the lower the fixed overhead per unit of output.

A flexible budget shows us what the overhead rate will be at various production levels. To illustrate, assume the following overhead costs are budgeted:

Annual fixed costs	$500,000
Variable costs per unit of output	4

Exhibit 13-4 plots the total anticipated overhead costs at various levels of activity. The curve is called the *budget line,* and it represents the following budget formula:

$$\text{Budgeted overhead} = FC + (VOH_o \times V_o)$$
$$= \$500,000 + (\$4 \times V_o)$$

where: FC = fixed costs
VOH_o = variable overhead per unit of output
V_o = volume expressed in units of output

We noted in Chapter 8 that an actual cost-accounting system may use a *predetermined* overhead rate to estimate the cost of the units produced. The calculation of this overhead rate uses a *standard volume,* which is the level

Exhibit 13-4
Flexible Overhead Budget

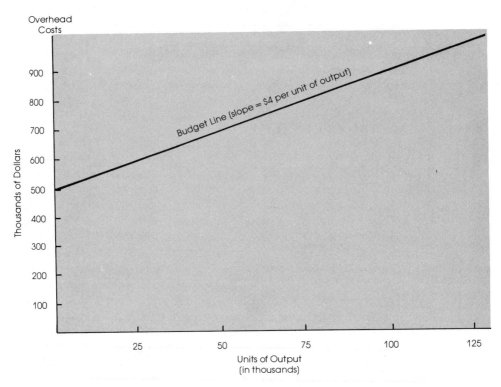

of production activity that can be anticipated under ideal (but attainable) conditions. The overhead rate figured at this level of activity sometimes is known as the *absorption rate*. If we assume a standard volume of 100,000 units of output, we can plot the *absorbed line* shown in Exhibit 13-5. The slope of the line represents the standard *overhead rate*, and is $9 of overhead per unit of output.

There are two reasons that actual overhead might vary from standard: first, because we did not produce at standard volume (overhead volume variance); or second, because we paid more or less for the overhead costs than anticipated (overhead spending variance). The formulas for these two variances are:

$$\text{Overhead volume variance} = A_bOH - BOH$$
$$\text{Overhead spending variance} = BOH - A_cOH$$

where:

BOH = budgeted overhead costs (at actual volume)
A_bOH = absorbed overhead costs
A_cOH = actual overhead costs

If we assume that the standard volume was 100,000 units, and actual production during the year 97,000 units, and actual overhead costs $902,000, we can calculate these variances as:

Exhibit 13-5

**Comparison of Budgeted and Absorbed Overhead
Based upon Output**

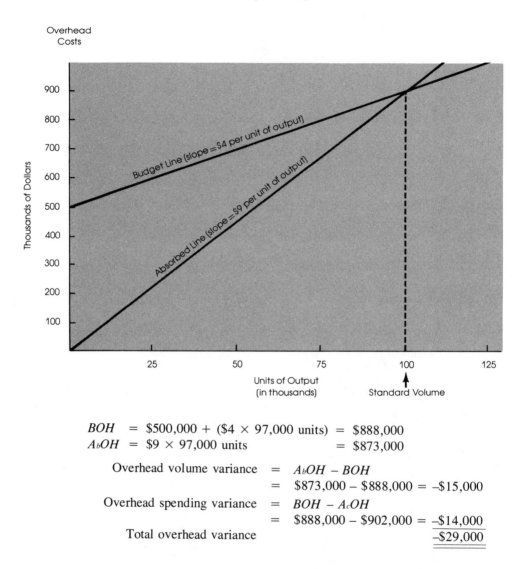

Overhead
Costs

Thousands of Dollars

Budget Line (slope = $4 per unit of output)

Absorbed Line (slope = $9 per unit of output)

900
800
700
600
500
400
300
200
100

25   50   75   100   125

Units of Output
(in thousands)

Standard Volume

$$BOH = \$500,000 + (\$4 \times 97,000 \text{ units}) = \$888,000$$
$$A_bOH = \$9 \times 97,000 \text{ units} \qquad\qquad = \$873,000$$

Overhead volume variance $= A_bOH - BOH$

$\qquad\qquad\qquad\qquad\quad = \$873,000 - \$888,000 = -\$15,000$

Overhead spending variance $= BOH - A_cOH$

$\qquad\qquad\qquad\qquad\quad = \$888,000 - \$902,000 = -\$14,000$

Total overhead variance $\qquad\qquad\qquad\qquad\qquad\quad \underline{-\$29,000}$

The sales manager (or other person responsible for keeping the factory operating at standard capacity) should be held responsible for the volume variance. This variance arises when we operate at any level other than standard volume because fixed costs must then be allocated over more or fewer units of output. The sales manager is normally charged with the responsibility of assuring that the company does operate at the planned level of activity. The spending variance should be broken into component parts according to responsibility center and the heads of these departments held accountable for differences between actual and budgeted amounts. The student should note again that the variance itself does not tell us *what* is wrong or even necessarily *who* is wrong. Instead, it tells us that something needs investigating (and possibly, explaining) and who in our organization is responsible for making that investigation.

Overhead Variances (Three Variances)

In the analysis of overhead just completed, we assumed that overhead was absorbed *on the basis of output* ($9 per unit of *output*). Often, overhead is absorbed according to an input factor, such as direct-labor hours. Where this procedure is used, the overhead variance may be broken into three parts: a volume variance, a spending variance, and an efficiency variance. This third variance is tied directly to the input factor upon which overhead absorption is based. Assume, for example, that the overhead is absorbed on the basis of direct-labor hours. If the workers spend too much time making the product (causing a negative labor efficiency variance), they will also use too much overhead (such as heat and power) thereby causing a negative overhead efficiency variance.

If overhead is absorbed (and budgeted) on the basis of input, our formulas for budgeted and absorbed overhead must be revised. To illustrate, assume the following budgeted amounts:

Annual fixed-overhead costs	$500,000
Variable overhead costs	$2 per *direct-labor hour*
Standard volume	200,000 *direct-labor hours*
Ratio of input to output (standard)	2 direct-labor hours per 1 unit of output

Our budgeted and absorbed costs are diagrammed in Exhibit 13-6 (p. 368). Note that the horizontal axis now reads direct-labor hours instead of units of output. The formulas for our budgeted and absorbed overhead costs become:

$$BOH = FC + (VOH_I \times AH)$$
$$A_bOH = SOH_I \times AH$$

where:

BOH = budgeted overhead costs at actual volume (hours)

A_bOH = absorbed overhead costs at actual volume (hours)

FC = fixed overhead costs ($500,000)

VOH_I = variable overhead costs per unit of input (direct-labor hours)

AH = actual direct-labor hours

SOH_I = standard overhead rate per unit of input (direct-labor hours)

If we assume actual overhead costs of $902,000, actual output of 97,000 units, and actual input of 198,000 direct-labor hours, we can calculate our budget and spending variances as:

$$BOH = FC + (VOH_I \times AH)$$
$$= \$500,000 + (\$2 \times 198,000 \text{ hours})$$
$$= \$896,000$$

$$A_bOH = SOH_I \times AH$$
$$= \$4.50 \times 198,000 \text{ hours}$$
$$= \$891,000$$

Overhead volume variance $= A_bOH - BOH$
$$= \$891,000 - \$896,000$$
$$= -\$5,000$$

Overhead spending variance $= BOH - A_cOH$
$$= \$896,000 - \$902,000$$
$$= -\$6,000$$

where:

BOH = budgeted overhead costs at the actual volume
FC = fixed costs
VOH_I = variable overhead costs per unit of input (direct-labor hours)
AH = actual direct-labor hours
A_bOH = absorbed overhead costs
SOH_I = standard overhead rate per unit of input (direct-labor hours)
A_cOH = actual overhead costs

In addition to the above variances, we can calculate the *overhead efficiency variance* because we are absorbing overhead on the basis of direct-labor hours instead of units of output. Unless the number of actual hours worked happens to agree with the number of hours that *should have been worked* to produce the actual output, we will have an overhead efficiency variance, which is calculated as:

Overhead efficiency variance $= (SH - AH) \times SOH_I$
$$= (194,000 - 198,000) \times \$4.50$$
$$= -\$18,000$$

where:

SH = standard hours (hours it *should* have taken to produce actual output) (2 hours per unit $\times$ 97,000 units)
AH = actual direct-labor hours (given)
SOH_I = standard overhead rate per unit of input (direct-labor hours)

Exhibit 13-6
Comparison of Budgeted and Absorbed Overhead
Based on Input

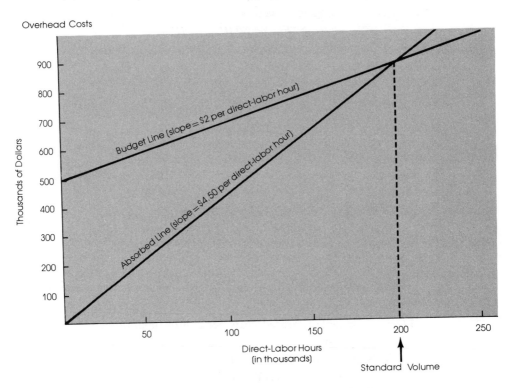

The three overhead variances may be summarized:

Overhead volume variance	−$ 5,000
Overhead spending variance	− 6,000
Overhead efficiency variance	− 18,000
Total overhead variance	−$29,000

This total variance agrees with the total shown under the two variance analyses presented earlier (page 365). All we have done is to break the total variance ($29,000) down into three parts (three causes) instead of two parts. There are other ways of subdividing overhead variances, which we will not attempt to present here. But you should understand that any variance breakdown should assist managers in fixing responsibility and in evaluating performance. Otherwise, it should not be calculated.

Establishing Standards

Standards should be established by carefully analyzing what it would cost to produce a given product under *attainable, efficient* production conditions. Engineering studies may be necessary to establish the best combination of ingredients. Careful analysis of materials, dimensions, and prices may be

368

necessary to arrive at the best combination of inputs. Layout men may assist in deciding just how the necessary parts must be cut or assembled to assure minimum waste. *Time-and-motion studies* may be made to determine the time required to perform a given task at maximum efficiency. In short, many management resources are brought to bear on the question of what it *should* cost to produce a given product when everyone performs efficiently.

Advantages of Standards

One advantage of a standard cost system is that it encourages managers to use the *management by exception* approach (see Chapter 11) and focus their attention on apparent inefficiencies. The variances generated help managers *identify* the problem areas, and thus direct their efforts toward solving the most damaging ones. Establishing standards helps management scrutinize the entire business operation to arrive at the best coordinated methods of production.

Recordkeeping is simplified with a standard cost system and, accordingly, cost data are more readily available and more easily calculated. Under this approach most of the cost flows are recorded at standard figures, and the various inventory accounts are carried at standard cost rather than actual. This practice greatly simplifies the perpetual inventory system, because no records need to be maintained for various unit costs. The records reflect quantities, *only,* which are later multiplied by the standard unit cost.

Limitations of Standards

It is neither easy nor cheap to establish accurate standards, and once set, they are still subject to change. When major changes occur in the product, in any of its components, or in the method of manufacture, the once valid standard becomes obsolete. Furthermore, standards have limited usefulness and little application where items are produced on a one-time basis or where the categories of items produced differ greatly from period to period.

Variances cannot be regarded as solutions to management problems; rather, they should be interpreted in light of the situation surrounding the operations during the particular period the variances arise. A price variance, for example, might have several causes: Quantities sufficient to take advantage of large order discounts may not have been ordered; a strike may have required a more expensive form of shipping; or substantial price increases may have been posted by suppliers. Unfortunately, experience frequently shows that variances can be easily misinterpreted. Instead of enabling management to pinpoint the problem, variances merely call attention to the general problem area. Solving the problem is left to the responsible manager.

Standard cost systems sometimes create problems in labor relations. For example, many unions resist attempts to measure efficiency. Also, workers sometimes fear that standards will become too rigid and thereby threaten their job security (unfortunately, these fears may be well-founded). Others fear that management may misinterpret the variance and, without giving the workers any chance to explain, use it as an ironclad decision rule for passing out rewards and punishments. It is well-known and understandable that an attempt to check on efficiency usually receives little enthusiasm or cooperation from the employees, and often does not provide meaningful results.

STANDARD COST SYSTEM ILLUSTRATED

The variance analysis described in the previous sections can be incorporated into a formal job-order or process cost system by recording costs at standard, paying the costs at actual, and then generating variance accounts as the goods flow through the manufacturing process. To illustrate, the Trivet Blivet Company uses a *process cost* system and has established the standards shown in Exhibit 13-7.

Exhibit 13-7
Standard Cost to Produce One Blivet

Materials, 40 pounds @ $2.00 per pound	$ 80.00
Labor, 27 hours @ $3.00 per hour	81.00
Overhead, 100% of direct-labor cost	81.00
Total cost	$242.00

Budgeted Overhead	Amount	Rate per Hour*
Fixed overhead per month	$ 5,400	$1.00
Variable overhead	10,800	2.00
Total	$16,200	$3.00

*Standard volume (per month) is 200 Blivets (requires 5,400 direct-labor hours)

Based on the standards in Exhibit 13-7 and other actual data, the following journal entries would be recorded:

1. 10,000 pounds of material are purchased on account at cost of $20,500.

Journal entry: Materials	20,000	
Material Price Variance	500	
Accounts Payable		20,500

The amount paid for the materials is entered in the Raw Materials account at $20,000. This amount represents the actual quantity purchased (10,000 pounds) at the standard price ($2.00 per pound). The Accounts Payable, of course, must be recorded at the actual cost of the material ($20,500). The difference represents the material price variance. This amount may be confirmed by utilizing the previously cited formula:

$$MPV = (SP - AP) \times AQ$$
$$= (\$2.00 - \$2.05) \times 10,000 \text{ pounds} = -\$500$$

2. The factory payroll, amounting to $15,325, was computed as: 4,800 direct-labor hours at $3.10 per hour, and 178 indirect-labor hours at $2.50 per hour.

Journal Entry: Direct Labor	14,400	
Direct Labor Rate Variance	480	
Manufacturing Overhead	445	
Payroll Payable		15,325

The Direct Labor account is charged with $14,400 which represents the actual direct-labor hours worked (4,800 hours) times the standard direct-labor rate ($3.00 per hour). The Manufacturing Overhead account is charged with the actual indirect-labor cost of $445 (178 hours at $2.50 per hour), while the Payroll Payable account is credited for the actual total payroll cost of $15,325. The balancing figure is $480, the Direct Labor Rate Variance, and may be calculated:

$$LRV = (SR - AR) \times AH$$
$$= (\$3.00 - \$3.10) \times 4,800 \text{ hours} = -\$480$$

3.   Overhead costs incurred during the month (in addition to the $445 indirect-labor recorded above) are:

   a.   Cost of electricity services consumed was $2,300 and was paid with cash.

   b.   Factory insurance expired during the month amounted to $1,450. The insurance has previously been recorded as prepaid.

   c.   Rent for the factory building for the month is due but unpaid in the amount of $6,000.

   d.   Machinery and equipment (factory) depreciation amounts to $5,000 for the month.

Journal entry: Manufacturing Overhead   14,750
                     Cash   2,300
                     Prepaid Insurance   1,450
                     Rent Payable   6,000
                     Accumulated Depreciation,
                       Machinery and Equipment   5,000

(No variances for overhead can be recorded until the figures regarding production for the period are available.)

4.   Production departments used 6,825 pounds of material to produce 175 equivalent units.

Journal entry: Work-in-Process   14,000
                     Materials   13,650
                     Materials Quantity Variance   350

The Work-in-Process account should be charged with only the standard cost of material that *should* have been used, that is, the equivalent production (175 units) times the standard quantity per unit (40 pounds) times the standard price ($2.00 per pound), or $14,000. The Raw Materials account must be credited for the actual quantity used (6,825 pounds) times the standard price ($2.00 per pound). The difference is a favorable (credit) variance of $350, calculated as:

$$MQV = (SQ - AQ) \times SP$$
$$= (7,000 \text{ pounds} - 6,825 \text{ pounds}) \times \$2.00 = \$350$$

5.   4,800 hours of direct-labor were worked to produce 175 equivalent units.

Journal entry: Work-in-Process   14,175
                     Direct Labor Efficiency Variance   225
                          Direct Labor   14,400

As was done with materials, the Work-in-Process account is charged with only the labor cost that *should* have been incurred to produce 175 units. According to the preestablished standard, we should have used $14,175 of labor (175 Blivets × 27 hours per Blivet × $3.00 per hour). The Direct Labor account should be credited for the actual direct-labor hours worked (4,800 hours) at the standard labor rate ($3.00 per hour), or $14,400. The difference of $225 represents a labor efficiency variance. The amount of this variance may be checked by utilizing the formula:

$$LEV = (SH - AH) \times SR$$
$$= (4,725 \text{ hours} - 4,800 \text{ hours}) \times \$3.00 = -\$225$$

6. Overhead is applied to production at a rate of 100 percent of direct-labor costs.

Journal entry:

Work-in-Process	14,175	
Overhead Spending Variance	195	
Overhead Volume Variance	600	
Overhead Efficiency Variance	225	
Manufacturing Overhead		15,195

Now that the production for the period is known (175 equivalent units), we can assign overhead costs to Work-in-Process and calculate three overhead variances. The debit to Work-in-Process is again determined by what *should* be charged according to the standards (175 units × $81 overhead per unit). The credit to Overhead is for the amount of the *actual* overhead costs recorded during the period ($445 + $14,750 = $15,195). The difference of $1,020 represents the *total* overhead variance which was broken down as follows:

Overhead Spending Variance

$$OSV = BOH - A_cOH$$
$$= (\$5,400 + (4,800 \text{ hours} \times \$2.00)) - \$15,195$$
$$= \$15,000 - \$15,195 = -\$195$$

Overhead Volume Variance

$$OVV = A_bOH - BOH$$
$$= (4,800 \text{ hours} \times \$3.00) - [\$5,400 + (4,800 \text{ hours} \times \$2.00)]$$
$$= \$14,400 - \$15,000 = -\$600$$

Overhead Efficiency Variance

$$OEV = (SH - AH) \times SOR$$
$$= (4,725 \text{ hours} - 4,800 \text{ hours}) \times \$3.00 = -\$225$$

7. 160 Blivets are completed during the period and transferred to the warehouse:

Journal entry:

Finished Goods	38,720	
Work-in-Process		38,720

In the previous entries the Work-in-Process account was charged only with standard costs. As units are completed, they are recorded in the Finished Goods inventory at the standard cost of $242 per unit.

8. 150 Blivets are sold on account for $400 per unit.

Journal entry:

Accounts Receivable	60,000	
Sales		60,000
Cost of Goods Sold	36,300	
Finished Goods		36,300

As goods are sold, they are removed from the Finished Goods inventory at standard cost ($242 per unit).

9. The variance accounts are generally carried on the books as deferred charges (asset) or deferred credits (liability) from month to month until they are closed to the Cost of Goods Sold account at the end of the year. The following entry would close the variance accounts. (Notice that the net effect of the variances was an $1,875 understatement of the product's cost.)

Journal entry:	Cost of Goods Sold	1,875	
	Material Quantity Variance	350	
	Material Price Variance		500
	Direct Labor Rate Variance		480
	Direct Labor Efficiency Variance		225
	Overhead Spending Variance		195
	Overhead Efficiency Variance		225
	Overhead Volume Variance		600

A SERVICE INDUSTRY APPLICATION

Standard cost systems and many other variations of profit improvement plans were first developed for manufacturing operations and have continued to be used more extensively by manufacturing firms than service industries. The concepts, nevertheless, have application beyond the confines of the production line. The following paragraphs will present an illustration of the use of these concepts outside the manufacturing framework—in a bank.

Work Measurement

The first task in any standard system is to establish meaningful standards. In this example, the initial step was to carefully analyze the tasks performed in the bank, which were then timed under carefully controlled circumstances.

In order to have a convenient unit of measure for all operations, elapsed time was measured in time measurement units (TMU). One TMU is equal to 1/100,000 hours, or 0.036 seconds. Each task was analyzed and a standard time established and expressed in TMUs.

In the Proof Department, for example, the employees receive large volumes of checks written by depositors of the bank. They must be prepared for computer processing, which deducts them from the various customer accounts. To avoid certain errors, the checks are input into the computer system as carefully controlled *batches,* or bundles. A task analysis sheet for a particular job in the Proof Department is shown in Exhibit 13-8. The standard time to "get checks" from the tray has been set at 44 TMUs while the standard time to "remove the rubber band" is 16 TMUs. The 4 steps shown on the task analysis sheet total 102 TMUs. This amount is transferred to an *operation summary sheet,* shown in the bottom portion, with the time to complete other tasks. Because an average bundle is known to contain 34 items, operation 1 (preparing bundle to *run*) shows a frequency of 1 per 34 items, or only 3 TMUs per item. Other operations are similarly converted according to the frequency with which they are expected to occur.

Performance Records

Each employee maintains a daily time record which shows the operations performed and the actual time spent on each of them. These data are accumulated on a weekly activity report, like the one shown in Exhibit 13-9 for Marion Evans, an employee of the Proof Department. Notice that only tasks subject to time measurement are included under "measurable time." Time

Exhibit 13-8
Task Analysis Sheet

ANY NATIONAL BANK	☐ OPERATION SUMMARY		APPROVED	CODE 402-1		
CLERICAL EXCELLENCE	☒ TASK ANALYSIS SHEET		ANALYST Baird	DATE Mar.'76	PAGE 2 OF 4	

DESCRIPTION   IBM-803 Clearing Items

Prepare Bundle to Run

DEPT. BRANCH Central Operations		SECTION Proof Department				
UNIT						

LINE NO.	DESCRIPTION	UNIT	REFERENCE	ELEMENT TIME TMU	FREQ.	TOTAL TMU
1	Get checks	Occ	CGB-TU-01	44	1	44
2	Remove rubber band	Occ	CPB-RR-01	16	1	16
3	Aside rubber band	Occ	CCA-OT-01	17	1	17
4	Aside checks to feed tray	Occ	CGA-OR-01	25	1	25
					TOTAL TMU	102

ANY NATIONAL BANK	☒ OPERATION SUMMARY		APPROVED	CODE 402		
CLERICAL EXCELLENCE	☐ TASK ANALYSIS SHEET		ANALYST Baird	DATE Mar.'68	PAGE 1 Of 4	

DESCRIPTION   IBM-803 Clearing Items

Per Item Handling

DEPT. BRANCH Central Operations		SECTION Proof Department				
UNIT						

LINE NO.	DESCRIPTION	UNIT	REFERENCE	ELEMENT TIME TMU	FREQ.	TOTAL TMU
1	Prepare bundle to run	Item	402-1	102	1/34	3
2	Process per item	item	402-2	47	1	47
3	Batch card - non add	item	402-3	49	¼	12
					TOTAL TMU	62

Exhibit 13-9
Weekly Activity Report

WEEKLY ACTIVITY REPORT

Employee Name ___Marion Evans___

Department ___Proof___

Employee Number ___091385___

Week Ended ___11/19/76___

		MONDAY	TUESDAY	WEDNESDAY	THURSDAY	FRIDAY	WEEKLY TOTAL
Chargeable Hours:							
Code	402	2.7	2.4	3.0			8.1
Code	407	3.4	3.1	2.2		2.7	11.4
Code	291	1.1		1.0		1.0	2.1
Code	470	.3		1.0		.8	2.1
Code	344		2.0				2.0
Code	380			.9		1.5	2.4
Code							
Code							
Code							
Code							
Unmeasured			.5				.5
Delay				.4			.4
Errors				7.5		6.0	24.5
Total Chargeable		8.0	8.0	7.5	0	6.0	24.5
Nonchargeable Hours:							
Absent						2.0	2.0
Vacation					8.0		8.0
Holiday							
Training							
Administration							
Other				.5			.5
Total Nonchargeable				.5	8.0	2.0	10.5
Grand Totals		8.0	8.0	8.0	8.0	8.0	40.0

spent on vacation, holiday, loan to other departments, and similar activities are not treated as "chargeable" items. Time wasted due to delay and errors, while chargeable to the department, is not subject to standardization, and is itemized separately. The employee's time on the job is expressed in hours and tenths of hours to facilitate recordkeeping. A computer program converts the hours and TMUs to a common basis for comparison.

In order to measure performance, we need to know not only the time spent on each task, but also how much was accomplished. This second item of information is reported on a daily time report prepared by the department head. The report indicates the number of times each task was accomplished by each employee. It would show, for example, the "number of bundles" prepared for run each day by Marion Evans as well as the number of times she performed each of the other tasks reported on her time sheet.

Performance Summary

Each week the section head is furnished an employee performance report, like the one shown in Exhibit 13-10. It is prepared by a computer program, utilizing the data from the employees' time reports (as shown on the weekly activity report), the department head's daily reports on performance, and the standards established by management (as shown on the task analysis sheet). Performance (based on the above inputs) is expressed as a percent of standard for the most recent 13-week period as well as for the current period. For example, Evans performed at 123 percent of standard (better than standard) during this past week, but has averaged only 89 percent over the past 13-week period.

Reports like this one can assist management at various levels in evaluating performance. To be effective, this standard system must be incorporated into an overall profit improvement system such as the one described in the first section of this chapter. The variances from standard must be analyzed into specific problem areas and interpreted with care because a variance could reflect: (1) a faulty or unrealistic standard, (2) an inaccurate measurement of actual performance, (3) the existence of unusual and noncontrollable factors, (4) poor performance, or (5) superior performance. Investigation into the problem area highlighted by the variances should enable management to pinpoint the problem and to initiate corrective action.

SUMMARY

Profit improvement can best be accomplished through a system which compares actual results against objectives. A system which: (1) sets specific profit improvement objectives; (2) establishes accounting reports that provide timely data regarding actual performance in each of these objective areas (the data base); (3) enables management to regularly compare actual performance against planned objectives to determine the variance or objective gap; (4) analyzes the variances into specific problem areas according to lines of responsibility; (5) enables management to plot specific corrective action

Exhibit 13-10
Employee Performance Summary

ANY NATIONAL BANK — WEEK ENDING 11

DIVISION NO. 2 SALT LAKE DIV	DEPARTMENT NO. 1 CENTRAL OPERATIONS	SECTION NO. 60 PROOF	SUPERVISOR NO. 1 J. HARMON

EMPLOYEE NUMBER	NAME		PERFORMANCE 13 Week	PERFORMANCE Cur. Wk.	STANDARD ALLOWED HOURS	MEASURABLE Measured	MEASURABLE Unmeas.	CHARGEABLE HOURS DELAY	CHARGEABLE HOURS ERRORS	CHARGEABLE HOURS PAID NOT WORKED	SERVICE AND ADMIN	TOTAL AVAILABLE	NON-CHARGEABLE LOANED	NON-CHARGEABLE APPROVED ACTIVITY	NON-CHARGEABLE ABSENCE VACATION HOLIDAY	TOTAL STRAIGHT HOURS
0013851	EVANS	P P	89	123	7.9	28.6	4.0	.5	.4			29.5		.5	10.0	40.0
0012788	MURDOCK	P P	94	115	9.7	8.4	2.4	18.3				30.7				30.7
0016750	BAGLEY	P P	92	115	17.1	14.9	.9		1.4			18.7				18.7
0011277	LLOYD	P P	111	112	31.5	28.1	1.6	.2	4.7			33.9				33.9
0015641	ELLING		102	111	28.2	25.3	5.8	.4	.7			28.0		1.0	4.0	32.0
0006921	HANSEN	P	105	110	30.2	27.5	4.6	3.6	2.1			39.0		6.7		40.0
0015757	BURK	P	107	110	16.8	11.6		8.4	.7			25.3				32.0
0006699	FOX	P	106	100	23.7	15.5	22.6	8.6				46.7				46.7
0016136	HOCKING	P	83	102	19.2	23.3	4.7	.3	.8			28.3				28.3
0016227	ELLSWOR		95	101	14.0	19.0	7.6					27.4				27.4
0014396	HATCH		53	95		14.8	8.1	1.1	1.3		21.0	24.0	16.0			40.0
0013778	CARLSON		71	94		17.0		.5	5.0			41.5				41.5
0016946	DUNN	P	89	89	23.3	26.2	1.7	6.1	2.6			41.5				41.5
0018199	MONSON		88	85	19.1	22.5	4.2	5.5	4.9	.3		34.5		1.0	3.0	43.5
0013876	MATHESON		88	83	26.5	31.9	3.9	4.8	2.3			43.2				43.2
0016235	LARSEN	P	81	75	16.8	22.4	1.3					27.1				27.1
0016300	TAYLOR	P	66	75	16.0	21.3	2.4	4.5	4.3			28.4		1.0		28.4
0012802	AMOTT		71	70	20.8	29.9	7.1	8.7	1.1			39.0		1.5		40.0
0014214	BROCK	P	78	70	23.0	32.7	.3	3.5	4.5			42.5				44.0
0013933	UTLEY		48	63	19.6	31.2	2.0	3.5	6.2			41.2				41.2
0010294	BROWN		48	58	19.3	33.7		1.5	2.5			43.1				43.1
0018967	MOSS		39	33		28.0						32.0			8.0	40.0
0000001	HUGHES		88								5.1	19.6				19.6
0003084	BARKER	O	109						14.0			18.5				20.0
0011202	MOORE	P P	78									22.0	21.5		20.0	40.0
0013455	TEMPEST															
0013914	WEST	P	69		17.0	17.0	4.2	.8			13.5					22.0
0019106	RAYMOND															
	TOTALS				420.9	530.8	89.9	80.5	59.5	.3	44.6	805.6	37.5	11.7	50.0	904.8

STANDARDS GOAL 90. — ACTUAL 83.

ADJUSTED TOTAL SAH 530.8

AVERAGE STAFF PERFORMANCE GOAL 85. — ACTUAL 83.

STAFF PERFORMANCE GOAL 89.9 — 79. ACTUAL

STAFF EFFECTIVENESS GOAL 77. — ACTUAL 77.

377

to reduce the variance; and (6) establishes a feedback system to monitor results and regularly update the data base and revise (when necessary) the objectives.

To be effective, a profit improvement system should establish *responsibility centers* that fix responsibility for specific profit improvement objectives. Four types of responsibility centers are commonly found: *Nonmonetary centers* are used when it is difficult to assign dollar values to tasks performed or to evaluate results in monetary terms. *Expense centers* are used when output can not be expressed in monetary terms but performance can be judged according to amounts expended. In a *profit center,* performance is evaluated in terms of profits generated (output is, therefore, expressed in dollar terms). *Investment centers* are special profit centers where the profits generated are compared with the funds invested to get a rate of return.

A standard cost-accounting system is an example of a profit improvement system used by many manufacturing enterprises to improve profits by controlling the costs of production. Standards are established to tell what a product should cost under ideal (but attainable) conditions. As production is accomplished, variances are generated to alert management to problem areas.

Three variances may be calculated for materials: material price variance, material quantity variance, and material mix variance. The purchasing agent is generally responsible for explaining the price variance while the foreman is held accountable for the other two.

Three similar variances are calculated for labor: the labor rate variance, the labor efficiency variance, and the labor mix variance. The head of the Personnel Department must account for rate variances while the foreman must explain the other two.

Overhead variances may be analyzed in either two or three parts depending on how the overhead costs are absorbed in production. When the absorption rate is based on output, an overhead volume and overhead spending variance may be calculated. When it is based on input (for example, direct-labor hours), one additional variance, the overhead efficiency variance, may be calculated. The plant superintendent is generally responsible for volume while the foreman is responsible for efficiency (both labor efficiency and overhead efficiency). The spending variance should be broken down by responsibility center and the heads of these departments should be held accountable for differences between actual amounts and budgeted amounts.

The concept of variance analysis (and the broader concept of profit improvement) have application far beyond the manufacturing enterprise. The details of the system will vary according to type of responsibility center, purpose of the organization, nature of the products or services sold, training and qualification of employees, and other factors. Nevertheless, the basic idea behind all these systems is that profit can be improved by establishing goals (standards) and regularly comparing actual performance with these goals.

QUESTIONS

1. What do we call the difference between actual performance and the profit improvement objective?

2. Of what value is *feedback* in a profit improvement system?

3. What is a responsibility center? How many responsibility centers should a company have?

4. If the variance in a profit improvement system is $500,000 and the data base shows $5,000,000, how much was the objective?

5. Explain why costs should not be *allocated* extensively to responsibility centers.

6. In what two different ways may information about costs be accumulated? What purpose is served by each type of accumulation?

7. What are the four types of responsibility centers described in the text? Explain how performance is judged in each type of responsibility center.

8. What three variances may be calculated for production inputs such as material and direct labor? Which of these is normally not calculated or reported in a standard cost system? Why is this variance not calculated separately?

9. In a production firm, who would be held responsible for a material usage variance? For a material price variance?

10. Under what circumstances would a firm calculate a mix variance? As a manager, how would you interpret a material mix variance?

11. Who should be held accountable for a labor efficiency variance? For a labor rate variance?

12. Define the term *standard cost* as used in accounting. What is the major purpose of a standard cost accounting system?

13. What overhead variances may be calculated when a firm budgets and absorbs overhead based on a unit of input (such as direct-labor hours)? Who should be held responsible for each of these variances?

14. What overhead variances may be calculated when a firm budgets and absorbs overhead based on a unit of output? Who should be held accountable for each of these variances?

15. Define *budgeted overhead?* What is the formula for budgeted overhead based on direct-labor hours?

16. What are the major limitations of a standard cost system?

17. Explain how the concepts of standards and variances may be used outside of the traditional manufacturing framework? Suggest several examples of nonmanufacturing enterprises to which these concepts might be applied.

EXERCISES

E13–1 *Material variances.* Polly Company uses a standard cost system which specifies that 6 units of *D* should be used to produce one unit of *J*. The standard cost of *D* is $2 per unit. During the month of December Polly Company purchased 1,200 units of *D* at a cost of $1.92 per unit. The company used 900 units of *D* to produce 175 units of *J*. Calculate the material price and material quantity variance.

E13–2 *Labor variances.* Given the following data regarding direct labor, calculate the labor rate variance and labor efficiency variance. What are some of the possible causes of these variances? Who should be held accountable for each variance?

Standard: 4 hours of direct-labor at a standard cost of $4.25 per hour.

Actual: Produced 492 units of output utilizing 1,950 direct-labor hours at a total cost of $8,443.50.

E13–3 *Mix variance.* Packer Products Company utilizes two classes of labor in the production of a small 2-man tent. The standard wage for a sewing machine operator is $4.20 per hour while the standard wage for the cutter is $3.00 per hour. When *bottlenecks* in production develop, sewing machine operators are shifted to cutting or cutters are required to operate sewing machines. This, of course, causes some inefficiency since workers are trained for a particular specialty. The standard cost system specifies 0.4 hours cutting and 1.2 hours sewing for each tent produced. During the month of January 1,821 tents were produced utilizing 1,000 cutting hours and 2,000 sewing hours. Calculate the mix variances.

E13–4 *Labor variances.* Refer to the data in E13-3 and the following data, and calculate the labor rate variances and the labor efficiency variance. Total payroll costs for cutting labor was $3,120 and for sewing hours was $8,360.

E13–5 *Overhead variances.* Turbo Tank Company's management established 80,000 tanks per month as the standard production level. Each of these tanks should require 8 hours to produce. Fixed overhead costs are expected to be $240,000 per month and variable overhead cost $0.70 per direct-labor hour. Actual overhead costs during the month of March amounted to $601,000, actual production 72,000 tanks, and 575,000 actual direct-labor hours. Calculate the total overhead variance and break that variance into 3 sub-variances.

E13–6 *Overhead variances.* Refer to the data in E13-5, but assume that overhead is absorbed on the basis of *output* (tanks produced) rather than *input* (direct-labor hours). The variable overhead rate is $5.60 per tank. Calculate the overhead volume and overhead spending variances.

E13–7   Overhead variances.   Walton Motor Manufacturing uses a standard cost system and absorbs overhead on the basis of $8 per direct-labor hour. During the month of April the overhead spending variance was zero, actual overhead costs $92,321, and 11,490 actual direct-labor hours. Did the company produce above or below standard volume? How much was the volume variance in April?

E13–8   Overhead variances.   Marco Incorporated absorbs overhead at the rate of $36 per unit of output. During the month of July the overhead volume variance was zero, the overhead spending variance –$9,422, actual overhead costs $313,406. How much was the absorbed overhead during July? How many units were produced during July? What is the standard volume (number of units)?

PROBLEMS

P13–1   Responsibility centers.   The Bedford Company has accumulated the following data regarding the activities of its four subdivisions during the first quarter of the current fiscal year:

	Purchasing Department	Office Custodial Department	Eastwood Mall Store	Shoe Department Tampa Store
Fixed assets	$ 8,000*	$ 3,000*	$ 82,000	$10,000*
Average inventory		50	44,000	
Average receivables			11,000	
Revenues			150,000	63,500
Direct expenses	62,294	11,440	138,000	47,400
Budgeted expenses		12,000		
Budgeted contribution				16,000
Budgeted output per hour	5 documents			
Documents processed	47,888 documents			
Direct hours worked	9,500 hours			

*Allocated share of building cost

Management is considering establishing responsibility centers but has not decided which type to use in each department or store.

Required:

a.   Select the kind of responsibility center which you think would be most appropriate for evaluating the performance of the various activities and explain your answer.

b.   How did each of the activities perform during the period based on the evaluation basis that you selected? (Show all calculations.)

P13–2 *Mix variances.* The Tropic Delight Company manufactures and markets a fruit drink, "F-S". The drink is composed of the juices of 5 fruits and water and sells for $0.75 per 20 ounce can. Shown below are the ingredients, the standard usage per can, and the standard price per ounce.

Ingredients	Standard Proportions	Standard Price per Ounce
Pineapple juice	6	$0.005
Cherry juice	2	0.020
Passion fruit juice	3	0.010
Grapefruit juice	5	0.015
Orange juice	2	0.030
Water	2	0.000

During the month of July the company produced and sold 10,900 cans of Tropic Delight. Purchases and quantities used of each input are summarized below:

	Quantity Purchased (in ounces)	Actual Price (per ounce)	Quantity Used (in ounces)
Pineapple juice	75,000	$0.006	60,000
Cherry juice	25,000	0.019	22,000
Passion fruit juice	40,000	0.011	33,000
Grapefruit juice	80,000	0.018	55,000
Orange juice	58,000	0.034	47,000
Water	1,000	0.000	1,000

Required:

Analyze material costs for the month of July and calculate all variances which you think will assist management in evaluating production performance.

P13–3 *Standard cost accounting.* The Astro Chemical Company uses standard costs in its cost accounting system. The unit standard cost of chemical PDQ is $22.40, computed as follows:

Raw Materials, 2 pounds @ $1.90/pound	$ 3.80
Labor, 3 hours @ $5.70/hour	17.10
Overhead	1.50
	$22.40

The following were the inventory balances on April 1:

Raw Materials (500 pounds)	$ 950
Work-in-Process (150 units, one-third complete)	1,120
Finished Goods (200 units)	4,480

Material, labor, and overhead are applied at the same rate in the production process, so that if the Work-in-Process inventory is 50 percent complete, it will have been charged with 50 percent of each type of cost. Overhead is absorbed in the production process on the basis of units of output; however, the company only calculates a single overhead variance.

The following activities took place during the month of April:

1. Purchases of 1,600 pounds of raw material were made at an average price of $1.96 per pound.
2. A total of 2,540 direct-labor hours were worked at an average rate of $5.80 per hour.
3. Actual overhead costs for the period totaled $1,250 (credit Various Accounts).
4. The company started 850 units during the period. At the end of the period 200 were still in-process and were on the average 50 percent complete. The April 30 inventory of raw material shows 240 pounds on hand.
5. The company sold 858 units during the period at an average price of $37.50. The company records the cost of goods sold at the time sales are made. Two-thirds of the sales were for cash.

Required:

a. Prepare an equivalent unit schedule.
b. Prepare journal entries to record the transactions that occurred in April.
c. Assume that the company closes its books (including the variance accounts) each month. Prepare the closing entries for April.

P13–4 Variances. The unit standard cost of Model UB2 of the United Sauces Corporation is $63.75 as follows:

Material, 9 units @ $2.50/unit	$22.50
Labor, 5 hours @ $3.30/hour	16.50
Overhead	24.75

During June the company purchased 11,150 units of material at an average cost of $2.70 per unit, and 4,805 units of material were used. A total of 2,454 direct-labor hours were worked at an average rate of $3.25 per hour. Overhead is absorbed on the basis of units of output ($24.75 for each unit of Model H produced). Actual overhead costs were $12,640. The number of units of Model H started and completed during the month was 500.

Required:

a. List the variances that can be calculated from the above information.
b. Calculate the amount of the variances.
c. Indicate whether the variances are favorable or unfavorable.

P13–5 *Overhead variances.* During the first quarter of the year, the Kat Manufacturing Company estimated that it would produce 50,000 Kiddie Kats. At normal operating capacity, the fixed overhead costs are expected to amount to $62,500, and the variable overhead should run to $0.75 per direct-labor hour. The company's standard cost system provides for the use of $4.00 of material and 2 hours of labor in the production of each finished unit.

The production records of the Kat Manufacturing Company disclosed that 62,000 Kiddie Kats were produced during the period. The company incurred actual overhead costs of $172,000, and the employees worked 125,000 direct-labor hours.

Required:

a. Prepare a *three*-variance overhead analysis.

b. Assume all facts the same as above except that overhead is budgeted according to units of *output* ($1.50 for each Kiddie Kat produced). Prepare a *two*-variance overhead analysis.

P13–6 *Standard cost accounting.* The Tenaco Production Company uses a standard cost-accounting system to control factory operations. The unit standard cost of Product T, one of Tenaco's main products, is $84.35, divided as follows:

Material 16 units @ $3.10/unit	$49.60
Labor 8.5 hours @ $2.50/hour	21.25
Overhead	13.50

During the month of July 18,000 units of material were purchased at an average price of $3.18 per unit, and 17,500 units of material were used. The total number of direct-labor hours worked, at an average rate of $2.65 per hour, was 9,075. Actual overhead costs for the month were $14,995. The number of units of Product T started and completed during July was 1,100.

Required:

Prepare journal entries to record the above information. Your entries should include the recording of 2 material variances, 2 direct-labor variances, and a single overhead variance.

P13–7 *Variances.* Pogo Manufacturing Company uses a standard cost-accounting system. Production of one unit of product Go has the following standards:

Material, 15 pounds @ $1.10/pound	$16.50
Labor, 12 hours @ $2.50/hour	30.00
Overhead, $3.75/direct-labor hour	45.00
	$91.50

During the month of December the company budgeted overhead costs of $31,500 for the production of 700 units of product Go. The fixed overhead is expected to be $16,800 for the month, and the variable overhead will be applied at the rate of $1.75 per direct-labor hour.

Production records for the month revealed that 650 units were produced during the month. A total of 9,725 pounds of material was used. The employees were paid $19,928.25 for 7,815 direct-labor hours.

During the month the company purchased 10,000 pounds of material for $11,200. Actual overhead charges incurred during the month were $32,600.

Required:

List and calculate seven variances from the above information.

P13–8 *Setting standards.*   The Insoluble Soap Company, an established firm in the detergent industry, has experienced declining profits in recent years despite the fact that sales have shown a steady increase. Stockholders and other interested parties have voiced concern over the poor earnings performance. Frank Lee, the company president, has decided the unfavorable earnings trend must be stopped and accordingly calls in T. M. Hymm, the controller, for an explanation. Somewhat defensively, Hymm suggests possible trouble areas, but cannot really provide the president with any answers. Wisely, Hymm asks for time to further investigate the probable problem, and Lee gives him two days to come up with some concrete evidence to support his explanations.

Back in his office, Hymm sets out to rectify a situation he was well aware of, but elected not to disclose. Insoluble Soap had established a standard cost system ten years ago, but in the last two years had failed to update or even use it.

Hastily, the controller puts several other accountants to work revamping standards and calculating current variances. In their search, the accountants uncover the following information:

1. The raw materials mix has changed since the last standards were set, thereby increasing the quality of detergent. This change in mix has, however, caused a 50 percent increase in the cost of raw materials. Quantity requirements per case have remained constant.

2. Labor costs have increased 18 percent due to a new 3-year union contract negotiated last year. Because new machinery was acquired last year, the hours of direct labor required to produce a product have decreased by 10 percent.

3. The company allocates overhead on the basis of direct-labor hours. The estimated number of direct-labor hours has increased by 80,000 since the standard was last revised. Mr. Hymm feels this increased volume, when added to the previous standard volume, represents a fair standard.

4. The estimated overhead costs at normal or standard volume have increased by $968,000 of which $584,000 constitutes fixed costs.

Selected Data for Past Year
(Standard)

Standard cost per case:

Raw material, 20 pounds @ $0.04/pound	$0.80
Direct labor, 0.20 hours @ $3.00/hour	0.60
Overhead	1.50
Total standard cost per case	$2.90

Standard annual volume: 1,760,000 direct labor hours
Total fixed costs at standard volume: $8,800,000

(Actual)

Raw materials used	200,490,000 pounds
Cost of raw materials used	$13,031,850
Direct labor hours worked	1,700,200 hours
Direct labor costs	$6,120,720
Actual overhead costs	$14,840,000
Actual output	9,780,000 cases

Required:

a. Calculate new standards for the company, assuming they plan to reestablish a standard cost system.

b. Based upon the new standards, calculate variances for the past year.

c. Having calculated the appropriate variances, suggest several possible causes for each.

d. What might be done to remedy the existing problems?

Section 4

Planning for the Long Run

It is not adequate to plan only for the next few years because tremendous opportunities may be lost through inadequate facilities. This section examines several management activities that must be considered if success is to be achieved in the more distant future.

Chapters 14 and 15 explain the capital budgeting problem as it relates to the acquisition of assets. Chapter 16 examines the other side of the coin by describing alternative means by which funds can be obtained for acquiring the assets. Chapter 17 delves into the impact of income and other taxes on the decision-making process.

14

The Fundamentals of Capital Budgeting

In previous chapters, we have been concerned with various decision situations and the usefulness of certain types of information for producing better results. Almost without exception, the situations have been *short-run* in nature, involving only one- or two-year time frames. In this chapter (and chapters 15 through 17) we will turn our attention to *long-run* decisions, which have effects that last over several, or even many, years. Characteristically, long-run planning requires the commitment of relatively large amounts of money and manpower. Thus, careful analysis before and during implementation can yield substantial benefits through avoided costs. Errors in long-term planning are more difficult to rectify, as American automobile manufacturers learned after consumer tastes shifted toward smaller models. Once momentum is established, it may take months or even years to accomplish a change in direction.

The information needs for long-range planning are just as important as for short-run, if not more so. The problem of providing it is made more difficult because predicted values tend to be more imprecise as the time frame lengthens. Also, more factors are variable in the long run, so that the decision models tend to be more complex and more sensitive to changes in assumptions. One major factor of variability that must be considered is the effect of time on the *value of money*. This effect can be treated as a variation in the size of future dollars, which makes quantitative comparisons of results more systematic and less intuitive.

As a simple analogy, consider the task of selecting the wealthier of two persons. One decision rule might tell us that the greater wealth would lie with the individual who had the larger quantity of bills in his or her wallet. The rule works very well if every bill in each wallet is the same denomination. The rule will work in some situations in which this condition is not met, such as when one person has ten $5 bills and the other has eight $1 bills. But reason tells us that in many situations, the rule will lead us astray, as when one person has one $10 bill, and the other has one $5 bill and four $1 bills.

The objective of this chapter is to demonstrate and explain one particular approach to providing information about money flows occurring over the long run. In some cases, as shown above, the approach is not necessary because the dollars are essentially all the same size. In other cases, the approach is useful because it allows us to arrive at a systematic, quantitative basis for our conclusion. It is possible to come to the right conclusion without the correct information, but over a series of decisions, we would be wrong more often than right. Specifically, the approach described in the following pages takes dollars from different points in time and expresses them in a constant size. In this sense, the model is similar to the general purchasing-power approach presented in Chapter 5.

TIME AS A FACTOR IN VALUE

If you were offered a choice between two alternatives, both of which would involve giving up $10 now and receiving $20 tomorrow, would it affect your decision if one alternative would return a $20 bill, and the other two $10 bills? Probably not, because there would be no economic difference in the outcomes. In both cases, you would sacrifice the same amount of purchasing power, and would receive the same amount of purchasing power.

Suppose, however, that one alternative would return $20 two years from now, instead of tomorrow. Which would you select? If you were rational, you would choose to have $20 tomorrow. Why would you make this choice? There are at least four reasons:

1. *Risk*—the longer the time lag, the less likely you are to collect the $20.
2. *Usefulness*—the sooner you have the $20, the sooner you can enjoy the benefits of spending it.
3. *Income*—the sooner you have the $20, the sooner you can invest it to earn income. The sooner you invest it, the more you make.
4. *Inflation*—$20 now will purchase more goods than $20 two years from now, if the economy experiences inflation (the opposite is true for deflation).

The first two reasons, *risks and usefulness,* will not be discussed at length in this text. Our decision to deemphasize these factors is not based on a lack of significance, but rather on a lack of appropriate decision models for dealing with their effects. The income factor is discussed in this chapter and in Chapter 15; inflation was dealt with in Chapter 5. The last section of Chapter 15 will examine the situation in which both the income and inflation effects occur simultaneously. It is your authors' opinion that the effects of these factors can best be described in terms of the differences of the value of the monetary measuring unit.

The Income Factor

There was little difficulty in choosing between $20 tomorrow and $20 two years from now, but what if the situation is subject to less intuition? Suppose you have three alternatives, which all involve a present sacrifice of $10. Would you select *A*, which will return $12 one year from now; *B*, which pays $14 after two years; or *C*, which will give you $16 after three years?

If you make the assumption that all the measuring units are the same size, you would select *C*. After all, it returns a larger number of dollars than either of the others.

How can we make a more rational choice among alternatives *A, B,* and *C*? The best way is to convert the dollars of *payoff,* which actually represent different types of dollars, into one common type (and size) of monetary unit. If we can accomplish this conversion, then we will be able to make a more informed selection.

WORKING WITH FUTURE DOLLARS

Taking into consideration the ability of something of value to earn more value, we can convert dollars of one time period to dollars of another time period by adding to the first amount the income (*interest*) it could earn in the meantime.

Throughout this discussion, we will refer to dollars of *cash,* or *cash flows.* In the U.S. system, cash itself is unproductive in that it can earn no income until we use it to buy another asset that *will* yield a return in the future, such as real estate, rare stamps, or an interest-paying savings account. Nonetheless, we will refer to *cash flows* as if they did involve the ability to earn funds *directly.* Cash can be readily used to earn *indirectly,* so no great harm is done by this simplification.

It is convenient and customary in business to refer to an investment's ability to earn income as its *rate of return,* or *interest rate.* This rate is expressed as a percentage of the amount of value invested in the asset. The percentage multiplied by the amount invested will yield the amount of income earned in the stated time period.

Thus, $100 invested at 5 percent will pay only $5, but $1,000,000 at the same rate will pay $50,000. However, these numbers mean little if we fail to specify the period of time required to earn the income. If the same $100 earned 5 percent every hour, it would yield more than the $1,000,000 that earned 5 percent every ten years. The time period customarily associated with a rate of return or interest rate is *one year.* An annual rate may be modified as needed to yield the appropriate rate for some other time period. For example, many credit cards carry an 18 percent annual interest charge on past-due balances. For computations, this rate is expressed as 1.5 percent monthly, which is the 18 percent rate divided by 12.

Another frequently encountered convention is *compounding.* Under this arrangement, any assets received as income from an investment are considered as *additional investments,* and earn income at the same rate as the original investment. A savings account usually involves compounding, as do some mutual fund plans that call for reinvestment of dividends.

Compounding also depends on a stated time period. The assets cannot be reinvested until you obtain title to them. For example, if a savings account compounds 5 percent *annually,* a $1,000 deposit will earn $50 the first year, with the result that $1,050 will be invested the next year. If the 5 percent annual rate is compounded *semiannually,* $25 will be earned the first 6 months and added to the original $1,000 at the end of that time. Thus, $1,025 will be invested for the next 6 months, and will earn $25.62. Total earnings for the year are $50.62, whereas annual compounding yields only $50. It should be observed that, with a constant interest rate, more frequent compounding yields more income over the same period of time.

An Algebraic Formula

The earning of income and the compounding of that income can be described in algebraic terms, a fact which may help the reader to understand the conversion process for changing dollars of different time periods to the same unit of measure.

If we invest a sum of money (X dollars), at interest (i) for one time period, at the end of that period, we will have our original investment plus the income that was earned. This amount may be described as:

$$X + (i)X$$

For example, $100 at 5 percent can be shown as:

$$\$100 + (0.05)\$100$$

or $105. Note that we can "factor out" X, and have the expression:

$$X(1 + i), \text{ or } \$100(1 + 0.05)$$

Thus we can consider an investment of $100 to be 100 investments of $1. Although this observation may seem trivial, it enables us to make simpler and quicker calculations. The results of those computations may be multiplied by the number of dollars we invest to get the total we will have on hand.

Suppose, then, that we have invested $1, at 5 percent, what do we have after one time period? Your answer should be [$1 + 0.05($1)], or $1.05. But what if we leave the interest and the investment to earn more interest during the next time period? We have:

(Original amount + Interest) + Interest on the (Original amount + Interest)

More easily, we can say:

$$(\$1 + \$0.05) + (5\% \text{ of } \$1.05)$$

or

$$\$1.05 + 0.05(\$1.05)$$

Factor out $1.05, drop the dollar sign, and we have:

$$1.05(1 + 0.05), \text{ or } (1.05)^2$$

Thus at the end of the second year, our investment would total $1.1025. What if we leave it invested another year?

$$(1.05)^2 + 0.05(1.05)^2$$

Factoring yields:

$$(1.05)^2 (1 + 0.05), \text{ or } (1.05)^3$$

This process can go on, with the result that the exponent gets larger by 1 for each additional time period we compound our investment. In general, we can say that $1 invested at i interest per time period, compounded each time period, for n time periods, will total:

$$(1 + i)^n$$

The quantity symbolized by this expression is known as the *future amount of $1*. We can think of it as converting a measure of the purchasing power of today's dollar into terms of the purchasing power of a dollar n time periods from now.[1]

Suppose that a piece of candy costs $0.05 and a kindly gentleman approaches you with two offers: He will give you 20 pieces of candy one year from now, or he will give you $1 now if you agree to deposit it in an account that pays and compounds 5 percent interest annually. The $1 is equal to 20 pieces of candy, so it might appear that there is really no difference between the two choices. However, if you invest the dollar, you will have enough cash after one year to buy 21 pieces of candy. Thus, $1 of today's earning power is equal to $1.05 of next year's earning power. If the kindly gentleman had expressed your alternatives as being either 20 or 21 pieces of candy, you undoubtedly would have chosen the latter because there is a clear superiority in the benefit obtained from that selection.

Let's return to the three alternatives described earlier:

> *A*: $12 paid one year from now
> *B*: $14 paid two years from now
> *C*: $16 paid three years from now

All three cost the same ($10), so that factor is not differential. How can we convert the payoffs expressed in three different sizes of dollars to the same measuring unit?

---

[1] To avoid confusion, we will refer to *purchasing power* in this chapter as *earning power*. The first term has been used extensively in accounting and economic literature to describe the effects of inflation and deflation on the dollar. The student should keep in mind that the two concepts are *similar but separate*. We have chosen to use *earning power* to emphasize that the ability to earn income affects the value of the dollar.

A straightforward approach is to convert the dollars of *A* and *B* to the dollars of *C*, using the compound interest effect. Suppose that you could earn interest, compounded annually, with your funds. The $12 from *A* could be invested two years, and the $14 from *B* could be invested one year. The following diagram may be helpful:

	Now	**1 year**	**2 years**	**3 years**
Time				
A:		$12 ⟶ + *interest* ⟶ ?		
B:			$14 ⟶ + *interest* ⟶ ?	
C:				$16

We will select the alternative that will accumulate the greatest amount of earning power *after three years*.

First, suppose that 5 percent interest can be earned and compounded annually: $1 from *A* will equal $$(1 + 0.05)^2$ three years from now, or $1.102. A $12 investment is the same as twelve $1 investments, so that the total from *A*, at the end of Year 3, will be $12($1.05)^2$, or $12($1.102), or $13.22. Thus, 12 Year 1 dollars are equivalent to 13.22 Year 3 dollars in terms of earning power.

B's payoff, in terms of Year 3 earning power, is $14($1.05)^1$, or $14.70. The $16.00 from *C* is already expressed in Year 3 terms, so no modification is necessary. Now we can compare the three alternatives and select *C* with confidence because it will provide the greatest amount of earning power after three years, if we can earn 5 percent with our invested funds.

But suppose that we can earn 15 percent compounded annually. *A*'s $12.00 will grow to be $12($1.15)^2$, or $12($1.322), or $15.86 in Year 3 earning power. *B*'s $14.00 will equal $14($1.15)^1$, or $16.10 in the same monetary unit. There is still no need to change *C*'s $16.00. Given that we can earn the 15 percent interest, we now slightly prefer *B* over the other alternatives because it promises to yield the most earning power at the end of the third year.

Finally, assume that we earn 25 percent compounded annually. We can calculate the payoffs as:

$$
\begin{array}{llll}
A: & 12(\$1.25)^2 & = & 12(\$1.562) & = & \$18.74 \\
B: & 14(\$1.25)^1 & = & 14(\$1.25) & = & \$17.50 \\
C: & 16(\$1.00) & = & 16(\$1.00) & = & \$16.00
\end{array}
$$

These three amounts are all expressed in terms of Year 3 earning power and we can conclude that *A* offers the greatest payoff, if the interest rate is 25 percent. Thus we have come to a conclusion contrary to our original intuition that *C* is the best choice because it provides the greatest return. (In fact, for any interest rate greater than 16 percent compounded annually, *A* pays the largest amount.) The following table summarizes our calculations. The payoff of the best alternative for each interest rate is circled.

Interest Rate:		0%	5%	15%	25%
Choices:	A	$12.00	$13.22	$15.86	($18.74)
	B	$14.00	$14.70	($16.10)	$17.50
	C	($16.00)	($16.00)	$16.00	$16.00

These payoffs are expressed in terms of *dollars available at the end of the third year*.

Future Amount Tables

It would be rather cumbersome to convert present dollars to future dollars through the use of our formula, $(1 + i)^n$, for a large n. Can you imagine computing the value of $(1.035)^{19}$?

Of course, we could use a computer to perform our calculation, if we happened to have one handy that would not need lengthy programming. Even without such a machine, there is a solution easier than multiplying a number by itself 19 times. Table A in Appendix II (page 610) shows the future amount of $1 invested at several interest rates for different numbers of years. To find the future amount of $12 invested two years at 5 percent, go to the $i = 5$ percent column and move down to the row representing $n = 2$. The number at that intersection ($1.102) represents the future amount of $1, which must now be multiplied by 12 to yield the future amount of $12. You should test your understanding of the table by verifying the numbers shown in the above tabulation.

Table A may be used to solve other types of problems involving future amounts. Notice that three factors exist for each entry in the table: n, i, and the *future amount* (FA). In the problem that we just worked, n and i were known, and we found the future amount at the intersection of the row and the column. If we know n and FA, we can solve for i. Or if we know i and FA, we can solve for n.

INTEREST RATE UNKNOWN

Suppose that we wanted to select among A, B, and C by finding the one with the highest interest rate. Remember that each one returned an amount greater than the $10 that was necessary to buy it. Look at this diagram.

Time	Now	1 year	2 years	3 years

A: $10 →+ *interest* →$12

B: $10 ————→+ *interest* ————→$14

C: $10 ——————————→ + *interest* ——————————→ $16

In each case, we know FA (A: $12, B: $14, C: $16) and we know the number of years the $10 will be invested and compounded (A: 1, B: 2, C: 3). We want to solve for i, which we can do with Table A.

$$A: \quad \text{Investment:} \quad \$10 = 10 \times \$1.00$$
$$\text{Future amount:} \quad \$12 = 10 \times \$1.20$$
$$n = 1$$
$$i = ?$$

Enter the table at the row where $n = 1$, move across until you find the value that is closest to $1.20. You should find that the annual interest rate paid by alternative A is 20 percent. Now, let's find the rate for alternative B.

$$B: \quad \text{Investment:} \quad \$10 = 10 \times \$1.00$$
$$\text{Future amount:} \quad \$14 = 10 \times \$1.40$$
$$n = 2$$
$$i = ?$$

This time enter the table at $n = 2$, and move across until you find a future amount equal or close to 1.40. You should find a table value of 1.440 in the 20 percent column. To find the actual interest rate paid by B, it will be necessary to *interpolate* between two known values.

In this case, we know that a $1 investment paying 15 percent will yield $1.322 after two years, while at 20 percent it will yield $1.440. The rate that will yield $1.40 is between those two. The interpolation is shown below:

Interest   **Future Amount**

$$\left.\begin{array}{l} 15\% \\ ?\% \\ 20\% \end{array}\right\} x \quad \left.\begin{array}{l}{} \\ {}\end{array}\right\} 5\% \qquad \left.\begin{array}{l} 1.322 \\ 1.400 \\ 1.440 \end{array}\right\} 0.078 \quad \left.\begin{array}{l}{} \\ {}\end{array}\right\} 0.118$$

$$\frac{x}{5\%} = \frac{0.078}{0.118}$$

$$x = \frac{5 \times 0.078}{0.118} = \frac{0.390}{0.118} = 3.3\%$$

Therefore, the rate of interest paid by B is $(15 + 3.3)$, or 18.3 percent. Finally, we can calculate the interest rate for alternative C.

$$C: \quad \text{Investment:} \quad \$10 = 10 \times \$1.00$$
$$\text{Future amount:} \quad \$16 = 10 \times \$1.60$$
$$n = 3$$
$$i = ?$$

Enter the $n = 3$ line of the table, and move across until you find 1.60. Because the closest values in Table A are 1.520 (at 15 percent) and 1.728 (at 20 percent), it will be necessary once again to interpolate:

Interest   **Future Amount**

$$\left.\begin{array}{l} 15\% \\ ?\% \\ 20\% \end{array}\right\} x \quad \left.\begin{array}{l}{} \\ {}\end{array}\right\} 5\% \qquad \left.\begin{array}{l} 1.520 \\ 1.600 \\ 1.728 \end{array}\right\} 0.080 \quad \left.\begin{array}{l}{} \\ {}\end{array}\right\} 0.208$$

$$\frac{x}{5} = \frac{0.080}{0.208}$$

$$x = 1.9\%$$

Thus, the interest rate paid by alternative C is $(15 + 1.9)$ or 16.9 percent.

The interest rate computed in this manner is frequently referred to as the *time-adjusted rate of return*. Under this approach, alternative A would have been selected because it yields the highest rate of return of the three.

NUMBER OF TIME PERIODS UNKNOWN

If we are given the future amount and the rate of interest, we can use Table A to determine how long it will take to earn enough interest to achieve that future amount. For example, assume that you have been given $1.00, and you would like to invest it in a savings account that pays 8 percent annual interest compounded quarterly. For how many three-month periods must you leave that $1.00 invested before your account balance will equal $2.00?

$$FA = \$2.00$$
$$i = 2\% \ (8\% \ \text{annual}/4 \ \text{quarters})$$
$$n = ?$$

Enter Table A at the column for 2 percent and move down until you find an amount equal to 2.00. You should find the value 1.999 for $n = 35$. We can be satisfied with this answer because it is sufficiently close. Therefore, the $1.00 (or any other amount) must be left on deposit for 35 three-month periods in order to be doubled, if 8 percent annual interest is compounded quarterly.

WORKING WITH PRESENT DOLLARS

In the previous section, we described a means of determining the amount of earning power that would be available at a future date, if a given amount were invested at the present. In this section, we turn that situation around and show how we can determine the amount of earning power that must be invested at the present in order to have a given amount available at a given future date. This procedure is called finding the *present value* of a future amount, and is based on the same interest-earning and compounding concepts just covered.

We have seen that:

$$FA = \text{Investment} \times (1 + i)^n$$

At this point, we want to solve for the investment (or *PV, present value*), given the future amount *(FA)*, *i*, and *n*. We can divide both sides of this equation by $(1 + i)^n$ to obtain:

$$PV = \frac{FA}{(1 + i)^n}$$

Thus in order to have $1 on hand after *n* time periods, it is necessary to invest $1/(1 + i)^n$ dollars at *i*, compounded each time period. To summarize, *the present value of a future sum is the amount of earning power that must be invested now in order to accumulate that future sum in the given number of time periods.*

For example, a kindly old gentleman offers to give you $12 one year from now. How much cash must he invest now at 5 percent to be able to give you $12 one year later? The future amount is $12, the interest rate is 5 percent, and *n* is 1. Therefore:

$$\text{Present value of } \$12 \; = \; \frac{\$12}{(1 \, + \, 0.05)} \; = \; \$11.43$$

Thus he must invest $11.43 now to have the $12.00 on hand next year.

Suppose he wishes to give you $100, two years from now, and he can invest his cash at 8 percent. What present value must he give up?

$$\text{Present value of } \$100 \; = \; \frac{\$100}{(1 \, + \, 0.08)^2} \; = \; \$85.73$$

You may test this computation by finding the future amount of $85.73 invested for two years at 8 percent compounded annually. You should find your answer to be $100. A slight difference may occur through rounding.

Present Value Tables

As you might imagine, tables have also been prepared showing the present value of $1 for combinations of i and n. The methods of using Table B (in Appendix II) to find the present value of $1 are virtually identical to those for Table A.

Test your understanding of Table B by solving this problem: What present value must be invested now to yield $100 after two years if it can earn interest at 8 percent compounded annually?

Go to Table B, enter at the 8 percent column, and read down to the $n = 2$ line. You should find the value 0.857. This number tells us that we would have to invest $0.857 now to have $1 in two years; $100 can be on hand if we invest ($100 × 0.857), or $85.70.

Business Applications of Present Value

The translation of future dollars into present dollars is particularly useful for the business manager making decisions about buying assets. His overall goal should be to assure that a purchased investment will produce an adequate amount of income. Seldom, however, does an asset begin producing income immediately after it is acquired, with the result that the purchase price is expressed in terms of dollars with more earning power than the dollars used to describe the income of future periods.

EXAMPLE 1

Suppose an individual is considering the purchase of a piece of real estate. He thinks that he will be able to sell it after three years for $10,000. The present owner wants $8,000 now. Our investor is wondering whether the price is too high. How can we advise him on what to do?

Intuitively it appears that he should pay the $8,000 and wait three years for a $2,000 profit. By now, you should be doubting that intuition, so let's go on. Suppose that our investor is cautious, and if he doesn't buy land, he'll put his $8,000 in a savings account paying 6 percent compounded annually.

How much cash would he have to deposit now, in order to have $10,000 on hand after three years? Or, what is the *present value* of $10,000, given $i = 0.06$ and $n = 3$?

Turn to Table B, go to the 6 percent column and move down to the third row. There you should find the present value of $1.00 to equal $0.840. The present value of $10,000 is thus equal to $8,400. How do we interpret this finding?

Our investor has two alternatives, both of which will yield $10,000 after three years: (1) to buy land, giving up $8,000, or (2) to deposit $8,400 in the bank. Clearly alternative 1 is preferable because it yields the same earning power in Year 3 that choice 2 would yield, but involves a *smaller* sacrifice. In fact, we can see that our individual is better off (all other things equal) paying any price up to $8,400 for the land.

Suppose, on the other hand, that our investor is a professional real estate developer, and has other possible investments that he knows will yield 12 percent compounded annually. Should he pay $8,000 for this land? How much would he have to invest now at 12 percent for three years to produce $10,000? Go to Table B for your answer.

You should compute the present value of $10,000, for $i = 12$ percent and $n = 3$, to be $7,120. Thus his two choices are: (1) to invest $8,000 to get $10,000, or (2) to invest $7,120 to get $10,000. In this case, he should *not* buy this particular piece of land at any price greater than $7,120.

What has this example shown? At the very least, it should demonstrate that the existence of a simple gain is not sufficient in itself to lead us to a decision to buy. We must take into consideration not only the magnitude but also the timing of the gain and the other opportunities available to us. This example shows how we can convert future dollars to present dollars and thereby make a more rational comparison. We know that our conservative investor, if he buys the land, is better off by 400 (8,400 − 8,000) of today's dollars. On the other hand, the professional investor is better off by 880 (8,000 − 7,120) present dollars if he does not choose to buy the land.

EXAMPLE 2

Suppose the seller makes another offer to our professional ($i = 12$ percent). He can pay $3,000 now and $5,000 after two years. He can still expect to receive $10,000 three years from now when he sells the property. Should he buy under these conditions? Let's take the same approach, and convert all the future dollars to present dollars.

We know that the present value of the $10,000 inflow is 7,120 present dollars. What is the present value that he must sacrifice to obtain this payoff? Using Table B, we can analyze the situation as:

First payment:	Already expressed in present dollars	$3,000
Second payment:	How much has to be invested now at 12% so that he'll have $5,000 on hand in two years?	
	(0.797) × ($5,000)	3,985
Total present value sacrificed		$6,985

In this case, his two alternatives are: (1) to invest $7,120 at 12 percent to have $10,000 in three years, or (2) to invest $6,985 now ($3,000 down, $3,985 at 12 percent for two years) to have $10,000 in three years. He will select the one representing the smaller sacrifice, and thus will buy the land.

EXAMPLE 3

Suppose the owner of another piece of land is offering it for sale for $8,000 to be paid now. Another investor, who can earn 12 percent in other places, is considering the purchase. He is a developer, and plans to sell the property in 3 stages, one at the end of each of the next three years. He expects to receive $4,000 for the first parcel, and $3,000 for each of the two smaller remaining parcels, for a total of $10,000. Can we give this developer the same advice to not buy that we gave his friend in the first example? After all, the total proceeds are the same.

But, there is a difference because some of the proceeds are received earlier. We know that he must sacrifice 8,000 present dollars to make the purchase. How much are the three future cash flows worth in present dollars? Turning to Table B, we find:

First sale:	How much must he invest now at 12% for one year to yield $4,000?	
	(0.893 × $4,000)	$3,572
Second sale:	How much must he invest now at 12% for two years to yield $3,000?	
	(0.797 × $3,000)	2,391
Third sale:	How much must he invest now at 12% for three years to yield $3,000?	
	(0.712 × $3,000)	2,136
Total present value sacrificed		$8,099

Thus his situation may be summarized in two alternatives: (1) to buy the land for $8,000 now and get yearly proceeds of $4,000, $3,000, and $3,000; or (2) to invest $8,099 elsewhere for 12 percent to get yearly proceeds of $4,000, $3,000, and $3,000. If (and that's a big *if*) all other things, such as risk and usefulness, are the same, our investor will choose the alternative that will cost less, and will buy the land.

To look at the situation another way, we can see that by buying the land for $8,000, our investor obtains an asset that is worth 8,099 present dollars. Despite the change in approach, we can see that he will prefer to buy the land.

EXAMPLE 4

Still another investor is contemplating two real estate deals which have been offered to him for $11,500 and $12,000. He has other opportunities available on which he can earn 10 percent compounded annually. Both parcels being considered will be developed into five lots. The first, Flatland Acres, will have identical lots, one of which will be sold at the end of each of the next five years for $3,000. The second, Highland Estates, will have five distinct lots selling for $5,000, $4,000, $3,000, $2,000, and $1,000. It is expected also that one of the lots will be sold at the end of each of the following years, in the order of most to least expensive. Which deal should he pick, if either?

Both arrangements will yield a total of $15,000 even though the purchase prices differ. Our investor once took an accounting course and remembers that cash received sooner is worth more than cash received later. He has therefore decided that the Highland deal is worth something more than Flatland but he is unable to figure out how much. Let's help him by taking the present value of the cash flows at 10 percent compounded annually. In other words, we're going to use Table B to convert the future dollars to present dollars, as shown in Exhibit 14-1.

Exhibit 14-1

Years Elapsed (n)	Table B Value ($i = 10\%$)	Flatland Acres		Highland Estates	
		Future Dollars	Present Dollars*	Future Dollars	Present Dollars*
1	0.909	$ 3,000	$ 2,727	$ 5,000	$ 4,545
2	0.826	3,000	2,478	4,000	3,304
3	0.751	3,000	2,253	3,000	2,253
4	0.683	3,000	2,049	2,000	1,366
5	0.621	3,000	1,863	1,000	621
	3.790	$15,000	$11,370	$15,000	$12,089

*Present dollars are calculated by multiplying future dollars by the appropriate factor from Table B.

From this information we can see that Highland Estates is worth 719 present dollars more than Flatland Acres. We have come up with a *quantitative measure* of the difference in the value of these two alternatives.

We can see also that by buying Highland Estates, our investor can obtain the equivalent of $12,089 for only $12,000, and we can recommend that he buy it. On the other hand, to purchase Flatland Acres at $11,500 would provide the equivalent of only $11,370 of present earning power. In conclusion, our investor should prefer Highland to Flatland, and should not even consider the purchase of Flatland if he were to have additional funds available for investment at 10 percent.

EXAMPLE 5

(Rate of Return Unknown). Suppose another investor can acquire an investment for $18,000. He knows that he can sell it in five years for $25,000, but he doesn't know what rate of return this gain would represent. Can we help him?

We can, by computing the time-adjusted rate of return for him from Table B. We simply ask: What interest rate (compounded annually) will turn $18,000 now into $25,000 five years from now? The present value of the

$25,000 is $18,000. The present value of $1 of those $25,000 is ($18,000/25,000), or $0.72. We know that $n = 5$, so enter Table B at line 5, and go across until we find 0.72; this column will give us the interest rate. In this case, we will have to interpolate to find that the time-adjusted rate of return is 6.8 percent.

FUTURE AMOUNTS AND PRESENT VALUES

It may be apparent that there is more than an accidental relationship between the future amount of $1 and its present value. It was demonstrated before that the future amount of $1 is equal to $(1 + i)^n$, when it is invested and compounded at i for n periods. It was also seen that the present value of $1 is $1/(1 + i)^n$, or the *reciprocal* of the future amount for the same i and n. A brief examination of Tables A and B will show that this relationship holds true.

For example, from Table A, we can find the future amount of $1 invested for three periods at 15 percent to be $1.520. From Table B, the present value of $1 under the same conditions is 0.658. The reciprocal relationship is demonstrated by the fact that $1/(1.520)$ equals 0.658, and that $1/(0.658)$ equals 1.520. Because of this relationship, many problems can be solved using either Table A or Table B. In Example 5 we used the present value table to find the unknown rate of return. Below we show the solution with the future amount table:

Future amount of $18,000 = $25,000
Future amount of $1   = $25,000/18,000 = $1.389
n = 5
i = ?

Interpolating between Table A values for $i = 6$ percent and $i = 7$ percent yields the solution of 6.8 percent as our time-adjusted rate of return.

Because the tables are rounded to only three decimal places, minor differences may occur in going from one approach to the other. However, for nearly all realistic applications of these tables, no difficulty will be encountered from the errors introduced by rounding.

Notice that for all $i > 0$ and all $n \geq 1$, the term $(1 + i)^n$ will be greater than one. Thus every entry in Table A is greater than one. Under the same conditions, the term $1/(1 + i)^n$ will always be less than one. Thus every entry in Table B is less than one.[2]

THE ANNUITY: A SPECIAL CASE

Businessmen frequently encounter situations in which a series of equal payments are involved. For example, an agreement to rent an asset will require the payment of periodic sums by the firm that uses the asset. A bondholder

---

[2] Because the present value of a future amount is smaller than that amount, the computation of present values is frequently called *discounting*. Accordingly, the interest rate is frequently called the *discount rate*.

receives equal-size interest payments semiannually. A homeowner may make monthly cash payments to the bank to cover the interest accrued on his loan and to reduce the principal balance of that loan. For ease of analysis, it is occasionally convenient to assume that an investment will generate a series of regularly occurring equal payments. For example, it may be convenient to assume that an additional retail outlet will return approximately $20,000 each month for two years. The return will probably vary from month to month, but the approximation may be sufficient for the decision maker.

Such a series of *equal-size, equally spaced* payments is called an *annuity.* In general, each payment is called a *rent,* regardless of the business purpose of the payment.

Because annuities involve cash flows from *different* points in time, it is inappropriate to add the dollars of the rents without adjusting them to the *same* dollar. Of course, we can convert them all to present dollars by computing the value that would have to be invested now to yield those cash flows *(the present value of the annuity).* As an alternative, we can convert the flows to future dollars by computing how much will be on hand at a given future date if the rents are invested *(the future amount of the annuity).*

Present Value of an Annuity

Look back to Example 4 (page 401) in which we compared the present values of the cash to be received from Flatland Acres and Highland Estates. Notice that the proceeds of the sale of the Flatland lots constitute an annuity (5 *rents* of $3,000 each, occurring one year apart). We computed the present value of this annuity by summing the present value of each of the 5 rents.

Look at Exhibit 14-1 again, and notice that we can compute the present value of the annuity by multiplying the rent by *the sum of the Table B values.* Our alternatives are:

$$
\begin{array}{rcl}
\$3{,}000 \times 0.909 &=& \$\ 2{,}727 \\
3{,}000 \times 0.826 &=& 2{,}478 \\
3{,}000 \times 0.751 &=& 2{,}253 \\
3{,}000 \times 0.683 &=& 2{,}049 \\
3{,}000 \times 0.621 &=& 1{,}863 \\
\hline
3.790 && \$11{,}370
\end{array}
$$

or

$$
\$3{,}000 \times (3.790) = \$11{,}370
$$

By taking the second route, we reduce the number of multiplications to *one,* and save a lot of effort.

But suppose we want to compute the present value of an annuity with *many* rents, or the present value for *several* possible interest rates. To look up that many table values, add them, and then multiply by the size of the rent would be not only time consuming but also likely to cause errors.

Turn now to Table D, in Appendix II, which is the *Present Value of an Annuity of $1,* for various *rates of return,* and various *numbers of rents.* Look up the present value of an annuity for $i = 10$ percent and $n = 5$ rents.

You should find 3.791. Multiply by $3,000, and you have computed the present value of the dollars to be received from the sale of the Flatland lots. With Table D we can compute the present value of virtually any annuity with only one multiplication and no additions. We have reduced the time consumed *and* the likelihood of error.[3]

To summarize, Table D values are equivalent to the sum of Table B values.[4] The annuity of $3,000 is equal to 3,000 annuities of $1, so we simply multiply the Table D value by the size of our rent.

Future Amount of an Annuity

Suppose that we wished to compute the *future amount* of the Flatland lots. That is, we want to know how many dollars will be on hand at the date of the last rent, assuming that each rent is invested at 10 percent interest. In Exhibit 14-2, we assume that each rent is invested on the date it is received, and is allowed to compound until the date of the last rent. At that date, we should have on hand:

$$FA_1 + FA_2 + FA_3 + FA_4 + \$3,000$$

Exhibit 14-2
Future Amount of The Annuity

Lot Number	Time	Now	1 year	2 years	3 years	4 years	5 years
1		$3,000 ———————→ + interest —————————→ FA_1					
2			$3,000 ———————→ + interest ————→ FA_2				
3				$3,000 —→ + interest ——→ FA_3			
4					$3,000 —→ + int. —→ FA_4		
5							$3,000

We can compute the various *FA*s by using Table A. We may multiply each rent by the table value (assuming that $i = 10$ percent), as shown in Exhibit 14-3.

Alternatively, we can multiply the *sum* of the Table A values by the *number of dollars in each*:

$$6.105 \times \$3,000 = \$18,315$$

As a third approach, we can turn to Table C, in Appendix II, for the *future amount of an annuity of $1*, and find a value for $i = 10$ percent, and $n = 5$. This table value (6.105) can be multiplied by the size of the rent to yield the future amount of this annuity:

$$6.105 \times \$3,000 = \$18,315$$

---

[3] If the frequency of the compounding of our investment (annually, semiannually, and so on) does not coincide with the frequency of the rent payments, then Table D cannot be used. In this case, we have to use the long approach with Table B.

[4] In our example, the sum of Table B values was $3.790, whereas Table D shows $3.791. The difference of $0.001 results from rounding and is insignificant.

Exhibit 14-3

Exhibit 14-3
Future Amount of the Annuity

Payment Number	Years Invested	Future Amount of $1*	Future Amount of $3,000 Payment
1	4	1.464	$ 4,392
2	3	1.331	3,993
3	2	1.210	3,630
4	1	1.100	3,300
5	0	1.000	3,000
		6.105	$18,315

*From Table A, i equals 10 percent.

Thus we see that Table C is the counterpart of Table D. The values in Table C are found by taking the appropriate sum of the values in Table A.[5]

The annuities on which Tables C and D are based are called *ordinary annuities*. They are characterized by the fact that the rent occurs at the end of the interest period.

In computing the future amount, no interest is earned in the first period because nothing has been deposited. The last rent date is the point in time that we are concerned with; therefore no interest accumulates on the last rent. The *number of rents* is one more than the *number of periods* between the first rent and the date of our computation.

In computing the present value, interest is earned in *every* time period, including the first. Thus, the number of rents is equal to the number of periods between the last rent and the date of computation.

The two time lines in Exhibit 14-4 demonstrate the differences between the future amount and the present value.

Exhibit 14-4
Comparing Future Amount and Present Value

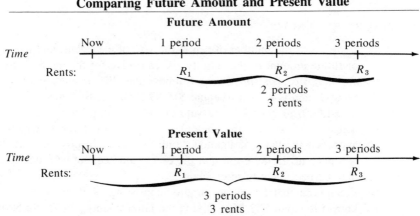

[5] Again, the compounding frequency must be the same as the rent frequency. However, notice that the reciprocal relationship seen between Tables A and B does *not* hold for Tables C and D.

Annuity Problems

There are several types of problems that can be solved using the future amount and present value annuity tables. For an annuity, there are four variables; when any three are given, the fourth can be computed from the table. The four variables are:

(1) i = the interest rate
(2) n = the number of rents
(3) R = the size of each rent
(4) FA = the future amount of the annuity, or
        PV = the present value of the annuity

Table C shows FA for various values of i and n, and Table D shows PV for various values of i and n. In both cases, it is assumed that R is equal to $1. Thus, FA or PV can be computed by multiplying the appropriate table value by the actual R. This procedure was followed in the Flatland Acres example.

FUTURE AMOUNT OR PRESENT VALUE UNKNOWN

The example of the $3,000 annuity of 5 rents showed how to solve for FA or PV. For the future amount we used Table C. We entered the table at i = 10 percent, went down until n = 5; found the table value (6.105), and multiplied by R ($3,000). The future amount of the annuity was found to be $18,315.

For the present value we used Table D. We entered at i = 10 percent, went down until n = 5; found the value (3.791), and multiplied by R ($3,000). The present value of the annuity was found to be $11,373.

These procedures may be used whenever i, n, and R are known. A situation in which we would want to compute FA would be the estimation of the future balance in a savings account. We might want to compute PV in determining whether or not a potential investment should be purchased.

INTEREST RATE UNKNOWN

If we know the number of rents, the size of each rent, and the present value or future amount of the annuity, we can solve for the interest rate (i), or, the *time-adjusted rate of return.* Suppose that PV of an annuity of 5 rents of $4,000 each is known to equal $15,972. Divide the known PV ($15,972) by R ($4,000) to get the table value (3.993); enter Table D at n = 5; and go across until you find the computed value. The column in which the number appears will show the unknown rate of return. In this case, the interest rate is 8 percent. In the event that the exact value cannot be found in the table, it may be necessary to interpolate.

Suppose that FA of an annuity consisting of 9 rents of $2,500 each is known to equal $32,552. Divide the latter quantity by R ($2,500) to get our computed table value (13.021); enter Table C at n = 9; and go across until you find the table value. The column will show the unknown rate of return. In this example, the annuity shows a 9 percent return.

This type of problem may be encountered in common circumstances. Suppose that a bank promised to deliver a certain amount of cash at a fixed future date in return for a fixed number of payments of a stated size. By this process, you could compute the rate of interest to be paid. Or, suppose that you were offered an investment that would yield a series of payments of a stated size. You could consider the purchase price as the present value of that annuity, and solve for the rate of return. Chapter 15 describes other situations where the time-adjusted rate of return should be computed.

RENT UNKNOWN

If we know the interest rate, the number of rents, and the future amount (or the present value) of the annuity, we can solve for the size of the rent (R). Suppose we know the rate is 5 percent, there are 12 rents and the *future amount* is $75,000. Enter Table C at $n = 12$ and go across to the column for $i = 5$ percent to find the table value (15.917). Divide the $75,000 by 15.917 to determine the size of the rent ($4,712).

Or if we know the rate is 14 percent, there are three rents and the *present value* is $6,200, we would enter Table D at $n = 3$ and go across to the column for $i = 14$ percent to find the table value (2.322). We would then divide the $6,200 by 2.322 to determine the size of the rent ($2,670).

A *sinking fund agreement* requires a firm to contribute assets to a separate fund, which is managed by a trustee to earn income, in order that a stated amount of cash will be on hand at a future date. Some bond agreements require the bond issuer to create a fund from which the maturity value of the bonds will be paid. Given the interest rate to be earned by the trustee, the number of payments, and the desired balance in the fund, we can compute the size of the periodic contributions that must be made to the sinking fund trustee by using Table C.

A borrower (such as a car or house buyer) may want to compute the size of the monthly payments that will be needed to repay the loan and the interest. The interest rate and number of payments will be stated by the lending institution, and the price of the asset may be considered to be the present value of the annuity of monthly payments. Such a problem may be solved by utilizing Table D.

Exhibit 14-5 shows a loan *amortization* table, which should demonstrate how a loan and the interest are paid off. The particular example is based on a loan of $11,373, with an annual interest rate of 10 percent, which is paid off in five annual installments. The first payment is due after one year.

Books of tables are available showing monthly payments for loans of various durations, sizes, and interest rates. Bankers and realtors find these tables much more convenient than one similar to Table D.

NUMBER OF RENTS UNKNOWN

Suppose that we know the interest rate, the size of the rent, and the future amount or present value of an annuity. Given these three items, we can determine the number of rents to be paid or received. To illustrate, assume

Exhibit 14-5
Loan Amortization

Payment Number	Amount Paid (A)	Interest Charged (B)	Balance Reduction (C)	New Balance (D)
Initial loan	$ –0–	$ –0–	$ –0–	$11,373
1	3,000	1,137	1,863	9,510
2	3,000	951	2,049	7,461
3	3,000	746	2,254	5,207
4	3,000	520	2,480	2,727
5	3,000	273	2,727	–0–
	$15,000	$3,627	$11,373	

A = Present value of annuity ÷ Table D value = $11,373 ÷ 3.791
B = Interest Rate × Loan balance = 10% × Previous D
C = Payment − Interest charged = $A − B$
D = Previous balance − Balance reduction = Previous $D − C$

the future amount is $48,027, the interest rate is 10 percent and the rents are $4,200 each. Divide FA ($48,027) by R ($4,200) to get the desired table value (11.435), enter Table C at the column for i = 10 percent, and go down until the table value is found. Then go across to find the number of rents to be eight.

On the other hand, if the *present value* is known, divide it ($22,407) by R ($4,200) to find our table value (5.335), enter Table D at the column for i = 10 percent, and go down until the table value is found. Then read across to find the number of rents (in this case, the answer is eight rents).

The situation may arise such that the number of payments is not a whole number. For example, if a borrower has a $10,000 loan, at 10 percent interest, which he wishes to pay off with $3,000 annual payments, he would compute a table value of ($10,000/$3,000) or 3.333. Entering Table D at the 10 percent column, he would find 3.333 to lie between 3.170 (n = 4) and 3.791 (n = 5). He would not need to interpolate to find the fraction of the payment that he would have to pay. The last installment would simply be larger than $3,000 if he elected to make four payments, or smaller than $3,000 if he elected to make five payments. Exhibit 14-6 presents amortization tables for these two plans.

By choosing the 4-payment plan, the borrower can avoid the additional $72 of interest that he must pay under the 5-payment arrangement.

This technique would be applicable for a future amount case in which a person puts aside a fixed amount of money each year in order to accumulate the down payment on a house. He knows the rate of interest that the savings can earn, the amount that he can afford to put aside each year, and the amount that he wishes to accumulate. With these three facts, he can compute how many deposits will be necessary to accumulate the desired amount.

The Annuity Due

Up to this point, we have worked only with *ordinary annuities*. Tables C and D are FA and PV tables for ordinary annuities of $1. Businessmen occasionally encounter annuity situations that do *not* meet the specifications of the ordinary annuity.

Exhibit 14-6
Loan Amortization

Payment Number	Amount Paid	Interest Charged	Balance Reduction	New Balance
Initial loan	$ –0–	$ –0–	$ –0–	$10,000
1	3,000	1,000	2,000	8,000
2	3,000	800	2,200	5,800
3	3,000	580	2,420	3,380
4	3,718	338	3,380	–0–
	$12,718	$2,718	$10,000	
Initial loan	$ –0–	$ –0–	$ –0–	$10,000
1	3,000	1,000	2,000	8,000
2	3,000	800	2,200	5,800
3	3,000	580	2,420	3,380
4	3,000	338	2,662	718
5	790	72	718	–0–
	$12,790	$2,790	$10,000	

The unordinary annuity is known as the *annuity due*. Whereas the ordinary annuity has the rent occurring at the *end* of the interest period, the annuity due has the rent occurring at the *beginning* of the interest period. Exhibit 14-7 demonstrates the differences for annuities of four rents. While we are not certain where this rather unusual name came from, it seems that the *due* indicates that the first payment is *due at once*.

In computing the *future amount of an annuity due*, we still work with the date at the end of the last interest period. The amount of the annuity due may be found by adding the interest for the fourth time period (after R_4) that will be earned by the total amount on hand on the date that R_4 is paid. This total should be recognized as the future amount of an ordinary annuity of 4 rents.

Thus, if R = $1,000, i = 10 percent, and n = 4:

$$
\begin{aligned}
FA_{due} &= FA_{ord} + i\ (FA_{ord}) \\
&= (1 + i)\ (FA_{ord}) \\
&= (1 + 0.10)\ (\$1,000 \times 4.641) \\
&= (1.10)\ (\$4,641) \\
FA_{due} &= \$5,105
\end{aligned}
$$

Exhibit 14-7
Ordinary Annuity versus Annuity Due

Ordinary Annuity

	Now	1 period	2 periods	3 periods	4 periods
Time					
Rents:		R_1	R_2	R_3	R_4

Annuity Due

	Now	1 period	2 periods	3 periods	4 periods
Time					
Rents:	R_1	R_2	R_3	R_4	

The only difference between the future amount of an annuity due of four rents and the future amount of an ordinary annuity of five rents is the size of one rent. Thus an alternative solution is to subtract one from the Table C value for $n + 1$ rents, and then multiply this adjusted factor by R. Given the same data as above, we can find the *future amount of the annuity due* of four rents as:

Table C value for 5 rents	6.105
Less: *FA* of fifth rent	(1.000)
Factor for annuity due of 4 rents	5.105

$$FA_{due} = R \times \text{Factor}$$
$$FA_{due} = \$1,000 \times 5.105 = \$5,105$$

The *present value of an annuity due* is computed on the date of the first payment. Thus the only difference between the present value of an annuity due of four rents and the present value of an ordinary annuity of three rents is one rent. In Exhibit 14-7 (page 409) we see that payments R_2, R_3, and R_4 can be treated as an ordinary annuity, and that we can compute their present value as of the beginning of the first time period from Table D. We can add to this number the size of R_1 to arrive at the present value of an annuity due of four rents of $1,000 each.

For example, we can find the present value of an annuity due of four rents, with $i = 10$ percent:

PV of R_2, R_3, and R_4:	
Size of rent	$1,000
Table D value	× 2.487
	$2,487
PV of R_1	+ 1,000
PV_{due}	$3,487

In equation form, this computation appears as:

$$(\$1,000 \times 2.487) + \$1,000$$

or,

$$(\$1000)(2.487 + 1).$$

Taking it back to the general case, our formula for the present value of an annuity due is:

$$PV_{due} = R \times [(\text{Table D value for } n - 1) + 1]$$

These manipulations are not necessary if we have *annuity due tables,* but they are uncommon. Exhibit 14-8 may help you identify and solve problems of these kinds.

Annuities due are encountered in many common business situations. For example, a sinking fund agreement may call for the last contribution to be made at a date one time period prior to the maturity date of the bonds. In

Exhibit 14-8
Formulas for Annuity Problems

	Ordinary Annuity		Annuity Due	
	Date	Computation	Date	Computation
Future amount	Last rent	$\left\{\begin{array}{c}\text{Table C value}\\\text{for } n \text{ rents}\end{array}\right\} \times R$	One period after last rent	$\left\{\left(\begin{array}{c}\text{Table C value}\\\text{for } (n+1) \text{ rents}\end{array}\right) - 1\right\} \times R$
Present value	One period before first rent	$\left\{\begin{array}{c}\text{Table D value}\\\text{for } n \text{ rents}\end{array}\right\} \times R$	First rent	$\left\{\left(\begin{array}{c}\text{Table D value}\\\text{for } (n-1) \text{ rents}\end{array}\right) + 1\right\} \times R$

that time period, the fund's trustee would be able to earn an additional year's interest with all the funds entrusted to him. Suppose the firm is to deposit an equal amount of cash at the beginning of each of the next five years so that $6,715 will be accumulated at the end of the fifth year. Let $i = 10$ percent.

We can find R as follows:

$$FA_{\text{due}} = R \times \text{Factor}$$

or

$$R = FA_{\text{due}} \div \text{Factor}.$$

From Exhibit 14-8:

$$\text{Factor} = (\text{Table C value for } n + 1) - 1$$

or, in this case:

$$\text{Factor} = (\text{Table C value for 6 rents}) - 1$$
$$\text{Factor} = 7.715 - 1 = 6.715.$$

Thus,

$$R = \$6,715 \div 6.715$$
$$R = \$1,000.$$

In another situation, a loan agreement may call for the first payment to be made *immediately*. Suppose that a loan of $8,340 is to be repaid in 5 installments, the first to be paid at once. If the interest charged is 10 percent, what is the size of the payment?

The general formula is:

$$PV_{\text{due}} = R \times \text{Factor}$$

or

$$R = PV_{\text{due}} \div \text{Factor}.$$

From Exhibit 14-8:

$$\text{Factor} = (\text{Table D value for } n - 1) + 1$$

411

or, in this case:

$$\text{Factor} = (\text{Table D value for 4 rents}) + 1$$
$$\text{Factor} = 3.170 + 1 = 4.170$$

Thus,

$$R = \$8,340 \div 4.170$$
$$R = \$2,000$$

An amortization table for this arrangement is seen in Exhibit 14-9.

Exhibit 14-9
Annuity Due Loan Amortization

Payment Number	Amount Paid	Interest Charged	Balance Reduction	New Balance
Initial loan	$ –0–	$ –0–	$ –0–	$8,340
1	2,000	–0–	2,000	6,340
2	2,000	634	1,366	4,974
3	2,000	497	1,503	3,471
4	2,000	347	1,653	1,818
5	2,000	182	1,818	–0–
	$10,000	$1,660	$8,340	

Two Brief Warnings

At this point, we want to give two warnings concerning the use of the annuity tables: First, be certain that you know the interest rate per interest period. Our examples have almost always used *annual* rates and *annual* rents. Annual rates must be converted to the appropriate rate when rents are paid and interest earned at a greater or lesser frequency.

Second, to use these tables to arrive at a precise number, the *interest-compounding period must be the same length as the rent period.* Thus if rents are received annually but interest is compounded semiannually, the tables cannot be used to find the precise present value or future amount of the annuity.

Fortunately, the size of the error that is injected in our computations from a lack of corresponding frequencies is not significant in most cases. We can *approximate* the present value or future amount by converting the interest rate to one corresponding to the rent period. Thus a 10 percent annual rate compounded semiannually is approximately equal to 10.25 percent compounded annually.

A PERSPECTIVE

This chapter has demonstrated that there are differences among monetary units of different time periods. One of the primary causes of the difference is the income-earning ability of value; that is, value received earlier can be used to earn income sooner than value received later. There are other sources of the difference, one of which, inflation, is discussed in Chapter 5.

This chapter also described methods of computing the *effect* of the time differences. The tools of *future amount* and *present value* computation are very precise, and can provide extremely useful information in solving many common business problems. The concepts can be applied with a great deal of precision in leasing and other financing decisions (see Chapter 16). They can be applied with a great deal of utility, but less precision, in comparisons or rankings of alternative investments (see Chapter 15). The tools have been incorporated in financial accounting. *APB Opinion No. 21* calls for the computation and disclosure of *effective* interest rates, and *APB Opinion No. 8* deals with the computation and disclosure of "past pension costs" on a present value basis.

We can see, however, that the application of these fundamentals to financial reporting is incomplete in that liabilities are shown at *maturity value* without regard to the maturity *date*. We have seen that a long-term liability of $1,000 constitutes a smaller debt than a short-term liability of $1,000, because we can invest substantially less than $1,000 now to have $1,000 on hand when the long-term debt matures. Thus, information about the present value of liabilities should be sought out by a manager in addition to their maturity value.[6]

Despite their relative freedom in comparison to financial accountants, management accountants have not unanimously applied compound interest concepts to their decision-aiding information. Unfortunately, one reason that has inhibited their use is a lack of understanding of how they work. We have included this chapter to help eliminate this deficiency.

But there are some other pitfalls and defects of the models that have inhibited their widespread use. Some of these are:

PREDICTIONS

We have assumed that future cash flows can be predicted precisely—clearly an oversimplification. Some managers and accountants feel that it is useless to apply precise tools to imprecise data. To your authors, it seems that the best ground lies somewhere between the two extremes. These techniques must be applied carefully and with the understanding that the accuracy of the output is related to the accuracy of the input.

INTEREST RATE

We assumed a single interest rate that could be earned by all investments made by the firm. This assumption is also an oversimplification, because a firm usually has a *portfolio* of investments which provide various rates of return. Consequently, to apply the model realistically, we have to rely on an

---

[6] See Robert T. Sprouse and Maurice Moonitz, *Accounting Research Study No. 3: A Tentative Set of Broad Accounting Principles for Business Enterprises*. (New York: AICPA, 1962), p. 39.

average rate of return which may be calculated in several different ways. A variation of one or two percentage points can produce significant differences in the output of the models. It is important that the user of these tools understand this weakness.

COMPOUNDING

It was our assumption that not only the original investment but also the interest received can earn interest at the same rate. Such a situation is not realistic. For example, a firm may build and equip a hotel at large cost, and begin to earn cash at a high rate of return. It is not necessarily true that this cash can be invested immediately to earn the same return as the hotel. On the other hand, there are a number of situations in which this assumption is quite realistic.

RISK

In the early part of the chapter, we occasionally qualified our decisions among investment alternatives with the phrase: *all other things equal*. One factor that can vary significantly is the degree of certainty of the cash payoffs. While investments X and Y may both seem likely to deliver $5,000 after two years, it is possible that X might return nothing at all, or even as much as $10,000. It is said that X entails more risk than Y, because its payoff is not as certain. Because risk is a perceived factor (its magnitude and impact vary from person to person), there are no precise methods for incorporating it in a decision model. Allowances for risk may be included in the decision model by altering the rate of return. The greater the discount rate is, the smaller the present value is. By requiring a higher rate of return of the risky ventures, we bias our model in favor of the more secure ones.

TIMING

We have also assumed that the cash flows occur at precise points in time. Such a simplification can be justified for instructional purposes and may be reasonable in some business situations. However, it is a mistake to lump an entire year's (or even a quarter's) cash flows into a single flow occurring at the end, beginning, or middle of the time period. Also, the analyst must be careful not to give in to the temptation to assume away significant variations in future cash flows in order to work with an annuity.

In summary, there are undeniable benefits gained from adjusting dollars of different time periods to a common size through compound interest computations, but there also are some weaknesses that compromise usefulness. It is just as important for your authors to point out these drawbacks as it is for a driving instructor to tell his student about the brake as well as the accelerator. We can use the models to put us in the right "ballpark," but we should not decide between two alternatives *simply* because of a small difference in the future amount or the present value of their cash flows. While the abstract concepts are perfectly valid, the inputs are not infallible.

COMPUTERS AND COMPOUND INTEREST

When a sufficient volume of computations justifies the expenditures necessary to develop the programs, computers can be extremely useful for dealing with compound interest problems. Many banks, for example, have been able to compute and pay compound interest on a daily, or even more frequent basis.[7] Such a task would, of course, be virtually impossible without the computer.

In terms of analyzing possible investment alternatives, software packages available from time-sharing services frequently contain programs that will perform the computations for the user. Many of these programs are designed so that the user need not have any knowledge of computer programming. Some programs may allow the analyst to perform *sensitivity* studies to determine the effects on the output by varying the input values.

If alternative *A,* for example, is preferable to alternative *B* for a wide range of discount rates, it should be selected. But if *A* and *B* change positions as the rate changes, special attention should be devoted to determining the appropriate rate.

Similarly, if variations in the size and timing of the cash flows produce different results, an effort should be made to establish the reliability of the estimates that are believed to be the best.

SUMMARY

Managers frequently face decisions in which cash flows are projected at different times in the future. The chapter shows that the dollar amounts of these flows cannot be rationally compared without conversion to a constant size. The conversion is made by considering the ability of cash received earlier to earn more income than cash received later.

Using the compound interest model, we can convert all cash flows to terms of the dollar at a future date (called the *future amount*) by using Table A in Appendix II. We also can convert the flows to terms of the dollar at the present time (called the *present value*) by using Table B in the same appendix.

A special situation is frequently found in business where there occurs a *series of equal sized cash flows at equal time intervals* (called an *annuity*). Because they occur at different points in time, the cash flows should be expressed in the same size dollar. By using Table C, we can convert the different dollars of an annuity to the dollars at the time of the last rent (*future amount*). By using Table D, we can convert dollars due beginning

---

[7] One bank, to our knowledge, compounds interest at the rate of once each heartbeat. If the bank's managers assume 72 heartbeats per minute, the amount of $1 invested for one year at 5 percent is:

$$\left(1 + \frac{0.05}{37,843,200} \right)^{37,843,200}$$

Incidentally, the final effective rate is only about 0.2 of 1 percent higher than 5 percent.

one time period hence to present dollars *(present value)*. In contrast to these *ordinary annuity* conditions, we may find *annuity due* situations, where the future amount is found at a point one period *after* the last rent or the present value at the date of the first rent. The chapter shows how these computations are made.

Before the techniques described in the chapter can be applied usefully, the manager should recognize their potential weaknesses. Difficulties can arise because of the limited accuracy of predictions, the selection of an interest rate, the compounding assumption, the impact of risk, and the timing with which cash is actually available to be invested. Nonetheless, the approach is a valuable analytical tool, as will be demonstrated in chapters 15, 16, and 17.

QUESTIONS

1. Provide two reasons for the added significance of planning in long-run, as opposed to short-run, decisions.

2. List and describe briefly four reasons for preferring present dollars to future dollars.

3. Using the income factor, explain how present dollars can be expressed in equivalent terms with future dollars.

4. What is an interest rate? What is compounding?

5. Give and explain the algebraic formula for the future amount of $1 and of $250, for *n* time periods at *i* interest per period.

6. Given these investment opportunities (all have the same cost), select the best one if you can invest elsewhere at 20 percent compounded annually:
   a. pays $250 after one year
   b. pays $300 after two years
   c. pays $400 after four years

7. Identify the three variables encountered in future amount tables.

8. What is the present value of a future sum?

9. Given the same choices as in question 6, which one or ones should you buy for $200 if you can earn interest elsewhere at 16 percent compounded semiannually? At 20 percent compounded annually?

10. What is the algebraic relationship between the present value and the future amount of a given investment?

11. What is an *annuity?* What is meant by the term *rent* in the context of an annuity?

12. What are the four variables associated with the tables of present values and future amounts of annuities? If an ordinary annuity has a present value of $6,811 and will pay $1,000 each year for 15 years, what is the time-adjusted rate of return?

13. What is the difference between an *ordinary annuity* and an *annuity*

due? Identify the dates at which the future amount and present value of each is computed.

14. What are the formulas for using ordinary annuity tables to work with annuities due?

15. List and describe five weaknesses of the earning-power model of describing future cash flows. Do these weaknesses merely modify the model's usefulness or do they destroy it?

16. How can computer capabilities be utilized in dealing with this model?

EXERCISES

E14–1 Compounding frequency. Find the interest rate (i) and the number of interest periods (n) for the following:

  a. 3 years, 10 percent compounded annually
  b. 7 years, 6 percent compounded annually
  c. 10 years, 6 percent compounded semiannually
  d. 5 years, 4 percent compounded semiannually
  e. 3.25 years, 6 percent compounded quarterly
  f. 1.5 years, 8 percent compounded quarterly
  g. 1.5 years, 8 percent compounded monthly
  h. 2 years, 12 percent compounded daily

E14–2 Future amounts. How much money will accumulate over the next five years if $20,000 is invested today under the following circumstances. (*Hint*: You will have to interpolate.)

  a. 10 percent compounded annually
  b. 10 percent compounded semiannually
  c. 10 percent compounded quarterly
  d. 10 percent compounded monthly

E14–3 Interest rate unknown. What is the time-adjusted rate of return of the following investment opportunities?

  a. Costs $1,000; yields $1,586 after 6 years; annual compounding
  b. Costs $3,300; yields $5,000 after 14 years; semiannual compounding
  c. Costs $15,000; yields $29,505 after 10 years; annual compounding
  d. Costs $1,500; yields $17,200 after 25 years; semiannual compounding

E14–4 Time periods unknown. How long will it take for the following investments to accumulate to the given future total?

  a. $3,000 to $6,000 at 15 percent compounded annually
  b. $1,000 to $2,500 at 8 percent compounded semiannually
  c. $2,000 to $3,000 at 8 percent compounded quarterly
  d. $4,500 to $6,060 at 12 percent compounded monthly

E14-5 *Present values.* How much must be invested now to yield:

a. $50,000 at the end of 3 years, if the going rate of return is 10 percent compounded annually?

b. $50,000 at the end of 3 years, if the going rate of return is 10 percent compounded semiannually?

c. $12,000 at the end of 4 years, if the market interest rate is 6 percent compounded quarterly? (*Hint:* You will have to interpolate.)

d. $100,000 after 2 years, if money is worth 12 percent compounded monthly?

E14-6 *Investment decision.*

a. An industrial firm's purchasing manager is faced with two choices concerning the purchase of a machine (which *must* be acquired):

1. The firm can pay $7,000 now.

2. The firm can pay $1,000 now, $3,000 after 1 year, and $4,000 after two years.

If the firm can earn 12 percent annually on its cash investments, which of the two arrangements should be accepted? Why?

b. If the earning rate is only 5 percent, does your answer change? Why or why not?

E14-7 *Annuities.*

Part 1:

Find the present value of the following ordinary annuities:

a. Rent is $2,000 each year for 10 years; the going interest rate is 6 percent.

b. Rent is $1,000 each year for 20 years; the current cost of money is 5 percent.

c. Rent is $100 each quarter for 6 years and 3 months; cash can be borrowed at 12 percent compounded quarterly.

d. Rent is $4,000 each year for 2 years; the interest rate is 10 percent compounded semiannually.

Part 2:

Find the future amount of each of the above ordinary annuities.

E14-8 *Annuities.* For each of the following ordinary annuities, use Tables C and D to find the missing factor:

	Future Amount	n	i	R
A	$?	15	10%	$ 1,000
B	944,600	?	7%	10,000
C	15,192	10	?	1,000
D	360,000	47	2.5	?

	Present Value	*n*	*i*	R
E	$ 9,000	12	5%	$?
F	18,000	?	25%	4,500
G	60,000	13	?	10,000
H	?	18	17%	850

E14–9 *Annuities due.* For each of the following annuities due, use Tables C and D to find the missing factor:

	Future Amount	*n*	*i*	R
I	$?	7	7%	$ 150
J	14,937	?	10%	1,000
K	11,996	36	?	250
L	1,003,884	17	5%	?

	Present Value	*n*	*i*	R
M	$ 126,888	26	15%	$?
N	?	9	10%	1,000
O	7,828	5	?	2,000
P	41,229	?	2%	4,500

PROBLEMS

P14–1 *Compounding frequency.* Compute the balance that would be on hand in a savings account after 4 years if an $8,000 deposit is left in and if the 6 percent annual interest rate is (interpolate as needed):

a.   compounded annually
b.   compounded semiannually
c.   compounded quarterly
d.   compounded monthly
e.   compounded biannually

P14–2 *Future amount.* On March 1, 1979, Fred Summers deposited $2,000 in a savings account that would pay and compound interest at 5 percent annually. On March 1, 1981, the interest rate was increased to 6 percent, and Summers added $3,000 to his account. On March 1, 1982, he withdrew $1,000. What will the balance be on March 1, 1984 if no further withdrawals or deposits are made?

P14–3 *An unusual problem.* David Vanderich, a coupon clipper, has come to you for advice. He has with him an advertisement from a local savings and loan that will give him a motor home in return for a $25,000 deposit. No interest will be paid on the account, and he cannot withdraw any of it until three years have passed.

Required:

a.   If the motor home can be purchased for $6,500 cash, and if Vanderich can earn 8 percent with his cash (compounded annually), should he make the deposit?

b.　For a $10,000 deposit to a passbook account paying 4 percent compounded quarterly, the savings and loan will give the depositor a stereo radio worth approximately $400. If the amount must be left on deposit 1 year, should Vanderich accept this offer?

P14–4　*Investment analysis.*　A firm has three investment opportunities, each of which will cost $4,000. The payoffs will be:

Opportunity 1: $6,000 after 2 years
Opportunity 2: $7,000 after 3 years
Opportunity 3: $8,000 after 4 years

Determine which, if any, of these three alternatives should be chosen if the firm can earn at a rate of:

a.　6 percent compounded annually
b.　15 percent compounded annually
c.　25 percent compounded annually

P14–5　*Investment analysis.*　Bill Williams is considering two large investments. He can borrow funds at 12 percent compounded annually, to acquire either or both of them. The following estimates have been made:

	A	B
Cost (cash paid now)	$14,500,000	$15,000,000
Cash returns:		
End of year 1	$ 6,000,000	$ 7,000,000
End of year 2	6,000,000	6,000,000
End of year 3	6,000,000	5,000,000
	$18,000,000	$18,000,000

a.　Because of the lower price, he is inclined toward A. What do you think?
b.　How, if at all, would your answer change if A were to cost $14,000,000 and B $14,500,000?

P14–6　*Future amounts and present value.*
a.　Using Table A, find the missing factors (interpolate as needed):

	Future Amount	i	n	Present Value
1.	$　?	6.5%	18	$ 10,000
2.	120,000	?	7	100,000
3.	120,000	10%	?	100,000
4.	98,000	7%	14	?
5.	75,000	?	23	10,335
6.	87,500	15%	?	14,223
7.	?	7.75%	8	11,000
8.	62,000	?	22	14,000

b.　Using Table B, find the missing factors in the above schedule.

P14–7 Investment analysis.

    a.   Leonard D. Velloper is evaluating several alternative land deals, and has narrowed his choice down to two: Country Club Estates and Mobile Home Haven. The first tract will cost $100,000, but will be sold after two years for $130,000. The second tract can be purchased also for $100,000 but it can be sold after only 6 months for $115,000. If Velloper can borrow cash at an annual 12 percent rate, compounded monthly, which (either, neither, or both) tract should he buy?

    b.   On the basis of time-adjusted rates of return, which investment will be the most desirable? (Ignore income taxes.)

    c.   Briefly discuss the relative risks inherent in this decision situation.

P14–8 Investment decision. A borrower can choose to pay off a $10,000 loan three years in advance for $8,000. If he can use cash to earn 10 percent compounded annually, should he retire the loan?

    a.   Solve this problem by comparing future dollars. How many future dollars will his choice save him?

    b.   Solve this problem by comparing present dollars. How many present dollars will his choice save him?

    c.   Reconcile the difference between the present and future dollar savings. (*Warning:* You will encounter rounding differences.)

P14–9 Investment analysis. The following information is known about three investment alternatives: *A, B,* and *C.*

	A	*B*	*C*
Cash outflows:			
Now	$40,000	$20,000	$16,000
End of Year 1		20,000	16,000
End of Year 2		10,000	16,000
Total	$40,000	$50,000	$48,000
Cash inflows:			
End of Year 1	$20,000		$10,000
End of Year 2	20,000		10,000
End of Year 3	20,000	$60,000	40,000
Total	$60,000	$60,000	$60,000

Required:

    a.   If the cash can be invested elsewhere at 10 percent, which of these (if any) should be acquired?

    b.   If the cash can be invested elsewhere at 16 percent, which of these (if any) should be acquired?

    c.   Apart from the compound interest factor, what other considerations should enter into our decision?

    d.   What are the weaknesses of the assumptions on which the compound interest analysis was based?

P14–10 *Future amount of an annuity.* Amalgamated Metals Company is planning to issue a group of 20-year bonds, for a total face value of $1,000,000. The bonds will mature on June 1, 1995. In order to make them more attractive to investors, a sinking fund will be established on June 1, 1985. Equal-size contributions will be made every June 1 from 1985 to 1995. It is expected that the sinking fund will earn interest at the rate of 8 percent compounded annually.

Required:

a. How large should each contribution be? (Round to the nearest $1,000.)

b. Prepare a schedule showing the amount of each contribution, the interest earned, and the balance in the sinking fund, for each June 1 from 1985 to 1995.

c. How large will each contribution be if all conditions are the same except that the last contribution will be made on June 1, 1994?

P14–11 *Loan amortization.* Chris Walker has found a four-wheel drive recreational vehicle that he would like to buy. The cash price of the truck is $8,000. His banker will loan him 80 percent of the required amount at an annual rate of 12 percent compounded quarterly for two years. Beginning three months from now, Walker will pay 8 equal-sized payments to cover the interest and retire the principal of the loan.

Required:

a. How large will each payment be (to the nearest dollar)?

b. Prepare an amortization table for this installment loan.

c. If Walker can retire the loan at any time without penalty, how much extra would he have to pay in order to do so on the day of the fifth payment?

d. Can you find the answer to c without referring to the amortization table? How?

P14–12 *Number of rents unknown.* Matthew Kirk recently borrowed $45,000 at an interest rate of 6 percent, which he will repay with annual installments of $10,000 each, except for the last. The first installment will be due exactly one year after the money is borrowed.

Required:

a. If he elects to have the last payment be greater than $10,000, how many payments will he have to make? Prepare an amortization schedule for this arrangement.

b. If he elects to have the last payment be less than $10,000, how many payments will he have to make? Prepare an amortization schedule for this arrangement.

P14–13 *An important decision.*   Harry Zonkem, a well-established professional football player, has received an offer from a team in the
newly formed Planetary Football League. If he accepts it, he will
play out the one remaining year of his present contract.

The general manager of the new team has presented the salary
offer in two ways:

1.   A $100,000 bonus at the end of the next season (January 1,
     1980) plus a $250,000 per year salary, payable on January 1 of
     each of the contract years (1980, 1981 and 1982). In the event
     an injury prevents his playing, he will still receive the pay-
     ments. If he wishes to play more than three seasons, a new
     contract will be signed.

2.   A $100,000 bonus on January 1, 1980, and $100,000 each
     January 1 thereafter until and including January 1, 1990. He
     will play only three seasons under this contract and will be
     entitled to receive all payments even if he is injured. If he
     wishes to play more than three seasons, he can negotiate a new
     contract without losing these deferred payments.

Under his present contract, he will receive a $100,000 salary
payment on January 1, 1980, and will have to negotiate a new contract for any future seasons.

Required:

Harry has come to you for help. As an accountant, your job is to
organize and analyze the situation to assist Harry in making his
decision. Because your client has his own values, he must make the
decision. You should prepare a brief analysis of the alternatives that
will enable you to assist him. Assume that he has come to you on
January 1, 1979 and that he expects to invest all funds (in excess of
those required for normal living expenses) at 10 percent. Be certain
to include an identification of the non-quantifiable factors affecting
the decision.

15

Planning Capital Asset Acquisitions

In order to manufacture a product, a firm acquires material and has labor efforts applied to it. The operations usually require the use of tools, machinery, and other physical devices. The terms *capital assets* and *fixed assets* are used to describe those facilities that enable production to be carried on more efficiently. In this chapter, we will discuss the decisions managers have to make concerning capital assets, and we will present several approaches to the analysis of the alternatives available in a particular situation.

THE ACQUISITION DECISION

The acquisition decision is critical for several reasons. First, the productive capacity of the organization is limited by the facilities available to it. A one-chair barbershop can provide only one haircut at a time. A bakery can produce only as much bread as its ovens can bake regardless of how many bakers it employs. An oil refinery is limited by the capacity of its catalytic "crackers," even though it may have plentiful crude oil supplies.

Second, the investment in fixed assets is often the largest figure on the balance sheet of a firm. Because of the size of the outlays, new funds frequently must be obtained through borrowing or through selling stock. Consequently, the responsible manager should be certain that his analysis is as complete and correct as the circumstances allow. To provide an indication of how significant capital asset acquisitions can be, General Motors invested over $2 billion in a single recent year. In the same period, the Exxon Corporation spent about $1.8 billion in capital outlays. This sum exceeded the earnings of the company by a substantial amount.

Third, fixed assets commonly last a relatively long period of time. If a mistake is made in acquiring an asset, the firm will feel the effects for several years. Consequently, the punishment for erring in a long-term commitment is more severe than for a short-run mistake.

Despite these compelling reasons, many managers make capital investment decisions on the spur of the moment without considering all the impacts of selecting a particular course of action over another. Occasionally, the situation is truly a crisis, and there is no real opportunity to perform an in-depth analysis of the alternatives available, for example, for replacing an inoperable machine that is preventing the assembly line from operating.

The following sections of this chapter provide fundamental information about analyzing investments from the *asset* side. Chapter 16 discusses the alternatives available for obtaining the funds to finance these acquisitions, and shows how they can be analyzed.

THE CAPITAL BUDGET

It is seldom appropriate to begin with the ending, but we feel that it will be meaningful to see an example of a *capital budget*. Typically, the capital budget includes plans for more than one year. The closer the time period is to the present, the more detailed the information. Our example, Exhibit 15-1 (page 426), contains a section showing several future periods as well as the upcoming one. These long-run plans encourage managers to continually watch for profitable acquisitions. Also, financial managers are alerted to the future needs for funds, and can begin laying the foundation for bond and stock issues. Despite the apparent simplicity of the capital budget, it should be noted that a substantial amount of analytical effort goes into the final selection of the projects.

THE ACQUISITION DECISION VARIABLES

As is true for any selection among alternative courses of action, it is useful to examine the differences that are likely to result from selecting one capital asset over others that might have been acquired. These factors that can assume different *values* are called the *decision variables*. The manager should determine which factors are most important and then see how each alternative affects those factors.

Cash Flows

The variable that is most universally analyzed by managers is the *cash flow* resulting from an asset. The negative flows *(outflows)* include such things as the purchase price, installation costs, and the operating costs (labor, material, and overhead). Notice that the financial accounting cost of using the asset *(depreciation)* is not a cash outflow. It is a delayed recognition of the effect of the purchase-price cash outflow on the reported net income of the firm.

The cash inflows associated with an asset are generally restricted to revenues coming from the sale of the output produced by it, and any cash re-

Exhibit 15-1
SUBURBAN DEPARTMENT STORES
Capital Budgets
Approved October 1979

Fiscal Year 1980

Land:			
Phoenix	$400,000		
Seattle	100,000	$ 500,000	
Buildings:			
Phoenix (new)	$744,000		
Denver (remodeling)	361,000		
Seattle (expansion)	170,000	1,275,000	
Store equipment:			
Phoenix	$178,600		
Denver	51,600		
Seattle	109,300		
Other stores	37,200	376,700	
Other equipment:			
Warehouse	$ 65,000		
Delivery	87,200		
Home office	23,100	175,300	
Total		$ 2,327,000	

Fiscal Year 1981

Land	$ 800,000
Buildings	1,600,000
Equipment	450,000
Total	$ 2,850,000

Fiscal years 1982–1985	$12,825,000
Fiscal years 1986–1990	$32,000,000
Fiscal years 1991–2000	$75,000,000

ceived upon its disposal. The relationship between an asset (for example, a delivery truck) and the resulting revenue can be extremely difficult to recognize. In these cases, or where the revenue will be essentially the same (*non-differential*) for all relevant alternatives, it is useful to deal with the cash savings achieved from one asset as opposed to another. Suppose that Machine *A* will produce the same amount of output as Machine *B* at a lower variable cost per unit, but it costs more to acquire. The difference between the purchase costs is the differential outflow, and the per unit savings is the differential inflow. Because the same product is produced in the same quantities, there is no differential revenue.

From the information in Chapter 14, it should be apparent that the *timing* of the cash flows is quite relevant to the investment decision. Cash flows of the same size occurring at different points in time should not be treated as equivalent. Cash received sooner (or spent later) can be used to earn more income.

It is a common alternative practice to use a financial accounting measure of net income to describe the net cash flow for a given time period. Although there are some cases in which this approximation can be fairly close, it is conceptually inferior to a pure cash-flow analysis because it will include some factors that are not cash flows. Depreciation has been mentioned; some other operating expenses may not involve cash flows in the same period. Also, there may be an *allocated* fixed-cost factor, assigned to the product or the period, which is not truly differential. Overhead costs are particularly susceptible to this weakness.

Whereas cash outflows associated with the purchase and installation of an asset can be identified fairly precisely, other outflows and nearly all inflows are estimates of future events, and are accordingly imprecise. The managers must be quite careful to avoid *spurious accuracy,* and should apply sensitivity analysis to observe the effect of different assumptions on the decision variables. This point is easily overlooked in the enthusiasm of applying a recently learned analytical tool.

Other Variables

In addition to the cash flows, there can be some very significant variables related to the capital-asset acquisition decision. The impact of each will depend on the particular situation faced by the firm. Difficulty is added by the fact that none of these variables is as easily quantified as cash flows, with the unfortunate result that they are often overlooked.

One factor to be considered in comparing alternatives is their flexibility. If one machine is adaptable to doing other tasks, we may prefer to buy it at a higher price, simply because there may be an opportunity to avoid another purchase later. This possibility should be considered in circumstances where it appears slack capacity will exist.

Some assets may be acquired in order to lend prestige to the firm and its products. A new computer might provide an opportunity for a public relations campaign. New delivery trucks may enhance the firm's image through the suggestion of success and high standards. On the other hand, a more economical vehicle could suggest cost consciousness and lower prices. It is extremely difficult to measure the monetary return of an attractive building, or landscaped grounds, or even plush carpeting in executive offices. Of course, not every firm requires that a full-scale analysis of the alternatives be made in every case.

As discussed in Chapter 10, a firm and its management face social responsibilities in addition to the fiduciary obligation to the stockholders. Meeting these requirements frequently causes capital outlays that do not promise to return a cash inflow sufficient to justify the outflow. Prime examples of such expenditures are pollution control or other environmental protection devices. On a cash flow basis, the firm and its stockholders may be better off if pollution is allowed to happen. However, some firms have actually obtained sufficient cash flows from the sale of extracted byproducts to pay for the devices. Others have been prompted by the workings of the law to acquire devices instead of being fined or taxed a larger amount. Still others have ignored the quantitative aspect, and installed controls as good citizenship or an image booster. Worker and consumer safety are similar factors in the management decision.

The significance of these nonquantifiable factors on the final decision depends upon the findings of the quantitative analysis. A strong preference on the basis of cash flow analysis will be difficult to reverse, but findings of indifference may result in one of these other variables swinging the tide. This point should be kept in mind throughout the following discussions of the quantitative tools of capital budgeting.

QUANTITATIVE CAPITAL-BUDGETING TOOLS

There are numerous approaches available for managers who desire quantitative information about investment decisions. Although it may appear that the final number produced by a model is sufficiently meaningful to support the decision alone, that is seldom true. The five models presented here are merely methods of processing data in order to increase the decision maker's comprehension of some of the information available to him. These five are not the only ones that can be used, and there are several variations of each that we have elected not to discuss.

Payback Period

Decision makers are frequently concerned with reducing the risk associated with getting returns from an investment. Risks are generally reduced when the cash flows are expected to be received sooner. Decision makers are also concerned with *liquidity,* or the availability of cash. The *payback period* is an analytical tool that provides useful information about both of these aspects.

The payback period can be computed in several ways. In any case, the result is expressed as a *number of years*. In application, the decision maker will prefer the investment alternative with the shorter payback period, as this project will tend to produce cash quicker than the other and will involve less risk.

A strength of this tool is its relative simplicity in computation, which can involve only the taking of a ratio. The numerator is the cost of the asset. The denominator is the annual differential cash inflow expected from its use. For example, if Machine *A* is expected to cost $75,000, and will produce $15,000 a year for at least 5 years, then the payback period is ($75,000/ $15,000 per year), or 5 years. In effect, we have computed a *breakeven point* —any cash received after 5 years will be *pure profit*. Accordingly, we can see why a manager would prefer the project that has the shorter payback period.

In the event that the cash flows from the investment are not expected to be constant from year to year, there are two computational approaches available. First, we can *accumulate* the cash flows until the cost is recovered, or we can work with an *average annual* cash flow. The latter approach is less accurate if the total time period used in computing the average is much longer than the payback period. The average is meaningless if it is computed for a total time period shorter than the payback period because there is no assurance that any income will be earned after the selected total time period.

Exhibit 15-2
Illustration of Payback Period

Year	Cash Flow	Accumulated Cash Flow to Date	Average Cash Flow to Date	Average Payback Period
1	$ 15,000	$ 15,000	$15,000	5.00*
2	20,000	35,000	17,500	4.29*
3	25,000	60,000	20,000	3.75*
4	30,000	90,000	22,500	3.33
5	20,000	110,000	22,000	3.40
6	10,000	120,000	20,000	3.75
7	5,000	125,000	17,857	4.20
8	5,000	130,000	16,250	4.62
	$130,000			

*Lacks significance because the average was computed for a time period shorter than the payback period.

Exhibit 15-2 shows the accumulation of cash flows as well as the computation of the average cash flow and payback period for a $75,000 project under consideration.

Under the *accumulation* approach, the payback point is found to occur somewhere in the fourth year of the asset's life. If it is assumed that the $30,000 will flow in on a constant basis during Year 4, we could interpolate and say that the payback period is 3.5 years. The average shows a different figure, but the difference does not become significant until the 6-year average is used. The 7- and 8-year averages are decidedly different and possibly misleading.

The payback period has two strengths: It is relatively easy to understand and it provides useful information when liquidity has a high priority. It is most meaningful for short-run projects. It is weak in that it generally ignores any cash flows occurring after the original investment is returned. For example, if assets A and B each cost $80,000, and A returns $20,000 per year, but B returns only $16,000 per year, we would prefer A to B because it would have 1 less year before being "paid back." This decision would have ignored the fact that A would return $20,000 for only 4 years, whereas B would return $16,000 for 20 years. While the decision in this case is clearly wrong and probably would not have been made, we can observe that the payback period technically ignores any later cash flows.

Also, the payback period treats all cash flows as if they are expressed in the same-size dollar. For example, assets C and D each cost $50,000, and promise to yield these cash flows:

Year	Asset C	Asset D
1	$12,500	$30,000
2	12,500	15,000
3	12,500	3,000
4	12,500	2,000
5	12,500	12,500
	$62,500	$62,500

On the basis of payback, we would be indifferent because they both have 4 years to go before they return a *profit*. It should be clear that D's cash returns are much more favorable because the dollars can be invested sooner.[1]

Despite these conceptual failings, many businessmen compute and rely on payback period extensively. We do not wish to state that the tool lacks usefulness, but we do encourage that it be used wisely as a supplement to other analyses.

Average Rate of Return

In order to give consideration to the cash flows received after the payback period, many managers compute the *average rate of return* that is to be earned from a project. The computation is relatively simple, but is based on some assumptions that can be unrealistic. Although the method is more applicable for long-range situations, it neglects the time value of money by using the average income rather than present values.

Basically, the calculation is another ratio. In this case, we divide *average* annual income from the asset by the *average* amount of investment during the asset's useful life. Notice that there is a departure from our stated concern with cash inflows. The interpretation supporting this concept is that some of the annual cash inflow represents a return *of* the investment (equal to depreciation) instead of a return *on* the investment. Accordingly, the size of the investment declines over the life of the asset.

There is some flexibility in selecting the figure for the average investment. One approach holds that in reality changes in book values occur continuously throughout any given year. Another idea is based on the bookkeeping practice of recording depreciation at the end of the year, and computes the average *book value* based on these year-end book values. To demonstrate, suppose that a $60,000 machine with a $10,000 salvage value is depreciated on a straight-line basis over 5 years. Applying the first concept, the average investment would be $35,000, computed by dividing the sum of the beginning and ending investments ($60,000 plus $10,000) by 2. Applying the second concept, the average investment would be the average book values for the years the asset was in use:

Year	Book Value
1	$ 60,000
2	50,000
3	40,000
4	30,000
5	20,000
	$200,000
Average	$ 40,000

When straight-line depreciation is used, the average investment can be found by dividing the sum of the first and last year's book values ($60,000 plus

[1] A modification of the approach is to compute the payback period using the *present value* of the future cash inflows. This method still suffers the weakness of ignoring post-payback cash flows.

$20,000) by 2. Compared to the continuous assumption, the average book-value approach is more easily applied when an accelerated method of computing depreciation is applied. Because the two approaches produce different average rates of return for the same investment, it is essential that the same one be used for analyzing all alternatives.

To demonstrate, suppose that Machine E will cost $20,000, will last 10 years, and will add $2,400 annually to profits. Suppose that Machine F will perform the same task, will cost only $18,000, will return $6,000 when it is salvaged after 6 years, and will add $2,600 annually to profits.

Applying the first approach to finding the average investment yields the following analysis:

	Machine E	Machine F
Initial investment	$20,000	$18,000
Ending investment	0	6,000
Total	$20,000	$24,000
Average	$10,000	$12,000
Expected return	$ 2,400	$ 2,600
Expected average rate of return	24%	21.7%

Thus our model would lead to a preference for Machine E.[2]

The relative strengths of the *average rate of return* model are that it is easy to understand and apply, that it is applicable to long-term projects, and that it considers returns after the payback period. It is weakened by the assumption about the *average* investment. It is also dependent on the meaningfulness of *average earnings*. If Machines G and H produced the earnings shown below, they would both yield an average annual return of $3,000. However, it is quite clear that H's cash flows would be more desirable because of the time value of money discussed in Chapter 14.

Year	Machine G	Machine H
1	$3,000	$5,000
2	3,000	4,000
3	3,000	3,000
4	3,000	2,000
5	3,000	1,000
	$15,000	$15,000

The other methods presented in this chapter do include the income earning effects of timing, and are conceptually more correct than the payback period or average return on investment.

Net Present Value

Under the *net present value* approach, the decision maker should select the alternative that has the greatest excess of the present value of the cash in-

---

[2] Using the alternate averaging method yields percentages of 21.8 and 20.0, and we would still select Machine E.

flows over the present value of the cash outflows. The discount rate used for the computations should be the *minimum rate of return* the firm must earn. This number might be found as the return on the next best available alternative investment (such as a savings account) or the interest cost of borrowing funds. The strengths of the analysis are its applicability to long- and short-run projects, its inclusion of all cash flows, and its consideration of the time value of money. A significant weakness is its higher level of conceptual and computational complexity, which tends to confuse and discourage some potential users. The selection of the discount rate is also critical to its proper functioning.

Exhibit 15-3 demonstrates how the net present value of alternatives are computed. The first section shows the unadjusted dollar inflows and outflows expected from Project *I* and Project *J*. The three following sections show the present values of the cash flows discounted at 10, 15, and 20 percent. Notice how our preference swings from *J* to *I* as the discount rate increases. This *sensitivity analysis* demonstrates how the selection of the rate is important to arriving at the right decision. If the computations produce a *negative* net present value, the project should be rejected offhand as inferior to our best alternative investment.

Exhibit 15-3
Net Present Values

Cash Flows Unadjusted:	Table B Factor	Project *I*	Project *J*
Purchase outflow		$(125,000)	$(120,000)
Net inflow Year 1		80,000	40,000
Net inflow Year 2		100,000	60,000
Net inflow Year 3		20,000	100,000
Salvage inflow		10,000	20,000
Discounted at 10%			
Purchase outflow	1.000	$(125,000)	$(120,000)
Net inflow Year 1	0.909	72,720	36,360
Net inflow Year 2	0.826	82,600	49,560
Net inflow Year 3	0.751	15,020	75,100
Salvage inflow	0.751	7,510	15,020
Net present value		$ 52,850	$ 56,040*
Discounted at 15%:			
Purchase outflow	1.000	$(125,000)	$(120,000)
Net inflow Year 1	0.870	69,600	34,800
Net inflow Year 2	0.756	75,600	45,360
Net inflow Year 3	0.658	13,160	65,800
Salvage inflow	0.658	6,580	13,160
		$ 39,940*	$ 39,120
Discounted at 20%:			
Purchase outflow	1.000	$(125,000)	$(120,000)
Net inflow Year 1	0.833	66,640	33,320
Net inflow Year 2	0.694	69,400	41,640
Net inflow Year 3	0.579	11,580	57,900
Salvage inflow	0.579	5,790	11,580
		$ 28,410*	$ 24,440

*Preferred investment

The same quantities can be expressed as *differential* cash flows, with the result that the number of calculations can be reduced. Shown below are the differential cash flows of *I* compared to *J*.

Year	Unadjusted	10%	15%	20%
0	$ (5,000)	$ (5,000)	$ (5,000)	$ (5,000)
1	40,000	36,360	34,800	33,320
2	40,000	33,040	30,240	27,760
3	(80,000)	(60,080)	(52,640)	(46,320)
3	(10,000)	(7,510)	(6,580)	(5,790)
Net		$ (3,190)	$ 820	$ 3,970

We prefer *I* to *J* at 15 and 20 percent because the net differential present value is positive.

A weakness of the net present value model is that it does not relate the size of the net present value to the size of the sacrifice necessary to acquire that present value. In order to deal with this shortcoming, it is advisable to use the *profitability index*.

Profitability Index

Suppose that a manager applies the net present value approach to two investment alternatives, *K* and *L*, which will produce the following cash flows:

	K	L
Purchase	$(50,000)	$(250,000)
Year 1	25,000	100,000
Year 2	20,000	100,000
Year 3	20,000	120,000

If they are discounted at 10 percent, the adjusted cash flows shown below are obtained:

Table B Values	K	L
1.000	$(50,000)	$(250,000)
0.909	22,725	90,900
0.826	16,520	82,600
0.751	15,020	90,120
Net	$ 4,265	$ 13,620

According to net present values, we can conclude that both of them are profitable, and that *L* should be preferred because it is worth 9,355 present dollars more than *K*. But notice that the cost of *L* is greater than *K*. We can take this factor into consideration by computing the *profitability index*, which is the ratio:

$$\frac{\text{Present value of cash inflows}}{\text{Cost of the investment}}$$

As with the net present value method the manager must first select a *cutoff* interest rate at which the cash flows will be discounted. If the profitability index calculation yields a value ≥ 1, the investment is expected to yield a return greater than or equal to the selected *cutoff* interest rate. A proposal for which the profitability index is less than 1 should normally be rejected because it will not provide a high enough yield.

The profitability index for alternatives K and L are:

$$K: \frac{\$54,265}{\$50,000} = 1.085$$

$$L: \frac{\$263,620}{\$250,000} = 1.054$$

Thus, because we prefer the project with the higher profitability index, we would select Project K. If we have $250,000 available to invest, we would be better off buying five Ks instead of one L. This strategy would yield a net present value of $21,325, as opposed to the $13,620 we would get from L. If our operations cannot justify the acquisition of, for example, five machines that do the same thing, we are faced with an *investment portfolio* problem, for which we will seek the best combination of all possible alternatives. The theoretical and practical aspects of portfolio management are well-developed, but further inquiry into them is beyond the scope of this text.

Time-Adjusted Rate of Return

Another time value model useful for capital-budgeting decision analysis involves the *time-adjusted rate of return* described in Chapter 14. In brief, the procedure is the search for the discount rate that will equate the present value of the cash outflows from a project to the present value of the cash inflows. The result of the search is a percentage rate of return. We will reject any project that will produce at a lower rate than our minimum rate elsewhere, or the interest cost of our funds. Furthermore, we can rank the projects according to the relative rates they promise to yield.

For example, investment M of $50,000 will return cash flows of $14,565 per year for 5 years. Investment N of $72,000 will return $19,539 per year for 6 years. Recall from Chapter 14 that if we divide the investment (PV) by the annual cash inflow (R) we get a table value. Thus,

$$\$50,000 \div \$14,565 = 3.433$$
$$\$72,000 \div \$19,539 = 3.685$$

Going to Table D and looking across the line where $n = 5$ for 3.433, we find the time-adjusted rate of return of 14 percent. Also, in Table D where $n = 6$, we note the factor 3.685 shows a time-adjusted rate of return of 16 percent.

INCOME TAX EFFECT

Before proceeding further, we need to introduce the effect of income taxes on the investment analysis. In the following example, the acquisition and use of Machine M will allow the firm to deduct depreciation expense in computing its taxable income, with a decrease in the cash outflow for income taxes.

Suppose that the machine can be purchased for $500,000, that it will last five years, that it will produce 6,000 units in that period, and that it can be sold at the end of that time for $50,000. The following estimates about each unit produced by the machine have been made:

Cash price		$ 500
Production costs:		
Variable cash expenses	$300	
Depreciation*	75	(375)
Pretax contribution		$ 125
Income taxes (40%)		(50)
Aftertax contribution		$ 75

*($500,000 – $50,000) ÷ 6,000 units

With these facts, we can project the per unit cash inflow in this manner:

Cash price		$500
Cash expenses:		
Production	$300	
Income taxes	50	(350)
Aftertax cash inflow*		$150

* Alternatively, we can take the aftertax contribution ($75) and add the noncash expense ($75) to come up with the same result ($150).

This table projects the cash inflows from the use of Machine *M* to produce its output, which are expected to be sold in the shown quantities.

Year	Unit Sales	Net Cash Inflow	Salvage Value	Total Inflow
1	200	$ 30,000		$ 30,000
2	1,000	150,000		150,000
3	2,500	375,000		375,000
4	1,500	225,000		225,000
5	800	120,000	$50,000	170,000

Our objective is to find the discount rate that will equate the present value of these five yearly cash flows to the present value of the purchase outflow ($500,000).

With a properly programmed computer, the search can be begun and completed with a relatively small effort. With a sophisticated hand calculator, the procedure is more complex. With a present value table, it is even more difficult. Because we cannot provide either of the first two devices, we will have to show you the third, which is demonstrated in Exhibit 15-4. We have proceeded on a trial-and-error basis to locate that percentage which will equate the Present Value of the expected cash inflows with the original cash outflow.

We begin the search with an arbitrary rate (10 percent), which yields a present value for the inflows of about $692,000. As this amount greatly exceeds $500,000, it is obvious that we need to discount them further by the use of a higher rate. The 40 percent rate is too high, as the present value drops to about $324,500. We continue this *trial-and-error search* by going halfway between 10 and 40 percent to 25 percent. This choice produces about $460,000, which is too low because we have discounted the inflows too much. We can next select 20 percent, which is too small, because the

Exhibit 15-4
Calculation of Time-adjusted Rate of Return

		Try 10%		Try 40%	
Year	Annual Cash Flow	Factor	Present Value	Factor	Present Value
1	$ 30,000	0.909	$ 27,270	0.714	$ 21,420
2	150,000	0.826	123,900	0.510	76,500
3	375,000	0.751	281,625	0.364	136,500
4	225,000	0.683	153,675	0.260	58,500
5	170,000	0.621	105,570	0.186	31,620
			$692,040		$324,540

		Try 25%		Try 20%	
Year	Annual Cash Flow	Factor	Present Value	Factor	Present Value
1	$ 30,000	0.800	$ 24,000	0.833	$ 24,990
2	150,000	0.640	96,000	0.694	104,100
3	375,000	0.512	192,000	0.579	217,125
4	225,000	0.410	92,250	0.482	108,450
5	170,000	0.328	55,760	0.402	68,340
			$460,010		$523,005

		Try 22%	
Year	Annual Cash Flow	Factor	Present Value
1	$ 30,000	0.820	$ 24,600
2	150,000	0.672	100,800
3	375,000	0.551	206,625
4	225,000	0.451	101,475
5	170,000	0.370	62,900
			$496,400

present value is too large (about $523,000). Going up to 22 percent yields a figure which is just under the desired goal ($496,400). We can conclude that the time-adjusted rate of return is slightly under 22 percent.

Keeping in mind the dangers of *spurious accuracy,* we can perform a linear interpolation between these two values:

Rate of Return					Present Value		
20%					$523,005		
	x		2%			$23,005	$26,605
?%					$500,000		
22%					$496,400		

$$\frac{x}{2\%} = \frac{\$23,005}{\$26,605}$$

$$x = 1.7\%$$

Time-adjusted rate of return = 21.7%

We would accept this proposal if funds could be borrowed at less than 21.7 percent interest, and if we had no project that could yield a higher rate.

A fourth method of solving for the time-adjusted rate of return depends on the use of higher order exponential equations, but its discussion is beyond the scope of this text. Curiously, this method can produce several discount rates that will equate the present values of the inflows and outflows for a given project.

A Perspective

Based on our discussion of the fundamentals of applying quantitative analysis models to capital budgeting decisions, it should be apparent that each of them has its relative disadvantages, and not one can stand alone. All are subject to the same limitation from the accuracy of the input data. The estimate of the size of the future cash flows is obviously subject to error. Furthermore, we presented our examples with the tacit assumption that the cash flows either occurred at once, or at one-year intervals in the future. Although this assumption produces an easily solved problem, it is decidedly invalid in virtually all real situations.

Finally, remember that *nonquantifiable* (sometimes called *qualitative*) factors can act to sway our decision from one alternative to another. No decision maker in the real world should ignore these additional aspects of the situation.

PROJECT SCREENING ILLUSTRATED

In order to demonstrate how these quantitative tools might be applied, suppose that the Ferber Company board of directors decided that each of the five members would independently analyze all proposals for capital expenditures, and then make a recommendation to his colleagues. By chance, each of the five members selected a different analytical model and developed his own decision criteria. The facts are shown in Exhibit 15-5.

Exhibit 15-5
Decision Criteria for Ferber Company
Board of Directors

Member	Model	Accept If:	Place In Second Priority If:	Reject If:
Gardner	Payback Period (PBP) in years	$PBP \leq 4$	$4 < PBP \leq 7$	$PBP > 7$
Hunterman	Average Rate of Return *(ARR)*	$ARR \geq 20\%$	$11\% \leq ARR < 20\%$	$ARR < 11\%$
Johnson	Net Present Value at 15% *(NPV)*	$NPV \geq \$10,000$	$0 < NPV < \$10,000$	$NPV \leq 0$
Randell	Profitability Index at 15% *(PI)*	$PI \geq 1.1$	$1.0 < PI < 1.1$	$PI \leq 1.0$
Young	Time-Adjusted Rate of Return *(TRR)*	$TRR \geq 20\%$	$11\% \leq TRR < 20\%$	$TRR < 11\%$

Joe Perry, the vice president of finance, distributed fact sheets about three new proposals, and the five directors agreed to have their analyses ready for the next meeting. The firm was operating in a 40 percent income tax bracket. Data about the projects and each member's analysis are presented below.

Project A

The following facts were known about Project A:

Cash price	$84,000
Salvage value	0
Service life	14 years
Depreciation method	Straight-line

Anticipated yearly income:

Cash revenues	$33,000
Cash expenses	(9,000)
Depreciation	(6,000)
Taxable income	$18,000
Income taxes	(7,200)
Aftertax income	$10,800

Anticipated yearly cash flow:

Revenues	$33,000
Cash expenses	(9,000)
Income taxes	(7,200)
	$16,800

PAYBACK PERIOD

Gardner computed the payback period as:

$$\frac{\text{Cost of project}}{\text{Yearly cash flow}} = \frac{\$84,000}{\$16,800} = 5.0$$

AVERAGE RATE OF RETURN

In order to make his analysis, Hunterman first had to find the size of the average investment. He decided to use the average annual book-value approach:

First year's book value	$84,000
Final year's book value	6,000
	$90,000

Average book value ($90,000 ÷ 2) = $45,000

On this basis, the average rate of return is:

$$\frac{\text{Average annual income}}{\text{Average investment}} = \frac{\$10,800}{\$45,000} = 24\%$$

NET PRESENT VALUE

After selecting his discount rate of 15 percent, Johnson referred to his copy of Table D and found:

Present value of inflows $16,800 × 5.724	=	$ 96,163
Present value of outflows $(84,000) × 1.000	=	(84,000)
Net present value		$ 12,163

PROFITABILITY INDEX

After making the same initial computation as Johnson, Randell found the profitability index:

$$\frac{\text{Present value of inflows}}{\text{Cost of the asset}} = \frac{\$96,163}{\$84,000} = 1.14$$

TIME-ADJUSTED RATE OF RETURN

Using Table D, Young set out to find the time-adjusted rate of return. He knew the present value of the outflows would be $84,000 for same i on the table. Thus, he formulated an equation:

$$\text{Table value} \times \text{Annual cash inflow} = \$84,000$$
$$\text{Table value} = \$84,000 \div \$16,800 = 5.000$$

Turning to his copy, he found the value of 5.008 under the column for 18 percent, which is the time-adjusted rate of return for Project A.

Project *B*

The following facts were known about Project B:

Cash price	$70,000
Salvage value	$14,500
Service life	4,000 units of output
Depreciation method	Units-of-production

Anticipated income per unit of output:

Cash revenues	$ 47.63
Cash expenses	(23.54)
Depreciation	(13.87)*
Taxable income	$ 10.22
Income taxes	(4.09)
Aftertax income	$ 6.13

*Depreciable basis ÷ Units of output = ($70,000 − $14,500) ÷ (4,000) = $13.87 per unit

Anticipated per-unit cash flows:

Revenues	$ 47.63
Cash expenses	(23.54)
Income taxes	(4.09)
Cash flow	$ 20.00

Anticipated yearly sales, aftertax income, and cash flows:

Year	Unit Sales	Aftertax income**	Cash flows†
1	500	$ 3,065	$10,000
2	1,000	6,130	20,000
3	2,000	12,260	40,000
4	500	3,065	10,000
	4,000	$24,520	

**Unit sales × per unit aftertax income: $6.13
†Unit sales × per unit cash flows: $20.00

PAYBACK PERIOD

Because the cash flows were irregular, Gardner used the "accumulations" approach, and determined that the $70,000 cost would be returned in cash by the end of the third year ($10,000 + $20,000 + $40,000).

AVERAGE RATE OF RETURN

Because the depreciation was not straight-line, Hunterman found the projected book value for each of the asset's four years with the following schedule:

Year	Preceding Year's Units of Output	Depreciation Expense	Book Value
1			$ 70,000
2	500	$ 6,935	63,065
3	1,000	13,870	49,195
4	2,000	27,740	21,455
			$203,715

$$\text{Average book value} = \frac{\$203,715}{4} = \$50,929$$

The average income from Project B is the total ($24,520) divided by four years, or $6,130 per year. Accordingly, Hunterman found the average rate of return:

$$\frac{\$6,130}{\$50,929} = 12.0\%$$

NET PRESENT VALUE

Again using 15 percent as the discount rate, but applying Table B, Johnson prepared the following schedule:

Year	Cash Flow	Table Value	Present Value
Purchase	$(70,000)	1.000	$(70,000)
1	10,000	0.870	8,700
2	20,000	0.756	15,120
3	40,000	0.658	26,320
4	10,000	0.572	5,720
Salvage	14,500	0.572	8,294
Net present value			$ (5,846)

PROFITABILITY INDEX

After the same processes, Randell found an unfavorable value for the profitability index:

$$\frac{\$64,154}{\$70,000} = 0.92$$

TIME-ADJUSTED RATE OF RETURN

Because there was no annuity of cash flows, Young had to use a trial-and-error basis to find the discount rate that would equate the present value of the five inflows to the $70,000 present value of the outflow. He first selected 10 percent, and found:

Year	Cash Flow	Table Value	Present Value
1	$10,000	0.909	$ 9,090
2	20,000	0.826	16,520
3	40,000	0.751	30,040
4	10,000	0.683	6,830
Salvage	14,500	0.683	9,904
			$72,384

As the cash flows had not been discounted sufficiently, he tried 12 percent in order to produce a lower present value:

1	$10,000	0.893	$ 8,930
2	20,000	0.797	15,940
3	40,000	0.712	28,480
4	10,000	0.636	6,360
Salvage	14,500	0.636	9,222
			$68,932

He concluded that the real rate must be somewhere between 10 and 12 percent, but slightly closer to 12. As this exact value was not critical, he simply concluded that it was about 11.5 percent (a linear interpolation yields the value of 11.4 percent).

Project *C*

This particular proposal was more complicated than the others, and required more intricate computations. The following facts were known:

Cash price	$73,000
Salvage value	$ 4,000
Service life	5 years
Depreciation method	Sum-of-the-years'-digits*

Anticipated yearly income for the five-year period:

	1	2	3	4	5
Cash revenues	$ 35,000	$ 35,000	$ 35,000	$ 35,000	$ 35,000
Cash expenses	(15,000)	(15,000)	(15,000)	(15,000)	(15,000)
Depreciation*	(23,000)	(18,400)	(13,800)	(9,200)	(4,600)
Taxable income	$ (3,000)	$ 1,600	$ 6,200	$ 10,800	$ 15,400
Income taxes (40%)	1,200**	(640)	(2,480)	(4,320)	(6,160)
Aftertax income	$ (1,800)	$ 960	$ 3,720	$ 6,480	$ 9,240

*Computed as 5/15, 4/15, 3/15, 2/15, and 1/15 of the asset's depreciable basis ($73,000 − $4,000)
**The reported loss can be deducted from other income and will reduce taxes by 40 percent of $3,000.

Anticipated yearly cash flows for the five-year period:

	1	2	3	4	5
Revenues	$ 35,000	$ 35,000	$ 35,000	$ 35,000	$ 35,000
Cash expenses	(15,000)	(15,000)	(15,000)	(15,000)	(15,000)
Income taxes	1,200	(640)	(2,480)	(4,320)	(6,160)
	$ 21,200	$ 19,360	$ 17,520	$ 15,680	$ 13,840

PAYBACK PERIOD

With irregular cash flows again, Gardner prepared a schedule of cumulative cash flows:

Year	Annual Cash Flow	Accumulated to Date
1	$21,200	$21,200
2	19,360	40,560
3	17,520	58,080
4	15,680	73,760

Thus, the $73,000 cost would be recovered in slightly less than 4 years. If it is assumed that cash flows in at a constant rate, the period would be 3.95 years.

AVERAGE RATE OF RETURN

Hunterman determined the average income by dividing the total for the 5 years ($18,600) by 5, which yielded $3,720 per year. He then computed the book value for each year:

Year	Preceding Year's Depreciation	Book Value
1	–0–	$ 73,000
2	$23,000	50,000
3	18,400	31,600
4	13,800	17,800
5	9,200	8,600
		$181,000

$$\text{Average book value} = \frac{\$181,000}{5 \text{ years}} = \$36,200$$

Thus the average rate of return on Proposal B is:

$$\frac{\$3,720}{\$36,200} = 10.3\%$$

NET PRESENT VALUE

Applying the factors from Table B, Johnson found the following net present value for Project C:

Year	Cash Flow	Table Value	Present Value
Purchase	$(73,000)	1.000	$(73,000)
1	21,200	0.870	18,444
2	19,360	0.756	14,636
3	17,520	0.658	11,528
4	15,680	0.572	8,969
5	13,840	0.497	6,878
Salvage	4,000	0.497	1,988
			$(10,557)

PROFITABILITY INDEX

Randell found that the present value of the future cash inflows was $62,443, and computed the profitability index:

$$\frac{\$62,443}{\$73,000} = 0.86$$

TIME-ADJUSTED RATE OF RETURN

Because of the irregular cash flows, Young again applied the trial-and-error approach. He arbitrarily selected 10 percent on his initial run-through:

Year	Cash Flow	Table Value	Present Value
1	$21,200	0.909	$19,271
2	19,360	0.826	15,991
3	17,520	0.751	13,158
4	15,680	0.683	10,709
5	13,840	0.621	8,595
Salvage	4,000	0.621	2,484
			$70,208

This rate discounted the inflows too far below the $73,000 outflow, so he tried again with 8 percent:

Year	Cash Flow	Table Value	Present Value
1	$21,200	0.926	$19,631
2	19,360	0.857	16,592
3	17,520	0.794	13,911
4	15,680	0.735	11,525
5	13,840	0.681	9,425
Salvage	4,000	0.681	2,724
			$73,808

Based on this information, he concluded that the real rate of return was slightly higher than 8 percent. Interpolation produces:

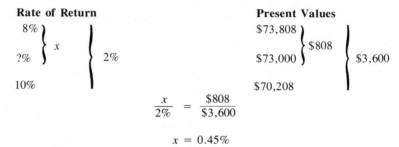

$$\frac{x}{2\%} = \frac{\$808}{\$3,600}$$

$$x = 0.45\%$$

Thus the time-adjusted rate is 8.45 percent.

The Board Meeting

The five members met again, each eager to present his analysis and recommendation concerning the three proposals. They were somewhat surprised, dismayed, and then amused as they learned what had happened. A summary of their findings is shown in Exhibit 15-6. The variety of conclusions shows that capital-budgeting tools are not ironclad. The differences arose because of two factors: the tools themselves and the criteria that each member independently selected.

Gardner's recommendations run counter to the others because he looked only at the original cost and those cash flows that happened before the

Exhibit 15-6
Summary of Analyses

Board Member	A Result	A Conclusion	B Result	B Conclusion	C Result	C Conclusion
Gardner— Payback period	5 years	Second priority	3 years	Accept	3.95 years	Accept
Hunterman— Average rate of return	24%	Accept	12%	Second priority	10.3%	Reject
Johnson— Net present value	$12,163	Accept	$(5,846)	Reject	$(10,557)	Reject
Randell— Profitability index	1.14	Accept	0.92	Reject	0.86	Reject
Young— Time-adjusted rate of return	18%	Second priority	11.4%	Second priority	8.45%	Reject

payback period was ended. He also failed to consider the timing of the cash flows during the payback period.

Notice the differences between Hunterman's and Young's analyses. Both were attempting to rank the three proposals by looking at a rate of return. They obtained inconsistent numbers, although their conclusions were quite similar. Hunterman's rates were uniformly higher than Young's because he considered that the incomes from the later years were expressed in the same-size dollars as those of the earlier years. Young did not make this conceptual error and produced a better measure of the real rate of return.

We would expect the three time-adjusted models to produce identical results. Indeed, we see that there is no difference between Johnson and Randell because their models are exactly the same, except for the last step. Johnson *subtracted* the present value of the outflows from the present value of the inflows whereas Randell *divided* the former into the latter. They would always reject the same proposals, but might find differences in those accepted or placed in the second priority. If Young had selected 15 percent as his *cutoff percentage* instead of 11 percent, his results would have coincided with the other two members. In effect, he set a very high standard in comparison to the others.

A firm would be usually mistaken to accept or reject a proposal even after this extensive analysis. No consideration has been given to possible variations of the cash flows from the predicted figures, nor to any of the qualitative factors described earlier in this chapter. It would also help to examine alternatives for each of these three in order to find the best. The decision is simply too complex to confidently make on such a small amount of information.

INFLATION AND TIME-ADJUSTED ANALYSIS

Both the income effect and inflation act to make the future dollar have a lower value than the present dollar. When income opportunities are available, today's dollar is more valuable because it can be used to earn more dollars sooner. If the purchasing power of the dollar is declining throughout the economy because of inflation, then the future dollar is less valuable than the present dollar.

Can we describe a model to help us compare future and present dollars, taking into consideration both these factors? Yes, we can, and in the next few paragraphs we will describe the computations that are necessary to do so.

Present Value from Interest

In the previous chapter; we demonstrated that we can describe the earning power of a future dollar by discounting it according to the formula:

$$\frac{1}{(1 + i)^n}$$

where i is the interest rate and n is the number of time periods, and where compounding occurs each time period. When i is greater than zero, the future dollar is worth less than today's dollar.

Present Value from Inflation

If inflation is described in terms of a percentage increase in the general price index, and if the inflation will occur at the same rate each time period, we can describe the present value of an inflated future dollar in terms of a very similar formula. Let f be the periodic rate of inflation and n the number of time periods, then the present value of a future dollar can be described as:

$$\frac{1}{(1+f)^n}$$

Thus we have discounted the future dollar for the effects of inflation.

Combining Interest and Inflation

Because these two effects occur simultaneously, the proper way to combine them is through multiplication. The present value of $1 must be described as:

$$\frac{1}{(1+i)^n} \times \frac{1}{(1+f)^n}$$

or

$$\frac{1}{(1+i)^n (1+f)^n}$$

For example, let $n = 3$, $i = 0.04$, and $f = 0.06$. Discounting for interest yields a present value for $1 of $0.89, while discounting for inflation yields a present value of $0.84. If we take these two effects together, the present value is ($0.89) $\times$ ($0.84), or $0.75. Table B may be used for these computations.

As a shortcut, we can *approximate* this dual effect simply by adding the interest and inflation rates. Our formula becomes:

$$\frac{1}{(1+i+f)^n}$$

Substituting our example data into this formula yields:

$$\frac{1}{(1+0.04+0.06)^3}$$

or $0.75. If our computations are carried out to more decimal places, we would discover a difference of about $0.0049.

This shortcut approximation works extremely well when i, f, and n are reasonably small. Exhibit 15-7 shows the different results obtained from the more precise computations and the estimation process for a variety of values of the variables. The deviation is surprisingly small, and the approximation may be used in many cases.

Finding the Real Rate of Return

In Chapter 14, we showed how we could determine the amount of dollars we could accumulate through investment. The formula is $(1+i)^n$, where i is the interest rate and n is the number of time periods.

Exhibit 15-7

Comparison of Actual with Estimated Present Values

	$i = 0.04$ $f = 0.04$		$i = 0.10$ $f = 0.08$		$i = 0.20$ $f = 0.15$	
	Actual*	Estimate**	Actual	Estimate	Actual	Estimate
$n = 1$	$0.925	$0.926	$0.842	$0.847	$0.725	$0.741
$n = 3$	0.790	0.794	0.596	0.609	0.381	0.406
$n = 5$	0.676	0.681	0.423	0.437	0.200	0.223
$n = 10$	0.457	0.463	0.179	0.191	0.040	0.050
$n = 20$	0.208	0.215	0.032	0.037	0.002	0.002

* $\dfrac{1}{(1 + i)^n (1 + f)^n}$

** $\dfrac{1}{(1 + i + f)^n}$

But we have just seen that inflation acts to discount those future dollars. The two formulas act simultaneously, so they must be combined by multiplication, yielding this formula for the future amount of *real purchasing power* from an investment of $1:

$$(1 + i)^n \times \frac{1}{(1 + f)^n}$$

or

$$\frac{(1 + i)^n}{(1 + f)^n}$$

Thus, if $i = 0.08$, $f = 0.06$, and $n = 1$,[3] the future amount of real purchasing power is:

$$\frac{(1 + 0.08)}{(1 + 0.06)} = 1.0189$$

The real rate of return is only 1.9 percent.

For another example, let $i = 0.15$, $f = 0.10$, and $n = 1$. The formula now yields:

$$\frac{(1.15)}{(1.10)} = 1.0454$$

In this case, the proposal will earn at a real rate of only 4.5 percent.

A shortcut computation is possible in this situation as well, although it is not as precise as the one we saw earlier. We can approximate the real rate of return by *subtracting the inflation rate from the interest rate*.

In our first example, this approximation would yield a real rate of return of $(0.08 - 0.06)$, or about 2 percent. This figure is only one-tenth of 1 percent larger than the more precisely computed solution. In the second example, our approximate real rate of return is $(0.15 - 0.10)$, or 5 percent, which is one-half of 1 percent larger than the number the more precise computation yields. Other examples would show that the shortcut computation will always produce an estimate that is slightly larger than the actual.

---

[3] The relationship will hold for *any* value of n. By using $n = 1$, we can determine the real rate of return without referring to Table A.

SUMMARY

The capital-asset acquisition decision is a very important one for all organizations because it sets the operating capacity, is large in size, and is long-lasting. Planning acquisitions is accomplished through *capital budgeting,* which should be the final step in the budgeting process. Capital budgets are detailed for the near term, and often cover 20 or more years of time.

There are numerous variables in the capital-asset acquisition decision. Foremost is the cash flow (in and out) from the projects. But other things need to be considered, such as the timing of the flows, flexibility, and social responsibilities. It is not unusual to find qualitative factors overriding cash-flow considerations.

The analysis of the situation can be aided by quantitative tools which boil down many data into one fact. Included in these tools are the payback period, average rate of return, net present value, profitability index, and the time-adjusted rate of return. The last three are *time-adjusted models,* and rely on the foundations established in Chapter 14. Each tool has its usefulness and its limitations. Care must be exerted in using any of the findings, and the qualitative factors should be included. A lengthy example shows how different models and different decision criteria can produce contrary results.

The effects of inflation on capital budgeting decisions cannot be safely ignored. Inflation reduces the value of future dollars and can be included in present value computations by adding the inflation rate to the discount rate. The time-adjusted rate of return should have an adjustment for lost purchasing power. The modification can be approximated by deducting the inflation rate from the rate of return.

QUESTIONS

1. What is a *capital asset*?
2. Describe three reasons why the capital-asset acquisition decision is critical.
3. Which of the acquisition decision variables is most widely analyzed? Why do you suppose it is?
4. Is depreciation expense a cash outflow? Explain.
5. Why is the accounting net income figure inferior to a measure of cash flow for analyzing an acquisition decision situation?
6. Name several other decision variables. Under what circumstances do the nonquantitative aspects outweigh the quantitative?
7. Basically, what is the *payback period* supposed to represent? Is it more desirable to have a lower or higher number?
8. Describe the two major weaknesses of the payback period. What are its strengths?
9. How is the *average rate of return* superior to the payback period as an analytical tool? What weakness does it have in common with the payback period?

10. Describe the two approaches to computing the average investment.
11. Is it more desirable to have a larger or smaller average rate of return?
12. What weakness of the payback period and average rate of return does the net present value approach attempt to overcome?
13. What is the meaning of a project's net present value? Is it more desirable to have a larger or smaller net present value?
14. If the discount rate is increased, what is the effect on the net present value of a project?
15. What weakness of the net present value does the *profitability index* attempt to overcome?
16. Is it more desirable to have a larger or smaller profitability index?
17. Even though the depreciation expense is not a cash flow, it can affect the amount of cash going out of the firm. Explain why this statement is true.
18. Is it more desirable to have a larger or smaller time-adjusted rate of return?
19. When inflation is considered, what happens to the time-adjusted rate of return for a given proposal?

EXERCISES

E15–1 Payback period.

    a. Project *A* will cost $12,000 and will return $5,000 each year for the next 6 years. How long is the payback period?

    b. Project *B* will cost $12,000 and will return $4,000 each year for the next 12 years. How long is the payback period?

    c. If this were the only analysis you performed (and you were fairly naive), would you prefer *A* or *B*?

    d. Project *C* will cost $25,000 and will return cash as follows:

Year	Amount
1	$10,000
2	12,000
3	4,000
4	2,000
5	1,000
6	1,000

Find the payback period for this project using (1) cumulative cash flows, and (2) average cash flows, as discussed in this chapter.

E15–2 Average rate of return.

    a. Project *D* is expected to cost $6,700. It will be depreciated on a straight-line basis, over a 5-year service life, assuming a salvage value of $700. It is expected that the annual net income for the 5 years (ignoring taxes) will be $860. What is the average rate of return for this proposal? (Assume that depreciation occurs continuously.)

b. Project E is expected to cost $10,000. It will be depreciated on a straight-line basis, over an 8-year service life, with no salvage value. It is expected that the annual net income for the 8 years (ignoring taxes) will be $230. What is the average rate of return for this proposal? (Assume that depreciation occurs continuously.)

c. Project F is expected to cost $9,600. Its salvage value after its 8-year life is expected to be one-sixth of the original cost. The estimates of the income it will produce over those 8 years (after allowing for straight-line depreciation) are:

Year	Amount
1	$1,200
2	1,200
3	1,600
4	2,000
5	3,000
6	4,000
7	2,000
8	1,000

What is the average rate of return from Project F? (Assume that depreciation occurs continuously.)

d. Perform the analysis of Projects D, E, and F with the average book value of the asset. Does the order of preference change from your first answers?

E15–3 Net present value.

a. Project G has a tentative price tag of $30,000. The cash flows from its implementation are expected to be:

Year	Amount
1	$12,000
2	20,000
3	25,000
4	10,000

If we have to pay 4 percent per year to borrow cash, what is the net present value of Project G? (Ignore income taxes.)

b. Project H is expected to cost $35,000 if we buy it. Our staff has estimated that the following cash inflows and outflows will occur during its useful life.

Year	Inflow	Outflow
1	$12,000	$7,500
2	9,000	8,000
3	25,000	5,000
4	25,000	4,000

If the minimum rate of return that we will accept on any proposal is 8 percent per year, what is the net present value of Project *H*? (Ignore income taxes.)

c. Proposal *I* has been brought to us by the plant manager. It will involve the purchase and installation of a new machine to replace an old one. The machine will produce at just the same rate of output as the old one, but it will use less labor and materials, and will not require as much maintenance. The plant manager has showed us the following figures to justify the $50,000 acquisition:

Year	Cost Savings
1	$ 5,000
2	10,000
3	10,000
4	20,000
5	20,000
	$65,000

If no further cost savings can be expected after 5 years, and if we have to earn 10 percent in order to be satisfied, should we buy this machine? (Use net present value to decide and ignore income taxes.)

E15–4 *Profitability index.*

a. Project *J* has been suggested to us, and before we accept or reject such a proposal, we will find its profitability index, using 6 percent per year as our discount rate. According to our best estimates, the project will provide the following cash flows over its 3-year life:

Year	Amount
1	$ 9,500
2	16,000
3	25,000

If it costs $40,000, what is the value of its profitability index? Should the project be accepted or rejected?

b. Project *K* is being analyzed prior to its being accepted by management. In general, if a proposal has a profitability index greater than 1.0, with a discount rate of 5 percent per year, it will be accepted.

The project calls for a cash outlay of $69,850, and will produce a net cash inflow of $15,000 each year for the next 6 years. What is the value of its profitability index? Should it be accepted?

c. Young Whitney R. Snapper was recently hired as a financial assistant for Mom's Old Fashioned Candy Corp. In his eager effort to make a lasting impression on his boss, he prepared a profitability index analysis of three capital expenditure opportunities. He is just completing his presentation: "So, Mother, you can see a clear-cut preference of *A* over *C* and *C* over *B*. Do you have any questions?"

His boss responds, "Have you tested your findings for different discount rates? You said that you assumed a 10 percent rate, but our experience in recent years has been as low as 6 percent and as high as 15 percent."

Young Snapper's data is shown below:

	A	*B*	*C*
Cost	$30,867	$21,798	$26,696
Cash inflows:			
Year 1	15,000	4,000	21,000
Year 2	15,000	8,000	17,500
Year 3	15,000	12,000	3,000
Year 4	15,000	20,000	7,000
Profitability index	1.54	1.51	1.52

Required:

1. Show how he found these values for the index.
2. Would the preference ranking be the same if the cost of capital fell to 6 percent? Show your work.
3. Would the preference ranking be the same if the cost of capital rose to 15 percent? Show your work.

E15–5 *Time-adjusted rate of return.*

a. Project *L* is under consideration for possible implementation. It will cost $5,000, which will be paid at once, and will yield the following cash flows:

Year	Amount
1	$2,150
2	2,470
3	922

Using a trial-and-error process, find the time-adjusted rate of return for Project *L*. (*Hint:* Start with 4 percent per year.)

b. Proposition *M* is being analyzed for acceptability. It will cost $565,000, but will yield an annual net cash flow of $100,000 each year for the next 10 years. What is the time-adjusted rate of return for this proposition?

c. Project *N* has an expected cost of $111,710. If it is implemented, it will result in the production of several thousand units of "Knarley." According to a revenue and cost analysis, the following figures can be reasonably expected to apply to *each unit* of Knarley:

Cash revenue received	$ 42.372
Costs:	
Variable cash costs	(20.857)
Depreciation	(13.939)
Pretax contribution	$ 7.576

Income taxes will be levied at 20 percent on all income. Sales of Knarley are expected to occur at the following rate:

Year	Unit Sales
1	2,000
2	2,500
3	3,000

The machinery can be sold at the end of the third year for $15,460.

Required:

What is the time-adjusted rate of return of this proposal? (*Hint:* Start your trial-and-error process with 12 percent per year.)

E15–6 *Various investment analyses.* Fudge Company is analyzing the decision to acquire a new machine which will cost $12,720. It is expected to last 6 years and have no salvage value at end of that time. It will be depreciated using the straight-line method. It is projected that $2,000 will be added to *net income* each year if the machine is used.

Required:

Ignoring income taxes, calculate:
a. the payback period
b. the average rate of return (assume continuous depreciation)
c. The time-adjusted rate of return (to the nearest 1 percent)
d. From the information given, can you decide whether the machine should be acquired? Explain.

E15–7 *Various investment analyses.* The Molasses Company is comparing two machines in contemplation of acquiring one of them. The two machines each cost $2,500, will last 5 years, and will be sold then for $500. If the company uses straight-line depreciation, the additional *net income* (ignoring income taxes), produced by each machine is expected to be:

Year	Grinder	Cruncher
1	$ 300	$1,500
2	500	1,000
3	1,000	–0–
4	1,000	1,000
5	1,000	100
	$3,800	$3,600

Required:

From the facts given, which one of the two would be preferred?

a. Use the payback period to decide (based on the accumulated cash).

b. Use the average rate of return to decide (based on continuous depreciation).

c. Use the net present value to decide (based on a 10 percent discount rate).

E15–8 *Net present value.* Wilson Window Works is in a position where it needs to acquire a new cutting machine. These facts are known about two possible makes that would be suitable from an engineering point of view:

	Ajax	Zjax
Initial cost	$240,000	$340,000
Service life	10 years	10 years
Salvage value	–0–	–0–

The only difference between the two in terms of operation is that the Zjax is more automatic, so it would not be necessary to pay the premium wages of a skilled cutter. This difference will produce an expected savings of $15,000 each year of the 10 years. The output capacity and quality of the two machines is exactly the same.

Required:

a. If Wilson's cost of borrowing is 5 percent per year, which machine will be preferred according to net present value (ignore income taxes)?

b. If Wilson's cost of borrowing is 12 percent per year, which machine will be preferred according to net present value (ignore income taxes)?

E15–9 *Various investment analyses.* The Tasty Candy Company's manager is trying to decide if the old mixer should be kept or replaced by a new one that will be easier to operate. Both the old and the new can handle the expected production volume over the next ten years. The old one could be sold for $50 if it is replaced now. The new one can be purchased for $2,500.

The old one will produce operating costs of $960 each year, whereas the new one will set the company back only $600 a year. Both will last until the manager sells the business in ten years and retires.

Required:

Ignoring income taxes:

a. What is the net present value of buying the new machine, if Tasty's minimum rate of return is 6 percent per year? Should the new machine be bought?

b. What is the profitability index of buying the new machine, if Tasty's minimum rate of return is 10 percent per year?

c. What is the time-adjusted rate of return of buying the new machine? If Tasty must earn 8 percent to justify buying the machine, should it be bought?

E15–10 Compound interest and inflation.

Part 1:

Find the present values of the future sums presented below, taking into consideration not only the earnings but also inflation. You should find the answer first by the precise method and then by the shortcut approach. (Be sure to utilize the tables in Appendix II.)

	Future Sum	Number of Periods	Interest Rate	Inflation Rate
1.	$ 1,000	3	4%	6%
2.	12,000	7	6	6
3.	4,700	12	18	12
4.	50,000	15	8	14

Part 2:

Using the shortcut method only, approximate the *real rates of return* for the following investments:

	Present Value	Future Amount	Number of Periods	Inflation Rate
5.	$10,000	$ 20,000	9	3%
6.	8,700	26,317	19	1
7.	21,500	115,025	12	9
8.	37,250	43,100	3	8

PROBLEMS

P15–1 Payback and average rate of return. George Henry, a noted concert pianist, is contemplating the acquisition of his own grand piano at a cost of $17,000. He expects, as a result of buying the piano, to earn additional money through higher paying concert dates. His agent has projected the following fees with and without the new piano:

Year	Without Piano	With Piano	Piano Depreciation
1	$ 6,000	$18,000	$3,400
2	12,000	23,000	3,400
3	20,000	30,000	3,400
4	9,000	3,000	3,400
5	3,000	–0–	3,400

The agent's fee is 15 percent of gross fees.

Required:

Ignoring income taxes:

a. What is the payback period of the piano, (using accumulated cash flows)?

b. What is the average rate of return of the piano (using average book value)?

P15–2 *Quantitative and nonquantitative factors.* Hopeful Enterprises is attempting to decide which of two real estate investments to acquire.

The Sunnybrook Acres development would cost $1,500,000, and would produce cash flows of $400,000 each year for 7 years. One disadvantage of the development is that it would turn a pleasant spot of grass and trees into a high-rise apartment complex.

The Sandy Acres development would cost $1,500,000, and would produce cash flows of $250,000 each year for 14 years. One advantage of Sandy Acres is that it would place an industrial development in an area that is undesirable for residential use because of its location and topography.

Required:

a. On the basis of the payback period alone, which of these two developments would you select?

b. On the basis of net present values alone (using 5 percent as the minimum rate of return), which of the two developments would you select?

c. Using the information in your answer to *B, and* the qualitative facts given, would *you* reach a different decision if you owned Hopeful Enterprises?

d. On the basis of net present values (using 10 percent as the minimum rate of return), which of the two developments would you select?

e. Using the information in your answer to *D and* the qualitative facts given, would *you* reach a different decision if you owned Hopeful Enterprises?

P15–3 *Various investment analyses.* Wesley Mathews recently inherited a small piece of property, which, fortunately for him, is located near the downtown area of a prosperous and growing city. The land is presently occupied by a group of vacant stores which are unsuitable for tenants. He faces three alternative courses of action:

1. He can sell the land outright for $400,000 cash, which he can invest in bonds that yield 10 percent interest per year.

2. He can enter into a 50-year lease agreement, whereby the lessee will clear the land and erect and operate a building. Under the terms of the lease, Mathews would receive $40,000 each

year for 50 years (net of expenses). At the end of that time, he (or his heirs) can sell the property for the existing market value, which should be $2,000,000.

3. He can tear down the buildings and operate a parking lot. It is estimated that the lot would yield a cash income of $30,000 each year for 5 years after which it could be sold for $500,000. A construction firm has agreed to tear down buildings and construct the lot in exchange for the salvaged materials.

Required:

a. Compare these three alternatives in terms of the average rates of return. Ignore income taxes and assume continuous appreciation.

b. Compare these alternatives in terms of the net present values. Ignore income taxes.

c. Compare these alternatives in terms of the time-adjusted rates of return.

d. What weaknesses in the compound interest models are apparent in this situation? Discuss them briefly.

P15-4 *Measuring and using cash flows.*   Aquanut Company manufactures swim suits and other beach wear. Although the company was very profitable for many years, it has suffered losses in each of the last two years. The president, Mr. Waters, has studied the situation and believes the reason for the losses is that Aquanut has not modernized its factory as rapidly as its competitors, and thus has lost sales through high prices. Much of the sewing at the Aquanut factory is presently accomplished on semiautomatic machines which have a physical life of another 8 years. Mr. Waters estimates that 8 machine operators, each with an annual salary of $9,500, could be released if the company were to purchase 2 new Whistler Model 88B automatic sewing machines. In order to compensate them for the loss, each of these workers would be paid $1,000 in separation pay. The company would scrap the 8 old semiautomatic machines, probably for about $500 each. These old machines are expected to have no salvage value if retained for another 8 years. The Model 88B sells for $200,000, at the Whistler factory. Freight charges to the Aquanut factory is estimated to be about $5,000 per machine, and installation costs are expected to be $10,000 per machine. Aquanut would depreciate the machines on a straight-line basis over an 8-year period, at the end of which time they would have an estimated salvage value of 20 percent of the original invoice price.

In addition to the labor savings mentioned above, the new machines should permit the company to expand production. Mr. Waters expects this added volume to make a net annual new-cash contribution of $20,000 (sales less the cash costs). For various reasons, you are to ignore taxes.

Required:

a.   Calculate the net cash outlay at the time the machines are purchased.

b.   Calculate the annual incremental net cash inflows.

c.   What is the value of the profitability index for this proposal, using an 8 percent annual discount rate?

d.   What is the time-adjusted rate of return?

P15–5   Profitability index.   The management of Investments Unlimited is considering the purchase of a newly constructed apartment building for a total price of $4.8 million. The building contains 200 virtually identical units. From similar investments, it has been observed that gross rent income typically falls as an apartment gets older. Vacancy rates increase, and rent rates are lowered to keep the old and to attract new tenants. The following table shows the expected average vacancy rates and apartment rent rates over the life of the building.

Years	Average Vacancy Rate	Monthly Rent per Apartment
1–5	1%	$300
6–10	2	280
11–15	3	250

Company practice has been to sell apartment houses after 15 years. At that time, the company expects to realize a salvage value of 25 percent of the initial cost. Cash expenses are expected to equal 20 percent of rent (net of vacancies). The building will be depreciated on a straight-line basis, and the company expects income tax rates to be 40 percent.

Required:

a.   Find the expected cash flows for each year of the building's life.

b.   Using the profitability index, find out if the company should buy the building, if 10 percent is the minimum rate of return to be earned each year.

c.   Calculate the most that should be paid for the building, if the minimum rate of return is 20 percent per year.

P15–6   Rates of return.   Mr. M. T. Head, the absent-minded chief executive of a small manufacturing firm, had called in two assistants at different times to analyze the same capital asset purchase. His memory worked sufficiently to get the following facts to them:

Cost of machine	$100,000
Salvage value after 10 years	$ –0–

Annual cash revenues	$ 40,000
Annual expenses	
Depreciation	(10,000)
Cash	(18,000)
Annual net income	$ 12,000

He also remembered to tell each of them that the firm was not interested in any project that would return less than a 20 percent annual return before income taxes.

Required:

a. Igor Beaver, management intern, analyzed the proposal on the basis of the average rate of return. He used the average book-value method to find the denominator of the ratio. Prepare the analysis using this technique.

b. Jack Armstrong, office boy, analyzed the proposal on the basis of the time-adjusted rate of return, and assumed that the revenues and expenses were paid at the end of each year. Prepare the analysis using this technique.

c. Compare the recommendations made by Beaver and Armstrong and explain why they agree or disagree. From the information in this chapter, which of the two methods is more correct on a theoretical basis? Explain.

P15–7 *Using decision criteria.* The Peter Pipe Company has instigated a more rigorous evaluation procedure for reviewing investment decisions. Henceforth, all proposals will be submitted to a five-way screening procedure, using the following methods and decision criteria:

Method	Accept
Payback	If less than 5 years
Average rate of return*	If greater than 20% per year
Net present value (8%)	If greater than $5,000
Profitability index (12%)	If greater than 1.2
Time-adjusted rate of return	If greater than 15%

*Using the average book value of the asset

The first proposal to be screened has the following conservative estimates:

Cost	$15,800
Life	10 years
Salvage value	$1,800
Depreciation method	Straight-line
Additional annual revenue	$6,000
Additional annual cash costs	$1,000
Income tax rate	50%

Required:

For each of the five methods, determine if the proposal will be accepted or rejected. Which decision would you make? Why?

P15–8   *Various investment analyses (with taxes).*   Konoko Corporation has limited funds available for capital expenditures. Top management is now considering three investment proposals but will not have sufficient funds to make all three investments.

The following information is available:

	Alternative		
	1	**2**	**3**
Expected annual cash revenue	$4,000	$15,000	$100,000
Expected annual cash expenses	1,000	10,000	95,000
Expected salvage value	0	3,000	4,000
Expected useful life	10 years	5 years	8 years
Depreciation method	Straight-line	Straight-line	Straight-line
Expected tax rate	40%	40%	40%
Expected color	Red	Green	Blue
Cost	$10,000	$18,000	$20,000

Required:

a.   Rank the proposals according to aftertax payback period.

b.   Rank the proposals according to profitability index (assume a 10 percent aftertax minimum return).

c.   What is the average rate of return for alternative 2? (Use aftertax income and assume continuous depreciation.)

d.   What is the aftertax time-adjusted rate of return for alternative 3?

e.   Can you think of any circumstances under which the color of one of the alternatives might determine the selection?

P15–9   *Compound interest and inflation.*

a.   Apart from earning income, how many of today's dollars would you pay to receive a $1,000 cash flow one year from now, if inflation is expected to occur at an annual rate of 8 percent?

b.   Apart from inflation, how many of today's dollars would you pay to receive a $1,000 cash flow one year from now, if earnings are expected to accrue at an annual rate of 7 percent?

c.   Considering both inflation and income, how many of today's dollars would you pay to receive a $1,000 cash flow one year from now, if earnings are expected to accrue at an annual rate of 7 percent and inflation is expected to be 8 percent?

d.   Under the same condition as in C, how much would you pay for the $1,000 cash flow if it is to occur three years from now?

P15–10   *Net present value and time-adjusted rate of return.*   The Gamma Corporation manufactures office equipment and distributes its products through wholesale distributors. Gamma recently learned of an opportunity to obtain the rights to a patent on the production of a semiautomatic paper collator. They can be obtained at a cost of $60,000 cash. The semiautomatic model would be superior to the manual model that the corporation now produces. At an additional cost of $40,000, present equipment could be modified to accommodate the production of the new semiautomatic model. These modifications would not affect the remaining useful life of 4 years or the salvage value of $10,000 that the equipment now has. Variable operating costs, however, would increase by $1 per unit. Fixed costs, other than the depreciation and amortization, would not be affected. If the equipment is modified, the manual model cannot be produced.

The current income statement relative to the manual collator appears as:

Sales (100,000 units @ $4)		$400,000
Variable costs	$180,000	
Fixed costs*	120,000	
Total costs		(300,000)
Net income before taxes		$100,000
Income taxes (40%)		(40,000)
Net income after taxes		$ 60,000

* All fixed costs arise directly from the production of the manual collator, and include depreciation on the existing equipment of $20,000 per year, calculated on the straight-line basis with a useful life of 10 years.

Market research has disclosed three important findings relative to the new semiautomatic model: First, a particular competitor will certainly purchase the patent if Gamma does not. If this were to happen, Gamma sales of the manual collator would fall to 70,000 units per year. Second, if no increase in the selling price is made, Gamma could sell approximately 190,000 units per year of the semiautomatic model. Third, because of the advances being made in this area, the patent will be completely worthless at the end of 4 years.

Required:

a. Prepare a schedule which shows the differential aftertax cash flows for the comparison of the two alternatives. Assume that the corporation will use the sum-of-the-years'-digits method for depreciating the cost of modifying the equipment.

b. Using the differential aftertax cash flows calculated in *a*, will Gamma, if it has a cost of capital of 18 percent, decide to manufacture the semiautomatic collator? Use the net present value decision rule and assume that all operating revenues and expenses occur at the end of the year.

    c.   Calculate the time-adjusted rate of return assuming that Gamma manufacture the semiautomatic collator.

    d.   What additional analysis, if any, would you consider before presenting a recommendation to management? Why?

(CMA Adapted)

16

Financing Decisions

Business enterprises obtain economic resources from three major sources: *creditors, owners,* and *customers.* When a firm borrows from a creditor, it has a *liability,* which is a claim against it that must be satisfied sooner or later. When a firm accepts an investment from an owner, or when its operations generate a net profit,[1] it has added to its *owners' equity,* which is also a claim against the firm. Unlike liabilities, the claims of the owners do not have to be satisfied in accordance with any predetermined schedule. Virtually every firm obtains its resources through some unique mixture of liabilities and owners' equity. Some rely heavily on borrowing, whereas others depend heavily on owners' investments and profitable operations. Banks characteristically have extensive liabilities, whereas small manufacturers tend to do little borrowing.

The ratio of debt (creditor provided funds) to equity (owner provided funds) determines the degree of financial leverage. As discussed in Chapter 3, financial leverage is the degree to which profits and losses are amplified by the existence of debt in the company's equity structure. The greater the proportion of debt-to-equity, the greater is the financial leverage and, thus, the profits or losses to stockholders will be multiplied over what they would have been had a lesser degree of debt been employed.

Financial leverage is also created by preferred stock issues because preferred dividends, like bond interest, are usually fixed in amount. It is the *fixed* feature of both interest and preferred stock that creates the leverage. Since the funds provided from these sources may be invested at a rate higher or lower than the fixed rate, the gain or loss accrues to the stockholders and

---

[1] Note that although profits are provided by customers, they belong to the owners and thereby increase the owners' equity.

adds to (or deducts from) the profits or losses that they have earned on their own funds.

The degree to which a firm employs financial leverage can be measured by the debt-to-equity ratio or debt-to-total-assets ratio. If the concept of financial leverage is not clear, refer again to Exhibit 3-5 (page 54) and the related discussion.

Let us now turn to the ways firms can obtain equity and debt funds.

EQUITY FINANCING

There are two means by which assets can be obtained from the owners of corporations: New stock may be issued for cash, or cash may be retained in the business instead of being paid out to the stockholders in the form of dividends. This latter source, called retention of earnings, has been the major source from which many U.S. corporations have obtained the funds required to finance their growth. An advantage of this approach is that the percentage interest of the present owners is not diluted. It is also easier and cheaper to retain funds already in the business than it is to seek funds from external sources.

Types of Stock

Many companies have different classes of stock, with each class having some special feature. When a firm has only one class of stock, it is called *common stock,* or *capital stock.* When there is more than one class, the "uncommon" shares are described as *preferred stock.* Generally, preferred stockholders precede common stockholders on claims for dividends. Not even the preferred stockholder, however, is *guaranteed* a dividend. Cash is paid to stockholders only when and if the board of directors decides to do so. The "preference" merely means that a dividend can legally be declared on common stock only after one has been declared on preferred stock. In exchange for the *preference,* the right to vote is generally withheld from the preferred stockholder.

CUMULATIVE VERSUS NONCUMULATIVE STOCK

Preferred stock may be *cumulative* or *noncumulative.* The former designation means that if preferred dividends are not paid in any particular year, they must be made up before the common stockholder can ever be paid a dividend. These preferred dividends that have not been declared are sometimes called *dividends in arrears.* The corporation is not obligated to pay dividends in arrears on *noncumulative* stock. If these dividends are not paid on schedule, they are lost, regardless of the future success of the corporation.

PARTICIPATING VERSUS NONPARTICIPATING STOCK

Generally, the annual dividend on preferred stock is expressed as a percent of its par value. When the preferred stock has no par value, the dividends are stated as a certain number of dollars per share. With *nonparticipating* stock, the indicated dividend is a maximum rate and acts as a ceiling. On the other hand, *participating* stock is able to share in increased dividends no matter how high a dividend is paid on common. Participating stockholders are entitled to dividends at the same percentage *rate* of par value as are the common stockholders, if such payment exceeds the regular preferred dividend rate.

CONVERTIBLE VERSUS NONCONVERTIBLE STOCK

A popular hybrid of preferred and common stock, convertible preferred stock offers an advantage to the holder over nonconvertible, and thus can be issued more easily and with a lower dividend rate.

Nonconvertible preferred stock pays a fixed amount of dividends each year, if the company is stable. The value of the stock is determined almost completely by the market rate of return. Thus, there is little opportunity for the value of the investment to increase (and little risk of a decrease).

Convertible preferred stock pays a fixed dividend each year (in precedence over the common stock) *and* can be exchanged for a stated number of shares of common stock. Thus, there is a greater chance that the value of the investment will increase. For example, if a share of preferred can be converted to 4 shares of common, and the common is worth $30 per share, then its value would be close to $120 (4 × $30). Suppose the value of the common drops to $20 per share. Is it likely that the preferred will be worth only $80?

The answer depends on the situation. If the share, for example, pays $8 per year as a dividend, and the market expects an 8 percent return, then the preferred will sell somewhere around $100 per share, because $8 is 8 percent of $100. So, the holder of convertible preferred enjoys a "floor" under the value of the investment below which it should not fall (barring catastrophes) but there is no "ceiling" limiting its upper value.

In the stock market, investors seeking the potential capital gain will accept a lower rate of return than they would for nonconvertible stock. Thus, the issuing company has a lower "cost" through the lower dividends it pays in return for the stockholders' money.

Retained Earnings

There are many complications associated with the issuance of new stock which make it a relatively infrequent source of assets for firms already in business. In most instances, stockholder approval is required and special documents must be submitted to the SEC. This process requires extensive legal and accounting work which greatly increases the cost of most issues. It may also be difficult to find a market for the new security. Many profitable companies therefore rely heavily on retained earnings as a source of capital, since the complications are avoided when currently owned assets are retained. The board of directors is free, within certain constraints, to limit dividends to relatively nominal amounts and to leave the balance of the assets in the company for growth.

Stock Dividends

Occasionally, corporations declare dividends that are settled by issuing additional shares of the corporation's own stock. These distributions are known as *stock dividends*. In effect, the stockholder receives nothing when a stock dividend is distributed because his percentage of the equity in the corporation remains the same as before. The only difference is that now there are more stock certificates (pieces of paper) symbolizing that identical interest. In ruling that stock dividends were *not* income for a stockholder, a judge stated that:

> A stock dividend really takes nothing from the property of the corporation and adds nothing to the interest of the stockholders. Its property is not diminished and their interests are not increased. . . . the proportional interest of each shareholder remains the same. The only change is in the evidence which represents that interest, the new shares and the original shares together representing the same proportional interests that the original shares represented before the issue of the new ones.[2]

Intuitively, the market value of an existing share of stock will fall proportionally when a stock dividend is declared. For example, if a person owned 100 shares of stock which were selling for $50.00 per share before a 10 percent stock dividend was declared, he could expect the price to drop to about $45.45 per share after the date of record.[3] It might be argued that the stock price will not fall proportionally because some of the stockholders might think they are getting something.

Because stock dividends add nothing to the interest of the stockholder and take nothing away from the corporation, you might wonder why companies declare them. First, the action might be taken to conserve the assets of the firm (for expansion or other purposes) and still get the favorable publicity associated with declaring a dividend. Second, the company may wish to decrease the market price per share and increase the number of shares outstanding as a means of increasing the activity (trading) of the company's shares. This increased activity may generate extra demand for the company's shares, and thus increase their selling price. Finally, the stock dividend may be used to convert so-called *temporary capital (retained earnings)* into *permanent capital (capital stock)* and thereby present a better picture to creditors.[4]

---

[2] Eisner v. Macomber, 252, U.S. 189.

[3] Total investment = $5,000; before dividend: $50/share × 100 shares; after dividend: $45.45/share × 110 shares.

[4] Accountants do not agree on the amount that should be transferred from Retained Earnings to Capital Stock; in other words, whether the par or market value of the stock should be used. The *Accounting Research and Terminology Bulletin*, Final Ed. (New York: AICPA, 1961) indicates that where the dividend is less than 20 to 25 percent, then, *market value* of

Stock Split

A *stock split* is similar to a stock dividend in that it merely changes the number of shares outstanding without changing the assets of the company or the shareholders' relative claims on those assets. In a regular stock split, the shareholder surrenders his old shares and receive more new shares. In a 2-for-1 split, for example, a shareholder owning 100 shares of $100 par stock before the split would own 200 shares of $50 par after the split. The market value of the new shares will usually fall to just half the market value of the old since the shareholder is really receiving nothing. Sometimes a *reverse split* is accomplished whereby the stockholder turns in more old shares than he receives in new shares. A reverse split would, of course, increase the market value of each share but would leave the total market value approximately the same as before the split.

DEBT FINANCING

Because of the advantage of financial leverage, many firms prefer to have *some* long-term debt financing. There are several factors which should be considered in deciding the particular form that this type of financing should take. In general, we should select the method that results in the lowest effective interest rate. In many instances, such as with a commercial bank loan, the effective interest rate is given by the lender: but the true rate is occasionally unclear. In these instances, we can utilize the principles of compound interest to place different forms of borrowing on a comparable basis in order to select the alternative with the lowest rate.

Bonds

A *bond* is a form of long-term debt consisting of two promises: (1) to pay the face (maturity) value at the specified maturity date, and (2) to pay given sums of money (interest) at regular intervals over the life of the bond. The amount of periodic interest is calculated by multiplying the face (coupon) rate times the face value of the bond. The face value, maturity date, and the face interest rate are all entered on the bond certificate at the time the documents are printed. The *true* (effective) interest rate, on the other hand, is a product of the supply of and the demand for money and cannot be known until the bonds are actually offered for sale in the market. The corporation must therefore have some means of adjusting the *coupon* rate to the *true* rate which the market demands. This adjustment is accomplished by adjusting the selling price of the bonds. The resulting interest rate is called the *effective yield*. If the selling price is below the face value, the bonds sell at a *discount* and the yield is greater than the nominal rate. If the selling

---

the stock should be used to determine the charge to Retained Earnings. If the stock dividend is greater than 20 to 25 percent, then the *par value* of the stock should be used. The apparent logic of the AICPA's position is that small stock dividends may be "looked upon" as having a value equal to the market value of the shares distributed in the dividend.

price is above the face value, the bonds sell at a *premium* and the yield is lower than the nominal rate.

If a $1,000 bond were to be issued at the price of 103, the company would receive $1,030 and be required to repay only $1,000. This extra $30, received at the time the bonds are issued, compensates the issuer for the extra interest it will pay over the life of the bond. Similarly, if a $1,000 bond were sold at a price of 94, the $60 discount would represent an adjustment of interest; the issuing company would receive only $940 but would be required to repay $1,000. The extra $60, which it would be required to repay the bondholder at maturity, would compensate for the failure to make sufficient interest payments over the life of the bond.

Thus, to know the cost of borrowing, a company must calculate the yield, or effective interest rate, on a bond issue. Because the proceeds of the loan are received *at the date of issue,* the face value is paid *at maturity,* and all other payments of interest come *at* points in time between these, it is most accurate to use compound interest concepts to recognize the time difference. In other words, it would not be accurate merely to apportion the extra interest in the various periods on a straight-line basis without any recognition of the time value of money.

To illustrate, assume that on January 1, 1977, the Kombo Company issues $100,000, face value of 8 percent, five-year bonds, at a price of $108,520. The bonds pay interest semiannually on June 30 and December 31 each year. The cash flows may be summarized as:

Date	Cash Inflow	Cash Outflow
January 1, 1977	$108,520	
June 30, 1977		$ 4,000
December 31, 1977		4,000
June 30, 1978		4,000
December 31, 1978		4,000
June 30, 1979		4,000
December 31, 1979		4,000
June 30, 1980		4,000
December 31, 1980		4,000
June 30, 1981		4,000
December 31, 1981		104,000

With a premium, the effective yield will always be less than the coupon rate. With a discount, the reverse will be true. The interest rate that will equate the cash inflow of $108,520 with the present value of the cash outflows is the true rate of interest inherent in the obligation. By referring to the present value tables in Appendix II (page 609), we learn by trial and error that the appropriate rate is 6 percent per annum (or 3 percent per interest period), as calculated:

Present Value of ordinary annuity at 3% per semiannual period for 10 rents ($4,000 × 8.530 from Table D)	$ 34,120
Present Value of $100,000 principal repayment (from Table B, $i = 3\%$, $n = 10$; $100,000 × 0.744)	74,400
	$108,520

Because bond yield computations are frequently needed, tables exist which allow us to find the effective yield directly. For example, the bond yield table shown in Exhibit 16-1 has its basis in the principles of compound interest. We can see that an 8 percent bond with a face value of $100, which matures in five years and zero months, and which sells for $108.53 (second column), will yield 6 percent per annum. Thus, our $100,000 bonds, if sold for $108,520 (slight rounding error), will also yield 6 percent.

Leases

One of the more important (and frequently encountered) management decisions is the choice between *borrowing* funds to purchase an asset or simply *leasing* the asset.

Some companies that specialize in leasing assets to users have added confusion by promoting the lease arrangement as a substitute for *buying* rather than as means of *borrowing*. Perhaps unwittingly, but generally unfortunately, many financial managers have used leasing without ever stopping to carefully analyze the differential costs of the alternative strategies. It is our objective in this discussion to identify the relevant factors for reaching an informed decision.

The choice between leasing and borrowing has been further clouded by the unwillingness of financial accountants (and their rule making boards) to disclose certain information about leasing agreements in a firm's financial statements. This issue involves a lack of distinction between the *operating* lease and the *capital* lease.

An *operating* lease is relatively short-term and usually can be canceled with little notice or penalty. Under this lease, the *lessor* (owner) is responsible for most of the costs normally associated with ownership. Generally, he does not depend on just one customer or lessee to recover the full cost of the asset. An airport car rental is an example of an operating lease. The customer typically rents the car only for a day or two and the leasing company assumes the responsibility for washing, cleaning, changing the oil, paying license fees, insuring the vehicle, and similar costs.

Exhibit 16-1
Bond Table, $100 Bond, 8% Coupon Rate

Yield	Matures in 5 Years and			
	0 months	2 months	4 months	6 months
5.75	109.66	109.92	110.20	110.48
5.80	109.43	109.69	109.96	110.23
5.85	109.21	109.46	109.72	109.99
5.90	108.98	109.22	109.48	109.74
5.95	108.75	108.99	109.24	109.50
6.00	(108.53)	108.76	109.00	109.25
6.05	108.31	108.53	108.76	109.01
6.10	108.08	108.30	108.53	108.77
6.15	107.86	108.07	108.29	108.52
6.20	107.64	107.84	108.06	108.28

A *capital* (or *financial*) lease, on the other hand, is a long-term agreement. The lessee normally leases the asset for most of its economic life and thereby returns to the lessor the entire investment. The lessee normally assumes the responsibilities (and costs) commonly associated with ownership even though the lessor is the legal owner of the asset. A capital lease of an automobile, for example, will typically cover a one- two-year period and the lessee will pay for gas, oil, insurance, maintenance, and similar costs. A capital lease normally contains the following features, which give it the characteristics of debt:

1. The decision to lease is based on financial considerations; that is, the lessor is really in the lending business and the lessee is really seeking financing.
2. The lease *cannot* be canceled (except under heavy penalty). Thus, the lease contract commits the user of the asset for a long period of time just as an installment purchase does.
3. The total lease payments are *more* than the purchase price of the asset. These rents are sufficient to recover the lessor's entire cost and provide a return on the investment. The lessor is in the same position as a bank providing an installment loan. The loan payments repay the entire loan plus the interest.
4. The lessee generally has the right to use the asset as long as desired, just as if he owned the asset. This is generally accomplished by giving the lessee the right to buy the asset at the end of the lease for a nominal sum or else continue to rent it at greatly reduced rentals. Thus, the right to use the asset is similar to what it would be if it were actually owned.
5. The lessee agrees to assume all costs normally associated with ownership such as maintenance, operating costs, taxes, insurance, and so on. His position in regard to these costs is identical to that of an owner.

The capital lease is a relatively new concept, enjoying wide usage only since the Second World War. Today it is difficult to find a fixed asset which is not available through leasing should the customer desire it. It has been estimated that the value of assets covered by financial leases in the United States exceeds $100 billion!

Up to this book's publication date, financial accountants have not fully endorsed the debt characteristics of financial leases, so that virtually none of the billions of assets nor the corresponding amount of liabilities arising from lease transactions have been reported in the body of the lessee's financial statements. Ironically, the assets are shown on the books of neither the lessee nor the lessor. This deficiency in financial statements has been the subject of much controversy among accountants and their governing bodies during the past 20 years. In August 1975, the FASB issued an exposure draft which was hotly debated. After a period of exposure, a new draft was issued in July 1976, and had not been adopted officially at the time of the publication of this book. Although this latest draft does contain compromises, it should, if adopted in its proposed form, eventually lead to proper disclosure of most capital leases. In order that the shock will not be too great on the financial community, the exposure draft provides for gradual recognition of these leases over a 3-year period. All new leases entered into after January 1, 1977, will be recognized as equivalent to debt, but leases entered into prior to that date are subject only to footnote disclosure. Beginning January 1, 1980, the statement is to be applied *retroactively* to all capital leases. The draft specifies that all future leases which meet one of the following characteristics should be described as *debt* instruments by a process referred to as *capitalization* of leases:

1.   The lease transfers ownership (legal title) to the lessee by the end of the lease term.

2.   The lease contains a bargain purchase option (i.e., the lessee can buy the asset at an unrealistically low price).

3.   The lease term is equal to 75 percent or more of the estimated economic life of the property.

4.   The present value of the minimum lease payments equals or exceeds 90 percent of the fair value of the leased property (i.e., the lessor essentially recovers his investment plus a return thereon).[5]

Analyzing a Capital Lease

In selecting among various forms of debt financing, the best choice is the alternative that has the lowest interest cost. A difficulty arises from the fact that leases do not usually state the rate of interest. Instead, the interest charges are part of the rent.[6] We should utilize the principles of compound interest to find the effective rate of interest in the lease.

ILLUSTRATION WITHOUT THE TAX EFFECT

The president of the Modern Company has decided a new automatic machine is needed but cannot decide how to finance the acquisition. The production manager has suggested that the machine be leased, while the controller feels that the machine should be purchased outright and the necessary funds borrowed from the bank. Facts related to the alternatives may be summarized as:

Lease: Five-year, noncancelable. Annual rents of $1,500 per year, payable at the beginning of each year. Lessee pays all costs of ownership (taxes, insurance, and so on).

Borrow: The company can borrow the necessary funds from its local bank at 6 percent interest, to be repaid in five equal annual installments, payable at the end of each year. The machine can be purchased for $7,500 and is expected to last 5 years at which time it

---

[5] Proposed Statement of Financial Accounting Standards *Accounting for Leases, Exposure Draft (Revised)* July 22, 1976 (Stamford, Connecticut: Financial Accounting Standard Board).

[6] Many leasing companies do not admit that leasing is a form of debt financing and therefore will not even admit interest is a factor, let alone tell the prospective lessee what the rate is.

should have a salvage value of $2,000. The company uses sum-of-the-years'-digits depreciation.

The cash flows, ignoring taxes, under the two alternatives may be summarized as:

	Cash Outflows	
Beginning of Year*	**Lease**	**Borrow**
1	$1,500	$ 0*
2	1,500	1,781**
3	1,500	1,781
4	1,500	1,781
5	1,500	1,781
6	2,000†	1,781

*The beginning of one year is considered the same as the end of the previous year.

**The payments on the loan constitute the amount necessary to repay the loan in 5 equal installments (the present value of an ordinary annuity of 5 rents, or $7,500/4.212). The terms of repayment of the loan are of no concern because the effective interest rate is already given in this instance. We are, on the other hand, concerned with the timing of the payments under the lease because no interest rate has been given, and we must calculate it.

†If the company leases the machine, then it must give up the machine at the end of the five years; whereas if it borrows, it gets to keep the machine. The salvage value must therefore be considered as a cash outflow under leasing. Or the salvage could be considered as a cash *inflow* under borrowing which would give an identical end result.

In the case of borrowing, all relevant facts for making the decision were given (the interest rate of 6 percent and the present value of $7,500). With the lease, however, the interest rate is unknown. If we equate the present value of the cash flows under leasing with the cash price ($7,500), we will have the effective rate of interest implicit in the lease. Thus, by trial-and-error use of Tables B and D, we find the rate of interest in the Modern Company lease to be 10 percent per year:

Present value of first rent	$1,500
Present value of other four rents ($1,500 × 3.170)	4,755
Present value of salvage ($2,000 × 0.621)	1,242
Total present value	$7,497
Desired present value	$7,500

Therefore, the effective interest rate equals 10 percent per year, and we should borrow and buy the machine.

ILLUSTRATION WITH THE TAX EFFECT

The previous example ignored the tax difference between leasing and buying. If Modern Company leases the machine, the rentals will be deductible from taxable income. If it owns the machine, the depreciation plus any interest paid on borrowed funds will be deductible. If the two deductions are not equal, the amount of taxes paid under the various alternatives will differ and the future cash flows will be affected. This effect can be described by calculating the *tax shield*, (an example is shown in Exhibit 16-2), which is the *advantage* (or *disadvantage*) arising from the difference in *timing of tax payments* that would occur under the different alternatives.

Exhibit 16-2
Exhibit 16-2
Calculation of Tax Shield: Lease or Borrow

Year	Deduction if Borrow Depreciation*	Interest**	Total	Deduction if Lease	Extra Deduction if Borrow	Tax Shield†
1	$1,833	$ 450	$2,283	$1,500	+$ 783	+$391
2	1,467	370	1,837	1,500	+ 337	+ 168
3	1,100	285	1,385	1,500	− 115	− 57
4	733	196	929	1,500	− 571	− 285
5	367	101	468	1,500	− 1,032	− 516
	$5,500	$1,402	$6,902	$7,500	−$ 598	−$299

 * Sum-of-the-years'-digits depreciation used.
** Interest calculations are shown below.
 † Tax shield assumes 50% tax rate. This column indicates the extra amount of taxes that will be paid (positive) or saved (negative) under the lease.

Calculation of Interest under 6% Loan

Year	Payment*	Interest	Principal	Remaining Balance
				$7,500
1	$1,781	$450	$1,331	6,169
2	1,781	370	1,411	4,758
3	1,781	286	1,495	3,263
4	1,781	197	1,584	1,679
5	1,781	102	1,679	−0−

*Loan repaid in five equal installments of $1,781 (7,500/4.212).

Calculation of *PV* of Tax Shield at 10%

Tax Shield	Factors (Table B)	Present Value
+$391	0.909	+$ 355
+ 168	0.826	+ 139
− 57	0.751	− 43
− 285	0.683	− 195
− 516	0.621	− 320
		−$ 64

Present value of lease rentals (from page 472)	$7,497
Less: tax shield	− 64
Net present value	$7,433

Note that the net effect of the tax shield in this case is only $64. The effective interest rate in the lease is actually *slightly* less than the nontax calculations show. The present value with the tax shield is only $7,433, whereas it was $7,497 without the shield. Since the correct interest rate will give us a present value of $7,500, we know that the 10 percent rate is slightly too high.

Although the effect of the tax shield in this problem is not significant, it could be in other circumstances. When the tax deduction is materially different under the various alternatives, the tax shield should be added (or deducted) from the lease rental in order to get the effective interest rate the company will pay if it leases. Our experience indicates that the tax shield is simply not significant in many financial leases.

Nonquantitative Factors in the Financing Decision

The true rate of interest *is* the *most important factor* influencing the choice between debt alternatives. It is not, however, the *only* factor that should be considered. Often there are significant restrictions placed upon the firm. For example, the lender may require the borrower to maintain a current ratio of at least 2-to-1 or to earn interest at least 5 times. If these restrictions are not met, for example, the firm may not be permitted to pay dividends on the common stock, or the bondholders may be allowed to elect directors to the company's board. Similarly, the amount of borrowing or the scope of the company's activities may be limited in order to provide extra security to the lender. These nonquantitative considerations must receive attention, especially when the interest rates are competitive, because they may be the factors on which the decision will hinge.

One particular nonquantitative advantage of leasing, mentioned previously, is the treatment that leases have been given in the financial statements. When an asset is purchased and the funds are obtained through debt financing, both the asset and the liability are shown on the balance sheet. When the asset is acquired through a capital lease, on the other hand, the accounting treatment has not been so clear. In the past, the disclosure has usually been limited to footnotes and accordingly many of the company's key financial ratios have been favorably biased. This "improvement" in the company's stated financial position has, no doubt, been regarded by many managers as a reason for leasing even when the interest rate calculations would dictate otherwise. As the proposed FASB requirements are implemented we can expect this apparent nonquantitative advance of leasing to disappear.

SUMMARY

Business enterprises have three sources from which they can obtain the necessary funds to acquire assets: *creditors* (debt), *owners* (investments), or *customers* (profits). The latter two sources are known as *equity financing*. The principle of financial leverage shows that some debt financing is desirable if the rate of return justifies it; that is, a firm should normally obtain some funds from debt and some funds from equity. Determining the proper balance between the two sources primarily hinges on the level and stability of the firm's earnings. Firms with relatively high and stable earnings can tolerate a greater degree of debt financing and thereby profit from financial leverage with less risk.

Corporations that finance new assets from owners' funds generally prefer to forego cash dividends rather than issue new stock for cash. When stock is issued, it may be either *common* or *preferred*. Preferred stockholders receive *preference* in payment of dividends and may have other advantages, including the right to accumulate dividends from year to year (*cumulative*), the right to participate with common shareholders in extra dividends (*participating*), and the right to convert the preferred issue into common stock (*convertible*).

Debt financing does not diminish voting control of the company. Many factors should be considered in deciding what form the debt financing should take, but the most important is the effective annual interest rate. In many instances, the *true* or effective interest rate is not immediately apparent. It is then necessary to calculate the effective interest rate on the particular obligation by utilizing the principles of compound interest.

To facilitate their issue, bonds are provided a *coupon rate* and then sold at a premium or discount to yield an effective interest rate consistent with current market conditions. Consequently, it is wise to calculate the *true yield* by equating the present value of all future cash flows (periodic interest payment plus the debt principal) with the issue price of the bonds. The interest rate that will equate these cash flows represents the true cost of the bonds.

A special form of leasing, known as a *capital lease,* is often used as a means of acquiring debt funds. The capital lease agreement is often complex and the effective interest rate is rarely disclosed by the lessor. The true rate of interest implicit in a lease agreement can be extracted by finding the rate that equates the present value of cash flows under the lease with the cash price of acquiring the same asset. The excess rents paid over the period of the lease (the amount paid above the cash price of the asset) really represent interest and should be recognized as such by management.

QUESTIONS

1. What are the three sources from which business enterprises obtain assets? Is there an ideal percentage that should come from each of these sources? Explain.

2. What is *financial leverage*? Explain what is meant by the statement that "financial leverage is a double-edged sword."

3. How does preferred stock differ from common stock? What *preference* does the preferred stockholder get? What does the preferred stockholder give up?

4. What are *dividends in arrears*? What feature must a stock have in order to accumulate dividends in arrears?

5. Why do some stocks contain a convertible feature? Into what is the stock convertible? Does such a feature make the stock more attractive to the potential investor? At whose option is the stock convertible?

6. Why are *retained earnings* often a more popular source of assets than issuing additional stock?

7. What is a *stock dividend?* What is a *stock split?* What similarities are there between stock dividends and stock splits? How do each affect the balance sheet? How do each affect the market price of the stock?

8. What is the *effective yield* on a bond? Is this rate normally the same as the face coupon rate? Why?

9. If a bond is selling at a premium what can we say about the interest rate? What if the bond is selling at a discount?

10. Distinguish between an *operating* and a *capital* lease. Give an example of each.

11. When considering a capital lease, why is it incorrect to label the decision as lease-or-buy? How could the decision be more correctly labeled?

12. List some of the important features of a capital lease.

13. What effect do income taxes have on capital leases? What costs are normally deductible for tax purposes if management chooses to lease an asset? What costs are normally deductible for tax purposes if management chooses to buy the asset and borrow the necessary funds?

14. What are some nonquantitative factors that might influence management when considering a capital lease?

EXERCISES

E16–1   *Allocating dividends.* Howell Instruments Company has outstanding 100,000 shares of $10 par common stock and 5,000 shares of $100 par 8 percent preferred stock. During 1977 the company declared and paid total dividends of $50,000; in 1978 they paid no dividends; and in 1979 the dividends totaled $250,000. How much went to common stockholders and how much went to preferred stockholders in each of the 3 years, assuming the preferred stock was noncumulative and nonparticipating? How much went to each class assuming the preferred stock was cumulative and nonparticipating? How much went to each class assuming the preferred stock was cumulative and participating?

E16–2   *Leases and taxes.* Dahl Doll Company plans to acquire a new hair-injection machine which will cost $63,000. It will last 6 years and is expected to have no salvage value. The company uses sum-of-the-years'-digits depreciation for tax purposes. If purchased, the entire $63,000 will be borrowed at 10 percent annual interest and will be repaid in 6 equal year-end installments. The company can lease the machine under a financial lease for $13,150 per year for the 6-year life with the rents due at the beginning of the year. The interest rate implicit in the lease contract is also 10 percent (ignoring any tax shield).

Required:

Calculate the tax shield assuming a 50 percent tax rate. Would the tax shield tend to lower or increase the aftertax interest cost of the lease?

E16–3 *Lease interest rate.* Monoco Corporation has just signed a capital lease for a new machine. If purchased for cash, the machine would have cost $9,977. It has an estimated life of 8 years with no expected salvage value. The lease is noncancelable during the 8-years, and requires annual rent payments in the amount of $1,980, payable at the beginning of the year. What is the interest rate implicit in this lease agreement?

E16–4 *Effective bond interest.* Standard Products Corporation is planning a new $3,000,000 bond issue. The bonds have a coupon rate of 10 percent and pay interest semiannually on January 1 and July 1 of each year. The bonds mature 20 years from the date of issue. An underwriting group has offered Standard $2,547,900 net for the entire bond issue. What is the effective annual interest cost (rate) to Standard Products Corporation?

E16–5 *Effective bond interest.* Shortly after the underwriting group acquired the Standard Products Corporation bonds (see E16-4), interest rates fell sharply on long-term securities. The underwriting group was able to resell one-sixth of the entire issue ($500,000 face value) for $598,825. Assume that the sale by the underwriting group occurred on the date of issue and that the bonds will be held to maturity. What is the effective yield (rate) to the new bondholders?

E16–6 *Selecting best lease.* Ellicot Company has decided to acquire a crane under a financial lease. A new crane, delivered to the company shops, would cost $27,630. Stateside Leasing Company has offered Ellicot a capital lease which requires annual rent payments of $6,000, payable at the beginning of each year. Central Leasing Company offers the same machine but requires quarterly rent payments of $1,631.53, payable at the end of each quarter. Both companies require a minimum term of 6 years after which the crane is expected to have no salvage value. Should the company lease from Stateside or Central? What is the effective annual interest rate under each of the proposed leases?

E16–7 *Lease or borrow.* Smokescreen, Inc., has been ordered by the State Pollution Control Board to install an electronic cleaner on the factory smokestack. The required air cleaner would cost the company $440,000 plus an additional $115,000 to install. The Good Neighbor Bank has offered to loan Smokescreen the money necessary to complete the project at an annual interest rate of 10 percent on the unpaid balance. This loan would be repaid in 10 equal annual installments. The manufacturer of the air cleaner will install and lease the cleaner for $92,055 per year, rents payable at the beginning of each year. The lease would be noncancelable for a 12-year period. The cleaner is estimated to have a useful life of 12 years and is expected to have no salvage value. Smokescreen would pay all maintenance and operating costs under either plan. Should Smokescreen lease the air cleaner or borrow the funds from the bank and purchase it? What is the effective interest rate implicit in the lease?

E16–8 *Allocating dividends.* Koleman Corporation currently has outstanding 8,000 shares of $100 par convertible 8% preferred stock. The stock is cumulative and nonparticipating and may be converted to common stock on a 1-for-4 basis (one share of preferred converts to four shares of common) at the option of the preferred stockholder. The company also has 50,000 shares of $20 par common stock outstanding. During 1976 the company earned $50,000 and paid no dividends. During 1977 the company earned $500,000 and paid dividends totaling $300,000. How much of the above dividends went to the preferred shareholders each year assuming they did not exercise their option to convert to common? How much would these same stockholders have received had they converted to common at the end of 1975?

E16–9 *Selecting best lease.* Leo Potter Company is currently constructing a new office building. When it is completed they expect to sell it to an insurance company and lease it back for 20 years. The building will cost $1,400,000 when complete. Two leases have been proposed: The first calls for rents of $167,344 per year for 20 years. The second provides for rents of $100,000 for 8 years and rents of $385,146 for the remaining 12 years. All rents under both leases are due at the beginning of the year. Which lease proposal should Leo Potter Company accept? Why?

E16–10 *Effective bond interest.* Tatum Tatoe Company plans to float a $1,000,000 bond issue. The bonds will have a coupon rate of 8 percent, pay interest once each year, and mature in 15 years. The entire issue will be sold to an underwriting group which will guarantee Tatum net proceeds of $847,480. What is the effective annual interest rate that Tatum will pay? What would the net proceeds of the issue be if Tatum were able to issue the bonds to yield an effective interest rate of 7 percent?

PROBLEMS

P16–1 *Leverage.* Latourrette Industries, Inc., is a family owned and operated manufacturing firm with several million dollars of assets. Management has been proud of its ability to operate without any borrowed capital. All capital expenditures have been paid "out of earnings," even if it has meant paying low dividends or delaying investments until such time as enough cash can be accumulated.

Consequently, something of an uproar has occurred at the suggestion of the firm's controller, Andrew Latourette, that

$1,000,000 be borrowed at an annual rate of 8 percent, to be paid back over 5 years. He has advocated this departure from tradition in order to enter a market that is relatively untouched. He has projected that it will take at least 2 years of small dividends and scrimping to accumulate the $1,000,000. By then, the market will have been captured by competitors, and the opportunity lost forever.

The money would be invested at once, and would yield annual aftertax cash flows of $280,000, each year for the next five years. The tax rate the company has used to calculate these aftertax earnings is 50 percent, a rate that has remained rather constant in recent years.

Required:

a. Explain why this radical financial policy should or should not be implemented. Use a language the board of directors will understand (i.e., dollars and cents).

b. One of the more liberal-thinking directors suggests that equity financing through the issuance of 7 percent preferred stock would raise the needed cash without incurring debt. What are the relative advantages and disadvantages of this approach (do not ignore income taxes).

c. This suggestion has finally brought the chairman of the board to his senses, and he offers the third proposal that common stock be sold in order to raise the $1,000,000. What are the relative advantages and disadvantages of this idea?

P16–2 **Lease or borrow.** Great Lakes Products Company furnishes each of its 10 salesmen with a new car every two years. This year management has decided to acquire 10 Chevrolet Chevettes, which list for $2,990 F.O.B. destination. The local Chevrolet dealer has agreed to allow a $1,500 trade-in allowance on each of the old cars that the company must dispose of. The new Chevettes should have an average salvage value of $1,600 at the end of the two-year period. If the cars are purchased, Great Lakes will borrow the necessary funds from a local bank under a *line of credit* agreement.

The company is currently being charged interest at the rate of 8 percent per annum on bank loans (calculated on the unpaid balance of the loan). One of the salesmen has suggested that the company lease the cars. He says that most of his friends drive leased cars because it's cheaper. Investigation reveals that identical Chevettes can be leased for only $66 per month per car, payable at the beginning of each month. The lease would be noncancelable for the 2-year period and would require the lessee to assume all costs normally associated with ownership (taxes, maintenance, gas, oil, insurance). A deposit of $100 per car is required when the lease is signed, but the entire deposit will be refunded at the end of the lease. If the Chevettes are leased, the old cars will be sold on the local auto auction. It is estimated that Great Lakes will net $1,200 per car if this is done.

Required:

Should the company lease the cars or should they purchase the cars and borrow the necessary funds from the bank? What is the interest rate implied in the lease? Show all supporting computations. You may ignore taxes.

P16–3   Bonds or bank loan.   The Supersport Boat Company has decided upon a $200,000 expansion for its plant; it plans to finance this expansion program with 50 percent equity and 50 percent debt financing.

The American State Bank has offered to lend the funds to Supersport on installment, with the following provisions: The Supersport Boat Company is to pay yearly installments of $10,000, starting 5 years after the date of the loan, and these payments are to be made for a period of fifteen years, at the end of which the balance of the loan will be due. The interest rate will be 7 percent on the declining loan balance. All yearly payments will apply first to the amount of accrued interest and the remainder to the principal.

A local brokerage firm has also offered to aid Supersport in obtaining the needed $100,000 through the issuance of 10-year bonds with a coupon rate of 5.5 percent. Interest on the bonds would be paid semiannually. An underwriting group has guaranteed Supersport a net price of $96,211.75.

Required:

Compute the true interest costs of these two alternatives. Which would be best? Show all computations.

P16–4   Effective bond interest.   Matheson Magic Company has decided to greatly expand their existing plant but needs $5,000,000 for the expansion. The directors have investigated floating a bond issue and a bond underwriting group has proposed the following:

Face amount	$6,000,000
Underwriting commission	1,000,000
Net proceeds to Matheson	$5,000,000
Coupon rate	8%
Interest dates	December 31, annually
Issue date	January 1, 1976
Term	20 years

Management has also investigated leasing the new plant. American Continental Insurance Company has proposed a financial lease under which American Continental would advance the entire $5,000,000 on January 1, 1976. The plant would be owned by American Continental and leased to Matheson for 20 years with annual rents of $448,462 per year, payable January 1 of each year. Since the new plant will not be completed until January 1, 1977—the first rent would be due on that date and the 20-year lease term would also begin that date. Under the lease Matheson must guarantee American Continental a *termination value* of $3,000,000 (Matheson has the option to buy at the end of the lease for $3,000,000 or they must guarantee American will receive at least that amount upon sale to another buyer at the end of the lease term). Both parties to the proposed lease agree that the $3,000,000 *termination value* is a fair estimate of the salvage value of the property at the end of the 20-year period.

Required:

Calculate the effective interest rate for each of the proposals. Should the company float bonds or lease? Ignore any tax shield.

P16–5 **Lease or borrow.** Kovar Company just completed a new office building at a total cost of $372,000, including the $50,000 cost of land. The building has an estimated useful life of 20 years after which it is expected to sell for $100,000 (including the land). The construction loan is due in 30 days and the company is looking for permanent financing. A local savings and loan has offered to finance the building with a mortgage loan at an annual interest rate of 10 percent. Because the building has an appraised value of $410,000, the savings and loan will finance the entire $372,000 amount. The loan would be repaid in 20 equal annual installments beginning 1 year from the date of the loan. Loan payments will be applied first to interest and then to principal, as is customary under such loans.

American Eastern Life Insurance Company has offered to sign a sale and lease-back agreement with Kovar. Under the agreement Kovar would sell the building to American at cost ($372,000) and then lease it back under a long-term capital lease with a minimum term of 20 years. Lease rents of $48,305 per year for the 20-year term are due at the beginning of each lease year, with the first rent due on signing the lease agreement. Kovar would have the option to purchase the building at the end of the 20-year term for $100,000 (its estimated salvage value).

Required:

a. Calculate the amount of the annual loan payment under the savings and loan proposal.

b. Calculate the effective rate of interest implied in the lease agreement.

c. Should the company lease or borrow? Support your answer with calculations in good form.

P16-6 **Lease or borrow.** East Coast Insulation Supply was formed by Cliff Hatch, Dick Flowers, and Frank Davis. All three owners had several years' experience in various phases of the insulation business. Dick and Frank would work as salesmen, with Dick taking the northern territory and Frank the southern. Cliff would be office manager and would handle all counter sales.

It is customary for firms in this industry to furnish cars for the salesmen. This presented a real problem to the owners because they were grossly undercapitalized and needed to invest as much of the company funds in inventory as possible. Cliff recently picked up a leasing company's brochure that made leasing cars sound very attractive.

Cliff was especially impressed by the following feature: "Leasing releases cash tied up in equipment or in reserves for replacement. The cash you realize in disposing of equipment you own is freed for you to put to more desirable uses. Leasing permits you to operate further on your own capital. Because your lease is not considered a loan, it protects your borrowing capacity."

The partners discussed the merits of leasing versus buying at great length. Frank agreed to contact Atlantic Leasing Company and see what he could arrange. The company was very cooperative and quickly drew up a draft copy of a lease agreement. It allowed the lessee to pick the exact car he wanted, including color and optional equipment. Although the company was talking in terms of leasing 3 identical cars, the draft was drawn up for only one, a Bentley Runabout. The leasing company said identical lease documents could be drawn up for the other vehicles. The lease is a *net* lease which would require East Coast to pay all operating costs including the $9 required to license the vehicle. A security deposit of $200 is due at the beginning of the lease but is refunded at the end of the lease provided all contract provisions are met. Monthly rentals of $120.25 are due at the beginning of each month. East Coast must either buy the cars at the end of the lease for $2,000 each or guarantee Atlantic this amount in a sale to an outside party.

Dick checked with the local Bentley dealer to see what sort of "deal" he could work out with him. A Bentley Runabout, identical to the one specified in the lease, had a window price, including destination charges, of $3,662. After considerable negotiation, the salesman agreed to a $150 per car discount. The discounted amount would be subject to state sales tax of 4.5 percent, and license and registration fees would amount to $9 per car. The Bentley dealer would finance each car purchased by requiring an initial payment of $493 ($484 down payment plus $9 for initial license and registration) and 24 monthly installments of $150 each, the first installment due 1 month after purchase. The Truth in Lending Act required the dealer to disclose the true annual interest rate of 12 percent.

a. Calculate the *true* interest rate implicit in the lease agreement. Ignore tax shield.

b.   Calculate the *true* rate of interest in the dealer loan. Did the dealer quote the true rate?

P16–7   Lease or borrow.   The Bull Frog Manufacturing Company has decided to acquire a new Model 3040 automatic lathe. The list price is $31,430 F.O.B. Bull Frog's factory. A $500 cash discount is available if they purchase the lathe directly from the manufacturer. The factory superintendent estimates that the lathe will have a useful life of 8 years, after which it should have a salvage value of $3,000. For a number of years, the firm has been in a critical cash position, because funds generated from operations have immediately been invested in plant, equipment, and inventories. Because of the tight cash position, no company funds are available for the new machine. The controller has investigated many possible sources of funds and has narrowed the choice down to two possibilities.

1.   A local leasing company has offered a Model 3040 lathe under a lease which requires Bull Frog to pay all maintenance and operating costs. The 8-year lease requires annual rents of $5,000 during each of the first four years and $4,000 per year for each of the remaining years. All lease payments are due at the beginning of the year. The lease has a purchase option which would allow Bull Frog to purchase the lathe at the end of the lease for $3,000.

2.   A loan company has agreed to advance the necessary cash on an 8 percent installment loan. The loan would be repaid in 8 equal year-end installments. Each installment on the note would be applied first to interest (8 percent of the unpaid balance) and the remainder to principal. The controller feels that the 8 percent interest rate is too high, but the bank has refused to extend more credit to Bull Frog.

Required:

Determine whether Bull Frog should lease or borrow; present calculations to support your recommendation. Ignore the tax shield.

P16–8   Allocating dividends.   Kundinger Corporation currently has 200,000 outstanding shares of $1 par common stock, 5,000 shares of $100 par Class A 10 percent preferred stock, and 40,000 shares of $10 par Class B 12 percent preferred stock. Earnings and dividend information are:

	1978	1979	1980	1981
Sales	$5,000,000	$6,000,000	$4,500,000	$8,000,000
Net income (loss)	200,000	400,000	(100,000)	900,000
Total dividends paid	100,000	–0–	200,000	500,000

Required:

a.   Assume Class A preferred stock is cumulative and nonparticipating while Class B preferred stock is noncumulative and participating. Calculate the dividends per share on each class of stock for each of the years given.

b. Assume Class A preferred stock is cumulative and participating and that Class B preferred stock is noncumulative and nonparticipating. Calculate dividends per share on each class of stock for each of the years given.

c. Assume Class A preferred stock is cumulative and nonparticipating and Class B preferred stock is noncumulative and nonparticipating. Class B preferred stock is convertible into common on the basis of 1 share of preferred for 2 shares of common. On January 1, 1980 half of Class B preferred stockholders convert their shares to common. Calculate the dividends per share on each class of stock for each of the years given.

P16–9 ***Lease or borrow or sell stock.*** Global Airlines has just received authorization from the authorities to open a new air route and will require $5,000,000 of new capital to finance this expansion. The company controller is opposed to more debt financing and recommended that the company raise the $5,000,000 by a new preferred stock offering. Underwriters will guarantee the company $5,000,000 for a 10 percent preferred stock issue. Because of the current market conditions, 60,000 shares of $100 par preferred stock would be issued in order for the company to net $5,000,000. The stock would have a cumulative feature and pay 1 annual dividend at year-end.

The company president prefers raising the necessary money by leasing new aircraft which the company would otherwise have to buy. Planes which could be purchased for $5,000,000 can be leased for 10 years under a financial lease plan. This would require annual rents of $735,000 per year with the lease payments coming due at the end of each year. The leased aircraft would be expected to have a salvage value of $500,000 at the end of the lease at which time Global could buy the planes for that sum, if they choose to do so.

The chairman prefers to issue 6 percent bonds which he feels should sell quickly because of the large discount that would be required. The company would issue $8,000,000 face value of bonds in order to net $5,537,280 to the company. The bonds would mature in 15 years and pay interest semiannually.

Required:

a. Calculate the effective annual interest rate for each of the proposals.

b. Which proposal do you favor? Why?

c. What are some nonquantitative factors that you think should be considered?

d. What effect would income taxes have on your decision?

17

Taxes and Business Decisions

Governments have been formed in our society to protect and nurture the citizens. These governments adopt laws and regulations which provide the economic environment in which the business must operate. Policies are undertaken by these governments which help determine: (1) the supply and demand for money (how much consumers will have available to spend); (2) the level of employment; (3) the rate of inflation; (4) the degree to which foreign goods and services are available (the balance of trade); and (5) the rate of economic growth. Without governments and their services, it would be impossible for a modern business to operate at all.

These services, of course, are not free! The governments must support themselves by levying taxes on the members of society. In our system of government, these taxes are numerous and the laws which govern them are very complex. In this chapter we will examine two major areas of taxation: the federal income tax laws and payroll tax laws. Our emphasis will be on how these tax laws influence business decisions.

INCOME TAXES

The major source of revenue for the federal government (and an increasingly important one for many state and local governments) is the *income tax*. In fiscal year 1973, the federal receipts from personal income taxes were over $103 billion and approximately *$36 billion* from corporate income taxes.[1] Thus, income taxes accounted for 60 percent of the federal government's receipts in fiscal year 1973. As income tax receipts have grown to be the

---

[1] *Economic Report of the President* (Washington, D.C.: U.S. Government Printing Office, February, 1974), p. 326.

major source of federal revenue, tax laws have become an increasingly important factor in the management decision-making process. It is commonplace for businessmen to call on CPAs and attorneys for advice on the tax consequences of various proposals.

The effect of income taxes on business decisions is too comprehensive to be covered completely in this text. In fact, the subject is so complex and ever changing that even those who devote *fulltime* to tax problems find themselves in need of constant updating. Nevertheless, the modern manager must be familiar with those major provisions of the tax law which provide for special choices. These provisions allow the taxpayer to choose among alternative tax methods which often have a significant impact on the amount of the tax liability, or at least on the timing of tax payments.

It is especially important to distinguish *tax planning* from *tax evasion*. Tax planning involves utilizing the provisions of the tax laws to avoid unnecessary taxes and to postpone other taxes to the full extent *permitted* by law. Sound tax planning is done in *complete compliance with the law* and generally follows closely the "spirit" of the law.[2] Tax evasion, on the other hand, disregards the provisions of the law. This practice is illegal and may subject the individual to fines and prison terms.

Tax Postponement

As we look at some of the provisions of the tax laws, you will become aware that many of the so-called *tax breaks* do not permit the taxpayer to avoid any taxes at all, but merely postpone the inevitable. They give the company a tax saving in one year which must be made up in a later year. Offhand, you might conclude that there is no advantage in postponing taxes, but, as the discussion of the time value of money in Chapter 14 brought out, a wise manager will take every opportunity to postpone taxes provided he can do so without penalty or interest. This strategy results in an interest free loan from the government. As we discuss provisions of the law which permit tax postponement, the reader should particularly note the present value effects of tax postponement.

The Taxable Unit

Even before a business unit is formed, consideration must be given to income taxes because the tax liability itself is affected by the legal form the business takes. If the business enterprise is organized as an individual proprietorship or as a partnership, the firm itself is not subject to any form of income tax.[3] On the other hand, if the firm is organized as a corporation, it

---

[2] Many tax provisions described by lay persons as tax *loopholes* are based on sound economic and social logic. For example, the investment credit was set up to stimulate investment at a time when the economy was facing a recession. Such a provision is probably good public policy. A company that takes advantage of the investment credit is not evading taxes but instead taking a risk (new investment) which is designed to provide public benefit (jobs).

[3] The *owner* or *owners* of the business (proprietor or partners) are subject to individual income tax on their shares of the earnings, whether or not these earnings are distributed. However, the business unit itself is not subject to any income tax.

is considered a separate taxable unit and is subject to the corporate income tax. One exception to this rule is the "Subchapter S" corporation, which will be discussed later in this chapter. This *taxability* is one of the prices a corporation pays for the special status it enjoys as a legal entity separate and apart from its owners. Because the corporation has always enjoyed special legal status as a "person created by law," it seems ironic that Congress has singled out this form of business as the only *business* unit subject to income taxes. William Paton, one of the great names in accounting history, observed:

> A review [of the history of federal income taxation] shows clearly that most members of Congress 50 years ago understood that the corporation was not an entity appropriately subject to this type of taxation; they were interested in the corporation primarily as a possible agent for withholding and remitting taxes levied on stockholders and employees as individuals. But, if these legislators were to sit in on the tax hearings and discussions going on in Washington these days, they would be startled to learn that through the invention of "Mr. Corporation," a taxable person has been found ostensibly capable of shouldering a large part of the burden that would otherwise fall on the individual citizen—the "people."[4]

The reader should recognize, of course, that the entire tax load eventually must be borne by the citizens. The corporate tax must be passed on to the individual members of society (employees, consumers, and owners) through lower wages, higher prices, and lower dividends. When the corporation is used as a device to funnel these taxes to the citizens, it is difficult to measure just how fairly this load is distributed. It appears that Congress continues to justify the practice because most voters do not seem to understand this shifting, whereas they would likely resist any attempt to raise the same revenue by means of a more direct tax.

CORPORATE INCOME TAX

Regardless of one's feelings about the merit or justice of the corporate tax, it must be recognized as an important factor in the decision-making process. The corporation is subject to two federal income taxes: the *normal* tax and the *surtax*. The former tax is levied against the corporation's entire taxable income while the latter tax is levied only on the taxable income in excess of $25,000 per year ($50,000 per year through 1977). In 1975, the tax law was revised to create two different levels of normal tax. When coupled with the surtax, this produced the following three-tier system:

First $25,000 of taxable income	20%
Next $25,000 of taxable income	22%
Taxable income in excess of $50,000	48%

Corporate tax rates have not changed very much during the last decade, but the manager should nevertheless always be alert for possible revisions. Some of the changes made in 1975 and 1976, for example, are scheduled to expire in 1977.

[4] William A. Paton, *Corporate Profits* (Homewood, Ill.: Richard D. Irwin, 1965), p. viii.

INDIVIDUAL TAX

Corporate dividends are included in the taxable income of the individual stockholders, and in this sense, corporate income is subject to *double taxation*. It is taxed to the corporation and, when paid out to the stockholders, is subject to individual income tax. In order to partially offset this double taxation, each taxpayer may exclude the first $100 of dividends received from qualifying corporations during the taxable year. This dividend exclusion is $200 for persons filing joint returns when both husband and wife each received dividends, or if the stock was jointly owned. All amounts in excess of the exclusion are combined with other items of ordinary income and taxed according to the individual's tax bracket. Current individual income tax rates vary from 14 to 70 percent. The effective rate the taxpayer pays depends on many factors including his gross income, number of dependents, age, deductions, and so on.

Partnerships are not subject to income tax but, nonetheless, are required to file an *information return* (Form 1065). This return reports the business profit and, more important, shows how the income was distributed among the individual partners. Each partner includes his share of the partnership income on his individual income tax return.[5] That portion of the partnership income representing ordinary income is then taxed according to the individual taxpayer's tax bracket. One important feature of partnership income is that it retains its "character" as it is passed through the partnership. That is, income which represents a capital gain is passed on to the partners as a capital gain and income which represents ordinary income is passed on as ordinary income. This provision does not hold for a corporation's income.

Proprietorships are likewise not subject to income taxes as a separate entity. The individual proprietor merely reports his business income on a supporting schedule which accompanies his individual tax return. All such earnings are taxed at individual rates, according to the owner's tax bracket.

SUBCHAPTER S CORPORATIONS

Subchapter S of the Internal Revenue Code allows the stockholders of certain corporations to elect to be taxed in a manner similar to the way partners are taxed. These corporations are commonly referred to as *Subchapter S* corporations and must meet these special requirements:

1. The corporation can have no more than 15 shareholders.
2. Shares can be of only one class.
3. All shareholders must consent to the election to be taxed as a Subchapter S corporation.
4. Only individuals and estates can be stockholders.
5. All shareholders must be U.S. citizens or resident aliens.
6. Not more than 80 percent of the firm's gross receipts may come from outside the United States.

---

[5] Note that the partner pays tax on his *share* of earnings (net income), *not* on the amount of cash he takes out of the business.

7. Not more than 20 percent of the firm's gross receipts may come from interest, dividends, rents, royalties, annuities, and gains from the sale of securities.

8. The election must be made within the first 30 days of the taxable year for which it will apply.

The Subchapter S election allows businesses that qualify under this provision to avoid double taxation. Each stockholder is subject to individual tax on his share of the corporation's earnings, but the corporation is not also subject to corporate taxes. Most corporations, of course, do not qualify for this special treatment. Even many that qualify do not make the election, primarily because the owners do not plan to pay dividends and therefore will not be subject to double taxation anyway. Instead, they plan to retain earnings in the business and grow.

Certain other corporations, including banks, trust companies, insurance companies, public utilities, regulated investment companies, nonresident foreign corporations, and nonprofit enterprises are given special tax treatment.

The Marginal Tax Rate

The *marginal tax rate* is that rate at which the next increment of income will be taxed. Suppose, for example, that an individual is currently at the top of the 40 percent tax bracket and that any additional income will place him in the 45 percent tax bracket. His marginal tax rate (over the entire range of this higher tax bracket) is 45 percent. Or, suppose a corporation already has earnings in excess of $100,000 and is therefore subject not only to the normal tax but also to the surtax. The corporation's marginal tax rate is 48 percent because any additional income will be taxed at this rate.

The marginal tax rate is significant to managers because, when they consider a particular course of action, it is the earnings (or savings) *after taxes* that are relevant. If an expenditure of $20,000 is tax deductible and the company's marginal tax rate is 48 percent, then the *net* cost to the company is only $10,400 ($20,000 less the *tax savings* of $9,600).

Suppose that a company has an asset with a book value of $75,000 which is now worth only $5,000 because of technical obsolescense. Management is considering selling the old asset for $5,000 cash and replacing it with a new modern version at a cost of $140,000. If the company's marginal tax rate for such losses is 48 percent, then how much additional cash will be required to purchase the new asset?

To answer this question, we must first calculate the tax loss. The tax loss would be the difference between the book value of $75,000 and the $5,000 proceeds from the sale, or $70,000. The *tax savings* which would accrue to the company by deducting the loss on its tax return would be $33,600 (the $70,000 loss multiplied by the 48 percent marginal tax rate). As the company makes regular payments to the government on its estimated income tax liability, it would simply deduct $33,600 from the check it sends to the government. The amount that the company *saves,* which would otherwise be paid in taxes, is equivalent to a cash inflow and reduces the amount of cash required to acquire the new machine. The additional cash required for the new machine would be only $101,400 ($140,000 less $5,000 proceeds from the old machine and less the $33,600 tax savings).

With the marginal tax rate, the manager can include the aftertax consequences of a planned course of action in the management decision process. In earlier chapters, as we considered the tax consequences of various courses of action, we just assumed a uniform tax rate. The student should note that the *appropriate* rate in each of these instances is the marginal tax rate which would apply to that particular gain, loss, or increment of income.

Net Income versus Taxable Income

Income taxes are levied on the *taxable income* as defined by the tax law. This *tax base* is not to be confused with reported *net income,* which is computed by applying generally accepted accounting principles. Taxable income is computed by following the provisions set forth in the Internal Revenue Code. Taxable income is defined by the legislative, judicial, and executive branches of government. The tax code is complex legislation and has been influenced by public policy, lobbyists of all political shades, court decisions, and, to a lesser degree, accounting principles.

There are two primary reasons why taxable income may not agree with the net income shown on the same company's income statement: *definitional differences* and *timing differences.*

DEFINITIONAL DIFFERENCES

There are some items which accountants regard as revenue or expense but which the tax law permanently excludes (by definition) from taxable income. For example, the interest earned on municipal bonds is not part of taxable income although the amount is included in accounting net income. Percentage depletion in excess of cost depletion, long-term capital gains deductions, and life insurance proceeds would similarly be included in accounting income but permanently excluded from taxable income. Penalty for late payment of taxes and fines for violation of the law, on the other hand, may not be deductible for tax purposes but would be properly deducted to arrive at net income. Items such as these are permanently excluded from taxable income calculations, and although the public policy behind these exclusions might be regarded as sound, it would not be good financial accounting to disregard the items in deriving the firm's net income.

TIMING DIFFERENCES

Other differences between a given year's taxable and net income are not permanent in nature, but merely represent differences in timing. That is, some items of revenue and expense are utilized in computations of both incomes but in different accounting periods. In other words, accounting principles and tax laws agree that the items should be considered, but they disagree as to *when* these items should be recognized. For example, a dance studio may receive $100 today in payment for a 52-week dance course to be offered over the next 12 months. The accountant would say that $100 is revenue, but that the total should be apportioned among accounting periods in proportion to the number of lessons provided. The tax officials would agree that the sum is revenue, but would require immediate recognition of the entire amount on the income tax return, regardless of when it may be earned and regardless of when the services are to be rendered. In addition, the costs of providing such services would not be deductible until the services were actually performed.

INCOME TAX ALLOCATION

If accountants used tax laws to measure annual tax expense, it is very likely that the expense would not be matched properly with the revenues reported in the financial statements. To deal with this problem, the practice of income tax allocation has become accepted and is a required accounting procedure for timing differences.[6] To illustrate, assume that the Randall Company earns $25,000 income each year *before* depreciation and taxes. The company uses straight-line depreciation to calculate net income, but uses the sum-of-the-years'-digits depreciation for tax purposes.[7] In all other respects, net income and taxable income are in agreement. The company's only depreciable asset is a machine which was purchased January 1, 1975, at a cost of $18,000. The company estimated that the machine would last five years and have a salvage value of $3,000. Depreciation on the machine would be:

	1975	1976	1977	1978	1979	Total
Per books	$3,000	$3,000	$3,000	$3,000	$3,000	$15,000
Per tax return	5,000	4,000	3,000	2,000	1,000	15,000
Extra tax deduction	$2,000	$1,000	$ –0–	–$1,000	–$2,000	$ –0–

Note that the extra depreciation the company is allowed for tax purposes in the first two years is exactly offset by reduced depreciation in the last two years. The difference is merely one of timing, and the effect of accelerated depreciation is to postpone the payment of some of the income taxes until later years.[8] If the matching guideline is used properly, the tax should be charged to expense in the period the income is recognized, regardless of

---

[6] Accounting Principles Board *Opinion No. 11: Accounting for Income Taxes* (New York: AICPA, December 1967). Also, Opinions No. 23 and No. 24 deal with some special problems in applying income tax allocation.

[7] This strategy will require that two ledgers be kept. This practice may seem devious, but it isn't. It is *inefficient* but it also is *profitable*.

[8] Remember that postponing taxes provides an advantage since money has time value. The company can invest the funds that otherwise would be used to pay taxes and thereby increase earnings.

when the tax is *actually paid*. This means that the current year's *Tax Liability* should be calculated according to *taxable income,* and the difference should be credited to the Deferred Tax Liability account. Such a practice more accurately matches revenue and expense, as illustrated:

	1975	1976	1977	1978	1979	Total
Net income before depreciation and tax	$25,000	$25,000	$25,000	$25,000	$25,000	$125,000
Depreciation per books	3,000	3,000	3,000	3,000	3,000	15,000
Net income before tax	$22,000	$22,000	$22,000	$22,000	$22,000	$110,000
Income tax expense (22%)	4,840	4,840	4,840	4,840	4,840	24,200
Net income	$17,160	$17,160	$17,160	$17,160	$17,160	$ 85,800

The amount debited or credited to the Deferred Tax Liability account would be calculated as:

	1975	1976	1977	1978	1979
Income tax expense	$4,840	$4,840	$4,840	$4,840	$4,840
Current tax liability*	4,400	4,620	4,840	5,060	5,280
Debit (credit) deferred tax liability	$ (440)	$ (220)	$ –0–	$ 220	$ 440

*The current tax liability would be 22 percent of taxable income:
    1975: 22% of $20,000 = $4,400
    1976: 22% of   21,000 =   4,620
    1977: 22% of   22,000 =   4,840
    1978: 22% of   23,000 =   5,060
    1979: 22% of   24,000 =   5,280

At the end of the machine's life, the timing differences would be offset, leaving a zero balance in the Deferred Income Tax Liability account.

Tax allocation enables the manager to get a more meaningful measure of profits and at the same time enjoy the benefits of postponing taxes. This benefit may be seen in our example, under the assumption that interest can be earned at 10 percent per year. The calculation of the present value of the tax postponement is:

Year	Taxes Saved (Extra Paid)	10% Table Factor	Present Value
1975	$ 440	0.909	$ 400
1976	220	0.826	182
1977	0	0.751	0
1978	(220)	0.683	(150)
1979	(440)	0.621	(273)
Net present value			$ 159

Accounting Methods

The tax law recognizes two primary methods of accounting: the *cash basis* and the *accrual basis.* For the most part, the accrual basis used for tax purposes is similar to that followed in accounting practice. Revenue is generally recognized as earned when the goods are delivered or the services rendered, and applicable expenses are then matched with the revenue. In some instances the IRS requires the taxpayer to modify the accrual method as with revenue received in advance, as in the dance studio example.

A taxpayer on the cash basis, on the other hand, recognizes revenue when the cash or its equivalent is received, regardless of when the goods or services are delivered. Expenses are similarly deducted when paid in cash, with certain exceptions which cannot be expensed in the period of cash payment. A taxpayer on the cash basis would be required to depreciate a fixed asset, for example, even though it is paid for in cash, because it has a useful life beyond the current tax year.

Many businesses use a modified cash basis to account for installment sales. When an item is sold on an installment contract and payments are received over an extended period of time, the *installment sales* basis of accounting enables the taxpayer to recognize the revenue *pro rata* over the period of collection and thereby defer the payment of taxes.

The installment sales method may be illustrated by reference to the following assumed facts regarding a machine which was sold on an 18-month installment contract on October 1, 1977:

Selling price	$5,000
Cost	2,900
Down payment	500
Monthly installment	250
Carrying charge	–0–

With a cost of $2,900 and a selling price of $5,000, the machine will provide a gross margin of $2,100, or 42 percent. Under the installment sales method, this gross margin is recognized *piecemeal, as the cash is collected,* rather than in the period of sale.[9] The tax effect of this method is to defer the payment of taxes which normally would be paid in the period of sale until the periods in which the cash is collected. Journal entries for 1977 would be:

1977

October 1	Installment Accounts Receivable	5,000	
	Inventory (Cost of Installment Sales)		2,900
	Deferred Gross Margin on Installment Sales		2,100
October 1	Cash	500	
	Installment Accounts Receivable		500
	To record down payment.		
November 1	Cash	250	
	Installment Accounts Receivable		250
	To record monthly payment.		
December 1	Cash	250	
	Installment Accounts Receivable		250
	To record monthly payment.		
December 31	Deferred Gross Margin on Installment Sales	420	
	Realized Gross Margin on Installment Sales		420
	To record realized gross margin of 42%		
	of collections during year.		

[9] Because the gross margin is the difference between sales and cost of goods sold, we are really deferring the Sales (revenues) and the Cost of Goods Sold (expense). Thus, the deferral of revenue is partially offset by deferral of the cost of goods sold.

By using this technique, the manager is able to temporarily postpone some of the taxes. In our illustration, only $420 (less applicable expenses) would be reported as taxable income in 1977. Had the manager not elected the installment sales method, then the entire $2,100 of gross margin (less the applicable expenses) would have been reported as 1977 income. If we assume a tax rate of 48 percent, a discount rate of 10 percent, and that all tax payments are made at the end of the year, we can calculate the net present value that would accrue to the company by choosing the installment sales basis over the accrual basis, as shown in Exhibit 17-1.

Exhibit 17-1

	Accrual Basis			Installment Sales Basis		
	1977	1978	1979	1977	1978	1979
Revenue	$ 5,000	–0–	–0–	$1,000	$3,000	$1,000
Cost of goods sold	(2,900)	–0–	–0–	(580)	(580)	(580)
Gross margin	$ 2,100	–0–	–0–	$ 420	$1,260	$ 420
Tax (48%)	$ 1,008	–0–	–0–	$ 200	$ 605	$ 202
Table B values	1.000	0.909	0.826	1.000	0.909	0.826
Present value	$ 1,008	–0–	–0–	$ 200	$ 550	$ 167
Total present value		$1,008			$917	

Through the present value analysis, we can see that the firm effectively saves 89 present dollars by electing the installment accounting method.

The Investment Credit

The investment credit was originally enacted as a temporary device to induce businesses to invest in new capital equipment. Since its inception, it has been suspended and reinstated from time to time as economic conditions have warranted. (Enacted in 1962, revised in 1964, suspended in 1966, reinstated in 1967, repealed in 1969, reenacted in 1971, increased in 1975).

The investment credit works effectively as a subsidy from the federal government to those businesses that make qualified investments. The amount calculated as an investment credit is deducted from the income tax *liability* and thereby directly reduces the amount of taxes paid. It is allowed in addition to depreciation deductions and does not reduce the tax basis of the property. The basic credit is 10 percent of the cost of the qualified property if the asset acquired had an estimated useful life of seven or more years; 6.67 percent if the estimated useful life is five or six years; 3.33 percent if the useful life is three or four years. No credit is allowed on assets which have a useful life of less than three years.[10] There are certain limits on the amount of investment credit allowed in any one year, as well as on the nature of the assets which qualify. Basically, it applics only to tangible personal property.[11]

---

[10] The maximum investment credit may be increased to 11½ percent if the company makes certain contributions to employee pension funds.

[11] *Real* property is land and anything attached to the land (e.g., building). *Personal* property is anything that is not real property. *Tangible* property has physical substance, as opposed to an *intangible* asset such as a patent or a copyright.

Accelerated Depreciation

The two major methods of accelerated depreciation used in accounting practice, sum-of-the-years'-digits depreciation and declining balance depreciation, are also acceptable (with certain limitations) for tax purposes. Either of
these methods will accelerate the depreciation deduction so that more is allowed in early years than in later years. Our illustration of tax allocation on
page 491 included an example of sum-of-the-years'-digits depreciation. It is
important to note that accelerated depreciation does not increase the total tax
deduction nor does it decrease total taxes. Instead, it changes the timing of
the total depreciation so that a larger proportion is deductible in earlier
years, thereby postponing the payment of taxes until later years.

Taxpayers also can elect to take an additional *first-year depreciation* deduction of 20 percent of the cost of certain taxable property. This election is
in addition to the regular first-year depreciation, but is limited to a maximum
of $2,000 ($4,000 on a joint return), and only applies to tangible personal
property with an estimated life of six years or longer. The extra depreciation
taken during the first year reduces the tax basis of the property so that the
regular depreciation is figured on the reduced amount. Thus, extra first-year
depreciation, like accelerated depreciation, does not increase total depreciation deduction, but merely increases the proportion taken during the first
year.

Percentage Depletion

In financial accounting, the term *depletion* is used to describe the process of
assigning the cost of natural resources (such as mineral deposits, timber-
lands, and similar property) to the accounting periods that benefit from their
use. Depletion is similar to depreciation and represents an expense of the
business. In tax accounting, there are two acceptable depletion methods: the
cost method and the *percentage method*. The cost method is similar to that
used in financial accounting. The depletion for any period is calculated by
multiplying the asset's cost by the ratio of units sold during the period to the
total estimated number of units which the property will produce (similar to
the unit-of-production depreciation computation).

The percentage depletion method, on the other hand, has no counterpart in
accounting theory. The authorized percentage is applied to the *gross income*
from the property without regard to its original cost. Under percentage depletion, the owner of the property (or the lessee) can obtain a tax deduction
in excess of the cost of the asset. To the extent that this excess is taken, the
percentage depletion allowance represents a subsidy to the particular taxpayer. The percentage allowed varies according to the type of mineral,
where the deposits are located, and the purpose for which the mineral or
wasting asset is used. The allowable percentages for some natural resources
are:

Oil and gas wells*	22%
Sulphur, uranium, lead, mercury, manganese,	
nickel, platinum, tin, and zinc	22%

*Following the oil crisis of 1974–1975, legislation was passed which repealed the percentage depletion
allowance for most oil and gas production.

Gold, silver, copper, and iron ore	15%
Coal and sodium chloride	10%
Building clay, peat moss, pumice, and sand	5%

Inventory Methods

The tax law permits taxpayers to use either FIFO or LIFO to price goods in inventory. The method selected for tax purposes need not correspond to the actual physical flow of the goods but the same method must be used on the tax return as is used in the financial accounting system.

The LIFO inventory method is often favored during periods of rising prices and has been adopted by many taxpayers during the periods of inflation experienced during the third quarter of this century. LIFO matches the *most recent* costs of goods purchased with revenue from the current sale of goods, which, during the periods of rising costs, reduces the firm's taxable income and tax liability. Firms with large inventories normally find LIFO inventory pricing an especially profitable tax election. To illustrate, assume that the Theide Corporation has 500 units of product on hand at the end of the fiscal year and that purchases during the period were:

400 units @	$50 each =	$ 20,000
800 units @	55 each =	44,000
200 units @	57 each =	11,400
300 units @	60 each =	18,000
250 units @	65 each =	16,250
		$109,650

If the LIFO inventory method were used, the goods on hand would be valued at $25,500 (400 units at $50, plus 100 units at $55), and the cost of goods sold would be $84,150 ($109,650 – $25,500). If the FIFO method were used, the ending inventory would be valued at $31,250 (250 units at $65, plus 250 units at $60), and the cost of goods sold would be $78,400 ($109,650 – $31,250). Thus, the taxable income would be $5,750 less under LIFO than under FIFO ($78,400 – $84,150).

The tax advantage of LIFO is that it effectively postpones the payment of taxes through a cost of goods sold higher than would be reported under alternative methods. The postponement lasts until the inventory is liquidated, if ever. If some unforeseen event (such as a strike) causes the lower cost LIFO *layers* to be used up, the delayed taxes will have to be paid.

Capital Gains and Losses

Gains realized on the sale of certain assets are frequently not taxed as ordinary income. The most important factors affecting the tax treatment are the nature of the asset, the use to which it is put, the type of taxpayer, and the time period over which the asset is held by the taxpayer. To qualify for the special tax treatment, the asset must meet the specifications of a *capital asset,* which is defined as any property held by the taxpayer *except:*

1. Inventory or goods held primarily for sale in the ordinary course of business.

2. Real or depreciable property used in a trade or business.

3. Copyrights and literary, musical, or artistic compositions created by the personal efforts of the taxpayer.

4. Accounts or notes receivable, generated through sale of merchandise or rendering services.

5. Certain discounted short-term government obligations.

Under special circumstances, property other than capital assets (such as depreciable business property) may be given capital gains treatment.

If the property is held *more* than twelve months, the gain (or loss) is referred to as *long term,* or, if it is held twelve months or *less,* as *short term.*[12] The distinction is important because short-term gains are treated as ordinary income. Net long-term capital gains, on the other hand, to the extent that they exceed short-term capital losses, are taxed at special rates. Currently, the maximum capital gains rate for corporations is 30 percent. For individuals the maximum rate is 25 percent on the first $50,000 of capital gains, with graduated rates up to 35 percent above that amount. The effective rate for individuals may be even lower because of a special deduction amounting to 50 percent of the net long-term capital gain. This capital gain deduction is *not* available to corporations.

Assume that Phillip Woolston sold the following securities during the taxable year 1977:

Number of Shares	Security	Date of Purchase	Cost	Date of Sale	Proceeds	Gain (Loss)
100	General Motors	February 15, 1976	$8,000	November 19, 1977	$9,010	$1,010*
50	Union Carbide	April 19, 1977	2,300	June 20, 1977	2,100	(200)
100	Piper Aircraft	September 3, 1976	4,900	October 25, 1977	4,275	(625)*
75	Combustion Engineering	August 30, 1977	5,115	December 10, 1977	5,225	110
200	Russ Toggs	May 23, 1975	4,600	October 14, 1977	9,440	4,840*

*Long-term

Inasmuch as the stocks of Union Carbide and Combustion Engineering were held less than twelve months, the loss and gain are short-term. The net short-term loss is $90 ($200 – $110). The other transactions are all long-term since the securities were held more than the required twelve months. Woolston has a net long-term capital gain of $5,225 ($4,840 + $1,010 – $625). The net gain from the sale of the capital assets is $5,135 (the $5,225 net long-term capital gain less the $90 net short-term capital loss). Mr. Woolston would be allowed a long-term capital gain deduction of $2,567.50, which is 50 percent of the $5,135 net gain. The other $2,567.50 would be taxed as ordinary income, but the tax is limited to 25 percent of the net gain of $5,135, or 50 percent of the amount included in taxable income. Thus, the net effect is that Woolston will pay less than 25 percent tax on long-term capital gains if his marginal tax rate is less than 50 percent. In any case, he is not required to pay more than 25 percent regardless of his bracket on net gains up to $50,000 in any one year.

[12] The holding period for long-term capital transactions increased to twelve months effective January 1, 1978.

If the preceding transactions were accomplished by a corporation (instead of an individual), the capital gains deduction would not apply. Instead, the tax on the gain from the sale of capital assets of $5,135 would not exceed 30 percent.

The reason behind special treatment for long-term capital gains is that to some degree, at least, they do not represent real economic gains, because they arise partially from changes in price levels. That is, the taxpayer is not as well off as the amount of the gain would suggest because the buying power per unit of the money he receives in the exchange has decreased below what he paid.

Had Mr. Woolston sustained a net loss on capital asset transactions, it could be partially offset against his ordinary income. First, the maximum amount of the loss that can be deducted is limited to $2,000 per year ($1,000 for married persons filing separate returns).[13] Second, while short-term losses are deductible in full (up to the limit), only 50 percent of a long-term loss (up to the limit) may be taken into account for the purpose of calculating the deduction from other income. Thus, a $1,000 long-term loss will produce only a $500 deduction whereas a $1,000 short-term loss will produce a full $1,000 deduction.

Involuntary Conversions

When property is stolen or destroyed by accident, the event is referred to as an *involuntary conversion*. If the property is insured and the proceeds from the insurance exceed the book value of the stolen or destroyed property, the transaction gives rise to an accounting gain. Such a gain is not immediately taxable, provided the insurance proceeds are reinvested in similar property within two years. The tax law allows this treatment in recognition of the fact that there has been no real economic change. If only a portion of the insurance proceeds are reinvested, the gain is taxable to the extent of the uninvested portion. Losses on involuntary conversions are generally deductible in full.

While the gain on the involuntary conversion may not be currently taxable, the *tax basis* of the new property must be reduced by the amount of any untaxed gain.[14] This requirement reduces the amount of depreciation which will be allowed on the new asset. Thus, the effect of the law is to postpone the payment of taxes until the periods in which the new asset will be used or sold.

To illustrate the tax effect of an involuntary conversion, assume that the Lund Corporation has a building which originally cost $250,000 and which is 50 percent depreciated. The building, which is fully insured at its current market value of $400,000, is completely destroyed by fire. This involuntary conversion would result in a book gain of $275,000 [$400,000 − ($250,000 − $125,000)]. Compare the tax consequences of the different uses of the insurance proceeds seen in Exhibit 17-2.

---

[13] The maximum deduction for losses from capital asset transactions will increase to $3,000 in 1978.

[14] The *tax basis* of a depreciable asset is the amount which is subject to depreciation for tax purposes. As depreciation is deducted, the tax basis is reduced. Any that remains when the asset is sold is deducted from the proceeds of the sale to determine the taxable gain or loss.

Exhibit 17-2
Involuntary Conversions Treatment under Various Assumptions

Situation	Cost of New Building	Taxable Gain	Nontaxable Gain	Basis of New Building*
1	$500,000	$ –0–	$275,000	$225,000
2	400,000	–0–	275,000	125,000
3	300,000	100,000	175,000	125,000
4	–0–	275,000	–0–	–0–

*Cost less nontaxable gain

Nontaxable Exchanges

Gains and losses from certain exchanges are not recognized at the time of the exchange but are postponed until the disposal of the property received. In such cases, the tax basis of the old property is assigned to the new property without regard to fair market values. When additional cash or other assets *(boot)* are received in the exchange, any gain would be taxable up to the amount of *boot* received. Generally, these exchanges take place between a corporation and a stockholder or the government and a bondholder.

A similar provision is followed when existing fixed assets are traded in on new ones. In this instance, no gain or loss from the trade is included in taxable income. Instead, the depreciated value of the old asset is added to the cash paid to arrive at the tax basis of the property. To illustrate, assume that a truck with a book value of $500 and a current market value and trade-in allowance of $800 is traded in on a new truck with a list price of $5,000. This transaction would result in a conventionally computed accounting gain of $300 (in effect, an asset with a book value of only $500 is sold for $800); however, the gain would not be included in taxable income. The tax basis of the new truck would be only $4,700 ($500 book value of the old truck plus $4,200 cash). The effect of this provision is to postpone the tax on the gain by reducing the depreciation deduction each year of the new truck's life. The total depreciation reduction will equal the untaxed gain.

Operating Loss Carryover

If a taxpayer sustains a loss from operating his trade or business, or from theft or casualty, the full amount can usually be deducted from ordinary income from other sources. To the extent that the loss *exceeds* other income, the amount may be offset against income of other years. The loss may be applied backward to income of the three preceding years *(carryback)* and, if any remains, ahead to the incomes of the next seven years *(carryforward)*. The carryback provision is optional but once the election is made the carryback must be applied to the oldest year first and then, to the extent any remains, forward to each succeeding year. This provision requires the taxpayer to recompute the tax liability for prior years to which the loss is applied, and thereby enables him to receive a tax refund.

Assume that Noah Count sustained a net operating loss of $30,000 in 1977; and that his taxable incomes for the three preceding years and the five subsequent years were:

1974	$10,000
1975	3,000
1976	1,000
1978	5,000
1979	8,000
1980	2,000
1981	10,000
1982	6,000

The loss would be carried back first to 1974 ($10,000) then to 1975 ($3,000), then to 1976 ($1,000), leaving $16,000, which would be carried forward first to 1978 ($5,000), then to 1979 ($8,000), then to 1980 ($2,000), and with the remaining $1,000 to 1981. The tax liability for the years 1974–1976 would be recalculated, and any tax refunds would be collected early in 1978.

PAYROLL TAXES

Payroll taxes are significant business expenses and an important source of revenue to governments. Unlike the complex income tax laws which lend themselves to tax planning, payroll tax laws are straightforward and provide little flexibility. Penalties are imposed for failure to account for and pay these taxes as required by law. These penalties reach out to the owners and managers (despite the shield of the corporate entity), who may be held *personally* liable if the taxes are not paid.

Some payroll taxes are imposed on the employer and represent operating expenses to the company; others are levied on the employee. These latter taxes are *not* expenses of the company; however, the company is required to act as a government agent in collecting them. Even though the expense of collecting these taxes is frequently large, the company is not compensated for acting as tax collector. All amounts collected must be promptly remitted to the government agencies. From the time collection is made until the sums are remitted, these amounts are liabilities of the company.

Taxes on Employers

There are three major payroll taxes levied against the employer. These are *Federal Insurance Contribution Act* (F.I.C.A.) taxes, *federal unemployment insurance tax,* and *state unemployment insurance tax.*[15]

EMPLOYER F.I.C.A. TAX

In the early 1970s, Congress passed a number of laws that have had a rather strong impact on the F.I.C.A. tax, and greatly increased the amount of it. These increases have been accomplished in two ways: First, the rate was

[15] In a sense, Workman's Compensation Insurance is also a payroll tax levied on the employer, although the premiums are often paid to private insurance companies rather than to a government unit. Most employers are required to carry insurance on all employees to protect the employee from economic loss due to on-the-job accidents. The premiums are generally based on the risk class of the employee (danger of his job) and the amount he earns.

increased from 2.5 percent to 5.85 percent. Second, the basis on which the tax is computed was increased from the first $4,800 to the first $15,300 of wages paid each employee. Legislation has also been passed which will gradually increase the rate to 7.45 percent. At this writing, legislation, which would increase both the rate and the base still further, is pending.

FEDERAL UNEMPLOYMENT INSURANCE TAX

The state and federal governments have joint programs for compensating unemployed workers who are *willing and able* to work. The federal portion of these tax funds is not used to pay unemployment benefits but is used to pay the cost of administering the joint programs. The state taxes are used to pay the actual unemployment benefits.

The federal unemployment tax is paid by the employer based on the earnings of his employees. The current federal rate is 0.7 percent of the first $4,200 of wages paid to each employee each year. The base upon which this tax is calculated will increase to $6,000 in 1978.

STATE UNEMPLOYMENT INSURANCE TAX

Each state has its own unemployment program, which is largely supported by taxes levied on employers. These state programs came into existence primarily because of a federal program, inaugurated in the 1930s, that provided assistance to the states that established their own qualifying programs. Accordingly, there is a great deal of similarity among the various state laws and a close alignment with the federal program. A *merit rating* plan often provides various tax rates according to employment experience. Employers with a stable payroll (essentially the same number of employees throughout the year) pay lower rates than those who experience seasonal peaks. This tax break encourages employers to stabilize employment. An example of a merit rating plan may be seen in the Utah state law that currently prescribes rates varying from 1.3 percent to 3.0 percent of the first $8,800 earned by each employee each calendar year.

Taxes on Employees

Employees are subject to two federal payroll taxes: the *F.I.C.A. tax* and the *withholding tax*. In many states, employees are also subject to a state withholding tax and, in some cases, even a city withholding tax. For each of these taxes, the employer acts as an agent of the government by withholding the amounts from the employees' checks and remitting them to the appropriate government agencies. These taxes *are not* direct expenses for the employer. However, they indirectly result in added expenses to the employer. First, the employer is required to keep extensive payroll records. Second, the employee tends to focus his attention on *take home pay*. As taxes are levied on wages, this amount goes down, resulting in additional demand for higher wages.

EMPLOYEE F.I.C.A. TAX

The F.I.C.A. tax is really two separate taxes: One levied against the employer and an equal one levied against the employee. The rates and the basis for calculating the two taxes are identical. In this respect, the employer and employee "share and share alike" in the social security program. As previously noted, the current annual F.I.C.A. rate is 5.85 percent of the first $15,300 earned by each employee, yielding a total rate of 11.7 percent.

FEDERAL WITHHOLDING TAX

In order to accelerate income tax collections, and, indeed, to ensure that they are collected, the withholding tax was inaugurated. Under this system, the employer deducts a specified sum from the employees' pay and remits it to the IRS at regular intervals. Each year, the employee is furnished with a W-2 form which shows the total tax withheld during the year. This form, when filed with each employee's tax return, serves as a basis for credit against the employee's income tax liability determined on his tax return.

The amount of tax withheld is generally determined from a table furnished by the IRS. The amount is based on both the number of exemptions claimed by the employee and the level of his income. Congress designed the withholding system to bring the amount withheld in line with the employee's ultimate tax liability.

STATE WITHHOLDING TAX

Many states recognized the advantages of the withholding system and passed laws similar to the federal statute. These taxes are collected by the employer, remitted to the state, and applied to the individual's state tax liability in the same manner as federal taxes.

Other Payroll Deductions

Many other organizations and agencies, and even employees themselves, have seen the advantages in having the employer make payroll deductions to assure that a designated organization will get the funds before the employee spends them elsewhere. Also, the cost of the collection process is shifted from the recipient to the employer. For these reasons, unions often require withholding of union dues, and employees elect withholding for savings bonds, retirement programs, club dues, charity drives, and the like.

SUMMARY

As members of society, business units are required to pay taxes to help the government provide the environment in which they operate. Even though all taxes must ultimately be paid by the people, some taxes are levied directly on business units. These taxes are expenses and, like wages and other costs, are passed on to society in the form of higher prices, lower wages, inferior products, and lower returns on investments.

Income tax laws are particularly important in the management decision-making process because of the opportunities these laws provide for planning. Of particular significance are those provisions in the laws which permit tax-payers to choose among alternative tax treatments in order to capitalize on special tax advantages. Some of the important areas in the federal tax laws with which the manager should be familiar are: taxable units; alternate accounting methods; the investment credit; accelerated depreciation; percentage depletion; alternate inventory methods; involuntary conversions; non-taxable exchanges; capital gains and losses; and the carryover of operating losses.

The corporation is the only form of business directly subject to income taxes. While proprietorships and partnerships are exempt from income taxes, the owners of these enterprises pay tax on their allocated shares of the earnings. The owners of corporations pay tax only on their shares of distributed earnings (dividends). The owners of Subchapter S corporations are exempt from this double taxation.

Net income is computed by application of generally accepted accounting principles but often does not coincide with taxable income as defined by the tax law. The differences between net income and taxable income can be classified as *definitional* (permanent) or *timing* (temporary). The matching concept requires that the accountant allocate the tax expense among the proper periods for timing differences.

The investment credit is used from time to time as a means of stimulating investment in capital assets through a subsidy for purchasing new equipment. The amount of investment credit has varied from 2.33 to 11½ percent of the cost of the new assets.

As opposed to straight-line, accelerated depreciation permits the taxpayer to expense more of an asset's cost during the early years of its life, thereby postponing the payment of taxes. Percentage depletion represents a special subsidy to industries engaged in the development of natural resources.

Businesses may elect to use either a LIFO or FIFO inventory method for tax purposes. By recognizing a larger cost of goods sold expense, the LIFO method has the effect of reducing the current tax liability.

Gains on *involuntary conversion* are not normally taxed at the time of conversion, but the taxpayer's basis in the new property is reduced below cost. Certain exchanges of "similar property" are likewise not taxed at the time of the transaction, but the basis in the old property is carried over to the new.

Gains realized on the sale of capital assets may be subject to lower tax rates than those applied to ordinary income. Operating losses may be carried back and, if applicable, carried forward to profitable years and offset against income to reduce the tax liability.

Income tax laws are complex and ever changing. The typical businessman cannot hope to become an expert in taxes while attending to other business matters. He must, however, be alert to changes in the laws and particularly to the election of alternative reporting procedures affecting business decisions. Knowledge in these areas must be sufficient to enable the seeking of advice from tax counselors.

Payroll taxes also are a significant cost to American business. These taxes tend to be uniform and do not allow for tax planning. Payroll taxes levied on employers include F.I.C.A. tax (often called social security tax), federal unemployment insurance tax, and state unemployment insurance tax. In addition to these, which are direct costs of the employer, the business is required by law to act as a government collection agency in withholding taxes (and other amounts) from employee wages. Payroll deductions of this nature for which the employer must account include employee F.I.C.A. tax, federal withholding tax, state withholding tax, union dues, and other employee requested deductions.

QUESTIONS

1. What difference does it make in regard to income tax treatment whether a firm is a proprietorship, partnership, or corporation? Does the size of the firm in terms of the number of stockholders have anything to do with the possible tax treatment?

2. Why is it sometimes said that corporate income is subject to double taxation? To what extent are individual stockholders freed from this double taxation?

3. What is a *Subchapter S* corporation? What tax option is available to corporations that qualify under this provision of the tax law?

4. Distinguish between *taxable income* and *net income*. What is the basis for calculating each of these figures? Who determines what should be utilized in the calculations?

5. What types of differences between net income and taxable income require tax allocation procedures? Give an example of such a difference.

6. What inventory method is most popular for tax purposes during periods of rising prices? Why?

7. What revenues and costs are deferred under the installment sales method of accounting? Does this method adequately match revenues and expenses?

8. What is the objective of the investment credit? How much would the investment credit be on a machine which cost $1,200 and has an estimated life of 10 years?

9. Comment on the statement: Accelerated depreciation is a tax loophole which provides certain large businesses with extra tax deductions. This provision should be eliminated from the tax law because it is tantamount to a subsidy to these companies.

10. What is percentage depletion? How does this differ from cost depletion as used in good accounting?

11. Define a *capital asset*. Distinguish between the treatment of a long-term and a short-term capital gain.

12. What is an *involuntary conversion*? How are gains and losses on involuntary conversions treated for tax purposes?

13. Define *boot*. What effect does *boot* have on the treatment of a nontaxable exchange?

14. How may operating loss carryovers be used to reduce the tax liability over a period of years? To what years may operating losses be carried?

15. What are the major payroll taxes levied on employers? What are the major payroll taxes levied on employees? Do all of these taxes represent expenses to the employer? Do they all result in liabilities to the employer? Explain.

16. What are the funds collected by the federal unemployment insurance tax used for? What is meant by the term *merit rating* when used in connection with unemployment insurance?

EXERCISES

E17–1 **Taxable units.** John Jay is sole owner of a business which last year earned $35,000 net profit (before deducting owner's compensation). Mr. Jay withdrew $15,000 for personal living expenses (owner's salary) and left the remaining $20,000 in the business for expansion. Mr. Jay is married and files a joint return; the Jays' average tax rate is 36 percent.

Required:

How much would the total taxes paid by the Jays (including his business and personal taxes) amount to under each of the following assumptions:

a. His business is a corporation but *does not* make a Subchapter S election.

b. His business is a corporation and does make a Subchapter S election.

c. His business is a sole proprietorship.

E17–2 **Tax allocation.** North Enterprises, Inc., acquired a new machine, at a cost of $45,000, which is estimated to have a useful life of 6 years and a salvage value of $3,000. The company uses straight-line depreciation for book purposes and sum-of-the-years'-digits for tax purposes. Income before deducting depreciation or income taxes is $90,000 in each of the 6 years.

Required:

Calculate the amount added to or taken from the deferred tax liability at the end of each of the 6 years. Assume a 40 percent tax rate.

E17–3 **Investment tax credit.** Servoss Service Company purchased a new automatic polisher during the year at an invoice price of $7,480. The current tax liability before making allowance for the investment credit is $49,700. Calculate the amount of the investment credit and the new tax liability under each of the following assumptions regarding the life of the machine:

a. 3 years
b. 5 years
c. 6 years
d. 7 years
e. 10 years

E17–4 Installment sales method entries. Mini Imports Company sold a new car to Jane Lloyd for $2,800. Jane paid $400 down and the balance in 24 equal $100 installments (the contract bears *no interest*). During the year of purchase, Jane paid 4 monthly installments in addition to the down payment. The car cost Mini Imports $2,100 and they account for the sale on an installment sales basis.

Required:
Prepare all entries on the books of Mini Imports Company (including year-end adjustments) related to the installment sale during the year of sale.

E17–5 Involuntary conversion. Heiner Hay Company purchased a building at a cost of $620,000, which was recently destroyed by fire. At the date of the fire, depreciation of $88,000 had been accumulated and the building had an appraised value of $800,000. The building was fully insured and the company suffered no direct loss.

Required:
Assume that all insurance proceeds are reinvested in a new building and calculate:

a. the accounting gain or loss
b. the taxable gain or loss
c. the accounting basis of the new building
d. the tax basis in the new building

E17–6 Payroll taxes. Turf Floor Coverings, Inc., has four employees with earnings to date as follows:

Joe	$ 2,500
Pete	4,000
Harvey	8,000
Gary	15,000

During the current month Joe earned $400, Pete and Harvey earned $600 each, and Gary earned $1,400. Using current tax rates (assume a state unemployment rate of 2.2 percent on the first $6,000 of wages and federal withholding rate of 20 percent on all employees, and ignore state withholding tax), calculate the amount of each tax levied on the employer and on the employee.

E17–7 **FIFO–LIFO.**   Condor Corporation sold 1,500 "Wing Dings" for $495 each during the first year of operations. Data related to Wing Ding purchases during the year are:

Date	Quantity Purchased	Cost per Wing Ding
January 2	400	$250
April 1	700	275
June 7	500	300
November 2	300	325

No units were lost or stolen during the year and no dividends were paid to any of the firms 50 stockholders. Operating (selling and administrative) expenses amounted to $265,000 for the year. The corporation is subject to income tax rates as listed in the text.

Required:

Prepare an income statement for Condor for the year, assuming:

a. FIFO inventory method.

b. LIFO inventory method.

E17–8 **Depletion.**   Gavison Clay Pits, Incorporated, extracts clay from a tract of land they purchased near the mouth of the canyon. They paid $1,200,000 for the 150-acre tract and expect to extract a total of 20,000,000 tons of clay after which they will sell the land to the city as a garbage dump. They expect to get about $1,000 per acre from the sale. During the year the company extracted a total of 2,500,000 tons which they sold to a local brick company at a price of $3.00 per ton.

Required:

Calculate the total depletion expense for the year:

a. Using generally accepted accounting techniques.

b. Using percentage depletion.

PROBLEMS

P17–1 **Involuntary conversion.**   The home office of the Moss Corporation was destroyed by fire on August 2, 1975. The building had been constructed by the company in the late 1950s at a cost of $242,000. It was first occupied on January 1, 1958. At that time the company estimated it would have a useful life of 40 years, after which it could be sold for $50,000. The company used straight-line depreciation for both tax and book purposes.

In each separate situation described below, the new building was purchased or constructed within two years:

1. The company carried no insurance on the building, and it completed construction of a new branch office building at a cost of $496,000.

2. The building was fully insured for its current appraised value of $329,000, and the entire proceeds were reinvested in a new branch office building.

3. The building was fully insured for its current appraised value of $329,000, and a new branch office building was purchased at a cost of $496,000.

4. The building was fully insured for its current appraised value of $250,000 and a new branch office building was purchased at a cost of $202,000.

Required:

For each situation:

a. Calculate the accounting gain or loss.

b. Calculate the taxable gain or loss.

c. Calculate the tax basis on the new property.

P17–2 **Tax allocation.** The Milme Truck Lines has a number of large semitrailers used to transport customers' goods across the country. It has been the company's practice to depreciate this particular equipment on a straight-line basis over a 6-year period because it is felt this method best matches the depreciation cost with the revenue. Several years ago, the company's CPA firm pointed out the advantages of sum-of-the-years'-digits depreciation for tax purposes. They said this technique would enable the company to accelerate the depreciation deductions thereby reducing the company's current tax liability. The company controller still felt the straight-line method enabled the company to more accurately measure income. The CPA firm indicated it would be acceptable to use sum-of-the-years'-digits for tax purposes and straight-line for book purposes, provided the company used proper tax allocation procedures. On January 3, 1977, 10 trailers were purchased at a cost of $35,000 each, with an estimated salvage value of $3,500 each.

Required:

Assume that the company uses straight-line depreciation for book purposes; sum-of-the-years'-digits depreciation for tax purposes; a marginal tax rate of 48 percent; and that prior to any deduction for depreciation, the taxable income and net income are $250,000 per year. Prepare a schedule which will show for each year the trailers will be used:

a. the income tax expense

b. the amount added to or deducted from the deferred income tax liability

c. the balance in the deferred tax liability account at the end of the year

P17–3 **Capital gains and losses.** During a recent year, Mr. Karl Konner completed these stock transactions:

Date	Transaction	Number of Shares	Company	Transaction Amount
January 8	Purchased	200	Malta Air Lines	$ 6,665
January 29	Sold	100	City Service	6,442
March 18	Sold	50	Allied Electric	2,894
March 24	Purchased	500	Western Pharmaceutical	26,500
April 30	Sold	200	Malta Air Lines	7,180
August 26	Purchased	1,000	Cannon Construction	1,215
September 30	Sold	250	Western Pharmaceutical	12,888

All sales relate to stocks purchased during the same year except for the City Service stock, which was acquired 4 years earlier at a cost of $4,521, and the Allied Electric stock, which was acquired January 19 of the prior year, at a cost of $3,420.

Required:

a. Calculate the gain or loss on each sale.

b. Calculate the net long-term capital gain or loss.

c. Calculate the net short-term capital gain or loss.

d. What amount would Mr. Konner include in his tax return as ordinary income?

P17–4 **Summary tax problem.** Leisure Time, Inc., was formed several years ago by a group of sports enthusiasts with the idea of capitalizing on the rapidly expanding recreation industry. The company reported taxable income of $10,000 in 1975; $17,000 in 1976; $22,000 in 1977; and $33,000 in 1978. Because profit trends had been favorable in recent years, management decided to greatly expand operations during 1979 and engaged in the following transactions:

1. On November 12, 1978, purchased a site for $49,000 on which the company planned to construct a miniature golf course. Several months later the state highway department announced construction of a freeway with an exit near this site. On December 10, 1979, the company accepted an offer from a national motel chain which wanted to build a motel on the site, selling the undeveloped property for $170,000.

2. On April 8, 1979, the company traded a bowling alley with a tax basis of $112,000 and a current appraised value of $325,000 for a larger bowling alley with an appraised value of $400,000. The difference in appraised values was paid in cash.

3. On April 25, 1979, the company purchased 1,000 shares of Winter Sports, Inc., at a total cost of $29,400. On September 1, 1979, Winter Sports announced sharply reduced earnings and the stock price began to fall. On December 15, 1979, Leisure Time decided to "bail out" and sold the entire 1,000 shares for only $10,220.

4. On July 9, 1979, a filling station was purchased at a cost of $100,000.

5. On September 1, 1979, General Motors stock was sold for $39,990. This stock had been acquired on August 20, 1978, at a cost of $38,810. The funds provided by this sale were used to buy a trampoline recreation center.

6. Operating profits for 1979 (excluding gains and losses from the foregoing transactions) were $38,000.

7. Early in February 1980 it became apparent that the firm's president had been spending far too much time "playing the stock market" and not enough time on company operations. On March 1, 1980, the president was fired, and the new president decided to freeze all investments and concentrate his efforts on the firm's deteriorating operating position. In spite of his efforts, the company sustained a $92,000 operating loss during 1980.

Required:

Using the corporate tax rates described in the chapter, calculate the company's adjusted tax liabilities for the years 1975 through 1980, inclusive. (Assume the firm elects the operating loss carryback provision.)

P17–5 **Taxable units.** Aaron, Barney, and Clyde are joint owners of an insulation business which operates under the name ABCO. The marginal personal tax rate for Aaron is 26 percent, 45 percent for Barney, and 40 percent for Clyde. During the year the partners' taxable income (after personal deductions and exemptions) from sources other than ABCO were Aaron $2,000, Barney $25,000, and Clyde $18,000.

Part 1:

Assume that ABCO is a partnership and that the partners have agreed to share profits by allowing a salary of $10,000 to Aaron (the managing partner) with the balance of the profits to be shared in the ratio 1:2:3 by Aaron, Barney, and Clyde, respectively. During the year, the partners withdrew the following sums: Aaron $10,000 (the agreed salary), Barney $1,000, and Clyde $2,000. The firm's net income (prior to any deduction for salary or other compensations to partners) was $85,000. What is ABCO's tax liability? What is the tax liability of each of the partners?

Part 2:

Suppose that ABCO is a corporation (instead of a partnership) not qualifying under Subchapter S. Aaron is allowed an $8,000 salary as manager and this amount is paid to him during the year. Dividends declared and paid during the year amount to $6,000: $1,000 to Aaron, $2,000 to Barney, and $3,000 to Clyde. The firm's net income (prior to any deductions for salary or other compensation to partners) was $85,000. Aaron and Clyde own their stock jointly with their wives, but Barney holds his stock in his own name. What is ABCO's tax liability? What is the tax liability of each of the partners?

Part 3:

How would your answer in Part 2 differ if ABCO had qualified under Subchapter S?

Part 4:

Which form of business would you prefer for ABCO if you were a partner? Would this method be equally desirable to all owners?

P17-6 *Various situations.*

Part 1:

Mr. Jim Javits completed the following transactions in his stock market account:

January 22
   Purchased 100 shares of NITCO common stock for $3,292.
January 30
   Sold 50 shares of Stuart Sales, Inc., common stock for $2,555.
March 13
   Sold the 100 shares NITCO for $4,820.
May 22
   Purchased 500 shares of Lightning Uranium Mines common stock for $500.
July 24
   Sold 200 shares of Mountain Motors common stock for $3,920.
October 15
   Sold 250 shares of Lightning Uranium Mines for $1,800.
December 2
   Sold 100 shares of Lightning Uranium Mines for $975.

The Stuart Sales, Inc., stock was acquired January 18 of the prior year for $3,200, and the Mountain Motors stock was acquired the previous April 29 at a cost of $2,340.

Required:

Calculate the tax liability associated with Mr. Javits' stock transactions assuming that his marginal tax rate is 22 percent.

Part 2:

Jack and Jill Johnson are married and file a joint return. Dividends that they received during the year were:

Stock	Owner	Dividend
General Electric	Joint	$25
Eastern Airlines	Husband	10
Litton Industries	Husband	18
RCA	Joint	44
Ford Motor	Husband	32
Sun Oil	Joint	14
J.C. Penney	Wife	20
Honeywell	Joint	52
Bethlehem Steel	Husband	30

What amount of dividends will be taxed as ordinary income on the Johnsons' tax return?

Part 3:

Wunderland Manufacturing constructed a factory building which was first occupied on July 1, 1968 at a cost of $2,400,000. The building was expected to last 40 years and have a salvage value of $400,000. The company uses straight-line depreciation on all assets and records fractional year depreciation to the closest full month. On February 27, 1978 the building was completely destroyed by fire. At the date of the fire, the appraised value was $3,000,000, but the building was only insured for $2,500,000. The company constructed a new factory at a total cost of $3,120,000 and moved into the new building on December 31, 1978. The new factory has an estimated life of 40 years and a $500,000 salvage value.

Required:

How much was the gain or loss? How much of the gain or loss is taxable in 1978? How much of the gain or loss is taxable in 1979? What is the tax basis of the new building?

Part 4:

Karl Reynolds is in the excavating business and has four 8-yard-capacity dump trucks. But, on many occasions he has needed a larger truck, and so he accepts an offer from a truck rental company to trade two of his 8-yard-capacity trucks for one 12-yard-capacity truck. Karl's trucks had a book value (tax basis) of $2,000 each, but had a current market value of $3,000 each. The larger truck was of similar age and condition as Karl's smaller trucks, and it had a current market value of $5,500.

Required:

What, if any, is Karl's recognized gain or loss on the transaction? What is his tax basis in the new truck?

P17–7 Payroll taxes.

a.   List separately those payroll taxes which are an expense to the employer and those which must be accounted for but are not an expense to the employer. What account is debited in each case when such taxes are accrued on the books?

b.   Smith and Smythe Management Consultants employ three salaried office workers, two of whom are paid $800 per month, and one $1,600 per month. Also, two parttime clerical workers are employed 40 hours each payroll period, each at $2.50 per hour. Pay periods end on the fifteenth and the last day of the month, payable on the tenth and twenty-fifth. The following are the applicable payroll tax rates, in percents:

Federal withholding	14
State withholding	2

F.I.C.A. (on employers and employees)   5.85 (up to $15,300)
Federal unemployment   0.7 (up to $ 4,200)
State unemployment   2.7 (up to $ 4,200)

Required:

Assuming that all employees have worked the entire year to date, calculate the amount of each payroll tax for all wages earned during the month of October (i.e., the payrolls paid on October 25 and November 10). Prepare a schedule which shows (for each of the above pay periods) the name of the tax, the amount of wages subject to tax and the payroll tax for that period.

P17–8   *Payroll taxes.*   The Sweetwater branch office of Houston Company has three office employees and a branch manager. The branch manager is paid $2,100 per month. The office employees are each paid $1,000 per month. Two of the office employees have been with the company for several years, but one was hired April 1 of this year. The following tax rates, in percents, are used for payroll taxes:

Federal withholding   14
State withholding   2
F.I.C.A. (on employer and employees)   5.85 (up to $15,300)
Federal unemployment   0.7 (up to $ 4,200)
State unemployment   2.7 (up to $ 4,200)

Required:

Assuming that each employee is paid at the end of the month, prepare a schedule showing the amount of each payroll tax the company will need to account for pertaining to the August payroll.

P17–9   *Comprehensive income tax problem.*   Appliance Sales, Inc., was formed in the early 1960s, specializing in the sale of washing machines. For many years the company operated as a discount outlet selling below retail prices but only on a C.O.D. basis. In 1978 to conform to the modern trend toward installment selling, the company changed its marketing strategy. Where all sales had previously been made for cash only, during 1978 all sales were made on installment contract. The company decided, therefore, to adopt the installment sales method of accounting. A trial balance, taken from the company books at December 31, 1978 (at the end of the taxable year), is shown on the following page.

Adjustments have not been made to record depreciation for 1978. All new equipment was purchased January 3, 1975 at a cost of $360,000. The company assumes that the equipment will have no salvage value and uses straight-line depreciation for book purposes, but sum-of-the-years'-digits depreciation for tax purposes. Except for this difference in depreciation methods and the resulting effect on the company's current tax liability, its net income and taxable income are in agreement.

The gain on sale of capital assets is the net result of three sepa-

APPLIANCE SALES, INC.
Trial Balance
December 31, 1978

Cash	$ 110,000	
Installment accounts receivable	900,000	
Merchandise inventory (January 1, 1978)	180,000	
Accumulated depreciation, Equipment		$ 135,000
Equipment	360,000	
Other assets	500,000	
Current liabilities		250,000
Deferred tax liability		36,000
Capital stock		400,000
Retained earnings		760,000
Purchases	1,040,000	
Cost of installment sales		1,010,000
Deferred gross margin on installment sales		790,000
Rent expense	85,000	
Salaries expense	185,000	
Other expenses	30,000	
Gain on sale of capital assets		9,000
	$3,390,000	$3,390,000

rate stock transactions. Stock of Motyke Corporation, purchased September 27, 1973 for $44,414, was sold on April 30, 1978 for $85,390. Stock of American Products Company was sold February 22, 1978 for $8,320. This stock was acquired on November 9, 1977 for $6,170. On November 23, 1978 the company sold Allgone Company stock for $27,074. This stock had been acquired in early 1970 at a cost of $61,200.

The directors of Appliance Sales are considering a cash dividend, and they are anxious to know the results of 1978 operations and to have a statement of financial position on that date. The profits earned during 1977 amounted to $221,000. Preliminary figures furnished by the sales manager indicate the number of units sold in 1978 (5,000 units) was 25 percent higher than in the previous year. With this encouraging news, the directors are looking forward to record profits this year. The president has been asked to report at the next director's meeting, and he asks you to prepare financial statements and other data that might assist him in making his report.

Required:

a. Prepare an income statement for 1978. Were profits up or down? Why? How can the president explain this?

b. Explain why it might be desirable to use different methods of depreciation for book and tax purposes. What impact does this difference have on the company's "deferred tax liability"?

Section 5

Other Management Tools

This section describes, at a very understandable level, the resources that are available to today's managers through mathematical analysis and computers. The objective of Chapters 18 and 19 is to more thoroughly acquaint the reader with the use of these tools. For those interested, references to more detailed and advanced sources of information are given.

18

Mathematical Aids to Management

As discussed in Chapter 1, the function of accounting is to provide quantitative information of a financial nature that is useful in making economic decisions.[1] Management accountants gather information to be used in the internal decision-making situations of planning and control. Together with other types of information, managers process accounting reports using the decision models described in the preceding chapters. There are many others in use, of course, but we could not begin to describe them all in the scope of this text.

We will introduce four of the most widely used *mathematical models: programming* models, *statistical decision* models, *network analysis,* and *inventory management* models.

As indicated by the name, these models depend upon abstract, quantitative relationships. Frequently, the mathematical basis for a model is beyond the understanding of all but the most highly trained expert. Nonetheless, to the inquisitive and ambitious businessman, they provide extremely useful assistance in beating out the competition and in earning greater profits. Many of these applications would be impossible without the speed and data handling capabilities of the computer (see Chapter 19). Time-sharing arrangements and conversational programs are lowering the barriers of complexity and making these models almost universally available.

The reason that a chapter of this kind should appear in a management accounting textbook is self-evident: Models must receive accurate input data from someone before they can produce valid output reports. Furthermore,

The authors are indebted to Dr. Reed Randall of The University of Utah for writing virtually all of this chapter.

[1] Accounting Principles Board, *Statement No. 4* (New York: AICPA, 1970), p. 17.   *517*

the output must be interpreted by someone who understands it. Both of these roles have been (and will continue to be) filled by management accountants. The level of the following discussions will be sufficiently high enough to describe the workings of the model for an accountant, but sufficiently low enough to be understood by a nonmathematician.

Before we get into specifics, let us look at the general concept of decisions and models.

DECISION MAKING AND MATHEMATICAL MODELS

A decision involves selecting one of several alternatives. Of course, if there are no alternatives our future action is self-evident and no decision has to be made. Unfortunately, there are very few business situations in which there is only one alternative. As discussed in Chapters 11 and 13, there are some identifiable steps in decision making. Whereas our context in those chapters was one of *planning* and *control,* in this section we present a generalized decision process.

There are three basic steps in the decision process: *problem definition, alternative evaluation,* and *alternative selection.* The most difficult is the first, which can be broken down into four parts. As we *define our problem,* we identify the following items:

1. The *objective*—the goal that we are seeking to accomplish. In most business situations, we seek to earn *satisfactory* or *maximum* profits. In other situations, our objective might be to stamp out a dreaded disease, to bring peace to the world, or to get elected to a high office. In mathematical modeling, we must seek a goal that can be expressed in quantitative measures, such as profits.

2. The *alternatives*—the various means by which we can attempt to achieve the objective. There is a nearly infinite set of *alternatives* for achieving a goal of satisfactory or maximum profits. Consequently, it is necessary to narrow the range of our alternatives to a manageable few.

3. The *problem factors*—the variable conditions within and outside the firm that influence the outcome of a particular alternative. Thus, if we are considering the manufacture of purses out of sows' ears, we must examine the behavior of such things as the demand for purses and the cost of sows' ears.

4. The *criterion*—the measure of the success to be obtained from an alternative. Each alternative should produce a result that can be measured against the others. Simple criteria, such as the size of profits or costs, or the number of votes, can be expressed in one quantitative dimension. More complex decision situations require multiple criteria, and there usually are tradeoffs among them. Therefore, we may have to examine not only the profits to be obtained from a factory but also such factors as ecological effects, the local economy, and working conditions.

After defining these factors, and identifying the available alternatives, we begin to narrow down the variety of possible actions by *evaluating* their effects on reaching our objective. A well-constructed criterion allows us to *select* the alternative that will most closely produce the desired result. Exhibit 18-1 is a flowchart of the decision-making process; note its similarity to the diagrams in Chapter 11.

Let us examine a simple situation where our *objective* is to maximize profits from a process to manufacture one product. Our *alternatives* are the various levels of production at which we can operate. Our *problem factors* are the demand for our product and the cost of running the factory. Our *criterion,* of course, is the difference between revenues and expenses. In mathematical notation, our goal is to achieve

$$\text{Max } P = R(Q) - C(Q)$$

where

Q	=	the decision variable representing the production level
$R(Q)$	=	the revenue resulting from production level Q
$C(Q)$	=	the cost resulting from production level Q
P	=	the profit, which we are trying to maximize

The equation is a model of the relationship, and we are seeking to achieve the greatest benefit from it. We *evaluate* each possible production level *(alternative)* in terms of its effect on profits *(criterion)*. We will select the alternative that promises the greatest profit *(objective)*.

There are two advantages of building a mathematical model: First, we are more or less forced into a *systematic analysis* of the decision situation and the problem factors related to it. The model should be a concise summary of

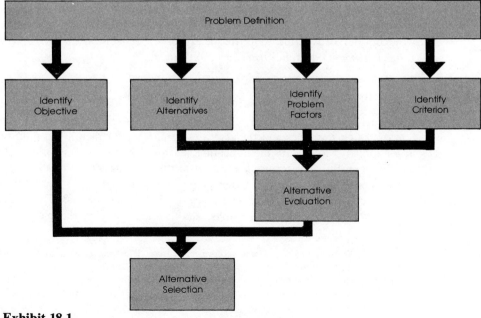

Exhibit 18-1
The Decision-Making Process

the relevant variables and their interactions. Second, the model can be tested and solved with mathematical processes. Thus, it is possible to examine several production schemes, for example, without ever actually manufacturing a single product. A mathematical model solution procedure (called an *algorithm*) is actually a systematic method of evaluating the alternatives and selecting the most desirable. In many cases, this selection can be made *without* evaluating each individual alternative.

The following quotation from a leading textbook will summarize this discussion:

> Constructing a model helps you put the complexities and possible uncertainties attending a decision-making problem into a logical framework amenable to comprehensive analysis. Such a model clarifies the decision alternatives and their anticipated effects, indicates the data that are relevant for analyzing the alternatives, and leads to informative conclusions. In short, the model is a vehicle for arriving at a well-structured view of reality.[2]

PROGRAMMING MODELS

One of the most important models is *mathematical programming,* which is used for planning future events. Some confusion in terminology has arisen because many people associate programming with computer instructions. As discussed in Chapter 11, every business firm should engage in planning of some kind; mathematical programming models are merely tools to assist the manager in preparing these plans. They are valuable in situations where there are so many alternatives to evaluate that they could never even be identified, much less evaluated within a reasonable time. In this section we will consider two of the tools frequently used by decision makers: *linear programming* models and *transportation* models.

Linear Programming

Like most economic models, linear programming (LP) deals with the allocation of scarce resources and the activities competing for them. The purpose of the model is to specify the allocation scheme that contributes the most to the firm's profits. The term *linear* refers to the fact that all the relationships in the model are *first order.*[3] Other programming models have been developed which do not have this requirement, but they cannot be as easily formulated or solved for realistic situations, and thus are not as applicable.

---

[2] Harvey M. Wagner, *Principles of Management Science: With Applications to Executive Decisions,* 2nd Ed. (Englewood Cliffs, N.J.: Prentice Hall, 1975), p. 7.

[3] In a linear equation, the independent variables are raised only to the first power. Thus, $y = a + bx$ expresses a linear relationship, if a and b are constants, and x is the independent variable. These equations are nonlinear: $y = a + bx^2$; $y = a + zx$ (where z is an independent variable), and $y = a + (b/x)$. In two-dimension space, a linear relationship can be described by a straight line on a graph.

MODEL STRUCTURE

The first part of an LP model is called the *criterion function,* which is a mathematical expression describing the objective whose value is to be minimized (such as costs) or maximized (such as revenues or profits). The criterion functions of our examples contain only a few variables whereas real world applications may require hundreds or even thousands. The second section of the model is many times larger than the first, and consists of a series of mathematical relationships called *constraints.* These relationships describe the use of scarce resources and other problem factors that affect our decision situation. Let us look at an example:

$$\text{Max } R = 4X_A + 3X_B + 5X_C$$
$$\text{Subject to:} \quad X_A + 2X_B + X_C \leqslant 10$$
$$2X_A + X_B + X_C \leqslant 12$$
$$X_A, \quad X_B, \quad X_C \geqslant 0$$

The variables symbolized by the X_i (X_A, X_B, and X_C) are the number of units of Products *A, B,* and *C* which are to be produced. The last constraint confines our solution to the real world—we must produce either none or some of a product. It is, of course, physically impossible to produce a *negative* quantity, and our last constraint makes it mathematically impossible to do so.

In the criterion function, we are seeking to maximize the benefit achieved from the production process. The coefficients of the X_i (4, 3, and 5) represent the excess of the selling prices of the three products over their costs. For example, if we sell two units of *A,* three units of *B,* and four units of *C,* our total net revenue *(R)* will be \$37 [(\$4 × 2) + (\$3 × 3) + (\$5 × 4)]. Our objective is to find that combination of outputs which will produce the greatest net revenue.

Of course, the greatest net revenue would come if we could produce and sell an infinite quantity of any or all three of our products. Naturally, we cannot operate at those levels because we are limited by the physical capacity of the factory, the demand for the product, and the supply of inputs. The constraints are mathematical interpretations of these limitations. Suppose the first constraint describes the amount of input material available for our products. Products *A* and *C* consume one unit of material for each unit made, while *B* requires two. Altogether, we must not consume more than 10 units of input. The second constraint may express limits on our production arising from the factory capacity available to us. It should be obvious that the usefulness of the LP model depends on the care, skill, and completeness with which these constraining factors are identified and expressed.

The optimal solution to this particular problem is to produce 10 units of Product *C,* and none of either *A* or *B*. This perhaps unexpected solution will produce a profit of \$50. The reader should try out various other combinations that will meet the constraints in order to prove that there is no other solution that will produce a greater profit. Notice that there are many *feasible* solutions, but only one is *optimal.*

MODEL FORMULATION

The value of the solution of a particular LP model depends completely on the care with which we construct the constraints and the objective function. This task is as much an art as it is a science. It requires not only knowledge of mathematics, but also insight into the environment and capabilities of the process being programmed.

One useful formulation technique is *dimensional analysis*. This procedure is especially helpful in developing the constraints. The dimensions of the left side of the constraint must be the same as the dimensions of the right side. Look at the first constraint in the preceding example, which told us that we could not use more than 10 units of the raw material. Thus, the dimension of the right side is "units of raw material." The dimension of the three decision variables (X_A, X_B, and X_C) is "units of product." We must construct the coefficients of the decision variables in such a manner that we convert the *units of product* to *units of raw material*. Our constraint appears below in a slightly different format:

$$(1 \times X_A) + (2 \times X_B) + (5 \times X_C) \leqslant 10$$

$$(? \times \text{Units of Product } A) + (? \times \text{Units of Product } B) +$$

$$(? \times \text{Units of Product } C) \leqslant (\text{Units of raw material})$$

The second line describes the dimensions of the constraint. Our task is to find the dimensions of the coefficients that will make everything work out to be the same. In this case, it is clear that the dimension of each coefficient should be "units of raw material per unit of product i." Let us look at the second factor in the constraint:

$$\frac{\text{Units of raw material}}{\text{Units of Product } B} \times \text{Units of Product } B$$

The denominator of the coefficient cancels out the dimension of the variable, with the result that the expression "$2X_B$" is a symbol for the number of units of raw material used.

While the particular approach used to describe a given situation may be unique, there are some general guidelines:

1. Problem definition
   a. Identify the decision alternative
   b. Identify the objective
   c. Identify the problem factors
2. Model formulation
   a. List the independent variables
   b. State the criterion function
   c. Construct the constraints
3. Model verification

In the following section, we will show how these steps can be applied.

AN ILLUSTRATION

Consider the following problem in which a manufacturer is trying to select the best *product-mix* to produce:

1. A small factory can produce three different products (A, B, and C) which can be sold (net of raw material, selling, and administrative costs) for $3, $3, and $2 each. Each product goes through a fabrication and finishing process.

2. The fabrication process payroll allows 2,000 man-hours per week. Each unit of product consumes the following man-hours: A, 0.3; B, 0.5; and C, 0.2. The cost per man-hour is $3.

3. The finishing process payroll allows 1,000 man-hours per week. Each unit of product consumes the following man-hours: A, 0.2; B, 0.1; and C, 0.1. The cost per man-hour is $2.50.

4. Management has estimated that the market can consume no more than 4,000 units of Product C in a week. There is a commitment to deliver 1,000 units of Product A to a special customer.

We can go through the phases of *definition:*

1. The decision alternatives are the many possible combinations of quantities of A, B, and C that can be produced.

2. The objective we want to achieve is maximum profits.

3. The problem factors are the revenues, the costs, the capacities of the two departments, and the market limitations.

Next, we turn to model *formulation:*

1. The independent variables are the quantities of each product that are to be produced, which we will symbolize by X_A, X_B, and X_C. This notation facilitates the accomplishment of the next two steps.

2. The objective function will describe the revenues received from the sale of the product less the costs incurred in its production. To simplify, we will compute the *contribution margin* per unit (which is frequently called the *profit margin*) for each product:

Product	A	B	C
Unit selling price (net)	$ 3.00	$ 3.00	$ 2.00
Unit labor costs			
Fabrication	(0.90)	(1.50)	(0.60)
Finishing	(0.50)	(0.25)	(0.25)
Contribution margin	$ 1.60	$ 1.25	$ 1.15

Thus we can describe our goal as:

$$\text{Max } 1.60X_A + 1.25X_B + 1.15X_C$$

3. The constraints will be based on the capacities of the two departments and the market situations, in particular:

Hours in fabrication	$0.3X_A + 0.5X_B + 0.2X_C \leq 2,000$
Hours in finishing	$0.2X_A + 0.1X_B + 0.1X_C \leq 1,000$
Contractual commitment	$X_A \geq 1,000$
Market saturation	$X_C \leq 4,000$
Nonnegativity	$X_A \geq 0$
	$X_B \geq 0$
	$X_C \geq 0$

After definition and formulation, we turn to testing the model, perhaps using the dimensional analysis approach. Of course, there might be other constraints arising from limitations on machine hours and raw materials. In the conventional LP format, our model would appear as:

$$\text{Max. Profit} = 1.60X_A + 1.25X_B + 1.15X_C$$
$$\text{Subject to:} \quad 0.30X_A + 0.50X_B + 0.20X_C \leq 2,000$$
$$0.20X_A + 0.10X_B + 0.10X_C \leq 1,000$$
$$X_A \geq 1,000$$
$$X_C \leq 4,000$$
$$X_A, X_B, X_C \geq 0$$

This model can now be solved using the *simplex algorithm,* for which many canned computer programs have been written. Because our emphasis has been on providing the input data, any discussion of this algorithm is beyond the scope of the text.

For this particular model, we find that maximum profits will be generated if the following quantities are produced and *sold: A,* 2,571.428 units; *B,* 857.143 units; and *C,* 4,000 units. This particular mix will result in the maximum profit of $9,785.71. If we substitute these values back into the constraints, we will see that we used the available manpower to its greatest capacity.

APPLICABILITY AND WEAKNESSES

LP models have been used extensively in a variety of situations, many of which require the use of hundreds of decision variables and literally thousands of constraints. However, we can identify six characteristics that should be met before applying this approach:

1. We must be able to define a single objective.
2. The objective and problem factors must be quantifiable.
3. The problem must allow several (at least) alternative courses of action.
4. The objective function and constraints must be linear.
5. The values of the independent variables must be able to take on fractional values.[4]
6. We can produce values for all the model coefficients.

[4]For example, an LP model might show we would have to produce 3.27 battleships, or 93.4 airplanes. In all but a very few cases, this factor is not prohibitive.

In practicality, there are very few actual situations that meet all these characteristics. It is possible to make assumptions that will allow us to apply the LP model, but we must interpret the results accordingly. Above all, we must pay particular attention to the *nonquantifiable* factors that may affect our decision environment. The accuracy of the output figures substantially depends on the accuracy of the input coefficients. If too many estimates must be made, the applicability of the approach is greatly diminished. Despite these weaknesses, the LP model serves as one of the very best techniques for dealing with programming problems, especially on the large scale.

Transportation Models

Transportation models are really only special cases of LP models, but they are unique and deserve a special discussion. Let's begin with an example:

A retailing firm maintains warehouses at three locations, each of which has a known quantity of one item in stock. The firm supplies three markets, and the demand in each market is known. Additionally, we know the cost of transporting a given item to a given market.

The term *transportation model* was attached to this approach because of its applicability to problems of this type. Specific information for our example is:

Warehouse	Units on Hand
A	50
B	100
C	65

Market	Units Demanded
East	55
South	70
West	60

Shipping Cost from Each Warehouse to Each Market
(Per Unit of Product)

To Market From Warehouse	East	South	West
A	$ 8	$7	$ 5
B	10	7	6
C	5	8	11

CRITERION FUNCTION

Our objective is to meet the demands of the three markets for the lowest possible shipping costs. The mathematical terminology will use the following subscripted variable:

X_{ij} = the number of units shipped from warehouse i to market j

Thus, i will be either A, B, or C, and j will be either E, S, or W. For example, X_{AW} will represent the number of units shipped from Warehouse A

to the West market, and $5X_{AW}$ will equal the cost of shipping those units to the market. In these terms, our objective is to:

$$\text{Min: } 8X_{AE} + 7X_{AS} + 5X_{AW} + 10X_{BE} + 7X_{BS} + 6X_{BW} + 5X_{CE} + 8X_{CS} + 11X_{CW}$$

CONSTRAINTS

Two problem factors have been identified: the existing quantities on hand and the amounts demanded. The form in which we express these factors is the *constraint,* just as we saw in the last section. The constraints for the warehouses are:

$$
\begin{aligned}
A: & \quad X_{AE} + X_{AS} + X_{AW} \leq 50 \\
B: & \quad X_{BE} + X_{BS} + X_{BW} \leq 100 \\
C: & \quad X_{CE} + X_{CS} + X_{CW} \leq 65
\end{aligned}
$$

To express these constraints verbally, we can not ship more items from a warehouse than we have on hand.

Similarly, we do not want to fail to meet the demand for an item in a market, so we set up market constraints in this manner:

$$
\begin{aligned}
\text{East:} & \quad X_{AE} + X_{BE} + X_{CE} \geq 55 \\
\text{South:} & \quad X_{AS} + X_{BS} + X_{CS} \geq 70 \\
\text{West:} & \quad X_{AW} + X_{BW} + X_{CW} \geq 60
\end{aligned}
$$

Of course, it is physically impossible to ship a negative quantity from a warehouse, so we constrain all of the X_{ij} to be greater than or equal to zero. Notice that the supply (215 units) is greater than the demand (185 units). This condition allows us to solve the problem.

TABLE FORMAT

Because of the way we have structured our model, we can express it in the table that appears in Exhibit 18-2. Each intersection of a row and column (called a *cell*) represents the quantity shipped from a warehouse to a market. The number in the corner is the *per unit shipping cost.* The totals around the outside of the table equal the total units on hand at each warehouse (the right side) and the total units demanded at each market (the bottom row). Notice that we added a column for *slack,* and these cells will represent the units that were not shipped anywhere because we did not expect to sell them.

If we were to apply a solution technique (beyond the scope of this discussion) to this table, we would find that the minimum transportation cost is $1,075, which we will achieve by shipping 50 units to the West from *A,* 70 units to the South from *B,* 10 units to the West from *B,* and 55 units to the East from *C.* Notice that the demand in each market has been satisfied and that we have left 20 units in Warehouse *B* and 10 units in *C.* (You should test this model against your own intuition by trying other possible solutions.)

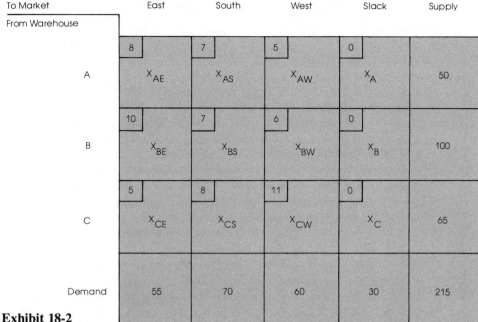

To Market / From Warehouse	East	South	West	Slack	Supply
A	8 X_{AE}	7 X_{AS}	5 X_{AW}	0 X_A	50
B	10 X_{BE}	7 X_{BS}	6 X_{BW}	0 X_B	100
C	5 X_{CE}	8 X_{CS}	11 X_{CW}	0 X_C	65
Demand	55	70	60	30	215

Exhibit 18-2
Transportation Model

APPLICABILITY AND WEAKNESSES

The transportation model is not restricted in application to distribution problems. It has been used successfully in planning production and inventory management. Whereas our example dealt with only one product and only one time period, we can expand it to deal with more realistic situations, including variations due to seasonal demand and supply functions. We can expand the concept of unit cost to include not only shipping costs but also expenditures for storage and production. Certain cells in Exhibit 18-2 would be effectively "crossed out" to prevent meeting a demand in one time period from a supply available only in a later period.

Many of the same restrictions that we saw in LP apply to transportation models, with the result that many of the same weaknesses exist. In particular, note that such factors as shipping costs, supply, and (especially) demand can only be estimated. Consequently, if reality differs from what is expected, it is possible that the optimum real solution may turn out to be somewhat different from our computed solution. Once formulated, the problem can be solved rather easily with a properly programmed computer.[5]

STATISTICAL DECISION MODELS

In the two preceding sections, we have dealt with *deterministic* models, to which we can assign definite values for the coefficients of the model. In the

[5] For further discussion of the model, the student should refer to: Richard I. Levin and Rudolph P. Lamone, *Linear Programming for Management Decisions* (Homewood, Ill.: Richard D. Irwin, 1969).

real world, of course, such conditions hardly ever exist and we are forced to deal with uncertainties about the future.

In these cases, we can frequently express the coefficient as a *probability distribution.* That is, we identify various possible values of the coefficient, and attach a measure of the likelihood (or *probability*) of each value's occurrence. For example, there might be a 0.2 chance of the coefficient being 20, 0.3 of being 25, and 0.5 of being 30. The total of the probabilities for a given coefficient will equal 1.0.

Statistical decision models (based on *Bayesian decision theory*) provide a method for solving problems that involve this element of uncertainty. In applying this approach, we must identify *alternatives, states of nature, payoffs,* and a *decision rule.*

An Example

Consider this problem:

A campus bookstore wishes to determine the number of copies of a particular accounting textbook it should order for the coming term. Copies not sold will have no value because a new edition will be published before the next term begins. The book costs $10, and sells for $17. If the bookstore sells out, the students must go without books.

It should be apparent that our decision depends on the demand for the textbook. If we can precisely estimate this amount, we would achieve maximum profits by ordering that quantity. If we order too few, we lose sales (and inconvenience our customers). If we order too many, we will lose because we have to pay for books we do not sell. As is true in virtually every business situation, we cannot tell exactly how many units we will sell.

We can formulate the problem by identifying the following factors:

1. *Alternatives*—a set of the possible actions that the decision maker can take. These factors are completely under the control of the decision maker, and, in this case, consist of the various sizes the textbook order might be.

2. *States of nature*—the possible future states of nature (or *events*) which are completely beyond the decision maker's control, and about which he is uncertain. He can identify the possible events, which should be *mutually exclusive* and *exhaustive* (that is, not redundant and complete), and he can assign a probability to each one. For the bookstore problem, the possible states of nature are the various levels of demand for the accounting text.

3. *Payoffs*—the result of taking a particular act when a particular state of nature occurred, or an *outcome.* Given our criterion variable (such as profit), we can produce a table which shows the payoff for each possible combination of act and event. In this example, we can compute the

profit that will result given the size of the order and the level of demand.

4. *Decision rule*—the means for selecting a strategy. Perhaps the most widely used rule in statistical decision theory is *Bayes' decision rule,* which selects the alternative that produces the best *expected value.*[6] In this situation, we will choose the strategy that produces the greatest expected profit.[7]

Against this background, and with specific items of information, let us formulate and solve the book ordering problem. To simplify, we have identified only three possible states of nature, which are sales levels of 250, 300, and 350 copies. It would be foolish to order less than the minimum sales or more than the maximum. Consequently, the possible acts are also to order 250, 300, or 350 copies. Exhibit 18-3 expresses the net profit that will accrue under each of the nine possible outcomes. These payoffs are calculated using a $7 profit for each sold book, a $10 loss for each unsold book, and a zero profit for each book that could have been sold if it had been ordered.

Events:	Sell		250	300	350
Acts:	Buy	250	$1,750	$1,750	$1,750
		300	$1,250	$2,100	$2,100
		350	$ 750	$1,600	$2,450

Exhibit 18-3
Payoff Table

Before we can select the best strategy, we must assign probabilities to each of the possible events. The assignment may be based on historical data derived from similar past situations, or we may turn to such things as faculty and student surveys, or preregistration rolls if these items are available on a timely and inexpensive basis. The more we rely on estimates, the more *subjective* our probability assessment becomes. In this case, suppose that we assign the following likelihood measures to the sales levels: 250, 0.3; 300,

[6] Other possible decision rules are known as *maximum likelihood, maximax,* and *maximin.* The Bayes rule is popular because it makes use of all the available information about possible outcomes for each act and event. For additional information on this subject see: H. Bierman, C. P. Bonini, and W. H. Hausman, *Quantitative Analysis for Business Decisions,* 4th ed. (Homewood, Ill.: Richard D. Irwin, 1973), Chapter 4.

[7] The disadvantage of this rule is that it does not necessarily reflect our attitude toward risk. It has been argued that a better criterion is *expected utility,* which is not always directly proportional to monetary payoffs. See: Bonini and Hausman, *Quantitative Analysis,* Chapter 17.

0.5; and 350, 0.2. The expected profit is found by taking the sum for each *act* of the products of each of its possible payoffs multiplied by the probability of their occurring. Refer to the figures below for clarification:

Act	Expected Profit
Order 250	$1,750(0.3) + $1,750(0.5) + $1,750(0.2) = $1,750
Order 300	$1,250(0.3) + $2,100(0.5) + $2,100(0.2) = $1,845
Order 350	$ 750(0.3) + $1,600(0.5) + $2,450(0.2) = $1,515

Thus, by our decision rule, we will order 300 copies. We would expect to earn $1,845 on the average if this situation could be repeated many times. By ordering 250 or 350 we would average only $1,750 or $1,515. Notice that this rule does not *guarantee* a profit of $1,845. Indeed, we will earn either $1,250 or $2,100, depending on the actual state of nature.

The Decision Tree

To evaluate the situation, we can describe our possible acts, the future events, and the corresponding payoffs on a *decision tree*. The tree is constructed to reveal the order in which an act is chosen and the true state of nature is revealed. By following a particular branch from left to right, we arrive at the outcome. Exhibit 18-4 shows our bookstore problem. Notice that each "event branch" is labeled with its probability of occurring.

In order to solve the problem with the decision tree, we take a *backward* approach. That is, we start with the payoffs on the right, multiply them by the probabilities to get the *expected value* of the main branch, and then select the act that leads to the greatest expected value. Thus, the expected value of the three forks are $1,750, $1,845, and $1,515, from top to bottom.

Sequential Problems

In reality, there are few problems as simple as our preceding example. In particular, we are frequently faced with a series of decisions occurring over several time periods. The situation is made more complex when a later decision depends on preceding decisions and states of nature. The decision tree serves as a relatively useful device for dealing with this type of sequential problem. Let us look at a slightly more complicated book ordering situation.

Assume that our bookstore manager is ordering an accounting text which is to be sold over two semesters. He is going to place one order prior to the beginning of each term. After the second semester, the revised edition will be used. Thus, any books not sold during the first term can be sold in the second; but any books left unsold after the second term will never be sold. To simplify our analysis (perhaps unrealistically), assign these probabilities to the possible states of nature during each semester:

	Sales	Probability
First term	300 books	0.7
	350 books	0.3
Second term	150 books	0.6
	200 books	0.4

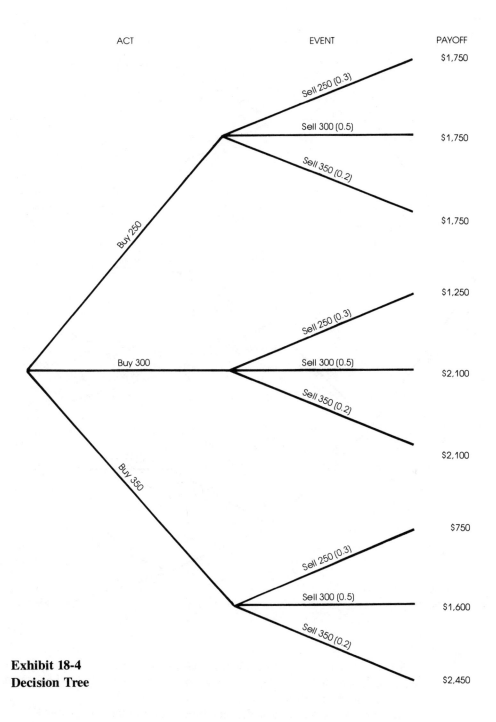

ACT	EVENT	PAYOFF

Sell 250 (0.3) — $1,750

Sell 300 (0.5) — $1,750

Sell 350 (0.2) — $1,750

Buy 250

Sell 250 (0.3) — $1,250

Buy 300 — Sell 300 (0.5) — $2,100

Sell 350 (0.2) — $2,100

Buy 350

Sell 250 (0.3) — $750

Sell 300 (0.5) — $1,600

Sell 350 (0.2) — $2,450

Exhibit 18-4
Decision Tree

The lower sales potential for the second term may be due to a drop in enrollment and/or to the availability of used copies. The tree for this situation is shown in Exhibit 18-5.

In this decision tree, we have simplified the event forks by eliminating the redundant outcomes. Thus, for example, if we buy and sell 300 books in the

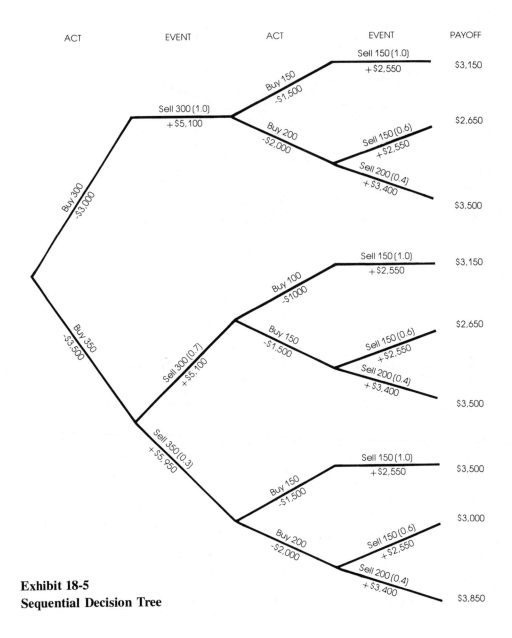

ACT   EVENT   ACT   EVENT   PAYOFF

Sell 150 (1.0)
+ $2,550
$3,150

Buy 150
-$1,500

Sell 300 (1.0)
+ $5,100

Buy 200
-$2,000

Sell 150 (0.6)
+ $2,550
$2,650

Sell 200 (0.4)
+ $3,400

$3,500

Buy 300
-$3,000

Buy 350
-$3,500

Buy 100
-$1000

Sell 150 (1.0)
+ $2,550
$3,150

Buy 150
-$1,500

Sell 150 (0.6)
+ $2,550
$2,650

Sell 300 (0.7)
+ $5,100

Sell 200 (0.4)
+ $3,400

$3,500

Sell 350 (0.3)
+ $5,950

Sell 150 (1.0)
+ $2,550
$3,500

Buy 150
-$1,500

$3,000

Buy 200
-$2,000

Sell 150 (0.6)
+ $2,550

Sell 200 (0.4)
+ $3,400
$3,850

Exhibit 18-5
Sequential Decision Tree

first term, and then buy only 150 for the second term, it does not matter
whether demand is 150 or 200. In either case we will sell only 150 books and
earn a profit of $1,050 for that term.

To assist in our analysis of the situation, the resulting cash outflows and
inflows are shown for each act and event. The payoff value shown on the
right side is the algebraic sum of these flows.

Notice also that our second sets of alternative acts differ, depending on the
results of the first act and event. Thus, if we end the first term with 50
unsold books on hand, we will need to buy only 100 or 150 in order to sell
150 or 200.

The optimal solution to this problem can be found by the same *backward* approach we saw before. Each of the right *event forks* can be replaced by its expected value. Then for each act fork we will choose the particular branch that has the greater expected value. We continue this process until we reach the beginning of the tree. Exhibit 18-6 is a simplified version of the same decision tree, and shows the expected value for each event fork at the begin-

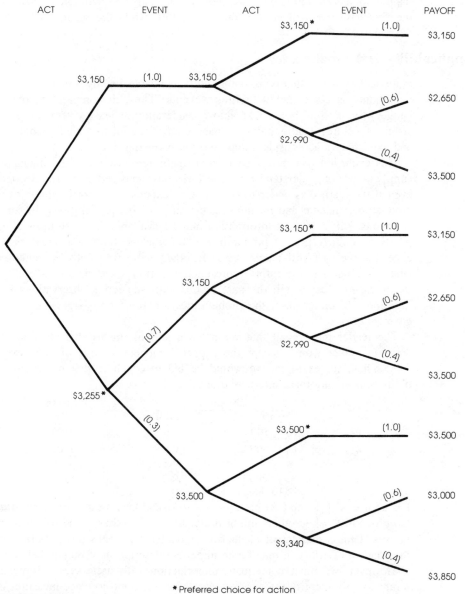

ACT	EVENT	ACT	EVENT	PAYOFF

$3,150 *   (1.0) $3,150

$3,150   (1.0) $3,150 $3,150 *

(0.6) $2,650

$2,990

(0.4) $3,500

$3,150 *   (1.0) $3,150

$3,150

(0.6) $2,650

(0.7) $2,990

(0.4) $3,500

$3,255 *

(0.3) $3,500 *   (1.0) $3,500

$3,500

(0.6) $3,000

$3,340

(0.4) $3,850

* Preferred choice for action

Exhibit 18-6
Decision Tree Solution

ning of the fork. The preferred expected value for an act fork is marked by an asterisk, and this value appears at the beginning of its fork.

This approach tells us that we should order 350 books for the first semester. For the second, we should order 150 copies, less however many copies are left on hand. Thus, if we sell only 300 copies in the first term (probability of this event is 0.7), we should buy 100 copies for the second term. If we happen to sell all 350 copies, we should order only 150 additional books. In the first case, we will earn a total of $3,150, while the second will yield $3,500.

Applicability and Weaknesses

Statistical decision theory is potentially applicable in any situation where uncertainty is associated with future events. Thus, the preparation of the budgets for a firm should take into consideration at least several different states of nature. Traditionally, managers have not incorporated probability and expected value considerations into the budgeting process.

This exclusion can be traced to two major reasons: First, the managers simply may not understand how the theory is supposed to work. Second, even if the method is understood, it is very expensive (if not impossible) to produce dependable and meaningful measures of the probabilities. In some situations, sufficient past information may be available that will allow computation of fairly precise probabilities. Nonetheless, there is no real assurance that the past will repeat itself. In other, more frequently encountered business situations, the future represents an entirely new circumstance, and the manager must weigh the past record with subjective observations and intuitions. In either case, the probabilities are subject to large margins of error.

The reader may recall that we made a simplifying assumption that the decision maker would accept the expected monetary value of each event fork. Thus, for example, we would be led to conclude that he would be indifferent among these alternative acts:

Act	Event Payoffs	Probability	Expected Value
1	+$ 100	1.0	$100
2	+$ 500	0.6	$100
	−$ 500	0.4	
3	+$40,500	0.2	$100
	−$10,000	0.8	

His choice will depend on his *aversion* to risk. Many would prefer the *sure thing* of $100, while others might prefer to choose either of the riskier alternatives. Unless the statistical decision model incorporates this idea through the concept of *utility,* it may be an imperfect description of human behavior.

However, we must not equate imperfection with uselessness. Some attempt to only identify the various acts and events, and to place measures on their payoffs and probabilities will undoubtedly lead to better decisions. The management accountant of tomorrow must be ready and able to provide information of this nature to his manager.

NETWORK ANALYSIS

Chapters 11 and 12 brought out and demonstrated the point that budgets can serve to facilitate the coordination of the various activities of a firm. In many cases, however, a budget is inadequate for planning and coordinating the specific physical steps that must be taken to complete a project. We may learn from the budget how much each step will cost, but we still need to know how long it will take to complete a certain task and which tasks must be finished before other tasks can begin. For example, a budget may tell us how much we will have to spend to build a house, and we may even have an estimate from each subcontractor on his fee. However, we still need to know when to call in each crew to perform its special task. For example, we would not put the roof up until we had erected the walls. Some of the plumbing work should come before pouring the foundation, and some should follow. Of course, the carpeting should not be put down until every other task is completed. Network analysis could be used to coordinate this project.

Of course, men constructed houses before anyone ever thought of a network analysis. Even large projects, like the construction of the pyramids, great cathedrals, and the Panama Canal, were completed without the use of a network for planning. However, could they have been built more cheaply and quickly? Probably so, and we want to examine briefly this technique for managing large efforts. In particular, it is aimed at these two questions:

A. How long will it take to complete the project?

B. How can we shorten this time?

The Planning Steps

To accomplish a network analysis, we must perform the following steps:

1. Identify the *activities* (jobs) involved in completing the project.
2. Identify the *precedence relationships* among these activities (that is, in what order must they be completed?)
3. Estimate the *time* needed to complete each activity.
4. Construct a *network* symbolizing the results of 1, 2, and 3.
5. Find the *critical path* through the network.

There are several ways in which the *network* can be depicted. Perhaps the most common approach is to use circles (*nodes*) and arrows *(directed arcs),* where the former represent activities, and the latter symbolize the precedence relationships among the activities. A network of this type is called an *activity-on-node diagram.* [8]

The *critical path* through a network is the set of precedence related tasks that will use the greatest amount of time in completion. The anticipated completion time for the critical path is the shortest time in which the *entire*

---

[8] An alternative format represents a single event (such as, "begin installing kitchen cabinets") as a node, and the arrow represents not only precedence but also the completion time of the task. A network of this type is called simply an *arrow* diagram.

project can be finished. Thus, if we wish to shorten our estimated time to finish, we should concentrate on those particular tasks that lie on the critical path. Subtleties arise in that we may create *another* critical path as soon as we alter some of the completion times.

Before we prepare a sample network, we will have to analyze our project. While our preceding references have been to construction applications, the network can be used for any project that can be broken down into identifiable tasks. Exhibit 18-7 presents the necessary data for our analysis of the preparation of a budget for a small manufacturer.

Exhibit 18-7
Preparing the Budget

Activity	Immediately Preceding Activity	Activity Duration (in weeks)
1. Sales forecast	——	4
2. Sales budget	1	3
3. Production schedule	1	2
4. Materials budget	3	1
5. Labor budget	3	3
6. Overhead budget	3	4
7. Cash budget	2,4,5,6	2
8. Budgeted financial statements	7	2

The number in the second column identifies the activity that must be completed before the desired job can begin. Notice that nothing precedes the sales forecast, and that everything else follows it. With this information, we can undertake the construction of the network diagram. Exhibit 18-8 is the network representation of this budget preparation project.

We have selected the *activity-on-node approach,* as it is the simplest. The numbers within each circle (such as 5;3) identify the job number (5), and its duration (3 weeks). (We will explain the numbers in brackets shortly.)

How can we find the longest time path through the network? For a project of such a small size, we can simply identify every possible path through the network from node 1 to node 8. It is apparent that the following paths exist:

Path	Total Duration
1–2–7–8	11 weeks
1–3–4–7–8	11 weeks
1–3–5–7–8	13 weeks
1–3–6–7–8	14 weeks

Thus, we can observe that the five tasks symbolized by nodes 1, 3, 6, 7, and 8 lie on the critical path. The entire project cannot be completed in less than 14 weeks.

Clearly, this approach would be extremely difficult if there were to be thousands of jobs and paths. Fortunately, there is another algorithm for identifying the critical path, one which is amenable to computerization. Indeed, without the computer, this approach would be virtually impossible to use. It would take nearly as long to draw and analyze the project as it would to complete all the tasks.

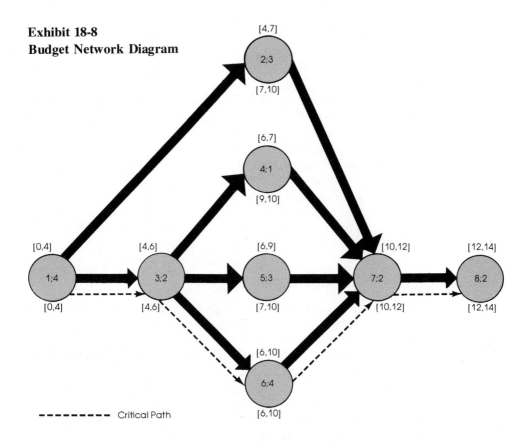

Exhibit 18-8
Budget Network Diagram

[4,7]
2;3
[7,10]

[6,7]
4;1
[9,10]

[0,4]
1;4
[0,4]

[4,6]
3;2
[4,6]

[6,9]
5;3
[7,10]

[10,12]
7;2
[10,12]

[12,14]
8;2
[12,14]

[6,10]
6;4
[6,10]

- - - - - - - - Critical Path

We can use the algorithm to produce useful management information. If we can identify the critical steps in the project, we can attempt to shorten the total completion time by hiring additional workers or acquiring additional equipment to work on those important phases. We also would want to assure that the supplies needed for these tasks are on hand when we need them. In the event that we can shorten the completion time of the critical path, we should perform another analysis in order to determine if there is another sequence through the network that will take longer, and thus become a new critical path.

A project manager must, of course, be concerned with those jobs that are not on the critical path. In particular, he may wish to temporarily assign workers to a critical task from one of the noncritical ones. Our analysis will tell him how long he can delay the completion of a noncritical step before he delays the entire project. In Exhibit 18-8, the numbers in brackets *above* each node represent the *early start* and *early finish* times (in terms of weeks from the beginning) for that activity. Thus, Job 2 cannot begin before 4 weeks have passed, and it cannot possibly be finished before the seventh week is over. Job 7 cannot begin until 10 weeks have passed. The *early finish* time for the last task is the *early finish* for the project. This information lets the manager know the earliest possible date at which work on a particular task can be begun.

The numbers in brackets *below* a node represent the *late start* and *late finish* times for that activity. The first number represents the latest possible time at which the task can be started without delaying the completion of the project. The second number is the latest possible time at which it can be finished without delaying the entire project.

The difference between the early and late start (or early and late finish) is a measure of the *slack* available to the manager for that particular activity. Thus, the manager could let Job 5 "slide" for a week before the project's completion is delayed. Notice that there is no difference between the early and late starts (or finishes) for the tasks on the critical path. The manager knows that any delay in starting or finishing one of them will delay the whole project.[9]

Two Approaches: PERT and CPM

Perhaps the two most popular and frequently used network approaches to project management are *PERT* and *CPM*. PERT was developed as a management aid for completing the Polaris missile project. Its name stands for *Project Evaluation and Review Technique*. CPM is quite similar to PERT. Its initials stand for *Critical Path Method*.

Probably the most significant difference between the two is their treatment of the job duration times. CPM takes the deterministic route, and assigns a particular *point estimate* to the amount of time it will take to complete each activity. PERT, on the other hand, takes the probabilistic route, and describes a probability distribution for the duration time. This approach causes us to use the *mean* of the distributions for the times associated with the activities. Additionally, it allows us to use the standard deviations of the distributions in making probability statements about the overall project completion time.[10]

CPM differs from PERT in that it allows consideration to be given to the relationship among the resources employed and the time needed to complete the project. That is, CPM is concerned with tradeoffs between time and costs.

Ideally, PERT is more appropriate for projects that occur only once (a research and development effort), while CPM is more often used for recurring projects (construction of apartment buildings). However, because of the practical problems associated with estimating three completion times for each project, the massive quantity of data, and the theoretical implications of

---

[9] More information on networks, their analysis, and their meaning, can be found in: Jerome D. Wiest and Ferdinand K. Levy, *A Management Guide to PERT/CPM* (Englewood Cliffs, N.J.: Prentice-Hall, 1970).

[10] PERT assumes a *beta distribution* of the activity times, which is assessed by estimating three parameters for each task:

t_o = optimistic completion time
t_m = most likely completion time
t_p = pessimistic completion time

The mean and standard deviation of the completion time for a task are computed by $(t_o + 4t_m + t_p)/6$ and $(t_o - t_p)/6$ respectively.

the use of the estimates, PERT is being applied more and more frequently with a single time estimate.[11] Similarly, there are practical problems in estimating the time-cost tradeoffs needed in CPM, and this feature is frequently deleted. Consequently, for most applications, PERT and CPM are essentially identical, and produce results much like we saw in our simple example above.[12]

The network analysis model is useful for project management if we can identify the jobs and predict their duration times. Because so much reliance is placed on what are really uncertainties, the network should be reviewed and revised almost constantly as the project progresses. This tool has been widely used in large-scale construction projects. Computer programs will allow the computation and presentation of event occurrence times in terms of calendar dates, and can take into consideration such things as weekends and holidays. This sophistication greatly increases the usefulness and applicability of the network.

INVENTORY MANAGEMENT MODELS

In Chapters 7 and 12, we emphasized the importance of properly managing inventories in not only retailing but also manufacturing firms. The importance derives from the mere size of inventories, as reflected in the current asset section of the balance sheet and the cost of goods sold item in the income statement. If inventory is managed improperly, losses through obsolescence, theft, spoilage, and shortages may mount up quickly. Because inventory is a non-interest earning item of working capital, prudence dictates keeping it at the lowest level consistent with meeting customer demands. On the other hand, if the inventory balance is kept too low, the firm may find itself with "rush" order problems with their added clerical and transportation expenses, and the loss of quantity discounts.

All of these problems can be consolidated into the following two questions:

A. How much should we order (or produce)?
B. When should we place an order (or start producing)?

Many of the problem factors described can be described in mathematical functions. Accordingly, models have been developed and used to assist the manager in answering these questions. We will now turn to a discussion of the simplest version of these models.

The Problem Factors

Without inventories, retailing and manufacturing firms could be viewed as *conduits* between suppliers and ultimate consumers. In order to avoid the

---

[11]For a more thorough discussion of the assumptions behind PERT, see: Elwood S. Buffa, Ed. *Readings in Production and Operations Management* (New York: Wiley, 1966), Chapter 30.
[12]Wiest and Levy, *PERT/CPM,* Chapter 8.

problems of specially ordering or producing goods, nearly all firms elect to stock up their inventories. Thus, the costs of having an inventory must be balanced against the benefits obtained (or the alternative costs that are avoided). The approach taken in most inventory models is to maximize the favorable gap between the benefits obtained and the costs incurred.

What costs are incurred? Among others, there are the costs of producing or acquiring the goods, of administering production or ordering, of holding an inventory, and of not having sufficient quantities to meet demand. Exhibit 18-9 classifies and summarizes these costs.

The relationships among the cost factors are important in terms of the *order quantity* (how much) decision. Basically, we would observe that, as the order quantity size *increased,* the holding costs would increase. On the other hand, with larger orders, we have to place them less often and the production setup or reordering costs would be less. Of course, as the quantity ordered *decreased,* the cost factors would behave in the opposite fashion.

Economic-Order-Quantity (EOQ)

These tradeoffs can be demonstrated more clearly through a simple inventory model, which is commonly referred to as the *economic-order-quantity* model. In order to begin our definition of the problem, we will make the following simplifying assumptions. We have a single product, and we know the annual demand for it. We feel that the costs of running out are so large as to cause us to consider them prohibitive. We also assume that we know how long it will take between placing the order and receiving the goods, called *lead time (L)*. While our example is expressed in a merchandising context, a manufacturing situation can be described by the same model if we assume that *no* output is available until *all* output is available.[13]

Exhibit 18-9
Inventory Costs

Production (reorder) costs
1. Production *setup* cost (or reorder *processing* cost)
2. Unit cost of items (labor, materials, overhead, purchase price, transportation, etc.)

Inventory holding costs
1. Storage space
2. Insurance
3. Property taxes
4. Obsolescence and/or spoilage
5. Opportunity costs (working capital unavailable for other production)
6. Handling and transfers

Costs of running out
1. Lost revenue from missed sales
2. Loss of goodwill (customer relations)
3. Costs of back order (extra production run, or special ordering)

[13] Clearly, every one of these assumptions is unrealistic. However, remember that our purpose is to demonstrate the general concept behind the model rather than show how it works under more realistic (and more complex) conditions.

The total cost that we are seeking to minimize thus consists of these three basic components: *reorder cost, holding cost,* and *unit cost.* Two other assumptions are necessary to describe the behavior of these factors:

1. The inventory holding cost is computed using the average inventory.
2. The acquisition or production cost per unit is constant (that is, there are no quantity discounts or economies of scale in the production process).

Before we examine these three components individually, we will establish the following notation:

$$S = \text{reorder cost per order}$$
$$I = \text{inventory holding cost per unit per year}$$
$$R = \text{total year's requirements (demand)}$$
$$C = \text{purchase cost per unit}$$
$$Q = \text{order quantity for each order}$$

The annual total reorder cost is found by multiplying the reorder cost per order *(S)* by the number of orders we place during the year. The number of orders we place during a year is computed by dividing the yearly demand *(R)* by the size of each order *(Q)*. Thus, the reorder cost for the year is $S(R/Q)$, and we observe that it will grow larger as Q gets smaller. We would expect this behavior because we would be ordering more frequently.

If we order Q units each time we order (and each shipment arrives just as we run out), then the average inventory will be $Q/2$, because we assume the demand occurs at the same rate throughout the year. Exhibit 18-10 is a graphic representation of the inventory level over time, and verifies this observation. From this point, we can go on to say that the yearly inventory holding cost is equal to $I(Q/2)$. Thus our holding cost is seen to increase as our average inventory level increases.

The total yearly purchase cost is equal to the quantity sold *(R)* multiplied by the unit cost *(C)*. This factor *(CR)* increases, of course, as the unit cost or the demand increases.

The *total* inventory cost is the sum of these three factors, as described by the following function:

$$\text{Total cost} = S(R/Q) + I(Q/2) + CR$$

Each of the factors and the total cost curve are shown in Exhibit 18-11. The total cost curve can be seen to be U-shaped, with the bottom part of the "U" representing the lowest total inventory cost. Our objective of minimizing total cost will be achieved if we can identify the reorder quantity Q^* that will put us at that lowest point.

There are two ways that we can solve for that quantity. First, if we draw the graph very carefully, we could find the Q^* by drawing a vertical line from the low point of the curve. Second, we could apply differential calculus, and take the first derivative of the total cost with respect to Q. We can set this expression equal to zero, and solve for Q^*:

Exhibit 18-10
Inventory Level Diagram

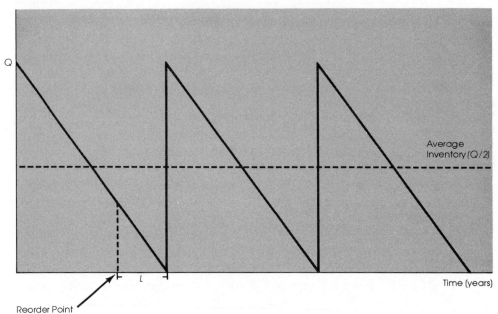

Inventory Level

Q

Average
Inventory (Q/2)

Reorder Point

L

Time (years)

Exhibit 18-11
Total Cost Curve

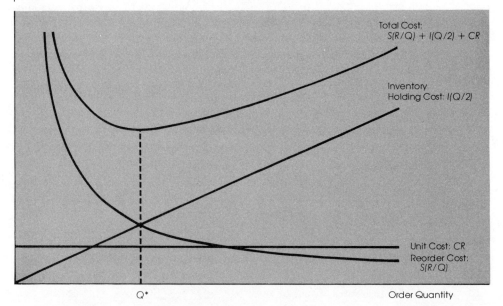

Cost
per Year

Total Cost:
$S(R/Q) + I(Q/2) + CR$

Inventory
Holding Cost: $I(Q/2)$

Unit Cost: CR
Reorder Cost:
$S(R/Q)$

Q^*

Order Quantity

$$\frac{d(\text{Total cost})}{dQ} = -\frac{SR}{Q^2} + \frac{I}{2}$$

$$-\frac{SR}{Q^{*2}} + \frac{I}{2} = 0$$

$$Q^{*2} = \frac{2SR}{I}$$

$$Q^* = \sqrt{\frac{2SR}{I}}$$

With this formula, we can answer the first question of *how much* should be ordered. Notice that the unit purchase cost does not affect our answer.[14]

To answer the *when* to order question, we have to turn our attention to the lead time between the placing of the order and its fulfillment. In this simple example, we would order at just the point in time where the inventory balance equals the number of units that will be demanded during the lead time. Thus, if the lead time is L years (which could be a fraction of a year), we will reorder when the inventory level reaches L times R. This approach is known as the *two-bin policy:* When the first bin is emptied, we place our order and use the second bin until the order arrives.

To deal with the uncertainties of lead time and irregularities in demand, firms carry an extra amount on hand (called a *safety stock*) to prevent any of the costs of being out-of-stock. These *stock-out* costs should be weighed against the carrying costs in order to arrive at the best level for the safety stock.

As we pointed out, the assumptions in this example are quite extreme, and the results of the analysis are not particularly useful for a real situation. However, we have demonstrated some of the fundamental elements of inventory management. As our assumptions become less restrictive and we deal with more complex situations (several products, several periods, uncertain demand, and lead times), our model becomes more sophisticated and descriptive.[15]

As a final comment, we must point out that it is very frequently inappropriate to isolate the inventory problems without considering the interactions

---

[14] In this special case, we can observe that the lowest point occurs where the holding cost line $(IQ/2)$ crosses the reorder cost line (SR/Q). By setting these two factors equal to each other, we can find the value for Q^* in terms of I, S, and $R:$

$$\frac{IQ^*}{2} = \frac{SR}{Q^*}$$

$$IQ^{*2} = 2SR$$

$$Q^{*2} = \frac{2SR}{I}$$

$$Q^* = \sqrt{\frac{2SR}{I}}$$

[15] The discussion on statistical decision theory described an inventory management problem under conditions of uncertain demand. *Simulations* have been used (applying Monte Carlo techniques) to deal with these uncertainties. For more information on other inventory models, see: Elwood S. Buffa and William H. Taubert. *Production-Inventory Systems: Planning and Control* (Homewood, Ill.: Richard D. Irwin, 1972).

with the rest of the firm. Most obviously, the production and inventory managers should not be allowed to operate independently because what is good for one (long production runs; low inventory levels), is not good for the other (high inventory levels; short production runs). As is true in so many cases, the entire firm must be evaluated as a system working toward a single, unified goal.

SUMMARY

This chapter has discussed the management decision process and the role that can be played by mathematical models in assisting the accomplishment of the organization's goals. The value of applying a mathematical model to a business situation comes from three sources:

1. A logical, systematic analysis of the problem.
2. A summary of the problem in a framework amenable for analysis.
3. A conclusion (arrived through solution of the model) that provides information about the problem.

In particular, we discussed *programming models* (including linear programming and transportation models), *statistical decision models, network analysis,* and *inventory management models.*

In addition to producing an optimal solution to the problem, a model may generate other useful information, especially through *sensitivity analysis.* Thus, if the actual values of the parameters in a problem are not known with certainty, we can solve the model several times with different values in order to see if a different strategy would be appropriate under different circumstances. If variation in a particular parameter produces variation in our apparently best decision, it becomes obvious that we are justified in putting out a significant effort to produce a valid estimate of that parameter.

The management decision process is a complicated one, and any device to improve its productivity is generally worth the cost. Mathematical methods have proven to be a useful tool in many cases, and have brought changes in the practices of management accountants. However, we are far from the stage where the models are sufficiently sophisticated to *replace* the mental skills of the successful manager.

QUESTIONS

1. What is the relationship between decision making and mathematical model building?
2. Identify the three steps of decision making.
3. Identify the four phases of problem definition.
4. How can mathematical analysis improve the management decision making process?
5. Define the term *linear programming.*
6. What is an *algorithm?*

7. What is meant by dimensional analysis? How does it aid you in mathematical model formulation?

8. What do you feel are the most critical assumptions behind the linear programming model?

9. What is the general type of problem the transportation model seeks to solve?

10. What are the basic elements of a statistical decision theory problem?

11. What is a *decision tree?*

12. Explain the *backward solution* method for solving a sequential decision problem under uncertainty.

13. How does *network analysis* aid in project management?

14. What is meant by the term *critical path* in network analysis?

15. Explain the following network terminology: early start time, early finish time, late start time, late finish time, and slack time.

16. What are the two basic questions of concern in inventory management?

17. What are three costs which are minimized in an inventory model?

18. What is the significance of safety stock in inventory management?

EXERCISES

E18–1 *Linear programming.* For the first LP example (page 000):

$$
\begin{aligned}
\text{Max} \quad R &= 4X_A + 3X_B + 5X_C \\
\text{Subject to:} \quad X_A + 2X_B + X_C &\leq 10 \\
2X_A + X_B + X_C &\leq 12 \\
X_A, \quad X_B, \quad X_C &\geq 0
\end{aligned}
$$

Show that the solution $X_A = 2, X_C = 8$ is a feasible solution, that is, it satisfies the constraints. What is the resulting profit? How does this compare with the solution indicated in the chapter?

E18–2 *Linear programming.* Assume the following data for the two products produced by Wagner Company:

	Product A	Product B
Raw material requirements (units)		
X	3	4
Y	7	2
Contribution margin per unit	$10	$4

If 300 units of raw material X and 400 units of raw material Y are available, what is the linear programming model for maximization of total contribution?

(AICPA Adapted)

E18–3 *Transportation model.* The solution for the transportation model in Exhibit 18-2 was indicated in the chapter. Suppose that instead of having 100 units of supply at Warehouse B, there are only 90. How would this change the solution to the problem? Why?

E18–4 *Transportation model.* Redraw Exhibit 18-2, to include a fourth market, North, which requires 25 units, with per unit shipping costs from Warehouse *A, B,* and *C* of $9, $7, and $4 respectively.

E18–5 *Statistical decision model.* In the bookstore example (page 528), we assumed that if the bookstore sells out, the students must go without books. Change the situation so that if the book supply is depleted, the bookstore will special order the book at an additional cost (absorbed by the store) of $2 per book. Recompute the payoffs of Exhibit 18-3 and find the best decision rule.

E18–6 *Statistical decision model.* If the probabilities for the second term in Exhibit 18-5 were switched (0.6 for 200 books and 0.4 for 150 books), how would the solution be changed?

E18-7 *Network analysis.* In Exhibit 18-8, if we shorten the activity time of activity 6 to 2 weeks, what is the new critical path and its completion time?

E18–8 *Network analysis.* For the budget preparation example in Exhibit 18-7, suppose that the overhead budget cannot be prepared until the materials and labor budgets are completed. Draw the network diagram for this revised problem and find the critical path. Leave all other aspects unchanged.

E18–9 *Inventory planning.* It is estimated that 1,125 units of an item will be required over the next 12 months. The costs of placing an order are $6, and the inventory holding cost per unit per year is $15. Find the optimum order quantity.

E18–10 *Inventory planning.* Find the minimum total annual inventory cost for E18-9, when the units cost $50 each.

PROBLEMS

P18–1 *Inventory planning.* The Robney Company is a restaurant supplier that sells a number of products to various restaurants in the area. One of their products is a special meat cutter with a disposable blade.

The blades are sold in packages of 12 blades for $20.00 per package. After a number of years, it has been determined that the demand for the replacement blades is at a constant rate of 2,000 packages per month. The packages cost the Robney Company $10.00 each from the manufacturer and require a three-day lead time from date of order to date of delivery. The ordering cost is $1.20 per order and the holding cost is 10 percent of the unit cost per year.

Robney is going to use the economic order quantity formula:

$$\text{EOQ} = \sqrt{\frac{2 \ (\text{Annual requirements} \times \text{Cost per order})}{\text{Holding cost}}}$$

Required:

Calculate:

a. The economic order quantity

b. The number of orders needed per year

c. The total cost of buying and carrying blades for the year

d. Assuming there is no reserve (safety stock) and that the present inventory level is 200 packages, when should the next order be placed? (Use 360 days equals one year.)

(CMA Adapted)

P18–2 Statistical decision model. Vendo, Inc., has been operating the concession stands at the University football stadium. The University has had successful football teams for many years; as a result the stadium is always full. The University is located in an area which suffers no rain during the football season. From time to time, Vendo has found itself very short of hot dogs and at other times it has many left. A review of the records of sales of the past five seasons revealed the following frequency of hot dogs sold.

Sales	Occurrences
10,000 hot dogs	5 times
20,000 hot dogs	10 times
30,000 hot dogs	20 times
40,000 hot dogs	15 times
Total	50 times

Hot dogs sell for $0.50 each and cost Vendo $0.30 each. Unsold hot dogs are given to a local orphanage without charge.

Required:

a. Assuming that only the four quantities listed were ever sold and that the occurrences were random events, prepare a payoff table (ignore income taxes) to represent the four possible strategies of ordering 10,000, 20,000, 30,000, or 40,000 hot dogs.

b. Using the expected value decision rule, determine the best strategy.

(CMA Adapted)

P18–3 Transportation model. Millson Corporation has three manufacturing plants that make their own unique product. The completed product is shipped to two regional warehouses for customer distribution. Warehouse 1 needs 50 units per week and Warehouse 2, 75 units per week. Plant 1 has a production capacity of 40 units per week with a variable manufacturing cost of $3 per unit. Plant 2 has a weekly capacity of 70 units and Plant 3, 60 units. The manufacturing costs per unit for Plants 2 and 3 are $1.50 and $2.00 respectively.

The unit costs of shipping are:

To warehouse	1	2
From plant		
1	$0.90	$1.30
2	1.10	1.20
3	1.00	0.85

Required:

Display the optimization problem for finding the least cost production-shipping schedule in a table (like the one seen in Exhibit 18-2).

P18–4 **Linear programming.** The Witchell Corporation manufactures and sells three grades, *A, B, C,* of a single wood product. Each grade must be processed through three phases—cutting, fitting, and finishing—before it is sold.

The following unit information is provided:

	A	*B*	*C*
Selling price	$10.00	$15.00	$20.00
Direct labor	5.00	6.00	9.00
Direct materials	0.70	0.70	1.00
Variable overhead	1.00	1.20	1.80
Fixed overhead	0.60	0.72	1.08
Materials requirements (in board feet)	7	7	10
Labor requirements (in hours)			
Cutting	3/6	3/6	4/6
Fitting	1/6	1/6	2/6
Finishing	1/6	2/6	3/6

Only 5,000 board-feet per week can be obtained. The Cutting department has 180 hours of labor available each week. The Fitting and Finishing departments each have 120 hours of labor available each week. No overtime is allowed.

Contract commitments require the company to make 50 units of *A* per week. In addition, company policy is to produce at least 50 additional units of *A,* 50 units of *B* and 50 units of *C* each week to actively remain in each of the three markets. Because of competition only 130 units of *C* can be sold each week.

Required:

Formulate and label the linear programming objective and constraint functions necessary to maximize the contribution margin.

(CMA Adapted)

P18–5 **Network analysis.** A construction company has contracted to complete a new building and has asked for assistance in analyzing the project. Using network analysis, the following has been developed:

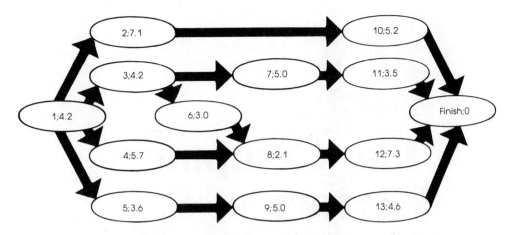

All nodes represent activities or processes that must be completed before the entire building will be completed.

Required:

a.   Find the critical path and the earliest project completion time.

b.   What is the slack time associated with activity or circle 2?

c.   What is the earliest time for reaching activity or circle 11? The latest?

(AICPA Adapted)

P18–6   Linear programming.   A company markets two products, Alpha and Gamma. The marginal contributions per gallon are $5 for Alpha and $4 for Gamma. Both products consist of two ingredients, D and K. Alpha contains 80 percent D and 20 percent K, while the proportions of the same ingredients in Gamma are 40 percent and 60 percent respectively. The current inventory is 16,000 gallons of D and 6,000 gallons of K. The only company producing D and K is on strike and will neither deliver nor produce them in the foreseeable future. The company wishes to know the numbers of gallons of Alpha and Gamma that it should produce with its present stock of raw materials.

Required:

Define the decision variables and formulate the objective function and constraints necessary to maximize the contribution margin.

(AICPA Adapted)

19

The Computer: Partner of Management

In several preceding chapters, brief descriptions of applications of computer technology to management accounting systems have been presented. This chapter provides a more detailed description of what a computer is, how it works, and how it can be used by managers. Clearly, it would not be possible to cover these topics completely in only one chapter. It is not our intent that the reader will become an expert in computing but rather that he will be prepared for further study, either in or out of a formal classroom.

Throughout this chapter, there is an emphasis on the *terminology* of computers to help bridge the communication gap between managers and computer experts.[1] We begin the chapter with a discussion of the characteristics of computing machinery *(hardware)*. This fairly long section is followed by brief introductions to computing languages and computer systems. The chapter closes with some comments on computer applications.

COMPUTERS IN GENERAL

Virtually everyone has a stereotype of what a computer looks like: gray metal, blinking lights, spinning wheels, and a long piece of paper spewing out. While some computer installations do present this kind of appearance, it is generally false when we consider all computers. The late 1960s witnessed miniaturization sufficient to produce very powerful computers of about the same size as a filing cabinet or home stereo. Many firms are marketing

[1] Perhaps no other field of study has developed such an intricate and completely new vocabulary as we see in computer science. The concepts of computing are new and the technology has been explosive in its ability to create new machines and techniques. These facts and the sense of humor of many experts have contributed to this new language.

highly specialized *microprocessors* that are literally small enough to fit in matchboxes.

Despite changes in size and appearance, computers today still operate in much the same way that they always have. The electronic fundamentals on which computers are built are relatively simple. Our technology has made utterly fantastic improvements in the means by which these fundamentals are applied.[2] Vast quantities of electronic circuits have been compressed and combined so that very few people actually understand how an entire machine works. It is ironic to observe that computer users cannot operate or repair one, computer engineers cannot operate or use one, and computer operators cannot repair or use one. It is not our intent in this discussion to describe the electronic workings of the computer and the other equipment. We intend only to provide enough information to allow the reader to recognize the various parts and their functions.

Components of a Computer

Basically, a *computer* is *a set of electronic and mechanical components that can perform a series of instructions very quickly and very accurately, without human intervention.* The conceptual center of a computer is called the *control* component. This part of the machine interprets the instructions and passes them along to the appropriate device for execution at the designated time.

The *arithmetic/logic* component is the place where most of the computer's operations are performed. Based on instructions from control, this unit finds numbers in storage, does things to them, and puts the new numbers in storage. Unfortunately, the use of the word *logic* in the title implies that the machine can "think through" a problem, like an electronic brain! In a sense, the machine *can* decide either "yes" or "no," but only in response to very carefully defined questions. It is not capable of doing anything it is not instructed to do.

Instructions, unprocessed data, and answers are kept in the *storage* component of the computer.[3] The computer user provides the instructions and data, which are converted into *binary code*. This code may be thought of as being composed of zeros and ones. Letters, numerals, and other symbols ($, ?, ., +, and the like) can be described in this binary code, and operated upon in accordance with the user's desires.

The user provides instructions and data to the storage component through the *input* component. There are numerous means of providing input, all of which have the common function of converting the user's code to the binary code of the computer.

The user receives answers (and some questions) through the *output* component of the computer. Upon receiving instructions from the control unit,

---

[2] It has been suggested that if comparable progress had been made in other industries, a three-bedroom home could be purchased for less than $0.05.

[3] For many years, the computer science term for storage was *memory*. To help eliminate the implication of intelligence, the more descriptive term *storage* has become preferred.

the output component takes the desired information from storage, translates it from binary form into the user's code, and makes it available to him. Thus, the user communicates with the computer only through translators.

Exhibit 19-1 presents a schematic diagram of the relationships among these components. Through input, the user notifies the control that he has something for the machine to do. The input channel is directed to accept the instructions and whatever other data are needed to carry out the task. The control and storage units work together to put this information where it can be found. The control unit finds the first instruction in storage and gives it to the arithmetic/logic section to execute. The instruction may require the acquisition of a data item from the storage section before it can be carried out. On the other hand, the instruction may be sent back to control for another action, such as (1) produce output, (2) provide more input, or (3) provide another instruction. When the output unit is to be used, the control component tells the storage unit to make the information available to output, and tells the output to translate it and make it available to the user. When both input and output have completed their tasks, they notify the control section of their availability for more work.

This discussion is, of course, extremely simplified, and expressed in humanistic terms. A computer should not be thought of as a *single* machine; it is really a *set* of machines, each of which is vitally important to the opera-

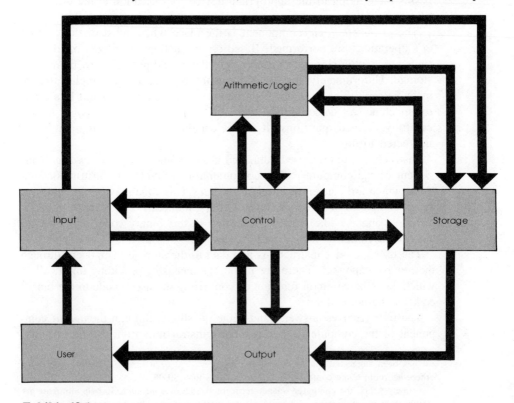

Exhibit 19-1

tion of the entire system. Each machine performs a specialized function which serves a purpose only in the context of the other machines. Furthermore, the computer does *only* and *exactly* what it is told to do by the user.

COMPUTER EQUIPMENT

A wide variety of devices has been developed to carry out the tasks of the various components of the computer. The following sections present brief descriptions of these devices that are intended only to acquaint the reader with their form and use.

Input

Input devices allow the user to communicate with the computer. In the early days of computing, the input process was very tedious and time consuming. The inefficiency did not matter because the computing process itself was very slow. As the speed of processing has increased, there has been a correlative need to improve input activities. The following paragraphs will show how this improvement has been manifested.

PUNCHED CARDS

Even those people who have not come into direct contact with computers are quite familiar with *computer cards*. These cards have mysterious little holes and an annoying admonition not to "staple, fold, or mutilate." Have you ever wondered what the computer does with these cards?

The position of the punched holes determines what the card means to the computer. The input device that processes the cards is called a *card reader.* The first punched card reader was invented in the last century by Herman Hollerith, and was used to tabulate data about the 1890 Census. For many years, a card was read by passing it between two sets of electrified "brushes." The presence of a hole allowed two of these brushes to touch and close an electrical circuit. Modern card readers utilize a bright light which shines on one side of the card. If a hole exists in a particular column, the light strikes a photoelectric cell which closes the circuit. Careful engineering results in these electronic "pulses" being translated into binary code, which the computer can "understand."

Too many varieties of punched cards exist to describe them completely in this chapter. The most common is the so-called *IBM card,* with 12 rows and 80 columns (see Exhibit 19-2). Its technical name is the *Hollerith card,* in recognition of the inventor.

Many firms notify their credit customers of the amount due by mailing punched cards to them. When returned, the card can receive additional holes to record the size of the payment remitted and then be processed by a card reader. This procedure eliminates several manual steps that could produce errors. If the card is damaged such that it has undesired holes or damaged edges, it cannot be processed without special treatment.

Exhibit 19-2
Hollerith Card

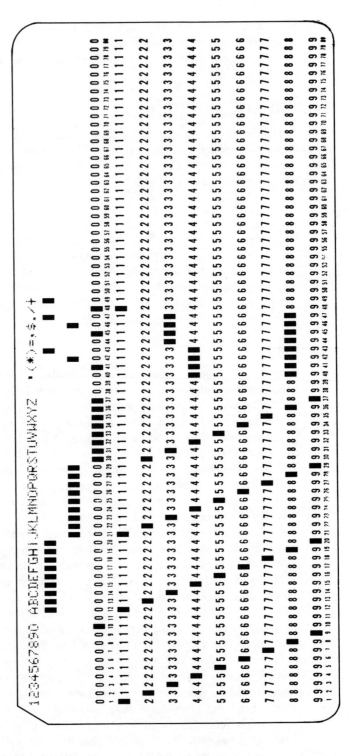

With the main exception of cards produced as output from the computer, most cards are processed *off-line* (by a machine not connected with a computer) using a *keypunch*. A keypunch is a very special typewriter that places the holes in the proper place on the card to get the desired instructions or data in a form that can be "sensed" by the computer.

Cards have been a popular medium for input because they are relatively cheap to produce and errors can be corrected relatively simply by removing the incorrect card from the deck and replacing it with a new one.

Several disadvantages make cards unacceptable in some circumstances. Once a card is punched, it cannot be used again, resulting in a high cost of wasted material. Also, the card must be processed by the card reader before the information can be used by the arithmetic component. Other input media avoid this intermediate step, with a savings in time. Additionally, because a deck of punched cards is bulky, it is awkward to handle, and consumes a great deal of storage space.

TAPES

Tapes are continuous media constructed of either paper or plastic. Some tapes are encoded with information by punched holes in a manner similar to that used for cards. One advantage of punched tape (usually paper) over cards is that virtually every available space is used. Even if a punched card has holes in only a few columns, all of it must be processed. On the other hand, items on a paper tape are separated by a special code, eliminating blanks, thus allowing the information to be processed more quickly. The same information also can be stored in a more compact physical space. Because the tape is continuous, there is no difficulty in keeping the information in the correct order. However, it is relatively difficult to correct an error on a tape without recopying it in entirety. Paper tapes are not as popular as punched cards, but they are especially useful in some situations.

We are all familiar with the appearance of *magnetic tapes (mag tape,* for short) from our use of cassettes, cartridges, or reel-to-reel devices at home or school. Of course, the tape itself is not magnetic. It is a continuous strip of plastic which is coated with a magnetizable compound. A magnetic field is imposed only on small sections of this substance by a *recording head,* which is really an electromagnet. The passage of the tape across a *reading head* generates an electric current which is amplified and processed by the computer or speakers. The tapes and *tape drives* used by computers are very precisely engineered to record a great deal of information in a very small space. The student should remember that computers work with binary digits *(bits)* to encode information. A spot on the magnetic tape receives one of two possible conditions, representing one or zero. The machines are so precise that literally hundreds of bits can be recorded on an inch of tape. For example, in only one minute a tape drive can read or record the same information that would be punched on a 30-foot high stack of cards.

Magnetic tape is an appropriate input device when a lot of information needs to be processed quickly by the computer. Most tapes are produced by computers as output, but many others are encoded by *key-to-tape* devices that are very similar to keypunches. Magnetic tapes are useful because they are relatively cheap, reliable, compact, and reusable. They are inefficient if there is only a small amount of information to be processed. Magnetic tapes are used most frequently for storage.

OPTICAL CHARACTER READERS (OCR)

Devices have been developed to interpret written or printed matter directly into computer code. Wide-scale use has been encouraged by the development of uniform symbols. Ideally, optical reading devices eliminate intermediate steps in converting data from a legible format to one that can be used by the computer. We can expect even more dramatic improvement in OCRs in the future.

MAGNETIC INK CHARACTER RECOGNITION (MICR)

Nearly everyone is familiar with the unusually shaped numbers (such as those seen below) that are found across the bottom of blank checks. These numbers are printed in a special ink that contains a magnetic substance. When the check moves across a reading head, the legible number is interpreted by the reader. The numbers on the checks are recorded on a magnetic tape, which in turn is processed by the bank's computer to update the balance in the customer's account. Using a special machine, the checks are sorted by account number so that they can be distributed in the monthly bank statements. Deposited checks can be quickly processed to determine what is due to the bank from other banks. These jobs could be performed by human clerks, but only with a great deal of tedium, time, and error. Most MICR applications have been in banking.

⑈1240⑈0222⑈ 65 120038 5⑈

REMOTE TERMINALS

Input, or user access, to computing facilities was revolutionized by the development of devices which allow communication of information to and from computers over relatively great distances (generally via telephone lines). Some of these *terminals* are designed for very specialized input applications, whereas others can be used for both *input and output (I/O).*

Input terminals have found a great deal of use in cost accounting systems. For example, a workman at a lathe may insert a unique identification card in the terminal and punch in the number of the job on which he is about to begin work. When he finishes, he hits the appropriate key on the terminal, and the computer has sufficient data for payroll accounting, job costing, and even planning maintenance on the shop equipment. Other applications involve the monitoring of production through sensors. For example, with the aid of a large number of remote terminals, it becomes possible for only a few men to operate a large refinery or chemical plant.

Terminals that can be used for both input and output visually resemble typewriters. The user enters data or program instructions through the keyboard. The output might be produced nearly instantaneously right before his eyes, or even at another location for someone else. Other (and presently more expensive) terminals utilize a *cathode ray tube* (CRT) rather than ink and paper. CRT, of course, is simply another name for a television picture tube. The information entered on the keyboard appears on the tube, as well as any responses from the computer. While they are more expensive, CRT terminals operate more quietly and quickly than printing terminals, and allow the presentation of output using pictures, or *graphics*. As a disadvantage, once the image is gone from the tube, it is effectively lost forever unless a *hard copy* (on paper) is made. It is reasonable to expect that most future terminals will utilize CRTs.

A third class of terminals, known generically and somewhat humorously as *intelligent terminals,* are programmable. In effect, they are small computers which can perform routine operations without requiring the attention of the main computer. This capability speeds responses and allows the utilization of many more terminals than might otherwise be handled. One major automobile rental company utilizes a computer system based on intelligent terminals. Many new cash registers are essentially intelligent terminals which not only perform routine calculations but also update inventory and sales records.

Computer Storage

We will turn now to a brief description of the devices and media that have been utilized by computer users and producers to provide storage capability. The usefulness of a certain device not only depends on its cost but also such variables as the frequency of access, the amount of data needed, the desired timeliness of the data, and the interval between the time the information is *desired* and the time it is *needed*. Programming needs may thus cause one device to be more desirable than another.

CARDS

Information to be used by a computer may be stored on cards. A box of punched cards can contain a great deal of information, but getting to it can pose a problem. Clearly, the response time between request and accomplished access is quite long. The box must be physically located, loaded in a reader, processed, and the information searched by the computer to find the needed item. Such a long interval makes cards unacceptable for most storage applications, although they are relatively inexpensive.

We may find data stored on *magnetic cards,* which are really shorter and stiffer versions of magnetic tape. Several ingenious machines have been developed which enable an item of information on a magnetic card to be found and made available within a relatively short period of time (one to five seconds). To find the item, it is necessary that the computer have an *index* to its *address*.

The address is a symbol for the location of the information, in much the same sense that each of us has an address where we can be found.[4] If the index is appropriately structured, and the device appropriately designed, we may be able to go directly to the address and get the needed information. Such an arrangement is called *direct* or *random access,* and typically involves a great deal of programming and an expensive machine. On the other hand, the address may start our search only in a particular area, and the machine must go through the equivalent of a door-to-door hunting trip. Such an arrangement is called *sequential* access because each address must be searched in order until we come up with the right one. As a compromise, we find the *indexed sequential* file, which involves an index that starts our search in a relatively smaller area of storage. A magnetic card storage device is usually employed with an indexed sequential file arrangement.

Such devices are much slower than random access machines, but still quite adequate for the majority of business applications. The slowness is counteracted by an immensely large data capacity, a relatively low cost, and a more than reasonable level of mechanical reliability.

DISKS AND DRUMS

Two very popular random access storage devices are high speed disks and drums. Both utilize a metal surface coated with a magnetizable substance. A disk has its flat surfaces coated, and spins about its axis (like a phonograph record) at several thousand revolutions per minute. A drum is a cylinder, with its outer surface covered with the magnetizable material. It is also spun about its central axis at a very high speed. Information is recorded on or read from these devices using a writing and reading head. The fastest disks and drums have a head for each track, whereas others have heads that must be centered over the desired track. Exhibit 19-3 presents schematic diagrams of these devices.

Disks and drums are appropriate storage media because of the extreme speed with which the desired data can be found and transferred to the computer. As a result of the need for careful and complex construction, these

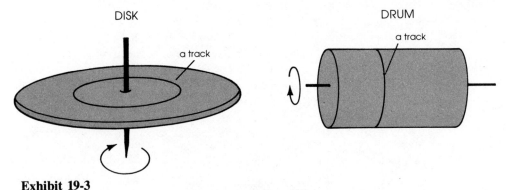

DISK   DRUM

a track   a track

Exhibit 19-3

[4]Of course, there are many times when we cannot be found there. But we possess a freedom of movement that computer information does not.

devices are relatively expensive. Although drums are used almost exclusively for on-line storage, some disks can be removed from the drive and stored on a shelf, like tape. These *disk packs* can be transferred from one location to another, or simply stored until needed. If the information is not used frequently, it is cheaper to utilize a tape for off-line storage.

CORES

Core storage is the fastest, but most expensive, storage medium in common use. It employs thousands of very small doughnut-shaped ferrite *cores*. A core is magnetized in one of two known directions when the appropriate amount of voltage is sent through wires that pass through the middle of it. Many, many of these small rings can be placed in a small space. Because the wiring is so intricate and expensive, core storage is impractical for wide-scale use. Consequently, most computers have only a limited amount of core storage which is exclusively utilized for executing programs. Unused data or instructions are temporarily stored on disks or drums until they are needed. The control component of the machine is carefully programmed to handle these problems, with the result that nearly all users of computers do not have to consider where their data and programs are stored.

The amount of core storage is such a critical factor in determining the capabilities of a machine that its core capacity is frequently included in its description. For example, a computer may be described as a "16K machine," indicating that it has a capacity for storing 16,000 computer words.

SOME EXPERIMENTAL MEDIA

The near future may see the introduction of new storage devices that will expand the capabilities of computers or make them more economical to operate. These may be variations on old versions (such as "floppy" disks) or utilize completely new concepts (thin film, integrated microcircuits, and lasers have been successfully used in experimental situations). Whatever the form, they will continue to meet the storage function that is so essential for the effective use of a computer.

Computer Output

Many of the devices listed under input and storage may do "double duty" as output media as well. The output function is to take the data from the machine and put them into a format suitable for further use, which may be more computer processing or interpretation by people.

Punched cards may be simultaneously printed with written information. This process is generally used in preparing customer billings. On other occasions, data may be output onto tapes, disks, or drums, and processed by another computer into legible copy. This procedure frees the main computer for more computations and leads to a more efficient use of resources.

PRINTERS

Most information that will be used by people is printed on paper by *printers*. Some printers can produce thousands of lines of output each minute, but most are much slower than that. The user may program the computer to produce the page and column headings, or he may elect to choose more attractive preprinted forms. The use of the latter requires careful design of a *format* to be certain that the correct information is typed in the correct place.

Printers have been used to prepare such various items as: bank statements, customer billings, checks, financial statements, advertising letters, mailing labels, and management reports. The computer user must determine not only the content and format of the report but also its timing and distribution. Care must be exercised to be certain that only people who use a report receive it, and that it is received soon enough to enable the recipients to do something with the information. Unfortunately, many users have misused the computer by producing too many copies. While the additional time consumed producing an additional copy is very low, the machine in the meantime is unavailable for other, perhaps more important, work.

GRAPHICS

One of the fastest growing applications of computer technology is the use of the machine to produce pictures. These *graphic* displays may be line or bar graphs, charts, or even pictures. Experimental work has produced animated simulations of motion. Graphics open up a very wide and nearly unlimited range of applications. Of particular interest is the use of a graphic display of architectural drawings of a building project. There have been extremely successful simulations of landing aircraft on carriers at sea.

Originally, graphic output was produced through slow and tedious *plotters*, which were operated off-line, using a magnetic or paper tape produced by the computer. Many applications now make use of CRTs, which enable the users to see the output more quickly. Some CRT terminals are *interactive*, which means that the user may enter input data to change the display, and see the results almost immediately. At the present, business applications of graphics are largely undeveloped.

OTHER FORMS

Other forms of output are growing in popularity, and new ones are being developed. One of the most promising involves *microfilm,* called *Computer Output Microfilm* (COM). The output data can be recorded much more quickly on the microfilm than it can be printed on paper. The microfilm can be loaded in a special printer that produces electrostatic copies at a very high rate. If the report is not needed immediately, or if a copy must be stored, the reel of microfilm takes up nearly negligible space in comparison to the bulky printed pages. Before the development of COM, microfilming followed printing, and was a much more expensive process.

An innovation that seems to have a great deal of potential involves the translation of computer output into *audible* tones. For example, a salesman may wish to know the number of units of a particular item in an inventory. With a special terminal, he can enter his request through the keyboard, and receive the response from a small speaker. The advantage of this arrangement lies in the simplicity of the output mechanism.

LANGUAGES AND SOFTWARE

We saw in the preceding section that input devices accept information from computer users. This information may include data to be operated upon, or it may include *programs.* A program is simply *a set of instructions that are to be executed by the computer.* Whereas the machinery of the computer is called *hardware,* the programs that a computer executes are called *software.*

Programs are written in many different *languages,* each of which is composed of a unique and precise set of rules regarding the meaning of symbols and groups of symbols. The rules specify not only the kinds of symbols and combinations of symbols that can be used, but also the relationship among the symbols and their context. In the following sections, we describe and contrast four major kinds of computer languages: machine, assembly, compiler, and user.

Machine Languages

Every computer program is eventually translated into instructions written in a so-called *machine language* before it is executed. A machine language utilizes *only* numbers, and is virtually unintelligible to anyone who is not a programming expert. In the early days of the computer, all programming was done in machine language because of the relatively primitive machines.

Machine language is said to be *machine dependent,* which means that one instruction must be provided for every action to be taken by the computer. Also, we say that a machine language is a *low level* language, which means that there is little or no relationship between it and a human language. Machine languages are also nonuniversal, in that different sizes and models of computers do not use the same language.

An example of a very simple machine language instruction would be: 130127. The 13 in the first two positions might mean *add.* The last four numbers, 0127, would specify the storage location or *address,* of the number that is to be added. The instruction tells the arithmetic/logic component that the number in location 0127 is to be added to a number that appears in a *register.* Other instructions might include the other arithmetic operations, "loading" the contents of an address in the register, "storing" the contents of the register in an addressed location, or "branching" to another instruction.

Normally, the instructions are executed sequentially. However, the programmer may wish a certain sequence of instructions to be executed only when special circumstances arise. The departure from the normal path is called *branching*. For example, we might want to compute service charges on past due accounts. We would instruct the computer to "decide" if a particular account was overdue. We would have to define our decision criterion very precisely, or the machine could not give us an answer. In this case, if today's date (which would be a *number*) is more than 30 larger than the number representing the date of purchase, then the bill might be past-due, and we could have the machine execute a series of instructions to compute the service charge. The *only* decisions that a computer can make are these: "is the number in the register *less* than, *greater* than, or *equal* to zero?" We frequently hear or read that a computer "says" that the weather will be cold, or that a computer "decided" to order 1,000 items for the inventory. These so-called "decisions" are really only the combined result of a number of very simple "yes" or "no" decisions, all of which are precisely defined in advanced by the programmer. The machine's ability to process a lot of data very quickly, our willingness to give it human characteristics, and the desire for brevity cause us and allow us to say the computer "decides." We must never fall into the trap of really believing that it does.

One more point is essential before going on. Even a machine language program must be translated into *binary digits* before it can be executed. If the instruction 130127 were to be translated into *bits* (assuming it is expressed originally in *octal*, or base eight, numbers), it would be 001011000001010111. Of course, it would be virtually impossible for a human being to work with such long numbers. We can rely upon the input device (hardware) to translate the instruction into binary form.

Assembly Languages

Assembly languages represent the next step up the ladder of complexity. They are at a *higher level* than machine languages, but they are certainly not the highest. They are still machine dependent, in that an instruction in assembly language must be written for each operation to be performed. Assembly language differs from machine language in that the programmer uses symbols other than numbers to represent operations and storage addresses. For example, the statement "ADD X" might instruct the computer to add the contents of memory location "X" to whatever was in the register. "STR X1" might tell the machine to store the contents of the register in location "X1".

Before we get too far, it must be pointed out that a computer can execute only those programs that are written in machine language in binary digits. How do we get from assembly language to machine language? The hardware can not do it; but more *software* can. A program written in assembly language is translated, or *assembled*, through the use of another, larger program called an *assembler*. In very simple terms, the assembler takes each statement in the assembly language program and converts it to the appropriate machine language instruction, on a one-for-one basis. Then, the machine language program is executed, and the desired information is printed or otherwise made available to the user. To the user, it appears that he provided a set of instructions in assembly language and data to the computer, and received his output. This diagram shows what he might think:

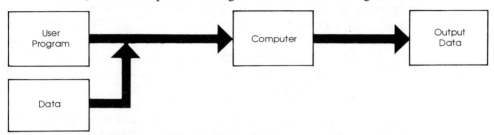

Actually, the process should be diagrammed this way:

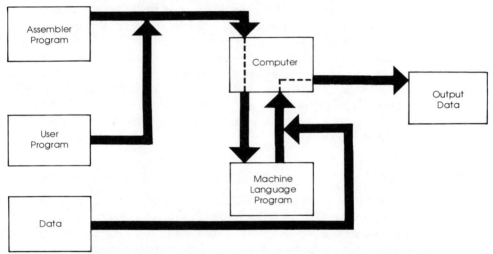

In effect, the user program is *data* for the assembler, which produces the machine language (or *object*) program as its output. The user's data are operated upon by the computer in accordance with the machine language program, and produces the desired output. Unless special instructions are given, the machine language program is never seen by the user, which is fine because he probably would not be able to understand it.

Compiler Languages

In most business and accounting applications, neither machine nor assembler languages are used by the programmer. Instead, he uses a *compiler* language, which is at a higher level than the other two. Some compiler languages are mostly mathematical in structure (such as APL and FORTRAN) while others are highly verbal (such as COBOL). One compiler language that has a little of each (BASIC) has grown immensely in popularity since the late 1960s. It is very likely that you will receive instruction in the use of BASIC before you graduate. Compiler languages are more universal than assembly languages or machine languages. Thus, if BASIC is learned on one type of computer, the programmer will be able to use it on virtually any other machine that has a BASIC compiler. The compiler program itself will differ from machine to machine because it must produce an object program in the language of the particular machine on which it is run.

A compiler language program is *machine independent,* which means that a single instruction will cause *one or more machine instructions* to be executed. This characteristic frees the programmer from a substantial amount of detail work, and allows him to prepare extremely complex programs with relatively few instructions.

The compiler language (or *source*) program is translated by a *compiler program* in essentially the same manner as an assembly language program is translated by the assembler. Because the compiler language is of a higher level, the *compiler program* is extremely complicated and rather expensive to produce. However, without the compiler, it would be necessary to train your programmer more extensively, which is also quite expensive.

The *compiling* of the source program is relatively slow in comparison to the *assembling* of an assembly language program because of the greater complexity of the process. However, the difference can be measured in a matter of a few seconds and is insignificant for humans. Of course, the object (machine language) program may be stored for later use, either on-line or off-line. This procedure eliminates the need for future compiling and saves some of the lost time.

User Languages

The late 1960s and the early 1970s saw the introduction and propagation of *data management systems.* The function of these systems is to facilitate the collection, storage, updating, and dispensing of data. A prime example of a successful data management system is the airline reservation system that allows the telephone customer to obtain confirmed seating on virtually any flight, and even to request special meals or surface transportation at his destination.

This particular system is remarkable not only because of its success and complexity, but also because it operates in the *on-line* mode. Thus, when a customer makes a reservation, that particular flight is updated to show one less seat available for future requests. The opposite of the *on-line* is the *batch* mode. Under this approach, requests for flights would be accumulated over a period of time and then processed in a group (or *batch*). This approach would not allow the confirmation of a reservation until a point substantially after the telephone request was made, and would introduce the problem of having to assign priorities to requests for the same flight when there are more of them than there are seats.

The airline reservation system is also an example of a *real-time* system. The customer receives his information within a short enough period of time to make a decision. The length of time that constitutes *real time* depends on the situation. The airline customer may be able to wait thirty seconds for a reply, whereas the pilot of an airplane or a moon-landing vehicle may need the response to his request for his altitude within a split second. On the other hand, an inventory manager may be able to wait hours, days, or even weeks before he has to decide whether to restock a particular item. Consequently, the designer of the data management system must know what the objective of the system is before he decides what its capabilities will be.

Data management systems generally utilize a unique, very high level language to enter the requests or to update the files of information. In many cases, a *user language* statement must be translated to a compiler language statement or statements, which in turn must be translated by the compiler program into machine language before the computer can execute the instructions and provide for the user's needs. It should be apparent that a user language system is the most expensive to implement, but it is the most efficient in terms of reducing training efforts. A large volume of usage can cause the savings to exceed the additional costs, and thus make the system economically feasible.

It is reasonable to expect that the costs of user oriented data management systems will be driven down in the future, with the result that they will become quite common not only in businesses but also in homes. Any further decreases in hardware costs will only accelerate this trend.

Flowcharting

A *flowchart* is useful in computer applications because it describes to the programmer what the computer program is to accomplish. The programmer utilizes a flowchart to design the program before he ever writes a statement in a programming language. Finally, after the program has been written, tested, and implemented, it is summarized in a flowchart to describe how it works.

In simplest terms, a flowchart is a systematically prepared diagram of the relationships among several activities. An activity is symbolized by a box, and relationships between two activities are shown by an arrow emanating from the first and entering the second. If an activity leads to one of several alternative activities, we have to show how the decision among them is made.

A flowchart is said to be *macro* if it does not describe many of the details of the program. It is called *micro* if it is more detailed. The flowchart in Exhibit 19-4 is a macro representation of a day in the life of a typical breadwinner. Major activities are shown in rectangular boxes and decisions are shown as diamonds. Notice that the activity boxes may have more than one entering arrow, but only one exit arrow. A decision must have more than one arrow emanating from it. Notice that each decision is very simple, and involves only one criterion. The activity of going to work results only if we answer "no" to both questions.

Exhibit 19-5 illustrates a typical situation faced by a firm that maintains accounts receivable. In this particular case, the customer gets a discount if he pays early, or incurs a penalty if he pays late. If the amount paid by the customer does not match the amount owed, then either a refund or an overdue notice will be prepared and sent. In converting this flowchart into

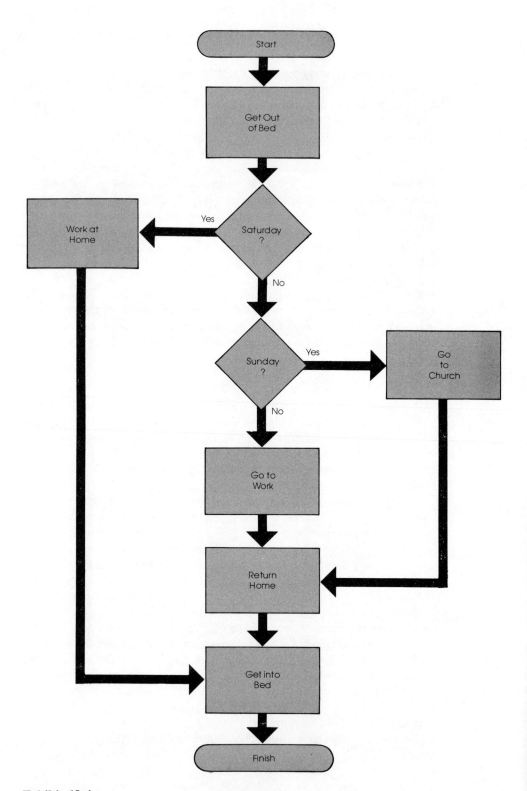

Exhibit 19-4

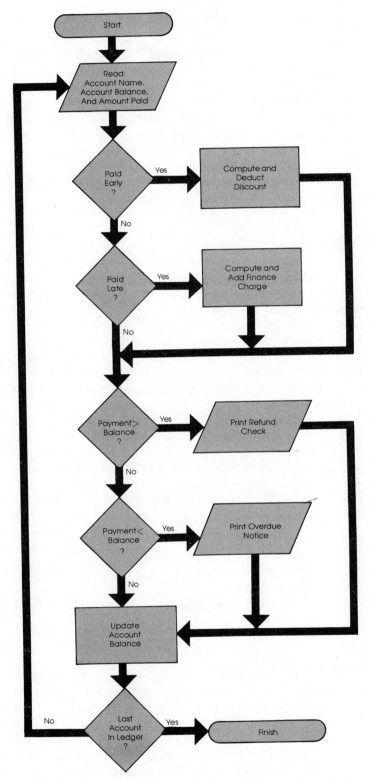

Exhibit 19-5

a computer program, numerous instructions will be required to determine the timing status of the payment, and the gathering of the data for the checks and overdue notices. The last step of the chart represents the repetition of the procedures for each customer.

There exist numerous sources for additional information about flowcharting, especially in computer applications. Flowcharts are also used to describe the movements of documents or material from one process to another. Auditors have found this approach to be useful in analyzing an existing system for weaknesses or redundancies. The interested student should consult his library for more information on this subject.

Documentation

An item concerning computer accounting systems that unfortunately receives little or no attention is the *documentation*. This neglect can be costly when a manager finds himself with a malfunctioning program but no programmer. Or a programmer may find it next to impossible to remember what he was trying to do in the two-year-old program that has developed a new defect, or *bug*. Documentation is a written and diagrammatic description of what a particular program or group of programs is supposed to accomplish. The complexity of the documentation should vary directly with the complexity of the project. It is not uncommon to find a large system described in several *tens* of volumes.

The documentation must describe not only the way the system or program operates but also how it can be implemented and what the output means. It may be presented in several tiers of detail, beginning with a broad statement of the system's objectives and macro flowchart. This section may reference other sections where more detail is available, which in turn may reference still other more detailed information. For example, we may find the following headings in the documentation of an accounting system:

        Basic purpose of the system
          The balance sheet accounts
            Managing current assets
              Controlling receivables
                Customer accounts
                  Billings
                  Receipts, normal
                  Receipts, past-due

Each successive tier should have an appropriately constructed flowchart and description of the inputs, outputs, and processes that occur in that area. Care should be taken to leave out none of the details, because it is in the details that the bugs appear.

To acquire a software package (whether a simple program, a compiler, or an entire data management system) without also acquiring the complete documentation would make as much sense as buying the software without having any hardware. The documentation should be studied carefully and completely before acquiring or implementing any type of software. To fail to do so is to flirt with disaster.

COMPUTER SYSTEMS

A wide variety of alternatives are available to the management accountant seeking the advantages of electronic data processing (EDP). We cannot hope to even begin to provide sufficient data here for choosing among them. Expert guidance should be sought before the choice is made. Major accounting and management consulting firms provide this service. Computer manufacturers usually do not charge anything specifically for a feasibility study, but the salesman's opinions can hardly be considered objective. There are four basic alternatives open to today's manager.

Service Bureaus

Even the smallest businessman can obtain EDP capabilities through a *service bureau*. This type of firm provides computer processing for its clientele, including such services as data pickup and preparation, processing, file maintenance, customer billing, and report generation. A service bureau may be a fulltime operation run by a small or a large firm, or it may be simply a sideline of a firm that owns a computer but lacks sufficient internal workload to utilize it fully.

This approach relieves the businessman of the need to acquire a computer or to learn very much about programming. It entails a risk in at least two ways: Valuable information is turned over to an outsider, and the failure of the bureau to survive may leave the client with no system at all. The history of service bureaus shows that this second risk is not minor.

Time Sharing

A variation of the service bureau approach is the *time-sharing* computer operation. Under this arrangement, many users can be connected to a single computer through local and long-distance telephone circuits. Because of the machine's ability to perform operations in microseconds,[5] or even less, each user may have his program executed within a matter of moments. Because of the transmission costs, a time-sharing arrangement is not desirable for an accounting system with lengthy input or output needs. Time sharing is highly suitable for the use of specialized programs for various types of analyses. Managers can use these programs to prepare analyses that we discussed in earlier chapters, involving such things as present values, cost-volume-profit relationships, alternative depreciation schemes, or cash budgeting.

[5] A microsecond is one-millionth of a second. A beam of light will move only 980 feet in one microsecond. Some machines can execute an instruction in several *nanoseconds,* one of which is one-billionth of a second. There are as many nanoseconds in one second as there are seconds in 32 years!

Flexibility is added with this system because the manager can choose to prepare and run his own program or to use a program available in the software package offered by the computer company. While it consumes more time, the former choice provides the manager the assurance of being familiar with the source of his information.

Time sharing has an additional disadvantage in the limited scope of its output capabilities. Unless the user is prepared to install a high speed printer (annual rental costs may run to several thousands of dollars), or wait several days to receive mailed output, he has to be content with the very slow but steady output rate of his terminal. The delay is costly in terms of the executive's time and the long-distance transmission charges.

Minicomputers

A new technology was born in the 1960s and boomed in the 1970s. Specifically, firms began to manufacture computers that do not consume as much space, energy, or money as larger machines.[6] Furthermore, the smallness factor allowed the computer user to design his system in *modules,* or sections. He could start out small and expand his hardware as his needs grew. Before this development, it was necessary for him either to buy a large machine and hope he would grow into it, or to buy a small machine and replace it with a larger one if he grew. This latter strategy could result in serious and expensive problems of software and data file compatability.

Peripheral equipment (such as tape and disk drives) available for use with minicomputers can greatly enhance their usefulness for managers of both small and large businesses. Many firms have found it more useful to buy several small computers, especially when their divisions are geographically dispersed. Such an arrangement tends to reduce the likelihood of catastrophic hardware failures, and helps avoid the organizational problems that have been experienced when a centralized data processing office has total responsibility for management information.

Multiprocessors and Others

One of the offshoots of the Space Age was the extremely large computer. Actually, several computers are combined to produce what is known as a *multiprocessor.* At the heart of the system is one extremely fast and powerful machine, called a *central processing unit* (CPU). It is surrounded in fact and in concept by a number of smaller machines. The only way that the CPU communicates with the user is through one of these *peripheral processors.* They perform no computations other than loading data and instructions into the CPU and receiving output from it. One of the peripheral processors has the specialized task of controlling all the others.

---

[6] Common practice dubbed these smaller machines *minicomputers.* Manufacturers of larger machines entered the market later and seeking to lend more dignity to their products, created the term *small computer.*

Multiprocessors are extremely rare, and are generally found only in universities, multinational corporations, and government agencies. Even in these cases, it is occasionally necessary to sell "time" to other users in order to utilize the full capabilities of the system.

Of course, there are machines that fit in the category between minicomputers and multiprocessors. They have some of the characteristics of each and range in cost from several tens of thousands of dollars to several million. So many varieties now exist that any firm can select the computer that it needs.

Some Ideas about Obsolescense

It is frequently seen in computer trade journals that certain machines or techniques have been made *obsolete* by the introduction of new machines or practices. The businessman must resist the temptation to immediately scrap his present system and get a new one. Computers are simply too expensive to change without substantial evidence that a cheaper alternative exists.

Frequently, the basic difference between the old and the new is a matter of time. It may be significant that one machine can do a task in a day that another one can do in three days. There is less significance if one can perform a job in an hour and the other in 5 minutes. While there is a large *ratio* measure of the difference (12 to 1), there is really only a very small *real* difference (55 minutes). In all but a few special cases, the fact that a new machine is faster than an old one does not make the latter unsuitable for its purposes. The businessman must not confuse technical advancement with practical inadequacy. The term *obsolescence* should be used only when the presently used system cannot perform its task as cheaply as a new one. Above all, the manager must resist any feelings of being out-of-date or behind-the-times that may be generated by salesmen or competitors that have shiny new equipment.

USING THE COMPUTER IN BUSINESS

Now that we have examined the computer and its components, it is important that we turn to the uses of the computer. Before deciding to acquire a computer, the manager should plan ahead to see how profits can be affected by the machine.

Many popular magazine and newspaper articles would have us believe that the major benefit to be obtained from a computer comes from eliminating numerous clerks and their ledgers and adding machines. Of course, this image is oversimplified and even misleading. The installation of a computer frequently *increases* the payroll expense. The clerks' jobs are only *changed,* not eliminated, and high priced specialists have to be hired to program, operate, and repair the computer. If this is a likely result, why would a manager go ahead with the installation?

In a word, the answer is *information*. If it is programmed and used correctly, the computer can process reports more quickly than a manual system, thus allowing decisions to be made sooner. Because of the dependability of its circuitry, the reports also are prepared more *accurately*. Furthermore, through its speed and capacity of data storage and processing, the computer can make available *new types* of information that simply cannot be prepared with a manual system. The following sections briefly describe some applications of computer technology to business management.

Bookkeeping and Accounting

Recordkeeping procedures are especially adaptable to computerization. They are characterized by frequent repetitions of a series of simple steps of recording, classifying, and copying, with a few noncomplex computations. Many of the early business applications of computers involved a simple transfer of these tasks from humans to the machine, with no changes. The machine can even be programmed to notify the manager when it is unable to process an unusual transaction, much in the same way that a clerk will turn to his supervisor to solve a nonroutine problem.

It is apparent that the computer can do much more in accounting than replace an existing system. Even a relatively slow machine, working at the rate of one operation per millisecond (0.001 seconds) could perform the entire bookkeeping function for a medium-size firm for a month in only a few hours. The quest was, has been, and will continue to be, to find new, profitable applications.

Some large firms have discovered that the computer will enable the consolidation of a number of geographically dispersed accounting offices. For example, one computer may be used to prepare payroll checks for all the employees of a firm with many local offices more quickly and with fewer errors than the individual branches could manage on their own.

Similarly, some firms have centralized their procedures for disbursing cash, so that all checks are drawn on one account. Consequently, the total cash balance of the firm is much less than might be required if 20, 50, or 200 branch offices had to maintain their own accounts. Other firms have consolidated their accounts receivable operations (especially retail chain stores), thereby improving the main office controls over credit terms, collections, and bad debts.

New markets have come into existence through computer data-processing ability. Bank credit cards are able to provide low interest terms to consumers because of the relatively low cost of maintaining an account on a computer file. It has been suggested that it would require many *millions* of man-hours of effort to operate the telephone system for one month, if there were no computers to handle the circuitry and the customer accounting.

Obviously, the computer does more than replace a few clerks.

Asset Management

Using the ability of the machine to store vast quantities of data in small places, and its ability to access and update this information, many firms have found it possible to improve their efficiency in managing their nonmonetary assets.

Perpetual inventory systems are much more economical and accurate when electronic capabilities are utilized. For example, the number of units of each item which a company carries in stock may be reduced, simply because the balance on hand can be monitored more closely. The savings of only a few dollars per item can produce a substantial savings when there are thousands of items in the inventory. Data gathered from the requests for items can be used to produce better estimates of future demands and to reduce costs through damage or shortages.

Firms that cover geographically dispersed markets have found it economical to establish regional warehouses in order to reach their customers sooner. The maintenance of a centralized computer file enables locating the nearest alternative source when the closest warehouse happens to run short. Careful programming also allows the analysis of each warehouse's market, in order to produce a "profile" of items most and least likely to be needed. Again, it is possible to reduce the amount of unnecessary investment in working capital. Military supply systems have utilized this approach to minimize the amount of time that the troops are without necessary consumables or equipment.

Fixed assets can be managed more productively with the computer's help. Data can be kept about the location and usage of each piece of equipment. Excessively idle items can be noticed by the program, and called to management's attention for possible deletion. Frequently used items can be noted, with the implication that more units should be acquired. In very large systems, records of maintenance activities can be kept, in order to facilitate the stocking of repair parts, the planning of prescheduled preventive maintenance, and even the selection of a more reliable model of the particular items. It would be essentially impossible to acquire, store, and utilize this information without electronic data processing.

Planning

The late 1960s and early 1970s saw the emergence of a new tool in management which would not have been developed without the capabilities of the computer. A *financial planning model* is a combination of several *thousands* of equations, and is intended to describe the relationships among the many variables that determine the net income of the firm over a period of time. The equations describe the effects of such factors as the general economic conditions, actions taken by competitors, advertising and other marketing strategies, production line modifications, increases in employee output, maintenance policies, and various unusual events, such as strikes, severe weather, or natural disasters. When the model is solved for a given set of values for the variables, the outcome will *simulate,* or approximate, what would have happened in the given time period under those conditions.

After the equations are designed and tested against actual historical data, one of these *simulations* can be run and evaluated in only a few minutes or hours. Thus, the manager can test alternative strategies to find which ones will most likely produce the best results. Without the computer model, he would have to rely on intuitive guesses, or at best, only very sketchy analyses. With the model, he can use trial-and-error methods without risking the firm's assets or his job.

It is reasonable to expect that the future will see extensive development of *generalized* planning models that will be available to even the smallest manager. Indications have appeared that firms will have to publish estimated future earnings, with the possibility that external auditors may have to attest to the propriety of the estimates. Reliable planning models should produce better projections and simplify the auditor's job.

Of course, the output received from one of these models is only as valid as the input data, and is useful when the manager recognizes that it is only a result of a large number of estimates. If the input data is faulty, we have a situation known affectionately as *garbage-in-garbage-out,* or GIGO. If the manager relies too heavily on the model to do his planning, he may forfeit his responsibilities to the programmer, and cease to react to those situations that demand his attention. The optimum benefit is obtained at the middle ground between the two extremes of unquestioning acceptance and total rejection.

Conclusion

The computer is a complex electronic device that offers many unique advantages to the businessman. If it is applied simply as a replacement for manual data processing, it is not being used to its full potential, with the result that the manager is wasting his money and losing some opportunities. On the other hand, if it is applied as a replacement for *personal judgment,* it is being used improperly, with the result that the manager is not earning his salary and still might be losing opportunities.

To use the computer properly (as an *augmentation* of his skills), the manager needs some basic understanding of how the machine works. He does not need to be able to program it in detail, but he must be able to tell his programming staff what he wants. To avoid sacrificing control over this aspect of his job, he needs to have confidence in, and the confidence of, his data processing staff. He must seek to educate himself, and should allow his programming director to participate in appropriate policy decisions.

The preceding sections have shown just a few ways that a computer can produce benefits for the businessman. The possibilities are endless, and tomorrow's successful manager must be ready to innovate. You cannot afford to pretend that the computer does not exist or that you can get by without it.

SUMMARY

This chapter has taken the reader through several areas of computer technology and applications. We saw initially that a computer has five conceptual components: *input, control, arithmetic/logic, storage,* and *output.* Each has its own function to perform before the computer can satisfy the needs of the *user.*

Descriptions were given of some of the devices that accomplish these functions. Among others, there were discussed such things as *cards, tapes, terminals, disks, drums,* and *printers.* Throughout this section of the chapter, the objective was to provide the student with a set of computer science terms that will enhance his understanding of later contacts with the subject.

The next major topic involved the *software* aspects of computers. This section discussed *machine, assembly, compiler,* and *user languages,* and the appropriate circumstances in which each is encountered. *Flowcharting* and *documentation* were described, with an emphasis on their importance for describing a computer application.

The next section dealt with four alternative approaches to computer systems: *service bureaus, time sharing, minicomputers,* and *multiprocessors.* The businessman should seek to find the particular configuration that meets the needs of his situation, and must avoid selecting one for any other reason.

The chapter concluded with brief descriptions of three major areas of computer usage in today's business world: *bookkeeping, asset management,* and *planning.* Other specific applications have been discussed in preceding chapters.

QUESTIONS

1. What is a computer?
2. Identify and describe briefly the five components of a computer. Which, if any, is the most important?
3. Name and briefly describe five devices used as input media.
4. Distinguish among magnetic cards, disks, drums, and cores, in terms of relative speeds and costs.
5. What are computer graphics? What is a CRT?
6. What is COM? What is its advantage over other output media?
7. What is binary code?
8. What is a computer program? A computer language?
9. Name four general kinds of computer languages.
10. How does a computer "make" a decision?
11. Contrast the apparent with the real processing of a program written in an assembly or compiler language.
12. Distinguish between an on-line and a batch system.
13. What is a flowchart?
14. Why is documentation of a program or system important?
15. Describe four alternative means by which a businessman may acquire computer capabilities.
16. Why are bookkeeping procedures amenable to computerization?
17. What is simulation? Why is it so useful in management of large organizations?

PROBLEMS

P19–1   General knowledge.   Identify the correct answer to each of the following:

a.   Which of the following is not a direct access storage device?
1.   disk
2.   core
3.   drum
4.   magnetic tape
5.   none of the above

b.   *Software* refers to:
1.   the peripheral equipment in a data processing installation
2.   pliable media, such as cards and tapes
3.   the CPU and its components
4.   the programming support of a computer system
5.   none of the above

c.   Which of the following applications would be least likely to be done on an on-line basis?
1.   airline reservations
2.   preparation of payroll checks
3.   a stock market quotation system
4.   a computerized traffic-light control system
5.   computer monitoring of coronary patients in a hospital

d.   Direct access storage devices are:
1.   basic to on-line operations
2.   supplementary to on-line operations
3.   harmful to on-line operations
4.   incompatible with on-line operations
5.   none of the above

(CMA Adapted)

P19–2   Flowcharting.   Prepare a flowchart that would enable someone to start a car's engine. Be sure to include several possible problems that a novice would be likely to encounter.

P19–3   Flowcharting.   Prepare a flowchart describing the process of reconciling a bank statement with the cash account. Assume that the only factors to be considered are outstanding checks, deposits in transit, and errors in addition.

P19–4   System design.   On the basis of:

a.   desired speed of response
b.   frequency of updating data base
c.   frequency of inquiries to data base

indicate whether the following data processing systems would be more appropriately arranged on an on-line or batch basis. Briefly explain your choice.

1. Processing of clerks' requests for approval of small purchases on established charge accounts.

2. Processing of credit managers' requests for credit related information on charge account applicants.

3. Processing bank officers' requests for credit related information on loans for purchase of large items.

4. Preparation of annual income statements.

5. Processing of checks and deposits on personal checking accounts.

6. Perpetual accounting system for an inventory of airline seats.

7. Perpetual accounting system for an inventory of auto parts.

8. Perpetual accounting system for an inventory of Minuteman missile parts.

9. Monitoring system for the flight status of Minuteman missiles.

10. Processing of orders for new automobiles.

11. Processing of cash receipts and customer billings.

P19–5 **Terminology.** Match the number of the term with the letter of the definition that fits it most closely.

1. Flowchart	14. MICR
2. Magnetic disk or drum	15. Minicomputer
3. Storage	16. Direct access
4. Assembly language	17. CRT
5. Documentation	18. Machine language
6. Cores	19. Output
7. Input	20. Service bureaus
8. Sequential	21. Assemblers and compilers
9. Arithmetic/logic	22. COM
10. User languages	23. Control
11. Program	24. Simulation
12. Time sharing	25. Terminal
13. Graphics	26. Herman Hollerith

a. A television picture tube

b. An alphanumeric, machine dependent language

c. Computer programs that translate source programs into object programs

d. Computer component that translates binary coded information into the desired readable format

e. An organization of computer storage that requires a step-by-step search for the desired item

f. An 1890 census taker

g. Agencies that process other peoples' data

h. Computer component that directs the activity of the other components

i. A symbolic representation of a process

j. An output device that exposes microfilm directly

k. Computer component that accepts information from the user and translates it into binary code

l. Computer output that utilizes more than alphanumeric symbols.

m. Computer input system that uses magnetic ink

n. The highest level computer languages

o. A set of instructions executed by a computer

p. A modeling method that uses the computer and mathematical relationships to test a process or to predict an outcome

q. Computer component that performs calculations and makes "yes" or "no" decisions

r. Computer component that accepts and reproduces information on command

s. An organization of computer storage that enables the finding of the desired item without a step-by-step search

t. The most expensive but fastest computer storage device

u. A device that allows remote communication with a computer

v. A written description of a program or a group of programs

w. A numeric, machine dependent language

x. A computer storage device that uses a rapidly spinning component

y. A system that allows many people to use the same computer without waiting

z. A type of computer that allows the system to be expanded easily

P19–6 Flowcharting. With the following flowcharts, you will be able to forecast tomorrow's weather like a computer might do it. Your model has only four variables, and only one observation is taken, whereas a real meteorologist's model would have many, many more. For each of the sets of data, you are to determine what the forecast will be.

	Barometric Pressure (BP)	Relative Humidity (RH)	Temperature (T)	Wind
a.	31	22	75	E
b.	30	55	12	S
c.	28	43	27	N
d.	31	75	37	S
e.	30	39	52	S
f.	30	60	75	E
g.	30	98	36	E
h.	31	81	85	W
i.	30	23	47	N
j.	30	47	−4	N

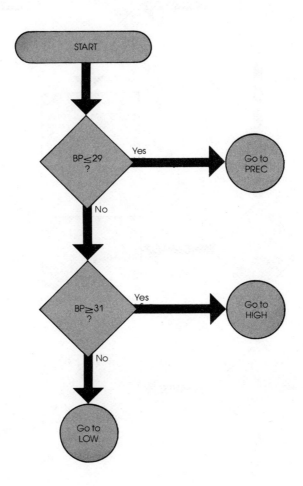

START

BP ≤ 29 ?

Yes → Go to PREC

No

BP ≥ 31 ?

Yes → Go to HIGH

No

Go to LOW

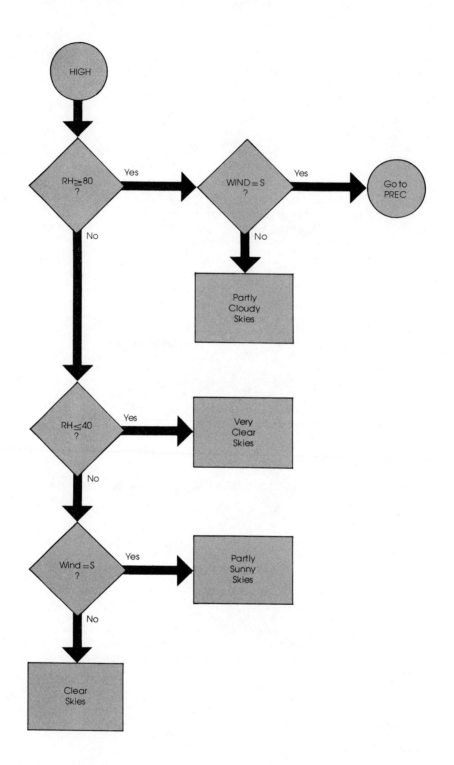

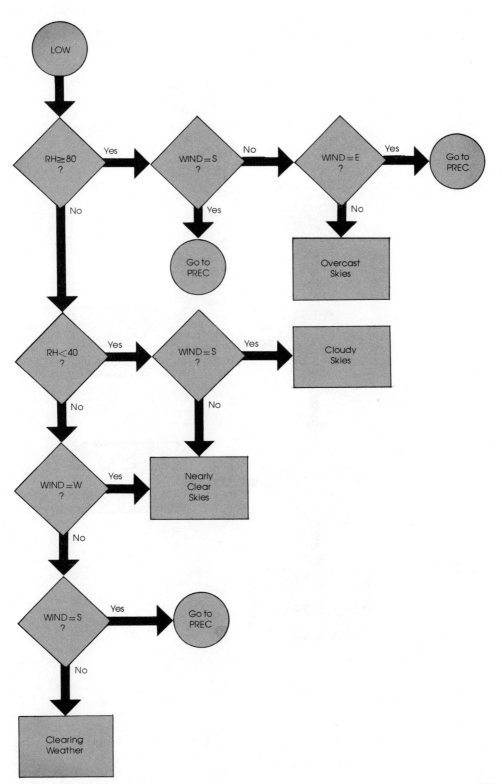

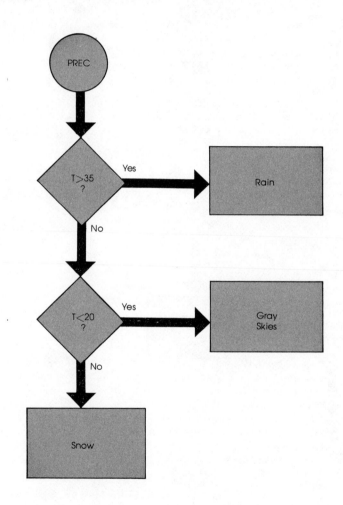

I

Double-Entry Accounting Procedures

This appendix has been included to provide a quick summary of commonly used recordkeeping procedures. Of necessity, many details have been deleted, but the essence of the subject has been preserved. This information, while not essential, will help the reader to more completely understand the subjects covered in this text.

THE OBJECTIVE OF ACCOUNTING

Chapter 1 established the fact that accounting exists to provide information to makers of economic decisions. Consequently, an accounting system is designed to provide economic data about an entity's condition and operations. For reasons of usefulness, simplicity, and tradition, financial accounting focuses on two dimensions of the entity: what it *owns* and what it *owes*. The things that it owns are called *assets,* and they are used to earn profits, pay bills, and give a return to the owners. The things that a firm owes are called *equities,* and are classified into two categories: *liabilities* and *owners' equity.* Liabilities are owed to people who are not owners, and usually arise because the firm has borrowed money from a lender, or postponed paying for an asset or a service. Owners' equity is owed to the entity's owners, and arises from two activities: First, owners frequently turn over some assets to a firm. Second, the firm uses those assets to earn *income,* which increases the assets of the firm and the owners' claims. Financial accounting is concerned not only with how many assets and equities exist at a particular time, but also with the *changes* that occur in them *over a period of time*. The financial statements are reports describing both of these aspects (as discussed in Chapters 2, 3, 4, and 5).

There are a great number of items of information about an entity that are useful to economic decision makers that are *not* included in the financial statements, simply because they cannot be expressed (with today's techniques) in terms of assets and equities. This fact should not be considered a shortcoming of accounting but should reflect the truth that economic decisions are very complex.

THE BUILDING BLOCK OF THE SYSTEM

The fundamental unit of the recordkeeping system is the *account,* which can be thought of as a symbol for a thing or an event. Each account has a *name* and a *balance.* The name is the same as the thing it symbolizes, such as Cash, Truck, Accounts Payable, Stockholders' Equity, Sales Revenue, or Income Tax Expense. The balance is a quantity of money, and is found by subtracting the recorded decreases in the account from the recorded increases. The computed balance should correspond to the actual amount of the item symbolized by the account.

In its simplest form, an account would be only a column of numbers:

	Cash
+	$1,000
–	300
–	250
+	400
–	700
+$	150

A more convenient format splits the account into two parts: One for recording increases and one for recording decreases. This version is shown below, and is called a *T account:*

Cash	
1,000	
	300
	250
400	
	700
1,400	1,250
150	

Another version, which is used very frequently in real business systems, produces the account's balance after each event, or *entry:*

Cash		
Increase	**Decrease**	**Balance**
1,000		1,000
	300	700
	250	450
400		850
	700	150

There are literally hundreds of possible formats for accounts, including holes punched in cards or tapes, or magnetized spots on tapes, cards, drums, or disks, which would be readable only by a computer. In any case, the account is still a symbol with a name, recorded changes, and a balance.

Using Accounts

To provide the information needed to produce the financial statements mentioned earlier, *three* main categories of accounts are used: *asset, equity,* and *changes in owners' equity.* Variations are used in special situations; others *could* be used if they were desired. These three are by far the most common, presumably because of their usefulness.

The Accounting Equation

It is an economic fact that what an entity *owns* is exactly equal to what it *owes,* and this fact serves as the foundation for double-entry accounting. This approach has been traced through history to the fifteenth century, when it was developed by and for Italian merchants. In its simplest form, the equation is:

(1)   Assets = Equities

There are two types of equities: those owed to nonowners *(liabilities)* and those owed to owners *(owners' equity).* Using this terminology, the equation can be re-stated as:

(2)   Assets = Liabilities + Owners' equity

Another version of the equation, which recognizes that the owners get what is "left over" after paying off the liabilities is:

(3)   Assets − Liabilities = Owners' equity

The form seen in equation **(2)** is the one that we will use to demonstrate how double-entry accounting works.

Transactions

The life of an entity witnesses the occurrence of economic events that alter the composition of assets and equities. The accountant's task is to devise a system that records not only the occurrence of these events *(transactions)* but also their effects on the assets and equities. While the variety of forms that transactions may take is very large, they can all be sorted into one of nine general types, five of which are much more common than the other four. Exhibit I-1 shows these nine types in terms of their effects on the assets and equities with an example of each. The symbols indicate that the particular category of accounts will have its balance increased (+) or decreased (−).

Exhibit I-1

	Transaction Type	Examples	Assets	Effect on Liabilities	Owners' Equity
1	Increase an asset; reduce another asset	Firm buys a truck for cash	(+)(−)		
2	Increase an asset; increase a liability	Firm borrows cash from a bank	(+)	(+)	
3	Increase an asset; increase owners' equity	Owner invests cash in firm; firm earns a cash revenue	(+)		(+)
4	Reduce an asset; reduce a liability	Firm retires a loan with cash	(−)	(−)	
5	Reduce an asset; reduce owners' equity	Firm pays cash to owner; or firm incurs a cash expense	(−)		(−)
6	Reduce a liability; increase another liability	Firm converts an Account Payable to a Note Payable		(+)(−)	
7	Increase a liability; reduce owners' equity	Firm incurs an expense to be paid later with cash		(+)	(−)
8	Reduce a liability; increase owners' equity	Bonds Payable converted to Preferred Stock		(−)	(+)
9	Reduce an owners' equity; increase another owners' equity	Preferred Stock converted to Common Stock			(+)(−)

Notice that the system results in the equation remaining in balance, regardless of the type of transaction.

To explain events 3, 5, and 7 more fully, a *revenue* is an increase in owners' equity resulting from providing a good or service for a customer. In a sense, it is a "reward." An *expense,* on the other hand, is a decrease in owners' equity resulting from providing a good or service for a customer. In a sense, it is an "effort" or sacrifice.

Debits and Credits

While the terms *increase* and *decrease* would be adequate for describing changes in the account balances, a more useful terminology is applied in accordance with the early Italian system. We can use the T-account format to show how the system works. Basically, *every* account is split into two parts, a *debit* and a *credit*. The left side of *every* account is the debit, and the right side of *every* account is the credit. If the sum of the numbers on the left side is greater than the sum of the numbers on the right side, the account is said to have a *debit balance.* The opposite condition produces a *credit balance.*

Purely by an arbitrary choice in the beginning, and by tradition since then, increases in *asset* account balances are recorded by entries on the *debit* side, and decreases by entries on the *credit* side. Applying this convention to recording transaction 1 in Exhibit I-1, the debit entry to the Truck account would equal the credit entry to the Cash account. *If the equality between debits and credits is not maintained, an error has occurred.*

If we apply the same conventions to transactions 2 and 3, an increase in an equity account must be recorded with a *credit entry.* Thus, if we maintain equality of debits and credits in each transaction, we will, at the same time, retain the balance in our accounting equation. Exhibit I-2 is the same as Exhibit I-1, except that the (+) and (−) symbols have been replaced by Debit or Credit as appropriate.

Revenues and Expenses

Accounts for revenues and expenses symbolize events rather than things. Specifically, they symbolize changes in owners' equity brought about by rewards from and efforts for providing goods and services to customers. Because a revenue is an *increase* in owners' equity, the event is recorded as a *credit* in a *revenue* account. For example, if transaction 3 is the receiving of cash in payment for the washing of a car, the entry would be a *Debit* to the Cash account (the balance is increased) and a *Credit* to the Washing Revenue account (the balance is also increased).

Exhibit I-2
Recording Effects of Transactions on:

Trans.	Assets	Liabilities	Owners' Equity
1	Debit-Credit		
2	Debit	Credit	
3	Debit		Credit
4	Credit	Debit	
5	Credit		Debit
6		Credit-Debit	
7		Credit	Debit
8		Debit	Credit
9			Credit-Debit

Because an expense is a *decrease* in owners' equity, the event is recorded as a *Debit* in an *expense* account. For example, if transaction 5 is the payment of cash for soap used in washing a car, the entry would be a *Debit* to the Soap Expense account (the balance is increased) and a *Credit* to the Cash account (the balance is decreased). While Debits to expense accounts do increase the balance of the expense account, expense accounts are really reductions in Owner's Equity. Thus, every time we increase an expense we are really reducing Owners' Equity.

The table below summarizes which type of entry is used to record increases and decreases in the five account categories, as well as the *usual* balance of each:

Account Category	Increase	Decrease	Usual Balance
Asset	Debit	Credit	Debit
Liability	Credit	Debit	Credit
Owners' equity	Credit	Debit	Credit
Revenue	Credit	Debit	Credit
Expense	Debit	Credit	Debit

Quantities

Up to now, we have talked only very generally in terms of account entries, and only in the sense of direction (that is, positive or negative). The size of the entry is extremely significant, and great deliberation frequently goes into determining which amount will be used. Let's examine each account type and see what amount is usually recorded.

ASSETS

Based on the assumption of an efficient marketplace and its result that the amount paid for an item is really its value, financial accounting requires that an increase in an asset account balance be recorded at cost (the amount sacrificed to obtain the asset). Subsequent changes in an asset's value (while it is owned by the entity) are treated inconsistently. Generally, if the value increases, no change in the account balance is made; however, if the value decreases, the account balance is also decreased. The end result is conservative, in that no risk of overstating value is taken, but the practice is nonetheless inconsistent.

LIABILITIES

Increases in liabilities are recorded at the amount that will have to be paid back when they mature, without providing for interest payments. Interest is considered to be an expense of the time periods in which the liabilities are outstanding. The amount to be paid back is equal to the amount received from the lender. Thus, the balance in a liability account equals the dollar value of the claim held by the lender.

OWNERS' EQUITY

Like a liability account, an owners' equity account symbolizes the claims that owners have against the firm. The claims arise from investment of assets and the earning of net income. Thus, the increases in the account balance are recorded at the same amount assigned to the assets invested, or for the excess of the revenues over the expenses. The total balance symbolizes the claims that the owners hold, which they could potentially collect if the liabilities were paid and the business dissolved. Intermediate distributions of assets satisfying part of these claims are called *drawings,* or *dividends,* and are quite proper if they do not damage the firm's ability to exist and earn profits. These distributions are recorded in the owners' equity accounts at the value of the assets taken out of the firm.

REVENUES

An increase in a revenue account is recorded at the amount of value received or to be received in the transaction. A revenue is recorded under good *accrual* accounting when the service or good is *provided,* whether or not the cash (if any) has yet been received.

EXPENSES

An increase in an expense account is recorded at the amount of value sacrificed or to be sacrificed in the transaction (that is, the amount *paid*). An expense is recorded under good *accrual* accounting when the effort is made, whether or not cash has yet been paid. In recording some expenses the "value" sacrificed is not precisely known, and the accountant must estimate the amount of the sacrifice. For example, when a truck is used to make a delivery, it is difficult to precisely identify the amount of the sacrifice.

A TYPICAL ACCOUNTING SYSTEM

Imagine the task faced by a firm that wishes to prepare financial statements,[1] when hundreds and even thousands of events affecting assets and equities take place every day. Without some organized set of procedures and forms, there would be little assurance that each significant event was acknowledged and recorded, or that any consistency existed in analyzing similar transactions. Consequently, a major task of the firm's accountant is to create and operate an *accounting system* which has the function of routinely "capturing" information about the transactions and their effects on the firm's assets and equities. By having routine procedures, consistency and efficiency are encouraged.

The Processing Steps

A series of steps in the operation of the system can be identified. Because of the repetitive nature of the procedures, the completion of all of the following steps is frequently referred to as the *accounting cycle:*

1. Recording the transaction
2. "Posting" the transaction to the accounts
3. Testing the posting efforts
4. Recording other changes
5. Preparing the income statement
6. "Closing" the income accounts
7. Preparing the balance sheet

[1] As pointed out in Chapter 1, no firm in today's society really has a choice between reporting or not.

Steps 1, 2, and 3 are carried out much more frequently than steps 4, 5, 6, and 7. It would therefore not be very meaningful to prepare new statements after each transaction.

1. RECORDING THE TRANSACTION

To have a chronological record of events and to have information about a particular event, typical accounting systems maintain some form of a daily *journal*. An *entry* in a journal consists of at least three components: a date, the accounts affected and the size of the effects, and a brief description of what happened (which may only be a reference to a file or document number). Presented below is an example of an entry that might be made in a manual system:

```
1978
August 23  Notes Payable                    10,000
               Cash                                    10,000
           Paid off loan from Ken Smith;
           see Voucher No. 78-814.
```

Two accounts were affected by this transaction—a liability and an asset—and both were reduced. Consequently, entries will be made to those accounts, reducing their balances. The debited account is listed first (a convention that is followed in this text and in nearly all systems), and the amount shown in the first column. Then with an indentation to distinguish it from the debit, the Cash account is credited, and the amount shown in the second column. The explanation is quite brief, and, as in this example, may refer the reader to another place where a more complete description can be found.

Notice that a journal entry can serve as a useful "shorthand" description of an event in terms of its effect on a firm's financial statements. For this example, see how the entry conveys quickly and completely that a debt was reduced and that available cash was diminished. In this book, we have occasionally used journal entries to show such effects. Presented below are journal entries to record the transactions shown in Exhibit I-1. For the sake of brevity, we have omitted the dates and the explanations, and entered "XX" instead of an amount.

```
1.  Truck                              XX
        Cash                                    XX
2.  Cash                               XX
        Notes Payable                           XX
3.  Cash                               XX
        Owners' Equity                          XX
    Cash                               XX
        Sales Revenue                           XX
4.  Accounts Payable                   XX
        Cash                                    XX
5.  Drawings                           XX
        Cash                                    XX
    Rent Expense                       XX
        Cash                                    XX
6.  Accounts Payable                   XX
        Notes Payable                           XX
7.  Utilities Expense                  XX
        Accounts Payable                        XX
8.  Bonds Payable                      XX
        Preferred Stock                         XX
9.  Preferred Stock                    XX
        Common Stock                            XX
```

Also, it is quite possible to have an entry that would record changes in several account balances. This "compound" entry would be made in order to record the payment of a loan plus interest:

Notes Payable	10,000	
Interest Expense	200	
Cash		10,200

To avoid errors, journal entries are often recorded daily. A variety of *specialized* journals are used in practice to record routine, similar transactions, such as cash receipts and payments, and sales on account.

2. POSTING THE TRANSACTION

In order to change balances in the accounts, journal entries are *posted,* or *copied,* from the journal into the *ledger,* which is the book (or other recording medium) that contains all the accounts. When a journal entry calls for the debiting of, for example, Notes Payable, by $10,000, that particular account has a debit entry posted to it, which thus reduces the balance by $10,000. Then, the credit half of the journal entry would be posted to the account listed, such as Cash.

This procedure is followed until all the journal entries have been copied into the ledger, and the account balances updated to symbolize the most recent state of the assets, equities, and income related events. To briefly demonstrate, suppose that the following account balances existed before the collection of a Note Receivable and Interest:

Cash		Notes Receivable		Interest Income	
3,475		13,000			

The note is collected, and this entry recorded:

Cash	7,575	
Notes Receivable		7,500
Interest Income		75

After posting this entry, the accounts would appear as:

Cash		Notes Receivable		Interest Income	
3,475		13,000			75
7,575			7,500		

3. TESTING THE POSTING EFFORTS

On a regular basis, the accuracy of the posting procedure should be tested by finding and listing the balances of *all* the accounts in the ledger. If the posting has been properly done (and the balances correctly computed), the sum of the debit account balances will equal the sum of the credit account balances. However, because it is possible that an entire entry may not have been posted, or that an incorrect account may have received the entry intended for another account, this *trial balance* can still show equal *debits* and *credits* when the posting is incorrect. If the trial balance does *not* balance, then it can be concluded that an error has occurred. Exhibit I-3 is an example of a trial balance, which is merely a list of the accounts and their balances as found in the ledger on the given date.

The trial balance is *not* a financial statement, even though much of its data will appear on the statements. It is strictly an internal test for bookkeeping accuracy.

Exhibit I-3

HYPOTHETICS, INC.
Trial Balance
December 31, 1978

	Debit	Credit
Cash	37,300	
Accounts receivable	17,500	
Land	23,000	
Building	47,200	
Machinery	83,500	
Accounts payable		13,000
Mortgage payable		60,000
Stockholders' equity		86,350
Dividends paid	3,450	
Sales revenue		140,000
Selling expense	37,250	
Administrative expense	50,150	
	299,350	299,350

4. RECORDING OTHER CHANGES

For two general reasons, it is necessary for the accountant to change account balances when there have been no new transactions. This *adjustment* process (which uses *adjusting entries*) occurs only when statements are to be prepared, and arises because of errors and shortcuts.

Errors

Errors may enter the accounting records through mistakes in arithmetic or classification, or through misapplication of accounting principles.[2] The process involves three steps:

1. Determine present balances in the affected accounts.
2. Determine desired balances in the affected accounts.
3. Deduce the entry that will change the balances from their present amounts to the desired amounts.

Suppose, for example, that the journal entry to record the purchase of a Fixed Asset shows a *debit* to the *Repairs Expense* account instead of the *Fixed Asset* account. The Cash account received the correct credit, so that no change in it is necessary. The incorrect accounts might appear as:

Fixed Asset	Repairs Expense
	5,000

Our analysis reveals that the fixed asset in question has a cost of $3,500, and that all other repairs expenditures had been recorded correctly. The balances *should* be:

Fixed Asset	Repairs Expense
3,500	1,500

To accomplish the correction, we must increase the fixed asset account and decrease the repairs account by $3,500 each. Our adjusting entry would be:

Fixed Asset	3,500	
Repairs Expense		3,500

[2] Inaccuracies arising from intentional efforts to mislead the financial statement reader are treated essentially the same as unintentional errors. The evildoer frequently will suffer some form of chastisement, of course. Our concern is with correcting the improper records.

This entry would be recorded in the journal, and posted to the ledger. After this posting, the accounts would appear as:

Fixed Asset		Repairs Expense	
		5,000	
3,500			3,500
Bal. 3,500		Bal. 1,500	

If the error had occurred in *posting* (that is, the original entry was correct), there would be no need to record an adjusting entry. We would simply erase or crossout the incorrectly posted *ledger* entries and write in the proper one, without making any notation in the journal.

Shortcuts

Many economic events transpire without the occurrence of an observable event. For example, the coverage provided by an insurance policy is used up without any further cash outflows subsequent to the payment of the premium. Property taxes accumulate throughout the year, even though the county government sends out a notice only once every twelve months. Fixed assets slowly but surely lose their productivity as they are used in production. While it *might* be possible to record these subtle changes as they happen, the value of the obtained results would probably be much less than the sacrifices made to obtain them. We compromise by recording these changes only "every so often," usually on a cyclical basis corresponding to the frequency with which we prepare the financial statements.

The student will recall from Chapter 1 that the intent behind the *matching rule* is to associate efforts with rewards in the appropriate time period. Some efforts occur after we pay out cash, while others precede the payment. Some rewards are earned after we receive cash, while others precede the receipt. Exhibit I-4 represents these four possibilities over a time line.

Exhibit I-4
Cash Flows, Efforts, and Rewards

	Last Year	This Year	Next Year *Time*	
1	Cash paid ────	►Effort made		Prepaid expense
2		Effort made ────	►Cash paid	Accrued expense
3	Cash received ──	►Reward earned		Unearned revenue
4		Reward earned ────	►Cash received	Accrued revenue

For the sake of simplicity, most accounting systems call for the *recognition* (recording) of expenses and revenues when cash is paid or received. Little trouble results if only a short time elapses between the *cash event* and the *economic event*. However short the time lag may be, good accounting practice calls for adjusting entries to record the proper amount of expense or revenue before financial statements are prepared. Let us look at four examples:

1. *Prepaid expense:* Cash paid *before* effort made.
    Suppose that office supplies are purchased for cash. The entry to record the event might take this form:

Supplies Expense	1,000	
Cash		1,000

A count of the supplies on hand at the end of the year shows that $400 worth are still on hand. Thus, we conclude that our efforts used up $600 of supplies, and we have $400 of unused supplies on hand. Our adjusting entry would be:

Office Supplies	400	
Supplies Expense		400

Notice that this entry not only adjusts the expense to the proper amount, but also recognizes the existence of an asset with a cost of $400.

2. *Accrued Expense:* Cash paid *after* effort made.

Suppose that our office workers are paid on the 15th day of the month for their work of the preceding month (for example, work done in June is paid for on July 15). As of December 31, we would have consumed the efforts of our office staff for one month, but no entry would have been made. Also, we would *owe* our workers for their month's labors. If our monthly payroll were $10,000, our adjusting entry to record the accrued expense would be made on December 31 in this manner:

Office Payroll Expense	10,000	
Office Payroll Payable		10,000

Notice that this entry records the expense in the proper year, and produces the correct balance in the liability account.

3. *Unearned Revenue:* Cash received *before* reward earned.

Suppose that we want to assure that a customer will accept a specially ordered item by having him pay us for it in advance of our delivering it to him. On a *cash basis,* this entry would be made on the day he paid us:

Cash	6,000	
Sales Revenue		6,000

But, because we have not delivered the product, we have not *earned* the revenue, and we are not justified in recording the payment as revenue. Additionally, we are indebted to the customer for the amount he paid in advance. The adjusting entry to be made (if he paid us before December 31, and we had not delivered by then) would be:

Sales Revenue	6,000	
Customer Advance		6,000

The Customer Advance account is a symbol of our liability to the customer. We can satisfy the liability by delivering the product or refunding his advance payment.

4. *Accrued Revenue:* Cash received *after* reward earned.

Suppose that a customer wishes to assure that we provide all the service he wants by not paying us until we finish the task (such as constructing a building). If the project is still "in process" at December 31, we would have recorded no revenues under the cash basis. However, we have earned that fraction of the revenue that corresponds to the percentage of the project we have completed. Thus, if we have done 25 percent of the work on a $40,000 house, we would record the following adjusting entry:

Receivable from Customer	10,000	
Construction Revenue		10,000

This entry not only records that portion of the revenue we have earned by our efforts to date, but also reflects the fact that our customer owes us 25 percent of the total fees.

Subsequent Entries

After recording adjusting entries of these types, we have to eventually account for the disposition of the assets and liabilities. The following entries are based on the above examples:

1. *Disposing of a prepaid expense.*
   When the Office Supplies are all used up, we could record an adjusting entry like this:

Office Supplies Expense	400	
Office Supplies		400

2. *Disposing of an accrued expense.*
   When the office workers are paid their December wages on January 15, we would make this entry:

Office Payroll Payable	10,000	
Cash		10,000

3. *Disposing of an unearned revenue.*
   When we delivered the product to our customer, we would record:

Customer Advance	6,000	
Sales Revenue		6,000

4. *Disposing of an accrued revenue.*
   When we completed the construction job, and received payment in full, we would make this entry:

Cash	40,000	
Receivable from Customer		10,000
Construction Revenue		30,000

Notice the dual nature of the cash receipt. It pays us for the efforts of last year ($10,000) *and* of this year ($30,000).

Certainly the most difficult part of the adjusting process is determining which accounts should be adjusted and for what amounts. This task falls on the shoulders of the accountant, who must be intimately familiar with the nature of the firm's revenues and expenses and the customary manners in which they are paid and received.

Alternative Approaches

In order to summarize the discussion of adjusting, we have prepared Exhibit I-5. Notice the alternative approach to recording, adjusting, and disposing of *prepaid expenses* and *unearned revenues*. The balances in the affected accounts are the same after adjustment under both approaches. The choice between the two is purely one of personal preference because it does not produce any difference on the financial statements.

DEPRECIATION

One of the most significant adjusting journal entries deals with the recording of the expense associated with using a fixed asset. The cost sacrificed to acquire a truck, or a computer, or a drill press, or a building, or something similar, remains *unexpired* until the asset is used somehow to earn revenues. If the asset's usefulness is consumed within one time period, its cost is totally *expired,* and we will record the

Exhibit I-5
Summary of Adjusting Entires

Items and Events	General Journal Entries		Alternative Procedures	
Prepaid Expenses				
(a) Pay $1,000 for insurance policy	(a) Insurance Expense	1,000	(a) Prepaid Insurance	1,000
	Cash	1,000	Cash	1,000
(b) Adjust for use of three months' coverage	(b) Prepaid Insurance	750	(b) Insurance Expense	250
	Insurance Expense	750	Prepaid Insurance	250
(c) Record use of the remaining coverage	(c) Insurance Expense	750	(c) Insurance Expense	750
	Prepaid Insurance	750	Prepaid Insurance	750
Accrued Expenses				
(a) Adjust to record estimated property tax expense	(a) Tax Expense	1,200	(a) Tax Expense	1,200
	Estim. Taxes Payable	1,200	Estim. Taxes Payable	1,200
(b) Pay the taxes	(b) Estim. Taxes Payable	1,200	(b) Estim. Taxes Payable	1,200
	Cash	1,200	Cash	1,200
Unearned Revenues				
(a) Collect $450 in advance	(a) Cash	450	(a) Cash	450
	Sales	450	Customer Advance	450
(b) Year-end adjustment	(b) Sales	450	(b) (No Entry)	
	Customer Advance	450		
(c) Deliver the product	(c) Customer Advance	450	(c) Customer Advance	450
	Sales	450	Sales	450
Accrued Revenues				
(a) Record unbilled services	(a) Accounts Receivable	750	(a) Accounts Receivable	750
	Sales	750	Sales	750
(b) Collect for services	(b) Cash	750	(b) Cash	750
	Accounts Receivable	750	Accounts Receivable	750

expenditure as an expense. On the other hand, if the asset lasts several years and its use contributes to profits in each of those years, we are faced with the problem of assigning part of the cost to each of those periods. That is, we should attempt to assign a measure of the expense of using the asset to the accounting period in which it is used.

This procedure of apportioning cost is called *depreciation*. In the accounting sense, depreciation is *not* the opposite of *appreciation*. Notice that depreciation does not represent the "setting aside of funds" for replacing the asset. We will depreciate an asset's cost in order to more properly describe net income, even if we do not intend to replace it when it is worn out.

Perhaps the reader can see that it is difficult (if not impossible) to determine precisely how much of an asset's usefulness is consumed in a particular period. In dealing with this problem, several methods have been developed for *systematically* computing the annual depreciation expense.

The simplest of these methods is called *straight line*. It involves determining the total expense to be incurred over the life of the asset (acquisition cost less salvage value), which is then divided by the number of years in its life to get the annual charge. For example, a $12,000 truck will be used for 4 years, and will then be sold for $2,000. The total expense (called *depreciable basis*) is $10,000. Over four years, we would record $2,500 each year as the annual depreciation expense. The adjusting entry to record this cost expiration would be:

Depreciation Expense	2,500	
Accumulated Depreciation		2,500

Notice that we use the Accumulated Depreciation account instead of directly crediting the asset account. The balance in this *contra* account would be deducted from the asset account on the financial statements, like this:

Truck	$12,000
Less: Accumulated Depreciation	2,500
Net book value	$ 9,500

If we sold this particular truck for $8,000, after using it for 2 years, our entry would be:

Cash	8,000	
Accumulated Depreciation	5,000	
Truck		12,000
Gain on Sale of Truck		1,000

Other popular approaches to depreciation computations involve taking unequal amounts over the life of the asset. In recognition of the observation that some assets provide better service and require less maintenance when they are new than when they are old, these *accelerated* methods deduct amounts that start out large but diminish steadily over the life of the asset. In any case, we cannot deduct more depreciation expense over the life of the asset than we paid for it originally.

5. PREPARING THE INCOME STATEMENT

After the adjusting entries have been recorded in the journal and posted to the ledger accounts, the income statement can be prepared by extracting the revenue and expense account balances, and placing them in the proper format (see Chapter 2). Basically, the sum of the expenses is subtracted from the sum of the revenues to yield the net income for the particular time period. The difference represents the net benefit of providing services or goods to the customer, and adds to the owners' claims against the firm. Exhibit I-6 shows the income statement for Hypothetics, Inc. (See Exhibit I-3 for this firm's trial balance.)

Exhibit I-6

HYPOTHETICS, INC.

Income Statement

For the Year Ended December 31, 1978

Sales revenue		$140,000
Selling expense	$37,250	
Administrative expense	50,150	
Total expense		87,400
Net income		$ 52,600

6. CLOSING THE INCOME ACCOUNTS

Because the revenue and expense accounts symbolize changes in owners' equity *during a particular period of time* (such as 1978), it would not be meaningful to add to their balances the results of transactions that occur in other periods. Thus, step 6 in the cycle is to shutdown, or *close,* these accounts after the particular period is ended. This is accomplished by entering in the account an amount that is equal to the balance, but on the opposite side, thus causing the new balance to be zero. A second result of this procedure is that the net income figure is added to the owners' equity. As part of the same process, any accounts used for other owners' equity transactions are also closed.

For Hypothetics, Inc., there would be the following four closing entries (notice the use of the temporary Income Summary account):

a.	*Expenses:*		
	Income Summary	87,400	
	Selling Expense		37,250
	Administrative Expense		50,150
b.	*Revenue:*		
	Sales Revenue	140,000	
	Income Summary		140,000
c.	*Net Income:*		
	Income Summary	52,600	
	Stockholders' Equity		52,600
d.	*Distributions:*		
	Stockholders' Equity	3,450	
	Dividends Paid		3,450

On completion of this process, a *post-closing trial balance* can be prepared. Exhibit I-7 shows such a trial balance for Hypothetics, Inc. The revenue and expense accounts now have zero balances and are ready for 1979's events, and the firm's balance sheet can be prepared.

Exhibit I-7

HYPOTHETICS, INC.

Post-Closing Trial Balance

December 31, 1978

	Debit	Credit
Cash	37,300	
Accounts receivable	17,500	
Land	23,000	
Building	47,200	
Machinery	83,500	
Accounts payable		13,000
Mortgage payable		60,000
Stockholders' equity*		135,500
	208,500	208,500

*Original balance plus Net Income less Dividends Paid: $86,350 + $52,600 – $3,450

7. PREPARING THE BALANCE SHEET

As the final step in the accounting cycle, the balances of the accounts in the post-closing trial balance, are classified and presented in the firm's *balance sheet*. This financial statement is a symbolic representation of the firm itself, at least in terms of its assets and equities, as of the particular date. Chapter 2 provides a great deal of information about the structure and format of the statement itself, and Chapter 3 explains how it can be interpreted. Figure I-8 presents Hypothetics, Inc.'s balance sheet as of December 31, 1978.

Exhibit I-8

HYPOTHETICS, INC.

Balance Sheet

December 31, 1978

Current Assets:		
Cash	$37,300	
Accounts Receivable	17,500	
Total Current Assets		$ 54,800
Fixed Assets:		
Land	$23,000	
Building	47,200	
Machinery	83,500	
Total Fixed Assets		153,700
Total Assets		$208,500
Current Liabilities:		
Accounts Payable		$ 13,000
Long Term Liability		
Mortgage Payable		60,000
Total Liabilities		$ 73,000
Stockholders' Equity		135,500
Total Equities		$208,500

Flowcharting the Cycle

Exhibit I-9 presents a flowchart of the accounting cycle described on the preceding pages. The first three steps are carried out over and over again during the year according to the arrangement that is most convenient for the firm. The last four steps are typically performed only once at the end of each year. *Interim*, or mid-term, adjustments and statements can be prepared if the system is designed accordingly.

SUMMARY

The objective of this appendix is to briefly describe the basic operation of a double-entry accounting system. The purpose of this system is to routinely capture information that will be meaningful and useful. The discussion is built around a financial accounting system, whereas the main body of the text is concerned with management accounting. There is no conceptual difference between the two orientations with respect to the operation of the information-gathering procedures.

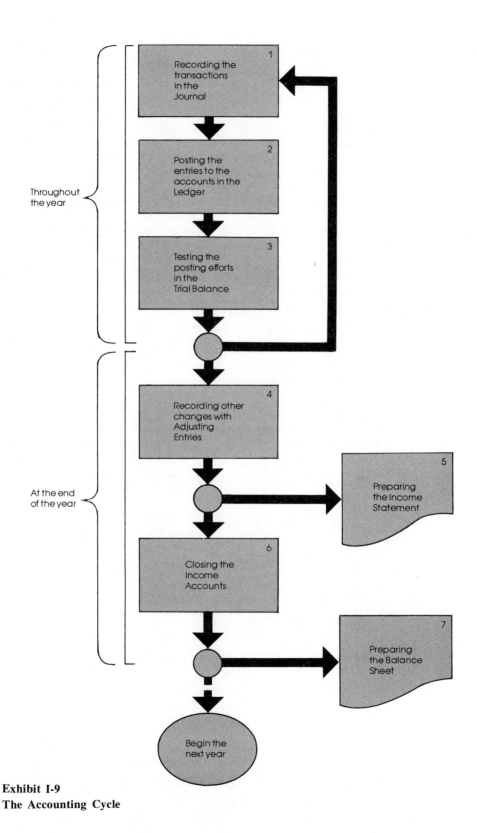

Exhibit I-9
The Accounting Cycle

The key element of the system is the *account,* which symbolizes (with a monetary amount) some important aspect of the entity. Accounts usually exist for assets, equities, revenues, and expenses because information about these particular items has proved useful. In addition to the accounts themselves (which are collected in the *ledger*), other documents are maintained. Specifically, a *journal* is kept in which each transaction is recorded in terms of which accounts are affected. Trial balances are occasionally taken to partially ensure that certain errors have not been made.

To correct errors or to make up for the effects of bookkeeping shortcuts, *adjusting* entries are periodically made by the accountant, usually to accomplish a more sound measurement of income. *Closing* entries are made in order to clear out the revenue and expense accounts (so that they can be used for the next period) and to properly update the amount of owners' claims against the firm.

From these data in the accounts and from other sources, the firm's financial statements can be prepared.

QUESTIONS

1. On which two dimensions of the entity does financial accounting focus?
2. What is the *building block* of the accounting system? What is its function? What forms can it assume?
3. What are the three main categories of accounts?
4. State and explain the *accounting equation.*
5. Identify nine types of transactions (see Exhibit I-1) and give an example of each.
6. What is a *debit*? What is a *credit*? How are they used in recording transactions?
7. What is a *revenue*? What is an *expense*? How are they recorded in accounts?
8. How is the size of the entry determined for:
   a. asset accounts
   b. liability accounts
   c. owners' equity accounts
   d. revenue accounts
   e. expense accounts.
9. What are the seven steps in the *processing cycle*?
10. What is *posting*?
11. What function is served by a *trial balance*?
12. Name and describe the two main reasons for making *adjusting entries.*
13. What is the time relationship between the economic and cash events associated with:
   a. prepaid expenses
   b. accrued expenses
   c. unearned revenues
   d. accrued revenues
14. What is *depreciation*? How is it recorded?
15. What account balances appear on the income statement?
16. What two results are achieved by closing the income accounts?
17. What account balances appear on the balance sheet?
18. Why is it inappropriate to close the balance sheet accounts?

EXERCISES

EI–1 ***Terminology.*** Examine the items or events in the list below. Determine whether they involve one or more of the following: (1) asset, (2) liability, (3) owners' equity, (4) revenue, or (5) expense. Explain each answer.

a. Truck purchased by the firm

b. Truck rented by the firm

c. Amount owed to employees for wages

d. Amount received from customer for services rendered to him

e. Amount received from customer for services to be rendered to him

f. Amount borrowed from the bank

g. Interest owed on loan in (f)

h. Amount invested in the firm by owners

i. Net income for the year

j. Payment of the loan in (f)

k. Payment to owners as return on investment

EI–2 ***The accounting equation.***

a. Write the accounting equation and explain why it will always balance if used properly.

b. Using the relationship described by the equation, determine what amount should be placed in the blanks to make it balance:

	Assets	Liabilities	Owners' Equity
1.	?	$15,000	$ 60,000
2.	$ 75,000	?	50,000
3.	80,500	40,200	?
4.	100,200	?	79,700
5.	?	68,230	112,150
6.	14,000	?	1,100
7.	75,000	85,000	?

EI–3 ***Cash versus accrual.*** Calculate the missing item in each of these cases.

a. Find the Insurance Expense for the year, if:
1. The beginning balance in Prepaid Insurance was $120
2. An annual premium of $275 was paid during the year
3. The ending balance in Prepaid Insurance (after adjustment) was $93

b. Find the ending balance in Prepaid Advertising, if:
1. The Advertising Expense for the year was $2,070
2. The beginning balance in Prepaid Advertising was $495
3. The advertising agency had been paid $2,200 during the year

c. Find the amount that customers had paid in advance during the year, if:
1. The beginning balance of the Customer Advances account was $79
2. The ending balance (after adjustment) in Customer Advances was $103
3. The appropriate Revenue for the year was $690

    d.   Find the beginning balance in the Accrued Wages Payable account, if:
1. The ending balance was $23,000
2. The Wage Expense for the year was $52,000
3. The cash paid to the employees during the year was $44,000

EI–4 **Trial balance.** The following errors were made in recording events in the life of Tower and Pusher Hauling Company. Explain whether or not the trial balance would have been out of balance because of the error. Also explain how the error should be corrected.

    a.   A $250 cash purchase of supplies was recorded as a debit to Cash and a credit to Supplies.

    b.   A monthly insurance premium was posted as a debit to Insurance Expense and a debit to Cash, both for $23.

    c.   The entry recording the purchase of a small machine for $189 was posted to Advertising Expense and Cash.

    d.   The journal entry to record the payment of $129 rent showed a debit of $129 to Rent Expense and a credit of $219 to Cash.

    e.   Wages of $1,260 were paid in Cash and recorded with a debit to Wages Expense and a credit to Wages Payable.

    f.   Trade association dues in the amount of $120 were paid and recorded with a debit to Dues Expense and a credit to Cash, both for $210.

    g.   The purchase of equipment was recorded correctly, but posted as credits to both Accounts Payable and Equipment for $237.

    h.   Hauling services performed for a customer were recorded with a debit to Revenue and a credit to Cash for the amount received, $200.

    i.   Hauling services performed for a customer were recorded with a debit to Cash for $262 (the right amount) and a credit to Revenue for $226.

    j.   Travel expenses of $120 were recorded with a debit of $12 to Travel Expense and a credit of $210 to cash.

EI–5 **Adjusting entries.** Account balances from the ledger of the Fly-By-Knight Air Express Company, before and after *adjustments,* are presented below:

	Before	After
Accumulated depreciation, office furniture	$ 548	$ 685
Accounts receivable	1,740	1,740
Advertising expense	350	295
Cash	985	985
Commissions payable	–0–	150
Commissions expense	1,620	1,770
Daniel Knight, capital (before closing)	12,137	12,137
Depreciation expense	–0–	137
Insurance expense	–0–	360
Interest earned	40	66
Interest expense	–0–	35
Interest payable	–0–	35
Interest receivable	–0–	26
Land	14,500	14,500
Notes payable	870	870
Office furniture	1,370	1,370

	Before	After
Office rent expense	$ 2,030	$ 1,720
Prepaid advertising	–0–	55
Prepaid insurance	450	90
Prepaid office rent	–0–	310
Revenue received in advance	–0–	230
Salaries expense	12,440	13,270
Salaries payable	–0–	830
Service revenue	23,890	23,660
U.S. government bonds	2,000	2,000

a. Prepare the unadjusted and adjusted trial balances.

b. From the changes in the account balances, determine what the adjusting entries were and why they were made.

EI–6 Depreciation. Record the depreciation that would be taken during 1978 for the following assets. Assume straight-line methods are in use.

	Date of Purchase	Cost	Salvage Value	Service Life
a.	June 1, 1968	$200,000	$25,000	14 years
b.	October 1, 1975	15,000	–0–	4 years
c.	January 15, 1976	75,000	50,000	3 years
d.	July 1, 1976 (retired July 1, 1978)	10,000	2,000	2 years
e.	April 1, 1978	62,500	7,500	6 years

EI–7 The accounting cycle. As of September 1, the following balances were outstanding on the books of the Bijou Theater:

	Debit	Credit
Cash	4,000	
Candy	100	
Loan		1,000
Owners' equity		3,100
	4,100	4,100

These events occurred during the month of September:

1. Paid the monthly rent in advance, $500. (*Hint:* This expenditure represents an unexpired cost, which will expire as the month passes.)

2. Purchased various Supplies costing $125, for Cash.

3. Rented a popular movie, *The Last Polka in Warsaw,* under the following arrangement:

First week	40% of admissions
Second week	25% of admissions
Other weeks	10% of admissions

During the first week $1,200 was collected; $800 during the second; $600 during the third; and $400 during the fourth.

4. Paid the usher, ticket seller, and projectionist $320 cash.

5. Candy sales were $130 and inventory costing $35 was still on hand.

6. Supplies costing $75 were still on hand.

Required:

a. Prepare journal entries in good form to record the events during the month of September in the life of the Bijou.

b. Post the entries to the needed ledger accounts.

c. Prepare a trial balance of the ledger.

d. Compute the net income for the month and present your findings in a neat tabulation.

PROBLEMS

PI–1 *The accounting cycle.* Prepare journal entries to record the events involving Sherwood Forest Enterprises as described below. *Post* (copy) the entries into a set of eight accounts and prepare a trial balance.

1. Mr. Robert Hood invests the following items in the firm: Cash, $5,000; Hideout, $10,000; 25 green suits, $500.

2. In a cash purchase, the firm acquires the following items: longbows, $1,000; arrows, $2,000; feathers for caps, $45.

3. In a credit purchase (with a promise to pay eventually), the firm acquires $2,000 of targets.

4. At a cost of $200 in arrows, 4 deer are obtained, prepared, and served at the weekly employee banquet along with 4 barrels of root beer, purchased from the monastery at $10 each.

5. The Earl of Nottingham pays $2,000 to the firm in return for services that saved his life.

6. A *Golden Arrow* is awarded to the firm; the market value is considered to be $10.

7. Half of the debt for the targets is paid in cash. The merchant agrees that the other half need not be paid because his life was saved by services rendered by the firm.

8. In order to finance his marriage to Ms. Marion, Hood withdraws $2,000 and the *Golden Arrow* from the firm.

PI–2 *The accounting cycle.* In general journal format, record the following transactions of Teddy Ryder's Leather Store. Use these accounts: Cash, Trucks, Building and Equipment, Merchandise, Receivables, Merchandise Liability, Building Liability, Owner's Equity, Revenues, and Expenses.

1. Teddy Ryder, proprietor, invested $10,000 cash by opening a checking account in the name of the firm.

2. Purchased 2 trucks, costing $4,000 each.

3. Teddy Ryder, proprietor, invested another $10,000 cash in the firm. He had obtained the funds by borrowing them from his brother-in-law.

4. Purchased a Building and Equipment by putting $11,000 Cash down and agreeing to pay the remaining $29,000 later.

5. Purchased Merchandise for $10,000 on credit, by giving an IOU.

6. Sold 80 percent of the Merchandise for $17,000 on credit, by taking an IOU. (*Hint:* There are two entries to be made.)

7. Paid $1,000 Cash towards merchandise debt.

8. Collected $15,000 Cash from Receivables.

9. Paid $3,000 on Building liability.

10. Teddy Ryder, proprietor, took home $2,000 to pay his personal bills.

11. Paid $800 to employees for work done.

12. Paid gasoline bills of $150.

Required:

Post the entries to accounts, and prepare a trial balance. Find the net income for the period.

PI–3 **Adjustments.** The trial balance (before adjustments) for the Arrow Collection Agency as of December 31, 1980 is presented below:

Cash		755
Accounts receivable		1,664
Office supplies		185
Prepaid insurance		1,020
Office equipment		840
Accounts payable		710
Revenue received in advance		1,200
Boland, capital		1,400
Boland, drawings	3,150	
Service revenue		47,910
Salaries expense	33,930	
Medical expense	5,290	
Meals expense	1,805	
Rent expense	1,425	
Telephone expense	836	
Miscellaneous expense	320	
	51,220	51,220

Items to be considered in making the adjustments are:

1. The office equipment was purchased May 2, 1980 for $840. It is expected to be useful for 10 years, with no salvage value.

2. The company pays its employees each Tuesday for the previous week's work. The daily payroll amounts to $130. The last day of the year fell on a Sunday. The employees worked 5 days in the preceding week.

3. Boland withdrew $280 on December 31, but failed to record it.

4. The firm had not reimbursed 2 of its employees for medical expenses incurred during December. These claims total $138.

5. The company insured all of its employees, and paid $1,020 on June 15 for 12 months coverage. No other insurance is carried.

6. Rent ($570) for 6 months was paid on October 1.

7. A client recently paid the agency $1,200 in advance to collect a group of accounts. Of the $37,500 that was expected to be collected, $9,375 had been paid in by December 31, 1980.

Required:

a. Prepare the necessary adjusting entries.

b. Prepare the necessary closing entries.

c. Prepare a post-closing trial balance.

PI–4 *Adjustments.* Consider these events in the life of the Brown Derby Hat Company:

1. On November 15 the firm paid $1,200 to Norman S. Hyster for legal fees in advance, for the next 12 months.
2. On December 20 a customer paid $50 in advance on an order of hats that would be delivered on January 15. The total order was for $150.
3. On December 27 the firm sold a hat to a customer on credit for $25. Such sales are customarily recorded at the time the bill is mailed to the customer, 10 days after the sale.
4. The average daily heating and lighting expense is $12. On December 15, the firm paid $350 for services from November 7 to December 7. On January 15 the firm paid $372 for services from December 7 to January 7.

Required:

a. Present journal entries to record these events initially, to adjust the balances as of December 31, and to dispose of the balances during the next year as necessary.
b. Post these entries to ledger accounts.
c. Where it is appropriate, use an alternative bookkeeping approach to recording, adjusting, and disposing of the balances for events 1, 2, 3, and 4.
d. Post these entries to ledger accounts.

PI–5 *The accounting cycle.* From the given adjusted trial balance:

1. Prepare and record closing entries.
2. Prepare an income statement for the year ended December 31, 1979.
3. Prepare a post-closing trial balance.
4. Prepare a balance sheet as of December 31, 1979.

X.M. PILL COMPANY
Adjusted Trial Balance
December 31, 1979

Cash	12,489	
Accounts receivable	23,711	
Inventory	41,200	
Machinery	25,400	
Accumulated depreciation		7,700
Accounts payable		25,800
Notes payable		10,000
X.M. Pill, Capital (January 1, 1979)		50,093
Sales		123,650
Other revenue		7,213
Cost of goods sold	75,719	
Wages expense	24,072	
Rent expense	12,000	
Insurance expense	4,250	
Tax expense	5,615	
	224,456	224,456

PI–6 *The accounting cycle.* On October 1, Peter Pilot founded the Pilot Print Shop. The subsequent events of that month were:

October 4: Deposited $10,000 in the bank account of Pilot Print Shop.

October 5: Purchased Printing Machinery for $5,000, paying $2,000 cash and agreeing to pay the rest after 3 months. The equipment was expected to last 5 years before falling completely apart.

October 6: Purchased $800 worth of supplies on account.

October 8: Paid $100 cash to Advertising, Inc., for services to be rendered during the rest of the month.

October 10: Completed printing job for Sharp Pencil Company, and collected $300 cash.

October 12: Paid $110 for rent for the months of October and November.

October 15: Completed a job for Donner and Blitzen, who agreed to pay the $450 later.

October 15: Paid $175 wages to his assistant. A similar amount would be paid on the first of the next month for services rendered after the fifteenth.

October 17: Withdrew $500 cash for personal expenses.

October 19: Agreed to pay $2,000 for another machine when it is delivered next month.

October 24: Paid $25 to the syndicate for protection during the first part of the month.

October 25: Billed the Underground Times $150 for a printing job.

October 27: Paid $400 on account for supplies purchased October 6.

October 28: Received $300 from Donner and Blitzen.

October 31: The supplies inventory was down to $550.

Required:

a. Record the above transactions in a general journal.

b. Post the entries to a general ledger.

c. Prepare, record, and post any adjusting entries needed at the close of business on October 31.

d. Prepare a trial balance.

e. Prepare an income statement for the month ended October 31.

f. Prepare, record, and post closing entries for October 31.

g. Prepare a post-closing trial balance.

h. Prepare a balance sheet as of October 31.

PI–7 *The accounting cycle.* The following events occurred in the life of the Sharp Pencil Company:

August 1: Tom Sharp invested $10,000 in the business by opening a checking account with a cash deposit.

August 3: Sharp signed a lease on a building to house the operations. On August 15, he would pay the first month's rent of $200 and move in.

August 15: Paid the $200 and moved in.

August 15:   Purchased 1,000 gross of pencils for $5,000 on account.

August 18:   Sold 400 gross of pencils for $3,000 cash.

August 23:   Sold 200 gross of pencils for $1,500 on account.

August 25:   Paid half of the account owed for the August 15 purchase.

September 4:   Received $3,000 for a special order of pencils to be delivered later.

September 10: Collected the $1,500 from the August 23 sale.

September 15: Paid the wages of his assistant for month's work, $250.

September 15: Received the bill from the power company for last month ($50).

September 15: Paid the next month's rent in advance.

Required:

a. Record the above transactions in a general journal.

b. Post the entries to a general ledger.

c. Prepare, record, and post any adjusting entries needed at the close of business on September 15.

d. Prepare a trial balance.

e. Prepare an income statement for the period ended September 15.

f. Prepare, record, and post-closing entries.

g. Prepare a post-closing trial balance.

h. Prepare a balance sheet as of the close of business on September 15.

II

Compound Interest Tables

Table A
Future Amount of $1

n	½%	1%	1½%	2%	2½%	3%	3½%	4%	5%	6%	7%	8%	9%	10%	15%	20%	25%
1	1.005	1.010	1.015	1.020	1.025	1.030	1.035	1.040	1.050	1.060	1.070	1.080	1.090	1.100	1.150	1.200	1.250
2	1.010	1.020	1.030	1.040	1.050	1.060	1.071	1.081	1.102	1.123	1.144	1.166	1.188	1.210	1.322	1.440	1.562
3	1.015	1.030	1.045	1.061	1.076	1.092	1.108	1.124	1.157	1.191	1.225	1.259	1.295	1.331	1.520	1.728	1.953
4	1.020	1.041	1.061	1.082	1.103	1.125	1.147	1.169	1.215	1.262	1.310	1.360	1.411	1.464	1.749	2.073	2.441
5	1.025	1.051	1.077	1.104	1.131	1.159	1.187	1.216	1.276	1.338	1.402	1.469	1.538	1.610	2.011	2.488	3.051
6	1.030	1.061	1.093	1.126	1.159	1.194	1.229	1.265	1.340	1.418	1.500	1.586	1.677	1.771	2.313	2.985	3.814
7	1.035	1.072	1.109	1.148	1.188	1.229	1.272	1.315	1.407	1.503	1.605	1.713	1.828	1.948	2.660	3.583	4.768
8	1.040	1.082	1.126	1.171	1.218	1.266	1.316	1.368	1.477	1.593	1.718	1.850	1.992	2.143	3.059	4.299	5.960
9	1.045	1.093	1.143	1.195	1.248	1.304	1.362	1.423	1.551	1.689	1.838	1.999	2.171	2.357	3.517	5.159	7.450
10	1.051	1.104	1.160	1.218	1.280	1.343	1.410	1.480	1.628	1.790	1.967	2.158	2.367	2.593	4.045	6.191	9.313
11	1.056	1.115	1.177	1.243	1.312	1.384	1.459	1.539	1.710	1.898	2.104	2.331	2.580	2.853	4.652	7.430	11.641
12	1.061	1.126	1.195	1.268	1.344	1.425	1.511	1.601	1.795	2.012	2.252	2.518	2.812	3.138	5.350	8.916	14.551
13	1.066	1.138	1.213	1.293	1.378	1.468	1.563	1.665	1.885	2.132	2.409	2.719	3.065	3.452	6.152	10.699	18.189
14	1.072	1.149	1.231	1.319	1.412	1.512	1.618	1.731	1.979	2.260	2.578	2.937	3.341	3.797	7.075	12.839	22.737
15	1.077	1.160	1.250	1.345	1.448	1.557	1.675	1.800	2.078	2.396	2.759	3.172	3.642	4.177	8.137	15.407	28.421
16	1.083	1.172	1.268	1.372	1.484	1.604	1.733	1.872	2.182	2.540	2.952	3.425	3.970	4.594	9.357	18.488	35.527
17	1.088	1.184	1.288	1.400	1.521	1.652	1.794	1.947	2.292	2.692	3.158	3.700	4.327	5.054	10.761	22.186	44.408
18	1.093	1.196	1.307	1.428	1.559	1.702	1.857	2.025	2.406	2.854	3.379	3.996	4.717	5.559	12.375	26.623	55.511
19	1.099	1.208	1.326	1.456	1.598	1.753	1.922	2.106	2.526	3.025	3.616	4.315	5.141	6.115	14.231	31.947	69.388
20	1.104	1.220	1.346	1.485	1.638	1.806	1.989	2.191	2.653	3.207	3.869	4.660	5.604	6.727	16.366	38.337	86.736
21	1.110	1.232	1.367	1.515	1.679	1.860	2.059	2.278	2.785	3.399	4.140	5.033	6.108	7.400	18.821	46.005	108.420
22	1.115	1.244	1.387	1.545	1.721	1.916	2.131	2.369	2.925	3.603	4.430	5.436	6.658	8.140	21.644	55.206	135.525
23	1.121	1.257	1.408	1.576	1.764	1.973	2.206	2.464	3.071	3.819	4.740	5.871	7.257	8.954	24.891	66.247	169.406
24	1.127	1.269	1.429	1.608	1.808	2.032	2.283	2.563	3.225	4.048	5.072	6.341	7.911	9.849	28.625	79.496	211.758
25	1.132	1.282	1.450	1.640	1.853	2.093	2.363	2.665	3.386	4.291	5.427	6.848	8.623	10.834	32.918	95.396	264.697
26	1.138	1.295	1.472	1.673	1.900	2.156	2.445	2.772	3.555	4.549	5.807	7.396	9.399	11.918	37.856	114.475	330.872
27	1.144	1.308	1.494	1.706	1.947	2.221	2.531	2.883	3.733	4.822	6.213	7.988	10.245	13.109	43.535	137.370	413.590
28	1.149	1.321	1.517	1.741	1.996	2.287	2.620	2.998	3.920	5.111	6.648	8.627	11.167	14.420	50.065	164.844	516.987
29	1.155	1.334	1.539	1.775	2.046	2.356	2.711	3.118	4.116	5.418	7.114	9.317	12.172	15.863	57.575	197.813	646.234
30	1.161	1.347	1.563	1.811	2.097	2.427	2.806	3.243	4.321	5.743	7.612	10.062	13.267	17.449	66.211	237.376	807.793
31	1.167	1.361	1.586	1.847	2.150	2.500	2.905	3.373	4.538	6.088	8.145	10.867	14.461	19.194	76.143	284.851	1009.741
32	1.173	1.374	1.610	1.884	2.203	2.575	3.006	3.508	4.764	6.453	8.715	11.737	15.763	21.113	87.565	341.821	1262.177
33	1.179	1.388	1.634	1.922	2.258	2.652	3.111	3.648	5.003	6.840	9.325	12.676	17.182	23.225	100.699	410.186	1577.721
34	1.184	1.402	1.658	1.960	2.315	2.731	3.220	3.794	5.253	7.251	9.978	13.690	18.728	25.547	115.804	492.223	1972.152
35	1.190	1.416	1.683	1.999	2.373	2.813	3.333	3.946	5.516	7.686	10.676	14.785	20.413	28.102	133.175	590.668	2465.190

Table A
Future Amount of $1 (continued)

n	½%	1%	1½%	2%	2½%	3%	3½%	4%	5%	6%	7%	8%	9%	10%	15%	20%	25%
36	1.196	1.430	1.709	2.039	2.432	2.898	3.450	4.103	5.791	8.147	11.423	15.968	22.251	30.912	153.151	708.801	3081.487
37	1.202	1.445	1.734	2.080	2.493	2.985	3.571	4.268	6.081	8.636	12.223	17.245	24.253	34.003	176.124	850.562	3851.859
38	1.208	1.459	1.760	2.122	2.555	3.074	3.696	4.438	6.385	9.154	13.079	18.625	26.436	37.404	202.543	1020.674	4814.824
39	1.214	1.474	1.787	2.164	2.619	3.167	3.825	4.616	6.704	9.703	13.994	20.115	28.815	41.144	232.924	1224.809	6018.531
40	1.220	1.488	1.814	2.208	2.685	3.262	3.959	4.801	7.039	10.285	14.974	21.724	31.409	45.259	267.863	1469.771	7523.163
41	1.226	1.503	1.841	2.252	2.752	3.359	4.097	4.993	7.391	10.902	16.022	23.462	34.236	49.785	308.043	1763.725	9403.954
42	1.233	1.518	1.868	2.297	2.820	3.460	4.241	5.192	7.761	11.557	17.144	25.339	37.317	54.763	354.249	2116.471	11754.943
43	1.239	1.533	1.896	2.343	2.891	3.564	4.389	5.400	8.149	12.250	18.344	27.366	40.676	60.240	407.386	2539.765	14693.679
44	1.245	1.549	1.925	2.390	2.963	3.671	4.543	5.616	8.557	12.985	19.628	29.555	44.336	66.264	468.495	3047.718	18367.099
45	1.251	1.564	1.954	2.437	3.037	3.781	4.702	5.841	8.985	13.764	21.002	31.920	48.327	72.890	538.769	3657.261	22958.874
46	1.257	1.580	1.983	2.486	3.113	3.895	4.866	6.074	9.434	14.590	22.472	34.474	52.676	80.179	619.584	4388.714	28698.592
47	1.264	1.596	2.013	2.536	3.191	4.011	5.037	6.317	9.905	15.465	24.045	37.232	57.417	88.197	712.522	5266.457	35873.240
48	1.270	1.612	2.043	2.587	3.271	4.132	5.213	6.570	10.401	16.393	25.728	40.210	62.585	97.017	819.400	6319.748	44841.550
49	1.276	1.629	2.074	2.639	3.353	4.256	5.396	6.833	10.921	17.377	27.529	43.427	68.217	106.718	942.310	7583.698	56051.938
50	1.283	1.644	2.105	2.691	3.437	4.383	5.584	7.106	11.467	18.420	29.457	46.901	74.357	117.390	1083.657	9100.438	70064.923
51	1.289	1.661	2.136	2.745	3.523	4.515	5.780	7.390	12.040	19.525	31.519	50.653	81.049	129.129	1246.206	10920.525	87581.154
52	1.296	1.677	2.168	2.800	3.611	4.650	5.982	7.686	12.642	20.696	33.725	54.706	88.344	142.042	1433.136	13104.630	109476.442
53	1.302	1.694	2.201	2.856	3.701	4.790	6.192	7.994	13.274	21.938	36.086	59.082	96.295	156.247	1648.107	15725.557	136845.553
54	1.309	1.711	2.234	2.913	3.793	4.934	6.408	8.313	13.938	23.255	38.612	63.809	104.961	171.871	1895.323	18870.668	171056.941
55	1.315	1.728	2.267	2.971	3.888	5.082	6.633	8.646	14.635	24.650	41.315	68.913	114.408	189.059	2179.622	22644.802	213821.176
56	1.322	1.745	2.301	3.031	3.985	5.234	6.865	8.992	15.367	26.129	44.207	74.426	124.705	207.965	2506.565	27173.762	267276.471
57	1.328	1.763	2.336	3.091	4.085	5.391	7.105	9.351	16.135	27.697	47.301	80.381	135.928	228.761	2882.550	32608.515	334095.588
58	1.335	1.780	2.371	3.153	4.187	5.553	7.354	9.725	16.942	29.358	50.612	86.811	148.162	251.637	3314.932	39130.218	417619.485
59	1.342	1.798	2.407	3.216	4.292	5.720	7.611	10.115	17.789	31.120	54.155	93.756	161.496	276.801	3812.172	46956.261	522024.357
60	1.348	1.816	2.443	3.281	4.399	5.891	7.878	10.519	18.679	32.987	57.946	101.257	176.031	304.481	4383.998	56347.514	652530.446
70	1.417	2.006	2.835	3.999	5.632	7.917	11.112	15.571	30.426	59.075	113.989	218.606	416.730	789.746			
80	1.490	2.216	3.290	4.875	7.209	10.640	15.675	23.049	49.561	105.795	224.234	471.954	986.551	2048.400			
90	1.566	2.448	3.818	5.943	9.228	14.300	22.112	34.119	80.730	189.464	441.102	1018.915	2335.526	5313.022			
100	1.646	2.704	4.432	7.244	11.813	19.218	31.191	50.504	131.501	339.302	867.716	2199.761	5529.040	13780.612			

Table B
Present Value of $1

n	1%	2%	3%	4%	5%	6%	8%	10%	12%	14%	15%	16%	18%	20%	22%	24%	25%	30%	35%	40%	45%	50%
1	0.990	0.980	0.970	0.962	0.952	0.943	0.926	0.909	0.893	0.877	0.870	0.862	0.847	0.833	0.820	0.806	0.800	0.769	0.741	0.714	0.690	0.667
2	0.980	0.961	0.942	0.925	0.907	0.890	0.857	0.826	0.797	0.769	0.756	0.743	0.718	0.694	0.672	0.650	0.640	0.592	0.549	0.510	0.476	0.444
3	0.971	0.942	0.915	0.889	0.863	0.840	0.794	0.751	0.712	0.675	0.658	0.641	0.609	0.579	0.551	0.524	0.512	0.455	0.406	0.364	0.328	0.296
4	0.961	0.924	0.888	0.855	0.822	0.792	0.735	0.683	0.636	0.592	0.572	0.552	0.516	0.482	0.451	0.423	0.410	0.350	0.301	0.260	0.226	0.198
5	0.951	0.906	0.862	0.822	0.783	0.747	0.681	0.621	0.567	0.519	0.497	0.476	0.437	0.402	0.370	0.341	0.328	0.269	0.223	0.186	0.156	0.132
6	0.942	0.888	0.837	0.790	0.746	0.705	0.630	0.564	0.507	0.456	0.432	0.410	0.370	0.335	0.303	0.275	0.262	0.207	0.165	0.133	0.108	0.088
7	0.933	0.871	0.813	0.760	0.710	0.665	0.583	0.513	0.452	0.400	0.376	0.354	0.314	0.279	0.249	0.222	0.210	0.159	0.122	0.095	0.074	0.059
8	0.923	0.853	0.789	0.731	0.676	0.627	0.540	0.467	0.404	0.351	0.327	0.305	0.266	0.233	0.204	0.179	0.168	0.123	0.091	0.068	0.051	0.039
9	0.914	0.837	0.766	0.703	0.644	0.592	0.500	0.424	0.361	0.308	0.284	0.263	0.225	0.194	0.167	0.144	0.134	0.094	0.067	0.048	0.035	0.026
10	0.905	0.820	0.744	0.676	0.613	0.558	0.463	0.386	0.322	0.270	0.247	0.227	0.191	0.162	0.137	0.116	0.107	0.073	0.050	0.035	0.024	0.017
11	0.896	0.804	0.722	0.650	0.584	0.527	0.429	0.350	0.287	0.237	0.215	0.195	0.162	0.135	0.112	0.094	0.086	0.056	0.037	0.025	0.017	0.012
12	0.887	0.788	0.701	0.625	0.556	0.497	0.397	0.319	0.257	0.208	0.187	0.168	0.137	0.112	0.092	0.076	0.069	0.043	0.027	0.018	0.012	0.008
13	0.879	0.773	0.680	0.601	0.530	0.469	0.368	0.290	0.229	0.182	0.163	0.145	0.116	0.093	0.075	0.061	0.055	0.033	0.020	0.013	0.008	0.005
14	0.870	0.758	0.661	0.577	0.505	0.442	0.340	0.263	0.205	0.160	0.141	0.125	0.099	0.078	0.062	0.049	0.044	0.025	0.015	0.009	0.006	0.003
15	0.861	0.743	0.641	0.555	0.481	0.417	0.315	0.239	0.183	0.140	0.123	0.108	0.084	0.065	0.051	0.040	0.035	0.020	0.011	0.006	0.004	0.002
16	0.853	0.728	0.623	0.534	0.458	0.394	0.292	0.218	0.163	0.123	0.107	0.093	0.071	0.054	0.042	0.032	0.028	0.015	0.008	0.005	0.003	0.002
17	0.844	0.714	0.605	0.513	0.436	0.371	0.270	0.198	0.146	0.108	0.093	0.080	0.060	0.045	0.034	0.026	0.023	0.012	0.006	0.003	0.002	0.001
18	0.836	0.700	0.587	0.494	0.415	0.350	0.250	0.180	0.130	0.095	0.081	0.069	0.051	0.038	0.028	0.021	0.018	0.009	0.005	0.002	0.001	0.001
19	0.828	0.686	0.570	0.475	0.395	0.331	0.232	0.164	0.116	0.083	0.070	0.060	0.043	0.031	0.023	0.017	0.014	0.007	0.003	0.002	0.001	
20	0.820	0.673	0.553	0.456	0.376	0.312	0.215	0.149	0.104	0.073	0.061	0.051	0.037	0.026	0.019	0.014	0.012	0.005	0.002	0.001	0.001	
21	0.811	0.660	0.537	0.439	0.358	0.294	0.199	0.135	0.093	0.064	0.053	0.044	0.031	0.022	0.015	0.011	0.009	0.004	0.002	0.001		
22	0.803	0.647	0.521	0.422	0.341	0.278	0.184	0.123	0.083	0.056	0.046	0.038	0.026	0.018	0.013	0.009	0.007	0.003	0.001	0.001		
23	0.795	0.634	0.506	0.406	0.325	0.262	0.170	0.112	0.074	0.049	0.040	0.033	0.022	0.015	0.010	0.007	0.006	0.002	0.001			
24	0.788	0.622	0.491	0.390	0.310	0.247	0.158	0.102	0.066	0.043	0.035	0.028	0.019	0.013	0.008	0.006	0.005	0.002	0.001			
25	0.780	0.610	0.477	0.375	0.295	0.233	0.146	0.092	0.059	0.038	0.030	0.024	0.016	0.010	0.007	0.005	0.004	0.001	0.001			
26	0.772	0.598	0.463	0.361	0.281	0.220	0.135	0.084	0.053	0.033	0.026	0.021	0.014	0.009	0.006	0.004	0.003	0.001				
27	0.764	0.586	0.450	0.347	0.267	0.207	0.125	0.076	0.047	0.029	0.023	0.018	0.011	0.007	0.005	0.003	0.002	0.001				
28	0.757	0.574	0.437	0.333	0.255	0.196	0.116	0.069	0.042	0.026	0.020	0.016	0.010	0.006	0.004	0.002	0.002	0.001				
29	0.749	0.563	0.424	0.321	0.242	0.185	0.107	0.063	0.037	0.022	0.017	0.014	0.008	0.005	0.003	0.002	0.002	0.001				
30	0.742	0.552	0.411	0.308	0.231	0.174	0.099	0.057	0.033	0.020	0.015	0.012	0.007	0.004	0.003	0.002	0.001	0.001				
40	0.672	0.453	0.306	0.208	0.142	0.097	0.046	0.022	0.011	0.005	0.004	0.003	0.001	0.001								
50	0.608	0.372	0.228	0.141	0.087	0.054	0.021	0.009	0.003	0.001	0.001	0.001										

Table C
Future Amount of an Annuity of $1
(Amount of $1 Deposited Annually for n Years)

n	½%	1%	1½%	2%	2½%	3%	3½%	4%	5%	6%
1	1.000	1.000	1.000	1.000	1.000	1.000	1.000	1.000	1.000	1.000
2	2.005	2.010	2.015	2.020	2.025	2.030	2.035	2.040	2.050	2.060
3	3.015	3.030	3.045	3.060	3.075	3.090	3.106	3.121	3.152	3.183
4	4.030	4.060	4.090	4.121	4.152	4.183	4.214	4.246	4.310	4.374
5	5.050	5.101	5.152	5.204	5.256	5.309	5.362	5.416	5.525	5.637
6	6.075	6.152	6.229	6.308	6.387	6.468	6.550	6.632	6.801	6.975
7	7.105	7.213	7.322	7.434	7.547	7.662	7.779	7.898	8.142	8.393
8	8.141	8.285	8.432	8.582	8.736	8.892	9.051	9.214	9.549	9.897
9	9.182	9.368	9.559	9.754	9.954	10.159	10.368	10.582	11.026	11.491
10	10.228	10.462	10.702	10.949	11.203	11.463	11.731	12.006	12.577	13.180
11	11.279	11.566	11.863	12.168	12.483	12.807	13.141	13.486	14.206	14.971
12	12.335	12.682	13.041	13.412	13.795	14.192	14.601	15.025	15.917	16.869
13	13.397	13.809	14.236	14.680	15.140	15.617	16.113	16.626	17.712	18.882
14	14.464	14.947	15.450	15.973	16.518	17.086	17.676	18.291	19.598	21.015
15	15.536	16.096	16.682	17.293	17.931	18.598	19.295	20.623	21.578	23.275
16	16.614	17.257	17.932	18.639	19.380	20.156	20.971	21.824	23.657	25.672
17	17.697	18.430	19.201	20.012	20.864	21.761	22.705	23.697	25.810	28.212
18	18.785	19.614	20.489	21.412	22.386	23.414	24.499	25.645	28.132	30.905
19	19.879	20.810	21.796	22.840	23.946	25.116	26.357	27.671	30.539	33.759
20	20.979	22.019	23.123	24.297	25.544	26.870	28.279	29.778	33.065	36.785
21	22.084	23.239	24.470	25.783	27.183	28.676	30.269	31.969	35.719	39.992
22	23.194	24.471	25.837	27.298	28.862	30.536	32.328	34.247	38.505	43.392
23	24.310	25.716	27.225	28.844	30.584	32.452	34.460	36.617	41.430	46.995
24	25.431	26.973	28.633	30.421	32.349	34.426	36.666	39.083	44.501	50.815
25	26.559	28.243	30.063	32.030	34.157	36.459	38.949	41.645	47.727	54.864
26	27.691	29.525	31.513	33.670	36.011	38.553	41.313	44.311	51.113	59.156
27	28.830	30.820	32.986	35.344	37.912	40.709	43.759	47.084	54.669	63.705
28	29.974	32.129	34.481	37.051	39.859	42.930	46.290	49.967	58.402	68.528
29	31.124	33.450	35.998	38.792	41.856	45.218	48.910	52.966	62.322	73.639
30	32.280	34.784	37.538	40.568	43.902	47.575	51.622	56.084	66.438	79.058
31	33.441	36.132	39.101	42.379	46.000	50.002	54.429	59.328	70.760	84.801
32	34.608	37.494	40.688	44.227	48.150	52.502	57.334	62.701	75.298	90.889
33	35.781	38.869	42.298	46.111	50.354	55.077	60.341	66.209	80.063	97.343
34	36.960	40.257	43.933	48.033	52.612	57.730	63.453	69.857	85.066	104.183
35	38.145	41.660	45.592	49.994	54.928	60.462	66.674	73.652	90.320	111.434
36	39.336	43.076	47.275	51.994	57.301	63.275	70.007	77.598	95.836	119.120
37	40.532	44.507	48.985	54.034	59.733	66.174	73.457	81.702	101.628	127.268
38	41.735	45.952	50.719	56.114	62.227	69.159	77.028	85.970	107.709	135.904
39	42.944	47.412	52.480	58.237	64.782	72.234	80.724	90.409	114.095	145.058
40	44.158	48.886	54.267	60.401	67.402	75.401	84.550	95.025	120.799	154.761
41	45.379	50.375	56.081	62.610	70.087	78.663	88.509	99.826	127.839	165.047
42	46.606	51.878	57.923	64.862	72.839	82.023	92.607	104.819	135.231	175.950
43	47.839	53.397	59.791	67.159	75.660	85.483	96.848	110.012	142.993	187.507
44	49.078	54.931	61.688	69.502	78.552	89.048	101.238	115.412	151.143	199.758
45	50.324	56.481	63.614	71.892	81.516	92.719	105.781	121.029	159.700	212.743
46	51.575	58.045	65.568	74.330	84.554	96.501	110.484	126.870	168.685	226.508
47	52.833	59.626	67.551	76.817	87.667	100.396	115.350	132.945	178.119	241.098
48	54.097	61.222	69.565	79.353	90.859	104.408	120.388	139.263	188.025	256.564
49	55.368	62.834	71.608	81.940	94.131	108.540	125.001	145.833	198.426	272.958
50	56.645	64.463	73.682	84.579	97.484	112.796	130.997	152.667	209.347	290.335
51	57.928	66.107	75.788	87.270	100.921	117.180	136.582	159.773	220.815	308.756
52	59.218	67.768	77.924	90.016	104.444	121.696	142.363	167.164	232.856	328.281
53	60.514	69.446	80.093	92.816	108.055	126.347	148.345	174.851	245.498	348.978
54	61.816	71.141	82.295	95.673	111.756	131.137	154.538	182.845	258.773	370.917
55	63.125	72.852	84.529	98.586	115.550	136.071	160.946	191.159	272.712	394.172
56	64.441	74.580	86.797	101.558	119.439	141.153	167.580	199.805	287.348	418.822
57	65.763	76.326	89.099	104.589	123.425	146.388	174.445	208.797	302.715	444.951
58	67.092	78.090	91.435	107.681	127.511	151.780	181.550	218.149	318.851	472.648
59	68.427	79.870	93.807	110.834	131.699	157.333	188.905	227.875	335.794	502.007
60	69.770	81.669	96.214	114.051	135.991	163.053	196.516	237.990	353.583	533.128
70	83.566	100.676	122.363	149.977	185.284	230.594	288.937	364.290	588.528	967.932
80	98.067	121.671	152.710	193.771	248.382	321.363	419.306	551.244	971.228	1746.599
90	113.310	144.863	187.929	247.156	329.154	443.348	603.205	827.983	1594.607	3141.075
100	129.333	170.481	228.803	312.232	432.548	607.287	862.611	1237.623	2610.025	5638.368

Table C
Future Amount of an Annuity of $1 (continued)

n	7%	8%	9%	10%	15%	20%	25%
1	1.000	1.000	1.000	1.000	1.000	1.000	1.000
2	2.070	2.080	2.090	2.100	2.150	2.200	2.250
3	3.214	3.246	3.278	3.310	3.472	3.640	3.812
4	4.439	4.506	4.573	4.641	4.993	5.368	5.765
5	5.750	5.866	5.984	6.105	6.742	7.441	8.207
6	7.153	7.335	7.523	7.715	8.753	9.929	11.258
7	8.654	8.922	9.200	9.487	11.066	12.915	15.073
8	10.259	10.636	11.028	11.435	13.726	16.499	19.841
9	11.977	12.487	13.021	13.579	16.785	20.798	25.802
10	13.816	14.486	15.192	15.937	20.303	25.958	33.252
11	15.783	16.645	17.560	18.531	24.349	32.150	42.566
12	17.888	18.977	20.140	21.384	29.001	39.580	54.207
13	20.140	21.495	22.953	24.522	34.351	48.496	68.759
14	22.550	24.214	26.019	27.974	40.504	59.195	86.949
15	25.129	27.152	29.360	31.772	47.580	72.035	109.686
16	27.888	30.324	33.003	35.949	55.717	87.442	138.108
17	30.840	33.750	36.973	40.544	65.075	105.930	173.635
18	33.999	37.450	41.301	45.599	75.836	128.116	218.044
19	37.378	41.446	46.018	51.159	88.211	154.739	273.555
20	40.995	45.761	51.160	57.274	102.443	186.687	342.944
21	44.865	50.442	56.764	64.002	118.810	225.025	429.680
22	49.005	55.456	62.873	71.402	137.631	271.030	538.101
23	53.436	60.893	69.531	79.543	159.276	326.236	673.626
24	58.176	66.764	76.789	88.497	184.167	392.484	843.032
25	63.249	73.105	84.700	98.347	212.793	471.981	1054.791
26	68.676	79.954	93.323	109.181	245.711	567.377	1319.488
27	74.483	87.350	102.723	121.099	283.568	681.852	1650.361
28	80.697	95.338	112.968	134.209	327.104	819.223	2063.951
29	87.346	103.965	124.135	148.630	377.169	984.067	2580.939
30	94.460	113.283	136.307	164.494	434.745	1181.881	3227.174
31	102.073	123.345	149.575	181.943	500.956	1419.257	4034.967
32	110.218	134.213	164.036	201.137	577.100	1704.109	5044.709
33	118.933	145.950	179.800	222.251	664.665	2045.931	6306.887
34	128.258	158.626	196.982	245.476	765.365	2456.117	7884.609
35	138.236	172.316	215.710	271.024	881.170	2948.341	9856.761
36	148.913	187.102	236.124	299.126	1014.345	3539.009	12321.951
37	160.337	203.070	258.375	330.039	1167.497	4247.811	15403.439
38	172.561	220.315	282.629	364.043	1343.622	5098.373	19255.299
39	185.640	238.941	309.066	401.447	1546.165	6119.048	24070.124
40	199.635	259.056	337.882	442.592	1779.090	7343.857	30088.655
41	214.609	280.781	369.291	487.851	2046.953	8813.629	37611.819
42	230.632	304.243	403.528	537.636	2354.996	10577.355	47015.774
43	247.776	329.538	440.845	592.400	2709.246	12693.826	58770.717
44	266.120	356.949	481.521	652.640	3116.633	15233.591	73464.396
45	285.749	386.505	525.858	718.904	3585.128	18281.309	91831.496
46	306.751	418.426	574.186	791.795	4123.897	21938.571	114790.370
47	329.224	452.900	626.862	871.974	4743.482	26327.286	143488.962
48	353.270	490.132	684.280	960.172	5456.004	31593.743	179362.203
49	378.998	530.342	746.865	1057.189	6275.405	37913.492	224203.754
50	406.528	573.770	815.083	1163.908	7217.716	45497.190	280255.692
51	435.985	620.671	889.441	1281.299	8301.373	54597.628	350320.616
52	467.504	671.325	970.490	1410.429	9547.579	65518.154	437901.770
53	501.230	726.031	1058.834	1552.472	10980.716	78622.785	547378.212
54	537.316	785.114	1155.130	1708.719	12628.824	94348.342	684223.765
55	575.928	848.923	1260.091	1880.591	14524.147	113219.011	855280.707
56	617.243	917.837	1374.500	2069.650	16703.770	135863.813	1069101.884
57	661.450	992.264	1499.205	2277.615	19210.335	163037.576	1336378.355
58	708.752	1072.645	1635.133	2506.377	22092.885	195646.091	1670473.943
59	759.364	1159.456	1783.295	2758.014	25407.818	234776.309	2088093.429
60	813.520	1253.213	1944.792	3034.816	29219.991	281732.571	2610117.787
70	1614.134	2720.080	4619.223	7887.469			
80	3189.062	5886.935	10950.574	20474.002			
90	6287.185	12723.038	25939.184	53120.226			
100	12381.661	27484.515	61422.675	137796.123			

Table D
Present Value of an Annuity of $1
(Present Value of $1 Received Annually for n Years)

n	1%	2%	3%	4%	5%	6%	8%	10%	12%	14%	15%	16%	18%	20%	22%	24%	25%	30%	35%	40%	45%	50%
1	0.990	0.980	0.970	0.962	0.952	0.943	0.926	0.909	0.893	0.877	0.870	0.862	0.847	0.833	0.820	0.806	0.800	0.769	0.741	0.714	0.690	0.667
2	1.970	1.942	1.913	1.886	1.859	1.833	1.783	1.736	1.690	1.647	1.626	1.605	1.566	1.528	1.492	1.457	1.440	1.361	1.289	1.224	1.165	1.111
3	2.941	2.884	2.829	2.775	2.723	2.673	2.577	2.487	2.402	2.322	2.283	2.246	2.174	2.106	2.042	1.981	1.952	1.816	1.696	1.589	1.493	1.407
4	3.902	3.808	3.717	3.630	3.545	3.465	3.312	3.170	3.037	2.914	2.855	2.798	2.690	2.589	2.494	2.404	2.362	2.166	1.997	1.849	1.720	1.605
5	4.853	4.713	4.579	4.452	4.329	4.212	3.993	3.791	3.605	3.433	3.352	3.274	3.127	2.991	2.864	2.745	2.689	2.436	2.220	2.035	1.876	1.737
6	5.795	5.601	5.417	5.242	5.075	4.917	4.623	4.355	4.111	3.889	3.784	3.685	3.498	3.326	3.167	3.020	2.951	2.643	2.385	2.168	1.983	1.824
7	6.728	6.472	6.230	6.002	5.786	5.582	5.206	4.868	4.564	4.288	4.160	4.039	3.812	3.605	3.416	3.242	3.161	2.802	2.508	2.263	2.057	1.883
8	7.652	7.325	7.019	6.733	6.463	6.210	5.747	5.335	4.968	4.639	4.487	4.344	4.078	3.837	3.619	3.421	3.329	2.925	2.598	2.331	2.108	1.922
9	8.566	8.162	7.786	7.435	7.107	6.802	6.247	5.759	5.328	4.946	4.772	4.607	4.303	4.031	3.786	3.566	3.463	3.019	2.665	2.379	2.144	1.948
10	9.471	8.983	8.530	8.111	7.721	7.360	6.710	6.145	5.650	5.216	5.019	4.833	4.494	4.192	3.923	3.682	3.571	3.092	2.715	2.414	2.168	1.965
11	10.368	9.787	9.252	8.760	8.306	7.887	7.139	6.495	5.937	5.453	5.234	5.029	4.656	4.327	4.035	3.776	3.656	3.147	2.752	2.438	2.185	1.977
12	11.255	10.575	9.954	9.385	8.863	8.384	7.536	6.814	6.194	5.660	5.421	5.197	4.793	4.439	4.127	3.851	3.725	3.190	2.779	2.456	2.196	1.985
13	12.134	11.343	10.634	9.986	9.393	8.853	7.904	7.103	6.424	5.842	5.583	5.342	4.910	4.533	4.203	3.912	3.780	3.223	2.799	2.468	2.204	1.990
14	13.004	12.106	11.296	10.563	9.899	9.295	8.244	7.367	6.628	6.002	5.724	5.468	5.008	4.611	4.265	3.962	3.824	3.249	2.814	2.477	2.210	1.993
15	13.865	12.849	11.937	11.118	10.379	9.712	8.559	7.606	6.811	6.142	5.847	5.575	5.092	4.675	4.315	4.001	3.859	3.268	2.825	2.484	2.214	1.995
16	14.718	13.578	12.561	11.652	10.837	10.106	8.851	7.824	6.974	6.265	5.954	5.669	5.162	4.730	4.357	4.033	3.887	3.283	2.834	2.489	2.216	1.997
17	15.562	14.292	13.166	12.166	11.274	10.477	9.122	8.022	7.120	6.373	6.047	5.749	5.222	4.775	4.391	4.059	3.910	3.295	2.840	2.492	2.218	1.998
18	16.398	14.992	13.753	12.659	11.689	10.828	9.372	8.201	7.250	6.467	6.128	5.818	5.273	4.812	4.419	4.080	3.928	3.304	2.844	2.494	2.219	1.999
19	17.226	15.678	14.323	13.134	12.085	11.158	9.604	8.365	7.366	6.550	6.198	5.877	5.316	4.844	4.442	4.097	3.942	3.311	2.848	2.496	2.220	1.999
20	18.046	16.351	14.877	13.590	12.462	11.470	9.818	8.514	7.469	6.623	6.259	5.929	5.353	4.870	4.460	4.110	3.954	3.316	2.850	2.497	2.221	1.999
21	18.857	17.011	15.415	14.029	12.821	11.764	10.017	8.649	7.562	6.687	6.312	5.973	5.384	4.891	4.476	4.121	3.963	3.320	2.852	2.498	2.221	2.000
22	19.660	17.658	15.936	14.451	13.163	12.042	10.201	8.772	7.645	6.743	6.359	6.011	5.410	4.909	4.488	4.130	3.970	3.323	2.853	2.498	2.222	2.000
23	20.456	18.292	16.443	14.857	13.488	12.303	10.371	8.883	7.718	6.792	6.399	6.044	5.432	4.925	4.499	4.137	3.976	3.325	2.854	2.499	2.222	2.000
24	21.243	18.914	16.935	15.247	13.798	12.550	10.529	8.985	7.784	6.835	6.434	6.073	5.451	4.937	4.507	4.143	3.981	3.327	2.855	2.499	2.222	2.000
25	22.023	19.523	17.413	15.622	14.093	12.783	10.675	9.077	7.843	6.873	6.464	6.097	5.467	4.948	4.514	4.147	3.985	3.329	2.856	2.499	2.222	2.000
26	22.795	20.121	17.876	15.982	14.375	13.003	10.810	9.161	7.896	6.906	6.491	6.118	5.480	4.956	4.520	4.151	3.988	3.330	2.856	2.500	2.222	2.000
27	23.560	20.707	18.327	16.330	14.643	13.211	10.935	9.237	7.943	6.935	6.514	6.136	5.492	4.964	4.524	4.154	3.990	3.331	2.856	2.500	2.222	2.000
28	24.316	21.281	18.764	16.663	14.898	13.406	11.051	9.307	7.984	6.961	6.534	6.152	5.502	4.970	4.528	4.157	3.992	3.331	2.857	2.500	2.222	2.000
29	25.066	21.844	19.188	16.984	15.141	13.591	11.158	9.370	8.022	6.983	6.551	6.166	5.510	4.975	4.531	4.159	3.994	3.332	2.857	2.500	2.222	2.000
30	25.808	22.396	19.600	17.292	15.372	13.765	11.258	9.427	8.055	7.003	6.566	6.177	5.517	4.979	4.534	4.160	3.995	3.332	2.857	2.500	2.222	2.000
40	32.835	27.355	23.114	19.793	17.159	15.046	11.925	9.779	8.244	7.105	6.642	6.234	5.548	4.997	4.544	4.166	3.999	3.333	2.857	2.500	2.222	2.000
50	39.196	31.424	25.729	21.482	18.255	15.762	12.234	9.915	8.304	7.133	6.661	6.246	5.554	4.999	4.545	4.167	4.000	3.333	2.857	2.500	2.222	2.000

Index